THE WANING OF MA´

The Waning of Materialism

Edited by
ROBERT C. KOONS AND GEORGE BEALER

OXFORD
UNIVERSITY PRESS

OXFORD

UNIVERSITY PRESS

Great Clarendon Street, Oxford OX2 6DP

Oxford University Press is a department of the University of Oxford.
It furthers the University's objective of excellence in research, scholarship,
and education by publishing worldwide in

Oxford New York

Auckland Cape Town Dar es Salaam Hong Kong Karachi
Kuala Lumpur Madrid Melbourne Mexico City Nairobi
New Delhi Shanghai Taipei Toronto

With offices in

Argentina Austria Brazil Chile Czech Republic France Greece
Guatemala Hungary Italy Japan Poland Portugal Singapore
South Korea Switzerland Thailand Turkey Ukraine Vietnam

Oxford is a registered trade mark of Oxford University Press
in the UK and in certain other countries

Published in the United States
by Oxford University Press Inc., New York

British Library Cataloguing in Publication Data

Data available

Library of Congress Cataloging in Publication Data
Library of Congress Control Number 2010920518

Typeset by Laserwords Private Limited, Chennai, India
Printed in Great Britain
on acid-free paper by
CPI Antony Rowe, Chippenham, Wiltshire

ISBN 978–0–19–955618–2 (hbk.)
978–0–19–955619–9 (pbk.)

1 3 5 7 9 10 8 6 4 2

Contents

PART III: INTENTIONALITY, MENTAL CAUSATION, AND KNOWLEDGE

PART IV: ALTERNATIVES TO MATERIALISM

Introduction

The twenty-three papers in this volume, both individually and collectively, help to show why and in what ways materialism is on the wane. By saying that materialism is on the wane, we do not mean that materialism is in the process of being eclipsed—nor do we mean that materialism is likely to be eclipsed at any point in the foreseeable future. Indeed, there is good reason to think that materialism is a perennial fixture of philosophy (not to mention cognitive science). After all, materialism is a readily intelligible monistic worldview, appealing in its apparent simplicity, and a natural complement to the impressive ongoing successes in the natural sciences.

In spite of this, materialism is waning in a number of significant respects—one of which is the ever-growing number of major philosophers who reject materialism or at least have strong sympathies with anti-materialist views. It is of course commonly thought that over the course of the last sixty or so years materialism achieved hegemony in academic philosophy, and this is no doubt right by certain measures—for example, in absolute number of self-identified materialist philosophers of mind or in absolute number of books and journal articles defending materialism. It is therefore surprising that an examination of the major philosophers active in this period reveals that a majority, or something approaching a majority, either rejected materialism or had serious and specific doubts about its ultimate viability. The following is just a partial sampling of these philosophers, more or less in order of birth.

Bertrand Russell, Rudolf Carnap, Alonzo Church, Kurt Gödel, Nelson Goodman, Paul Grice, Stuart Hampshire, Roderick Chisholm, Benson Mates, Peter Strawson, Hilary Putnam, John Searle, Jerrold Katz, Alvin Plantinga, Charles Parsons, Jaegwon Kim, George Myro, Thomas Nagel, Robert Adams, Hugh Mellor, Saul Kripke, Eli Hirsch, Ernest Sosa, Stephen Schiffer, Bas van Fraassen, John McDowell, Peter Unger, Derek Parfit, Crispin Wright, Laurence BonJour, Michael Jubien, Nancy Cartwright, Bob Hale, Kit Fine, Tyler Burge, Terence Horgan, Colin McGinn, Robert Brandom, Nathan Salmon, Joseph Levine, Timothy Williamson, Mark Johnston, Paul Boghossian, Stephen Yablo, Joseph Almog, Keith DeRose, Tim Crane, John Hawthorne, Richard Heck, David Chalmers.[i]

---

i For all the people listed, we have documentation that they either rejected materialism or harbored serious and specific doubts about its ultimate viability. All the living philosophers listed (Putnam, Searle, Plantinga, Parsons, Kim, Nagel, and all those following) have given us explicit permission to include them on the list (under the description used in the sentence preceding this one). Limitations on space prevent us from giving a thorough presentation of citations; in the Bibliography, however, we cite relevant works by many of these philosophers. A comment about Russell and Carnap will be helpful here. Russell espoused, at different times, phenomenalism and robust neutral monism,

Materialism plainly has not achieved hegemony when it comes to philosophers of this high caliber.

Here, then, is one respect in which materialism has been on the wane. We will identify two further respects in a moment. But, first, it will be useful to say a few more words about what we mean by materialism.

MATERIALISM

Although the term 'materialism' has been used in diverse ways in philosophy, it traditionally has had a comparatively precise use within philosophy of mind. In this context, materialism is a certain view, or family of views, in the metaphysics of mind. Specifically, materialism is a certain view, or family of views, on the Mind-Body Problem, which concerns the ontological status of, and fundamental metaphysical relationship between, the mental and the physical—between, for instance, mental properties and physical properties, mental relations and physical relations, mental events and physical events, people and their bodies. (For simplicity, we will hereafter focus primarily on mental and physical properties (and relations); understanding their relationship arguably provides a key to resolving the entire problem.)

Historically, materialism was just the reductionist position that mental properties are identical to—and in that sense are nothing but—physical properties. (Idealism was the competing reductionist answer to the Mind-Body Problem, reducing physical properties to mental properties.) Throughout most of the history of philosophy, materialism took the form of what today we call the Identity Theory, according to which mental properties are identical to internal bodily properties, whether they be the properties associated with Democritean atoms, Hobbesian motions in the body or, in our period, electrochemical interactions at the neurological level. (Of course, nothing prevents such a theory from incorporating environmental factors in order to accommodate content externalism; for us, this kind of extended theory would still count as a materialist ontological reduction.) In the first half of the Twentieth Century another form of materialist reductionism emerged, namely, Behaviorism, according to which mental properties are identical to behavioral properties (dispositions of the body to behave in certain ways in certain circumstances). In the 1960s and '70s a third form of reductionism gained prominence, namely, functionalism, according to which our standard mental properties and relations (being conscious, thinking,

each of which is antithetical to Reductive Materialism and also to the thesis that physical properties are metaphysically prior to—and hence are a supervenience base for—mental properties. See, e.g., Russell (1956). The young Carnap (of the *Aufbau*) was a phenomenalist. The mature Carnap (of 'Empiricism, Semantics, and Ontology') endorsed a form of anti-realism incompatible with the sort of materialism prominent over the course of the last sixty or so years. Like the young Carnap, Nelson Goodman and Benson Mates were also phenomenalists, not materialists.

etc.) are identical to (and hence reducible to) second-order properties: specifically, mental properties are held to be definable in terms of the characteristic interactions of their first-order 'realizer' properties with one another and the external environment—where in the actual world, and perhaps all possible worlds, these first-order realizer properties are physical properties (presumably, the sort of physical properties invoked by the Identity Theory).[ii] On a strong version of this view (hereafter called 'Functionalism'), the realizers of mental properties are *necessarily* first-order physical properties, from which it follows that mental properties are necessarily second-order physical properties and therefore belong to the general ontological category of *physical* property.[iii] Like the Identity Theory and Behaviorism, Functionalism qualifies as a form of Reductive Materialism.

There is a weaker version of functionalism according to which, even though mental properties are reducible to second-order properties and even though their realizer properties in the actual world are physical, it is not *necessary* that the realizer properties be physical. If this view were correct, however, mental properties would not belong to the ontological category of physical property. To see why, consider a world in which the realizer properties are not physical (a possibility implied by this version of functionalism). Plainly, the inhabitants of such a world would be mistaken if they were to assert that mental properties belong to the ontological category of physical property. Therefore, since properties cannot change ontological category, it follows that it would, in the actual world, likewise be a mistake for *us* to assert that mental properties belong to the ontological category of physical property; on the contrary, mental properties would need to belong to an entirely different ontological category. Given this, this weak version of functionalism does not count as a form of Reductive Materialism, unlike

---

ii David Lewis construes his functionalism as a form of first-order Identity Theory. This construal is dependent on his implausible view that our paradigmatic mental expressions are non-rigid designators of mental properties and relations. This view of these expressions fails for all of our core mental verbs and verb phrases: 'thinks', 'believes', 'perceives', 'experiences', 'senses', 'feels', 'is aware of', 'is conscious of', etc. By applying the operation of relation-abstraction to these expressions, we get the following relation-abstracts: 'the relation of thinking', 'the relation of believing', etc. Such expressions are rigid designators, as Lewis himself acknowledges, and they denote core mental relations (the relation of thinking, the relation of believing, etc.). Analogously for verb phrases such as 'thinks that human beings exist': the associated property abstract 'the property of thinking that human beings exist' rigidly denotes the property of thinking that human beings exist. Expressions like 'pain', by contrast, do not even denote properties. On two core uses of the expression 'pain' (*the* core uses, we believe), 'pain' functions as a count noun which applies to pains, and it also functions as an associated mass noun for more or less pain (more or less in intensity or extent) or for some pain (some amount of pain). The mental property associated with the count-noun use is the sortal property of being a pain, and the mental property associated with the mass-noun use is the property of being some pain. The associated property-abstracts 'being a pain' and 'being some pain' are rigid designators of these properties. On Lewis's functionalism, therefore, all of the above mental properties and relations (the property of being a pain, the property of thinking that human beings exist, the relation of thinking, etc.) are rigidly designated second-order properties and relations. That is, Lewis's functionalism is just another instance of functionalism, as it was characterized in the text.

iii Putnam (1970) proposed this reductive version of functionalism but has since renounced it.

the strong version described in the previous paragraph. There is another weak version of functionalism that is like this one except that it simply remains neutral on the question of whether it is necessary or contingent that the first-order realizers of mental properties be physical properties. This version does not *on its own* count as a form of Reductive Materialism (but only in conjunction with the independent thesis that it is necessary that the first-order realizers of mental properties be physical).[iv] We will call these two weaker versions of functionalism Minimal Second-order Functionalism, or Minimal Functionalism for short.

Beyond the three forms of Reductive Materialism, there is an altogether different form of materialism, namely, Eliminative Materialism, according to which there simply are no mental properties—or, at least, no instantiated mental properties. It turns out, however, that there are extremely few full-blown Eliminative Materialists. Most philosophers who identify themselves as eliminative materialists do so simply because they reject some central *subcategory* of mental property. For example, Paul and Patricia Churchland reject propositional-attitude properties, but they nevertheless accept that there are experiential properties (regarding which they adopt a certain form of reductionism).[v] Moreover, although they deny that there is a propositional attitude of knowing, they hold that there is knowledge. Another radical view is that there is no consciousness whatsoever (and so, in particular, no conscious experiential properties); but among the few philosophers of mind who have held this view, most have accepted that there are at least nonconscious propositional-attitude properties.[vi] The fact is that it is difficult to think of any major philosopher today who is thoroughgoing eliminativist, who holds that there are absolutely no (instantiated) mental properties—no knowing, no experiencing, no consciousness.

Besides Reductive Materialism and Eliminative Materialism, there has been one further rallying point for materialists, namely, Supervenience. In the setting of the Mind-Body Problem, this is the thesis that, whether or not mental properties are identical to physical properties, they in any case supervene on them (if only as a brute fact). Approximately, and in slogan form, mental properties supervene on physical properties if and only if it is necessary that any two objects that are alike in their physical properties are also alike in their mental properties (i.e., it is necessary that any two objects that differ in their mental properties also differ in their physical properties). Since the Mind-Body problem concerns the metaphysics of mind, the relevant modality here is metaphysical necessity, not mere nomological necessity; when we speak of supervenience, we will *always* mean metaphysical supervenience. Naturally, there are other notions

---

iv A great many (perhaps most) functionalists adopt one or the other of these two weaker versions—for example, David Lewis, Frank Jackson, Sydney Shoemaker, Robert Cummins, and many others. (More recently, Shoemaker (2001) abandoned this version of functionalism in favor of a thoroughgoing nonreductive functionalism in the sense of Chapter 6 below.)

v See, e.g., Churchland (1979).   vi See, for example, Rey (1982).

of metaphysical supervenience besides the one just articulated in slogan form, some stronger and others weaker; and associated with each of these notions is a corresponding supervenience principle (more below).

We will say (relative to a chosen notion of metaphysical supervenience) that mental properties *logically supervene* on physical properties if they not only supervene on them but do so as a logical consequence of relevant definitions (including perhaps a posteriori scientific definitions).[vii] Logical Supervenience is the thesis that mental properties logically supervene on physical properties (relative to some chosen notion of supervenience). The appeal of Logical Supervenience is that (if correct) it guarantees that there is an *explanation* of why the underlying supervenience principle holds: it holds because it is a logical consequence of certain relevant definitions. For example, if Reductive Materialism is correct, mental properties will have reductive definitions that yield, as a logical consequence, a supervenience principle for each supervenience notion, regardless of strength. In this way, Reductive Materialism (if correct) provides explanations of why these supervenience principles hold. This, of course, is no surprise. But suppose that Reductive Materialism fails. This does not rule out the possibility of other instances of Logical Supervenience. For instance, Minimal Functionalism (discussed two paragraphs above) provides second-order definitions of mental properties that yield, as logical consequences, certain weak supervenience principles, for example, principles relativized to the actual world (more below); therefore, even though Minimal Functionalism is not a form of Reductive Materialism, it would (if correct) guarantee that there is an explanation of why these weak supervenience principles hold. And there are still further forms of logical supervenience.[viii] Suppose, however, that Minimal Functionalism is incorrect; and suppose, more generally, that all forms of Logical Supervenience fail. It would nevertheless be at least coherent to maintain Brute Metaphysical Supervenience (Brute Supervenience, for short): the thesis that not only do mental properties supervene on physical properties but they do so as a brute synthetic necessity (or as a consequence of brute synthetic necessities which are as much in need of explanation a this supervenience itself).[ix] Of course, Brute Supervenience comes at a price: supervenience would then be an

---

vii Thus, we do not use the term 'logically supervene' as a synonym of 'metaphysically supervene', as some people do.

viii For example, there might be supervenience principles that are logical consequences of (a) thoroughgoing nonreductive definitions of mental properties (in the sense of Chapter 6) plus (b) definitions of various meta-theoretic notions such as nomological necessity, causation, explanation, the notion of a realizer property, and even the notion of a property itself. (Shoemaker (2001) constructs an instance of this form of Logical Supervenience built around a novel definition of the notion of a realizer property.) But, in fact, almost all advocates of Logical Supervenience base their case on the kind of definitions provided either by Reductive Materialism or by Minimal Functionalism.

ix If there is some promising intermediate position between Logical and Brute Metaphysical Supervenience, we are not aware of it.

unexplainable mystery (this will be relevant to the issue of complexity in the next section).

As already indicated, for Reductive Materialists, Supervenience is just a trivial corollary of their view. Likewise, for Eliminative Materialists: Supervenience is a trivial corollary since it is vacuously true on their view. But for Nonreductive Materialists—that is, materialists who deny both Eliminative and Reductive Materialism (in most cases, these materialists are advocates of the sort of Logical Supervenience associated with Minimal Functionalism or they are advocates of Brute Supervenience)—Supervenience has some promise of filling a crucial gap in their materialism. For suppose some supervenience principle (or a cluster of supervenience principles) provides a sufficient condition for materialism. In this case, our Nonreductive Materialists would be in a position to give a characterization of materialism that does not require the truth of Eliminative Materialism or Reductive Materialism and so does not trivially exclude from the start their own form of materialism. The envisaged characterization may be put as follows: materialism is the doctrine that one of Eliminative Materialism, Reductive Materialism, or Supervenience Materialism holds. For this strategy to succeed, the requisite supervenience principle or principles must meet two requirements: (1) they must be strong enough to provide a sufficient condition for materialism, and (2) they must be weak enough to avoid easy refutation. In service of goal (1), some materialists have gone beyond 'intraworld' supervenience (i.e., the sort of principle articulated in slogan form two paragraphs above) and have proposed instead a stronger 'interworld' supervenience principle.[x] Others have gone beyond this and have proposed an outright entailment principle.[xi] The problem with both proposals is that they seem to threaten goal (2). That is, they appear open to possible counterexamples: for example, the metaphysical possibility of a disembodied being—a possibility that is accepted by many self-identified materialists (e.g., David Lewis, Frank Jackson, Jerry Fodor, and many others). To lessen the threat of such counterexamples, the most common strategy has been to propose certain weaker supervenience principles, namely, principles that are relativized to the actual-world. For example, Jackson has proposed the following principle: if a world is a minimal physical duplicate of the actual world, it is a duplicate of the actual world simpliciter and so, in particular, is a duplicate in all mental respects. (A minimal physical duplicate is a world that (a) duplicates all the actual physical facts and (b) contains nothing else beyond what it *must* contain in order to satisfy (a).) But, then, the worry is that these

---

[x] That is, for all possible worlds w and w', and any possible individuals x and x', if x in w and x' in w' are alike in their physical properties, they are alike in their mental properties.

[xi] For example, Kim once proposed the following strong entailment principle (but calling it 'strong supervenience'): for all mental properties M, necessarily, whatever has M has some physical property P such that, necessarily, whatever has P has M (i.e., P is such that P entails M). This principle implies that mental properties M can be defined as infinite disjunctions of such properties P. It does not imply, however, that mental relations can be defined this way (see note 25, Ch. 6).

principles might now run into trouble with goal (1): that is, they might be too weak to provide a sufficient condition for materialism and hence fail to provide the desired characterization of materialism.

There are good reasons to think that this strategy for characterizing materialism by resorting to the indicated actual-world relative supervenience principles does not succeed; in particular, there are reasons to think that such principles do not provide a sufficient condition for materialism. Here is one style of counterexample. The envisaged principles do not on their own rule out (i.e., they are consistent with) the existence of possible worlds (remote from ours) in which there are disembodied beings. For the same reason, these principles do not on their own rule out *your existing* in one of those remote worlds in a wholly disembodied state. Thus, these principles do not on their own rule out there being a difference between the modal properties possessed in the actual world by you and those possessed in the actual world by your body (after all, your body cannot exist in a wholly 'disembodied' state in any world); and this is all that is needed to establish a thesis of substance dualism. Since substance dualism is paradigmatically anti-materialist, none of these supervenience principles on its own provides a sufficient condition for materialism.[xii] This is just one style of counterexample; there are several others.

These considerations indicate that the suggested Supervenience approach faces an in principle problem. Our Nonreductive Materialists are committed to the falsity of Reductive Materialism; so, for them, there must be possible counterexamples to the biconditionals associated with the reductive definitions proposed by Reductive Materialists.[xiii] In the case of the Identity Theory, for example, there must be either a possible failure of the necessity condition (e.g., a disembodied being, in the extreme case) or a possible failure of the sufficiency condition (e.g., a zombie, in the extreme case); there are far less extreme possibilities that suffice for the same purpose. But once such possibilities are admitted, they may then serve as counterexamples to the strong supervenience principles described above, thus forcing our Nonreductive Materialists to adopt the proposed 'local' actual-world relative supervenience principles. In that context, however, the same possibilities may then be used (as they were in the preceding paragraph) to construct new, 'distant-world' counterexamples to the claim that the 'local' supervenience principles provide sufficient conditions for materialism.

---

xii Perhaps the conjunction of one of these weak supervenience principles and some additional kind of metaphysical principle would rule out such counterexamples, but then the additional principle would itself need to be incorporated into the envisaged sufficient condition. Supervenience alone does not do the job.

xiii For analogous reasons, an advocate of Brute Supervenience must deny the truth of Minimal Functionalism and, hence, is committed to the existence of possible counterexamples to that doctrine; these additional counterexamples will in turn lead to additional trouble for the supervenience principles that the advocate of Brute Supervenience may choose to invoke.

The situation is even worse for advocates of Brute Supervenience. Consider an analogy between this thesis and a broadly Moorean brute supervenience thesis about aesthetic properties. According to the latter thesis, aesthetic properties (being beautiful, elegant, etc.) do not reduce to physical properties (they are neither first-order nor second-order physical properties) and, more generally, they do not logically supervene on physical properties; instead, they brutely supervene on them. No one in Moore's day, however, would have said such a view is a form of materialism about aesthetic properties.[xiv] Quite the contrary, this brute supervenience thesis was universally considered an instance of anti-naturalism. But, according to virtually everyone—both in Moore's day and today—materialism is just a special case of naturalism. In view of this, it difficult to see what could justify counting the above wholly analogous Brute Supervenience thesis about mental properties as a form of materialism.

Taken together, these considerations cast doubt on the above strategy for building Supervenience into the account of what materialism is, thus lending support for the view that there is only one coherent notion of materialism, according to which materialism is the doctrine that either Eliminative Materialism or Reductive Materialism holds. We find this view quite compelling even if we are not ready to endorse it here. A number of contributors to this volume, however, do endorse this view. That said, most of the contributors to the volume are willing, at least for sake of argument, to count various supervenience theses as forms of materialism. The majority of these contributors believe, however, that there are convincing arguments against such supervenience theses; for this reason, they are simply much less concerned about whether such theses really should be counted as forms of materialism.

Thus, 'materialism' is used in two main ways in this volume, one stronger and one weaker. According to the stronger use, materialism is the doctrine that either Eliminative Materialism or Reductive Materialism holds. According to the weaker use, materialism is the doctrine that one of Eliminative Materialism, Reductive Materialism, or Supervenience Materialism holds.[xv] (The best policy for readers is to refer to the individual papers to understand how the author is using the term.)

One final terminological point. Among the philosophers of mind who reject Reductive Materialism, Eliminative Materialism, and Supervenience Materialism, many believe that the instantiation of mental properties is nevertheless determined by the instantiation of physical properties, where the hypothesized determination

---

xiv Terence Horgan gives a quite similar argument in this collection against counting Brute Supervenience as a form of materialism.

xv A certain number of people on the list given at the outset were included because they reject strong materialism (i.e., Eliminative and Reductive Materialism); they include van Fraassen, McDowell, Salmon, Williamson, Yablo, Almog, and Heck, among others. Some of these philosophers accept some form of metaphysical supervenience and, hence, accept weak materialism; others are agnostic on this question.

relation is a *contingent* relation—for example, a contingent causal or contingent nomological relation (in which case either the physical events would cause the mental events, or it would be nomologically necessary that, if the physical facts are such as they are, the mental facts would be as well). These views, however, are not positions in the metaphysics of mind; they are instead contingent scientific theories and as such are not versions of materialism, at least not on the primary use(s) of 'materialism' in traditional philosophy of mind. (Dualists from René Descartes to the present have held just such contingent-determination views of sensory experience, for example.) In any case, this is how we are using the term when we speak of the waning of materialism.

THE WANING OF MATERIALISM

Over the last fifty or so years, materialism has been challenged by a daunting list of arguments (some inspired by classical arguments from the history of philosophy and others, wholly new) beginning with the Chisholm-Geach-Putnam attack on Behaviorism and fortified by Kripke's attack on the Identity Theory, followed by a host of others: the multiple realizability argument, the disembodiment argument, the certainty argument, the zombie (or nonconscious automaton) argument, the absent qualia argument, the knowledge argument, the inverted spectrum argument, the argument from the special sciences, the explanatory gap argument, the anti-individualism argument, the self-consciousness argument, the mental causation argument, and many, many more. Taken together, these arguments and sophisticated variations on them constitute a significant prima facie threat to the success of materialism.

How does the list of problems facing anti-materialism stack up against the list of problems facing materialism? As far as we can see, there are only three main worries confronting anti-materialism.[xvi]

(1) *Complexity.* The first worry is that it lacks the ontological simplicity of Eliminative Materialism and Reductive Materialism (this of course is not so in the case of Nonreductive Materialism); for, other things being equal, a theory with

---

xvi In general, we use 'anti-materialism' to refer to the disjunction of a certain cluster of views incompatible with materialism: namely, dualism (property dualism or substance dualism); robust neutral monism (neither physical properties nor mental properties have metaphysical priority over the other); anti-reductionist versions of hylomorphism; anti-reductionist accounts of normativity; 'liberal naturalism' (as opposed to reductive naturalism); idealism (e.g., phenomenalism); epistemic stalemate (the materialism/anti-materialism debate ultimately ends in a draw); enigma (the Mind-Body Problem has no solution); various anti-realisms (including those that deny the legitimacy, or even the intelligibility, of the Mind-Body Problem). In the next few paragraphs, however, we will focus on property dualism, as if it is the view most representative of the views in this cluster, and we will use 'anti-materialism' as if it refers just to property dualism. The thought is that, if property dualism fares well with regard to the problems facing it, the disjunction of views in the cluster will fare well with regard to the problems facing it.

a simpler ontology is to be preferred to a theory with a less simple ontology. So are other things equal? Two preliminary points. First, at present a large number problems confront materialism; until it is known whether materialism is, or is not, able to solve these problems, no one will be able to give a determinate answer to our question. Second, suppose materialists in the end have no way to deal with their various problems besides appealing to some mystery tenet or tenets. Such principles, however, would as a matter of overall theoretical simplicity cancel out any gain provided materialism's greater ontological simplicity; so until the nature of materialism's solutions to its problems is known, no one will be able to give a determinate answer to our question of whether 'other things are equal.' It seems, therefore, that the best anyone can do today is to make a (provisional) case-by-case examination of the other problems facing the two positions. Are the two remaining problems facing anti-materialism as bad as (or worse than) the long list of problems facing materialism?

(2) *Psychophysical regularities.* It is sometimes thought that, if anti-materialism (property dualism, for example) were true, then the mental would be so different in nature from the physical that it would be impossible for them to be related to one another nomologically (lawfully), causally, or explanatorily; yet without positing some such relations anti-materialism would be unable to account for obvious psychophysical correlations. Here are two responses. First, physics (which is the scientific backdrop of materialism) admits lawful relationships among physical entities that are extraordinarily diverse in nature and, in turn, admits relations of causal influence and law-grounded explanation among these entities. Physics allows, moreover, that some of these lawful relationships are brute facts having no further explanation. If such relations are tolerated in physics, why not psychophysics?[xvii] Second, the alleged problem has little force in a neo-Humean intellectual context (which is the context within which physics has been operating successfully since the Seventeenth Century), wherein it is allowed that, for any regularity among contingent entities, it is metaphysically possible that the regularity be a *lawful* regularity. (Analogously, for causal and explanatory relations.) This principle, however, would allow anti-materialists to posit lawful psychophysical regularities, thus solving the problem.[xviii]

---

xvii The following, for example, might be among the psychophysical laws: all beings with mental properties have bodies (where it is understood that a being has a body only if there is a regular correlation between the being's mental properties and the body's physical properties).

xviii Suppose Reductive Materialism and Logical Supervenience are unable to surmount the problems confronting them. Then Brute Supervenience would be the only haven for materialists (assuming that this is a form of materialism). But absent a compelling argument or intuition, it is an affront to simplicity of theory to posit brute supervenience relations rather than brute nomological relations. The reason is that brute supervenience relations impose restrictions on modal space far exceeding what is needed for the explanatory tasks at hand; brute nomological relations do the job just fine while imposing far weaker restrictions on modal space. Absent compelling argument or intuition, brute supervenience relations are always extravagances lacking epistemic warrant.

(3) *Mental Causation.* Anti-materialism is alleged to be unable to accommodate the possibility of mental causation without violating the causal closure of the physical. But this is not at all clear when causal closure is formulated in its most plausible form, as follows: for every physical event e that has a cause, there is a physical event c such that it is nomologically (or causally) necessary that if c occurs, e occurs. Suppose that physics requires, and provides justification for, this weak causal closure principle. But obviously this weak principle does not imply the following stronger closure principle: for every physical event e that has a cause, there is a physical event c such that c is a sufficient *cause* of e.[xix] Failure to appreciate the distinction between weak causal closure and strong closure principles has led many philosophers to the conclusion that mental causation is untenable in an anti-materialist setting, whereas in fact there are very promising accounts of mental causation compatible with anti-materialism. For example, there is an account that is built around nonreductive functional definitions of mental properties which is compatible with both materialism and anti-materialism.[xx] There are also promising probabilistic accounts compatible with anti-materialism.[xxi]

There is also the so-called pairing problem, which arises in the context of substance dualism. The pairing problem may be put as a question: how, if substance dualism were correct, could there to be a determinate fact about which mental substances are paired with which bodies (i.e., which mental substances have which bodies).[xxii] Two points are in order. First, even if the pairing problem were a problem for substance dualism, it is simply not a problem for *property dualism* and so, therefore, is not a problem for anti-materialism generally. Second, the first account of mental causation mentioned in the previous paragraph is compatible with the denial of substance dualism, but it is also compatible with substance dualism and, in that setting, is able to provide a solution to the pairing problem. According to this solution, the network of causes identified by this account is sufficient to settle the question whether a given being has a body and if so which body it is. If this is correct, the pairing problem would turn out to be just a special case of the problem of mental causation rather than a further type of problem for anti-materialism.

How does mental causation look on the materialist side? If the Identity Theory were correct, accounting for mental causation would at least initially seem fairly straightforward. Things are not so clear, however, in the case of Behaviorism, Functionalism, and Brute Supervenience. It is possible that the accounts of mental

---

xix Nor does it imply the following still stronger closure principle (which is an immediate consequence of the conjunction of Kim's closure and exclusion principles; Kim (2005)): for every physical event e that has a cause, there is a physical event c that is the unique sufficient cause of e (except in genuine cases of overdetermination).

xx See Bealer (2007).   xxi One such account is Usher's (2006).

xxii See Kim (2001).

causation that seem to work well in the context of these forms of materialism are just those accounts that appear to be open to anti-materialists. If so, the problem of mental causation is at least a wash in the materialist/anti-materialist debate, if not a point in favor of the anti-materialist side.

Let us tally the results. Anti-materialism's greater ontological complexity would be a problem if other things were equal—that is, if the challenges facing anti-materialism were as serious as those facing materialism. But it is far from clear that other things are equal: arguably the problem posed by psychological regularities has little or no force, and the problem posed by mental causation is at worst a wash. This is how things stand on anti-materialism's side of the scorecard. But, as indicated above, on materialism's side we find an unusually long list of challenging problems. (Why is there this disparity? Presumably the short answer is that the very features that make anti-materialism ontologically more complex than materialism enable it to deal with the various phenomena that materialism finds difficult to accommodate.) The upshot is that, as things stand today, materialism is at least on the defensive. In this respect, materialism is on the wane.

This seems to be reflected in the attitudes of a many contemporary philosophers of mind. A growing number—among them prominent philosophers who once had strong materialist sympathies—have come to the conclusion that at least some of the arguments against materialism cannot be overcome.[xxiii] True, certain materialists believe that they already know how to answer all of the arguments against their position. But many materialists would acknowledge that the extant responses are at best inconclusive. Others admit that they do not yet know how to dispel all of the aforementioned worries, though they nevertheless remain convinced of the truth of materialism, taking it as an article of faith that at some point in the future they, or someone else, will find ways to do so. But such a conviction clearly does not rise to the standard of epistemic justification needed for theoretical knowledge. Still other philosophers, who initially had strong materialist sympathies (for example, Thomas Nagel (1986) and Colin McGinn (1999)), have seriously entertained the possibility that it might well be beyond the intellectual capacity of human beings to discover, and understand, answers to all of the arguments against materialism. Although it might be natural for a materialist who takes this possibility seriously to remain convinced of the truth of materialism, this conviction will have lost its epistemic standing; it certainly falls far short of theoretical knowledge. In any case, a great many materialists familiar with the arguments against materialism admit that these arguments constitute a genuine threat and that they need to be taken very seriously. In fact, a number of very prominent materialists acknowledge that the materialism/anti-materialism debate could well be a draw or at least that anti-materialism is a sensible position that they can see rational people believing. Here is William Lycan:

xxiii For example, Kim (2005)

Being a philosopher, of course I would like to think that my [materialist] stance is rational, held not just instinctively and scientistically and in the mainstream but because the arguments do indeed favor materialism over dualism. But I do not think that, though I used to. My position may be rational, broadly speaking, but not because the arguments favor it: Though the arguments for dualism do (indeed) fail, so do the arguments for materialism. And the standard objections to dualism are not very convincing; if one really manages to be a dualist in the first place, one should not be much impressed by them. My purpose [in this essay] is to hold my own feet to the fire and admit that I do not proportion my belief to the evidence.[xxiv]

And Jerry Fodor:

I think it's strictly true that we can't, as things stand now, so much as imagine the solution of the hard problem [of explaining consciousness]. . . . I would prefer that the hard problem should turn out to be unsolvable if the alternative is that we're all too dumb to solve it.[xxv]

These cracks in the ranks of materialists constitute another respect in which materialism is on the wane.

Given the fixity and asymmetry in the lists of respective problems, it is natural to predict that, among the major mature philosophers in the future, a significant portion (perhaps sometimes a majority) will reject materialism. Even among those who start out as materialists in their youth, a significant number are likely to end up doubting materialism's ultimate viability or suspecting that the materialism/anti-materialism debate is moot, and in either case recognizing that some versions of anti-materialism have rational credentials at least as good as materialism's. Thus, even though it is likely that in the future the ranks of materialists will continue to see new recruits, especially among newcomers to philosophy, the character of the problems facing materialism will continue to inspire very serious doubt. If this is the case, materialism will in one respect continue to wax; in another, it will continue to wane.

THE PAPERS

I. Consciousness

The first paper, 'Against Materialism' by Laurence BonJour, serves as an overview of the entire volume. BonJour argues that the positive case for materialism is quite weak. He argues, using a new version of Frank Jackson's 'knowledge argument,' that the most popular materialist explanation for consciousness, namely, functionalism, fails to provide an adequate account of the qualitative content of consciousness ('qualia'), and that materialist accounts of the intentionality of the

xxiv Lycan (2009), p. 551.   xxv Fodor (2007).

mental have also failed for similar reasons. BonJour concludes that some form of property dualism offers the best hope for an adequate philosophy of mind.

Adam Pautz argues, in 'Consciousness: A Simple Theory of Approach,' for *primitivism* about sensory consciousness: the thesis that the relation of sensory consciousness cannot be reduced to or constituted by physical or functional features. He does not rely on the usual a priori arguments, such as the knowledge argument, but instead upon certain philosophical claims about the structure of consciousness, together with empirically discovered facts about its physical basis in the brain. Pautz presupposes a broadly relationalist account of sensory consciousness, a category that includes sense-datum, disjunctivist and intentionalist accounts. Pautz refers to empirical evidence that our phenomenology is badly correlated with external properties that we might bear some causal relation (such as the 'optimal cause' relation) but strongly correlated with internal features of our neural processes. These facts give us good reason to believe in the possibility of 'coincidental variation': cases in which the individuals involved have different sensory experiences despite bearing the same causal relations to the same external properties. Pautz argues that the only possible explanation of such coincidental variation is primitivism. Finally, although Pautz admits that primitivism is consistent with the metaphysically necessary supervenience of the mental on the physical, he argues that the truth of primitivism would leave us without any good reason for positing such a brute metaphysical necessity.

Charles Siewert, in 'Saving Appearances: A Dilemma for Physicalists,' takes as his target 'ambitious physicalism': an approach that aims to provide an explanatory reduction of consciousness to a physical and functional base. Siewert uses a range of cases involving the phenomenon of 'blindsight' to argue for the reality of phenomenal appearances of such a kind that cannot be accounted for by the standard physicalist theories, whether eliminativist, functionalist, or representationalist. Siewert argues that the physicalist faces a dilemma: either denying the reality of phenomenal appearances by trying to identify those appearances with something manifest and describable in non-phenomenal terms, or facing an unavoidable arbitrariness in deciding which hidden features should be assigned metaphysically necessary and constitutive status with respect to conscious phenomena. Siewert argues that the cost of abandoning ambitious, reductive physicalism is not high, since we can still study the systematic relations between phenomenal appearances and physical conditions. The persistent failure to find an ultimate explanation of the real 'nature' of consciousness does not threaten the explanatory completeness of science.

In 'The Property Dualism Argument,' Stephen L. White argues that materialism cannot provide an explanation of the possibilities of a posteriori identities between phenomenal qualities and physical or functional properties that satisfies what he calls 'Frege's constraint.' Frege's constraint requires that we explain the possibility of a rational person's ascribing contradictory properties to a thing in terms of distinct 'modes of presentation,' in such a way that these modes can provide a rational justification of the person's beliefs, attitudes, and actions at a personal level. White argues that satisfying Frege's constraint requires our recognition of both representational and nonrepresentational modes of presentation. The latter must be properties that are instantiated in *the world as a person represents it to himself.* These properties must be so finely individuated that they are incapable of having any empirically discoverable real essence (they must be 'thin' properties), and the connection between such properties and the predicates that express them must be a priori, or else we would be unable to account for the rational justification of the person's beliefs in terms of how the world appears to him or her. To deny these constraints is to embrace what White calls 'local eliminativism' about mental contents, a position that he argues is no more defensible than the elimination of the mental tout court. Avoiding local eliminativism through accepting these Fregean constraints prevents the materialist from making good on the claim that we could discover an a posteriori identity between any mental property (such as pain) and any physical or functional property, without thereby positing *another*, higher-order mentalistic property, one needed to explain the possibility of rationally denying the identity. An infinite regress can, therefore, be avoided only if, at some level, a mentalistic property is instantiated that could not be identified a posteriori with any other property. White defends his argument against recent challenges by Richard Boyd and Brian Loar and distinguishes it from Jackson's knowledge argument and Levine's explanatory gap.

In 'Kripke's Argument against Materialism,' Eli Hirsch elucidates Saul Kripke's argument against the possibility of a posteriori identities between phenomenal and physical properties. As is well known, Kripke provided powerful arguments for thinking that all identity claims involving terms that pick out their referents essentially are necessarily true, if true at all. However, if claims of the identity of the properties of pain and of the firing of C-fibers are necessarily true, and if our use of 'pain' to refer to pain depends only on features of our epistemic situation, then necessarily anyone in our epistemic situation who believes this identity believes something that cannot be false. How, then, could the identity fail to be a priori? Moreover, how could we explain our resilient modal intuition that either one could occur in the absence of the other? Hirsch fills a lacuna in Kripke's argument: responding to the objection that, unlike 'pain', 'the firing of C-fibers' does not pick out its referent essentially. Hirsch argues that, unless we embrace an extreme version of structuralism about physical properties, we must acknowledge the possibility of constructing terms that pick out any relevant physical property essentially. In addition, Hirsch re-formulates the Kripkean argument in terms of supervenience (rather than identity), enabling him to replace the singular term 'C-fiber firing' with quantification over all physical properties.

In 'The Self-Consciousness Argument: Functionalism and the Corruption of Content,' George Bealer targets functionalism as the most cogent form of contemporary materialism. In particular, he takes aim at Reductive Functionalism and Minimal Functionalism: theories that attempt to specify the essences of mental, in a non-circular fashion, by means of properties functional definitions (i.e., by means of the Ramsification of causal theories of the mind). Bealer points out that functionalism must account for thoughts (such as introspective thoughts) that have psychological attitudes embedded within them. For example, John may attribute to himself the property of being in pain. When Ramsified, the resulting proposition asserts that John is in the R_1 relation to the proposition that he has the R_2 property (where R_1 and R_2 are the first-order physical properties that 'realize' thinking and being in pain). However, no one self-attributes by introspection the physical property R_2 (i.e., having firing C-fibers or whatever physical property R_2 is). Bealer effectively sets asides worries that the intensionality of the context of thought renders the argument invalid. He also draws attention to the devastating consequences of the other strategies for avoiding the dilemma, including language-of-thought functionalism. When the language-of-thought theorists attempt to define the content-of relation, they face a dilemma concerning the content of psychological predicates in the language. The language-of-thought theorist must either accept a definitional circularity incompatible with materialism, or resort again to Ramsified definitions that misdescribe the contents of self-conscious thoughts. In addition, such language-of-thought functionalism readily leads to epiphenomenalism. Finally, attempts to avoid the definitional circularity by means of something like a Tarskian hierarchy of distinct psychological attitudes founder on the type-free nature of introspection. Bealer concludes that the only viable functionalism is a non-reductive one that accepts mental properties as ontologically primary, on a par with physical properties.

II. The Unity and Identity of Persons

David Barnett, in 'On the Significance of Some Intuitions about the Mind,' defends the thesis that the simplicity (non-compositeness) of the mind is the best explanation for the fact that it is impossible for a pair of persons to constitute a single subject of experience. Barnett uses thought experiments to out the alternative explanations: an insufficient number of immediate parts, the wrong nature or structure, or some combination of these.

In 'Persons and the Unity of Consciousness,' William Hasker argues that the materialist cannot account for undeniable datum of conscious unity. Moreover, he shows that this datum is not defeated by careful consideration of such empirically based problem cases as commissurotomy or multiple personality syndrome. Hasker concludes that a form of emergent dualism is most consistent with both the datum of unity and the empirical facts about the problem cases.

In 'An Argument from Transtemporal Identity for Subject–Body Dualism,' Martine Nida-Rümelin argues that a subject of experience cannot be either identified with or constituted by the human body, on grounds that only the thesis of Subject–body dualism can explain the substantive difference between contrasting hypotheses about personal identity in duplication thought experiments. She argues that this substantive difference exists only when it is the transtemporal identity of self-conscious beings (in contrast to artifacts or associations) that is at stake. Nida-Rümelin contends that any form of materialism, including functionalism and four-dimensionalism, will be committed to what she calls 'the illusion theory' about personal identity: the theory that there is, despite appearances, no real fact of the matter about which ensuing individual, if any, continues the existence of the original person in the duplication cases, a theory fundamentally at variance with our self-conception as conscious beings.

III. Intentionality, Causation, Knowledge

In 'Burge's Dualism,' Bernard Kobes shows that Tyler Burge's anti-individualism about mental content leads to a form of 'dualism,' broadly conceived. Kobes argues that Burge's methodological stance, which relies on our actual explanatory practices and which rejects the presumption of physicalism, is defensible. Burge's anti-individualism, his claim that mental contents are individuated in terms of features of the individual's physical, social, and historical environment, undermines any type identity between mental representations and neurophysiological or localized functional states. Given the failure of localized supervenience, Kobes argues that the Burge thought-experiments provide strong grounds for rejecting even token identity claims about mental and physical events. Burge dismisses Kimian worries about mental causation, on the grounds that our scientific and commonsense knowledge of the efficacy of the mental is more secure than any metaphysical argument to the contrary. According to Kobes, Burge effectively challenges weaker versions of materialism, such as the claim that mental events are constituted by physical events, on the grounds that our concepts of composition lack any clear application to events and similar entities. Kobes closes by defending Burge's position against a number of objections and challenges.

In 'Modest Dualism,' Tyler Burge begins by stating and defending his argument against the token identity of physical (neural) and mental events, based upon the dependency of mental content on distal causes. Burge then turns to the weaker formulation of materialism given by Kobes: the thesis that mental events are composed or constituted by physical events. Burge argues that such a thesis of the material composition of the mental finds little support from common sense or empirical psychology, especially where propositional thought and consciousness are concerned. In contrast to Kobes, Burge does not think that the compositional model can be rejected simply on the grounds that psychological kinds cannot be demarcated on the basis of physical patterns alone, since the same thing is true of biological kinds, for which a material composition model seems secure. Burge agrees, however, with Kobes in thinking that the issue diachronic causation is critical: in particular, can the mental and neural kinds be 'correlated in a manner familiar from sciences that make use of causal aspects of material components to illumine causal aspects of higher-level composed kinds?' Burge insists that psycho-physics provides us with no such causation-illuminating correlations. In the case of propositional thought, with its essential connections to the norms of reason, the prospects of the discovery of such explanatory connections are especially bleak.

Neal Judisch, in 'Descartes' Revenge Part II: The Supervenience Argument Strikes Back,' argues that Jaegwon Kim's argument, which purports to show that nonreductive materialism cannot account for mental causation (on the hypothesis of the causal 'closure' or sufficiency of the physical), can in fact be turned against Kim's own position (reductive functionalism). Kim's argument entails that a theory of mind preserves the possibility of mental causation only if, on that theory, mental properties (i) multiply realizable, (ii) have instances that are efficacious in virtue of being instances of those mental properties, and yet (iii) are physically reducible. Judisch argues that these three constraints are mutually inconsistent. Thus, Kim's argument actually supports the *incompatibility* of mental causation with the assumption of the causal sufficiency of the physical realm.

Timothy O'Connor and John Ross Churchill, relying on a causal-powers metaphysics of properties, defend Kim's argument for the incompatibility of mental causation and non-reductive materialism in 'Nonreductive Materialism or Emergent Dualism? The Argument from Mental Causation.' After critically reviewing proposals by Shoemaker and Gillett, they develop and defend their own version of emergent dualism.

In 'Epistemological Objections to Materialism,' Robert Koons argues that materialism is vulnerable to two kinds of epistemological objections: transcendental arguments, that show that materialism is incompatible with the very possibility of knowledge, and defeater arguments, that show that belief in materialism provides an effective defeaters to claims to knowledge. Koons constructs objections of these two kinds in three areas of epistemology: our knowledge of the laws of nature (and of scientific essences), our knowledge of the ontology of material objects, and mathematical and logical knowledge. Koons concludes that these epistemological weaknesses place the materialist in a dialectically weak position in respect of ontological identity claims, since the materialist cannot know the causal powers or persistence conditions of material objects. Finally, Koons argues that the materialist can provide no non-circular account of epistemic normativity. Anti-realist accounts of normativity are unavailable because normativity is already implicated in all intentionality. Moreover, Koons argues that materialists face a fatal dilemma in attempting to carry out an etiological reduction of teleological norms, since neither Humean nor anti-Humean accounts of causation yield defensible results.

IV. Alternatives to Materialism

The distinction between this section and the preceding three is not hard and fast: the chapters in the final section do contain arguments (some involving appeals to phenomenal consciousness, personal identity, and mental causation) in support of their favored alternatives. However, none of them is purely negative or critical: each puts forward and defends a specific alternative.

Terry Horgan, surveying the current state of the philosophy of mind in 'Materialism, Minimal Emergentism, and the Hard Problem of Consciousness,' argues that the position of minimal emergentism is one that must be taken seriously. Horgan defines materialism as a position ruling out both metaphysical and nomological 'danglers': the instantiation of properties and relations over and above those involved in the instantiation of fundamental, physical properties, and relations. The minimal emergentist accepts the nomological closure of the physical realm and posits no fundamental, non-physical properties. Minimal emergentism comes in two forms: nomological and Moorean, depending on whether the necessity involved in the supervenience of the mental on the physical is physical or metaphysical necessity. Horgan argues that there are two enduring problems for materialism: the irreducibility of phenomenal qualia, and the explanatory gap between the mental and the physical. The existence of the explanatory gap between functional and qualitative properties provides grounds for a good abductive argument for the existence of zombies and phenomenal inverts, contrary to materialism. In addition, Horgan argues that the 'new wave materialism' of Hill, Loar, and McLaughlin, which provides a novel account of directly referential 'phenomenal concepts,' offers no solution to these problems, since it cannot account coherently for the uniquely self-presenting character of phenomenal qualia. Horgan also argues the problem of phenomenal qualia is much broader than is often acknowledged, affecting the viability of materialists' accounts of intentionality and agency no less than their accounts of sensation. Finally, Horgan suggests that the fact of mental causation provides no argument for materialism, even given the nomological closure of the physical realm, since minimal emergentists can legitimately make use of the very same, suitably weakened notion of 'causal efficacy' that the materialist must use in allowing for the efficacy of mental properties (given the fact of multiple realizability).

In 'Dualistic Materialism,' Joseph Almog defends a position that is both dualistic (recognizing the distinctness and the difference in nature between mental and physical events) and materialistic (in the sense of positing a natural or essential *connection* between the two types of phenomena). Almog insists that our common sense (or 'marketplace') view embraces both a duality and a necessary connection intuition, unlike either substance dualism or philosophical materialism. On Almog's view, there can be (contra Hume) necessary connections between distinct existences, whenever the distinct existences have *correlative* or *coordinated* natures. Almog provides examples from mathematics of correlated natures linking distinct numbers or sets to one another, or sets to non-sets (such as singleton sets and their members). The correlated natures of biological species and their individual members provide another example. Almog argues that, since there is only one cosmos, the nature of each type and token must be correlated with that of the generative process responsible for its coming into being, providing just the sort of necessary connection between mental and physical phenomena required by common sense.

Michael Jubien, in 'Dualizing Materialism,' offers a novel, ontological argument against token-token identity claims involving mental and physical states and events. Jubien defends a Kimian object-property-time conception of the identity conditions of events and states. Jubien proposes that intentional properties, such as the property of *thinking about the moon*, are complex properties—properties that contain other properties (the relation of *thinking about* and the property of *being the moon*) as literal parts. Jubien concludes by arguing that there is no reason not to expect to find psychophysical causal laws.

In 'Varieties of Naturalism,' Mario De Caro focuses his attention on what he calls 'scientific naturalism,' the thesis that science and science alone should dictate the terms of our ontology (including what particulars, properties, events, and processes there are). De Caro defends an alternative, 'liberal' naturalism, that insists (with John McDowell) that there is a 'space of reasons' that cannot be understood exhaustively in scientific terms. In contrast to De Caro, Angus J. L. Menuge advocates the rejection of any kind of naturalism, even at the level of scientific methodology, in 'Against Methodological Materialism.' Menuge concedes that science must deal with proximate, and not metaphysically ultimate, causes. Consequently, appeals to supernatural agency (such as divine fiat) would be inappropriate. However, recognizing this limitation does not exclude the positing of irreducibly teleological causes *within* nature, as in Aristotle's biology. Menuge appeals to the question of the possible functional role of 'junk DNA' as an example of the methodological fruitfulness of a teleological stance within science.

Uwe Meixner offers a version of Cartesian dualism that draws on the resources of a Husserlian account of intentionality. For example, Meixner argues that I can locate myself at the point in space from which I am looking at the world (my 'center of perspective'), and Meixner relies on empirical phenomenology to show that this location that does not correspond to my body or any part of it. Finally, Meixner argues that the self's endurance through time calls for explanation in terms of patterns of psychophysical causation or interaction.

Brian Leftow adumbrates a Thomistic theory of mind/body relation in 'Soul, Mind, and Brain.' He defends the Thomistic theory from the familiar charge of inconsistency, showing how it is possible to assert simultaneously that the human being is a single, unitary substance, that the soul is the 'form' of the human body, and yet that the soul can exist without the body, by virtue of being an immaterial particular. As Leftow explains, Aquinas's view of the embodied souls avoids being *dualistic* by denying that the human body is a separable substance in its own right. What combines with the soul to produce a substantial human thing is not one thing but a plurality. Moreover, Leftow explains that Aquinas's claim that human thought has no bodily 'organ' does not entail the natural independence of our cognitive functions from the physical condition of the brain. It does, however, imply that mental content cannot be *fully and determinately* encoded in the brain's physical condition.

In 'Substance Dualism: A Non-Cartesian Approach,' E. J. Lowe defends a dualism, not of minds and bodies, but of persons (or subjects of experience) and merely physical objects. Unlike Descartes, Lowe supposes that persons have both mental and physical properties. Lowe takes the central argument for substance dualism to be the difference in identity or persistence conditions between persons and their bodies. Neither the body as a whole, nor any part of it, is a plausible candidate for an entity with the persistence conditions of a person. Lowe concludes his essay with considerations that undermine the case for the causal closure of the physical.

RECURRING THEMES

1. The Primitiveness of Consciousness

Several recurring themes run through more than one chapter. One such theme is the existence of an irreducible and 'primitive' consciousness relation. BonJour, Pautz, Siewert, Hirsch, White, Horgan, and Jubien all provide reasons, based on the self-presenting character of phenomenal qualities within consciousness. BonJour, Horgan, and Jubien all argue that this argument can be extended to cover all intentionality. In his critique of functionalism, Bealer defends an analogous thesis concerning self-conscious intentional states—being conscious of one's own conscious intentional states.

2. The Ontology of the Human Person/Body

In the second recurring theme, several authors charge materialism with having inadequate resources for an adequate ontology of the human being or the human body. Ontology must account both for the synchronic composition of a single whole by the numerous parts of the human body, and the diachronic unity of the body over time. Barnett and Hasker focus on the synchronic problem, with both providing a priori arguments for the ontological unity of the person, while Hasker defends this conclusion against empirical challenge. Nida-Rümelin,

Leftow, and Lowe all argue that the diachronic identity conditions for conscious persons are incompatible with materialism, and Koons argues that materialism undermines the necessary conditions for human knowledge of the ontology of material things, putting materialists in a dialectically weak position from which to argue for mind/body identity.

3. Psychophysical Causation

The possibility of psychophysical causation is a theme that runs through much of the volume, unsurprisingly, since accounting for mind/body interaction has been a perennial problem for every kind of dualism. The views expressed by contributors fall into a spectrum of positions, depending on how far each is willing to depart from the principles of the causal closure and nomological completeness of the physical, At one end, Terence Horgan defends a position of metaphysically necessary supervenience of the mental on the physical, and he argues that such a position can accommodate mental causation in a somewhat attenuated form, but a form no more qualified than that which physicalists must settle for. E. J. Lowe's position would seem to be similar, except that he requires only nomological connections between physical and psychological properties. Lowe offers a counterfactual account of causation and argues that, at least in an indeterministic universe, psychological properties could figure in fact-causal (if not event-causal) relations to physical facts.

Tyler Burge's view is also similar to Horgan's, in that Burge is favorably disposed to the global supervenience of the mental on the physical, and he is confident that mental causation is compatible with 'gapless' chains of physical causation. He and Bernard Kobes see no serious threat of overdetermination looming, since purely physical and psychophysical causal explanations occur at different 'levels,' with mental and physical events being individuated in radically different ways.

At the other extreme, several contributors express doubts about the secure status of the supposed principles of causal closure and nomological completeness (even in their weakest forms). Laurence BonJour, for example, argues that the inductive argument from the apparent nomological completeness of physics for observations made on inanimate and unconscious things provides little support for the extrapolation of this principle to conscious things. William Hasker, Timothy O'Connor and John Ross Churchill, Michael Jubien, and Uwe Meixner explicitly endorse the search for novel causal laws of consciousness as an emergent phenomenon, and Angus Menuge argues that the actual practice of biology (as opposed to the official, materialist gloss on that practice) relies on the positing of non-physical teleological causes. These emergentists find the attenuated sort of mental causation endorsed by Horgan subject to the charge of type epiphenomenalism that has been lodged against Davidson's anomalous token-identity theory.

The broadly Aristotelian conception of causation in evidence in the causal powers metaphysics of O'Connor and Churchill and in the Thomistic metaphysics of Brian Leftow points to another sort of solution. This solution would also be available to those who place the ontological simplicity of the person at the center of their anti-materialist strategy (such as Hasker, Barnett or Lowe). When physical particles come to compose a person (or other organism), many (if not all) of the ordinary physical powers of those particles are absorbed by the whole. The particles no longer exercise in every case their own, autonomous causal powers: instead, the action and interaction of the particles in some cases is a result of the organism exercising its causal powers (with the particles serving only as instruments or occasions of causation). The interactions within the living body are, therefore, no longer really *governed* in all cases by the ordinary laws of physics, although they might in fact continue to *conform to* those laws. Mental properties of the whole person contribute their own, distinctive causal powers, even if the resulting behavior of the incorporated particles is empirically indistinguishable from the behavior of autonomous particles (in inanimate matter). The Aristotelian could thus embrace a principle of the 'quasi-completeness' of physical law, in the sense that each collection of particles behaves *as if* it were governed exclusively by ordinary physical laws, even though the causal powers that are in fact exercised are holistic, non-physical powers of the whole person.

I

ARGUMENTS
FROM CONSCIOUSNESS

1

Against Materialism

Laurence BonJour

Recent philosophy of mind has been dominated by materialist (or physicalist) views: views that hold that mental states are entirely material or physical in nature, and correlatively that a complete account of the world, one that leaves nothing out, can be given in entirely materialist terms.[1] Though (as the title of this volume suggests) this may be changing to some extent, philosophers of mind who are willing to take seriously the possibility that materialism might be false are still quite rare.

I have always found this situation extremely puzzling. As far as I can see, materialism is a view that has no very compelling argument in its favor and that is confronted with very powerful objections to which nothing even approaching an adequate response has been offered. The central objection, elaborated in various ways below, is that the main materialist view, quite possibly the only serious materialist view, offers no account at all of *consciousness* and seems incapable in principle of doing so. But consciousness, as Nagel pointed out long ago,[2] is the central feature of mental states—or at the very least a feature central enough to make a view that cannot account for it plainly inadequate.

Supposing, as I will try to show below, that this assessment is correct, why have materialist views been so dominant? Part of the answer is that it is far from clear that dualist views, at least those that go much beyond the bare denial of materialism, are in any better shape (see the last section of this chapter for some elaboration of this). But it must be insisted that the inadequacies of dualism do not in themselves constitute a strong case for

---

[1] Admittedly, the rather stark simplicity of this formulation is not to everyone's taste. There are those who prefer a formulation in terms of the *supervenience* of the mental on the physical, and some (one variant of the recently popular view known as 'non-reductive materialism') who want to interpret such a formulation in a way that gives the mental some sort of ontological independence. (For a recent discussion, see Antony (2007). I have no space here to sort out the twistings and turnings of that discussion and will simply assume that any genuine ontological independence of the mental would amount to a kind of epiphenomenalism (see further below) rather than genuine materialism, and thus that a genuine materialism must be committed to the formulation in the text.

[2] In his classic 1974 paper 'What Is It Like to Be a Bat?' *Philosophical Review* 83:435–50.

materialism: arguments by elimination are always dubious in philosophy, and
never more so than here, where the central phenomenon in question (that
is, consciousness) is arguably something of which we still have little if any
real understanding. Instead, materialism seems to be one of those unfortunate
intellectual bandwagons to which philosophy, along with many other disciplines, is so susceptible—on a par with logical behaviorism, phenomenalism,
the insistence that all philosophical issues pertain to language, and so many
other views that were once widely held and now seem merely foolish. Such a
comparison is misleading in one important respect, however: it understates the
fervency with which materialist views are often held. In this respect, materialism often more closely resembles a religious conviction—and indeed, as I
will suggest further in a couple of places below, defenses of materialism and
especially replies to objections often have a distinctively scholastic or theological
flavor.

In what follows, I will try to substantiate this indictment of materialism by
doing the following things. First, I will look at some of the main considerations
that are advanced in favor of materialism in general, as opposed to particular
materialist views, attempting to show that these are surprisingly insubstantial and
rest mainly on assumptions for which no real defense is offered. Second, I will
look at the overwhelmingly dominant materialist view, namely functionalism,
arguing that it is deeply inadequate in relation to the problem of consciousness.
Third, I will look at what is widely regarded as the most serious specific
problem for materialism in general and functionalism in particular, namely
the problem of qualitative content or qualia, focusing here on a somewhat
modified version of Frank Jackson's well-known "knowledge argument" and
trying to show that the objection to materialism that results is still extremely
compelling. Fourth, I will look at a problem that functionalism is claimed
to handle more successfully, the problem of intentional states, arguing that
there are clear cases of *conscious* intentional states which materialism in general
and functionalism in particular can handle no better than qualia—and for
essentially the same reasons. Fifth, and last, I will ask what lessons, if any, for
a more adequate account of conscious mental states can be derived from all
of this.

1. THE CASE FOR MATERIALISM

One of the oddest things about discussions of materialism is the way in
which the conviction that *some* materialist view must be correct seems to
float free of the defense of any particular materialist view. It is very easy to
find people who seem to be saying that while there are admittedly serious
problems with all of the specific materialist views, it is still reasonable to pre-
sume that *some* materialist view must be correct, even if we don't know yet

which one, or that the seeming force of the objections to particular mater-ialist views must be balanced against the strength of the underlying case for materialism. But why is this supposed to be a reasonable stance to take? What arguments or reasons or otherwise compelling intellectual considerations are there that could yield a strong background presumption of this sort in favor of materialism (or create a substantial burden of proof for opponents of materialism)?

There are, of course, arguments *against* particular versions of dualism, mainly against the interactionist version of Cartesian substance dualism. For reasons already mentioned, I will set these aside as not constituting in themselves an argument *for* materialism. There is also the inductive generalization from the conspicuous success of materialist science in a wide variety of other areas. This undeniably has some modest weight, but seems obviously very far from being enough to justify the strong presumption in question. Inductions are always questionable when the conclusion extends to cases that are significantly different from the ones to which the evidence pertains, and even most materialists will concede that conscious phenomena are among the most difficult—indeed, seemingly the most difficult of all—for materialist views to handle. Thus the fact that materialism has been successful in many other areas does not yield a very strong case that it will succeed in the specific area that we are concerned with.

Beyond this, there seem to be only two related sorts of grounds that are offered for a strongly pro-materialist presumption, both of which are quite flimsy, when subjected to any real scrutiny.

1.1. The 'Principle' of Causal Closure

The first and clearer of these two grounds appeals to the thesis that the material universe is *causally closed*: that material things are never causally affected by anything non-material (so that, as it is often put, physical science can in principle give a completely adequate explanation of any physical occurrence, without needing to mention anything non-physical). This thesis is commonly referred to as a "principle," a characterization that leaves its status rather obscure. (Philosophers often seem to describe something as a "principle" when they are inviting their readers to accept it as a basis for further argument, even though no clear defense of it has been offered.)

The closure principle does not by itself entail that materialism is true. It leaves open both the possibility of non-material realms that are causally isolated from the material world and also the possibility that epiphenomenalism is true: that conscious phenomena are side-effects of material processes that are incapable of having any reciprocal influence on the material world. But, assuming that the non-material realm in the first possibility is supposed to be the locus of conscious phenomena, both of these possibilities are extremely unpalatable, even paradoxical, in essentially the same way. The main problem is not, as is often suggested, that they are incompatible with the general common sense intuition that conscious states causally affect bodily behavior. A more specific and serious problem is that if either of these possibilities holds, then it becomes difficult or seemingly impossible to see how verbal discussions of conscious phenomena—such as this chapter and many others—can be genuinely about them in the way that they seem obviously to be. How can people be talking about conscious states or saying anything significant about them if completely adequate causal explanations of their verbal behavior can be given that make no reference to such states? Even without invoking any specific version of the causal theory of reference, it is hard to see why verbal discussions that are entirely unaffected by what they purport to be about should be taken seriously. Thus while a number of philosophers have in recent times been seemingly tempted by epiphenomenalism, it appears that they can have been genuinely advocating such a view about conscious states only if the view itself is false.[3]

For these reasons, the argument from the principle of causal closure to the truth of materialism is quite strong, even if not fully conclusive. But why is the principle of causal closure itself supposed to be so obviously correct? Clearly this 'principle' is not and could not be an empirical result: no empirical investigation that is at all feasible (practically or morally) could ever establish that human bodies, the most likely locus of such external influence, are in fact never affected, even in small and subtle ways, by non-material causes. We are told that scientists accept this principle, and often that most philosophers accept it as well. But do they have any compelling reasons for such acceptance? Or is this vaunted principle nothing more than an unargued and undefended assumption—a kind of intellectual prejudice, in the literal meaning of the word?

Taken in the abstract, apart from any appeal to a specific account of conscious mental phenomena, I have no idea whether the principle of causal closure is true or not. More importantly, I cannot imagine how to rationally decide whether it is true without *first* arriving at a defensible account of conscious mental states. It seems utterly obvious that mental states do causally affect the material realm: probably by causally affecting the actions of human bodies in general, but (as just argued) at least more narrowly by causally affecting verbal discussions of these matters. *If* a materialist account of conscious states is correct, then the principle of causal closure seems likely to be true. But if no such account is correct, then the principle is almost certainly false. Thus to argue for the truth of materialism or for a strong presumption in favor of materialism by appeal to the principle of causal closure is putting the cart in quite a flagrant way before the horse.

---

[3] This problem seems to be the main reason for Jackson's abandonment of his previous anti-materialist stance. (Jackson never took seriously the possibility that the non-material qualia for which he was arguing might causally affect the material world.)

1.2. The Appeal to 'Naturalism'

A second sort of defense of a general presumption in favor of materialism appeals to the general idea of *naturalism*. Here again we have a view, like materialism itself, to which many, many philosophers pay allegiance while offering little by way of clear argument or defense, but here the view itself is much harder to pin down in a precise way. Indeed, even more striking than the absence of any very clear arguments is the fact that many recent philosophers seem so eager to commit themselves to naturalism—to fly the naturalist flag, as it were—while showing little agreement as to what exactly such a commitment involves. Thus naturalism seems to be even more obviously an intellectual bandwagon than materialism. (In addition, naturalism, for some of those who use the term, seems to just amount to materialism, which would make an argument from naturalism to materialism entirely question-begging.)

Is there any genuine support for a materialist presumption to be found in the vicinity of naturalism? One version of naturalism is the idea that metaphysical issues—or philosophical issues generally—should be dealt with through the use of the methods of natural science. If this is accepted, and if it is true that following the methods of natural science leads plausibly to an endorsement of materialism, then at least some presumption in favor of materialism might follow. But both of the needed suppositions are in fact extremely dubious, to say the least. There is simply no good reason to think that the methods of natural science exhaust the methods of reasonable inquiry—indeed, as has often been pointed out, there is no plausible way in which that claim itself can be arrived at using those methods. Nor is there any very clear reason to think that applying the methods of natural science to the question of whether materialism is true, assuming that one could figure out some reasonably clear way to do that, would lead to the conclusion that materialism is correct. Such a conclusion is obviously not within the purview of physics, but it is also not within the purview of psychology, especially as currently practiced. As was true with closure, there is no doubt that many (but not all) natural scientists *assume* the truth of materialism, but the question is whether they have any good reason for such an assumption—a reason that would itself have to transcend their strictly scientific claims and competence.[4]

Thus, while the murkiness of the discussions of naturalism makes it harder to be sure, naturalism, like closure, does not seem to yield an independently defensible presumption in favor of the truth of materialism. If there is any better

---

[4] Lurking here is the difficult issue of what sorts of entities or properties count as material or physical. Is there any good way to delimit the realm of the material that does not preclude further discoveries in physics, but also does not trivialize the category by allowing it to include anything that people in departments labeled "Physics" might eventually come to study? This is anything but a trivial problem, but I have no space here to pursue it further.

reason or basis for such a presumption that is prior to and independent of the defense of some particular materialist view, I have no idea what it might be.

2. FUNCTIONALISM AND CONSCIOUSNESS

The upshot of the previous section is that the case for materialism must rest almost entirely on the defense of particular materialist views and not to any substantial extent on any background presumption. So what materialist views are there? The answer, I think, is that once both logical behaviorism and various versions of eliminativism are set aside as too implausible to be taken seriously—something that I will assume here without any further discussion—there is only *one* main materialist view, namely functionalism, with no very serious prospect that any others will emerge. And the fundamental problem for materialism, I will suggest, is that functionalism offers no account at all of consciousness and seems in principle unable to do so.

What gives rise to the mind–body problem in the first place and poses the essential problem that any adequate version of materialism must solve is the fact that conscious mental states, as we are aware of them, do not present a material appearance—do not seem as we experience them to be material in their makeup in any apparent way. Thus a view which holds that everything that exists is material must either (a) deny the very existence of such states, as eliminativism does, or else (b) explain how states and correlative properties that do not initially seem to be material in nature can nevertheless turn out to be so. A view that takes the latter alternative must give an account of the nature of such states and properties that both accurately reflects their character as experienced and explains how they can nonetheless be entirely material in their makeup. And this, I suggest, is something that has never been successfully done.

The starting point for modern versions of materialism was the central-state identity theory, particularly the version advocated in a famous paper by J. J. C. Smart (1959). Smart recognized that the truth of materialism can only be an empirical discovery, not something knowable a priori. For this to be so, he argued, the various mental states in question must be conceived in a *topic-neutral* way: a way that makes it *possible* for them to be merely material in character, without implausibly *requiring* that this be so. Only in relation to such a conception would it be possible to discover empirically that such a state is in fact a neurophysiological state of some kind.

But for this to work, it is crucially important that the topic-neutral conception in question be adequate to capture the essential features of mental states—something about which Smart was less clear than he might have been. For only if this is so will it be the case that showing that the conception offered can be realized by a material state can establish that mental states might in fact be merely material states, thereby allowing the rest of the argument to proceed on grounds of simplicity, as Smart suggests. Whereas if the proposed topic-neutral conception leaves out essential features of mental states—such as consciousness—then the fact that material states can satisfy that conception will be insufficient to explain how mental states might just be material states. (Smart's own attempt at a topic-neutral characterization fails to distinguish conscious mental states from whatever else might be "going on" in the person under a particular set of circumstances.)

As in Smart's view, functionalism in effect attempts to offer a topic-neutral characterization of mental states, one which will allow but not require that they be essentially material in character.[5] The more general functionalist characterization is in terms of *causal role*: a mental state is characterized by its causal relations to sensory inputs, behavioral outputs, and other mental states of the same sort. The functionalist then proceeds to argue that the states thus characterized could perfectly well be material states, even though the functional characterization does not require this. A further, widely discussed, aspect of the view is that different material states could satisfy the functionalist characterization of a particular mental state in different sorts of creatures or even in the same creature at different times, so that (on the most standard version) a material state *realizes* a functionally characterized state but is not strictly *identical* with it.

But the deepest problem for the functionalist is that the characterization of mental states in terms of causal role says *nothing at all* about consciousness or conscious character. There is no apparent reason why a state that realizes a particular causal role would thereby need to have any specific sort of conscious character (the point made by the familiar reversed spectrum cases)—or indeed any conscious character at all. Thus to point out that a physical state could realize such a causal role really does *nothing at all* to explain how a conscious state could be (or be realized by) a merely physical state. In this way, functionalism fails utterly to offer any explanation or account of the most important and conspicuous feature of mental states—or, at the very least, of a very important and conspicuous feature.

It may seem hard to believe that a view that has been held by so many people for so long can be so easily shown to be inadequate in a fundamental way, but I think that this is nonetheless so. The only solution would be

---

[5] This way of looking at functionalism is explicit in David Lewis's discussion of one of the earliest versions of the view in his 1966 paper 'An Argument for the Identity Theory,' *Journal of Philosophy* 63: 17–25, see p. 20.

to offer some supplementary account of what material features give rise to conscious experience. But I know of no such account, at least none with any real plausibility.[6]

This difficulty with materialism in general and functionalism in particular has of course occasionally been recognized.[7] But it still seems to have had remarkably little impact on the widespread acceptance of materialist views. I have no very good explanation to offer of this, though part of the reason is perhaps the prevailing tendency to approach the philosophy of mind from a third-person, neo-behaviorist perspective, in which consciousness is largely or entirely ignored. (But on this issue, it is hard to distinguish the chickens from the eggs.)

My basic case against materialism is complete at this point: there is no good reason for any strong presumption in favor of materialism; and the main materialist view fails to offer any real explanation of a central aspect of mental states, namely their conscious character, meaning that there is no good reason to think that it is correct as an account of such states. But though this very simple argument seems to me entirely compelling, I will elaborate it further in the next two sections by focusing on the two main specific kinds of mental states. The version of the argument that applies to states with qualitative content is very familiar, even though I think that its full force has still not been generally appreciated. In contrast, the application of essentially the same basic argument to conscious states with intentional content has received far less attention.

3. THE PROBLEM OF QUALITATIVE CONSCIOUSNESS: MARY REDUX

Though functionalism fails to adequately account for consciousness of any sort, perhaps the most conspicuous aspect of this failure pertains to qualitative content: the sort of content involved in experiences of color and sound, and of things like pains and itches. This point has been made in many ways, but the most straightforward and compelling in my view is still the so-called "knowledge argument," initially suggested by Thomas Nagel in relation to the experiences of bats and later developed by Frank Jackson using his famous example of black-and-white Mary, on which I will mainly focus here. (As most will know,

---

[6] One possibility is the so-called higher order thought theory, which holds that consciousness arises when one mental state is the object of a second, higher order mental state. I have no room here to consider this view in detail. But the basic—and obvious—problem with such a view is that there is no reason why there could not be a hierarchy of sort, even one with many more levels, in which there was no consciousness involved at all. (For some elaboration, see my contribution to BonJour and Sosa (2003), pp. 65–8.)

[7] See, for example, Colin McGinn (1989); David Chalmers (1995); and David Chalmers (1996).

Jackson has changed his mind about this argument and now rejects it, though his reasons seem to me unpersuasive.)

I will assume here that Jackson's original version of the saga of Mary is familiar enough to require only a brief summation. Mary is a brilliant neurophysiologist, who lives her entire life, acquires her education, and does all of her scientific work in a black-and-white environment, using black-and-white books and black-and-white television for all of her learning and research. In this way, we may suppose, she comes to have a complete knowledge of all the physical facts in neurophysiology and related fields, together with their deductive consequences, insofar as these are relevant—thus arriving at as complete an understanding of human functioning as those sciences can provide. In particular, Mary knows the functional roles of all of the various neurophysiological states, including those pertaining to visual perception, by knowing their causal relations to sensory inputs, behavioral outputs, and other such states. But despite all of this knowledge, Mary apparently does not know all that there is to know about human mental states: for when she is released from her black-and-white environment and allowed to view the world normally, she will, by viewing objects like ripe tomatoes, learn what it is like to see something red, and analogous things about other qualitative experiences. 'But then,' comments Jackson, 'it is inescapable that her previous knowledge was incomplete. But she had all the physical information. Ergo there is more to have than that, and Physicalism is false.'[8]

Despite the initial force of this rather simple argument, materialists have not been persuaded, and the literature comprising materialist responses to the Mary example is very large.[9] One thing to say about these responses is that few if any of them are even claimed to have any substantial independent plausibility; instead they are put forward in a way that takes for granted the sort of general presumption in favor of materialism and correlative burden of proof for anti-materialist views that I have argued does not genuinely exist. A full discussion of these responses is impossible here, but there are some main themes that can be usefully dealt with in a general way.[10] One of these is the suggestion that although Mary undeniably acquires something new when she leaves the black-and-white room, what she acquires is not a knowledge of a new *fact* (or facts), but rather something else. A second is the suggestion that what she does acquire is instead something like a new *ability*, perhaps more specifically a new conceptual or representational ability. And if these two themes are combined, it is claimed, the

---

[8] Frank Jackson (1982), p. 130; see also Frank Jackson (1986).

[9] Many of these discussions are collected in Ludlow, Nagasawa, and Stoljar (2004).

[10] For a useful taxonomy of the various possible materialist responses, see Robert Van Gulick, 'So Many Ways of Saying No to Mary,' in Ludlow, Nagasawa, and Stoljar (2004), pp. 365–405. (This is of the places where the materialist discussion bears a striking similarity to scholastic theology: one can easily imagine a complacent theist writing an article entitled 'So Many Ways to Answer the Problem of Evil.')

result is that there is nothing about the Mary example that is incompatible with the truth of materialism.

Particularly in light of the general materialist failure to provide an account of conscious experience, I doubt very much whether any response of this sort would seem even mildly convincing to anyone who was not already determined to adhere to materialism come what may. But the first of these two themes does at least point to a kind of lacuna in Jackson's original account of the case: if Mary learns new facts, what exactly are they? Indeed, in his response to an early version of this suggestion, Jackson is reduced to invoking the problem of other minds as a (very!) indirect basis for thinking that factual knowledge of some sort is involved.[11]

It is, however, surprisingly easy to modify the original case in a way that makes it utterly clear that there are facts that Mary does not know while she is in the black-and-white room and will learn when she emerges. Suppose that while she is still in the otherwise black-and-white environment, two color samples are brought in: one a sample of a fairly bright green, approximately the color of newly mown grass, and the other a sample of a fairly bright red, approximately the color of a fire engine. Mary is allowed to view these samples and even to know that they are two of the 'colors' that she has learned about in her black-and-white education. She is not, however, told the standard names of these colors, nor is she allowed to monitor her own neurophysiology as she views them.

We now remind Mary of two specific cases that she has studied thoroughly and about which she knows all the physical/neurophysiological/functional facts. One of these is a case where a person was looking at newly mown grass, and the second is a case where a person was looking at a newly painted fire engine. We tell Mary that one of these people had an experience predominantly involving one of the colors with which she is now familiar and that the other person had an experience predominantly involving the other color, but of course not which was which. If we call the colors presented by the samples *color A* and *color B*, Mary now knows that one of the two following pairs of claims is true:

(1) The experience of freshly mown grass predominantly involves color A, and the experience of a newly painted fire engine predominantly involves color B.

(2) The experience of freshly mown grass predominantly involves color B, and the experience of a newly painted fire engine predominantly involves color A.

But can she tell, on the basis of her black-and-white knowledge, together with her new familiarity with the two colors, whether it is (1) or (2) which is true? (Notice carefully that there is no apparent problem with her *understanding* of these claims.)

[11] See Jackson (1986: 294).

Though we have made things vastly easier for Mary by focusing on two cases involving colors with which she is now familiar, rather than asking her to figure out on the basis of her overall physical/neurophysiological/functional knowledge what color experiences in general are like, it still seems quite clear, for essentially the same reasons that were operative in the original case, that she will have no more success with her much more limited task. Just as there was nothing in the physical account that could tell her what an experience of red was like, so there is still nothing in the physical account of the fire engine case that could definitively pick out the color of one of the samples as opposed to the other.[12] And yet whichever of (1) and (2) is true states a *fact* (or facts) in as robust a sense as one could want—a fact that Mary will learn when she emerges from the black-and-white room and is allowed to view ordinary objects of various kinds.

Moreover, if there are *abilities* that result from experiencing the two colors in question, Mary presumably can acquire them on the basis of the samples. Consider, for example, Harman's suggestion[13] that what Mary acquires in the original case, when she leaves the black-and-white room and sees red for the first time, is a *perceptual concept* of red, one that essentially involves being disposed to form perceptual representations involving it in the presence of causal stimulation of the right sort—so that she cannot acquire *that* concept in the original version of the black-and-white room. There is much that is questionable about the idea of such a concept, but if there is indeed such a thing, then Mary in the new version of the case presumably can acquire it by viewing the red sample. (Perhaps more than one sample is for some reason required, but it would be easy enough to modify the new version of the case to allow for that.) So, we may suppose, Mary has the perceptual concept of red and the perceptual concept of green, but she still cannot figure out from her physical knowledge which of these concepts is being employed by the people in the cases she has studied. Yet this too is a fact, and if materialism is true, an entirely physical fact. So why can't she know it?

Here, as far as I can see, there are only two possible moves for the materialist which are even marginally worth considering. One is the suggestion that Mary *already* knows the facts in question, as a part of her overall physical knowledge, but that she knows them under a different 'guise' or 'mode of presentation' than that under which she will come to know them when she leaves the black-and-white room. This idea can be developed in different ways and with enormous technical ingenuity. But does it really have any serious plausibility? Imagine that

---

[12] As Jackson emphasizes in Jackson (1986: 295), it is not enough for Mary to be able to conjecture or guess at the answer to this question. For physicalism to be true, the fact in question must actually be *contained* in her physical knowledge.

[13] Gilbert Harman (1990), 'The Intrinsic Quality of Experience,' *Philosophical Perspectives* 4: 31–52, at pp. 44–5. Harman does not actually mention the Mary case as such, focusing instead on a person who is blind from birth but still learns 'all the physical and functional facts of color perception.' But he does cite Jackson (along with Nagel) as the source of the objection he is discussing.

Mary, in our modified version of the case, having finally experienced real colors, is eager to find out more about these intriguing features of the world about which she has been kept in ignorance. She wants very much, for example, to know whether it is (1) or (2) that captures the relevant facts about cases of that sort—and is seriously frustrated about being kept in ignorance any longer. Suppose that we respond to her frustration by informing her that she already knows the very facts that she is so eager to learn. Surely she would not be satisfied. How might she respond?

I think we can imagine Mary saying something like this:

You philosophers are really amazing! The idea that I *already* know the facts I am interested in—indeed all facts of that general kind—is simply preposterous. I know all of the physical details, but none of them tells me which of the properties I have just experienced, on the basis of the samples, is realized in each of the two cases. If you suggest to me that there aren't really novel properties, but rather novel concepts or ways of representing or whatever, then (while finding that suggestion itself pretty hard to swallow) I would still insist that *which* concept or way of representing is involved in each case is still something that my physical knowledge doesn't give me any clue about. Perhaps, as you say, there is some clever or complicated way in which the things I want to know are related to the physical things I do know—maybe there is even some metaphysically necessary connection between them (assuming that it is kosher for materialists to believe in such things!). Anything like that, however, just *adds* to the list of facts that my physical knowledge doesn't reveal to me. I am a scientist and not a philosopher, so I'm not really sure which conception of a fact is the right one. (All of the ones you suggest seem pretty weird.) But there is undeniably something that I want to know—something that is true about the world—that can't be learned on the basis of all my physical knowledge. And that means that the physical story isn't in fact the whole story!

Not surprisingly, I think that the response I have imagined for Mary is exactly right—that any way of understanding or individuating facts according to which some piece of Mary's physical knowledge and either (1) or (2) above turn out to be formulations of the same fact is a conception of fact that is simply too intuitively implausible to be taken seriously.

The other possible materialist response is to grant that Mary will learn new facts when she emerges from the black-and-white room in the modified version of the case, but to insist that these are nonetheless still *physical* facts. On this view, what the case shows is that it is impossible for Mary to acquire complete physical knowledge in the black-and-white room. One way to put it is to say that while she can learn all the *objective* physical facts, there are still certain *subjective* physical facts[14] that she can't learn. One can learn what it feels like subjectively to be an organism of such-and-such a general physical description in such-and-such a specific physical state only by actually realizing that condition. But that it feels

---

[14] See Van Gulick (2004) for one version of this suggestion.

a certain way or involves a certain sort of conscious experience is still, on this view, an entirely physical fact.

I have to admit that I find it nearly impossible to take this response seriously. The only argument for it seems to be an appeal to a background presumption in favor of materialism that is so strong as to make it allegedly reasonable to claim that any fact there is *must* be a material fact, even if we can't see in any clear way how it could be a material fact. Materialism, as we have already seen, offers no real account or explanation of consciousness and so also no reason for thinking that there is any subjective experience at all involved in being in a certain material state. Thus to advance a view of this sort is in effect just to insist that no fact of any sort can be allowed to refute materialism and thus that any possibility of this sort must simply be absorbed into the materialist view, however inexplicable in materialist terms it may be. (It is not much of a stretch to imagine the materialist saying that we must first believe in order that we may understand.)

Thus the modified version of the Mary case seems to present an objection to materialism in general (and functionalism in particular) that is about as conclusive as philosophical arguments ever get. However exactly they should be characterized, there are facts that Mary cannot know on the basis of her complete physical/neurophysiological/functional knowledge, even when she is given the sort of limited experience needed to understand the claims in question and to acquire any abilities that might be relevant. These facts do not seem to be material facts, and there is no basis that is not utterly arbitrary and question-begging for supposing that they are. Thus we have the strongest of reasons for holding that the materialist account of reality is incomplete and hence that materialism is false.

4. THE PROBLEM OF CONSCIOUS INTENTIONAL CONTENT

Qualia of the sort involved in the Mary case are widely recognized to pose a serious problem for materialist views, and it is not too hard to discern occasional misgivings in this respect under the façade of materialist confidence. But, as already mentioned above, it is widely assumed that materialism is in much better shape with regard to intentional mental states: propositional attitudes and other states that involve "aboutness." I believe, however, that this is almost entirely an illusion—that the problems for materialism are just as serious in this area, with consciousness being once again the central focus.

Materialist accounts of intentional states tend to focus mainly on dispositional states, such as beliefs and desires. Given the central role of such states in explanations of behavior, this is in some ways reasonable enough. But such a focus tends to neglect or even ignore the existence of *conscious* intentional states—even though having conscious thoughts that *P* is surely one of the central things that having a dispositional belief that *P* disposes one to do. A focus on belief in particular also has the unfortunate effect of making externalist accounts of intentional content seem more plausible than they possibly could if the emphasis were on conscious intentional states.

For these reasons, I will focus here explicitly on conscious thoughts. As I sit writing this chapter, a variety of conscious thoughts pass through my mind. Many of these involve the assertion or endorsement of various propositions: that materialism cannot account for consciousness, that the trees outside my window are very bare, that the weather looks cold and dank, that the situation in the Middle East looks grim, and so on. Other thoughts are also propositional, but in a way that does not involve assertion: my conscious desire to get several pages written before lunch, the hope that the stock market will continue to rise, and so on. It is doubtful that conscious thought must always be propositional in character, but it will in any case simplify the issues to be discussed if we largely ignore the propositional aspect of these various thoughts and focus simply on their being conscious thoughts *of* or *about* various things or kinds of things: materialism, the trees, the Middle East, the stock market, and so on.

One crucial feature of such conscious thoughts is that when I have them, I am in general consciously *aware of* or consciously *understand* or *grasp* what it is that I am thinking about (and also what I am thinking about it). When I think that the trees outside my window are bare, I consciously understand that it is certain *trees* that I am thinking about (and along with this, what sort of thing a *tree* is, and *which* trees I have in mind). What exactly this conscious grasp of the object of thought involves varies from case to case and is sometimes not easy to precisely specify. Moreover, as will emerge, it is something of which I think we presently have no real explanatory account of any substance. But its existence is, I submit, completely undeniable. Indeed, being able in this way to consciously think about things, to have them in mind, is in many ways the most central and obvious feature of our mental lives.

It is obvious that a person's conscious grasp of the object of their thought, of what they are thinking about, can vary on a number of dimensions: it may be more or less precise, more or less detailed, more or less clear, more or less complete. But contrary to what is sometimes suggested, it is rarely if ever merely *disquotational* in character. *Perhaps* (though I doubt it) there are cases where a scientifically untutored person is thinking about, e.g., electrons, and where their sole grasp of what they are thinking is that it is what is referred to in their society or community by the word 'electron'—so that what they are thinking about is in effect: "electrons" (whatever *they* are). But this is surely not the ordinary situation when we think about various things.[15]

---

[15] Notice that even a thought about what the relevant *societal experts* mean by "electrons" would have to involve a non-disquotational element in the reference to those experts and also in the reference to the word: to think about 'whatever it is that the societal experts mean by "electrons"'

Moreover, the existence of conscious intentional content is perfectly compatible with the existence of an externalist dimension of thought content—though not with the view that *all* content is external. If, as in Putnam's famous example, a person is thinking about earthly water at a time prior to the discovery of its chemical composition, there is no reason to deny that they are, in a sense, thinking about H_2O. But in such a situation, the aspect of being about H_2O will obviously not be part of their conscious, internal grasp of what they are thinking about in the way that the more superficial aspects of water will.[16] And in a somewhat parallel way, the person in Burge's famous example who thinks he has arthritis in his thigh and to whom our standard belief-ascription practices ascribe a belief about *arthritis* (where this is, among other things, a disease that only occurs in joints) obviously does not consciously grasp the disease that he is thinking about in a way that involves this specific feature of it.[17] But it is nonetheless impossible to describe either example in a convincing way without presupposing that the people in question do have *something* consciously in mind: a substance having the superficial properties of water in Putnam's example; and a disease having certain fairly specific features in Burge's. Thus while it is possible to dispute the relative importance of conscious, internal thought content and external thought content of which the subject is not conscious, examples of this sort provide no basis at all for denying that conscious internal content exists.

The issue I want to raise here is whether a materialist view can account for the sort of conscious intentional content just characterized. Can it account for conscious thoughts being about various things in a way that can be grasped or understood by the person in question? In a way, the answer has already been given. Since materialist views really take no account at all of consciousness, they obviously offer no account of this particular aspect of it. But investigating this narrower aspect of the issue can still help to deepen the basic objection to materialism.

Here it will be useful to bring the brilliant neurophysiologist Mary briefly back onto the scene, even though the black-and-white aspect of her situation is no longer relevant. Suppose that Mary studies me as a subject and comes to have a complete knowledge of my physical and neurophysiological makeup as I am thinking these various thoughts. Can she determine on that basis what I am consciously thinking about at a particular moment?

One thing that seems utterly clear is that she could not do this merely on the basis of knowing my *internal* physical characteristics—as it is sometimes put, knowing everything physical that happens inside my skin. There is no reason

is not the same thing as thinking about 'whatever is meant by "electrons" by whatever is meant by "the societal experts."''

[16] See Hilary Putnam (1975a). (Cambridge: Cambridge University Press), pp. 215–71.
[17] See Tyler Burge (1979).

at all to think that the internal structure of my physical and neurophysiological states could somehow by itself determine that I am thinking about weather rather than about the Middle East or the stock market.

A functionalist would no doubt say that it is no surprise that Mary could not do this. In order to know the complete causal or functional role of my internal states, Mary also needs to know about their external 'causal relations to various things. And, it might be suggested, if Mary knows all of the external causal relations in which my various states stand, she will in fact be able to figure out what I am consciously thinking about at any particular time. No doubt the details that pick out any particular object of thought will be very complicated, but there is, it might be claimed, no reason to doubt that in principle she could do this.

Here we have a piece of materialist doctrine that again has a status very similar to that of a claim of theology. It is obvious that no one has even the beginnings of an idea of how to actually carry out an investigation that would yield a result of this kind—that the *only* reason for thinking that this could be done is the overriding assumption, for which we have found no cogent basis, that materialism *must* be true. Among a multitude of other difficulties, Mary would have to be able to figure out the content of thoughts that are confused or inaccurate, or thoughts about imaginary or fictional entities or supernatural entities. It is, to say the least, *very* hard to see how she could do this on the basis of a knowledge of causal relations to more ordinary sorts of things.

But the problem for materialism is in fact even worse than that. For, as already emphasized, it is an undeniable fact about conscious intentional content that I am able for the most part to consciously understand or be aware of what I am thinking about 'from the inside.' Clearly *I* do not in general do this on the basis of external causal knowledge: I do not have such knowledge and would not know what to do about it if I did. All that I normally have any sort of direct access to, if materialism is true, is my own internal physical and physiological states, and thus my conscious understanding of what I am thinking about at a particular moment must be somehow a feature or result of those internal states alone. Causal relations to external things may help to *produce* the relevant features of the internal states in question, but there is no apparent way in which such external relations can somehow be partly *constitutive* of the fact that my conscious thoughts are about various things in a way of which I can be immediately aware. But if these internal states are sufficient to fix the object of my thought in a way that is accessible to my understanding or awareness, then knowing about those internal states should be sufficient for Mary as well, without any knowledge of the external causal relations. And yet, as we have already seen, it seems obvious that this is not the case.[18]

---

[18] It is worth noting that the same thing is really true in the case of qualia as well. A person's awareness of one color rather than another when he or she looks at newly mown grass obviously

Thus we have the basis for an argument that is parallel to Jackson's original argument about qualia: Mary knows all the relevant physical facts; she is not able on the basis of this knowledge to know what I am consciously thinking about at a particular moment; but what I am thinking about at that moment is as surely a fact about the world as anything else; therefore, complete physical knowledge is not complete knowledge, and so materialism is false.

One way to further elaborate this point is to consider how it applies to what is perhaps the most widely held materialist view of intentional content: the view, popularized by Jerry Fodor and many others, that intentional mental states employ an internal *language*, a "language of thought."[19] Fodor calls this view 'the representational theory of the mind,' though it might better be called 'the symbolic theory of the mind.' For the crucial feature of the view is that the language of thought, like any language, is composed of *symbols*: items that do not stand for anything by virtue of their intrinsic properties, but whose representative character depends instead on the *relations* in which they stand to other things—for Fodor, the sorts of causal relations that are captured in the idea of a causal or functional role.[20] Just as the word "dog" could in principle have stood for anything (or nothing at all) and in fact stands for a kind of animal rather than something else only because of causal relations that arise from the way it is used, so also the symbols in the language of thought stand for whatever they stand for only by virtue of analogous sorts of relations and not in virtue of their intrinsic physical and neurophysiological properties. Their intentional character is thus *extrinsic*, not *intrinsic*.

Proponents of the language of thought rarely have much to say about conscious thoughts of the sort that we are focusing on here. But it is clear that on their view, what happens when I am consciously thinking about, say, the Middle East is that in some appropriate location in my overall cognitive operations there occurs a symbol (or set of symbols) that refers to the Middle East. This symbol, like the surrounding context in which it occurs, is some neurophysiological state or some constellation of such states. No one, of course, has at present any real knowledge of the concrete nature of such symbols or their larger contexts, but it will do no harm to follow Fodor in thinking of a mental "blackboard" on which mental symbols are inscribed in appropriate ways. Thus for me to be consciously thinking about the Middle East is for me to have the mental symbol that refers to

does not depend in a constitutive way on external causal relations, even though it may be causally produced by them. Thus in that case too, a knowledge of the person's internal physical and neurophysiological states alone should enable Mary to pick out one color rather than the other as the right one. But it is even more obvious than in the original case that this is not so.

[19] See, e.g., Jerry Fodor, 'Propositional Attitudes' and 'Methodological Solipsism Considered as a Research Strategy in Cognitive Science,' both reprinted in his 1981 book *Representations* (Cambridge, MA: MIT Press).

[20] See, for example, Jerry Fodor (1987), chapter 4. Fodor has subsequently refined this view in various ways, but none that affect the issues being raised here.

the Middle East inscribed in the right way on this "blackboard." But the symbol's reference to the Middle East, to repeat, depends not on its intrinsic physical or neurophysiological character alone, but also on the relations in which it stands to other such symbols and, directly or indirectly, to the external world.

Suppose now that Mary is studying my cognitive operations. Suppose that she has somehow isolated what amounts to my mental "blackboard" and the various symbols "written" on it. Obviously this will not in itself tell her what I am thinking about. Even if she could somehow focus on the specific symbol that refers to the Middle East and tell that it is functioning in a way that determines the object of my conscious thought (even though there is no reason to think that she could in fact do these things), she will not on this basis alone be able to tell what it is that this symbol in fact refers to. Nor is there any plausibility to the idea that Mary could figure out the reference or meaning of the various mental symbols simply by examining their internal relations to each other.[21] Thus she will need once again to appeal to external causal relations of various sorts.

But how then am I able to be aware of or understand "from the inside" what I am thinking about? Once again I have no knowledge of those external relations (and would be very unlikely to be able to figure anything out from them even if I did). All that I plausibly have access to is the mental symbol or symbols and the surrounding system of states, and this is apparently not enough to determine the object of my thought.

The only very obvious recourse here for the proponent of a language of thought is to construe my understanding or awareness of what I am thinking about disquotationally in relation to the language of thought. When thinking about the Middle East, I do so by using some mental symbol. And when I understand or am aware of what I am thinking about, it might be suggested, I in effect use that very same symbol: what I am aware of is that I am thinking about 'the Middle East' (whatever that is—that is whatever that symbol in fact refers to). If the symbol in question did succeed in referring to the Middle East, then this specification of what I am thinking about will refer to the Middle East as well and so will be correct. But it is intuitively as obvious as anything could be that my awareness of what I am thinking about normally involves more than this: involves actually understanding (at some level of precision, detail, etc.) what the Middle East is in a way that goes beyond merely repeating the same symbol. Assuming for the moment that there really is a language of thought, I *understand* my language of thought in a way parallel to the way in which I understand my own public language—and not in the merely disquotational way that could just as well be applied to a language of which I have no understanding at all.

Here a proponent of the language of thought may want to reply that the difference in the public language case is merely that one language is a language

---

[21] Such an idea has sometimes at least apparently been suggested. For more discussion, see my 1998 book *In Defense of Pure Reason*, pp. 174–80.

that I successfully use—and that the same is true of my language of thought. On this view, the intuition that I understand what I am thinking about—or what I am talking about—in any stronger sense, one that is not merely disquotational, is merely an illusion. But here again we have a view that it seems to me would appeal to no one who was not motivated by the conviction that materialism must be true.

My conclusion is that the language of thought view has nothing useful to say about the most obvious sort of intentional content: the intentional content that is involved in having something explicitly and consciously in mind. Nor do I know of any other materialist account that does any better in this regard. There is perhaps room for dispute about just how important conscious intentional content is in relation to the causation and explanation of behavior, but no plausible way to deny that it genuinely exists. Thus with respect to intentional content, as with the case of qualitative content, materialism seems to be utterly bankrupt as a general account of mental states and to be held merely as an article of faith.

5. WHAT IS THE ALTERNATIVE?

The last two sections serve merely to strengthen and deepen the fundamental objection to materialism already offered in section 2: consciousness genuinely exists; materialism can offer no account that explains consciousness (or of the specific varieties thereof) or shows it to be merely material in character; therefore (at least in the absence of any strong antecedent argument or presumption in favor of materialism), the indicated conclusion is that materialism is false. There is more in heaven and earth than is dreamt of in materialist philosophy.

But what do I mean by more? Here, as I see it, there is very little that can be said in our current state of knowledge, so that the main result is that we have very little understanding of consciousness—or, given the arguably central role of consciousness, of mentality in general.

In the first place, there is no clear way in which the objections that I have raised against materialism support the classical substance dualist position. Positing a separate mental substance that is characterized in almost entirely negative terms does nothing very obvious to explain consciousness in general, or qualitative and intentional content in particular. As far as I can see, the main appeal of substance dualism is that the account of the supposed mental or spiritual substances is far too vague and sketchy to provide the basis for any very clear argument that such substances could *not* be the locus of consciousness. But this negative point hardly counts as an argument in favor of such a view.

The obvious alternative is 'property dualism': the view that human persons and perhaps other kinds of animals have non-material or non-physical properties in addition to their physical ones, with at least the main such properties being the various kinds of consciousness, including the central ones that have been discussed here. In a way, this view seems obviously correct. The properties in question genuinely exist and seem, on the basis of the failure of materialism to explain or account for them, to be clearly non-material in character. But without some further explanation of what such properties amount to or of how they could be properties of a mostly material organism—or, for that matter, of an immaterial substance—the property dualist view yields little in the way of real understanding and hardly counts as a serious account of the nature of mental states.

One somewhat more definite result can, I think, be derived from the discussion of conscious intentional thought. If when I think consciously about things, I am able to know what it is that I am thinking about without knowing anything further about external relations, then what the states in question are about must apparently be an *intrinsic* feature of them: they must have *intrinsic intentionality*, as opposed to an intentionality like that of language (including a language of thought) that is derived from external relations. When I am consciously thinking about, say, trees, there must be something about the intrinsic character of my state of mind that makes it about trees (and in a way that is immediately apparent to me). Here we have a conclusion that very few would accept and that many would regard as virtually absurd. All I can say is that it seems to me clearly required by the facts of the situation.

But how could the intrinsic character of a state definitively pick out something external to it in this way? I do not claim to have anything like a clear answer to this question, but I will indulge in a bit of what seems to me initially plausible speculation. First, I offer the surmise that what is needed to account for intrinsic intentionality in general is an account of two sorts of intrinsically intentional elements: first, intrinsic reference to *properties* of various kinds; and, second, intrinsically *indexical* content.

About the latter of these, it is reasonably plausible to suppose that indexical content of all kinds can be reduced to an indexical reference to the self, with other things, including other places and times, being indexically specified by appeal to their relations to the self. Such a view has sometimes been suggested by others as well,[22] but I have no space to develop it further here.

Intrinsic reference to properties seems more difficult. Including anything in a state that merely in some way *stands for* or *represents* a property does not seem to yield intrinsic intentionality, since the reference to the target property will also depend on the external relation between this representing element and that property itself. Having a symbolic element that stands for the target property in question obviously will not work, for reasons that we have already seen in the earlier discussion. But having a representing element that *resembles* the target property also seems inadequate. If the representing element resembles the target

---

[22] See, for example, David Lewis (1979a).

property by having some other distinct property, then the connection to the target property seems to depend on the relation of resemblance in a way that makes the reference to the target property no longer intrinsic. It is also hard to see how someone who has direct access only to the resembling property would be able to be aware that they were thinking of the target property (or of something else that was picked out by appeal to the target property). Such a person would seemingly have only the resembling property and not the target property explicitly in mind.

Thus what seems to be required is that the intrinsically intentional state actually involve, in some way, the target property itself. Nothing else seems adequate to make the reference to that property both intrinsic and in principle accessible to the person having the thought. Obviously though this cannot in general involve the intrinsically intentional state or some component of it literally instantiating the target property, for obviously we can think about lots of properties that are not literally instantiated in our intentional states. Elsewhere I have speculated that what might be involved is the state or some component instantiating a *complex universal* that has the target property as an ingredient in some appropriate way.[23] But while this proposal seems to have in a way the right sort of structure, I do not really claim to have even an initial understanding of what it would involve or how it would work.

My conclusion remains almost entirely negative. We can see that consciousness exists, and we can see what this specific sort of consciousness in particular would have to involve—namely intrinsic intentionality. And seeing what intrinsic intentionality in turn would require makes it, if anything, even clearer that there is no reason at all to think that a merely material state could have this characteristic. But how consciousness in general or intrinsic intentionality in particular can be explained and accounted for is something about which, if I am right, we know almost nothing.

[23] See BonJour (1998: 180–6).

2

A Simple View of Consciousness

Adam Pautz

I will argue for *primitivism* about sensory consciousness. On primitivism, sensory consciousness cannot be fully reductively explained in physical or functional terms. Others have defended primitivist views of color, personal identity, the intentionality of thought, semantic properties, and goodness.

My argument for primitivism will not be based on the usual a priori considerations, for instance the knowledge argument, the explanatory gap, or the thesis of revelation. Instead, the argument will be based on a philosophical claim about the structure of consciousness together with an empirical claim about its physical basis. The philosophical claim is that having an experience with a certain phenomenal character is a matter of bearing a 'consciousness relation' to a certain item external to the subject. For instance, intentionalism about sensory consciousness holds that having an experience with a certain phenomenal character is a matter of standing in an intentional relation to an intentional content into which external properties enter. The empirical claim is that phenomenology can vary due to internal differences. These two claims create a puzzle and I will argue that the only solution to the puzzle involves adopting the view that the consciousness relation is a simple relation—one that cannot be analyzed in terms of an individual's physical or functional relations to the external world.

Primitivism does not automatically lead to the rejection of physicalism—at least if physicalism is a mere thesis of supervenience. G. E. Moore held that goodness is primitive, yet supervenient on the natural as a matter of metaphysical necessity. Likewise, one could hold that the consciousness relation is primitive, yet supervenient on the physical as a matter of metaphysical necessity.

My plan is as follows. In sections 1 and 2 I introduce the two claims that will play a significant role in my argument. In sections 3–11 I develop the argument. Finally, in section 12 I briefly address the prospects for the view that the consciousness relation is primitive yet supervenient on the physical with metaphysical necessity.

1. THE RELATIONAL STRUCTURE OF SENSORY CONSCIOUSNESS

The first claim that will play a significant role in the argument is that a *relational view* of sensory consciousness is correct. Suppose you have a visual experience as of a tomato. A natural view is that having an experience with this phenomenal character is a matter of standing in a relation to an item that somehow involves the property of being red and the property of being round. Maybe the relevant item is a sense datum instantiating the properties, or the tomato instantiating the properties, or an intentional content that merely attributes the properties. In any case, the properties are not properties of your experience or your brain. Instead, they are properties of the object of your experience, if they are properties of anything at all. The relational view endorses this natural conception of experience. Say that a property is *external* iff it is not instantiated by an individual's experience or brain. Then the relational view holds that, for some types of experience, to have an experience with a certain phenomenal character is to stand in a certain relation to an item involving certain external properties; the phenomenal character of the experience is determined by the external properties that figure in the item. The argument I will be developing requires that the relational view applies to color experience, taste experience, and pain experience.

The relational view goes beyond the uncontroversial claim that in non-hallucinatory experience we are related to external items. On the relational view, phenomenal character is at least sometimes *constituted by* our relations to external properties, rather than by properties of our brains or experiences. For instance, on typical *sense datum theories*, having a visual experience with a certain phenomenal character is a matter of sensing mental objects whose properties determine the phenomenal character of the experience, for instance color and shape properties. These properties qualify as external in my sense, since they are not instantiated by the experience itself or by the brain. *Disjunctive theories* hold that the property of having an experience with a certain phenomenal character is the disjunctive property of standing in a certain relation to physical objects instantiating certain external properties *or* being in some other state. Disjunctive theories are akin to sense datum theories in holding that in some cases phenomenal character is determined by our relation to objects having external properties. *Intentionalist theories* are importantly different from sense datum and disjunctivist theories, but still count as relational in my sense. Whereas sense datum and disjunctivist theories hold that the determinants of phenomenology are *concreta* involving external properties, intentionalist theories hold that they are *abstracta* involving external properties. In particular, intentionalist theories have it that the determinants of phenomenology are *intentional contents* which involve external properties in the sense that the contents attribute them to external objects. On most versions of intentionalism, the relevant contents are *propositions*. On another version of intentionalism, the *property-complex theory*, the contents are not propositions but *complex properties* or *property-structures* built up from external properties and spatial relations. In non-veridical cases the property-structures are not instantiated before one, but one is still related to them. I favor intentionalism and in this chapter I will be working with the property-complex version of intentionalism for convenience.[1]

There are also prominent theories which reject the relational view. The *identity theory* is one. On this theory, having an experience with a certain phenomenal character does not incorporate *any* external properties; it is necessarily identical with the property of being in a certain internal neural state. Phenomenal differences are always constituted by differences in non-relational neural properties.

One argument for the relational view of phenomenology is semantic: it provides the best explanation of why we use expressions for external properties, expressions such as *round, red*, or *in my foot*, to characterize phenomenology. For instance, we might truly say of two individuals undergoing hallucinations that one is conscious of every shape the other is conscious of; and the truth of such a report seems to supervene on the phenomenal characters of their experiences alone. We need a relation to serve as a semantic value of the expression *x is conscious of y* which occurs in this statement. Another argument is introspective: the relational view agrees with the transparency observation that when we try to focus on what our experiences are like we focus on external properties ostensibly instantiated by external objects or bodily regions. I think that the best argument is epistemic: the relational view is required to explain why merely having an experience with a certain phenomenal character necessarily grounds the capacity to have beliefs involving external properties, for instance shapes, colors, and properties ostensibly located in bodily regions. These are certainly not properties of our experiences or brains. I will not develop these arguments here. Suffice it to say that there are strong arguments for the relational view.[2]

As mentioned, I favor intentionalism and in this chapter I will be working with the property-complex version of intentionalism for convenience. I will call the relation we bear to the properties the *consciousness relation* and I will call the external properties the consciousness of which determines phenomenal character the *sensible properties*.

Some comments. First, I hold that the relational view is correct for all aspects of sensory phenomenology. But some disagree, holding for instance that the relational view is incorrect in the case of *blurriness*. And some hold that the

---

[1] For a defense of intentionalism, see Pautz (2007a) and Pautz (2008). For the property-complex theory in particular, see Johnston (2004).

[2] For a defense of the relational view, see Pautz (2007a) and Pautz (2008).

relational view fails for some types of non-sensory experiences, for instance moods and emotions. But, as we shall see, such exceptions would not matter to the argument. It is enough that the relational view is correct for color, taste, and pain experience. This is why above I equated the relational view with a restricted thesis only about these types of experiences. Second, some hold that the colors, tastes, and pains presented in experience are *response-dependent properties* in the sense that they are properties of objects or bodily regions concerning how they affect the nervous system. I will remain neutral on this view, but at one point my argument requires that this view cannot be extended more generally to all the sensible properties (see the discussion of the manifestation relation in section 7). The argument for this assumption is that having a series of visual experiences, even hallucinatory, is enough to give one the capacity to have beliefs involving *geometrical properties*, which evidently cannot also be identified with response-dependent properties of this form. So the epistemic argument for the relational view supports the additional claim that not all the sensible properties are such response-dependent properties.

2. THE PHYSICAL BASIS OF SENSORY CONSCIOUSNESS

There are obviously actual cases of perceptual variation, and they are much discussed by philosophers. The second claim that will play a large role in my argument for primitivism about sensory consciousness is that a certain type of perceptual variation is possible, but it is not one of the uncontroversial types of variation which philosophers typically discuss. Further clarification will be provided later on, but to a first approximation my second claim is that there are possible cases in which individuals bear the consciousness relation to different ostensible external properties of objects *even though their physical relations to external properties are the same*. In these cases the individuals involved are conscious of different external properties owing to internal differences between them. Now in the present section I only intend to introduce the claim; exactly how this claim will contribute to the case for primitivism will be revealed in the next section of the chapter, section 3.

I said that my second claim is that there are possible cases in which individuals bear the consciousness relation to different ostensible external properties of objects even though their physical relations to external properties are the same. In particular, I will argue that there are possible cases in which two individuals bear the consciousness relation to different ostensible external properties of objects even though they bear the *optimal cause relation* to the same properties of those objects. I choose to focus on the optimal cause relation because, as we will see in section 3, some philosophers have attempted to reduce the consciousness relation to this relation. The optimal cause relation may be defined as follows:

The optimal cause relation: x is in a state that plays the e-role and that would be caused by (for short, would track) the instantiation of external property y were optimal conditions to obtain.

The *e-role* is the functional role characteristic of brain states that realize experiences. On one view, the e-role is being poised to influence the formation of beliefs and desires. The notion of *optimal conditions* might be defined in different ways. Here I will equate them with conditions in which the sensory systems operate in accordance with design and result in adaptive behavior.

My argument that the relevant type of variation is possible will not be based on intuition. Indeed, because there are no a priori links between phenomenal and physical concepts, I do not think that issues concerning the physical basis of consciousness can be decided a priori. Rather my argument will based on the empirical finding that the phenomenology of our experiences is poorly correlated with the external properties we bear the optimal cause relation to when we have those experiences, and is much better correlated with the internal neural goings-on taking place in us then. I will express this by saying that there is *bad external correlation* and *good internal correlation*. I will provide examples involving color, pain, and taste experience. Then I will clarify the relevant type of variation, and argue that the empirical findings support its possibility.[3]

First, consider color experience. Some color experiences are of *unitary* colors. Some shades of red, green, yellow, and blue are unitary colors: they do not contain any hint of any other shades. All other color experiences are of *binary* colors: shades of orange, for instance, contain hints of red and yellow, and shades of purple contain hints of red and blue. In addition, color experiences resemble one another more or less closely, depending on the degree to which the colors presented in them resemble. But psychophysics has revealed that there is no simple relationship between the character of color experience and the reflectance properties we bear the optimal cause relation to when we have those color experiences. When we have unitary experiences there is nothing unitary about the reflectance properties that we then bear the optimal cause relation to, and when we have binary ones there is nothing binary about the reflectance properties we then bear the optimal cause relation to. And resemblances among color experiences are not matched by resemblances among the reflectance properties we bear the optimal cause relation to when we have those color experiences.

By contrast, neuroscience has revealed a very modest relationship between the activity of red-green (R-G) and yellow-blue (Y-B) neurons in the lateral geniculate nucleus (a kind of halfway house between the eyes and the visual cortex) and the character of color experience. Some models have it that in the

---

[3] The empirical results concerning color vision I will present come from Werner and Wooten (1979), Hunt (1982), Hardin (1988), De Valois and De Valois (1993); those concerning taste come from Stevens (1975), Borg *et al.* (1967), and Smith *et al.* (2000); and those concerning pain come from Stevens (1975) and Coghill (1999).

visual cortex there is a much better correlation. Granted, the details remain poorly understood. But given that the explanation of color structure is not to be found in the physical properties we bear the optimal cause relation to, the explanation must lie in the brain. When one has a unitary experience there is something special about the processing occurring in one then, and when one has a binary experience there is something binary about the processing occurring in one then. And resemblances among one's color experiences are matched by resemblances among the processing occurring in one then, even though they are not matched by the reflectance properties one then bears the optimal cause relation to.

In the case of pain, the situation is much the same. First, there is bad external correlation. Psychophysics has revealed that in the case of pain there is response expansion. There is a non-linear, exponential relationship between intensity of bodily disturbance and pain intensity. So if John's pain is twice as great as Jim's, then the bodily disturbance that John bears the optimal cause relation to might well be much *less than* twice as great as the one that Jim bears the optimal cause relation to. Why then is his pain twice as great? In the case of pain the evidence of good internal correlation is stronger than it is in the case of color vision. The neural response is amplified further downstream. So John's somatosensory neural discharge rates are twice as great as Jim's. It is only in the brain that we find a nice correlation between pain intensity and anything in the physical world. Indeed, there is a linear relationship between pain intensity and neuronal discharge frequency rates in many areas of the primary somatosensory cortex.

Likewise, in the case of taste, there is a non-linear correlation between the character of our taste experiences and the character of the chemical properties we then bear the optimal cause relation to. By contrast, there is a linear correlation between perceived sweetness and neural response, and resemblances among tastes are matched by resemblances among so-called *across-fiber patterns* in the brain.

In general, when we have experiences the external properties we bear the optimal cause relation to are a mess. The nervous system transforms the mess into something more manageable, and it is only in the brain that we find a nice correlation between experience and anything taking place in the physical world. I will now develop a two-stage argument from this to the second claim that will play a significant role in my argument for primitivism. This is the claim that there are possible cases in which individuals bear the consciousness relation to different ostensible external properties of objects *even though their physical relations to external properties are the same.*

In the first stage, I will argue for *the physical possibility of coincidence cases.* These are cases in which the following two physical conditions co-obtain. *First,* the properties two individuals bear optimal cause relation to (in a certain sense-modality) exactly coincide. *Second,* at the same time the individuals vary

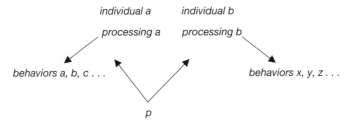

Fig. 2.1. The structure of a coincidence case.

profoundly in neural processing and functional organization. In particular, they are in quite different neural states, which play quite different output oriented functional roles with respect to behavior (see Figure 2.1). The possibility of such cases should be uncontroversial. Note that the first stage will be neutral on whether the individuals in such cases have the same experience or different experiences. This issue will be left open until the second stage.

In the second stage, I will use 'good internal correlation' and 'bad external correlation' to argue that, given that the individuals in coincidence cases differ profoundly in neural processing and functional organization, the most reasonable view concerning these cases is that in at least *some* of them an additional phenomenal condition obtains, namely, that the individuals also have different experiences. This is so despite the fact that they bear the optimal cause relation to the same external properties. Given good internal correlation and bad external correlation, the internal and functional differences are better evidence of phenomenal difference than the sameness of tracking is evidence of phenomenal sameness. This will provide an argument that does not rely on untutored intuition for the claim that experience can vary independently of optimal cause relations and other such relations to external properties. I will call this *coincidental variation*.

We begin, then, with the first stage. Unfortunately there are no obvious actual coincidence cases. As noted at the outset, the form of variation argued for here is importantly different from the forms of actual variation that philosophers typically discuss. To see this, consider *interspecies variation* first. Humans and pigeons differ profoundly in color processing and functional organization. But, since they have different receptor systems, they bear the optimal cause relation to *different* ranges of reflectances. So the second condition of coincidence cases, namely that the properties tracked are the same, is not met in this case. Consider *standard variation* next. On viewing a color chip with a certain reflectance property, Jack and Jill are put into different opponent processing states and differ functionally. So, in this one case, the neural states they are in are caused by the same reflectance property. Since, we may suppose, the differences are within the range of normal, optimal conditions obtain, this looks like a coincidence case. But it might be argued that if we look at how their neural states respond to external properties under *all* optimal conditions, we find that under those conditions those neural states track *overlapping but distinct* ranges of reflectances. If so, then, on viewing the color chip, they might be in states that are *actually* caused by the same reflectance property, but they bear the *optimal* cause relation to distinct but overlapping reflectance properties. So these are not obviously coincidence cases.[4] Fortunately, it should be uncontroversial that there are *possible* coincidence cases, and this is all my argument will require. I will describe three. In the rest of the chapter, I will make essential use of all three of these cases in my argument for primitivism.

Mabel and Maxwell. Mabel and Maxwell occupy the same possible world but belong to different species that evolved on separate continents. By chance, Mabel and Maxwell evolved identical receptors systems. On viewing a fruit, they bear the optimal cause relation to exactly the same reflectance property, r. However, the fruit is an important food-source to Maxwell's species but not to Mabel's. So they evolved different postreceptoral wiring, with the result that r normally produces quite different color processing in Mabel and Maxwell. For instance, we might suppose that r normally produces 'unitary' opponent processing in Mabel that might underlie a vivid unitary color experience (for instance a unitary red experience), while it normally produces 'binary' opponent processing in Maxwell that might underlie a dull binary color experience (for instance, a desaturated red-yellow experience). We may also suppose that Mabel is easily able to pick out the fruit from the background foliage, while Maxwell has difficulty in this task. I will call the opponent channel state Mabel is in u and the different opponent channel state Maxwell is in b, because I will argue in the second stage of the argument that in at least some scenarios of this kind Mabel has a unitary color experience while Maxwell has a binary one.

Likewise in general. On viewing the same objects, Mabel and Maxwell bear the optimal cause relation to exactly the same ranges of reflectances, but they are put into neural states which differ in two ways. First, they differ in whatever neural respect underlies the distinction between the experience of unitary colors like red and the experience of binary colors like red-yellow. Second, they fall into different internal resemblance-orderings. So, for instance, if both Mabel and Maxwell look at the same two objects consecutively, Mabel might be put into two radically different neural states, while Maxwell is put into two similar neural states. In consequence, they differ markedly in their sorting, discrimination, recognition and other color-related behavior with respect to the

---

[4] This is explained more fully in Pautz (MSb); see also section 4 of the present chapter. It follows that, contrary to Byrne and Tye (2006: 250), coincidence cases such as the one developed in Pautz (2006) cannot be assimilated to cases of standard variation.

same objects. But when they track the same properties by way of different internal processing, optimal conditions obtain. Their visual systems operate differently, but when they do so they are operating exactly as they were designed by evolution to operate. And their behavioral dispositions, although different, are adaptations to different selection pressures. Thus, Mabel and Maxwell constitute a coincidence case, because they bear the optimal cause relation to properties that exactly coincide, but they vary profoundly in neural processing and functional organization.

Yuck and Yum. Yuck and Yum belong to different species. If they taste the same foodstuff under optimal conditions, then their taste systems respond to the same chemical property of that foodstuff, *c*. So, they bear the optimal cause relation to the same property, *c*. However, the foodstuff is poisonous to Yuck but not poisonous and indeed an important food-source to Yum. In consequence, they so evolved as to respond to *c* with different across-fiber patterns (which, as we saw above, are well-correlated with taste experiences in the actual world) and different affective reactions. For instance, Yuck withdraws from it violently, while Yum is drawn to it. I will call the across-fiber pattern Yuck undergoes *d* and the one Yum undergoes *p*, because the second stage of the argument I will argue that in at least one scenario of this kind the patterns realize a displeasing and pleasing taste experience, respectively.

Likewise in general. When Yuck and Yum taste the same foodstuffs, they bear the optimal cause relation to the same properties of those foodstuffs, but they undergo quite different across-fiber patterns and exhibit different taste-related affective and sorting behaviors. The neural and behavioral differences do not impugn the assumption of optimality. These differences evolved naturally. Moreover, they are adaptive, since the same foodstuffs have different nutritional values for Yuck and Yum. I believe that there are actual cases of roughly this kind. But, to avoid controversy, I will continue with the hypothetical case.

It may be said that in this scenario Yuck and Yum do not bear the optimal cause relation to exactly the same properties, contrary to what I have said. In particular, on tasting the foodstuff, Yuck bears the optimal cause relation to the dispositional property of being poisonous for Yuck and Yum bears the optimal cause relation to the dispositional property of being healthy for Yum. But this is ruled out if we make an additional supposition. Suppose that the foodstuff has two chemical properties, *c* and *c'*. The property which is responsible for the foodstuff's being poisonous for Yuck and for its being healthy for Yum is *c'*. However, *c'* has no causal effect on their taste systems. *A fortiori*, the foodstuff's being poisonous or healthy has no causal effect on their taste systems. Instead, only the other chemical property *c* has a causal effect on their taste systems. Since the optimal cause relation is defined in causal terms, it follows that Yuck and Yum do not bear the optimal cause relation to the foodstuff's being poisonous or healthy. Instead, they only bear the optimal cause relation to the causally relevant chemical property *c*, as originally stipulated.

Mild and Severe. Two communities of pain-perceivers evolve separately. Mild belongs to one community and Severe belongs to the other community. Both occasionally experience bodily disturbance d in the leg. In Mild's community, d is not very dangerous. So d normally puts his primary somatosensory cortex into state m involving a certain mild rate of firing of neurons. Recall that in our own case there is a linear correlation between the neural discharge frequencies of the relevant neurons and pain intensity. By contrast, in Severe's community, d is much more dangerous. For instance, maybe it is more susceptible to dangerous infections in this community because the community occupies an environment in which bacteria are more plentiful. In consequence, in Severe, d normally causes somatosensory state s, involving a rate of firing of somatosensory neurons which is twice as great as that which is involved in m. As a result, Severe attends to his leg with greater urgency than does Mild. But optimal conditions obtain in each case, because the different behaviors are completely adaptive given the noted difference in the significance of the damage to them. So, Mild and Severe bear the optimal cause relation to the same property, d, but they differ radically in pain processing and behavior.

Of course, there are indefinitely many such possible cases in which two individuals differ profoundly in neural processing and functional organization but bear the optimal cause relation to the same external properties. Everyone must accept the physical possibility of coincidence cases, for these two physical conditions are certainly compossible. The real question is not whether such cases are possible, but whether the individuals in some such cases have the same or different experiences.

Now for the second stage of the argument. I will argue that the best view is that in at least *one* such coincidence case an additional phenomenal condition obtains: the individuals involved have different experiences. This is so despite the fact that they bear the optimal cause relation to the same properties. This yields *coincidental variation*. Of course, I think that this is true in many such cases. But, as we will see in section 4, my argument only requires that it is true in one. I offer two arguments for this claim.

First, as we have seen, experiential properties are very well correlated with neural properties and very poorly correlated with the external properties we bear the optimal cause relation to. This suggests that, if two individuals stood in the optimal cause relation to the same external properties but differed in the relevant neural properties, then they would have different experiences. In other words, translating from counterfactual language into the language of possible worlds, in at least some nearby possible worlds in which coincidence cases actually obtain, the individuals have different experiences, even though they bear the optimal cause relation to the same properties. What is being invoked here is a general principle: if we know that magnitudes x and y are well correlated but x and z are not, then we have some reason to believe that, if two objects differed on y but were the same on z, they would still differ on x.

Second, the individuals in the cases exhibit robust and systematic differences in color-related, taste-related, and pain-related behavior. We may suppose that the differences are not learned but innate. And we may suppose that they are widespread in the relevant populations.[5] To explain these behavioral differences, the opponent of coincidental variation might say that the individuals involved have experiences with the same phenomenal characters, but have systematically different beliefs and desires about the same objects. But this is a poor explanation because the behavioral differences are supposed to be innate and widespread. Further, if the individuals involved do not have different experiences, there would be no explanation of why they have systematically different beliefs and desires about the same objects. The only reasonable explanation is that in at least some of the cases they have different experiences, in accordance with coincidental variation.

The alternative to accepting coincidental variation is holding that the individuals *in every possible coincidence case* have the same experiences in spite of the vast neural and behavioral differences between them (or else are Zombies who have no experiences at all, a possibility I will ignore). This is simply unbelievable. Imagine meeting Yuck and Yum, Mild and Severe, or Mabel and Maxwell. To say that they have the same experiences in spite of all the evidence against this would be unreasonable.

Coincidental variation says that, in *some* possible coincidence cases, internal and functional *differences* are accompanied by phenomenal *differences*. It would be a mistake to confuse coincidental variation with the much-discussed thesis of internalism. Internalism says that only internal factors are relevant to phenomenology, so that, in *every* possible case, internal *sameness* guarantees phenomenal *sameness*. As we will see at the end of section 7, some might say that there are functionalist reasons to doubt this pure internalism. Coincidental variation is quite consistent with the externalist view that sensory consciousness is somehow determined jointly by the properties tracked on the input side, internal factors, and behavioral dispositions on the output side. This would yield a form of externalism, but with internal as well as external factors playing a role. My argument for primitivism only requires coincidental variation. The issue of internalism is not relevant here, and I am neutral between pure internalism and some form of externalism.

Coincidental variation says that in at least one coincidence case the individuals involved have different color, taste, or pain experiences in spite of bearing the optimal cause relation the same external properties. On a non-relational view such as the identity theory, their having different experiences simply consists in their having different internal neural states. This is not so on a relational view. For instance, on the property-complex version of intentionalism assumed here, their having different experiences consists in their bearing the consciousness relation to

---

[5] My thanks to Fred Dretske for pointing out that the argument is stronger if it is supposed that the behavioral differences are innate and widespread.

different external color, taste, or pain properties. (Coincidental variation is neutral on the issue of whether these different properties are different response-dependent properties of objects and bodily regions, or different projected properties that the objects and bodily regions do not actually have.) So, on a relational view, coincidental variation means that in at least one coincidence case two individuals, *a* and *b*, bear the *consciousness relation* to *different* color, taste or pain properties *x* and *y*, despite bearing the *optimal cause relation* to the very *same* property *p*. Those who combine the relational view and variation will say that this is somehow *owing to* the internal or functional differences between them. Diagramatically:

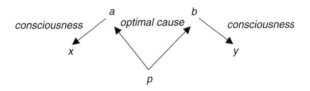

Fig. 2.2. The relational view and coincidental variation entail that the depicted situation obtains in some coincidence cases.

On a non-relational view such as the identity theory, coincidental variation is not puzzling. On such a view, the individuals' having different experience simply consists in their being in different neural states. By contrast, the combination of a relational view and coincidental variation creates a puzzle. On this combination of views, two individuals can be conscious of different *external* properties owing to *internal* or *functional* differences between them. In other words, the consciousness relation is at once externally directed and internally sensitive. Now I do not say that this is incoherent. On the contrary, since we have good reasons to accept both the relational view and coincidental variation, I believe that it is true. That it is not incoherent may be brought out with an analogy. The relation *x has mass-in-grams y* is a relation between objects and numbers which are "external" to objects, but what numbers objects bear this relation to is sensitive to the "internal" mass properties of those objects. Still, I admit that the combination of the relational view and coincidental variation is puzzling. I will argue that the only solution to the puzzle involves adopting a primitivist view of sensory consciousness according to which the consciousness relation is a primitive relation that cannot be analyzed in terms of an individual's physical or functional relations to the external world.

The argument applies to any version of the relational view. It may seem that the argument does not apply to disjunctivism because the disjunctivist has a radically externalist view of consciousness that is inconsistent with coincidental variation. Elsewhere I attempt to show this is not the case: the argument applies to disjunctivism as well.⁶ The disjunctivist can and indeed must accommodate coincidental variation, and the only way they can do so is by adopting a primitivist view of consciousness. However, as noted in the previous section, here I will focus on how the argument plays out on the type of intentionalist view I favor.

3. THE STRUCTURE OF THE ARGUMENT

By *primitivism* about a property (or a relation, that is, a polyadic property) I just mean the denial of reductionism. *Reductionism* about a property holds that it is a complex property constructible from the fundamental physical and functional properties of the world. Here I will use 'physical property' to mean all and only such complex properties. So I understand reductionism broadly to include the various forms of functionalism, even though others would consider them to be non-reductionist views. And I understand primitivism about sensory consciousness to be the strong claim that some properties or relations involved in sensory consciousness are properties or relations over and above all those constructible from the fundamental physical and functional properties of the world. How do the relational view and coincidental variation create an argument for primitivism about sensory consciousness? In the present section, I will indicate the structure of the argument that I will be developing.

On a relational view, every episode of sensory consciousness has two components: the consciousness relation and the complex of sensible properties to which we bear this relation. In the history of philosophy perceptual variation has often been used to draw conclusions about the nature of the sensible properties. By contrast, I will use a unique type of perceptual variation, coincidental variation, to draw a conclusion about the nature of the *consciousness relation*, namely that it is primitive. I will set aside the second component of sensory consciousness, the sensible properties that are *relata* of the consciousness relation. I will give to the reductionist about sensory consciousness any view of the sensible properties they wish: they might identify them with response-independent physical properties, response-dependent physical properties, or primitive properties. My argument will be entirely neutral on this issue.

The argument for primitivism about the consciousness relation will take the form of a dilemma. We may divide all physical relations into two categories. Our most promising reductive theories of the consciousness relation identify it with a physical relation that the individuals in coincidence cases bear to the *same* properties. For example, one such theory identifies the consciousness relation with the optimal cause relation. I will call such physical relations *A-type relations*.

---

⁶ See section 12 of Pautz (2007b).

The idea is that the mind's capacity to be conscious of the external items can be explained in terms of a causal process from those items to minds. Indeed, it is very difficult to see *how else* we might reductively explain the consciousness relation. But, as we will see, there are also physical relations that the individuals in coincidence cases bear to *different* properties. I will call such physical relations *B-type relations*.

I will argue that there is principled reason to believe that the consciousness relation cannot be an A-type or B-type relation. Since these exhaust all physical relations, this will be an argument against reductionism and for primitivism. The argument will unfold as follows. Previously, I argued for a relational view of sensory consciousness and for coincidental variation. These two claims entail that there is a consciousness relation with the following two properties:

Relationality In at least some cases, the consciousness relation holds between individuals and external properties, for instance shapes, colors, pains felt in bodily regions, and tastes felt in the tongue.

Variation The consciousness relation is such that *some* pairs of individuals in coincidence cases bear it to different external properties.

These properties yield constraints on the reduction of the consciousness relation. Evidently, they immediately entail that the consciousness relation is not an A-type relation, thereby ruling out our most promising reductive theories of this relation. Such relations satisfy the relationality constraint: they are relations between individuals and external properties. But, by definition, they do not satisfy the variation constraint. For instance, in at least some coincidence cases two individuals bear the *consciousness relation* to *different* sensible properties, but they bear the *optimal cause relation* to the very *same* property (see Figure 2.2). So far, I have focused on the optimal cause relation. But I will generalize the argument to other A-type relations. This will be the easy part of the argument.

The larger and more difficult part of the argument will involve showing that the consciousness relation cannot be identified with a B-type relation. To rule out B-type relations, the relationality constraint and the variation constraint will be insufficient. By definition, B-type relations satisfy the variation constraint. And, as we will see, some satisfy the relationality constraint as well. So we will have to rely on considerations that have not yet been introduced. I will argue that these relations are ruled out by two other properties of the consciousness relation:

Scrutability The consciousness relation is the subject of our talk and thought about consciousness.

Extensionality The consciousness relation has a certain actual-world extension—individuals bear it to countless shapes, colors, and so on.

As we will see, B-type relations may be subdivided into two categories: those defined in *internal terms* and those defined in *functional terms*. I will argue that there is principled reason to think that B-type relations defined in internal terms

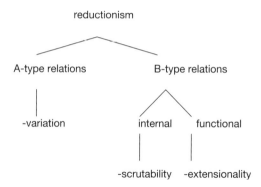

Fig. 2.3. The structure of the variation argument against reductionism and for primitivism.

fail to satisfy the scrutability constraint and B-type relations defined in functional terms fail to satisfy the extensionality constraint. So the complete structure of the argument is represented in Figure 2.3.

Coincidental variation plays a key role in this argument. It rules out our otherwise most promising theories of the consciousness relation, namely A-type theories. For this reason I will call it the *variation argument* for primitivism.

4. A-TYPE RELATIONS FAIL TO SATISFY THE VARIATION CONSTRAINT

The most common reductions of the consciousness relation are A-type. The idea is that sensible properties like colors, tastes, and pains are physical properties that external objects and bodily regions actually possess. And the consciousness relation is some A-type relation between individuals and such properties. Here are several A-type relations that the consciousness relation might be identified with:

The optimal cause relation: x is in an internal state that plays the *e*-role and that would be caused by the instantiation of external property y were optimal conditions to obtain.

The indication relation: x is in an internal state plays the *e*-role and that has the biological function of indicating external property y.

The asymmetric relation: x is in an internal state that plays the *e*-role and whose tokening asymmetrically depends on the instantiation of y.

The input–output relation: x is in an internal state that plays the *e*-role and that under optimal conditions tracks the instantiation of y and that in turn enables x to distinguish objects that have y from objects that do not.[7]

---

[7] For these relations, see, respectively, Tye (2000), Dretske (1995), Fodor (1990), and Armstrong (1968).

Actual forms of variation are not a problem for these theories. Consider a case of standard variation. On viewing a chip, John and Jane bear the consciousness relation to different color properties, namely unitary blue and green-blue, owing to internal differences. But, as we saw in section 2, it might be said that John and Jane also bear the optimal cause relation to *different* but overlapping reflectance properties *r* and *r′* of the chip. Likewise for the other A-type relations on the list. This would mean that this case is not a coincidence case in my sense. And it would mean that the case is not a problem for the view that the consciousness relation is the optimal cause relation. The optimal cause theorist could say that the consciousness relation is the optimal cause relation, that *r* is unitary blue, and that *r′* is green-blue. This entails that the chip is unitary blue and green-blue, and that John is conscious of the first color while Jane is conscious of the second color. In general, the combination of the relational view and *actual* cases of standard variation is not problematic because it can be said that what is going on is that every object has a set of multiple colors, and on viewing the objects different individuals bear the optimal cause relation to colors in the set.[8] The same strategy applies to interspecies variation and indeed all actual forms of variation in color experience. On this view, colors are response-independent properties, and objects have many of them. So this is a kind of *color pluralism*.[9] One could imagine similar views of taste and pain.

By contrast, the relational view and hypothetical coincidence cases create a decisive argument against A-type theories. This argument is just the two stage argument for coincidental variation presented in section 2. The first stage established *the physical possibility of coincidence cases*: there are possible coincidence cases in which two individuals bear the optimal cause relation to *exactly the same* properties, but vary profoundly in internal neural processing and behavior. The idea is that, even though objects and bodily regions have multiple properties, the individuals in these cases bear the optimal cause relation to the very same properties of those objects or bodily regions. A moment's reflection will reveal

---

[8] See Pautz (MSb). This is how the intentionalist who accepts the optimal cause theory can solve Johnston's (MS, chapter 5) selection problem.

[9] For color pluralism about interspecies variation cases, see Byrne and Hilbert (2003) and Tye and Bradley (2001). For color pluralism about standard variation cases such as John and Jane, see Byrne and Hilbert (1997: 273) and Tye (2000: 91). It should be noted that, while these philosophers continue to accept color pluralism in cases of interspecies variation, they now reject it in cases of standard variation: they now maintain that different minimal colors within human color space are incompatible, so that in these case at least one individual must get it wrong. Pautz (MSb) argues these philosophers would do better to accept color pluralism in both cases, as they once did. For, as we have seen, in both cases color pluralism follows from the optimal cause theory; indeed, it follows from all available reductive theories of our consciousness of colors. But, as I am about to explain in the text, color pluralism does not help the reductionist about the consciousness relation when it comes to hypothetical *coincidence cases*. For in these cases, even if objects have many colors, the individuals involved bear A-type physical relations to exactly the same colors of objects, yet it is reasonable to suppose that they bear the consciousness relation to different ostensible colors of those objects.

that the individuals also bear the other A-type relations listed above to the same properties. The first stage of the argument should be uncontroversial. The second stage argued for *coincidental variation:* in view of the profound neural and behavioral differences, the most reasonable view is that in at least *one* such case the individuals involved have different experiences and so bear the consciousness relation to *different* properties. The most reasonable view, then, is that the consciousness relation is not identical with the optimal cause relation or any of the other A-type relations on the list (see Figure 2.2). This is an argument against A-type theories that does not rely on the mere *intuition* that phenomenology could vary independently of A-type relations.[10]

It might be objected that the optimal cause relation and the other relations on the list are vaguely specified. Maybe, then, there is some precisification of the optimal cause relation or one of the other relations on the list that is not vulnerable to the argument. In response, what we have here is a general

---

[10] Kalderon (2007) has taken up the view that Byrne and Hilbert (1997, 2003) and Tye (2000) once accepted (see the previous note): color pluralism in cases of both interspecies variation and standard variation. He also accepts *selectionism*, which is a view concerning what determines what colors of objects we are conscious of. He writes that 'the relation between object, perceiver, and circumstances of perception . . . determines the perceptual availability of [one of the many colors of an object]' (2007: 577). Later he says that the determination proceeds by way of something about color similarity: 'given the nature of Norm's visual system, Norm's visual system selects certain relations as relations in color similarity and, hence, which colors are perceptually available to Norm' (2007: 593). The selectionist component of Kalderon's view is difficult to understand, but I think that coincidence cases may create a problem for it. What is it to select a relation as a relation of color similarity? And how precisely does the visual system determine what colors are perceptually available *by* determining what relations are relations of color similarity? In the first quote, Kalderon speaks of a relation between the object and the perceiver as determining what color of the object the perceiver is conscious of, but does not specify what this relation is. On one natural interpretation of selectionism, the relevant relation is a *causal relation:* the mechanism of selection is causation. Then selectionism is very similar to Tye's optimal cause theory. Humans and pigeons are conscious of different colors of the same objects because, owing to their different receptor systems, their visual systems are causally sensitive to different colors of those objects. The pigeons but not the humans are causally sensitive to ultraviolet light (Tye and Bradley 2001). The optimal cause theory entails a similar story about cases of standard variation such as John and Jane, as I explained in the text. (In the previous note, I explained that Tye previously accepted such a parallel pluralist view of standard variation, but that he now rejects it in favor of an inegalitarian view, even though this seems inconsistent with his optimal cause theory.) But if selectionism is explained in terms of causation (and it is hard to see how else it might be explained), so that it is like the optimal cause theory, then it is also refuted by coincidence cases, in which two individuals are relevantly causally related to exactly the same color properties of objects and relations among objects, but it is nevertheless reasonable to hold that they bear the consciousness relation to different ostensible color properties of those objects. Of course, the two views endorsed by Kalderon are separable. One could accept a pluralist response-independent view of color and reject a selectionist view of color-consciousness (if such an account is indeed inconsistent with coincidental variation). Instead, one could combine color pluralism with a broadly internalist view of color consciousness. By a *broadly internalist* view, I mean one that entails that, on viewing the same objects, Maxwell and Mabel bear the consciousness relation to different colors owing to internal differences, even though their visual systems respond to the same chromatic properties of those objects. (As noted in section 2, such an account is not committed to pure internalism.) But I believe that, once we accept a more internalist view of color-consciousness, an epistemic problem arises for the pluralist response-independent view (see note 21).

recipe for refuting the view that the consciousness relation can be identified with *any* relation of this kind. Let *r* be any physical relation within the general ballpark of the relations listed above. There will always be a class of possible cases in which two individuals bear *r* to the *same* external properties, but differ profoundly in neural processing and functional organization. The claim that the individuals in at least one of these cases have different experiences and so bear the consciousness relation to *different* properties will always be more plausible than the philosophical theory that the consciousness relation is identical with *r*.[11]

5. ARE THE CASES POSSIBLE?

Responding to an earlier presentation of this argument directed specifically against the optimal cause theory, some commentators have objected that coincidence cases are *impossible*.[12] Presumably, they do not mean to reject *the physical possibility of coincidence cases*: that there are possible cases in which two individuals track the same properties under optimal conditions while differing profoundly in internal processing and functional organization. As we saw in the first stage of the argument of §2, this claim ought to be uncontroversial. On the only reasonable

---

[11] Lycan (2000), who says he tends to accept the present argument against the optimal cause theory, helpfully made the suggestion of presenting the argument in this way: the argument is that the claim of coincidental variation that in at least some coincidence cases the individuals involved have different experiences is more plausible than any philosophical theory, such as the optimal cause theory, which delivers the contrary verdict.

[12] The earlier presentation is Pautz (2006; see also Pautz (2003) and the commentators are Byrne and Tye (2006). Byrne and Tye raise four further objections to the earlier presentation of the argument, the first two of which rely on misunderstandings. First, in the earlier presentation, I introduced the thesis of *Dependence* and said that it has the consequence that in coincidence cases the individuals involved have different experiences. Byrne and Tye consider two interpretations of Dependence and argue that on neither does it have this consequence. My reply is that neither of these interpretations is correct. On the correct interpretation, Dependence is *equivalent to* the thesis that in coincidence cases the individuals involved have different experiences, so that the entailment is trivial (Pautz 2006: 207). Here I have used the more appropriate title of *coincidental variation* for this thesis, and I have offered a different, two-stage formulation of my argument for this thesis and against A-type theories such as the optimal cause theory. Second, Byrne and Tye object that the failure of existing A-type theories would not show that externalism about phenomenology is false and internalism is true because externalism is not committed to any particular reductive theory (2006: 251). This objection, too, relies on a misunderstanding, because in the earlier presentation of the argument I did not take myself to have shown that externalism is false and internalism is true, but only that all of the versions of externalism I considered in the paper are false (2006: 228). Given my language in the earlier presentation, the misunderstanding was natural. I now call these theories *A-type theories* to remove the impression that my target is externalism in general. In fact, in my (2006) and in the present chapter, I take no stand on the issue of externalism *versus* internalism (see section 2 of the present chapter). Third, Byrne and Tye (2006: 252) point out that A-type theories are often vague, which makes it unclear whether they are refuted by coincidental variation. I addressed this objection at the end of section 4 in the present chapter. Fourth, Byrne and Tye argue that the failure of every existing reductive theory of the consciousness relation would not show that reductionism fails (2006: 252). In other words, we could take the view that the correct reductive theory is unknown. I call this view *mysterian reductionism* and argue against it in section 11.

interpretation, they are rejecting *coincidental variation.* In other words, they are rejecting the further claim argued for in the second stage of the argument that in some of these cases an additional phenomenal condition obtains: the individuals involved bear the consciousness relation to *different* sensible properties. If they are right in rejecting this claim, then of course my argument fails. Their rejection of coincidental variation requires their acceptance of the radical view that in every coincidence case the individuals involved bear the consciousness relation to the same sensible properties in spite of the profound neural and functional differences between them. (I ignore the view that the individuals are not conscious of any sensible properties at all.)

Of course this radical view follows from the philosophical theory that the consciousness relation is the optimal cause relation, but one would like a non-question-begging argument for it. The argument seems to be as follows. If, for instance, Mabel and Maxwell bear the consciousness relation to different color properties on viewing the fruit, then at least one of them must be conscious of a color that the fruit does not have, because such color properties are mutually exclusive. But this is incompatible with the condition that they track the same external properties *under optimal conditions.* According to the objection, contrary to coincidental variation, the only verdict compatible with this condition is that they bear the consciousness relation to the very same color and so have the same color experience. This is so despite the fact that there are profound differences between them in opponent processing and color-related behavior. So this is the verdict we should accept. Call this the *argument from error* against phenomenal variation in coincidence cases.

Now, since coincidental variation (and hence my argument against the optimal cause theory) only requires phenomenal variation in *one* coincidence case, the argument from error against coincidental variation is successful only if it is general. For instance, it must also be assumed that, if Yuck and Yum bear the consciousness relation to different tastes on tasting the same food, one must be wrong about the food's true taste, so that this verdict is inconsistent with the optimality condition. In that case, as against coincidental variation, we must accept the implausible verdict that they are conscious of the same taste, in spite of the radical neural and behavioral differences between them.

One problem with the argument from error against coincidental variation is the implausibility of its key assumption that phenomenal variation in these cases requires error. Those who provide pluralistic theories of color would deny this in the case of color vision. Indeed, as I explained in section 4, I think that the optimal cause theorists themselves should deny that variation requires error in cases such as John and Jane. For my part, I hold that phenomenal variation requires error in the case of color vision because I accept a general color exclusion principle. Indeed I accept a projectivist theory of color according to which all color experience involves error. But I reject the assumption in the cases of taste and pain. Here the assumption is very implausible. Why couldn't individuals from different communities have different taste or pain experiences in response to the same stimulus, and yet both have true beliefs about the tastes of things in their communities or about the pains they feel in their bodies? So the argument from error against coincidental variation cannot succeed because the assumption that phenomenal variation entails error does not hold in general.

But I think that there is a more basic problem with the argument from error that applies even if the assumption is granted. The problem is that the optimality condition and error are incompatible only if optimal conditions are defined as conditions in which there is no error, that is, in which individuals are conscious of properties that objects actually have. But, since the defender of the optimal cause theory is attempting a reduction of this intentional relation, they cannot define optimal conditions in terms of notions such as error which are explained in terms of that very relation. Instead, they must define optimal conditions in terms notions such as adaptive fitness, design, and so on.[13] So even if we grant the implausible assumption that phenomenal variation would in every case entail error on the part of one of the parties involved, there is no reason to think that it is inconsistent with their tracking the same properties under optimal conditions. Indeed, we can imagine many possible cases of adaptive error. So why cannot coincidence cases be cases of this kind? Of course, if the optimal cause theory were correct, there could not be cases of this kind, for it is a kind of verificationist theory of sensory content according to which tracking under optimal conditions is inconsistent with error. But I am offering an argument against this theory. In view of the arguments offered in section 2, the claim that there is phenomenal variation in at least some coincidence cases is the most reasonable one to make, even if it means that at least one of the individuals is in error. It is much more reasonable than the alternative view that in all such cases the individuals involved have the very same experiences in spite of the radical neural and functional differences between them.

So the original argument succeeds. The individuals in coincidence cases bear the optimal cause relation and the other A-type relations to the *same* properties. But, in view of the profound internal and functional differences between them, the most reasonable view is that some such individuals have different experiences and so bear the consciousness relation to *different* properties. So the consciousness relation cannot be identical with the optimal cause relation or any other A-type relation.

6. NO B-TYPE RELATION SATISFIES THE OTHER CONSTRAINTS

This brings us to B-type relations. The individuals in coincidence cases bear such relations to different properties. So such relations satisfy the variation constraint

---

[13] For this point, see also Chalmers (2005).

on the reduction of the consciousness relation. This means we need another argument to rule out B-type relations.

As I already mentioned, my argument is that B-type relations either fail to satisfy the scrutability constraint or the extensionality constraint. The individuals in coincidence cases differ only in two respects. First, they differ internally, in particular in neural processing. Second, they differ functionally, in particular in how their internal states guide their behaviors. So B-type relations fall into two categories. The first category contains B-type relations defined in internal terms and the second category contains B-type relations defined in functional terms. I will provide general reasons to think that B-type relations belonging to the first category fail to satisfy the scrutability constraint and those belonging to the second fail to satisfy the extensionality constraint (see again Figure 2.3).

7. RELATIONS DEFINED INTERNALLY

The view that the consciousness relation can be identified with such a relation is very unpromising and to my knowledge no one has advocated such a view. But we must get the view out of the way before considering the view that the consciousness relation can be defined functionally.

An initial hurdle is to see how a relation defined in internal terms might satisfy the relationality constraint. Consider:

The brain state relation: x is in a brain state that plays the e-role and that has internal neural property y.

The problem with this relation is the reverse of the problem with A-type relations. It satisfies the variation constraint and hence is a B-type relation. But it fails to satisfy the relationality constraint. The semantic, introspective and epistemic arguments mentioned in section 1 show that to have an experience with a certain phenomenal character is to stand in a relation to shapes, colors, pains felt in bodily regions, tastes felt in the tongue, and so on. These properties are not all neural properties instantiated in the brain. If they are instantiated at all, they are instantiated by external objects or bodily regions, not by parts of the brain. So the consciousness relation at least *sometimes* holds between individuals and external properties. By contrast, the brain state relation *never* holds between individuals and external properties; it always holds between individuals and neural properties of their own brains. So the consciousness relation is distinct from the brain state relation.[14]

---

[14] Alex Byrne proposed in discussion that the optimal cause theorist could handle the cases of Yuck and Yum and Mild and Severe by claiming that these individuals bear the optimal cause relation and hence the consciousness relation to different neural properties instantiated by their own brains. The trouble is that, like the brain state view, this proposal violates the relationality constraint, because it entails that the phenomenology of experience is always constituted by the

To obtain a relation that satisfies both the relationality constraint and the variation constraint, the reductionist needs an algorithm that goes from internal states to *external* properties and that is sensitive to the internal or functional properties of those states. We are now after an algorithm that is sensitive to the internal properties of those states. I do not suppose that the algorithm must be specifiable in some relatively compact way. But I do require that it satisfies all four constraints on the reduction of the consciousness relation.

The reductionist might rely on the analogy with the mass-in-grams relation mentioned at the end of section 2. It is a relation between objects and numbers which are 'external' to objects, and yet it is sensitive to the 'internal' mass properties of objects. And it can be defined in terms of a kind of structural isomorphism between masses and numbers. Likewise, the reductionist might claim that there are structural isomorphisms between our internal states and the external properties we are conscious of, and claim that the consciousness relation is definable in terms of these isomorphisms. As noted in section 2, neuroscience has revealed a very modest relationship between the activity of R-G and Y-B neurons in the lateral geniculate nucleus and the degree to which the colors we are conscious of are reddish, greenish, yellowish and bluish. And there appears to be a linear relationship between neural discharge frequencies of neurons in the primary somatosensory cortex and the intensity of the pains we are conscious of. Now, presumably, there are infinitely many or at least very many possible but non-actual sense modalities, and corresponding to each of them there might be a different algorithm of this kind. We could truly say of any creature possessing such an alien sense-modality that it is conscious of properties that we are not conscious of. This leads to the idea that the consciousness relation might be identified with:

The infinitely disjunctive relation: x is in a color state c and $f(c) = y$ or x in is in a pain state p and $g(p) = y$ or x is in some alien state a and $h(a) = y$ or x is in some alien brain state a' and $i(a') = y$ or . . . and so on for every possible sense-modality.

However, there are a few reasons to doubt that there are any such modality-specific algorithms as $f, g, h, i, \ldots$ First, neuroscience has only revealed a very imperfect relationship between the activity of R-G and Y-B neurons in the lateral geniculate nucleus and the degree to which the colors we are conscious of are reddish, greenish, yellowish and bluish. Some hold that the discrepancies are corrected further downstream, but there is no evidence of this. If anything, it is more confusing as we move to the cortex. Second, sensible properties are not

consciousness of internal rather than external properties. So it is inconsistent with the arguments for accepting a relational view such as intentionalism mentioned in section 1: the semantic argument, the phenomenological argument, and the epistemic argument. The proposal is especially implausible in other cases. For instance, it would be very implausible to suggest that colors are neural properties and Mabel and Maxwell have different color experiences because they bear the optimal cause relation and hence the consciousness relation to different neural properties of their own brains.

easily quantifiable, so it is difficult to believe that there might be algorithms concerning them. Think of tastes and sounds, for instance. Third, we are not merely conscious of sensible properties; we are conscious of *property-structures* in which properties are presented at various locations. So the relevant algorithms would have to go from intrinsic neural properties to spatially arrayed property-structures. But it is very hard to imagine such algorithms. In humans, there is topographical mapping, but it is much too rough to provide such an algorithm.

The absence of algorithms would obviously not be inconsistent with my claim in section 2 that internal factors explain some aspects of phenomenology, so that internal differences, when accompanied by functional differences, are evidence of phenomenal differences. Here I take no stand on whether or not there are such algorithms.

If it should turn out that there are no algorithms, then the reductionist who hankers after an internal definition of the consciousness relation has no choice but to define the conscious relation in terms of an infinitely long list:

The infinitely disjunctive relation II: x is in total internal state b_1 and y = property structure s_1 or x is in total internal state b_2 and y = property structure s_2 or . . ., and so on for every possible property-structure.

So now we have before us two infinitely disjunctive relations. Evidently there are relations of this kind which satisfy the relationality constraint, the variation constraint and the extensionality constraint. When individuals are in different internal states b_1 and b_2, they bear this relation to different property structures s_1 and s_2, which might involve different external color, taste, or pain properties.

Could the consciousness relation be identical with either of these relations? The problem is that these relations do not satisfy the scrutability constraint. There are many infinitely disjunctive relations $r_1, r_2, r_3, . . .$ with different extensions. For instance, consider the brain state b' of a creature, Blurg, we have never before encountered. These different infinitely disjunctive relations $r_1, r_2, r_3, . . .$ map b' onto different sensible properties. The problem is that none of the infinitely disjunctive relations $r_1, r_2, r_3, . . .$ could be the semantic value of our predicate x *is conscious of y*. This follows from a theory that the semantic value of a predicate is the most natural property or relation that fits our use of the predicate.[15] For all of these relations $r_1, r_2, r_3, . . .$ fit actual use, and they are equally natural because they share the same very low degree of naturalness. What could make it the case that the semantic value of x *is conscious of y* is one of these relations to the exclusion of the others? Indeed, none of these relations is a relation we *could* think about. By contrast, the consciousness relation is evidently the semantic value of x *is conscious of y*. And it is a relation we can think about. So the consciousness relation cannot be identical with any one of these infinitely disjunctive relations. Nor would it do to say that x *is conscious of y* indeterminately refers to all of these

---

15 This is an oversimplified version of Lewis (1983a).

relations, so that there are no determinate truths about what properties Blurg is conscious of. There are such truths, even if we do not know what they are.

At this point, the reductionist seeking a definition of the consciousness relation in internal terms might appeal to a trick in order to avoid infinitely disjunctive relations. In particular, he or she might adopt a kind of global response-dependent theory according to which the sensible properties one and all are relational, dispositional properties of the form *normally causes internal state s*. If the external properties we are conscious of are relational properties whose *relata* are internal states, then it is easy to specify an algorithm going from internal states to such properties. In particular, the consciousness relation might simply be identified with:

The manifestation relation: x is in internal state s that plays the e-role and $y =$ the property of normally causing s.

In other words, the idea is that we can simply say that a person is conscious of such a sensible disposition just in case they are in the internal state which is the manifestation of that sensible disposition. On this view, when Mabel is in u and Maxwell in b, Mabel bears the manifestation relation to *normally causing u* and Maxwell bears the manifestation relation to *normally causing b*. The colors they are conscious of are identical with these relational, dispositional properties. Likewise for Yuck and Yum and Mild and Severe. So this is a B-type relation that satisfies the variation constraint. Further, one might think that it could be the semantic value of x *is conscious of* y and hence could satisfy the scrutability constraint, on the grounds that it is the most natural relation that fits our use of this expression.

The problem is that this relation does not satisfy the extensionality constraint. As noted at the end of section 1, it is a fact about the actual extension of the consciousness relation that not all the properties we are conscious of are response-dependent properties of the form *normally causes internal state s*. For instance, having an experience with a certain character is enough to ground the capacity to have thoughts involving shapes. And shapes are not properties of this form, since it is obvious that objects might have shapes while entirely lacking such properties. For instance, objects might have had shapes, even if creatures with internal states had never evolved. And, in the actual world, objects that are too small to have an effect on perceivers have shapes but lack properties of this form. So this trick fails and the original conclusion stands.

Therefore there is a *principled* reason to think that relations defined in internal terms are bound to fail to satisfy the scrutability constraint. The reason is that there is an abundance of equally natural infinitely disjunctive algorithms going from the internal properties of an individual to external properties.

There is another potential problem with the view that the conscious relation is definable in internal terms. Those with functionalist intuitions will say that the idea that our internal neural properties *alone* determine what properties we are conscious of is somewhat implausible. Consider a twist on the case of

Mild and Severe. Two species are hardwired so that the *same* rate of firing among somatosensory neurons produces in them radically different pain-related behavior, and in general plays quite different functional roles in them. Theories according to which the consciousness relation is definable in purely internal terms entail that they are conscious of the same pain. Or consider a brain in a vat belonging to no actual species with no sense organs or motor-output system, and so without even the potential to act on the world. Theories according to which the consciousness relation is definable in purely internal terms entail that the brain in a vat has a vivid inner life. Or imagine some somatosensory neurons firing in a Petri dish, completely functionally isolated. Some (but not all) theories according to which the consciousness relation is definable in internal terms might entail that the Petri dish is conscious of pain properties! Reductionists with functionalist tendencies will reject such theories and adopt a theory according to which the consciousness relation is defined at least in part in functional terms.

Whereas the problem with relations defined in internal terms was that they fail to satisfy the scrutability constraint, the chief problem with relations defined in functional terms will be that they fail to satisfy the extensionality constraint. I will consider the consumer relation and the interpretation relation.

8. RELATIONS DEFINED FUNCTIONALLY: THE CONSUMER RELATION

On the *consumer theory*, the consciousness relation is identical with:

The consumer relation: x is in an inner state s that plays the e-role and that represents property y, where s *represents* a property y iff, in the past, when an object was present with property y, and the consumer devices used s to perform output behaviors $a, b, c, \ldots$ these behaviors frequently had advantageous results *because* an object with property y was present, so that now individuals have consumer devices that might use s to perform $a, b, c, \ldots$ [16]

This relation is defined in functional terms inasmuch as it appeals to how our internal states are used to guide behavior. Unlike many of the A-type theories we have considered, it is not an entirely input-based theory.

The stock illustration of this theory is the frog. A frog state b is caused by flies and causes tongue-darting. On the consumer theory, it does not represent the property of being a black dot. The instantiation of this property does not enter

---

[16] See Millikan (1989) for a consumer theory of intentional relations in general. Lycan (2006) says that the consumer theory is likely to deliver the correct verdict that in coincidence cases the individuals are conscious of different properties. Against this, in what follows I argue that the consumer theory does not deliver correct verdicts in coincidence cases. I should mention that Lycan does not go so far as to defend the consumer theory. Instead, he appears to endorse what I will call in section 12 *mysterian reductionism*.

into an explanation of why tongue-darting was beneficial in the past. Rather, it represents the response-dependent, biologically significant property of being frog-food. It is this property which enters into the explanation.

The evaluation of the consumer theory is complicated by the fact it is very difficult to see what types of properties individuals bear the consumer relation to in more complex cases, in particular in coincidence cases. There are two interpretations. On the first, the consumer relation fails to satisfy the variation constraint. On the second, it fails to satisfy both the variation constraint and the extensionality constraint.

On the first interpretation, the individuals in coincidence cases bear the consumer relation to the same response-independent physical properties, that is, the same reflectance properties, chemical properties, and bodily disturbance properties. The idea is that, although they exhibit different behavioral patterns, the same external properties enter into the explanation of the evolution of those behavioral patterns.

This interpretation is arguably incorrect. For instance, Mabel is in u and Maxwell is in b. By contrast to the frog's internal state, in the past, these states were used to perform a great variety of behaviors, such as picking out a fruit, finding a mate, avoiding a predator, and so on. Intuitively, on none of these occasions was the behavior advantageous *because* the presented food or individual had reflectance property r. This is simply not a true because-statement. Maybe r is *correlated with* properties that enter into true because-statements, such as being healthy food, being a potential mate, being a predator. But r itself does not enter into such a true because-statement. The same problem applies in the cases of Yuck and Yum and Mild and Severe.

Nevertheless, suppose this interpretation is correct for the sake of argument. Then the consumer relation is just another A-type relation which fails to satisfy the variation constraint. On this interpretation the individuals in coincidence cases bear the consumer relation to the same response-independent physical properties, just as they bear the optimal cause relation to the same response-independent physical properties. But the most reasonable view is that in at least some coincidence cases the individuals involved bear the consciousness relation to different properties. So on this interpretation the consciousness relation is not identical with the consumer relation.

On a second interpretation, on tasting the foodstuff, Yuck bears the consumer relation to the response-dependent property *being poisonous to his kind* and Yum bears it to the response-dependent property *being healthy to his kind*. The consumer theorist might say that these properties *just are* the different taste properties they are conscious of. Then, in this case at least, the consumer relation satisfies the variation constraint.[17]

---

[17] The suggestion that the different properties Yuck and Yum are conscious of are properties of this sort was made by Andy Egan in discussion.

This interpretation is more plausible than the first. Intuitively, it is these biologically significant properties which explain why in the past avoidance-behavior was advantageous to members of Yuck's species and why pro-behavior was advantageous to members of Yum's species. And this interpretation is in better accord than the first with what consumer theorists say about the frog. The frog does not represent the response-dependent property *being a black dot* that his visual system tracks, but the untracked response-dependent property *being food for frogs* which enters into the explanation of the relevant behavioral pattern.

But under the second interpretation the consumer relation fails to satisfy the variation constraint in cases other than Yuck and Yum. For instance, what different coarse-grained response-dependent properties do Mabel and Maxwell bear the consumer relation to as they view the fruit? Indeed, they arguably do not bear the consumer relation to *any properties at all.* As noted above, in the past, u and b were used to produce a variety of behaviors. And a variety of different properties explained why these different behaviors were advantageous. There is no *single* property which frequently explained why these behaviors were advantageous. So in this case there is *no* property which satisfies the consumer theorist's formula.

Consider next Mild and Severe. What different properties do they bear the consumer relation to? *Being a dangerous case of bodily damage* and *being an even more dangerous case of bodily damage?* These do not seem to be very good candidates for the different properties they are conscious of.

Finally, consider *adaptively neutral* coincidence cases. It is obvious that a creature's internal processing and overall functional organization are not rigidly determined by selection pressures. So we can imagine cases in which two creatures respond to the same external properties, and are under roughly the same selection pressures, but in which they evolved different internal processing and functional organizations by chance. In these cases, the same objects have the same coarse-grained, biologically significant properties with respect to the two creatures. On the second interpretation, then, the individuals involved cannot bear the consumer relation to different such properties. But the most plausible view is that they bear the consciousness relation to different properties.[18]

Another problem with the consumer relation under the second interpretation is that it fails to satisfy the extensionality constraint. To see this, suppose as before that Yuck tastes a foodstuff with chemical property c and undergoes across-fiber pattern d. But now suppose that Yuck takes another taste of the foodstuff, this time from a different part of the same foodstuff which has a slightly different chemical property c'. We might suppose that c is the property of having a certain concentration of a certain type of molecule and that c' is the property of having a slightly greater concentration of the same type of

---

[18] For an *adaptively neutral* coincidence case involving color vision, see Pautz (2003) and Pautz (2006).

molecule. As a result, Yuck now undergoes slightly different across-fiber pattern *d'*, and withdraws from the foodstuff even more violently than before. On the second interpretation, in each case Yuck bears the consumer relation to the same coarse-grained response-dependent property, namely *being poisonous to his kind*. But, in view of his different internal processing and behavior, the best view is that on the different occasions he bears the consciousness relation to slightly different taste properties, the second more displeasing than the first. There are actual cases of this kind. For instance, on the second interpretation, when a bird takes two bites of a poisonous dart frog and gets a greater concentration of batrachotoxin on taking the second bite, the bird bears the consumer relation to the same property *being poisonous to its kind* on both occasions, but arguably bears the consciousness relation to slightly different tastes.

It may be said that there is a third interpretation of the consumer theory. On this interpretation, individuals bear the consumer relation to *fine-grained* response-dependent properties. For instance, in the case just mentioned, on the different occasions, Yuck bears the consumer relation to the property of normally causing across-fiber pattern *d* and then the property of normally causing across fiber pattern *d'*. So on this interpretation the consumer relation might satisfy the extensionality constraint. But this interpretation cannot be correct. Consider the case of color vision. Previously, I argued that *no* external properties satisfy the consumer theorist's formula in the case of color vision, because there are no properties that frequently explained the advantageousness of the many behaviors we used the color vision system to perform in our evolutionary past. If so, then on viewing objects individuals bear the consciousness relation to a myriad of colors, but there are no properties at all that they bear the consumer relation to. In particular, they do not bear the consumer relation to such fine-grained response-dependent properties as the property of normally causing opponent channel state *u* or the property of normally causing opponent channel state *b*. Or consider the case of Yuck again. Here again the interpretation fails. In the past, *d* was used by members of Yuck's kind to avoid the relevant foodstuff. But this behavior was never advantageous *because* the foodstuff had the property of normally causing that very brain state, *d'*. There is simply no sense in which this is a true because-statement. If anything, it was advantageous because it had the property of being poisonous to Yuck's kind. Therefore, when he undergoes across-fiber pattern *d* Yuck certainly does not bear the consumer relation to the property of normally causing that very brain state, *d*. If Yuck bears the consumer relation to any property, it is the property of being poisonous to Yuck's kind, as on the second interpretation. But, as we have seen, on this interpretation, the consciousness relation cannot be identified with the consumer relation, for the reasons explained previously.[19]

---

[19] The *success theory* of Papineau (1993) has some similarities to the consumer theory. In the case of the belief relation, it holds that *A has a belief according to which state s obtains* just in case *s* is

9. RELATIONS DEFINED FUNCTIONALLY: THE INTERPRETATION RELATION

On the interpretation theory, the consciousness relation is identical with:

The interpretation relation: x is in internal state s and the best interpretation of the members of k (where k is the kind or species to which x belongs) assigns to s the experience of y, where the best interpretation of the members of k is the one that best satisfies the constraints on interpretation, given the functional roles of their internal states.[20]

This needs to be unpacked. Functional roles are second-order properties of internal states to do with their interactions with the external world, their interactions with other inner states, and their interactions with behavior. Constraints on interpretation are principles taken from our common sense theory of persons about how mental states change as a result of evidence from the external world, and how they combine to produce behavior. They include the following general principles. *Rationalization:* assign beliefs, desires and other mental states so as to rationalize behavior. *Humanity:* assign beliefs that are reasonable on the evidence, and desires that reflect sane values. *Eligibility:* all else equal, assignments are to be preferred that assign contents involving natural properties. Roughly, the best interpretation is the assignment of mental states—beliefs, desires, and experiences—to the internal states of members of k which best satisfies the constraints on interpretation, given the functional roles of those states.

I have formulated the interpretation theory in a way that requires a unique best interpretation. The interpretationist might instead claim that there might be several interpretations that are tied for best. But I will continue to assume a formulation in terms of a unique best interpretation. Afterwards we will see that the problems I will raise apply even if we allow for multiple best interpretations.

In coincidence cases, the individuals involved exhibit radically different color-related, taste-related and pain-related behaviors on the output side. So they differ functionally on the output side. This will mean that, *if* there are such things as best interpretations of them, they will assign to their brain states experiences of quite different external color properties, taste properties, and pain properties, despite the fact that they track the same properties on the input-side. Whether

---

the state of the world which would guarantee that A's belief, in combination with different desires, would lead to actions that satisfy those desires. But the theory does not apply to the consciousness relation. When a person is conscious of a shade of orange, he or she has no desires that are so specific that their satisfaction requires that the viewed object instantiate that very shade of orange. Even if he or she did—for instance, even if he or she had the desire to have an object with *that very color*—its content would derive from the content of his or her experience. So, one could not without circularity explain the fine-grained content of his or her experience in terms of the fine-grained content of such a desire.

[20] See Lewis (1983b).

these properties are response-dependent properties, primitive properties, or whatever, need not concern us. So it might be thought that the interpretation relation satisfies both the relationality constraint and the variation constraint.

But there are four problems. The first is familiar. Let *unique functional role* be the claim that, for every different possible experience, there is a unique functional role that belongs to it necessarily. There are reasons to think that this is false. Two individuals might have different experiences that have the same functional roles. For instance, there might be functionally identical individuals with different color experiences, as in spectrum inversion. Or there might be two simple creatures who have different pain experiences, but who are so wired that their pain experiences play exactly the same input–output functional role. Since the detail in sensory experience is so vast (think of listening to music, for example), it seems easy to imagine other cases of phenomenal differences between individuals without even potential functional differences. Even if functional role contributes to determining what properties we are conscious of, it is not the whole story. Internal factors play a role as well. But if *unique functional role* is false and such cases are possible, then the consciousness relation cannot be the interpretation relation. For, since the best interpretation of a population of individuals is only sensitive to the functional roles of their states, the best interpretations of the individuals in such cases would assign the individuals experiences of the same properties. So they would bear the interpretation relation to the same properties but bear the consciousness relation to different properties.

The second and third problems are independent of the well-trodden problem posed by spectrum inversion and other such problem-cases for *unique functional role*. If the functionalist rejects the relational view of sensory consciousness, and only recognizes monadic experiential properties, then once he or she establishes *unique functional role* the functionalist is home free. For then he or she can identify these monadic experiential properties with properties of the form: being in a state which plays functional role f. By contrast, on a relational view, even if *unique functional role* is true, the functionalist with reductive aspirations faces a difficult further issue. For, on a relational view, there also exists a dyadic consciousness relation to external properties which is involved in every sensory episode. As we have seen, there are good semantic, phenomenological, and epistemic reasons for believing that there is such a relation. Here I have been assuming an intentionalist version of the relational view according to which the relevant relation is an intentional relation between individuals and contents, in particular property-structures. So, on a relational view, the truth of *unique functional role* would not automatically vindicate reductionism about sensory consciousness. There would remain the problem of reducing the consciousness relation. The reductive functionalist must make it plausible that there is a relation defined in terms of functional role that satisfies the four constraints on the reduction of the consciousness relation, so that the consciousness relation might be identified with it. To make this plausible, he or she must be able to at least gesture at an algorithm, *a*, for going from the functional roles of any actual or possible individual's internal states to the external properties the individual is conscious of. Then the reductive functionalist may say that the consciousness relation is identical with a relation of the following form: *x* is in a state with some functional role *f* and *a(f)* = *y*. The only way to define such an algorithm is *via* the notion of the *best interpretation* of a population. So the interpretation relation is the only relation of this form with which the consciousness relation might be identified. The second and third problems concern the notion of a best interpretation.

The second problem is that the interpretation relation is defined in terms of the property of being the best interpretation. But it is not even clear that there is such a property. So it is not even clear that there is such a relation as the interpretation relation.

Some philosophers have advocated best system theories of laws. Systems of generalizations vary in simplicity and strength. Since simplicity and strength are variable magnitudes, we might think that there is such a property as being the best system, although there are serious problems concerning when the virtues of simplicity and strength add up to an overall best system. But what variable magnitude do candidate interpretations of persons vary along such that the best interpretation may be defined as the one that maximizes this magnitude?

Let me rule out some suggestions. First, the interpretationist cannot identify the property of being the best interpretation with the property of being the correct interpretation, on pain of circularity. Second, some interpretations are more reasonable than others, so one might think that the property of being the best interpretation is the property of being the most reasonable interpretation light of the functional evidence. But this would undercut the reductive aspirations of the theory, for now it is appealing to an unreduced notion of reasonableness of interpretation. In addition, this would make the interpretation theory very implausible, for we may imagine cases in which the most reasonable interpretation is mistaken. For instance, if an unfortunate species is so wired up that when it has an experience of an object straight ahead, it is disposed to reach slightly to the right, the most reasonable interpretation will be mistaken. Third, the property of being the best interpretation might be identified with the property of doing the best job overall of conforming to the constraints on interpretation. But this is not much of an advance. Since the constraints on interpretation are *ceteris paribus* (indeed, they are so vague it is not even clear that they express propositions), it is clear that different interpretations, which are intuitively not equally good, might all satisfy the few constraints on interpretation. So we would need an explanation of the key notion invoked here, the notion that some interpretations *better* conform to the constraints on interpretation. Since there is no account of the property of being a best interpretation, I think that the interpretation theory cannot even get off the ground. Nevertheless, I will raise a third and final problem, which applies even if this initial problem can somehow be overcome.

The third problem is as follows. Grant that there is such a property as the property of being the best interpretation, and so such a relation as the interpretation relation. I will argue that there is no interpretation of any human or non-human population that has the property of being the unique best interpretation. Since the interpretation relation is defined in terms of the notion of the best interpretation, it follows that individuals do not bear it to any properties. In other words, it is entirely without application. But, of course, individuals bear the consciousness relation to many properties. So even if there is such a thing the interpretation relation, it fails to satisfy the extensionality constraint.

Consider humans first. For example, suppose Mabel is disposed to sort two objects together. There are many different interpretations: she is conscious of two shades of red and desires to sort red objects together; she is conscious of two shades of green and desires to sort green objects together; she is conscious of two unitary colors and desires to sort objects with unitary colors together. In fact, once we remember that interpretations can differ in fine-grained ways—one might assign the experience of red_{17} and another might assign the experience of red_{18}—we see that the number of different possible interpretations that rationalize the sorting behavior perfectly well is fantastically large. There are two reasons to believe that none of these interpretations has the property of being the uniquely best interpretation. *First*, it is simply unbelievable. True, exactly one of the interpretations has the property of being the correct interpretation. However the property of being the best interpretation cannot be the property of being the correct interpretation, on pain of circularity. So the interpretation theory requires that there is some *other* property such that exactly one of the interpretations has this property and all the others lack it. But it is clear that there is no such property. *Second*, by their nature, the constraints on interpretation are insufficient to whittle down the interpretations to a single best interpretation. It is well-known that *Rationality* is insufficient on its own. If a man goes to a bar, one interpretation that rationalizes his behavior is that he wants a saucer of mud and believes he can get one at a bar. To rule out such perverse interpretations, defenders of the interpretation theory must appeal to another constraint, *Humanity*. We should assume that individuals have reasonable beliefs given the evidence available to them, and that they have desires that reflect the same values that we have. But in the case of sensory content this fix fails. As we have seen, in the case of sensory content as in the case of belief and desire content, there are indefinitely many interpretations that rationalize the individuals' behaviors. And here *Humanity* is inapplicable because it makes no sense to say that certain experiences are unreasonable on the basis of an individual's evidence while others are reasonable. So there is no constraint on interpretation available to whittle down all of these interpretations to a single best interpretation.

The problem extends to animals and aliens. Imagine that we discover a species on earth or on an alien planet that has sophisticated sensory systems and exhibits behavior that is finely tuned to its environment. But suppose its sensory systems and behavior are radically different from ours. For instance, sometimes members of the species turn purple and expand. Now there is reason to believe that a member of this population, for instance *Blurg*, is conscious of indefinitely many fine-grained sensible properties, perhaps ones belonging to alien quality spaces. In the formal mode, if we were to say *Blurg is conscious of indefinitely many fine-grained sensible properties*, we would express a truth. So if *x is conscious of y* picks out the interpretation relation, as defenders of the interpretation theory say, then Blurg must bear this relation to indefinitely many fine-grained sensible properties that we cannot imagine. That is to say, the best interpretation of Blurg and the others in the population must assign to their brain states experiences of indefinitely many sensible properties. But, again, there is no such thing as the best interpretation. There are many interpretations that rationalize the bizarre behavior more or less well. Some differ radically: they assign experiences of different sensible properties from entirely disjoint quality spaces to the same brain states. Some interpretations differ less radically: they assign experiences of quite different sensible properties from the same quality space to the same brain states. Others differ less radically: they assign experiences of sensible properties that differ only in fine-grained ways to the same brain states. Nevertheless, many of these different interpretations could rationalize the strange behavior equally well. For the same two reasons given above in connection with humans, it is simply unbelievable that the functional roles of their brain states and the constraints on interpretation could determine that among these interpretations one that stands out as the uniquely best one.

The defender of the interpretation theory might reply that, in the human case and the alien species case, exactly one interpretation has the property of being the unique best interpretation, and attempt to explain our reluctance to believe this by saying that what interpretation has this property is deeply epistemically opaque. But this does not answer the problem. What could this nebulous property *being the best interpretation* be? As we have seen, exactly one interpretation has the property of being the correct one, but the defender of the interpretation theory cannot explain the property in this way, on pain of circularity. What the interpretation theory requires is that there is some *other* property that exactly one interpretation has and all the others lack. For the two reasons given above, the claim is completely unbelievable, and the present reply does nothing to make it more believable.

Another reply is that the best interpretation is determined by input-oriented functional role. Mabel and Maxwell bear the optimal cause relation to r, Yuck and Yum bear the optimal cause relation to c, and Mild and Severe bear the optimal cause relation to d. According to the present reply, the best interpretation will accordingly assign to them experiences of r, c, and d. But evidently this will not be the best interpretation. *If* there is a best interpretation, it will assign to them experiences of different external properties of objects and bodily regions, so as to provide the best rationalization of their radically different behaviors on the output side. (Incidentally, it is unclear what these different properties of the objects and bodily regions might be: response-dependent properties, primitive properties, or whatever.) As we have seen, there is no best interpretation of this kind.

I have formulated the interpretation theory in terms of a unique best interpretation. The interpretationist might instead claim that there can be several different interpretations that are tied for best. An initial problem with this proposal is that, even if there were a unique set of interpretations that are tied for best, the arguments given previously show that they could radically differ as regards what properties an individual experiences. Depending on what the interpretationist says about such cases, the interpretation theory would entail that the individual is conscious of no properties at all, or that the individual is conscious of many properties, or that it is radically indeterminate what properties the individual is conscious of. None of these consequences agrees with fact. But there is a more serious problem. Not only is there no such thing as a single best interpretation, there is no such thing as a single set of interpretations that are tied for best. There will simply be many interpretations that rationalize individuals' behaviors. For the two reasons given above, no subset of these stands out as the interpretations that are tied for best.

So the third problem is that, even if the second problem can be overcome and some account of the property of being the best interpretation can be provided, individuals do not bear the interpretation relation to any properties at all. But, of course, individuals bear the consciousness relation to many properties. So even if there is such a relation as the interpretation relation, it fails to satisfy the extensionality constraint.

I conclude that there is *principled* reason to think that relations defined in functional terms will fail to satisfy the extensionality constraint. The problem with relations defined in purely internal terms was that there is no *scrutable* algorithm from the purely internal properties of any actual or possible individual to the external properties that the individual is conscious of. The problem with relations defined in purely functional terms is that there is *no algorithm at all* for going from the functional roles of any actual or possible individual to the external properties the individual is conscious of. The only possible algorithm proceeds *via* the defunct notion of a best interpretation. It might be said that I have forgotten algorithms defined in terms of both internal factors and functional factors. But such algorithms will simply face both of these problems.

10. HOW A PRIMITIVE RELATION MIGHT SATISFY THE CONSTRAINTS

By contrast, a primitive relation might easily possess all four of the properties possessed by the consciousness relation: relationality, variation, scrutability, and extensionality. This, together with the fact that there are systematic reasons to think that no physical relation possesses these properties, gives us excellent reason to think that the consciousness relation is a primitive relation.

A primitive relation could obviously be a relation between minds and external property-structures. So it could satisfy the relationality constraint. In addition, what property-structures we bear it to might partly depend on internal and functional factors, and not depend only on what properties are tracked in the external world. (Whether the dependence here holds with metaphysical or merely nomological necessity is an issue addressed in section 12.) So, unlike A-type relations, it could also satisfy the variation constraint. The fine-grained internal processing and functional organization of an individual might fully determine what fine-grained properties the individual bears the relevant primitive relation to. So, unlike B-type relations defined in functional terms, it might satisfy the extensionality constraint. Finally, unlike an infinitely disjunctive B-type relation defined in internal terms, a primitive relation might satisfy the scrutability constraint. On one view, which was mentioned in section 7, the semantic value of x *is conscious of y* is the most natural relation that fits our use. The relevant primitive relation fits our use. And it is perfectly natural. Of course, it might *supervene on* an infinitely disjunctive, extremely unnatural relation of the kind discussed in section 7. On a more externalist view, it might *supervene on* a combination of internal factors and external factors. But the relation itself, as opposed to its supervenience-base, is perfectly natural. Since it is bound to be the most natural relation that fits our actual use of x *is conscious of y*, it is bound to be the semantic value of this expression. Once use plus naturalness determine that the expression x *is conscious of y* refers to this primitive relation, we will then be able to use it to state truths about instantiation of this relation in cases such as the case of Blurg (discussed in sections 7 and 10) which lie outside of actual use.

For reasons that I will not go into here, primitivism about the consciousness relation goes best with primitivism about colors, tastes, and pains. In principle, it might be combined with any of three versions of primitivism. In the case of color, they are as follows. First, *response-independent primitivism*. On this view, objects have certain response-dependent primitive colors, and they had these primitive colors prior to the evolution of color vision. However, this view faces an epistemic problem. On an A-type theory, misperception under optimal conditions is not possible. If we evolved so that we bear the optimal cause relation to a color of an object, we are bound to be conscious of that color. But, given coincidental variation, such A-type theories are mistaken. Internal factors play some role in determining what colors we are conscious of, so that misperception under optimal conditions is possible. For instance, if we evolved so that we bear the optimal cause relation to a dull color of an object, we might be conscious of a bright color, owing to our internal processing. That might be so if the object is an important food source. Now what internal wiring we evolved is insensitive to the response-independent primitive colors that objects had prior to the evolution of color vision. Instead, it was determined by the unique set of selection pressures that operated on our ancestors, determined by their habits, dietary needs, and environments. So if we evolved internal wiring that makes us conscious of colors that occasionally coincide with the true response-independent colors of objects, then this can only be a lucky accident. Intuitively, this means that response-independent primitivism has the drawback of entailing that we cannot be credited with *knowledge* of the response-independent colors of objects in our environment, even if by a lucky accident we so evolved that we occasionally have true beliefs about the colors of those objects. In addition, response-independent primitivism is implausible for tastes and pains. Second, *response-dependent primitivism.* On this view, necessarily, an object has a primitive color just in case it is disposed to cause individuals to bear the consciousness relation to that primitive color under normal conditions. So, for instance, if on viewing a fruit Mabel is conscious of unitary red and Maxwell is conscious of red-yellow, then the fruit instantiates both of those primitive colors. Color vision and the primitive colors of external objects co-evolved. This view avoids the consequence of response-independent primitivism that we can only veridically perceive by accident, and so is compatible with the claim that we know the colors of things. But it violates our intuitions about color incompatibility, and it is unattractively complicated. Third, *projectivist primitivism.* On this view, which is the view I favor, we bear the consciousness relation to primitive colors, but nothing at all instantiates them. Colors live only in the contents of our experiences. I take a similar view of tastes and pains. It may be the common sense view that experience provides us with knowledge of the mind-independent sensible properties of things. On none of these three versions of primitivism about the sensible properties is this common sense view correct. The failure of the common sense view is an inevitable consequence of the combination of the relational view and coincidental variation.[21]

---

[21] For response-independent primitivism, see Campbell (1993). For response-dependent primitivism, see McGinn (1996). For projectivist primitivism, see Pautz (2006: 235), Pautz (MSa), Pautz (MSb), and Chalmers (2006). It should be noted that the epistemic problem raised in the text for the response-independent view applies equally to a pluralistic version of this view according to which before the evolution of color vision every object had a *cluster* of similar response-independent colors, but not every single color: for instance, on this view, an object might have various shades of red, but no shades of green, yellow, or blue (Kalderon 2007: 581). Given the role of internal factors in determining color-consciousness, we might have so evolved that, on viewing an object, we bear the consciousness relation to color properties that lie entirely outside of its color cluster. And if we so evolved that occasionally we bear the consciousness relation to properties lying within the color clusters of objects, this must be counted a lucky accident. So this view entails that we can never be said to have knowledge of the colors of things. (Of course, the problem is avoided by an even more radically pluralist response-independent view which makes veridicality assured by holding that every object has *every* color, but such a view is not to be taken seriously.) The pluralist version also violates our intuitions about color-exclusion because it holds that objects have all the colors different normal perceivers perceive them to have. One possible reply is that different perceivers are always conscious of colors from disjoint color families, and that color exclusion only holds within a color family (Kalderon, 2007: 583). But since some of the primitive colors one person perceives will exactly resemble some of the primitive colors another person perceives, this view goes against the principle

11. WHAT SHOULD WE CONCLUDE?

There are principled reasons to think that reductionism about the consciousness relation is false and primitivism is true. But sometimes it is not reasonable to follow an argument wherever it leads. The reductionist might say that the argument for reductionism is stronger than the argument I have presented against it. There are two reductionist views which might be adopted in face of the variation argument: mysterian reductionism and compromise reductionism.

Mysterian reductionism is the conjunction of three claims. First, there is a consciousness relation, and the constraints on its reduction I have put forward are correct. Second, reductionism is correct: there is a physical relation which satisfies the constraints, and with which the consciousness relation is identical. Third, we cannot even gesture at what this physical relation is because we are still in the early days of the reductionist program.[22]

To evaluate this response to the variation argument against reductionism, we must consider the argument for mysterian reductionism and the argument against it. The chief argument for mysterian reductionism is that the rival view of primitivism requires danglers (brute laws connecting the internal and functional properties of individuals with what sensible properties they bear the primitive consciousness relation to) and faces problems with mental causation. So even if we cannot come close to finding a physical relation that satisfies the four constraints, maybe we should simply conclude that we have not looked hard enough.

Another argument is that existing theories show promise in handling simple cases and this provides reason to think a suitably elaborate and detailed descendant of one of these theories will work for the more complicated examples.[23] Consider the optimal cause theory. And consider a simple case concerning belief rather than sensory consciousness. Jack and Jill view a cow. Jack sees it from close up and says *that is a cow*. Jill sees it from far away and says *that is a horse*. Intuitively, the right verdict in this case Jack and Jill bear the belief relation to different propositions. The optimal cause theory applied to belief accommodates this intuition. In the case of Jack, optimal conditions obtain, so the content of *that*

that for universals exact resemblance entails identity. And in any case it is not clear how it answers the intuitive objection. To take an example from section 4, intuitively, the unitary blue color that John is conscious of and the green-blue color that Jane is conscious of *exclude*, even if we say that they are from different families. These problems cast doubt on the claim that color pluralism is the best view of variation consistent with our pretheoretical conception of colors (Kalderon 2007: 584). Further, in its primitivist version, it is extremely complicated, requiring a kind of dualism at the surfaces of objects. Again, in my view, projectivism is the most reasonable view on color.

[22] For mysterian reductionism, see Byrne and Tye (2006: 252) and Lycan (2006). This form of mysterianism must be distinguished from that of McGinn (1989), which is instead a view about a priori deducibility.

[23] See Byrne and Tye (2006: 253–4).

is a cow in his belief-box is that there is a cow there. In the case of Jill, optimal
conditions do not obtain. She is viewing the cow from far away. But if they did,
that is a horse would only be tokened in her belief-box if there really had been
a horse there, so this is the content of this sentence in her belief-box. But this
provides no reason to believe that the optimal cause relation satisfies the variation
constraint in the coincidence cases I have presented. In the case of Jack and Jill,
the optimality clause saves the day. Not so in coincidence cases. For in these
cases the relevant individuals track the same properties *under optimal conditions*.
This is so however the vague notion of optimal conditions is elaborated. But
the most reasonable view is that in at least some of these cases the individuals
involved bear the consciousness relation to different properties. So even if the
optimal cause theory handles simple cases, there is absolutely no chance that a
suitably elaborate version will handle coincidence cases.

So the chief argument for mysterian reductionism is that the rival view of
primitivism requires danglers and faces problems with mental causation. But
there is also an argument against it. As we have seen, all the physical relations we
can think of fail to satisfy one or another of the four constraints (see Figure 2.3).
So mysterian reductionism requires that the alleged macro-level physical relation
which satisfies the constraints, and with which the consciousness relation is
identical, is a relation which we cannot presently think of. And there is a problem
with this view. Occasionally, mysterians about the mind–body link say that
we cannot form concepts of certain hidden *micro-level* physical properties, the
categorical bases of microphysical dispositions. This is not entirely implausible
because there is a sense in which the categorical bases of microphysical dispositions
are undetectable. But the mysterianism being contemplated now is implausible
because *macro-level* physical relations are perfectly detectable. So the mysterian
reductionist's claim that the consciousness relation is identical with a macro-level
physical relation that we cannot think of is very implausible. What could prevent
us from thinking of it?

In response, the defender of mysterian reductionism might attempt to provide
an alternative explanation of why we cannot think of the alleged hidden physical
relation which satisfies the four constraints. The explanation is provided by the
fantastic complexity of the sensory systems, the fact that there are huge gaps in
our knowledge of how sensible properties are represented in the brain, and of the
selection pressures driving the evolution of sensory systems.[24]

Against this, no discovery of what happens in the brain will enable us to
think of a physical relation between individuals and external properties that
we could not think of before and with which the consciousness relation might
be identified. Such discoveries may tell us a great detail about the details of
the neural content-carriers; but they will not tell us anything about how these
content-carriers get their contents. Consider an analogy: no amount of studying

---

[24] This is almost a direct quote from Byrne and Tye (2006: 252).

of the shapes of Chinese characters will enable one to discover what makes it the case that those characters carry the meanings they do among Chinese speakers. As for discoveries of the selection pressures driving evolution, it is impossible to see how they might reveal anything relevant here. In coincidence cases, the relevant differences are adaptations to different selection pressures, so that the sensory systems of the relevant individuals, although different, operate in accordance with design. Surely such cases are possible. Nothing we could discover about our actual evolutionary history could cast doubt on the claim that such cases are possible. I conclude that mysterian reductionism must be rejected.

Compromise reductionism is more concessive than mysterian reductionism. The compromise reductionist grants an inconsistency between the four constraints and reductionism about the consciousness relation. There is, on this view, no unknown physical relation that satisfies all the constraints. Since the extensionality constraint and the scrutability constraint are non-negotiable, this means we must choose between the relationality constraint, the variation constraint, and reductionism. But, whereas I hold that the most reasonable course is to keep the relational view and coincidental variation and give up reductionism, the compromise reductionist holds that the most reasonable course is to keep reductionism and give up the relational view or coincidental variation. For instance, he or she might keep reductionism and give up the relational view. Then the compromise reductionist would have no problem with coincidental variation. In particular, he or she might say that experiences are necessarily identical with internal brain states, which differ between the individuals in coincidence cases. Or he or she might keep reductionism, and reject coincidental variation rather than the relational view. In particular, the compromise reductionist might say that the consciousness relation is an A-type relation such as the optimal cause relation that is held constant in coincidence cases. This would entail that coincidental variation is false. In every possible coincidence case, on this view, the individuals involved bear the consciousness relation to exactly the same properties and have exactly the same experiences, in spite of the radical neural and functional differences between them.

But we cannot make sense of the phenomenological, semantic, and epistemic facts about sensory consciousness unless we accept the relational view. And I cannot bring myself to deny coincidental variation. Imagine meeting Yuck and Yum, Mild and Severe, or Mabel and Maxwell. To say that they have the same experiences in spite of all the evidence against this would be unreasonable. So the case for combining the relational view and coincidental variation is over-whelming.[25] By contrast, reductionism is an extremely speculative metaphysical

[25] This is one problem with combining a relational view such as intentionalism with an A-type reductive theory of the consciousness relation such as the optimal cause theory. Bad external correlation creates another, independent, problem that does not involve hypothetical coincidence cases. Given bad external correlation, a person might judge that one of his or her pains is twice as

claim. The chief argument for it is that it avoids danglers, providing a pleasingly simple view of the world. But it would be dogmatic to suppose that our world *must be* simple in this respect. So given the conflict between the relational view, coincidental variation and reductionism, I believe that the reasonable course is to keep the relational view and coincidental variation and to reject reductionism.

12. CONCLUDING REMARK

Primitivism does not automatically lead to the rejection of physicalism—at least if physicalism is a mere thesis of supervenience. G. E. Moore held that goodness is primitive yet supervenient on the natural as a matter of metaphysical necessity. Likewise, one could hold that the consciousness relation is primitive yet supervenient on the physical with metaphysical necessity. On this view, Zombies are impossible. This would yield what we might call *primitivist physicalism*. On this view, the consciousness relation is not a physical relation in the sense introduced at the beginning of section 3. It is not a complex relation constructible from the fundamental physical and functional relations of the world. It is an *extra* relation. But if primitivist physicalism is true, then the consciousness relation qualifies as physical in a broader sense because on this view it supervenes with metaphysical necessity on the physical way the world is. Alternatively, once one accepts primitivism, one could hold that the primitive consciousness relation supervenes on the physical with only nomological necessity. On this view, Zombies are possible. This would yield *property dualism*. Ontologically, primitivist physicalism and property dualism are identical, since both admit that the consciousness relation is an extra element of the world. They differ only modally. Which of these views should the primitivist adopt?

Some hold that reductionism about manifest properties fails in general in the sense that manifest properties cannot be identified with hugely complex properties built up from the fundamental physical and functional properties of the world. As noted, Moore held that reductionism fails in the case of the property of being good. And some would say that it fails even in the case of such

---

great as a second pain, even though the bodily disturbance the person bears the optimal cause relation to in having the first pain is *less than* twice as great as the bodily disturbance he or she bears the optimal cause relation to in having the second pain. Even under optimal conditions, there is *response expansion* (section 2). On a relational view such as intentionalism, truths about phenomenology are truths about content. So this combination of views runs the risk of entailing that John's introspective judgment about the phenomenal relationship among his pains is *false*. Since there is bad external correlation in general, the problem is general. For instance, such a combination of views also runs the risk of entailing that our introspective judgments about the resemblances among our color experiences and their unitary-binary structure are false. For a reply to this problem in the case of the unitary-binary character of color experience that involves complicated non-linear functions, see Tye and Bradley (2001). They do not explain how their reply applies to judgments about *resemblances* among color experiences or colors; nor do they address the problem as it arises for pain and taste.

unexciting properties as the property of being a mountain. But they still believe that there is an argument for believing that they supervene (with metaphysical necessity). Likewise, it might be said that, even if sensory consciousness fails to reduce, there is an argument for believing that it supervenes.

But this is a mistake. I do not think that the property of being good or the property of being a mountain fails to reduce. But if even we knew that they fail to reduce, we would have an a priori justification for believing that they supervene. It is inconceivable that a world that is a physical or natural duplicate of our world should differ from our world with respect to pattern of instantiation of the property of being a mountain or the property of being good. But consciousness is an exception. In the case of consciousness, we lack such a priori justification for supervenience.

In fact, I believe that reflection reveals that in the case of consciousness the only possible argument for supervenience proceeds by way of reduction. In slogan form: no justification without reduction. The argument from simplicity (avoiding danglers) and the causal exclusion argument might give us reason to accept reductionism about consciousness in a broad sense that includes reduction to functional properties. And reductionism entails supervenience. These arguments do not support supervenience independently of reductionism; they do not support primitivist physicalism. For, since primitivism is like property dualism, it faces the same problems about danglers and mental causation, as we shall see.

Now I have argued that reductionism about sensory consciousness fails. Even if one rejects my argument, one must at least admit that we are not overall justified in accepting reductionism. At the very least, we should suspend judgment. So if the only argument for supervenience proceeds by way of reductionism, we are left without any argument for accepting supervenience in the crucial case of consciousness. So we are left without any argument for even a minimal form of physicalism. We are also left without an argument for accepting what we might call *mysterian primitivist physicalism,* which has recently been defended by some philosophers.[26] This view combines primitivist physicalism with the claim that the supervenience of consciousness on the physical is not a priori to us now but would be a priori if only we knew more about the physical world. (Of course, this view must be distinguished from mysterian *reductionism* discussed in section 11.) Once we accept primitivism, there is no argument for accepting this view because there is no argument for accepting supervenience in the first place.[27]

---

[26] McGinn (1996) defends primitivist physicalism, and McGinn (1989) defends mysterianism.

[27] One might think that I have overlooked an argument: all other properties and relations of the manifest image supervene with metaphysical necessity, so we have inductive reason to think that the consciousness relation supervenes as well—even if it fails to reduce. This argument fails for two reasons. First, it is not clear that all other properties and relations of the manifest image supervene with metaphysical necessity. Consider sensible properties like color, sound, and taste: the gap between the ostensible sensible properties of external objects and physical properties is

In fact, I think we can say something stronger. Once we accept primitivism, there are two reasons for preferring property dualism over primitivist physicalism. First, we have the intuition that Zombies are possible. On any view, this provides *some* evidence that supervenience fails. Now, typically, defenders of supervenience respond that we have countervailing reasons to accept supervenience and to doubt this intuition. But, as we have seen, once we accept primitivism, we have no countervailing reasons to accept supervenience. So we no longer have any reason to doubt this intuition. Second, there is the Humean dictum against necessary connections between wholly distinct existences. Perhaps there are counterexamples to this dictum (for instance, being red seems to necessitate being extended), but one might think that in those cases where we have no reason to believe that distinct existences are necessarily connected we are justified in believing that the connection is only contingent.

But I should say that I do not find the modal issue between primitivist physicalism and property dualism very interesting, because these views are very similar and face the same problems. Property dualism requires nomological danglers: fundamental laws that dangle from the rest of the body of nomological truths. Primitivist physicalism requires modal danglers: necessary connections between wholly distinct properties that dangle from the rest of the body of modal truths. So the views seem on a par with respect to complexity. And, unlike some reductionist views, both views face the dilemma between overdetermination and epiphenomenalism. Of course, there are proposals on how to dodge this dilemma, but they seem available to the property dualist as well as the primitivist physicalist.[28]

In my view, the real interesting issue is the one that divides reductionism and primitivism. The views provide radically different pictures of our world. Here I have argued for the relational view and coincidental variation, and I have argued that these claims lead to primitivism.[29]

---

just as wide as the gap between consciousness and physical properties. Second, the properties of the manifest image that supervene also arguably reduce. So once we accept primitivism about the consciousness relation, we are admitting that it is very different from other properties and relations of the manifest image, and this considerably weakens the inductive inference.

[28] See Bealer (2007).

[29] Earlier versions of this chapter were presented at the New York University Friday Forum in 2002; at the universities of Michigan, Iowa, Texas, Arizona, Massachusetts, and Colorado in 2004; and at the inauguration of the Centre for Consciousness at the Australian National University in 2004. Thanks to the audiences on those occasions. I would especially like to thank David Barnett, George Bealer, Anna Bjurman-Pautz, Ned Block, David Chalmers, Rob Koons, Stephen Schiffer, and Michael Tye for comments and other help.

3

Saving Appearances: A Dilemma for Physicalists

Charles Siewert

1. INTRODUCTION

The sort of physicalism or materialism I will criticize finds expression in slogans of the form: '*X* is *nothing but*—or *nothing over and above*—*Y*.' What goes in for '*X*' is, for example, consciousness, or some type of experience—at any rate, it is something mental or psychological. Such views are plausibly described as 'reductionist.' By purporting to tell us what every mentalistic X *is*, they promise to *explain* it in physical terms. But just what makes something physical in the relevant sense is not obvious, and partly for this reason it is hard to see how precisely to characterize these views as a group. However, that does not matter too much for my purposes, as long as the difficulty I will spell out does in fact arise for views I will describe, whatever general category might unite them.

I have advertised the issues broadly (using 'consciousness,' 'mental,' and 'experience'), but my discussion will not remain this general. Rather I will concentrate more specifically on the notion of *visual appearance*. I will describe scenarios contrasting the occurrence of visual appearance in a certain sense with its absence. This will provide us with both a way to clarify our understanding of visual appearance and a test for theoretical recognition of its reality (and, by implication, of the reality of phenomenal consciousness generally). This then will motivate a challenge to 'ambitious' or reductive physicalist/materialist theories. Roughly speaking, the problem will be that, depending on the form they take, they either ultimately run into trouble acknowledging the reality of appearances, or else, to save appearances while holding onto their ambitions, they purport to discover deep necessities where warrant for these eludes us. If this dilemma is not resolved, then we should abandon ambitions to reduce consciousness to something physical. The question that finally confronts us then is whether this gives us any cause for regret.

2. 'LOOKS' IN A SENSORY, PHENOMENAL SENSE

To understand the challenge I want to pose, we must put off discussing the theories in question for awhile, and first try patiently to clarify the relevant notion of visual appearance. By 'a visual appearance' I mean an instance of something's *looking somehow to someone.* The use of 'looks' I want to invoke can be found in sentences of the form '*x* looks *F* (e.g., green or oval) to S.' But it is not confined to these. It can be found when I make claims like 'It looks to me as if this figure is larger than that one,' or: 'That one looks to me changing in shape, and *this* one looks to me to be staying the same shape,' or: 'That looks to me like a hat.'[1] When thinking of such examples, note that it is a *sensory* (visual) sense of 'looks' to which I wish to make appeal. Not all 'looks' are sensory. There is a (non-sensory, non-visual) sense in which we can speak of how it looks to us even when we have our eyes closed in a dark room, or if we are totally blind—as when someone says, 'It looks to me as if the next election's going to be very close.'[2]

Now I want to focus on a sense of 'looks' and 'visually appear' that is not only *sensory,* but *phenomenal.* To clarify this, I will not contrast a phenomenal sense of 'looks' with a non-phenomenal one, but with a non-phenomenal sense of 'vision.' One can be said to have *visual perception* or form *visual representations,* or have *vision,* even in the *absence* of visual appearances. There is a sense in which you might be said to *see* things, even when they do not *look* any way to you. Let me try to make clear how this could be by reference to the phenomenon of 'blindsight.' Psychologists and philosophers have extensively discussed experimental work on 'blindsighters'—subjects who have retained some visual functioning while suffering certain kinds of damage to their visual

---

[1] I do not mean to deny any logical distinction among sentences of these forms. For example, 'It looks to me as if that's a green one and that's a yellow one' does not entail 'That one looks green to me, and that one looks yellow to me.' For the first statement may be true in a situation where, in a very dimly lit room, one item merely looks darker to me than the other—and on that basis (plus some background assumptions) I'm inclined to judge the one is green, the other yellow. In that case, it would be wrong to say simply, 'one looks green to me, the other yellow.' (I adapt this example from Maund 2003.) However, one can grant such observations, while holding that the use of 'looks' in each of the sentences above counts as '*phenomenal.*' It seems I would disagree with Maund, in that I don't think reports of how something looks to us in a sensory and phenomenal sense have to be confined to a specific grammatical form, and I would not contrast 'phenomenal' with 'intentional.' Many phenomenal visual features we ordinarily enjoy are in my view inherently intentional.

[2] Here I take no position on the question of whether only *sensory* appearances (e.g., what's reported by 'looks' in a sensory sense) are phenomenal. Elsewhere (Siewert 1998: chapter 8) I argue that non-sensory conceptual thought is phenomenally conscious.

cortex. But not everyone describes such subjects in just the same way. I want to make explicit a way of understanding the condition of blindsight subjects that will help illuminate the notion of visual appearance at issue. This will take a little while to set out fully.[3]

We start with this. To consider the condition of a blindsighter, suppose you are seated before a screen, in a well-lit room with your eyes open, and in various locations on the screen various relatively simple figures and arrangements of lines are briefly presented — such as Xs and Os, or rows of either horizontal or vertical lines. Now suppose that because of damage to your brain, a change has occurred in your reports about what you see when such stimuli are presented. On some portion of the screen (on the left, let's say), where, with gaze fixed, you formerly would have reported seeing an X or an O (or horizontal or vertical lines), now, post-trauma, you no longer report seeing anything at all. When an X is flashed there, and you are asked what you see there, you say 'Nothing.' Nonetheless, when asked which of two figures (X or O) was presented there, and *required to make a choice*, you turn out to answer correctly at levels significantly above chance. Somehow the effect of the light from the stimulus on your eye and brain has enabled you to make this sort of 'forced' or 'prompted' discrimination of the presented figures. There is, it seems, a sense in which we can regard this as a case of 'visual' discrimination. This is blindsight. That such cases are actual has been made clear by the research of Weiskrantz (1986, 1997) and others.

You might understand a bit more specifically just what this condition involves in the following way. Suppose that, in the situation just described, the stimuli in that area where you deny seeing anything do not, in fact, *look* or *visually appear* any way at all to you — in a sense in which, elsewhere in the area before you, things still *do* look to you somehow. If you were to say that *nothing in that region of the screen looked any way at all to you*, you would be speaking the *truth*. And so, provided that talk of 'seeing' is interpreted so as to entail that you can't *see* what doesn't *look* any way to you, your denial that you see anything there would also be correct. Still, your brain's visual system enables you to make forced choice discriminations of the shapes or orientations of these figures, and so perhaps we should say there is also a sense in which you 'see' or 'visually perceive' them. Thus: in one sense you are *blind* to the figures (they don't look any way to you); in another sense you *see* them (you somehow discriminate and perhaps represent them by means of your brain's visual system) — hence you have

---

[3] My discussion here adapts, revises and condenses core aspects of my earlier discussion of blindsight and consciousness (Siewert 1998: chapters 3–6) — with a focus here on 'looks' and 'visual appearance' rather than 'phenomenally conscious.' What I say (now and before) bears similarities to Block's (2007) use of blindsight to explain the phenomenal concept of consciousness, but there are notable differences. For instance, I do not rely on his concepts of 'access' and 'monitoring' consciousness, and my Linda character is not described in the same way as his 'superblindsighter.'

'blindsight.' At any rate, this is an intelligible way of conceiving of the condition of blindsight.[4]

This shows we can conceive of states that are in *some* sense visual (and thus sensory) that are, however, not *phenomenal* visual states—not visual *appearances*. One may suppose that there is some *visual* state (some state of the visual system)—even one we may regard as 'representational' or 'information-bearing'—that is present in blindsight, and enables one to make, when prompted, discriminations of the figures one denies seeing. To grasp the contrast between vision of this sort, and that in which something looks some way to you (in the sensory sense) is to take a crucial step in grasping what I mean when I say visual appearance is phenomenal.

Now let's refine our understanding of visual appearance further, by altering the features of the blindsight situation a little, so as to consider a *hypothetical* form of it. Note that discriminations made in the sort of blindsight just discussed are elicited by means of 'forced choices'—prompting with a choice 'X or O?' offered to subjects who regard their responses as mere 'guesses.' However, it is not very difficult to conceive of a form of blindsight in which the discriminations, as revealed in verbal reports, button-pressings and the like, arise *spontaneously and unprompted by others' multiple choice questions.* Suppose that—while it remains true that the stimuli in your upper left quadrant do not look or visually appear any way to you—still, you find yourself disposed to judge, without having a choice forced on you, that a figure of a certain shape or orientation is or was just there—for some (perhaps not very extensive) range of shapes, orientations, and locations. For example, it just spontaneously occurs to you (perhaps in response to a self-posed question, perhaps not) that there is an X there, say. And you feel confident that this is true, as you might feel confident in your spontaneous and direct answer to the question, 'What day of the week is today?' And we may suppose: you are inclined to point to where you think the stimulus is, and adjust your gaze so as to look *at* it (in which case it *does* then *look* X-shaped to you, and you thereby confirm your judgment). So you also have this *non-verbal* responsiveness to the stimulus. Thus, to interpret 'looks' in the phenomenal manner, I ask you to conceive of this sort of spontaneous visual response to a stimulus that does *not* look any way to you, and contrast this with a case in which it *does*.

But here please note: I am *not* asking you to assume that spontaneous blindsight judgment is compatible with the principles governing vision (e.g.,

---

[4] I am deeply indebted to Weiskrantz's research on blindsight. But it seems to me he goes awry when he talks about consciousness, by suggesting that all his subjects are missing for visual consciousness is some monitoring function—'comment-ability'—with respect to a type of vision that may take either conscious or unconscious forms. Weiskrantz's discussion encourages one to think of blindsight as a condition in which one sees, but is 'blind' to the fact that one does. By contrast, I conceive of it as a condition in which the subject is, in a sense, *blind*, and (in another) *sees*. The subject is 'blind': the stimulus doesn't look anyhow to him or her. But the subject 'sees': he or she discriminates it via his or her visual system. What is crucial is to acknowledge the intelligibility of the latter (my) interpretation.

human neuropsychology) in the actual world. Maybe it is not—and the case is 'purely hypothetical.' However, I do assume that for the purposes of clarifying how we understand an expression, we can consider how it would apply (or not apply) in at least some hypothetical cases, without needing to be confident that the situations described wouldn't demand the natural world somehow be other than it actually is.

To get clearer about how to understand this hypothetical case, I need to make this explicit. I am not asking you to suppose that *what* is judged, the *content* of spontaneous judgments made in the two situations—with and without visual appearance—would be *in every way indistinguishable*. That might be impossible. To see this, consider: you may have no way of thinking specifically of the peculiar shape you see something to have on a given occasion, but demonstratively, as: *this shape*. And how you understand *which* shape *this* one is may depend on the stimulus right then and there *appearing* to you a certain way. You might articulate this way of understanding by saying that *this* shape is the shape that *this now looks* to you. Similarly we might say that you can judge a stimulus to have a certain *color*—*this shade*—where your understanding of what you mean by 'this shade' depends on its looking some way to you then and there: *the shade this now looks to me*. Thus I may understand which shape or shade I take a stimulus to have, in a way properly expressed by speaking of its concurrently *looking* somehow to me.

But it seems that your spontaneous blindsight discriminatory judgment could not have just the content identified relative to this way of understanding. For, *by hypothesis*, you are then *lacking* the visual appearance required. And plausibly, you cannot understand which shape you are thinking of, in a manner to be articulated as: *the shape this now looks to me*—if in fact *this* now *looks to you no way at all*. The point is: when we consider the scenario of spontaneous blindsight discrimination, we don't assume that we can entirely *duplicate* in blindsight all the very same judgments about visual stimuli that phenomenal vision affords. For we may wish to recognize a class of 'directly appearance dependent' judgments. These would be judgments where an expression of *what is judged* is understood by the subject in a manner that requires that it look or visually appear somehow to the subject at the very time of judgment. Subjects *lacking* the relevant appearances (like blindsighters) obviously could not make such judgments, or engage in behavior expressive of them.[5]

Clearly though, there will be *some* ways of classifying stimuli that can figure in spontaneous visually triggered judgments that are *not* 'directly appearance-dependent' in the way just illustrated. You can, of course, somehow understand what you mean by an assertive utterance of 'O-shaped,' or 'vertical,' or 'green,'

---

[5] My talk of 'appearance-dependent ways of understanding what is judged' is intended to leave open just how we should interpret, or even whether we should admit, the notion of distinctive 'phenomenal concepts.'

or 'brighter,' or 'larger,' or 'above'—without its *then and there* looking to you in ways thus reportable, in the sense we supposed absent in blindsight. And this remains so, even in the case where something looks O-shaped to you, and you judge it to be O-shaped: here too your understanding of what you mean by 'O-shaped' does not require that something then and there look O-shaped to you. For you understand what you mean by this term in the same way when you close your eyes. Your understanding of classifications (both in the blindsight and in the normal cases) can thus be at least *relatively* independent of current visual appearance, in the sense that they are not directly appearance-dependent.

You have so far supposed that you possess a power of spontaneous judgment to discriminate at least some features in part of your visual field where you would correctly report that nothing *looks* any way to you. Now however, to simplify further discussion, make the part of your visual field in which nothing looks any way to you encompass its *entire extent*. *Nothing at all* looks any way to you. It follows of course that the way you understand the terms by which you would express any spontaneous judgment about the stimuli—'X,' 'O,' 'vertical line,' 'horizontal line'—is *at least relatively independent* of visual appearance. (They are 'at least relatively independent' if they aren't *directly dependent*, and in this case they can't be directly dependent on your enjoying visual appearances, because you *haven't got any*.)

Now—compare this kind of blindsight case with a rather seriously degraded sort of phenomenal vision. Suppose nothing in your visual field looks any way to you, *except* what occurs in this relatively small part, and what appears there looks very blurry, and your vision is severely lacking in acuity. Still you would say correctly that something *looks* some way to you—perhaps you can say whether some patch of light looks brighter or darker, larger or smaller, moving or stationary. But stimuli there do not look distinctly X-shaped, O-shaped, etc., and the lines whose orientation you are asked to judge are not distinctly apparent to you. There seems now to be no obstacle to supposing that the range of spontaneous *blindsight* judgments you can make, in the case where nothing looks anyhow to you, are not overall inferior to those one can make in the latter 'blursight' case, in terms your understanding of which is not directly dependent on visual appearance. In fact, we can suppose that the judgments made with blindsight (e.g., of shape, size, and orientations) would be in some ways better (more discriminating) than the relatively appearance-independent judgments made with phenomenal blursight.[6]

So the contrast here is between a subject to whom nothing (sensorily) *looks* any way at all, and one to whom only stimuli in a relatively small area before her

---

[6] This hypothetical scenario appears to have been partially realized in Weiskrantz's subject D.B. (Weiskrantz 1986). At one stage D.B. reported regaining limited blurry sight in part of his formerly 'blind' field. But Weiskrantz found that his discriminations of stimuli in this area were by certain measures actually less acute than his blindsight discriminations.

look any way at all—and then only very blurrily, and in a manner that affords only relatively crude discriminatory judgments. One can conceive of the former subject (let's now call her 'Linda') having powers of blindsight that enable her to make unforced discriminatory judgments that are in some ways better than the relatively appearance-independent judgments made by the latter (call her 'Glenda').

Now for one more twist. We have recognized interpretations of 'visual,' 'vision,' and 'sight' that allow these to apply where there is discrimination of stimuli wherein what is 'seen' does not *look* or *visually appear* to the sighted person. But if we can make such a notion of 'the visual' available to ourselves, there is no reason we cannot make it available to the subjects in our scenarios. Suppose now that Linda can also classify the judgments she makes as 'visual' in the sense we have just recognized. Much as, seemingly without inference, she is able to tell when she is *judging* that something is so, as opposed to *wondering whether* it is, she is also able to classify her blindsight judgments as *visual* ones. We might say then that Linda not only enjoys a spontaneous blindsight—her blindsight is '*reflective*' in this sense: she can make discriminatory judgments not only about the visual stimuli but about these very discriminatory judgments as well, and thereby classify them as visual.

Glenda, meanwhile, though she can say that things look somehow to her when they do, has no inclination to employ *this* concept of the *visual* in her judgments about herself. Instead she is disposed to say that things do or don't *look* some way to her, and that they are thus and so, because of how they look to her, and that she judges that things look some way to her—where her use of 'look' is to be interpreted in line with our previous remarks. In this respect, I might add, Glenda and I are not so different. For my ordinary reflective first-person judgments about vision are about things *looking* some way to me, or about my *seeing* this or that (in a sense of 'see' that implies visual appearance). Although on reflection I can acknowledge a way of understanding 'vision' and 'seeing' divorced from looking, that is not a concept of 'visual' I ordinarily employ in thinking about my own vision.

The immediate point of this exercise was to explain how to interpret 'looks' and 'visual appearance' in a certain way. If it was successful, you recognize a sensory, phenomenal sense in which things look to you somehow, which allows you to contrast the situation of Linda (to whom things don't look any way) with that of Glenda (to whom things do, but only quite blurrily)—while nevertheless Linda is able to make unprompted discriminatory judgments of somewhat greater range than the 'relatively appearance-independent' judgments Glenda can make of shape, size, etc. Of course, one may refuse to cooperate in this exercise. But if you show a little patience, I don't think you need find any insuperable difficulty in interpreting 'looks' or 'appearance' in the manner I suggest.

3. A TEST FOR PHENOMENAL REALISM

In order to pose my problem for ambitious physicalism, I need to make a couple of points explicit. Recall that I have not been asking you to assume that the occurrence of two subjects such as Linda and Glenda is consistent with the principles governing the occurrence of visual perception in the actual world. Let us say that if their occurrence is *not* consistent with those principles, then the contrast described between Linda and Glenda is 'nomologically impossible.' That is, in that case it would be nomologically impossible for two subjects to differ as they were said to differ with respect to the visual appearances they enjoyed while otherwise being just as they were said to be.

Now, it seems that acceptance of certain claims about what we *mean,* what we *have in mind,* or what *concepts* we use, when we describe something in a certain way, would commit us to saying that certain scenarios are *inconceivable* for us in a sense that would have us regard them as *more than just nomologically impossible.* If I asked you to conceive of a situation in which Linda did not differ from Glenda in height, but Glenda was taller by an inch, you might reasonably respond that this is inconceivable for you. For when you say 'x is taller than y' part of what you mean or part of what you have in mind is that x and y *do* differ in height. Or it is part of your concept of *being taller than* that they would differ in height. In saying this, you would not be saying just that the occurrence of two such subjects is inconsistent with principles you accept governing the conditions under which objects in the actual world vary or are similar in size. You would not just be saying you regard the scenario as nomologically impossible.

Similarly, switching from talk of *meaning* and *concepts,* to talk of *natures, properties,* and *constitution*—if you said that differing in height belongs to the *property of being taller,* or is part of *what it is to be taller,* or partly *constitutes being taller,* then you would be saying something stronger than just that, as things are in the actual world, things that differ in tallness differ in height. You would be saying more than just that it is nomologically impossible to differ with respect to the one without differing with respect to the other. Now perhaps 'the right sort of' principles of nature secure truths about the identity of properties, natures, or what constitutes what. But the sheer fact that there is a nomological relationship between F and G (even one that says you get F *just when* you get G) is not by itself sufficient to secure such truths. So it seems that there is more than a mere nomological necessity and possibility invoked when one speaks of the identities of properties, what the nature of something is, or what constitutes what. And if this cannot somehow be accounted for in terms of what is conceivable, or *conceptually* necessary and possible, we may wish to speak here, as one sometimes does, of 'metaphysical' possibility—the sense in which it has been claimed that it is *metaphysically* impossible to have water without H_2O.

I rehearse these points because I am concerned that certain views about mind apparently (if not always explicitly) put themselves in the business of making either conceptual or metaphysical assumptions that would commit one to claims of more than nomological impossibility. Such theories would commit us to saying that the contrast I have invited us to consider between Linda and Glenda is more than just nomologically impossible—it's somehow rationally *inconceivable*, or perhaps *metaphysically* impossible. But that is not a conclusion I think we should accept lightly. For I believe that the way of interpreting 'looks' manifest in considering that contrast is not arbitrary, but provides a way of articulating and refining an understanding of ordinary talk of things looking this or that way to us. But if we do understand 'looks' in this manner, and yet it turns out that this interpretation should be deemed somehow conceptually incoherent, or that Linda's form of blindsight not only can't happen, given actual world psychology, but in some more fundamental way *couldn't* happen ('in any possible world'), then it turns out that our belief that things look somehow or other to us is deeply confused—there is no difference, of the sort we suppose, between the presence and absence of visual appearance; we literally don't know what we're talking about, when we say things look somehow to us. If the sort of contrast we seem to draw between Linda and Glenda really should be regarded as inconceivable, or if there is just nothing in reality that will permit any such contrast, then visual appearance is a cognitive illusion, and phenomenal vision is not real.

So I would propose that a theory's conceptual and metaphysical tolerance for the contrast between Linda's blindsight and Glenda's impoverished phenomenal vision provides a test for recognition of the reality of phenomenal vision itself. If acceptance of a theory would deprive you of the ability even to conceive coherently of this contrast, or it would commit you to regarding this contrast as deeply (more than nomologically) impossible, then it implicitly denies the reality of phenomenal vision.

4. PHYSICALISM CHALLENGED

Now I want to explain why some views don't seem to me to pass this test. Consider some of the remarks made by Daniel Dennett. He warns us against the 'trap' of thinking that, in vision, there is any appearance to be reckoned with—any 'seeming'—over and above one's 'judging' in some way that something is so. So when faced with a case of visual color illusion, in which the spaces between lines in a grid seem pink, he says it would be a mistake to think there is 'a phenomenon of really seeming—over and above the phenomenon of judging in one way or another that something is the case' (Dennett 1991: 364). The manner of judging in question is likened to a 'presentiment': it just occurs to you 'that there is something pink out there, the way it might suddenly occur to you that there's somebody standing behind you.' So: if you think that, in vision, things look some way to you, where this is distinguishable from your somehow spontaneously judging them to be some way, then you're wrong. This is important for Dennett because much of the point of his book *Consciousness Explained* is to persuade the reader that there is in reality nothing of the sort that people confusedly suppose a theory of consciousness needs to explain. We shouldn't ask a theory of consciousness to explain 'real seeming,' since there *just isn't any such phenomenon.*

But it is not always so clear exactly what Dennett is denying with his 'nothing over and above' talk. It seems he is not denying that we can conceive of someone spontaneously judging a visual stimulus is there, when it does not visually seem any way to her. (He agrees that a form of spontaneous blindsight is conceivable.) Rather, it seems he's saying that the contrast between such judgment and a visual appearance is *really nothing but a contrast between two species of judgment*—differing in the fineness of their content. For what he says he finds inconceivable is that *what is judged*—the *contents* of a spontaneous blindsighter's judgments—might surpass the *'limited and crude'* sort found in actual blindsight. To help motivate this, he suggests that we consider the 'talents' that actual blindsighters, with their crude and limited repertoire, lack with regard to the visual stimuli they deny seeing. Then he contends 'that what people have in mind when they talk of 'visual consciousness,' 'actually seeing,' and the like, is nothing over and above some collection or other of these missing talents.' (Dennett 1993: 151) So, it seems the claim is that 'all we have in mind' (or perhaps: all we *should* have in mind) when we contrast visual appearance with its absence is this difference in talents that goes with a difference in the relative 'fineness' or 'crudity' of the contents of judgments.

But at this point recall: Glenda, to whom we supposed things do look some way, has a pretty limited and crude content repertoire. And the only contents we supposed she had in her repertoire that Linda lacked were those the understanding of which depended on things looking somehow to her, in a sense of 'looks' specified by way of contrast with spontaneous verbally expressible judgment. But the contents of Glenda's judgments were not generally *finer*, or *less crude*, than Linda's. In fact, in some respects, Linda had a greater range of contents available for judging. Glenda's judgments differed from Linda's not in *greater general refinement.* They differed in depending on stimuli *looking* somehow to her—because they were judgments understood by her in a manner she might express by saying, e.g., 'the size (or shape or brightness) *this looks to me.*' However, it seems as if Dennett is saying a difference in how talented one is with respect to visual stimuli, how finely or crudely one's judgment distinguishes them, is all we do or should have in mind when we talk about visual appearance and its absence. But if we accept this, our scenario becomes incoherent. We tried to conceive of a scenario in which one subject (Glenda) is *not* superior to another (Linda) in respect of certain talents, when really all we had (or should have had) in mind when we distinguished them is that the first is more talented than the second in those respects. Belief in Dennett's view of consciousness would in that case render inconceivable the contrast wherein our grasp of the notion of visual appearance is evident, and so implicitly deny the reality of phenomenal vision.

Similar points might be applied to the general strategy for thinking about the mind, sometimes explicitly used for defending a physicalist or materialist perspective, known as functionalism—for Dennett's view might be seen as a variant of this strategy. There is great diversity in what may be regarded as a functionalist theory of mind. But I take the basic idea to be that differences in what mental states you have amount to differences in what 'functional roles' are being played or realized in you—where great variation is allowed in the physical nature of the structures or mechanisms that can play or realize such roles. In the case of visual appearance, the proposal would be that the difference between something's looking somehow to you, and its looking some other way to you (or not at all), is accounted for entirely in terms of some 'functional' difference, plus whatever physical mechanisms realize just those functions. The functionalist will say there is nothing to vision over and above exercising certain 'multiply realizable' functions (i.e., they can be realized in a physically very diverse range of entities), which functions can be understood ultimately in non-phenomenal terms—without employing 'looks' or 'visual appearance' in the sense to be accounted for. Once you have explained what these functions are, and what physical mechanisms carry out these functions in a particular case (or a particular 'population')—you have explained everything about visual appearance.

This suggests that functionalism will also have trouble passing the test for phenomenal realism. If there is to be really *wide* variation in the internal physical make-up of entities that realize the functions in question, it will seem that the character of the functions will have to be, in a sense, 'manifest,' not 'hidden.' That is, they will be the sort of functions one can have warrant for thinking are being somehow realized in oneself or someone else, even without internal, beneath the surface examination of the entity in whom they are realized—as one could have warrant for regarding Linda as capable of crude spontaneous visual discrimination without directly or indirectly observing her brain. But now if the functions that constitute vision (or our concept of it) are entirely *manifest* (only their physically variable realization is hidden), then it will be hard to see how to avoid rendering the contrast between Linda and Glenda either inconceivable or more than nomologically impossible.

For consider: if functionalism maintains a strong claim of multiple realizability, then it would seem to need to hold at least one of two claims. The 'conceptual' functionalist would hold that 'all we really have in mind' (or 'all we mean') by saying that things would look some way to Glenda but not to Linda, is that Glenda implements a certain manifest function (talent, disposition) absent in Linda. And a 'manifest property' functionalist would hold that the subjects' difference in experience would *consist in nothing but* Glenda's implementing a manifest function, absent in Linda. The worry then is that we conceived of Linda and Glenda in a manner that seems to leave us no way to spell out what we mean by saying it looks somehow to one but not the other, or what constitutes this difference, in terms of some manifest functional superiority on the part of Glenda, *without resort to the phenomenal difference between them.* For once we see that Glenda's phenomenal vision is not functionally superior to Linda's blindsight, with respect to the general fineness of discrimination it affords, we will find that the only manifest differences that would cling to such subjects, *relevant* for differentiating them phenomenally, are those whose characterizations depend on thinking of its *looking* somehow to Glenda but not to Linda. No one would or should maintain, for instance, that all we *mean* by or what *constitutes* the difference between them is the difference in the phonological properties by which they express the difference in appearance-dependent attitudes. That is, no one should hold that Glenda's *phenomenal* superiority lies in her being disposed to utter *types of sounds* the Linda is not disposed to utter. And we shouldn't think we can conjure a difference in whether things look somehow to the two subjects *purely* out of the fact that they merely *think* there is that very difference between them. We shouldn't think that what gives Glenda something more—visual appearances—than Linda, is simply that Glenda *thinks* she's got something more.[7] So to locate a functional superiority, we are ultimately thrown back on the fact that Glenda has attitudes of a sort that can be had only by someone to whom something *looks* somehow. But to rely ineliminably on differences so characterized (i.e., phenomenally) would be to reduce the theory to triviality. The *functional* difference in terms of which the *phenomenal* difference was to be identified would then be itself identified partly in terms of the phenomenal difference in question. Thus to confine ourselves to the resources for thinking about the mind to which a *non-trivial* manifest functionalism would restrict us would be to render inconceivable or deeply impossible the contrast between Linda's and Glenda's vision. So, unless we can point to some manifest functional difference in the contrast that would supply a reasonable candidate for capturing the phenomenal difference in non-phenomenal terms, we should think that such functionalism does not pass the test for phenomenal realism.[8]

We can see perhaps more clearly how this sort of problem arises if we consider certain views that are rather more specific than the generic, programmatic functionalism just considered. I have in mind here accounts whose authors (or

---

[7] Or so I argue in Siewert (1998: 130–3).

[8] It should be clear that I believe this problem arises whether we take functionalism as a conceptual thesis (as in Armstrong 1968 and Lewis 1972) or as a 'scientific essentialist' thesis about properties (as in Putnam 1967). Notice also that my argument here is *not* the 'absent qualia' argument, if that is supposed to rest on the claim that two subjects who are *completely manifestly functionally equivalent* might nonetheless differ experientially.

critics) tend to classify as 'reductive representationalist' theories of phenomenal character. These appear to come in two general varieties: 'first-order' representationalist, and 'higher order' representationalist. The first would hold that visual appearance—its looking somehow to someone—can be reduced to (and thereby *explained as*) a special form of mental representation of objects and features in one's environment ('first-order' representations). The second sort of view would hold that phenomenal vision requires (and is to be explained as) a certain way of representing one's own visual states (hence 'higher order' mental representations). These views' explanatory ambitions would bring them under the vague rubric of physicalism insofar as they promise to fit phenomenal sensory states into a general 'naturalistic' theory of mental representation that accounts for this in physical terms. I will take as an example of 'first-order' reductive representationalism the theory articulated and defended in some detail by Michael Tye (1995, 2002), while my 'higher order' representationalist will be David Rosenthal (2002), who has developed his 'higher order thought' version of the idea in detail.

According to Tye, the phenomenal character of sense perception is explained by reducing it to what he calls 'poised, abstract, non-conceptual intentional content,' which he refers to by the acronym 'PANIC.' The theory holds that something looks somehow colored and shaped to you—thus you have experience with a certain 'phenomenal character'—just when your brain forms a kind of fine-grained and unified representation of color and shape that represents in a 'map-like' fashion (by contrast with the 'sentence-like' manner of *conceptual* representations), and which is 'poised' to affect your beliefs (that is, available to have a direct impact on your beliefs by, e.g., disposing you to judge that there is something of a certain color and shape before you).

But now, if we adopt this theory, and think that its looking somehow to you is nothing but your being in a 'PANIC' state, how will we conceive of the contrast between Linda's blindsight and Glenda's blursight? What has Glenda got that Linda hasn't? Linda's blindsight is no worse overall than Glenda's poor phenomenal vision in what it affords by way of spontaneous discrimination of visual stimuli. So we would seem to have just as much call to think that Linda has encoded in her head a map-like representation of the visual stimuli to which she responds, which is not less detailed and unified than any we would be entitled to attribute to Glenda. And Tye himself would admit that there is nothing to prevent one from forming this sort of non-conceptual representation of what looks no way at all to one—otherwise there would be no need to introduce the 'poise' condition for PANIC. So would they differ with respect to *poise*? Recall that our two subjects are both disposed to spontaneous judgments, verbally and otherwise expressible, about what types of stimuli are before them. And so there would seem to be nothing relevant to distinguish their 'poise'—except that Glenda would be disposed to judgments about (e.g.) shape and color, her understanding of which would be articulated by talking about how things looked to her. But we don't want to have the theory characterize the special sort of representational content that allows us reductively to explain things looking to us as they do by saying—'and it's the kind of content that can be had only when things *look* to one somehow.' That kind of circularity would undermine the theory's right to claim it *explains* visual appearance. So, if we are to distinguish the two subjects content-wise, it will need to be with some 'phenomenally purified' notion of their contents. But once we set aside the difference in their appearance-dependent judgments, the two subjects are not to be distinguished in terms of the 'fineness of grain' of content.

What are we to conclude? Linda would have 'non-conceptual representations' of what's before her affecting their eyes, poised to affect her beliefs, crude but generally no less fine in content than Glenda's, except insofar as Glenda's grasp of the content of her belief is conceived to depend on things *looking* somehow to her. To be sure, Glenda enjoys more finely grained *visual appearances* than Linda, and makes more finely grained judgments dependent on these than she does, since Linda does not enjoy visual appearances at all. But the adoption of first-order reductive representationalism about phenomenal vision would not allow us ineliminable appeal to a difference in how things look to the subjects, in order to conceive of the difference between them (on pain of abandoning the theory's explanatory ambitions). Thus, its adoption would leave us no resources for supposing that things don't look any way to Linda, but do to Glenda. Moreover, the theory would tell us that the two subjects, given their visual talents, would have all they needed to be subjects of phenomenal vision—it would look somehow to both of them—by force of *metaphysical necessity*. There is no possible world in which things look blurry to Glenda on the left, but no way at all to Linda. Thus adoption of the theory would render the contrast between the two subjects inconceivable to us, and would declare the contrast itself a metaphysical impossibility. So the theory does not pass my test for phenomenal realism.

Now higher order reductive representationists would have something to say about what goes wrong in Tye's sort of theory. They would say he fails to recognize the need for the subject to *represent her own visual state*. For *that* is what constitutes the difference between things looking blurry to her and their looking to her no way at all. Following Rosenthal's account, we would say something like this. Phenomenal vision consists in the union of two otherwise dissociable aspects: the state of having *sensory (visual) qualities*, and the having of *seemingly non-inferential, assertoric thoughts* to the effect that one is in such a visual state ('higher order thoughts'). Visual qualities (and sensory qualities generally) are understood to be qualities of sensory states, in virtue of which we can distinguish and classify them, instantiable in the absence of phenomenal vision (or phenomenal sense experience generally). For as Rosenthal conceives it, the condition that enables subjects to discriminate stimuli in blindsight (or in subliminal perception) has visual qualities. (Similarly, for him your state of being 'in pain' has a sensory quality of some sort, even when (because of distraction) it doesn't *feel* any way to you to be in pain.) And so, since we're interpreting 'look' in such a way that things don't look any way to the blindsighter, possession of visual qualities is insufficient for having things look somehow to you. If we adopt the Rosenthal view, we need to say that what would make the blindsighter, possessed merely of visual qualities, someone to whom things look some way, would be the addition of seemingly non-inferential assertoric thoughts to the effect that she is in a state so visually 'qualified.'

Recall again the contrast we imagined between Linda and Glenda. Linda we supposed to be a *reflective* blindsighter: she spontaneously judges that her discriminations of stimuli are 'visual'—in the sense of 'visual' we recognized when we said that there can be a sort of vision in the absence of visual appearance. Glenda, on the other hand, we imagined inclined to no judgments about her own visual condition other than those to which I said I was ordinarily inclined: we are both disposed to say things look to us somehow or other, or that we do or don't see them (in a sense in which their looking no way to us precludes our seeing them). But even if there is vision without visual appearance in this sense, that's not a kind of vision she and I ordinarily attribute to ourselves.

But now what does adoption of the Rosenthalian higher order thought theory tell us about this scenario? Unless we can find some reason to suppose that the visual judgments we imagined Linda making would lack 'visual quality' in Rosenthal's sense, we should have to conclude that she would have everything she could possibly need for phenomenal vision. She's got the visual quality, and she's got the higher order thought: thus things would *have* to look somehow to her. Glenda on the other hand, would seem to be missing an essential element. For she would be missing the crucial 'higher order thoughts' that are supposedly needed to go from merely having the sort of visual qualities found in blindsight to things looking some way to a person. To be sure, she (sometimes) has higher order thoughts of a kind: she thinks, e.g., that it 'looks brighter to me *there*,' and she thinks that in this sense she sees something there. But those are not the thoughts she *needs*, according to the theory: she needs to attribute to herself a 'visual quality,' of the sort present when 'looking' or visual appearance as she understands this, is absent. So adoption of this higher order thought theory results in a *curious reversal* of our original scenario. Linda, the blindsighter, whom we were conceiving of as bereft of visual appearance, *has everything she could possibly want for having it*, and Glenda, to whom we said things *do* look some way, couldn't enjoy visual appearances—*she* must be the blindsighter.

But all this is just to say that adoption of the Rosenthal account would render our original scenario inconceivable to us, incoherent: we would have to conclude that each subject both was and was not a blindsighter. We might add: if this theory is supposed to tell us what the 'nature' of phenomenal vision is—what 'constitutes' seeing phenomenally, it would seem to tell us that either Linda must *have*, or that Glenda must *lack* phenomenal vision—or both—where 'must' has more than merely nomological force—the force, perhaps, of metaphysical necessity. And so, by my test, adoption of this higher order representationalist theory of consciousness makes visual appearance intellectually disappear.

If these difficulties are acknowledged, it seems that the following three options emerge for the ambitious physicalist. Option one: stick with the theory, and firmly deny that we enjoy visual appearances in the sense that would leave open the intelligibility and, in a broad sense, the possibility, of a contrast between Linda's blindsight and Glenda's blursight. An examination of the reasons one might offer in support of such an attitude is more than I can do here (though I do consider this elsewhere in detail).[9] For current purposes, I just want to note that a strong justification for this line is needed. If you are going to maintain that scenarios whose conceivability seems to embody a cogent understanding of visual appearance should be regarded (when we adopt the true theory of vision) as downright *logically incoherent or unintelligible*, or that they would then run counter not just to real world psychology, but *transgress the very limits of metaphysical possibility*, then you need to offer some very compelling reasons. And with respect to the latter claim, invocation of stock examples of 'a posteriori necessities' plausibly established by thought experiment is not enough to justify the needed analogy.

A second sort of response would be simply to disavow any claim to discover more than nomological necessities here. For example, you do not say *that all we have in mind* when we contrast things looking some way to Glenda, though not to Linda, is that Glenda can make spontaneous discriminations of a greater range than Linda. Rather more modestly you say that, in the world as it actually is, those to whom things look a certain way can make more and better spontaneous visual discriminations than blindsighters. Or else, you could limit yourself to saying that it is nomologically impossible for blindsight vision to give one's beliefs the 'poise' that visual appearance does, or to supply the range of discriminations afforded by any non-conceptual appearances of what is in one's visual field. Or you could confine yourself to saying that, in the actual world, it just so happens that subjects to whom colors or shapes look somehow are also always spontaneously *thinking* at the time that something looks somehow colored or shaped to them.

These more modest claims (especially the last) would not be beyond challenge. But the point I wish to make here is that such modesty would abandon the explanatory ambitions of the original views. For example, we were originally told, in effect, that it would explain phenomenal vision, and reveal its nature to us, if we accepted that one's conscious visual states are continually objects of one's own thoughts. But if one maintains no more than that, wherever phenomenal

---

[9] In Siewert (1998: chapter 5, and 2003).

vision occurs, it is targeted by higher order thought, then we will lack reason to think that the presence of higher order thought *explains* the fact that things look somehow shaped and colored to people. We may say: 'If anything explains anything here, it's the fact that things *look* thus and so to people that explains the fact that they *think* they do.' Similar remarks hold in the other cases. It will be the fact that varying shapes and colors look different to us that explains our talent for discriminating them in judgment—not the other way around. And it will be the manner in which things visually appear that explains why such appearance is non-conceptual in nature (if it is). And if visual appearance nomologically coincides with some functional role, we should conclude that the appearance *plays* the role, not that it *is* the role. To rest content with nomological claims would be to give up the original explanatory ambitions of the theories I've mentioned.

A third response to the challenge I've raised would hold onto the explanatory ambitions, and continue to search out some deeper necessity that will sustain them, but *alter or amend the theory*. For this, one might look to some difference between actual normal human vision and blindsight, on which our contrast between Linda and Glenda seems to be silent—i.e., it does not suggest they would be *alike* in this respect. After all there will be many such differences, since normal human visual subjects and blindsighters differ enormously simply in virtue of the fact that the latter have, to put it crudely, *big holes in their brains*. And in conceiving of Linda and Glenda, no suggestion was made that our subjects did not differ considerably in terms of what was literally in their heads. Now then: perhaps we should point to some such difference to get our story about what constitutes phenomenal vision. We can say of some such internal hidden feature: anyone such as Glenda enjoying blurry limited visual appearances *must have* that, and anyone such as Linda (to whom things look no way at all) *must lack* it. For that feature, together with other features we can characterize in appearance-free terms just *constitutes* visual appearance. Thus one might hope to sail through my test for phenomenal realism.

If one took this approach, we may ask how far one should go in making the theory's conditions for phenomenal vision dependent on the specifics of our psychology. Do we continue to honor the traditional functionalist idea that mental states are realizable in a very *physically diverse* range of beings? How similar must one be to normal human subjects to have what's minimally sufficient for phenomenal vision? One way to go here is illustrated by Peter Carruthers. His general view of phenomenal consciousness (Carruthers 2000) bears similarities to the two forms of reductive representationalism just considered. For he takes phenomenality to require both a 'fine-grained' content, and a layer of higher order mental representations. But he responds to the challenge posed by hypothetical Linda-style blindsight with an appeal to the idea that in *actual* blindsight, the subject's discriminations (e.g., of shape or orientation) are generated partly by reliance on certain motor pathways in the brain, whose activity serves as a kind of 'unconscious cue' to the character of the visual stimulus, disposing the subject to give certain answers to questions about what shape or orientation was found in the 'blind' field (Carruthers 2001).[10] This suggestion apparently is that it forms part of the nature of *phenomenal* vision that no such reliance on motor cues is involved. What would constitute the difference between the situation in which the stimulus doesn't look anyhow to the subject, but is discriminated only via spontaneous low-grade blindsight, and the case where it does look somehow to her, if only blurrily—is that in the latter, phenomenal case, discrimination is carried out in the absence of such motor cues.

But even granting that our discriminatory response in phenomenal vision does not actually rely on these motor cues, why suppose that this is anything more than a fact about how phenomenal vision happens to work in human beings? Why suppose there is some deeper, 'constitutive' relationship here, of a kind that would tell us it is metaphysically impossible for stimuli to look any way to a subject whose motor pathways contribute in a certain way to his or her capacity to make spontaneous visual discriminations? The point is not to suggest that there need be *no further* respect—beyond the presence or absence of visual appearance, together with whatever essentially appearance-dependent attitudes one admits—in which two subjects *must* differ, which is necessarily sufficient to make them thus differ phenomenally. The question is—what justifies us in choosing some specific difference as a *constitutive* difference? Maybe the absence of these motor cues is not constitutively necessary—but at most necessary only in some weaker sense (perhaps it is nomologically necessary in human vision). And why could there not be other creatures that have non-phenomenal vision (blindsight) without the use of these motor cues?[11] Perhaps then the constitutive difference is to be sought in some *other* aspect of the actual neuropsychological differences between the brains of normal human subjects and blindsighters. Just how do we distinguish the merely nomologically necessary from the constitutive?

One might say that awarding *some* differences constitutive status would wrongly delimit the range of physical diversity in the possible realizations of phenomenal vision. But once we have admitted that our understanding of

---

[10] I respond to Carruthers in Siewert (2001).

[11] Carruthers would perhaps reply that some creatures (young children and non-human animals) *do in fact* have non-phenomenal vision without reliance on motor cues, because they lack the disposition (which he thinks essential for phenomenal perception) to think higher order thoughts about their sensory condition. But this would just make matters worse, for two reasons. First, it seems he will need to say that what is allegedly essential are dispositions to think higher order thoughts attributing lower order potentially non-phenomenal sensory states (like Rosenthal's quality states). But things look somehow to *me* even though I am not generally disposed to attribute to myself such blindsight-compatible states. Second, even if (as seems plausible) young children and non-human animals lack cognitive skills necessary for thinking about their own minds, *it does not follow* that they never *feel pain*, and that nothing *looks* any way to them. But, by some kind of necessity, it *would* follow, if Carruthers were right.

the difference between the presence and absence of phenomenal vision is not exhausted by a difference in manifest functional roles, it becomes unclear just what entitles us to draw the bounds of possible realizations in a definite manner. If all we really had in mind when contrasting visual appearance with its absence were some difference in manifest 'talents,' then it would be a form of human neuro-*chauvinism* to suppose that some hidden physical aspect of how those talents are realized in us constitutes this difference quite generally. But once this sort of functionalism is exposed as a lack of realism about phenomenal vision, a less liberal approach can no longer be dismissed as chauvinist. At least *some* degree of *conservatism* is called for, if we are to remain realists, while sticking with ambitious physicalism. The problem though is—just how are we non-arbitrarily to select out some particular actual hidden difference and privilege it with 'constitutive' or 'metaphysically necessary' status?

This brings us finally to the dilemma that I announced at the outset—one that seems to arise for efforts to justify an ambitious form of physicalism. Ambitious physicalists are not content with the supervenience thesis that there can be no mental difference without a difference of a kind that can be captured in the vocabulary of physics. And it would not be enough for them to say that each experiential type (or consciousness generally) is identical with *some physical property or other*. They want to make more specific explanatory claims about the 'physical nature' of (for example) vision, committed to more than just nomological necessities. But then they face a dilemma. Either they fail the test for phenomenal realism when they try to absorb visual appearance entirely into something *manifest* and described in *wholly other terms*, or else they search for specific *hidden* features to which they can award deeply necessary or constitutive status. And in the latter case they risk being either too liberal or too conservative in the diversity allowed subjects of phenomenal vision, without justifying a clear standard by which to avoid excess in either direction, so as to ground their claims to the deep necessities they purport to discover.[12]

5. LIFE WITHOUT PHYSICALIST AMBITIONS

Naturally, more should be said about whether some form of 'ambitious physicalism' can resolve the dilemma posed. But if, as I think, the dilemma is deeply rooted, one should ultimately give up on such doctrines. Is the prospect of life without such physicalist ambitions so worrisome? You may be reluctant to abandon them, if you think they offer the only way to honor the success of the natural sciences, or to subordinate philosophical thought properly to empirical research, or to avoid some collection of supposed horrors associated

---

[12] One might say that this is another way of raising the general problem originally articulated in Block (1978): how to justify a theory's claim to be neither excessively 'liberal' nor 'chauvinistic.'

with dualism. But a robust phenomenal realism need bear no hostility to experimental science just because it wants nothing to do with conceptual and ontological theses vulnerable to the dilemma posed above. Nor is it even clear we need then embrace dualism in any definite sense. At least the argument so far leaves one free to endorse some physicalist supervenience thesis and a 'some-physical-property-or-other' identity claim, should that provide any metaphysical comfort.[13]

But maybe it seems that limiting oneself to a modest physicalism, or forsaking physicalism altogether, ultimately means giving up on any scientific explanation of facts about phenomenal experience. This seems to me an exaggerated worry. Without any help from the semantic or metaphysical theses of reductionist philosophy, we may hope to discover systematic enough relationships between what can be judged to occur by first-person reflection, and what can be discovered by probing our hidden features through brain science, that we can answer questions about why, for example, a person is subject to certain chronic feelings of pain, well enough to satisfy what ordinarily motivates such questions. Imagine that we can respond to such questions well enough to have a systematic means of predicting, altering, and eliminating in a highly targeted way various sorts of pain in human beings, with reference to fine-grained details in the activity and structure of the central nervous system. Suppose someone then complains that we still have no *real explanation* of why a given subject is or is not feeling pain, because we still cannot say why our world should not have been a pain-free, non-phenomenal 'zombie world,' type identical at the level of fundamental physics: 'Why is there consciousness rather than mere matter?' But perhaps we will—perhaps we should—find our lack of an answer to *this*, and other similar, residual mysteries, no more deeply threatens the explanatory powers of science than a persistence of the question, 'Why is there something rather than nothing?'

Finally, we need not fear that abandoning physicalist ambitions would deprive philosophy of mind of any positive content or aims. For our attempts to discover something systematic in the relationship between what is hidden inside our bodies and what is manifest in our experience are only as good as our understanding of the terms by which we conceptualize the latter. But the quality of that understanding is constantly threatened by obscurities and confusions that can be exposed and dispelled only by the sort of searching, independent-minded critical dialogue that will look for all the world like *philosophy*. And the clarity that may

---

[13] However, I am not convinced even modest physicalism can fend off the combined force of the conceivability and knowledge arguments defended by Chalmers (1996). But it also will not be clear to me that anti-physicalism should be a *dualism*, until it is clear to me that the types by which I understand my actions, and by which I identify perceptible things, can be clearly parceled out into purely mental and purely physical components.

result from such dialogue (however incomplete and tenuous) can be of value not only in framing a conception of what a science of consciousness is out to explain. It can also help us to respond to philosophical questions about knowledge, meaning, ethics, and aesthetics—and, generally, to examine our lives. So there can be more to philosophy of mind than arguing over physicalism.

4

The Property Dualism Argument

Stephen L. White

1. THE EXPLANATION OF A POSTERIORI IDENTITIES

Suppose that Smith's pain at t is identical with Smith's C-fiber firing at t. More specifically, suppose that the token state or event that has the property at t of being Smith's only pain also has the property at t of being his only C-fiber firing.[1] Assume that this identity is an empirical fact, discoverable only a posteriori. Then as used by Smith at t, the expressions 'my pain' and 'my C-fiber firing' will be coreferential, but will not (in any intuitive sense) mean the same thing. We must, therefore, explain how a mentalistic expression and a physicalistic expression could refer to the same event while at the same time satisfying the following desiderata.

(1) We explain how an identity such as 'My pain is identical with my C-fiber firing' could be a posteriori, i.e.,

(1′) we explain the difference in the cognitive significance of such expressions as 'my pain' and 'my C-fiber firing', i.e.,

(1″) we explain how a subject could be fully rational in believing what he or she would express by saying such things as 'I am in pain' and also in believing what he or she would express by saying things such as 'It is not the case that my C-fibers are firing,' and, more generally, anything of the form 'It is not the case that I am in a state of kind D' where 'D' stands in for a physical and/or functional description.

(2) We satisfy Frege's constraint in what I shall call its ordinary version (OVFC): If x believes y to be F and also believes y not to be F, then (to the extent that

---

[1] On such a supposition, the event of Smith's being in pain at t—i.e., the event of his C-fibers firing at t—is what Donald Davidson has called an unrepeatable or dated particular. See 'The Individuation of Events,' 'Events as Particulars,' and 'Eternal vs. Ephemeral Events,' in Davidson (1980: 163–203). For the view of events as property exemplifications see, Kim (1976), and Goldman (1970: chapter 1). This alternative view of events is addressed in the discussion of property identities in sections 4–5.

x is rational) there must be distinct representational modes of presentation *m* and *m'* such that *x* believes *y* to be *F* under *m* and disbelieves *y* to be *F* under *m'*).[2]

(3) We satisfy Frege's constraint in what I shall call its strong version (SVFC): We satisfy (1) and (2) by satisfying the following conditions.

    (a) The representational modes of presentation referred to in (2) provide a rational justification of the subject's beliefs, intentions, and actions.

    (b) The justification is available to the subject at the personal level.

    (c) The justification takes the form of a characterization of the way the world presents itself to the subject or the way the world is given from the subject's point of view.

As it is used in the literature, 'mode of presentation' is ambiguous between something on the side of language and content, such as a description, concept, or some form of nonconceptual content,[3] and something on the side of the world, such as a property.[4] Thus in the conditions above and in what follows, I distinguish between representational modes of presentation (on the side of content) and nonrepresentational modes of presentation (on the side of the world).

What the strong version of Frege's constraint adds to versions such as OVFC is an explicit acknowledgment of the justificatory role that modes of presentation in both senses are required to play. Modes of presentation are not postulated simply to explain behavioral and/or functional dispositions—for example, a subject's disposition to produce the sound associated with 'yes' in response to 'Are you in pain?' and that associated with 'no' in response to 'Are your C-fibers firing?' For this role a difference in the causal chains connecting the subject's pain to tokens of the word 'pain' on the one hand and to tokens of 'C-fiber firing' on the other (and a resulting difference in the causal role of the two terms in the subject's functional economy) would suffice. But such a difference in the causal chains and the functional roles associated with different linguistic expressions is one to which the subject need not have access. Thus, in the absence of some personal-level manifestation, such a causal difference could not play the justificatory role for which modes of presentation are slated.

Why, though, should we hold out for a justificatory as opposed to explanatory role for modes of presentation? The first reason is that conditions (3a)–(3c) are already implicit in conditions (1) and (2). Thus a justification of the latter conditions will provide a justification of the former as well.

---

    [2] Schiffer (1978: 180). See also Loar (1981: 99–100) and Peacocke (1983: 109).

    [3] On nonconceptual content see Peacocke (2001).

    [4] Schiffer's version of Frege's constraint suggests that modes of presentation belong on the side of language and content. Brian Loar sometimes means by 'modes of presentation' representations such as descriptions or concepts and sometimes the things connoted or expressed by such representations, such as properties. See Loar (1997: 600).

Condition (1) is a given in this context and is accepted on all sides; (1′) and (1″) are intended as elucidations of (1). Furthermore, (1′) and (1″) (and thus (1)) will be accepted by anyone who takes modes of presentation seriously and thus by anyone who takes Frege's constraint seriously in its ordinary version. Moreover, as I shall argue below, condition (2), Frege's constraint in its ordinary version, should be accepted by anyone who is serious about belief ascription. The same argument, which appeals to the constitutive role of charity and rationality in the ascription of intentional states, is sufficient to justify (3a) as well. And it is clear, as we have seen, that such rational justification must take place at the personal level (as (3b) requires).

To support the claim that the kind of rational justification in question proceeds by characterizing the way the world presents itself to the subject (i.e., (3c)), we need simply note that beliefs (and such other intentional entities as intentions and actions) are justified by appeal to other beliefs and intentional states and other representational contents—including, possibly, nonconceptual contents. Hence they are justified by reference to the way the world presents itself or the way in which it is given. But we have already seen that rational justification is a matter of what is available to the subject at the personal level. Hence rational justification is a matter of the way the world presents itself to the subject or the way it is given from the subject's point of view.

Condition (3), SVFC, has a second, related source of support. To suppose that differences in the modes of presentation required by Frege's constraint could consist merely in causal differences unavailable to the subject at the personal level is to adopt a position that I shall call *local eliminativism*. Just as the eliminativist regarding intentionality eschews talk of content altogether in favor of an explanation of behavior in terms drawn from the natural sciences, so the local eliminativist (regarding intentionality) eschews such talk in what we might call the *Fregean contexts* (i.e., the contexts in which SVFC would require the postulation of representational modes of presentation available to the subject in question). But local eliminativism is not a tenable position. The *point* of ascribing intentional content is to characterize the world as it presents itself to the subject, thereby providing a rational justification of the subject's beliefs, intentions, and actions. When we do so I shall say that we *rationalize* those intentional states (and to that extent their subject). In fact, rationality is constitutive of the project of intentional ascription, as is evidenced by the constitutive role of the principle of charity in radical interpretation.[5] Indeed, it would be a mistake to think of our commitment to Frege's constraint and to the principle of charity as independent. They are more appropriately seen as different manifestations of our fundamental commitment to the rationality of the subjects of intentional states.[6]

---

[5] Davidson (1984). Lewis (1983*b*).

[6] See my 'Narrow Content and Narrow Interpretation' (1991: chapter 2). Condition (3) and the subsequent explanatory remarks constitute, in effect, a commitment to a thoroughgoing internalism

Local eliminativism should be rejected in favor of full-blown eliminativism by those who are skeptical about intentional ascription altogether. Those who are not should hold out for the higher standard that SVFC entails.

2. THE ARGUMENT FOR PROPERTY DUALISM

I shall now outline the property dualism argument,[7] some points of which will receive further elaboration in subsequent sections. Notice first that although the explanations required by conditions (1)–(3) call for the rational justification of the beliefs, intentions, and actions ascribed to the subject, this is not to say that the contents of such intentional states play no explanatory role. The contents ascribed to such subjects must explain the subjects' access to the referents of their expressions. For example, to provide the explanations called for by (1) regarding the identity statement 'My pain is identical with my C-fiber firing' while satisfying OVFC, the two expressions involved must pick out the objects they do under distinct representational modes of presentation. And corresponding to these representational modes of presentation there must be properties (i.e., nonrepresentational modes of presentation) *in virtue of which* the representations pick out the object in question. Moreover, the representational and nonrepresentational modes of presentation must be appropriately related; indeed *the relation must be a priori*. That is, the property must be one that the subject could (in principle) ascribe to the object solely on the basis of an understanding of the representational mode of presentation in question, and it should involve nothing more than is ascribable on that basis.

This condition on the relation between representational and nonrepresentational modes of presentation presupposes a commitment to what we might call *thin* properties—those with respect to which we know or can infer all there is to know about their intrinsic (nonrelational) nature merely in virtue of understanding the predicates that express them. Thin properties, then, confer no empirically discoverable essence or nature on the objects that instantiate them.[8] Such properties, of course, are not necessarily phenomenal properties. Other types of thin

---

in one important sense of the term—a sense motivated by the kinds of intuitions that give rise to Frege's constraint and such notions as internal justification and the subject's point of view.

[7] This argument was first presented (in a much more compressed form) in my 'Curse of the Qualia,' (1986). It was inspired by an argument of J. J. C. Smart's which he attributes to Max Black, though a number of the important points in the present argument are not found in Smart's or, indeed, in my own earlier version. See Smart (1959). The property dualism argument is discussed in Hill (1991: 98–101), McConnell (1994), Hill (1997), McLaughlin (1997), Clapp (1998), Balog (1999), and Perry (2001). For closely related arguments see Colin McGinn, 'How Not to Solve the Mind–Body Problem', Terence Horgan and John Tienson, 'Deconstructing New Wave Materialism', and Brian McLaughlin, 'In Defense of New Wave Materialism: A Response to Horgan and Tienson,' all in Gillett and Loewer (2001: 284–330).

[8] Although there is an obvious connection to a proposal broached by Alvin Goldman according to which 'properties $\emptyset$ and $\emptyset'$ are identical just in those cases where they are expressible by

properties include (among others) mathematical properties, (arguably) functional properties, such as being a telephone, (some) observable properties, such as being a medium sized object within reach, common sense properties, such as being a hill or an island, and common sense psychological properties, such as being angry or brave. Indeed we could say that thin properties correspond not to natural kinds but to 'definable kinds,' were we willing to take a sufficiently relaxed view of definition.

For a subject who believed that a fortnight was a period of ten days, for example, the representational mode of presentation (description) in question would not correspond a priori to the property of being a period of fourteen days. So it would not be in virtue of this property of a fortnight that the subject's term picked it out.[9] Of course, the route from the linguistic expression to the referent may involve many representational modes of presentation, each with its corresponding property. If so, then along the route from expression to referent, each link must be either an a priori connection or an a posteriori connection grounded in the beliefs of the particular subject in question. And the reason is obvious. The route to the referent must explain how the *subject's* term succeeds in picking out the object in question.

Consider the analogy between the pain/C-fiber firing example and the Morning Star/Evening Star example. In both cases we have two linguistic descriptions that are coreferential but not coreferential a priori. In the case of 'the Morning Star' and 'the Evening Star' this is unproblematic. There are two properties corresponding to the two descriptions of Venus—the property of being the last heavenly body visible in the morning and the property of being the first heavenly body visible in the evening—properties that could have been instantiated by different objects. Thus the fact that one could fail to realize that a single object had both properties explains how one could believe—and be rational in believing—something of Venus under the description corresponding to the first property ('the last heavenly body visible in the morning') and fail to believe it or believe the contrary under the description corresponding to the second ('the first heavenly body visible in the evening').

Now there is no difficulty about the modes of presentation (either representational or nonrepresentational) that tie 'my C-fiber firing' to its referent. The term

---

synonymous expressions' (Goldman 1970: 12) there is no commitment on the present account to a notion of synonymy, a concept likely to yield controversial results in those cases where it is needed most. Indeed, there is no commitment to a notion of meaning (in the sense of a systematic semantics for all the relevant terms) shared by all competent speakers of a language. What is at issue is not the meanings of the relevant terms, but the modes of presentation under which individual speakers hold their beliefs about the referents of those terms—in short, the requirements imposed by Frege's constraint. In this respect the appeal to thin properties differs in its motivation from David Lewis's appeal to properties as classes of possibilia in order to satisfy the requirements of a systematic semantic theory of a language. See Lewis (1983a).

[9] For this kind of example, see Burge (1978). For the subject who is mistaken about the meaning of 'fortnight', the route might go through the description 'the period referred to by "fortnight" in this community'. Nothing here, however, turns on the account of parasitic reference.

'C-fiber firing' is connected a priori with a certain causal role and the causal role (we can assume) is connected a posteriori (for the subject in question) with the perception of instrument readings and the like. The difficulty is with the modes of presentation of the token brain state as it is given 'from the inside' to normal subjects, who determine that they are in pain without the aid of any special apparatus. There is a problem, that is, regarding one of the nonrepresentational modes of presentation of the token state that is both the pain and the C-fiber firing. What is the *property* in virtue of which one has one's normal, first-person access to such states? If we answer the question by analogy with the case of 'C-fiber firing', the route to the C-fiber firing will go through the property of being a pain and the property of hurting or having a certain phenomenal feel. And these are, on the face of it, mentalistic properties. Can we, then, provide a route that does not involve such mentalistic properties? It is evident that we cannot. No physical or neurophysiological property could play the role played by these ostensibly mentalistic properties in providing a route to the referent. For any such physicalistic property, a perfectly rational subject can believe that he or she is in pain and not believe (or indeed disbelieve) what he or she would express in using a description connoting that property to characterize one of his or her internal states. We must then continue to appeal to a mental property—such as the property of being one's state that is hurtful at t—in order to produce an analogue of the Morning Star/Evening Star example.

But does the Morning Star/Evening Star example provide the general pattern for a posteriori identities, or is it merely one pattern among others, an option not a requirement? The suggestion that the pattern is optional seems clearly false. Recall that we want to rationalize the relevant beliefs, intentions, and actions of the subject who believes what he or she would express by saying 'I am in pain' and 'My C-fibers are not firing.' Or, to put it another way, we want to say what the subject imagines or believes who is disposed to deny sincerely the identity of pain and C-fiber firing. And the answer must take the form of a specification of a possible world. First, suppose there were no such world (and nothing relevantly similar, such as a partial world or situation[10]) that was completely describable without contradiction and that captured what it was the subject imagined in imagining that pain was not identical with C-fiber firing. Suppose, that is, that every attempt to describe such a world ended in the revelation of a hidden contradiction. Then the identity would be a priori, contrary to our assumption. By the same token, a subject who failed to believe or who disbelieved such an identity would be irrational. Thus we could not, for example, characterize the content of the relevant beliefs of the subject in terms of 'impossible possible worlds' since such a characterization could not do justice to the subject's rationality, but would merely reveal the subject as *irrational*. What, though, would such a possible world be like, given that it could not be one at

[10] See, for example, Barwise and Perry (1983).

which pain $\neq$ C-fiber firing since (by hypothesis) there are none? Such a world would have to be one at which (intuitively speaking) what the subject would mean in asserting the negation of the identity was actually the case. This means that there must be a world in which the properties that are definitive of the content (for the subject) of the two modes of presentation are not coinstantiated.

Even if this is how it works in the case of the Morning Star and the Evening Star, however, is it clear that it *must* work this way? The answer is yes. We need properties in order to characterize the way the subject takes the world to be, since we are specifying the *content* of the subject's belief, not merely something about its vehicle (such as its functional or syntactical role). In other words, we are specifying a possible condition of the world, not merely a possible condition of the subject. We could derive the same conclusion by saying that we need properties of the world because, as we have already seen, local eliminativism is unacceptable and because it is the connection between properties and concepts that gives content to those concepts.

But if we need properties, is it clear that we need *thin* properties? Again the answer is yes. If the properties are to provide the content (*for the subject*) of the belief that he or she would express by saying 'Pain is not identical to C-fiber firing,' then their principle of individuation must be sufficiently fine-grained that they can be appealed to to explain the difference in cognitive significance between 'my pain' and 'my C-fiber firing'. Moreover, it must be fine-grained enough to capture and explain the difference in cognitive significance of 'my pain' and *any* (explicitly) physicalistic expression, since for any such expression we can imagine a subject who believes what he or she would express using a sentence of the form 'My pain is F and it is not the case that P is F' where 'P' stands in for the referring expression couched in a purely physicalistic vocabulary. But this is just another way of saying that the property that provides the content (for the subject) of 'pain' is connected to the subject's use of the term a priori—i.e., the property's obtaining entails nothing more about the world than the subject could (in principle) infer on the basis of his or her understanding of the relevant representational mode of presentation. Thus we have the condition that the connection between the properties and the subject's expressions must be a priori in the relevant sense.

Is it really obvious, though, that there must be an a priori connection between the subject's representational modes of presentation and nonrepresentational modes of presentation (properties) in order to avoid local eliminativism? Consider the alternatives. First, the inferential roles (and their underlying functional realizations) of the expressions that figure in a subject's descriptions are not sufficient to provide their semantic content. Unless there is something to take us outside the circle of word-to-word connections, inferential roles, regardless of how extensive, could never provide more than an uninterpreted calculus. The system of contents must contain some demonstrative element, and the question is where that element is to come from. As we have seen, bare causal connections to things in the world cannot, by themselves, provide the answer, since they are connections to which the subject need have no access.

But if inferential roles coupled with bare causal connections are not sufficient to provide content what is? A theory of meaning as use would be no help to the physicalist, since even if mental states are identified with physical states, the meanings of the physicalistic concepts will in turn be explained in terms of the contributions they make to our actions and practices—notions that themselves are mentalistic. Thus, if bare causal connections are unacceptable because they are connections to which the subject need have no access, then the explanation of content must involve a type of connection that rules out any such possibility. And this is exactly what justifies the claim that nonrepresentational modes of presentation (properties) must be individuated thinly and that the connection between such properties and the predicates that express them must be a priori in the sense defined.

We could not, then, fill out the analogy between the pain/C-fiber firing example and the Morning Star/Evening Star example simply by opting for an ostensibly mental property—e.g., being the state (or token event) of the relevant subject's that is hurtful at t—but claiming that it is identical with a neurophysiological property. Were we to do so, we would not have provided an explanation as to how a rational subject could believe that he or she was in pain and in a state that was hurtful and not believe that he or she was in *any* relevant neurophysiological state. This is because there is no logically possible world at which the subject could be in a state that was hurtful and not be in the neurophysiological state in question.[11] Thus we could not describe the subject's beliefs, including the routes from the subject's referring expressions to their referents, in such a way as to satisfy (1)–(3).

We *could* satisfy (1)–(3), however, if we supposed that the first order property of being hurtful (which, we are assuming, is identical with a neurophysiological property) itself has two second order properties—a mentalistic property (e.g., the property of involving a certain phenomenal feel) in virtue of which the property of hurting has an a priori connection with the property connoted by 'my pain at t' and a physical-functional property in virtue of which it could be picked out as the neurophysiological property that it is. Thus in order to satisfy (1)–(3), we are led to a dualism of second order properties. And if we address this problem

---

[11] The relevant notion of possibility here is logical or conceptual possibility—describability without contradiction. The appeal to logical possibility, however, must be understood correctly. As Kripke has argued, possible worlds are ways the actual world could have been. Moreover, in moving from the actual world to its possible alternatives, we keep our language fixed. In the present context this means that if the property of being hurtful, say, is identical with some neurophysiological property, then there is no logically possible alternative to the actual world at which they are distinct. Thus the possible worlds with which we are dealing are genuinely possible and not merely epistemologically possible. They correspond, then, with what at least some have meant by 'metaphysically possible worlds'.

by identifying the ostensibly mentalistic second order property with another neurophysiological property, we have no way of avoiding an infinite regress.

We can summarize, then, by addressing the claim that Frege's constraint is satisfied by the distinction between the two *concepts*—the concept of a state that is hurtful and the concept of a neurophysiological state of type N. On this suggestion, no distinction is required at the level of *properties*: we simply have two distinct descriptions and concepts that pick out the same referent in virtue of the same (thick) property. First, as we have seen, we need to explain how the subject's expressions pick out the object in question. Now the property of being a neurophysiological state of type N explains how 'my neurophysiological state of type N' picks out the subject's C-fiber firing. But how does this property explain the fact that the subject's expression 'my state that is hurtful' picks out the same state? It must be in virtue of a different aspect of this property than the one in virtue of which the physicalistic expression picks out its referent. Thus the property of being a neurophysiological state of type N must itself have second order properties, and unless we postulate a mentalistic property at some higher order, the threatened regress will occur.

Second, in order to justify rationally the subject's beliefs, intentions, and actions, we have to be able to say how the world presents itself to that subject (condition (3c)). But to say how it presents itself to a subject is to specify a condition of the world; it is not a fact about the subject's concepts but about the *contents* of those concepts—i.e., about what they represent. Thus it will be a fact about the properties of the internal state in question. And these properties will have to be individuated finely enough to explain how the subject could be rational in believing what he or she would express by saying 'I am in a state that hurts and not in a neurophysiological state of type N.'

Third, we have to explain what it is in virtue of which the two concepts—the concept of being a state that is hurtful and the concept of being a neuro-physiological state of type N—*are* distinct (at least as regards their cognitive significance). If it is claimed that they are distinct merely in virtue of a difference in functional roles and/or different causal chains to external objects, then we have local eliminativism. Since, however, there is nothing special about this local context, there is no principled way of avoiding eliminativism across the board, and this will seem to most too high a price for an objection to the property dualism argument.

Suppose it is admitted, however, that the difference in the cognitive sig-nificance of the corresponding descriptions 'my state that is hurtful' and 'my neurophysiological state of type N' for a subject is determined by the properties they connote. Then it is clear that the properties in virtue of which such descrip-tions pick out the objects they do must be given a priori. In other words, since the properties in virtue of which such descriptions pick out their referents provide the descriptions' (and the corresponding concepts') cognitive significance, those properties must be available to the subject solely on the basis of an understanding of the descriptions in question. Thus the properties connoted will be too thin to allow the kind of case proposed. That is, they will be too thin to allow a case in which the property of being hurtful *is* (unbeknownst to the subject) the property of being a neurophysiological state of type *N and* there is no genuinely mentalistic property not identical to a physicalistic property at the second or higher order.

3. BOYD'S ANTIKRIPKEAN ARGUMENT

It is sometimes claimed that the property dualism argument is vulnerable to an objection of Richard Boyd's to Saul Kripke's argument for dualism.[12] Kripke's argument stems from the claim that we can imagine pain without any C-fiber firing (and vice versa), though he acknowledges that we can, or think we can, also imagine water without H_2O, even though they are the same. Kripke argues, however, that the cases of pain and water are not parallel. In the case of water and H_2O, there is a plausible explanation of our thinking we can imagine water without H_2O, when in fact we cannot (since if water is *identical* with H_2O, there is no such possibility). According to Kripke we confuse the case in which at some possible world water exists and H_2O does not (which we cannot imagine) with the case in which at some possible world a liquid other than H_2O plays the role that water plays at the actual world. On Kripke's account, however, there is no analogous explanation where pain and C-fiber firing are concerned. For there is no distinction between pain and the appearance of pain analogous to the distinction between water and the water role or the observable manifestations of water. As Kripke points out, whatever has the appearance of pain—i.e., whatever feels like pain—is pain. Thus, the intuition that we could have pain without C-fiber firing (and vice versa) stands as an objection to the identity theory.

Boyd objects that on Kripke's account, a possible explanation of our thinking (falsely) that we can imagine pain without C-fiber firing has been overlooked. Although there is indeed no distinction between pain and the appearance of pain, there is an obvious distinction between C-fiber firing and the way *it* manifests itself. Thus according to Boyd, we *do* have an explanation of our conviction that we can imagine pain without C-fiber firing: what we imagine is not pain without C-fiber firing but pain without the appearance of C-fiber firing. And this, Boyd maintains, is exactly analogous to the explanation of our believing that we can imagine water without H_2O. If the analogy holds, we could explain the apparent conceivability of pain without C-fiber firing, and hence the a posteriori character of their alleged identity, without postulating any mentalistic properties. Thus, according to Boyd, the fact that we seem capable of imagining

---

[12] See Hill (1991: 101). Kripke (1980: 144–55), Boyd (1980).

pain without C-fiber firing is no more an objection to the identity theory than is the corresponding possibility regarding water and H_2O an objection to their identity.

Boyd's argument, however, does not supply the basis for skepticism about the original intuition (that we could have pain without C-fiber firing) in the way that Kripke's does for the intuition that we could have water without H_2O. Let us consider more carefully the nature of the alleged confusion on Kripke's account and its counterpart on Boyd's. On Kripke's account the confusion is over the question whether 'water' is a natural kind term or one that denotes anything that plays the water role. That is, it is over the question whether, with regard to any possible world, 'water' picks out the natural kind that plays the water role at the *actual* world, or, with regard to any possible world, it picks out whatever plays the water role at *that* world. However, once we fix the meaning of 'water' (as a natural kind term) and the fact that H_2O plays the water role at the actual world, the source of confusion disappears. Under these circumstances it is no longer even possible to *think* we can imagine water without H_2O. This is not so in the pain case. Suppose we make explicit to ourselves that we are using 'pain' *not* as a natural kind term, but in such a way that whatever feels like pain *is* pain. Imagine also that we make it perfectly clear to ourselves that 'C-fiber firing' is being used as a natural kind term (and not, say, as an operational concept such that anything that satisfies the standard tests for a C-fiber firing is one). Even with complete clarity on these points, we have no difficulty in imagining pain without C-fiber firing (and not merely in imagining pain without the standard evidence of C-fiber firing). If this is the case, however, Boyd's claim—that confusion over what we are imagining contributes to the intuition that pain is not identical with C-fiber firing—does not undermine the Kripkean argument against the identity theory. For in this case, unlike the case of water, the intuition remains even when the source of the alleged confusion is eliminated. Since it does, the need to postulate different routes to the referent of 'pain' (in accordance with (1)–(3)) provides the premises on which the property dualism argument depends.

The general principle to which we appeal in this reply to Boyd's argument is that for a true identity statement, if neither of the referring expressions that flank the identity sign connote (pick out their referents in virtue of) contingent properties of those referents, the statement cannot be a posteriori. What we have shown, in effect, is that when we eliminate the contingency in the way water is picked out (by specifying that 'water' denotes a natural kind and that the natural kind that realizes the water role at the actual world is H_2O), we eliminate the a posteriori character of water's identity with H_2O. Since this is not the case for the identity statement connecting 'pain' and 'C-fiber firing', Boyd's argument fails. It is appropriate, then, that we turn to an objection to the property dualism argument that calls this principle (the so-called Semantic premise discussed below) into question.

4. LOAR'S ARGUMENT AGAINST ANTIPHYSICALISM

Brian Loar's account of phenomenal states does not address the property dualism argument by name. It does, however, purport to address an 'antiphysicalist line of reasoning that goes back to Leibniz and beyond' and of which Frank Jackson's knowledge argument and Kripke's antiphysicalist argument are instances (Loar 1997: 598). Moreover, (together with a similar argument of Block's) it provides the most sophisticated response available to this class of arguments and one that includes a detailed positive alternative to the antiphysicalist position.[13] Let us, then, follow the usual practice in calling such antiphysicalist arguments *conceivability arguments* and consider whether Loar's criticisms of the other members of this class are effective against the present argument for property dualism.[14]

Loar has both an interpretation of the assumptions behind conceivability arguments and a refutation of the arguments so interpreted. He has, in addition, a positive physicalistic account of the meanings and referents of phenomenal terms such as 'pain' which, were it adequate, would undercut any conceivability argument for the postulation of mentalistic properties. I shall set out Loar's objections to conceivability arguments as he interprets them in this section and his positive views in section 5. (It should be noted that whereas the property dualism argument concerns the identity of token events, Loar's discussion concerns the identity of properties. Since in both cases largely the same considerations apply, I shall refer to the difference explicitly only when necessary.)

Loar accepts Kripke's claim that the phenomenal concept of pain conceives of it directly and essentially but rejects the conclusion that pain cannot be identical with a physical property. According to Loar, the inference depends on an implicit assumption:

(Semantic premise) A statement of property identity that links conceptually independent concepts is true only if at least one concept picks out the property it refers to by connoting a contingent property of that property. (Loar 1997: 600)

(Pairs of conceptually independent property concepts are just those that give rise to a posteriori property identity statements.) Loar's objection to the antiphysicalist position is that 'a phenomenal concept can pick out a physical property directly or essentially, not via a contingent mode of presentation, and yet be conceptually independent of all physical-functional concepts' (Loar 1997: 600). Thus there could be a true statement of property identity linking a physical-functional concept and a conceptually independent phenomenal concept such that neither concept picks out the physical property in question by connoting a contingent

---

[13] I shall consider Block's variation on this argument elsewhere.

[14] In the conclusion I shall distinguish two different forms that conceivability arguments might take.

property of that property. In other words, Loar's objection simply amounts to a denial of the Semantic premise.

Whether Loar's analysis of the antiphysicalist argument provides a fully adequate account of Kripke's or Jackson's position is a question I shall not try to answer. It would not, however, be an adequate characterization of the property dualism argument. Loar depicts the antiphysicalist commitment to the Semantic premise as based on the following intuition, which I shall call the *intuition of transparency*.

Phenomenal concepts and theoretical expressions of physical properties both conceive their references essentially. But if two concepts conceive a given property essentially, neither mediated by contingent modes of presentation, one ought to be able to see a priori—at least after optimal reflection—that they pick out the same property. Such concepts' connections cannot be a posteriori; that they pick out the same property would have to be transparent. (Loar 1997: 600)

I shall defend a version of this intuition below. But one needn't accept this intuition in order to see the force of the Semantic premise. Rather, the Semantic premise emerges (in a weakened and modified form) as the conclusion of an argument.

As we have seen, the proponent of the property dualism argument begins with a commitment to the strong version of Frege's constraint (SVFC). This involves a commitment to rationalizing the subject's intentional states and actions—to providing them with a rational *justification*, in part by characterizing the world as the subject conceives it. This commitment is constitutive of the project of radical interpretation and intentional ascription. Furthermore, it involves a commitment to antieliminativism. This is obvious where the global elimination of intentional states is concerned but less obvious where the eliminativism is local and part of an ostensibly antieliminativist program.

The argument, then, for what I shall call the Weakened modified semantic premise is as follows. Assume that 'water = H_2O' is a true identity. And assume that it is knowable only a posteriori; in other words, the concepts 'water' and 'H_2O' are conceptually independent in Loar's sense. Thus there could be a perfectly rational subject who believed what he or she would express by saying 'Water fills the lakes and reservoirs' and also what he or she would express by saying 'H_2O does not fill the lakes and reservoirs.' There must, then, be a possible world—one describable in complete detail without a contradiction—which justifies this belief. The possible world that rationalizes and justifies the subject's beliefs, however, needn't be one at which water ≠ H_2O. After all, our commitment is to making the subject's beliefs *rational*. (By and large. We can ascribe irrationality, but only against the background of largely rational relations between intentional states.) There is no such commitment to showing that the beliefs are possibly *true*. If there are necessary truths known only a posteriori, then a rational subject could form beliefs incompatible with them—beliefs that would be false at every possible world—and yet be rationally justified.

But what kind of world would justify the belief that the subject expresses at the actual world by saying 'water is not H_2O'? And what kind of world would justify a subject's (say Smith's) willingness to contribute to what is described as 'research into the nature of water,' which he believes necessary to sustain all life, but not to contribute to what is described as 'research into the nature of H_2O,' which he believes is an extremely rare and inert substance, irrelevant to biological life? Clearly the notion of worlds at which Smith's beliefs are justified needs some explanation. There is a sense, after all, in which one's belief that a theorem of mathematics is false is justified by a world in which it is publicly shared by the most prominent mathematicians. The existence of worlds of this kind, however, does nothing to justify rationally one's belief, since its falsity is knowable a priori and hence is, in the relevant sense, *irrational*. Thus we cannot demonstrate Smith's rationality by finding worlds at which his beliefs are *true*, since there are none, and we cannot do so by finding worlds at which they merely *seem true*, since this is not sufficient for justification in the relevant sense. What then could we possibly hope to find?

It would be sufficient that there be a world (possibly with different physical laws) at which the terms 'water' and 'H_2O', though they are tied to the same (representational and nonrepresentational) modes of presentation as Smith's words, pick out two different substances with precisely the properties Smith ascribes to them. The answer, therefore, is that we are looking for possible worlds at which the *narrow contents* of Smith's beliefs are accurate or veridical, where narrow content is simply understood as the content that satisfies (all the relevant versions of) Frege's constraint—or, equivalently, the content that fully captures the cognitive significance of the subject's beliefs. (We say that the narrow contents are accurate or veridical rather than true because 'true' has long since been co-opted by proponents of broad content.) Indeed, this is all we *could* be looking for. The worlds that demonstrate the subject's rationality are the worlds that show that contents which fully reflect the cognitive significance of the subject's beliefs *could* all have been realized.[15]

---

[15] See my account of notional content in White (1991). This appeal to narrow content plays a role analogous to that of Chalmers' appeal to what he calls the 'primary intention' of a proposition. See Chalmers (1996: 57–65). Chalmers' account of primary intentions is itself similar to an earlier account of mine of narrow content in 'Partial Character and the Language of Thought,' *Pacific Philosophical Quarterly* 63 (1982): 347–65, reprinted as chapter 1 of *The Unity of the Self*. The difference between my earlier account and Chalmers' turns on whether narrow content should be represented in terms of a certain kind of two-dimensional matrix or the diagonal of that matrix. This difference needn't concern us here, since the more recent account of notional content seems preferable to either in taking Frege's constraint as *constitutive* of narrow content. (Though the nonequivalence of my two accounts is obvious, some readers have evidently been misled by my failure to make this point explicit (see McLaughlin 1997)). So long as an account of narrow content satisfies Frege's constraint, however, nothing in the present context depends on the details.

Thus, Smith's belief need not be unjustified or irrational, even though there is no possible world at which water $\neq$ H_2O. A world at which 'water' and 'H_2O' pick out different substances with the properties that Smith ascribes to them will be sufficient. All we need to assume is that the properties that Smith associates with water—being colorless, odorless, tasteless, filling the lakes, etc., are instantiated by some substance other than H_2O.[16] But this is just to say that Smith's term 'water' has its meaning and picks out its referent in virtue of being associated with properties that are contingently connected with H_2O.[17]

If an identity is a posteriori, then, it might seem that there must be contingent modes of presentation (both representational and nonrepresentational) associated with at least one of the designating expressions that flank the identity sign. Suppose, however, that we consider Kripke's theory according to which the properties of having originated from a certain egg cell and having originated from a certain sperm cell are necessary properties of a person. Imagine an artificial fertilization process that includes a pair of egg cells named '*A*' and '*B*' and a pair of sperm cells named '*Y*' and '*Z*'. When the process is complete, one of the researchers involved says correctly that the person who originated from A (call her Eve) is the person who originated from *Z*. But this is an a posteriori identity linking conceptually independent concepts. (It is an empirical fact, discoverable only a posteriori, that *A* was combined with *Z* rather than *Y*.) Thus we have a violation of the Semantic premise (or its analogue for individuals) since the two descriptions in a true, a posteriori identity statement pick out Eve in virtue of their connoting two of her necessary properties. And this is evidently a straightforward counterexample to the Semantic premise, since even if Kripke is wrong about the necessity of origins for persons, we could define entities for which the thesis is correct.[18] The way of handling the counterexample, however, is also straightforward. In place of Loar's version we should substitute:

(Modified semantic premise) A statement of property identity that links conceptually independent concepts is true only if the concepts pick out the property they refer to by connoting contingently coextensive properties of that property.

[16] The question may arise why, in addition to the thin properties and the a priori connection between representational and nonrepresentational modes of presentation to which we appealed in the discussion of the Morning Star/Evening Star example, we need a notion of narrow content. The answer is that in the Morning Star/Evening Star case and its pain and C-fiber analogues it is assumed that the subject refers successfully to an actual object. In the general case in which we rationalize a subject's intentional states, however, we cannot make this assumption.

[17] It may well be incompatible with the basic laws of physics that a substance other than water could have all of its observable or macro-level properties or that water could have failed to have them. But even if it is, the basic laws of physics are not themselves conceptually necessary. Thus in the relevant sense of 'possible', it is not merely the case that there is a possible world in which the substance with the macro-level properties of water is not H_2O. There is also a possible world in which H_2O does not have the macro-level properties of water at the actual world.

[18] I am grateful to Ned Block for pointing out the significance of this example.

Thus although there is no world at which Eve lacks either of the two properties connoted by the researcher's descriptions, there are worlds at which the properties are instantiated by other individuals than Eve. Thus the Modified semantic premise is satisfied, and we have an appropriate explanation—one that satisfies conditions (1)–(3)—of the a posteriori character of the identity. Thus we have the argument for (a slightly modified version of) Loar's Semantic premise.

Recall, however, that the claim was that there was an argument for a *weakened* version of the premise. In what sense is what we have derived weaker than the premise Loar rejects? Consider once again the identity 'pain = C-fiber firing', and assume that it is true. Assume also that 'pain' picks out its referent because pain has the property of being hurtful. Suppose now that the physicalist allows this point but claims that being hurtful is itself a neurophysiological property. Does this possibility violate Loar's version of the Semantic premise? The obvious answer is yes, since we have a statement of property identity that links conceptually independent concepts and is assumed to be true, while neither concept picks out the property it refers to by connoting a *contingent* property of that property. But is this case compatible with SVFC? Again the answer is yes. It is true that the situation as described *so far* does not explain how a rational subject could believe what he or she would express by saying 'I am in pain' and what he or she would express by saying 'I am in no relevant neurophysiological state.' But the fact that the situation described does not *yet* explain the a posteriori character of the identity does not show that this aspect of the identity *cannot* be explained in a way that is compatible with everything that we have assumed. The a posteriori character would be explained if the second order property itself had two different kinds of third order properties—one in virtue of which it is the neurophysiological property it is and one in virtue of which it involves the feeling it does.

The point, then, can be put as follows. The strong version of Frege's constraint does not force a dualism of properties upon us at any *particular* level. It requires only that there be *some* level at which there is such a dualism of properties. Thus the semantic premise for which we have argued is not Loar's but:

(Weakened modified semantic premise) A statement of property identity that links conceptually independent concepts is true only if the concepts pick out the property to which they refer by connoting contingently coextensive properties of that property, or contingently coextensive properties of a property of that property, etc.

5. LOAR'S ALTERNATIVE TO ANTIPHYSICALISM

Loar's positive position has two basic components. First Loar holds that we can have true identities like 'the property of being pain = the property of being a C-fiber firing', where the designating expressions flanking the identity sign express conceptually independent concepts and where the identities are therefore a posteriori. And Loar believes that for any genuine psychological state, it is such an identity that captures the relation between that state and the subject's neurophysiological basis. Thus, for example, Loar rejects analytical functionalism. Second, Loar wants to maintain that this is possible even though neither of the designating expressions involved picks out the common referent by connoting a contingent property of that referent.

How does Loar reconcile these two claims? According to Loar, phenomenal concepts are type demonstratives—hence they pick out their referents directly. And Loar has an answer to the critic who says that

if the phenomenal concept is taken to discriminate some physical property, it then does so via a phenomenal mode of presentation . . . the phenomenal concept does not pick out a physical state *nakedly* . . . But that conflicts with your assertion that phenomenal concepts refer directly, with no contingent mode of presentation. (Loar 1997: 604)

His response is to say that phenomenal concepts have two kinds of *non*contingent modes of presentation.

(1) A phenomenal concept has as its mode of presentation the very phenomenal quality that it picks out. (Loar 1997: 604)

(2) Phenomenal concepts have 'token modes of presentation' that are noncontingently tied to the phenomenal qualities to which those concepts point. (Loar 1997: 604)

By (2) Loar apparently means that particular (token) feelings of pain can focus one's conception on the type of feeling to which those token feelings belong. Fundamentally, then, Loar's reply concerns phenomenal qualities or properties, and his claim is that the physicalist can say exactly what the antiphysicalist would say—that the phenomenal property (which is a physical-functional property) picked out by a phenomenal concept is its own mode of presentation. As Loar says 'the idea that one picks out the phenomenal quality of cramp feeling by way of a particular feeling of cramp . . . is hardly incompatible with holding that the phenomenal quality is a physical property' (Loar 1997: 604–5). And he adds that 'the main point is by now more than obvious. Whatever the antiphysicalist has said about these cases the physicalist may say as well' (Loar 1997: 604).

Loar's basic strategy is to point out that the antiphysicalist wants to say that there is no distinction between the phenomenal quality and its mode of presentation and to ask why the physicalist should not say exactly the same thing. The point that this obscures, however, is that the physicalist and the antiphysicalist have radically different reasons for making what is only superficially the same claim. The antiphysicalist makes this claim on the basis of what we might call the *acquaintance sense of direct reference*. The account is this. Visual sense-data (to take the clearest and most carefully worked out example), like other modes of presentation, are postulated to explain and describe the way the world presents itself to the subject. Thus visual sense-data have all and only the visual properties that seem to be instantiated. If Neo hallucinates a woman in red, then there is no physical object of his visual perception that explains the character of his visual experience. However, there is, on this view, a mental entity—a portion of his visual field, say—that actually has the shape and colors that seem to occur in the actual world.

Moreover, in line with the assumption of a strong analogy between one's visual field and such pictorial media as paintings and photographs, such pictorial properties are assumed to exhaust the properties of sense-data. Unlike a table (but like a picture of a table), the corresponding visual sense-datum has no hidden sides. Sense-data have all the properties they seem to have, and they have only those properties; we cannot be mistaken in thinking a visual sense-datum has a property of the appropriately pictorial sort, and none of their properties go unnoticed. Thus we explain the way the world presents itself visually in experience by postulating a special class of mental objects that actually have the visual properties that the world seems to instantiate. And we should notice explicitly the analogy between sense-data and the primarily descriptive Fregean modes of presentation with which we have been concerned. Both are intended to characterize the world as it presents itself to the subject in order to justify rationally the subject's beliefs, intentions, and actions.

These characteristics of sense-data make it clear why they were (and ordinary objects were not) appropriate referents of Russell's logically proper names. Russell appealed to definite descriptions to provide the representational modes of presentation necessary to solve the Frege problems that arise for the use of ordinary proper names in a range of contexts, including a posteriori identities. In such examples as 'Hesperus = Phosphorus', the difference in cognitive significance between 'Hesperus' and 'Phosphorus', the fact that one could be perfectly rational in believing what one would express in saying 'Hesperus is F and Phosphorus is not F,' and the fact that the identity is not a priori are all explained by the fact that 'Hesperus' and 'Phosphorus' are associated with different descriptions (e.g., as above, 'the first heavenly body visible in the evening' and 'the last heavenly body visible in the morning', respectively). As Russell certainly recognized, however, this cannot be the whole story. If every referring expression got its connection to the world by being associated with a definite description, we would be caught in another infinite regress. And such a regress would clearly be intolerable; we would never get outside the circle of language-to-language connections to establish a connection between language and the world.

Such a regress is halted, on Russell's account, by the existence of logically proper names—that is, designating expressions whose only semantic function is to pick out their referents directly, without the mediation of descriptive content. And postulating sense-data as the referents of these logically proper names was a move ideally suited to bring this regress to a halt. First, since the sense-data in question are visual in nature, their connection to objects in the external world—sometimes alleged to involve a natural relation of resemblance—is radically different from that of linguistic expressions. Thus, because they introduce no further linguistic or descriptive content, they allow us to break the circle of language-to-language connections.[19]

Second, because like the images in paintings and photographs they have no hidden sides, they are their own modes of presentation. Therefore they stop another potentially infinite regress—this time of modes of presentation in general.

Third, given that logically proper names refer to sense-data, there are no a posteriori identities involving such names. Since there is no distinction between sense-data and their modes of presentation, they are not presented in virtue of any contingent properties that might have been instantiated by something else. Thus there is no possibility that two routes to the referent that in fact converge might have picked out different objects and hence no possibility of an a posteriori identity. And this is exactly what we find. If we think we refer directly to our own current sense-data, it seems obvious that we know whether we refer to two different images or to the same one twice. Moreover, this would be true of anything to which we could refer directly in the acquaintance sense. (And notice that this is precisely the sort of transparency that Loar disparages and that I claimed earlier that we would see emerge as the conclusion of an argument. Nothing I say, however, commits me to the existence of visual sense-data, as I shall make clear below.) The result is that logically proper names referring to sense-data could be used by Russell (in conjunction with his theory of descriptions) to solve Frege's problems while terminating what would otherwise be an infinite regress of descriptive contents. And Russell did so by appeal to a class of entities that raised no new Frege problems of their own.[20]

Of course, as I have argued elsewhere, visual sense-data as understood by Russell do not exist.[21] But what is crucial in the present context is Russell's strategy for reconciling direct reference with a solution to the relevant Frege problems: his limiting such direct reference to objects that are nothing over and above their modes of presentation. And there is nothing in my arguments against visual sense-data to prevent our treating pains and/or their phenomenal properties in Russell's way. That is, there is nothing to prevent our supposing that they, like visual sense-data according to Russell, are nothing over and above their modes of presentation. And this, of course, is exactly what we do normally

---

[19] Russell (1971: 201).

[20] These semantic arguments, which are completely independent of any prior epistemological commitments, were never (to my knowledge) presented explicitly by Russell. As R. M. Sainsbury's discussion indicates, however, there are good reasons to suppose that Russell was committed to all of the premises of the arguments advanced above. See *Russell* (1979: 76–88, esp. 87–8).

[21] 'Consciousness and the Problem of Perspectival Grounding,' presented at the Workshop on Consciousness Naturalized, Certosa di Pontignano, Siena, May 28, 1999 and 'Subjectivity and the Agential Perspective,' in De Caro and Macarthur, eds., *Naturalism in Question* (Cambridge, MA: Harvard University Press), pp. 201–70.

suppose. We assume that at least in one sense of 'pain' or 'hurts', we only experience pain and it only hurts as long as we notice it and that if we believe that it hurts we cannot be mistaken.

The upshot is this. The antiphysicalist has a story to tell about how pains, understood as irreducible mental entities analogous to visual sense-data, could be nothing over and above their modes of presentation. Thus the antiphysicalist can explain direct reference to pains, so understood, without leaving any relevant Frege problems unsolved. Loar makes what are superficially the same claims: that reference to phenomenal properties is direct and that phenomenal properties are their own modes of presentation. And on this basis he claims that whatever the antiphysicalist can say, the physicalist can say as well. But the antiphysicalist and physicalist claims, though they are couched in the same language, are radically different. When Loar says that reference to pains or to phenomenal properties is direct and that they are their own modes of presentation, what he means is the following. The referring expressions that pick them out do so in a way that is unmediated by descriptive content. Thus the expressions do not connote properties of those phenomenal properties or pains. There will be a causal chain in virtue of which the linguistic expression is connected with its referent, but the connection is not mediated by representational or nonrepresentational modes of presentation distinct from the referent itself. There is in this account no counterpart of the antiphysicalist's claim that pains or phenomenal properties are nothing over and above the way they are given to the subject from the first person or subjective point of view.

What, then, is the conclusion? The problem for Loar is that ordinary demonstratives used to pick out ordinary objects (and not, for example, sense-data) *do* raise Frege problems—even in cases where it is clear that the subject has no access to a descriptive expression that could replace the demonstrative in singling out the referent. In the two tubes problem, for example, David Austin imagines a subject who, capable of focusing his eyes independently, looks with each eye through a separate tube at a red screen before him. Since he cannot tell exactly how the two tubes are oriented, he wonders whether 'that (referring to the red circular area that he is in fact seeing with his left eye) is identical with that' (referring to the circular area that he is in fact seeing with his right eye). These descriptions of the circular areas, however, are unavailable to the subject. This is because he cannot tell which area is seen with which eye—either because his ability to focus his eyes independently means that there is no unified visual field, or because he believes that he may suffer from a condition in which objects seen with the left eye appear on the right and vice versa.[22] Thus even cases in which a demonstrative reference is irreplaceable with an identifying description raise Frege problems.

---

[22] In addition to Austin's discussion of the two tubes problem, see his discussion of Sarah, the pharmacist-astronaut, both of which are found in *What's the Meaning of "This"?* (Ithaca: Cornell University Press, 1990), pp. 20–5 and 42–51.

It follows that even cases of demonstrative reference to ordinary objects that are not via identifying descriptions are not direct in the sense in which reference to a sense-datum using a logically proper name would be. In contrast to the case of acquaintance, ordinary demonstrative reference, whether or not we call it direct reference, requires, as the existence of the Frege problems demonstrates, representational and corresponding nonrepresentational modes of presentation in order to satisfy SVFC and avoid local eliminativism. Thus Loar's talk of direct reference does nothing to show how we could do without representational and nonrepresentational modes of presentation in cases such as these, unless we were willing to pay the cost and embrace the eliminativist option.

Furthermore, the physicalist cannot make sense of the idea that a neuro-physiological state is its own mode of presentation. At best the physicalistic could say that some *aspect* of such a state provides its nonrepresentational mode of presentation, but in this it is like any other objective entity. As such it is available from any number of points of view, and there are an indefinite number of aspects of the state to which the subject (of, e.g. a 'pain) has no access. Thus there is no counterpart of the assumption that pains have only the properties they seem to have or of the assumption that we cannot be wrong in ascribing them the phenomenal properties we do. As a result, the possibility of a posteriori identities arises (as it doesn't for sense-data) and with it the possibility of Frege problems generated by the fact that different routes can converge on the same referent in ways that can be established only by empirical investigation.

The conclusion, then, is that Loar's strategy fails. The physicalist cannot say that our reference to pain or to phenomenal properties is direct in the same sense in which the antiphysicalist makes this claim. When the antiphysicalist says this, he or she means that our normal access to our own pains or phenomenal properties is via Russell's notion of acquaintance. And, as we have seen, this approach is compatible with SVFC. When the physicalist says that our access is direct, this means merely that there is no *descriptive* mode of presentation of the state or property. But appealing to this fact to describe the mode of presentation of the physical property alleged to be identical with the characteristic feeling of pain involves the physicalist in a dilemma. Assume that there is a representational mode of presentation available to the subject. (If not, if there is just a causal chain or process, then we have local eliminativism.) Then either the pain and the phenomenal properties are nothing over and above the mode of presentation and we have antiphysicalism, or this is not the case and we lack a solution to the Frege problems. And the suggestion that there might be some other mode of presentation (besides descriptive, causal, and via acquaintance) involves exactly the same dilemma. If the referents we pick out in virtue of such alternative modes of presentation are nothing over and above their modes of presentation, we have antiphysicalism, and if not, we have the Frege problems (and hence the property dualism argument) all over again. Thus I conclude that Loar's reply cannot be made to work.

6. CONCLUSION

This account of the property dualism argument is an expansion of the version in 'Curse of the Qualia.' (White 1986) Though the current version adds substantially to the earlier one—particularly as regards the role of Frege's constraint, antieliminativism, and the threat to reductionists of an infinite regress, the conclusions differ only in this: while both versions of the argument yield the same disjunctive proposition, I have opted for a different disjunct in each case. The disjunction is that *either* there are irreducibly mentalistic properties *or* the connections between mentalistic and physical and/or functional concepts are conceptual and a priori. Since the second disjunct does not seem even remotely plausible for qualitative concepts and physical concepts, this comes down to the following: either there are irreducibly mentalistic properties, or analytic functionalism is true. In 'Curse of the Qualia' I opted for the latter alternative. This now strikes me as less plausible than it did, and in this chapter I have simply ignored analytic functionalism as a live option. Those who hold this view are entitled to point out that nothing I have said here provides a substantive reason for abandoning it.

If the property dualism argument is correct, then, (and the assumption about analytic functionalism is justified) we are committed to the existence of irreducibly mentalistic properties. (Nor would such properties supervene on the physical properties.) Does this mean that we must take such qualitative properties as being a pain, hurting, feeling like *that*, and so forth as beyond the reach of any sort of explanation or analysis? The answer is no. The property dualism argument requires mentalistic properties but not necessarily qualitative properties. Thus it is compatible with an attempt such as Michael Tye's to reduce the qualitative to the intentional.[23] And the implausibility of analytic functionalism does not automatically translate into an argument for the implausibility of such an intentionalistic reduction. This translation would only be available if the proponent of an intentionalistic reduction were also committed to an analytic reduction of the intentional to the physical or the functional. In the absence of this further commitment, however, there is no reason why we could not treat such so-called qualitative states as pain as representational and attempt to illuminate their ostensibly qualitative character on the basis of their representational properties. (I have given a sketch of a nonreductive account of intentionality and consciousness elsewhere (White 1999).)

The final issue is the relation of the property dualism argument to other recent conceivability arguments—Jackson's knowledge argument and Kripke's modal argument—and to Joe Levine's explanatory gap argument.[24] Though some are inclined to see these arguments as standing or falling on the basis of the same

[23] Tye (1990: 223–39).   [24] Jackson (1986), Kripke (1980: 144–55), and Levine (1993).

considerations, a number of reasons suggest that among conceivability arguments and those that appeal to similar assumptions, the property dualism argument has a special status. Jackson and his critics, for example, seem to have reached an impasse over the question whether a subject with a complete knowledge of all the physical facts but no experience of colors acquires a new piece of knowledge or merely a new set of skills when he or she first encounters a red object.[25] And although there are important objections to those critics of the knowledge argument who claim that only know how and not factual knowledge is acquired, these objections have not proved conclusive.[26] Moreover, in the light of the property dualism argument, we can see why this should be the case. The issue between Jackson and his critics is whether the chromatically deprived subject gains a new belief content in his or her first encounter with a red object. And it is plausible to think that the ultimate court of appeal on issues of this sort resides in the principles of radical interpretation that constitute and govern all content ascription. That is, the ultimate appeal is to appropriate versions of the principle of charity and of Frege's constraint, to the principles of theoretical and practical rationality, and so forth. And a typical instance of such an appeal would be the claim that the subject who opts to contribute to research described as 'water research' and not to equally important projects described as 'H_2O research' must have two modes of presentation of water—i.e., two distinct contents under which the same object figures in the subject's beliefs. By its very nature, however, the example that supports the knowledge argument seems to rule out an appeal to first principles where content is concerned. The general form of such an appeal is that content is required to rationalize what would otherwise be interpreted as irrational or self-defeating behavior. However, precisely because Jackson's subject has access to all the physical facts—including the facts about when and why normal subjects would use the color vocabulary and which such uses would be correct—he or she will never be guilty of the kind of apparent practical irrationality that would ground an appeal to Frege's constraint or to the principle of charity. Thus Jackson's argument is constructed in such a way as to preclude the appeal to first principles that provides the most important ground for the ascription of content in the context of the property dualism argument.

As a candidate for being the most fundamental argument in this area, Levine's explanatory gap argument seems equally problematic. Levine himself makes a case that the explanatory gap argument has this fundamental status when he attempts to explain the conceivability of a creature's occupying any given physical or functional state and its lacking any sort of qualia in terms of the lack of an *explanation* of the nature of the qualia in physical and functional terms.

It is *because* [my italics] the qualitative character itself is left *unexplained* by the physicalistic or functionalist theory that it remains conceivable that a creature should

---

[25] Jackson's critics include Lewis (1988) and Nemirow (1989).
[26] See Loar (1997: 607–8).

occupy the relevant physical or functional state and yet not experience qualitative character.[27]

But this surely gets things backwards. Even if we had an explanation of the qualitative character of pain, say, in physical or functional terms, it would remain conceivable that a creature should have the physical or functional states in question while lacking the qualitative experience and have the qualitative experience while lacking the physical or functional states in question—or indeed any relevant physical or functional states whatsoever. This is so for the same reason that it is conceivable that H_2O should fail to produce the macro-level properties of water on Earth and that those macro-level properties might exist on the basis of a different microstructure or none at all. There are, after all, possible worlds at which the laws of nature are different, and logical or conceptual possibility is what ultimately governs the relevant distinctions between what is conceivable and inconceivable, a priori and a posteriori. It is the lack of an *analysis* of qualia in terms that would make it a suitable explanandum of a causal/physical explanation that is crucial, and not the lack of an explanation itself. Thus in this domain it is conceivability that is basic, and this fact is amply reflected in the structure of the property dualism argument.

Finally, although Kripke's modal argument seems most closely related to the property dualism argument, even here the latter seems to provide some advantage. In its appeal to Frege's constraint and to antieliminativism, the property dualism argument supplies a grounding for what some of Kripke's critics (e.g., Loar) have seen as unmotivated and unsupported intuitions. By locating the basic issues in the theory of the ascription of content rather than in the logic and metaphysics of modality, the property dualism argument grounds the intuition of transparency and a version of the Semantic premise in a way that Kripke's discussions thus far have not. Thus in this domain it is the property dualism argument with which I believe physicalists will have to come to terms.

If the property dualism argument is understood as a conceivability argument, however, it is likely to be objected that conceivability is not always a reliable guide to possibility and that there has been no argument that it is so here. But this would be to misconceive the nature of the argument. The argument is that if pain were identical with C-fiber firing this identity would be a posteriori and one could be rationally justified in believing something that one would express in a statement of the form 'Pain is F and C-fiber firing is not F'. But making coherent sense of the possibility of such a rationally justified belief requires that we postulate either irreducibly mentalistic states or

---

[27] Levine (1993: 548).

irreducibly mentalistic properties of first or higher order. And we are committed to the existence of the entities required to make coherent sense of our other commitments. Thus we are committed to the existence of irreducibly mentalistic properties.[28]

[28] Earlier drafts of this chapter were presented at the NYU Language and Mind Colloquium, April 4, 2000 and at the Workshop on Conceivability and Possibility, University of Fribourg, Switzerland, December 8, 2001. I am grateful to the audiences on both occasions. I have also benefitted from discussion of the property dualism argument with Jody Azzouni, Ned Block, Davor Bodrozic, Wei Cui, Martin Davies, Joseph Levine, Thomas Nagel, Martine Nida-Rumelin, Christopher Peacocke, Ullin Place, Mark Richard, Stephen Schiffer, Gianfranco Soldati, Richard Swinburne, Michael Tye, and Stephen Yablo.

5

Kripke's Argument Against Materialism

Eli Hirsch

I

Although Kripke presents an argument designed to show that (a certain form of) materialism is a priori necessarily false, he allows that there are on the other side some 'highly compelling' arguments in favor of materialism. The issue is therefore for him 'wide open and extremely confusing.'[1] My aim in this chapter is to defend Kripke's argument. This does not necessarily imply criticism of philosophers who acknowledge the force of the argument and admit they do not know how to answer it, but continue to accept materialism.

The central idea of the argument is the following principle:

(K) If the terms '*a*' and '*b*' both pick out their referents essentially then, if the identity sentence '*a* is *b*' is true, not only is it (metaphysically) impossible for *a* not to be *b*, but it is impossible for people in our (actual) epistemic situation to be mistaken in asserting the sentence '*a* is *b*.'[2]

People are in the same epistemic situation in the relevant sense if their 'qualitative' evidence is the same. Two people looking at different but qualitatively indistinguishable tables are in the same epistemic situation in this sense. When considering issues related to certain terms (for example, the terms playing the roles of '*a*' and '*b*' in the principle (K)) people are said to be in our epistemic situation if their qualitative evidence for applying the terms is the same as ours. I take this to imply that these people are phenomenologically (introspectively, subjectively) like us in all ways that might be relevant to their use of the terms.

---

[1] Kripke (1980: 155, note 77). I address in this chapter only materialism at the level of types, not tokens. This includes the type-type identity thesis, but also a more general materialist position, as I will explain.

[2] See Ibid.: 151–2. A formulation that may be in some ways clearer is given in Kripke (1971: 162–3); reprinted in J. Kim and E. Sosa (eds.), *Metaphysics* (Oxford: Blackwell, 1999), 85. Subsequent page references to this article will be to the Kim and Sosa volume.

The term '*a*' picks out the referent *x* essentially if *x*'s being the referent of '*a*' is determined by *x*'s essential properties rather than by any contingent facts about *x*. In particular, *x*'s being the referent of '*a*' does not depend on any contingent facts about how *x* affects us. (Where *x* is a general property the idea is that *x*'s being the referent of '*a*' does not depend on any contingent facts about how instances of *x*, or instances of other properties in terms of which we can define '*a*', affect us.) It follows that if '*a*' picks out the referent *x* essentially then people in our epistemic situation, whose basis for applying '*a*' is relevantly the same as ours, must use '*a*' to pick out *x*, regardless of any contingent differences in how *x* affects them and us.

We can readily understand the rationale for (K). The term 'heat' is rigid, but it does not pick out its referent essentially. If some other phenomenon (e.g., some magnetic phenomenon) affected people's senses in the way heat affects ours, they could be in our epistemic situation and use 'heat' to refer to that other phenomenon. Heat is the referent of 'heat' not because of its essential nature, but because of contingent facts about how it affects our senses. This is why, although it is impossible for heat not to be molecular motion, people in our epistemic situation might be mistaken in asserting the sentence 'Heat is molecular motion.' The term 'pain,' on the other hand, picks out its referent essentially, without dependence on any contingent facts about pain. It's therefore impossible for people in our epistemic situation to use the term 'pain' to refer to something other than pain. The principle (K) implies, therefore, that if an identity sentence of the form 'Pain is such and such a physical property' were true, where the second term of the identity is filled in with a term that picks out some physical property essentially, then it would be impossible for people in our epistemic situation to be mistaken in asserting this sentence.

(Kripke typically talks about pain and heat as '(types of) phenomena,' but I often find it easier to talk in terms of properties. It is to be understood that throughout this chapter properties are individuated coarse-grainedly (as in Kripke (1980: 138)): The property *P* is identical to the property *Q* if it is necessary that something has *P* iff it has *Q*. For terminological ease, allow me to ignore the difference between 'pain' or 'heat' and 'having pain' or 'having heat,' the latter more properly designating properties.)

As Kripke says (Kripke (1980: 143–4, 150–1)) the most obvious case of non-essential reference concerns a rigid designator whose reference is fixed by a contingent description of the referent. The case of 'heat' fits this model. But I think it is clear that Kripke will consider a typical proper name such as 'Aristotle' to pick out its referent non-essentially. Although in this case it may be impossible to specify the contingent facts about Aristotle that determines him to be the referent of 'Aristotle,' it is nonetheless obvious that we could have been in the same (qualitative) epistemic situation and picked out someone else as 'Aristotle' (if a different baby had been there at the initial baptism, etc.). In David Kaplan's work a term is said to have 'stable character' if its referent does not vary with the context of its utterance. But Kaplan seems to consider only actual contexts, and therefore counts terms like 'heat' and 'Aristotle' as having stable character. For a term to pick out its referent essentially it must be context-free in the more radical sense of having a reference that does not vary with actual or possible changes in the context of utterance.[3]

Kripke's main target is indeed the kind of materialist who asserts an identity sentence of the form just mentioned ('Pain is such and such a physical property'), the kind of materialist, that is, who wants to identify mental properties (or types) with physical properties. Assuming that both terms of the identity sentence pick out their referents essentially, the principle (K) presents this materialist with two serious problems (or perhaps two formulations of what is at bottom a single problem). (Kripke focuses on the second one.) Since it follows from (K) that, if the materialist's identity sentence is true, it is impossible for people in our epistemic situation to be mistaken in asserting this sentence, this is tantamount to saying that our (qualitative) evidence guarantees that in asserting the identity sentence we are asserting the truth. But typical materialists surely do not want to accord to their identity sentence the epistemic status of being immune from error. The typical materialist's position is rather that the sentence affirming the identity of the mental and the physical, like the sentence affirming the identity of heat and molecular motion, is a plausible theoretical hypothesis, not something about which we couldn't possibly have been mistaken, given our evidence.

Let me mention here a related point that I will try to clarify later. If it is impossible for people in our epistemic situation to be mistaken in asserting the materialist's identity sentence, then the truth of this sentence might be knowable by us a priori. But no one is presumably claiming that the materialist's identity sentence might be known a priori to be true.

But suppose materialists do claim (most implausibly, it would seem) that, given our epistemic situation, it follows necessarily that in asserting the sentence 'Pain is such and such a physical property' we are asserting the truth. The second problem then is that they have no way of explaining why it seems intuitively obvious that the physical property could occur without pain occurring, and vice versa. We have an analogous intuition in the case of heat and molecular motion, but in that case we can explain why the intuition is illusory by appealing to the point that 'heat' does not pick out its referent essentially. Our initial intuition that heat and molecular motion are only contingently connected is dispelled once we come to realize that what we really meant to say was that, given our epistemic situation, the referent

---

[3] Kaplan (1989). I suggest a definition of essential reference similar to the one given here in Hirsch (1986). A related notion of 'semantic stability' figures in George Bealer's 1994 argument in 'Mental Properties,' *The Journal of Philosophy* 91: 201; it is clear that Bealer requires more for 'stability' than Kaplan does.

of 'heat' might not have been the referent of 'molecular motion.' But in the case of the materialist's identity sentence, since both terms pick out their referents essentially, there seems no analogous approach to explaining away the intuition that pain and the physical property are only contingently connected. If pain and the physical property are identical then, given our epistemic situation, the terms of the identity sentence that pick them out essentially would have to have the same referent.

In some literature this second problem has been minimized by responding that perhaps the illusion of contingency between the mental and the physical can be explained as resulting from our being muddled about modal matters in certain ways. That response seems to me to miss the point. It would be like someone's saying: 'The solution to Zeno's paradox is that Achilles really does overtake the tortoise, and the reason why Zeno's argument seems to show otherwise is that we are muddled.' That is not a solution to the paradox. To answer the second problem one has to show how things come out straight after reflection. That is what happens in the case of heat and molecular motion. After reflection we have the intact intuition that there is indeed an element of contingency in this case, but it's located a bit differently from where we originally supposed. Once we realize this everything seems intuitively okay. ('Oh, it's all clear now. That phenomenon that in actuality produces the sensation didn't have to, but it had to be molecular motion, since that's what the phenomenon is.') We cannot apparently achieve this result in the case of the materialist's identity claim. If that is so, we are left here with an intuitive problem that we cannot answer. If considerations that favor materialism are deemed to trump the force of this problem, then we may indeed be required to acknowledge that some of our modal intuitions are incorrigibly misguided, but that is not to have answered Kripke's argument.

Our modal 'intuitions' are the source of our a priori judgments about modal propositions.[4] Reflection may cause some intuitions to be corrected, and in that way to be dispelled in their initial form. Kripke's argument purports to show that our intuitions contrary to materialism cannot be corrected. If someone says, 'All things considered I remain committed to materialism, even though I can't make any intuitive sense of how a physical property can necessitate a mental property,' then this person has not expressed any criticism of Kripke's argument. One has not found some fault in an argument if one states that, though everything in the argument seems perfectly right, one has some reason not to trust one's judgment. A criticism of Kripke's argument must involve showing how it can make good intuitive sense to say what the materialist says.

Kripke's talk of explaining (away) the illusion of contingency has, I think, misled some philosophers into thinking that a relevant critique of Kripke's

---

[4] See George Bealer (2004).

argument is to come up with an explanation of why we lack the capacity to get things intuitively right with respect to materialism.[5] But our purported incapacities do not constitute an alternative explanation of the sort Kripke is talking about. By explaining the illusion he means explaining it in a way that *corrects* it. What Kripke seeks is an account of the relationship between the mental and the physical that at the end of the day seems intuitively intelligible. Kripke is saying:

1. It seems initially obvious that C-fiber stimulation could occur without pain occurring.
2. On more careful reflection this continues to seem completely obvious.
3. Therefore, we have a strong reason to believe that C-fiber stimulation could occur without pain occurring.

He contrasts this with:

1'. It seems initially obvious that molecular motion could occur without heat occurring.
2'. But on more careful reflection this is not really obvious at all.
3'. Therefore we have no reason to believe that molecular motion could occur without heat occurring.

His discussion about 'explaining the illusion' is a matter of explaining why we have 2 in one case and 2' in the other. Questions about trusting our (considered) intuitions don't enter at all.[6]

To repeat: If one is led by Kripke's argument to say that materialism seems after the most careful reflection to be intuitively absurd, then one has in the relevant sense *accepted* the argument, whether or not one then goes on also to accept materialism.

In the light of (K) the materialist's identity sentence should be compared with the following identity sentence: 'The feeling of dizziness is a slight burning sensation in the back of the tongue.' Suppose that scientists discover that, for deep neurological reasons, people feel dizzy when, and only when, they have a slight burning sensation in the back of the tongue. The reason why people generally don't notice this outside of experimental setups is that the salience of the dizziness drowns out the slight sensation. (Or perhaps they do notice it but, for deep neurological reasons, immediately forget it.) I think almost everyone will agree that even if there should turn out to be this correlation between the dizziness and the burning sensation, it would be absurd to identify the two. The principle (K) explains why this would be absurd in a way that it is not absurd to identify heat and molecular motion. It is absurd because both 'the feeling of

---

[5] An especially clear critique of this sort is developed in Hill (1997).
[6] See Bealer (2004) for more specific problems with the kind of critique of Kripke's argument that appeals to our incapacities.

dizziness' and 'a slight burning sensation in the back of the tongue' pick out referents by their essential natures, not by some contingent properties.[7] Kripke's argument imposes on the materialists the burden of explaining why their identity sentence is any less absurd.

II

The most significant response to Kripke's argument in the literature is that the principle (K) does not really apply to the materialist's identity sentence. Kripke explains why 'pain' picks out its referent essentially, but he pays little attention to the second term of the identity sentence. In Kripke (1980) this sentence is represented as 'Pain is C-fiber stimulation.' In order for (K) to apply to this sentence, 'C-fiber stimulation' must pick out its referent essentially. But it seems extremely plausible to suppose that 'C-fiber stimulation' picks out its referent by the contingent causal relations in which C-fiber stimulation stands to various other things (e.g., certain neurological instruments). People in our epistemic situation might therefore have been mistaken in asserting the sentence 'Pain is C-fiber stimulation,' because, although pain is necessarily C-fiber stimulation, they might be using 'C-fiber stimulation' to refer to something other than C-fiber stimulation (= pain).[8]

Kripke's attitude about this question comes out most clearly in his remarks in Kripke (1971: 85).

In fact, it would seem that both the terms, 'my pain' and 'my being in such and such a brain state' are, first of all, rigid designators. . . . Second, the way we would think of picking them out—namely, the pain by its being an experience of a certain sort, and the brain state by its being the state of a certain material object, being of such and such molecular configuration—both of these pick out their objects essentially and not accidentally, that is, they pick them out by essential properties. Whenever the molecules *are* in this configuration, we *do* have such and such a brain state. Whenever you feel *this*, you do have a pain. So it seems that the identity theorist is in some trouble, for, since we have two rigid designators, the identity statement in question is necessary. Because they pick out their objects essentially, we cannot say the case where you seem to imagine the identity statement false is really an illusion like the illusion one gets in the case of heat and molecular motion . . .

It is clear that Kripke is not making any claim about the specific term 'C-fiber stimulation.' His point is rather that a materialist who says that pain is C-fiber

---

[7] I am assuming that even if '(being a) tongue' does not pick out its referent essentially, 'a slight burning sensation in the back of the tongue' does.

[8] This objection, in one form or another, appears in many places, perhaps first in Boyd (1980: 84–5).

stimulation must be committed to the truth of an identity sentence of the form 'Pain is such and such a molecular configuration,' where the second term of the identity picks out its referent essentially.[9] But any such sentence will be subject to the problems mentioned earlier: it will seem implausible to suppose that people in our epistemic situation could not possibly be mistaken in asserting the sentence, and there would be no way to explain away the intuition that there is only a contingent relation between pain and the mentioned molecular configuration.

My impression is that many commentators on Kripke's argument pay insufficient attention to the passage just cited (nor to the corresponding formulation in Kripke 1980). And this often goes together with their overestimating the importance of a certain formulation Kripke gives of the difference between 'heat' and 'pain.' He says that whereas there is a distinction between heat and the experiences by which we pick something out as being heat, there is no distinction between pain and the experience by which we pick something out as being pain; the experience by which we pick something out as being pain is pain itself. I think some commentators have taken this to imply that a necessary condition for a term '*a*' to pick out a certain kind of phenomenon essentially is that there is no distinction to be drawn between the phenomenon *a* and the experience by which we pick something out as being *a*. It may seem to follow immediately that no term of the form 'such and such a molecular configuration' can pick out its referent essentially, since there will certainly be a distinction to be drawn between the configuration and the perceptual experiences by which we pick it out. The same point would hold for any physicalist description of a property.

Kripke's position must be understood differently. His famous formulation of the difference between 'pain' and 'heat' in terms of there being no distinction between pain and the experience of pain may perhaps imply that a *sufficient* condition for a term '*a*' to pick out a certain kind of phenomenon essentially is that there is no distinction to be drawn between the phenomenon *a* and the experience by which we pick something out as being *a*. But he certainly cannot mean that this is a necessary condition, for his argument would then obviously not get off the ground. As the quoted passage indicates, Kripke is in fact well aware that his argument requires him to say that certain physicalist descriptions pick out their referents essentially. It is true that Kripke pays a lot more attention to explaining why 'pain' picks out its referent essentially than to explaining why 'such and such a molecular configuration' does. My guess is that it never occurred to him that materialists might want to say that they cannot grasp the essential nature of the physical phenomena on which they pin all their hopes. Let me elaborate on this point.

---

[9] In Kripke (1980: 149), Kripke says, '[I]f "C-fiber stimulation" is not a rigid designator, simply replace it by one which is . . .' He also means that if it does not pick out its referent essentially, replace it by one that does.

C-fiber stimulation, as Kripke says, is a certain molecular configuration. This means that it consists of certain complex spatiotemporal and causal relations between molecules. Let's suppose for the moment that the term '(being a) molecule' picks out its referent essentially. Then it would seem that we could in principle construct a term that picks out C-fiber stimulation essentially if the relevant spatiotemporal and causal relations can be picked out essentially. Let's focus on a particular spatial relation: one thing being enclosed within another. Does our term '(being) enclosed' pick out this relation essentially? The intuitive test is this: Can we imagine people in our epistemic situation—people who are phenomenologically just like us—who say 'One thing is enclosed within another' but who are not thereby referring to the relation of being enclosed? That seems intuitively hard to imagine.

If we say that '(being) enclosed' does not pick out its referent essentially, then we are saying that it picks out the relation of being enclosed by virtue of certain contingent facts about that relation, most obviously, contingent facts about how the presence of things so related typically affect our senses. If we say this about '(being) enclosed' then we will presumably say the same thing about all of our most fundamental physicalist vocabulary. None of this vocabulary serves to pick things out by their essential natures. Bertrand Russell seemed to hold such a view. Russell said: 'The physical world is only known as regards certain abstract features of its space-time structure—features which, because of their abstractness, do not suffice to show whether the physical world is or is not different in intrinsic character from the world of mind.'[10] Since we don't know what the intrinsic or essential natures are of the basic physical properties we refer to, there is nothing to prevent it from turning out that certain complex properties built up out of the basic physical properties are identical with mental properties.

Glover Maxwell dubbed Russell's position 'structural realism,' but it may be questioned whether the position deserves to be called 'realism' at all.[11] It may strike one as having more of the feeling of a kind of Kantian idealism. If we cannot pick out a property essentially, but pick it out only by how it contingently affects us, then in an important sense that property is something-we-know-not-what that affects us in a certain way. We are left at bottom with no more than a kind of Ramsified description of physical reality: 'There are things $x, y, z, \ldots$, and properties $P1, P2, P3, \ldots$, and relations $R1, R2, R3, \ldots$, such that x has $P2$, and z has $P1$, and x stands in $R3$ to y, etc., and these facts relate causally to our experience in such and such ways.' Insofar as we have no idea what these Ps and Rs amount to, this description may seem to differ little from a Kantian

---

[10] Russell (1948: 224).   [11] Maxwell (1970).

formulation in which physical reality is something X that somehow produces our experience.[12]

This conclusion may of course be resisted. We are not simply saying that there is this unknowable X. We are saying rather that there are a multiplicity of properties and relations and a multiplicity of things making up a certain specifiable abstract structure. I don't want to go down the road of Putnam's paradox. I'll assume that the required kind of Ramsified description can somehow escape that problem. Perhaps the escape is by way of taking 'causality' as picking something out essentially and not being treated as a relation-we-know-not-what. Or perhaps the second order property of being natural is not Ramsified, and it is assumed that the Ps and Rs are natural. Even if that paradox can be escaped, so that the 'structural' description is not demonstrably vacuous, it seems intuitively too abstract and rarified to qualify as anything we would normally want to call a description of physical reality.

Let me mention a more specific problem, though I'm not sure how much weight to place on it. It seems plausible to say that if our understanding of a term 'a' depends on our understanding of a term 'b', then 'a' picks out its referent essentially only if 'b' does. Now according to an old doctrine going back to Aristotle our understanding of the individuation of physical objects depends on our understanding of objects being located in different places. This implies that our understanding of the term '(being a) different physical object than' depends on our understanding of the term '(being) located at.' Since structural realists say that the latter term does not pick out its referent essentially, neither can the former term. But then the abstract structure of the physical world itself cannot be picked out essentially, for the components of that structure are supposed to be different physical objects ('x has $P1$, and y has $P2$, and x is a different object than y, etc.'). If the abstract structure itself is something-we-know-not-what then this is surely no different from the Kantian X that produces our experience.

Structural realists may reject the claim that our understanding of the individuation of physical objects depends on our understanding of spatial location. Their position may then be coherent but, I think, very hard to believe. The intuitive idea, the idea that is surely implicit in the attitude of both scientists and ordinary people, is that such fundamental physical properties as *being enclosed in something* do not have for us the status of properties-we-know-not-what that affect us in certain ways, but that we grasp the essential natures of these properties, and through them have some understanding of what physical reality

---

[12] A version of structural realism is presented in Carnap (1966: chapter 26); Carnap apparently takes the position to be a form of 'instrumentalism' (p. 255), which is generally thought of as a kind of anti-realism. A view that seems closely related to structural realism is sketched in Putnam (1981: 60–1); in Putnam this position is taken to be a form of Kantian idealism.

is like. If structural realism is the only answer to Kripke's argument then the argument shows that materialism requires an extremely counterintuitive view of physical reality.

III

It might be suggested, however, that the answer to Kripke's argument does not require anything as extreme as structural realism. Perhaps many fundamental physical properties can be picked out essentially but some cannot. Kripke implies that C-fiber stimulation can be picked out essentially as a certain kind of spatiotemporal and causal configuration of molecules. For this to be the case the property of being a molecule must be picked out essentially. Might one hold that this property cannot be picked out essentially, though various other fundamental physical properties can? If that were so then C-fiber stimulation could not be picked out essentially as a certain molecular configuration. (And then, to recapitulate the main issue, the principle (K) would not apply to the materialist's identity sentence, and Kripke's argument would fail.)

A molecule, one might suppose, is simply a bit of matter made up of bits of matter having certain geometric properties and standing to each other in various spatiotemporal and causal relations. If we are not structural realists why can't we pick out these properties and relations essentially and thereby pick out the property of being a molecule essentially? One potential problem has been raised by George Bealer.[13] It seems plausible to suppose that for something to be a molecule its *size* must fall within a certain range. We pick out a particular size as 'such and such (milli-)meters,' and we pick out a meter as, say, the size of a particular stick. Since we can't pick out the stick essentially (we must pick it out by how it contingently relates perceptually and spatially to us), we cannot pick out a particular size essentially. We therefore cannot pick out the property of being a molecule essentially, and therefore cannot pick out C-fiber stimulation essentially.

I think Bealer's point is that particular sizes cannot possibly be picked out essentially. If it were just that we can't pick them out essentially but other possible people could, it's not clear that this would adversely affect Kripke's argument. If Bealer is right the property of being a certain size is ineffable in a certain sense. (I think this a good ordinary use of 'ineffable,' but readers who disagree should simply take the previous sentence as stipulating that 'ineffable' in this discussion is short for 'something that can't be picked out essentially.') And it can of course be suggested that other physical properties may be ineffable in this sense. Perhaps there are different kinds of matter, where each specific kind cannot possibly be picked out essentially. Pain is a certain kind of molecular

---

[13] Bealer (1994: 208).

configuration only because our molecules are made up of the special kind of matter we happen to encounter. Our epistemic replicas in a different possible situation might encounter a different kind of matter, and they would therefore be mistaken in asserting any sentence of the form 'Pain is such and such a molecular configuration.'

Whether it is really plausible to suppose that there are ineffable properties that figure in science is an interesting question that I will not go into.[14] It seems to me that the problem Bealer is raising can be circumvented by presenting a slightly different version of Kripke's basic argument. Doing so will at the same time respond to another problem that comes out of Bealer's discussion. This is that many current materialists do not endorse the kind of identity thesis that Kripke criticizes. The more popular current materialist view is formulated in terms of supervenience rather than identity. The current materialist might not claim that pain is identical with any physical property, but may claim instead that there is a physical property such that necessarily anything that has it has pain. Kripke's argument in the form that I have so far presented does not address that kind of supervenience claim.

Here is something Kripke says at the end of Kripke (1980: 155).

Materialism, I think, must hold that a physical description of the world is a *complete* description of it, that any mental facts are 'ontologically dependent' on physical facts in the straightforward sense of following from them by necessity. No identity theorist seems to me to have made a convincing argument against the intuitive view that this is not the case.

For Kripke too the basic materialist target of his argument is the supervenience claim, the claim that physical facts necessarily entail mental facts. The identity theory was primarily addressed because it seemed to be the most promising development of the supervenience claim. Let us now put the identity theory aside and recast Kripke's argument as directly targeting the supervenience claim. We will see that by so doing we also put aside objections about ineffable properties.

The target now is this (still sticking to the example of pain):

(M) There is a physical property such that necessarily if something has that property it has pain.

Evidently the principle (K) cannot apply directly to (M). Let us generalize (K) as follows:

(K*) If a sentence contains only terms that pick out their referents essentially then, if the sentence expresses a necessary truth, it is impossible for people in our epistemic situation to be mistaken in asserting the sentence.

---

[14] If *being the same size as that stick* counts as a (natural) property then it may be trivial that there are ineffable properties, but it's not clear that such properties figure in science.

In order to allow (K*) to apply to sentences containing general terms, let me stipulate that if the singular term 'the property of being F' picks out a certain property essentially, the general term '(is) F' will also be said to pick out that property essentially. The rationale for (K*) is no different than that for (K). Suppose that S is a sentence that expresses a necessary truth and that all of the terms in S pick out their referents essentially. And let w be a possible world in which people in our epistemic situation assert S. Since S contains only terms that pick out their referents essentially, these terms as uttered in the context of w will pick out the same properties that they pick out in our context. It follows that the truth conditions of S as uttered in the context of w is the same as the truth conditions of S as uttered in our context.[15] As uttered in our context S expresses a necessary truth and hence is true with respect to w. Therefore as uttered in w, S is true with respect to w. This means that the people in w are not mistaken in asserting S.

Even if we believe in ineffable properties, we should agree, I think, that the sentence (M) contains only terms that pick out their referents essentially. The only term in (M) that might be questioned is 'physical property.' But if we are not extreme structural realists, why would we not regard that term as picking out essentially the (second order) property of being a physical property? Suppose we stipulate that a 'physical property' is a property that can be constructed out of (natural) properties and relations falling under the following list: (being) matter; the part–whole relation; the causal relation; various spatiotemporal properties and relations; and perhaps various additional ineffable properties and relations. If someone thinks that something is missing from this list (e.g, that 'force' or 'energy' pick out properties that are not ineffable), or that some of the items mentioned (e.g., (being) matter) are ineffable, then let him adjust the list accordingly. These possible refinements aside, my point is that we will wind up with a definition of 'physical property' acceptable to the materialist in which definition all of the terms (if we are not extreme structural realists) will be viewed as picking out their referents essentially. It should then be agreed that (M) contains only terms that pick out their referents essentially. Indeed, if one wishes one can replace (M) with the sentence: 'There is a property P such that necessarily if something has P it has pain, and P can be constructed out of: (being) matter; the part–whole relation; the causal relation; various spatiotemporal properties and relations; and perhaps various additional ineffable properties and relations.'[16] Unless we are extreme

---

[15] I assume that logical constants do not alter their meanings in any relevant sense when they are moved from our context to the context of w. One can put this point, if one wishes, in terms of essential reference: 'negation' ('conjunction,' 'existence') pick out negation (conjunction, existence) essentially.

[16] Perhaps we should add, 'where these ineffable properties and relations do not themselves allow for the construction of a property Q such that necessarily if something has Q it has pain.' Materialism in any familiar form implies that, for pain to supervene on P, P requires for its construction some of the mentioned ingredients other than simply the 'additional ineffable properties and relations.' Let

structural realists we should regard this sentence, and therefore the sentence (M), as containing only terms that pick out their referents essentially.

If that is right, then (K*) will apply to (M) if (M) is necessary. Assuming that if a (physical) property exists, it necessarily exists (as a physical property), it immediately follows that (M) is necessary if it is true. If one wants to do without that assumption, simply replace (M) by a sentence that results from appending the words 'it is possible that' at the beginning of (M), and this will give us a sentence held by materialists, but not by their opponents, that is certainly necessary if true. I will stick to (M) as it stands and assume that it is necessary if true.

The materialist is then committed to holding that (M) is a necessary truth. It follows from (K*) that it is impossible for people in our epistemic situation to be mistaken in asserting the sentence (M). And that generates the same problems for the materialist that were indicated earlier with respect to the identity theory. First, the materialist will have to say that it follows necessarily from our qualitative evidence that in asserting sentence (M) we are asserting the truth, which seems extremely implausible. Second, the materialist will have no way of explaining away the intuition that (M) is not a necessary truth, since we cannot straighten this intuition out by saying that what we really meant was that our epistemic replicas might be mistaken in asserting (M).[17]

Kripke's discussion assumes from beginning to end that there are strong intuitions that run counter to materialism. It seems on the face of it completely obvious that, for any physical property and any mental property, there could possibly be entities having that physical property without having that mental property. I myself think that philosophers who simply do not acknowledge the force of such intuitions are beyond the pale of serious discussion about the mind–body problem.[18] But even strong intuitions might be rejected at the end of

me note that, since I want to leave the structural realist version of materialism behind at this point, I will not try to determine whether (K*) presents additional intuitive problems for that position, as it very well may.

[17] Bealer (1994) uncovers a surprising asymmetry between (1) 'Necessarily, if something has pain it has C-fiber stimulation,' and (2) 'Necessarily, if something has C-fiber stimulation it has pain,' an asymmetry that leads him to conclude that the Kripkean argument works only against (1) but not against (2) (pp. 201–2, 207–8). We can find a term '*a*' that picks out its referent essentially such that 'Necessarily, if something has C-fiber stimulation it has *a*' is true, while 'Necessarily, if something has pain it has *a*' is counter-intuitive. (Bealer's example of '*a*' is 'the property of containing parts that have 74,985,263 or more functionally related nonconscious parts.') Since Kripke's argument works against the latter sentence, which is entailed by (1), we thereby refute (1). On the other hand, because of ineffable properties that are constitutive of C-fiber stimulation, we cannot find a term '*b*' that picks out its referent essentially such that 'Necessarily, if something has *b* it has C-fiber stimulation' is true, while 'Necessarily, if something has *b* it has pain' is counter-intuitive. (2), therefore, does not entail any sentence against which Kripke's argument can work. My answer to this is to go up one logical level: (2) entails (M), against which Kripke's argument does work.

[18] Nozick (1981: 458), suggests that perhaps such philosophers lack subjective experience.

the day. This can happen for two different kinds of reasons. The initial intuitions might be revealed as confused and capable of being corrected. Kripke's argument shows that this apparently cannot happen for the anti-materialist intuitions. Or the intuitions, though they remain incorrigibly strong, might be trumped by competing considerations that are even stronger. As to whether this may happen in the case of materialism, Kripke leaves that open.

IV

In this final section I want to briefly consider a number of further issues coming out of Kripke's argument.

A. Epistemic Situations and a Priori Knowledge

To say that it's impossible for people in our epistemic situation to be mistaken in asserting a sentence is not, of course, to say that the sentence expresses a necessary truth. Assuming that the reference of the word 'heat' is rigidly fixed by the description 'the phenomenon that normally causes the sensation of heat,' then it's impossible for people in our epistemic situation to be mistaken in asserting the sentence 'Heat is the phenomenon (if there is one) that normally produces the sensation of heat.' The sentence, however, expresses a contingency, since something other than heat might have normally caused the sensation. This sentence is one of Kripke's examples of a priori contingency.

One might be tempted to suggest that to know a priori that a sentence is true is just to know that it is impossible for people in our epistemic situation to be mistaken in asserting the sentence, but that cannot be quite right. Since some of us have headaches accompanied by dizziness, it is impossible for people in our (actual) epistemic situation to be mistaken in asserting the sentence 'Some people have headaches accompanied by dizziness,' but one does not consider our knowledge of that truth to be a priori. The intuitive idea is that a priori knowledge must not describe people's contingent mental states, but must instead reflect our understanding of what follows from our concepts or rules of language. If it's impossible for people in our epistemic situation to be mistaken in asserting a certain sentence, and the sentence does not describe people's contingent mental states, then the sentence might be called a 'conceptual truth.' In these cases, it is the cognitive or conceptual aspect of our epistemic situation that makes it impossible for people in our epistemic situation to be mistaken in asserting the sentence. A priori knowledge, it may be suggested, is knowledge that a sentence is conceptually true. (It goes without saying that none of this is clear-cut.)

A simple thought now is that any conceptual truth is knowable a priori. That idea is threatened, however, by such examples as Goldbach's conjecture. If that conjecture is true then the sentence expressing it is a conceptual truth (it's impossible for people in our epistemic situation to be mistaken in asserting the sentence, and the sentence does not describe people's contingent mental states), but it's not clear that it is possible even in principle to know a priori that the sentence is true. A more cautious formulation of a connection between conceptual truth and a priori knowledge might be this:

(APR) If a sentence is conceptually true then it is impossible to rule out a priori the possibility of knowing a priori that it is true.

Even if the truth of Goldbach's conjecture is not knowable a priori, it doesn't seem that we can know a priori that this is the case.

If (APR) is accepted we can recast Kripke's argument in a form that seems especially powerful. It follows from (K*) that (M), if true, is a conceptual truth. It then follows from (APR) that we cannot a priori rule out the possibility that the truth of (M) is knowable a priori. But is seems a priori evident that the truth of (M) is not knowable a priori. It follows that (M) is false.[19]

B. Jackson's Knowledge Argument

In Frank Jackson's famous example the scientist Mary is raised in a black and white room, and learns all of the physical facts about color. When she steps out of the room and has her first experience of chromatic color it seems clear that she will learn something new. She will learn what the colors look like, which she did not previously know. This shows that there are mental facts over and above the physical facts accepted by materialists.[20]

I find Jackson's argument (as stated) hard to understand. Why would materialists have a problem in saying that Mary of course learns something when she leaves her room, but what she learns follows necessarily from what she previously knew? Materialists have no special views about what constitutes a 'new (or different) fact.' They can plausibly maintain that, since Mary learns something that follows necessarily from what she already knew, what she learns is in one sense a 'new fact' but in another sense not a 'new fact.' There seem to be many examples of that sort. Suppose that Sarah counts eighteen rows and eighteen columns of coins on the table. Since she doesn't know how to multiply those numbers, and she wants to know how many coins there are on the table, she counts them, and finds there are three hundred and twenty-four. She has thereby learnt something, but what she learnt follows necessarily from what she already knew. In a sense she has learnt a 'new fact,' but in a sense she hasn't. Why would it be a problem for materialists to say that Mary is like Sarah?

---

[19] This argument is related to Bealer's (1994: 204–7) 'reformulated certainty argument,' and to the version of Kripke's argument that I give in Hirsch (1986).

[20] Jackson (1982).

Jackson indicates his awareness of this question in his later paper 'What Mary Didn't Know.'[21] He says that Mary's lack of knowledge before she leaves her room can't be explained as merely being a matter of her 'not being sufficiently logically alert to follow the consequences through. If Mary's lack of knowledge were at all like this, there would be no threat to physicalism in it.' It seems clear, as Jackson says, that Mary could not even in principle have derived what she subsequently finds out just by reasoning from what she previously knew. That does indeed reveal a relevant difference between Mary and Sarah. But Jackson seems to be ignoring the phenomenon of a posteriori necessity. Suppose that Hannah, who has no idea that heat is molecular motion, perceives that there is heat in a certain object. She is then told that there is molecular motion in the object. (She is not told that heat is molecular motion or that the molecular motion causes the sensation of heat; she is just told that there is molecular motion in the object.) She has learnt something that follows a posteriori necessarily from what she previously knew. The obvious position for the materialist seems to be that Mary is like Hannah. Jackson, as far as I can tell, has not said anything (in the cited papers) to indicate why this would be a problem for the materialist.[22]

The only way I am able to understand Jackson's argument is that it is implicitly the version of Kripke's argument I sketched in the last sub-section. Jackson seems to be presupposing that: (1) Mary expresses her initial physicalist knowledge in terms that pick out their referents essentially; (2) Mary expresses her subsequent mentalist knowledge in terms that pick out their referents essentially; (3) if her physicalist knowledge necessarily entails her mentalist knowledge, as is required by materialism, it follows from (K*) that this is a conceptual truth; (4) it then follows from (APR) that it can't be ruled out a priori that Mary could have a priori derived her subsequent mentalist knowledge from her previous physicalist knowledge; but (5) it is a priori evident that no such derivation is possible.[23]

---

[21] Jackson (1986: 5).

[22] There are of course familiar problems about the opacity of intentional contexts that apply to Mary, and also the question about whether to say that Mary winds up knowing a 'new (or different) fact.' But those problems apply as well to the examples of Sarah and Hannah, and pose no special threat to materialism. Essentially this criticism of Jackson's argument is given in a number of places. See, e.g., Horgan (1984); and Tye (1986). Lewis, on the other hand, responds to Jackson's argument by suggesting that when Mary leaves her room and discovers what it is like to experience color, she only acquires a new 'ability.' See Lewis (1988). The 'ability' view may be found by some materialists to be plausible in its own right, but I don't see why Lewis thinks that Jackson's argument pressures materialists into saying anything more than that Mary is like Hannah.

[23] Condition (2) is needed. This is so even though, as Chalmers shows (in his two-dimensionalist terminology), if P is a physicalist sentence all of whose terms pick out their referents essentially, and materialists claim that any true sentence X is a necessary consequence of P, it follows that it is impossible for people in our epistemic situation to be mistaken in asserting the conditional sentence 'If P then X,' regardless of whether or not the terms in X pick out their referents essentially.

C. Chalmers' Two Dimensionalist Argument

Another famous recent anti-materialist argument is David Chalmers'.[24] I do not, however, see any substantive difference between Chalmers' argument and Kripke's. Certainly Chalmers' discussion contains a number of significant and novel insights. And he redirects Kripke's argument away from the identity thesis, focusing on the central materialist claim that the mental supervenes on the physical. I have done the same in this chapter. My point is that his core argument seems to me to be essentially Kripke's argument in different words.

I am not addressing here the general topic of two-dimensional semantics, which ranges over a wide variety of issues in semantic high theory. Whereas Chalmers suggests that Kripke implicitly endorses his brand of two-dimensionalism, Soames maintains that there are actually three different kinds of two-dimensionalism, with Kripke holding the ('benign') kind that is correct, and Chalmers holding one of the two other kinds that are incorrect.[25] Those subtleties, however, have no significant bearing on Chalmers' argument against materialism. My narrow focus here is on only those aspects of Chalmers' two-dimensionalist framework that are directly relevant to his argument.

Let me give a brief sketch of that framework. He applies it to both terms and sentences, but it is easier to start with the latter. It will be convenient to think of a proposition as a set of possible worlds, as in Lewis. A sentence can be associated with two sets of possible worlds. A sentence's *primary* proposition is the set of worlds in which the inhabitants could correctly assert the sentence as being true (with respect to that world). If the reference of 'heat' is rigidly fixed by the description 'the property that normally produces the sensation of heat,' then the primary proposition of the sentence 'Some things have heat' is the set of worlds in which some things have a property that (in that world) normally produces the relevant sensation. A sentence's primary proposition cannot vary from one context of utterance to another. Its *secondary* proposition can. A

(Chalmers (1996: 132–3); I follow the explanation of Chalmers' argument in Scott Soames, *Reference and Description* (Princeton, NJ: Princeton University Press, 2005), pp. 246–7). But Mary's situation is different. The physicalist sentence *P* that she initially knows to be true is not supposed to necessarily entail every truth, but just truths 'about color.' Whatever exactly is meant by a 'truth about color,' it seems clear that we can find a sentence *X* about color such that in our context Mary's known sentence *P* necessarily entails *X*, but the entailment need not hold for people in our epistemic situation in other possible contexts. For example, let *X* be the sentence, 'Objects generally look blue when they have *dthat* (the color that is either the color blue in a world containing an even number of molecules or the color red in a world not containing an even number of molecules).' Supposing that our world contains an even number of molecules, so that in our context the *dthat* expression refers rigidly to the color blue, the sentence *X* ought to be a necessary consequence of Mary's known *P*, but there is surely no requirement that Mary be able to derive *X* a priori from what she knows about color.

[24] Chalmers (1996). See also his 'Consciousness and its Place In Nature,' in D. Chalmers (2002).
[25] Soames (2005).

sentence's secondary proposition relative to a given context of utterance is the set of worlds with respect to which it holds true. The secondary proposition of 'Some things have heat,' as uttered in our context, is the set of worlds in which some things have molecular motion. Those worlds, and only those, are worlds in which some things have heat, whether or not some things in the world have a property that normally produces the sensation of heat. A terminological oddity that takes some getting used to is that the proposition that would normally be said to be *expressed* by a sentence is the secondary proposition, not the primary one (as Chalmers notes on p. 64).

I abstract here from many complications: How does the framework deal with cases involving indexicals and demonstratives in which the context of utterance must be more finely grained than whole worlds? Must the worlds in the primary proposition contain people? Must these people be in our epistemic situation? I ignore these complications, of which Chalmers is well aware.

There is clearly a close connection between Chalmers' account of primary and secondary propositions and Kripke's explanation of why some necessary truths may initially appear to be contingent. Here is how Kripke puts it at one point (Kripke 1980: 142), 'In the case of some necessary a posteriori truths . . . we can say that under appropriate qualitatively identical evidential situations, an appropriate corresponding qualitative statement might have been false.' What Kripke is here calling the qualitative statement corresponding to a sentence is a statement that expresses what Chalmers calls the sentence's primary proposition. Chalmers explains the illusion of contingency as applying to cases in which a sentence expresses a necessary truth (its secondary proposition is necessary) while it primary proposition is contingent. That is very close to Kripke's explanation. The basic idea on both formulations is that, although the sentence in our context expresses a necessary truth, people who in some (internalist) sense mean the same thing we mean by the sentence might in their context assert it falsely.

In terms of Chalmers' framework the central points of Kripke's argument against materialism can be reformulated. If a sentence contains only terms that pick out their referents essentially, there is no distinction between its primary and secondary proposition. In these cases the worlds with respect to which the sentence as uttered in a given context holds true are just the worlds in which the sentence can be truthfully asserted. Chalmers' distinction between the primary and secondary intensions of terms is more complicated. For my immediate purposes the only point that needs to be understood is that if, and only if, a term picks out its referent essentially, there is no distinction between its primary and secondary intension. Therefore, the primary/secondary distinction vanishes at the level of a sentence if it vanishes at the level of the terms in the sentence. Corresponding to Kripke's assumption that much of our fundamental physicalist and mentalist vocabulary picks out their referents essentially is Chalmers' assumption that with respect to this vocabulary (and the sentences built up from them) the primary/secondary distinction vanishes.

The central claim in Chalmers' development of his argument is a principle that might provisionally be put as follows:

(C) If a sentence expresses a necessary truth but its truth is not knowable a priori, then the sentence's primary proposition is contingent and its secondary proposition is necessary.

(C) immediately implies that the primary/secondary distinction must apply to any a posteriori necessary sentence. In Kripkean terminology the implication of (C) is that a sentence cannot be a posteriori necessary if all its terms pick out their referents essentially. It is perplexing that in repeatedly seeming to appeal to (C) throughout his discussion Chalmers ignores the problem posed by such examples as Goldbach's conjecture. When he finally addresses that problem (p. 139) he evidently retreats from (C) to a weaker principle, but it's not clear to me what exactly that principle is. Probably it is something like this:

(C′) If a sentence expresses a necessary truth but initially seems intuitively not to express a necessary truth, the reason for this modal confusion is that the sentence's primary proposition is contingent and its secondary proposition is necessary.

(C′) implies that if the primary/secondary distinction does not apply to a sentence, and the sentence seems intuitively not to express a necessary truth, then there is no modal confusion, and the sentence can be presumed not to express a necessary truth. That is essentially the import of (K*) when we add Kripke's explanation that the only reason why we may initially have an illusory intuition that a sentence does not express a necessary truth is that it is possible for people in our epistemic situation to be mistaken in asserting the sentence. (Another possibility for Chalmers is to emend the principle (C) in a way that brings it close to the conjunction of (K*) and (APR): If a sentence expresses a necessary truth but its truth is knowable a priori to be not knowable a priori, then the sentence's primary proposition is contingent and its secondary proposition is necessary.)[26]

Assuming that (C′) is the principle Chalmers ultimately appeals to, his argument proceeds from (C′) in essentially the same way that Kripke's argument

---

[26] It appears that in Chalmers (2002: sections 5–6), Chalmers again ignores examples like Goldbach's conjecture and is thereby led to a formulation equivalent to the faulty (C). I think that an underlying problem is that Chalmers seems often to slip into conflating the following two senses of 'It is conceivable that p': (1) 'It cannot be ruled out a priori that p' and (2) 'The primary proposition associated with the sentence "p" is possibly true' (alternatively, 'It is possible for people in our epistemic situation to assert the sentence "p" truthfully').

The same conflation seems to figure in a criticism of Kripke given in Brian Loar (2002), 'Phenomenal States,' in Chalmers (2002: 295–310). Loar states that Kripke's argument against materialism depends on the principle: 'A statement of property identity that links conceptually independent concepts is true only if at least one concept picks out the property it refers to by connoting a contingent property of that property,' (p. 297) It is made clear in Loar's discussion that he intends this principle to mean that if 'a' and 'b' pick out their referents essentially then, if the identity sentence 'a is b' is true, its truth is knowable a priori. But Kripke does not hold this principle, and his argument does not depend on it.

on my formulation proceeds from (K*). He takes the materialist to hold that there is in principle a sentence *P* couched in the fundamental physicalist vocabulary such that for any sentence *M* couched in the fundamental mentalist vocabulary the conditional sentence 'If *P* then *M*' expresses a necessary truth. Since the primary/secondary distinction cannot apply to this sentence (in the Kripkean formulation, every term in the sentence picks out its referent essentially) it follows from (C′) (in the Kripkean formulation, it follows from (K*)) that, if the sentence seems intuitively not to express a necessary truth, it does not express a necessary truth. The sentence does seem intuitively not to express a necessary truth. So it does not express a necessary truth, and materialism is wrong.[27]

Is there any virtue to recasting Kripke's argument in Chalmers' terminology? Of course if one is already invested in the two-dimensional framework developed by Chalmers, one will naturally be interested in formulating an argument within that framework. But it is, I think, at bottom just Kripke's argument.

There is one remark Chalmers makes in trying to distinguish his argument from Kripke's that puzzles me. He says: '[Kripke's] essentialist metaphysics is inessential, except insofar as the feel of pain is essential to pain as a type—but that is just a fact about what 'pain' *means*.' I think, on the contrary, that every move in Chalmers' argument depends on essentialism. Forget about the 'feel of pain': the argument requires it to be agreed (contrary, it seems, to David Lewis) that pain itself is something such that nothing other than it could have been pain. And that heat is something such that something other than it might have produced the relevant sensation. If these are facts about what the words 'pain' and 'heat' *mean*, then Kripke's essentialism is part of a theory of meaning. The distinction, I think, is moot.

D. Meanings in the Head

When we use a term to pick out a property essentially we do so without dependence on contingent facts about how (instances of) the property (or properties in terms of which we can define it) affect our experience. We use a term to pick out essentially a certain kind of configuration of matter (molecules), in Kripke's example. This property is picked out simply by virtue of what is going on in our minds. That is why if people are phenomenologically indistinguishable from us they must be thinking of that same kind of configuration of matter, regardless of what contingent differences there may be in how configurations of

---

[27] Chalmers addresses structural realism (p. 135), but he seems to ignore the threat to his position posed by Bealer's suggestion that certain physical properties (e.g., specific sizes) cannot be picked out essentially, which implies that the primary/secondary distinction must apply to any term that picks out such a property. My response to Bealer's question, recast in Chalmer's terminology, is that the primary/secondary distinction does not apply to the sentence (M).

matter affect them and us. In the case of picking properties out essentially what we mean is in a sense 'in our heads.'[28]

It is ironic that some of the most hard-nosed causal theorists of reference take Kripke as their inspiration. It is of course true that Kripke's analyses inject a causal element into the semantics of many ordinary words, including both proper names and certain general words. But it seems clear that a non-causal semantic model of some sort is at work in Kripke's idea that our mentalist vocabulary and some of our fundamental physicalist vocabulary pick out their referents essentially. Even in the case of proper names and certain general words whose references are said by Kripke to be determined by a causal chain going back to an initial baptism the baptism itself will involve picking out some properties essentially, e.g., as 'the kind of stuff over there that looks and behaves like such-and-such,' where 'stuff' and 'looks and behaves like such-and-such' pick out their referents essentially. Kripke seems often to be deliberately vague and non-committal about which words he would count as picking out their referents essentially (see especially p. 128, note 66), and it may be that in the first two lectures of Kripke (1980) he is not concerned with the specific commitments in this regard required for his anti-materialist argument to go through at the end of the third lecture. Some of his remarks may suggest that many traditional words for primary qualities pick out their referents essentially, whereas many words for secondary qualities do not (see Kripke 1980: 139–40 and note 71). On the other hand, the fact that he often has recourse to talking about 'such-and-such' properties may suggest that he thinks it is not easy to find words in English that unambiguously function to pick out their referents essentially. Despite these complications it seems clear to me that Kripke's overall semantic picture contains a central non-causal component.

If what is going on in our minds determines that we are thinking about a certain configuration of matter, this should not be understood in the manner of Locke as implying that an idea in our minds is 'similar to' a configuration of matter. Berkeley seemed to get it right when he insisted that only an idea can be similar to an idea. Nor need we be committed to a full dose of the 'magic' of Brentano's thesis of irreducible intentionality. That thesis seems to imply that when we pick out a property essentially there is in each mind a mental act or episode that independently of all other events in that or other minds picks out the property. I tend to doubt that this is Kripke's view. He always talks about people in *our* epistemic situation. The picture is perhaps of a community of people each of whose members is the phenomenological replica of one of us. The causal interactions between these minds, and within each mind, may be a

---

[28] I assume that if people are phenomenologically just like us then they are in Kripke's sense in our (qualitative) epistemic situation. This is not to attribute to Kripke the Cartesian view that our knowledge of external reality must be inferred from our introspective states. Our perceptual judgments (or some of them) may provide us with non-inferential knowledge. But hallucinators who are phenomenologically like us are in the relevant sense in our epistemic situation (they have the same 'evidence of the senses'), although they lack our perceptual knowledge.

necessary condition for any of these minds to pick out properties essentially or to have any understanding.

Although a full dose of 'magic' is perhaps avoided, I think it must be admitted that what Kripke implies about picking out properties essentially requires something in the way of irreducible intentionality. What is going on in our minds determines that when we use a certain term we are picking out a certain kind of configuration of matter, regardless of how that kind of configuration contingently affects our experience. The connection between the term and the configuration is not causal. It is something peculiar to language and understanding. If this seems too mysterious, one has to consider whether the alternative is less mysterious. An important corollary of thinking through Kripke's argument is that if one rejects the notion of picking out certain physical properties essentially then one is left with structural realism, which is often one small dialectical step away from a form of idealism. One need not resolve the mysteries of intentionality to appreciate the force and significance of Kripke's idea that some terms pick out their referents essentially.[29]

[29] For helpful comments my thanks to Dan Kornman, Beri Marusic, Jerry Samet, and Palle Yourgrau.

6

The Self-Consciousness Argument: Functionalism and the Corruption of Content

George Bealer

What exactly is the relationship between physical and mental properties?* On this question materialist philosophers and cognitive scientists have a very limited range of basic alternatives (short of rejecting mental properties as real properties; cf. Churchland 1981). Broadly speaking, these alternatives are: some form of behaviorism, some form of the identity theory,[1] and some form of functionalism. In recent years, however, compelling criticisms have been made against the various forms of behaviorism and of the identity theory—leaving functionalism, in one or another of its many guises, as the most promising alternative upon which philosophers and cognitive scientists can pin their materialist aspirations.

Today, functionalism unifies and animates much of materialist philosophy of mind and cognitive science, at least as its tacit conceptual framework. Broadly functionalist sentiments have been articulated at one time or another by a long list of notable philosophers and cognitive scientists. Here is a small sampling of the philosophers: Lewis (1966), Putnam (1970), Harman (1973), Fodor (1981), Lycan (1987), Shoemaker (1981), Jackson (2003). And a small sampling of the cognitive scientists: Pylyshyn (1984), Gardner (1985), Minsky

---

* In writing this paper I benefitted from numerous insightful comments and suggestions from Iain Martel, John Bengson, and especially Marc Moffett. I also benefitted from a lengthy correspondence with Sydney Shoemaker on the Self-consciousness Argument. My thanks to Leslie Wolf for his meticulous work on the proofs.

[1] I will take the identity theory to be the doctrine that standard mental properties (thinking, being in pain, etc.) are identical to first-order physical properties (e.g., being in such and such neural state); I give my reasons for rejecting the identity theory in Bealer (1994; see also note 26 below). Here and in what follows I mean by standard mental properties the sort designated by canonical gerundive phrases 'thinking', 'being in pain,' and so forth (for more on this point, see note 3). As a terminological convenience, here and elsewhere I use 'property' for both properties and relations; I will use 'relation' when the context requires. It turns out that mental relations will be central to the debate.

(1985), Chomsky (1988), Johnson-Laird (1988), Newell (1990), Jackendoff (1992; 1997). Because of functionalism, a great many philosophers and cognitive scientists now acquiesce in the belief that there are no serious conceptual obstacles to a broadly materialist understanding of the mind and that the remainder of the story is largely empirical. To put the point another way, since the cognitive revolution (since our renewed efforts to peer into the "black box"), cognitive scientists are once again willing to implement robust realist mental notions in their theories—but to no small degree because functionalism has been thought capable, at least in principle, of explaining those notions within a broadly materialist framework. In this way, functionalism has served to clear the intellectual conscience of philosophers and cognitive scientists seeking a materialist understanding of the mind.

If, therefore, there is a principled barrier to functionalism, this vision of materialist philosophy of mind and cognitive science is put in jeopardy. In this chapter I argue that there is such a barrier created by self-conscious intentional states—conscious intentional states that are about one's own conscious intentional states. As we will see, however, this result is entirely compatible with a scientific theory of mind, and, in fact, there is an elegant non-reductive framework in which just such a theory may be pursued.

1. WHAT IS FUNCTIONALISM?

Functionalism has earned its role by promising to resolve, in the words of Jerry Fodor, a "nasty dilemma" in the materialist program in cognitive science—specifically, by preserving the virtues of behaviorism and the mind–brain identity theory while disavowing their shortcomings. In his well-known *Scientific American* article Fodor (1981) summarizes the historical situation thus:

> On the one hand the identity theorist (and not the logical behaviorist) had got right the causal character of the interactions of mind and body. On the other the logical behaviorist (and not the identity theorist) had got right the relational [dispositional] character of mental properties. Functionalism has apparently been able to resolve the dilemma.

(It should be emphasized that Fodor's "computational language-of-thought" functionalism is only one of a wide spectrum of functionalist theories. Nothing in this chapter turns on accepting Fodor's version.)

The identity theory is thought to be right in that it treats mental properties (states) as real properties having genuine causal efficacy. But it is thought mistaken because it identifies mental properties with *particular* physiological properties, whereas plainly nothing prevents them from being realized in a multiplicity of different ways from species to species and perhaps even from individual to individual. For example, the property of being in pain can be realized by firing "C-fibers" in one sort of creature, firing "D-fibers" in another, etc. (where 'C-fiber,' etc. are being used as mere *dummy terms* for whatever properties physiology ultimately settles upon). Intuitions of this sort are simply overwhelming in the case of intentional properties, for example, the intuition that intelligence, knowledge, and thought can be realized in a multiplicity of different ways in different species. It would be completely unscientific and ad hoc to insist that this is not so. The functionalist response is that what is common across species are, not first-order physiological properties, but rather the functional roles of such properties.

Behaviorism, on the other hand, is thought to be right in that it treats mental properties (states) as having an essential dispositional character, where those dispositions are ultimately anchored in observable inputs and outputs. But it is thought to be incorrect in that it treats mental states as being fixed *entirely* in terms of inputs and outputs, disregarding their essential interaction with one another. That interaction, however, is thought to be required to account for the fact that two organisms could in principle have the same input–output functions and yet have different mental states. And treating mental states as physically realized internal states is thought to be required to explain rational behavior (resulting from means–ends reasoning) and the sort of peculiarly human linguistic phenomena celebrated by Chomsky (1959) and many others.

Against this historical background, Fodor (1981) states:

[The cognitive sciences] have in common a certain level of abstraction and a concern with systems that process information. Functionalism, which seeks to provide a philosophical account of this level of abstraction, recognizes the possibility that systems as diverse as human beings, calculating machines, and disembodied spirits could all have mental states. In the functionalist view the psychology of a system depends not on the stuff it is made of (living cells, mental or spiritual energy) but on how the stuff is put together.

An account of what mental properties are falls naturally out of this view.

According to functionalism, thinking, being in pain, and other such mental properties are *second-order*: they consist in there being *other* properties, namely, first-order *realizations* that have appropriate interactions with one another and the external environment.[2] Accordingly, functionalists hold that such mental properties can be defined wholly in terms of this general pattern of interaction of their realizations (the PATTERN, as I shall call it for brevity).[3] Because there

---

[2] For a gloss on 'first-order' and 'second-order,' see Putnam (1970). For now, suffice it to say that first-order properties are properties definable in terms of *specific* primitive properties of individuals. Second-order properties are not first-order properties but are definable by quantifying over (i.e., by speaking *generally* about) first-order properties. For example, the property of being square is a first-order geometric property, and the property of having *some* first-order geometric property or other is a second-order geometric property. These notions of first- and second-order underlie the ramified type theory presented in *Principia Mathematica*.

[3] This characterization of functionalism clearly fits standard "American" functionalism (advocated at one time or another by Putnam, Fodor, Block, Harman, Shoemaker, Loar, Lycan, Cummins, and many others). It also fits "Australian" functionalism (advocated by Armstrong, Lewis, Jackson,

can be more than one system of realizations that fits the PATTERN, functionalism is compatible with the intuition that a given mental property—say, being in pain or thinking—can be realized in a multiplicity of different ways. What such realizations have in common is precisely that they fit the PATTERN in the way definitive of being in pain, thinking, and so forth. (See, e.g., Block (1990) for further elaboration.)

The legacy of behaviorism is that behavioral input–output relationships provide the observable anchors in the PATTERN. The legacy of the identity theory is that the first-order physiological realizations underwrite the flow of causes and effects within the PATTERN. At the same time, this entire picture is, by design, consistent with the powerful collateral thesis that the internal transitions within the PATTERN are *computational* in character. Although a number of *philosophical* functionalists remain neutral on this computational requirement, a great many *scientific* functionalists embrace it and, indeed, use it to guide their (traditional or connectionist) research. What I have to say will apply equally to both versions of functionalism—explicitly computational and computationally neutral.

No doubt the major conceptual attraction of functionalism is that, if correct, it provides a very ingenious solution to the Mind–Body Problem. How? By making the relation between physical and mental properties completely transparent and unmysterious. For, when functional definitions are substituted into the following:

If a thing has some system or other of first-order physical realizations that fit the PATTERN, then it has the associated mental properties as well.

Braddon-Mitchell, Pettit, and others). True, the latter functionalists hold that *pain* is contingently identical to a certain first-order realization, namely, the occupant of the "pain-role" (say, firing C-fibers). But Lewis (1966) says, "I take 'the attribute of having pain'. . . as a *non-contingent* name of that state or attribute Z that belongs, in any world, to whatever things have pain in that world...." By parity, he, and his fellow Australian functionalists, would need to hold that the property of *being in pain* is necessarily identical to the property of having a first-order property which is an occupant of the pain-role. After all, like the gerundive phrase 'having pain,' the gerundive phrases 'being F,' 'having G,' etc., are also *non-contingent* names (i.e., they are rigid designators: they designate the same thing in counterfactual situations as they do in actual situations). Therefore, being in pain would have to be a second-order property definable in terms of the PATTERN of first-order realizations, just as in the general formulation in the text. (Note that, since being in pain is multiply realizable, it would not be identical to any one first-order physical property (e.g., having firing C-fibers). Therefore, the identity theory—as it is glossed in note 1—would be mistaken on Australian functionalism. I will return to this fact in the course of the argument.)

In this chapter, I will be primarily concerned with propositional-attitude psychology and intentional relations. These relations are expressed by standard propositional attitude verbs (e.g., 'thinks') and are designated by the associated canonical gerundive phrases ('the relation of thinking' or 'the thinking relation' or simply 'thinking'). The Self-consciousness Argument will focus on conscious intentional relations (and, in particular, the thinking relation). The argument will employ the premise that functionalism is committed to the following tenets: (1) the indicated gerundive phrases ('thinking,' etc.) rigidly designate second-order relations (thinking, etc.); and (2) there are associated first-order physical relations, which together with first-order physical properties, fit the PATTERN. Lewis commits himself to these two tenets, and so, it seems, do Armstrong, Jackson, and the other Australian functionalists.

the result is a tautology:

If a thing has some system or other of first-order physical realizations that fit the PATTERN, then there is some system or other of first-order physical realizations that fit the PATTERN and the thing has them.

In this sense, the body–mind relationship may be viewed entirely as a matter of logic and definitions (i.e., as analytic, in Frege's sense).[4] No puzzling non-logical (synthetic) relations need to be posited; at the same time, behaviorism and the identity theory are avoided. Moreover, functionalism is compatible with the following elegant form of materialism: even though mental properties might in principle be realized non-physically (is anyone certain that they cannot be?), they are in fact realized only physically; and, therefore, (given the truth of functionalism) all properties that are instanced in actual individuals are either first-order physical properties or higher-order properties that are logical consequences of them.[5]

Functionalism has many virtues, but there are also many prominent objections: anomalism (Davidson 1968); subjectivity and "what-it's-like" (Nagel 1974; Jackson 1986); inverted-spectra, absent qualia, Chinese nation, homunculus head (Block 1978); externalism and anti-individualism (Putnam 1975, Burge 1978); Searle's Chinese Room (Searle 1980); eliminativism (Churchland 1981); utopianism (Putnam 1988); consciousness and zombies (Chalmers 1996). I believe, however, that none of these is conclusive—that, at the very least, each can be rendered moot by a clever functionalist. Indeed, functionalism might well be wholly successful were it not for a central type of conscious intentional state, namely, *self-conscious thought* (thinking that one thinks *q*, desiring that one desires *q*, thinking that one desires *q*, being self-consciously aware that one feels pain, etc.). For this reason, I believe that self-conscious thought poses the most

---

[4] According to "psychofunctionalism" (Block 1978) these definitions must be discovered by empirical science and so are not a priori. And whether a given thing actually has a given system of first-order physical realizations is taken to be a contingent fact. Note that, both here and in what follows, 'physical realization' (and 'physical property') may be understood widely so as to include relevant physical facts about the external environment and perhaps even physical laws themselves.

[5] This is not to say that these higher order properties are physical *by nature*. For our purposes, a second-order property is physical by nature only if it can be expressed by some second-order formula in which all talk of properties is explicitly restricted to first-order *physical* properties. A great many functionalists (e.g., Putnam, Lewis, Fodor, etc.) reject the idea that mental properties are physical by nature, for they accept that it is possible for mental properties to be realized nonphysically. Accordingly, in their second-order definitions of mental properties, they would prohibit restricting the relevant quantifiers to first-order physical properties.

There is nevertheless a weak sense in which a higher-order property may be deemed physical. Suppose that in a typical second-order functional definition of a mental property, talk of properties is not explicitly restricted to first-order physical properties. And suppose that the first-order realizations of the mental property turn out to be physical as a contingent fact. Then, functionalists might deem the mental property to be *physical as a contingent fact*. Throughout this chapter, when I speak of physical properties, I will not mean physical in this weak sense but rather *physical by nature*. This is the dominant use of 'physical' in the literature.

formidable threat (and the only rigorous internal threat) to functionalism on all its familiar formulations.

The threat posed by self-conscious thought is especially apt today in light of the flurry of interest in the experiential aspects of consciousness (for example, Block 1978, 1995; Lycan 1987, 1997; Baars 1988, 1996; Crick and Koch 1990; Strawson 1994; Chalmers 1996; Jackson 2003). There is a growing tendency to think that all problems of intentionality (believing, thinking, desiring, deciding, etc.) have already been solved by traditional functionalism and that the only "hard problem" results from conscious experience (Strawson 1994; Chalmers 1996).[6] In this connection, consciousness is often actually equated with phenomenal experience, neglecting what traditionally (as far back as Descartes) was wholly central to consciousness—namely, conscious thinking (as in the *Cogito*). Plainly, conscious thinking and conscious experiencing have something in common, namely, consciousness itself. And this is no pun. The idea (Block, Strawson, Chalmers) that conscious thinking has a reductive explanation and conscious experiencing does not (or vice versa) yields an implausibly fragmented picture of consciousness (and, indeed, of the mind and the self).

The problem of self-conscious thought may be put as a dilemma. Either the standard functional definitions admit the wrong sorts of things as typical contents of one's conscious thoughts about one's current conscious states (since those contents would have to be propositions involving first-order *realizations* rather than mental properties themselves), or else the definitions are circular and so do not even count as definitions. The only way out of this dilemma is to abandon the primary tenet of functionalism (that mental properties can be defined wholly in terms of the PATTERN of their realizations) and to replace the standard reductive functional definitions with non-reductive counterparts. But doing this, we shall see, undermines functionalism's explanation of the relation between physical and mental properties and in turn its solution to the Mind–Body Problem itself.

2. FUNCTIONAL DEFINITIONS AND SELF-CONSCIOUS THOUGHT

In what follows I try to be faithful to the formulations of functionalism in the published literature, and I believe I succeed at this. If the argument is correct, those formulations of functionalism contain a serious internal difficulty. Functionalists therefore need to find a way to *revise* their view. I believe that this cannot be done without violating the central tenets and aims of functionalism.

---

[6] Galen Strawson introduced the term 'The Hard Problem' in his 1994 book. David Chalmers uses the term in his 1995 paper "Facing Up to the Problem of Consciousness" and in his 1996 book.

The most clear and precise formulations of functionalism are those based on the idea of "Ramsification."[7] Here a whole theory is converted into a definition by replacing its 'theoretical' (in this case, psychological) predicates with variables bound by the existential quantifier 'there exist.' As noted, psychological theory describes the PATTERN of interaction of the standard mental properties and relations with one another and the external environment. Let A be a comprehensive psychological theory specifying the PATTERN. A results from A by replacing psychological predicates with associated predicate variables 'R_1,' 'R_2,' . . . . Let 'R' be short for '$R_1, R_2, ...$' Then, assuming that 'is in pain' is the first psychological predicate occurring in A and 'thinks' the second, functionalists then propose the following standard functional definitions:

x is in pain iff$_{\text{def}}$ there exist first-order realizations R satisfying A and x has R_1.

x thinks q iff$_{\text{def}}$ there exist first-order realizations R satisfying A and x is related by R_2 to q.

Consider the second definition. We know that the thinking relation is characterized by a number of quite distinctive interactive principles. For example, the following *Self-intimation Principle*: if a person is thinking something and engaging in introspection, he or she will think that he or she is thinking something. Perhaps qualifiers need to be added—for example, 'engaging in thorough and attentive introspection,' '*ceteris paribus*,' 'probably.' (If you prefer, 'is thinking something' could be replaced with 'is in pain,' 'is sensing red,' etc., in the antecedent and in the embedded occurrence in the consequent. But it is convenient to stick with 'is thinking something' because self-embedded attitudes—and also cross-embedded attitudes such as thinking that you are desiring—will prove to be of special interest later on.) The point is that some such principles, with or without qualifiers, would belong to psychological theory A, given that A is comprehensive. As Sydney Shoemaker (1994: 59) says, "[I]n many cases it belongs to the very essence of a mental state (its functional nature) that, normally, its existence results, under certain circumstances, in there being such awareness of it." David Lewis (1966) expresses much the same point thus:

[Functionalism] allows us to include other experiences among the typical causes and effects by which an experience is defined. It is crucial that we should be able to do so in order that we may do justice, in defining experiences by their causal roles, to the introspective accessibility which is such an important feature of any experience. For the introspective accessibility of an experience is its propensity reliably to cause other (future or simultaneous) experiences directed intentionally upon it, wherein we are aware of it.

---

[7] Ramsey (1931: 212–36) proposed a technique, not for defining "theoretical" terms, but rather for eliminating them by means of existentially quantified predicate variables. To my knowledge, the idea of using existentially quantified predicate variables to construct the kind of definition described in the text is first found in R. M. Martin's (1966: 1–13). Martin's idea or variants on it were subsequently advocated by Putnam (1970), Lewis (1970), and a long list of others (Harman, Loar, Shoemaker, Block, Cummins, Jackson, etc.).

For simplicity, suppose that A_0 is a conjunction of some complex clause Q and the above Self-intimation Principle. The formula Q results from Q by replacing psychological predicates with predicate variables as before. Assume that 'introspects' is the third psychological predicate occurring in A. Then, stated in greater detail, the above standard functional definition of the thinking relation would be:

x thinks q iff$_{\text{def}}$ there exist first-order realizations R such that (i) they satisfy Q; (ii) if x R_2s something and x R_3s, then x will be related by R_2 to the proposition that he R_2s something; and (iii) x R_2s the proposition q.

Clause (ii) results from the Self-intimation Principle by replacing 'thinks' with 'R_2' and 'introspects' with 'R_3.' (To see that this is intensionally correct, see below.)

We can now pinpoint the problem: this functional definition implies that first-order realizations of the thinking relation (rather than the thinking relation itself) would be among the typical contents of our everyday self-conscious thoughts. To see why, suppose x is both thinking something and engaging in introspection. Then, by the left-to-right directions of the functional definitions of thinking and introspecting, there would be first-order realizations R which satisfy A such that: x R_2s something and x R_3s. Since this conjunction is the antecedent of clause (ii) and since (given that R satisfies A) R_2 and R_3 satisfy clause (ii), it follows by modus ponens that: x is related by R_2 to the proposition that he R_2s something. But the right-to-left direction of the definition of thinking implies that, if x is related by such a first-order realization R_2 to an arbitrary proposition q, then x thinks q. So, given that x is related by R_2 to the proposition that he R_2s something, it follows that x thinks that he R_2s something. But R_2 is not the relation of thinking (i.e., the relation expressed by the predicate 'thinks' and denoted by the associated gerund 'thinking'; see note 3), which according to functionalism is a second-order relation; rather, R_2 is a first-order physical realization of the thinking relation. The upshot is that the functional definition admits the wrong sorts of things into the contents of our everyday self-conscious thoughts.[8]

One response to this argument is to "bite the bullet," that is, to hold that propositions involving such first-order physical realizations really are typical objects of the thinking relation. But this is wholly implausible once it is realized that we are talking about the relation of conscious explicit thinking. This is a highly *focused* relation. When a person is consciously and explicitly thinking that he or she is thinking something, typically the person will not be consciously

---

[8] Another possibility is that there simply are *no* first-order realizations that display the sort of self-embeddability characteristic of mental relations. In this case, functionalists would be committed to holding that there is *no* sequence of first-order realizations R satisfying A. If so, the right-hand side of the definition would be null and therefore would not correctly define the thinking relation. Hence, it only helps functionalists to suppose that there are first-order realizations R satisfying A.

and explicitly thinking *two* propositions, one involving the relation of thinking (i.e., the relation expressed by the predicate 'thinks' and rigidly denoted by the associated gerund, cf. note 3) and the other some first-order physical realization of the thinking relation, say, R_2.

Would it make sense to reply that, although there is indeed just one of these propositions you are thinking when you are thinking that you are thinking something, it is really the proposition involving a first-order realization, rather than the thinking relation itself? More specifically, is it really the proposition that you R_2 something? Obviously not. Indeed, the former proposition does not even entail the latter: after all, it is possible that someone think something even if no one bears R_2 to anything. Look at the question this way. Suppose a creature in a species with a different physical make-up is thinking that it thinks something. Then, by a simple one-step existential-generalization inference, both you and the creature could arrive at a single proposition on which you *agree*, namely, that *someone* thinks something. But this obvious possibility would be out of reach if the respective propositions you and the creature were originally thinking involved, not the thinking relation itself, but instead *distinct* physical realizations of the thinking relation (your R_2 and the creature's S_2).[9]

The most common worry about our main argument concerns intensionality—specifically, the fact that the embedded occurrence of 'thinks' in the Self-intimation Principle was replaced with an existentially quantified predicate variable. Was it right to do that?[10] Yes, but before explaining why, let me put the argument in the form of a dilemma for functionalists: either they accept that the pivotal existential generalizations are valid or they do not. If they do, then some version of the argument goes through. If they do not, then the resulting functionalist "definition" of thinking will not even qualify as a definition, for the undefined psychological expression 'thinks' would still occur on the right-hand side.[11] Thus, functionalists may go one of two ways on the intensionality issue, but whichever way they go, their Ramsified definitions are unsatisfactory.

---

[9] In view of these considerations, it should be clear that our main argument applies against both American and Australian functionalism. Each implies that, when you are thinking that someone thinks something, the proposition that you are thinking involves a first-order realization, rather than the relation of thinking itself. Likewise for the creature in the other species. Consequently, on both versions of functionalism, you and the creature would not agree that someone is thinking something. Some Australian functionalists might reply that the creature—suppose it is a Martian—is not thinking (but rather is M-thinking). It is a truism, however, that intelligence requires thinking well. Hence, if the Australian functionalist were correct, it would follow that the creature is not intelligent. But this is absurd: the existence of extraterrestrial intelligence cannot be disproved so easily. It follows, therefore, that Australian functionalism is mistaken.

[10] For more extended discussion of the intensionality issue, see Bealer (1997 and forthcoming b). Note that Lewis would agree that there is no intensionality problem (see Lewis 1972: note 8).

[11] Definitions of the following sort escape both horns of this dilemma:

The relation of thinking $=_{def}$ the unique relation T such that, necessarily, (for all x and q) x Ts q iff for some first-order properties R, (i) R satisfies Q; (ii) it is causally or metaphysically necessary that, if x R_2s something and x R_3s, then x R_2s the proposition that x Ts something; and (iii) x R_2s q.

In fact, however, the intensionality worry is unfounded. True, *singular terms* occurring in intensional contexts cannot be existentially generalized. For example, even if '*x* thinks that the smartest spy is a spy' is true, its existential generalization 'For some *y*, *x* thinks that *y* is a spy' might well be false. The intensionality worry is that the argument overlooks this familiar point. But there is an important difference between our main argument and the above example involving 'the smartest spy.' Specifically, when we Ramsified in our argument, we existentially generalized, not on a singular term ('the smartest spy'), but rather on an embedded *predicate* ('thinks'). This existential generalization is on a par with the following inference: *x* thinks that he or she hurts; therefore, for some *R*, *x* thinks that he or she, *R*s. This is valid in the logical settings in which functionalists themselves intend to Ramsify.

Look at the matter this way. The proposition that is the semantic value of 'he thinks something' in the antecedent of Self-intimation Principle is the same as the proposition that is the semantic value of the 'that'-clause 'that he thinks something' in the consequent. In each case, it is the proposition *that he thinks something.* This is why the following truism holds: 'he thinks something' means *that he thinks something.* The correct logical analysis of this proposition is given in terms of the thinking relation, the relation (i.e., intension) expressed by the psychological verb 'thinks.' Since functionalists intend their predicate variables to replace psychological verbs and since each occurrence of 'thinks' is semantically correlated with one and the same relation (intension), functionalists would have us replace each occurrence with one and the same predicate variable '*R₂*.' This is what we did in the argument. So our argument goes through and involves no equivocations over intensionality.[12]

The entire issue of intensionality does not even arise in the case of the psychological relation of self-attribution (which Lewis (1979) and Chisholm (1981) focus upon). On analogy with the Self-intimation Principle, the following

But this is not the sort of definition allowed by functionalism, for the intended value of its quantified predicate variable '*T*' is the thinking relation itself, not a first-order realization of it. Instead, this definition is a special case of what I will call a nonreductive functional definition (see sections 4–5).

[12] Some people have tried to avoid the Self-consciousness Argument by proposing an intensional logic that deals with both properties (attributes) and concepts. In such a setting one of two things happens to the original Self-consciousness Argument. Either a version of that argument still goes through but is somewhat more complicated (see Bealer 1997: 83). Or else the new Ramsified definitions turn out to be nonreductive (in the sense isolated in section 4). In the latter case, those definitions might well be correct, but if they are, functionalism's solution to the Mind–Body Problem collapses in the manner discussed in section 5. For now, suffice it to say that invoking concepts does not help to avoid the problem in the case of the psychological relation of self-attribution (cf. the next paragraph in the text). For it is undeniable that ordinary people attribute to themselves the *attribute* of being in pain. The relation of attribution clearly relates people to properties (attributes) not concepts. So the self-consciousness argument applies just as it did before; the more complicated apparatus of both concepts and properties (attributes) does nothing to prevent it.

principle partially characterizes the self-attribution relation: if x has the property of being in pain and x has the property of introspecting, then x will self-attribute the property of being in pain. Here the occurrences of 'the property of being in pain' following 'has' in the antecedent and following 'self-attributes' in the consequent are both plainly extensional. So, uncontroversially, the Ramsification of this principle is: if x has R_1 and x has R_3, then x is related by R_2 to R_1. Then the rest of the self-consciousness argument goes through *mutatis mutandis*. The absurd conclusion follows, namely, that it is commonplace for ordinary persons x to attribute to themselves first-order realizations of the property of being in pain (say, the property of having firing C-fibers), rather than the property of being in pain itself.[13] For this reason, the standard style of Ramsified definition does not work generally: it fails in the case of the psychological relation of self-attribution.[14]

To avoid our argument, what functionalists need is a way of blocking the quantification of embedded mental predicates ('thinks,' etc.) in psychological theory A, and they must do this in a way that does not leave them with undefined psychological expressions on the right-hand sides of their definitions. This can be accomplished by treating embedded predicates as standing for mere syntactic entities—mere linguistic *representations*. Language-of-thought functionalism is designed to do just this. But it does not solve the underlying problem; it only hides it.

3. LANGUAGE OF THOUGHT

Language-of-thought functionalism resembles a common two-step technique of giving functional definitions. According to this technique, one first attempts to give functional definitions of mental state-types; that is, one attempts to define what it is for a state to be a state of thinking, a state of desiring, etc. Following that, one attempts to define what it is for a mental state of a given type to have p as its content; that is, to define what it is for a state of thinking to have p as its content, what it is for a state of desiring to have q as its content, etc. Putting the two steps together, one then obtains fully general definitions of what it is for x

---

[13] With this simpler argument in mind, it is easy to see that a wholly analogous argument shows that it would also be commonplace for ordinary people to self-attribute first-order realizations of the property of thinking something (rather than the property of thinking something itself).

[14] Against this argument it might be objected that self-attribution is a nonbasic mental relation which is to be defined, not by means of Ramsification, but rather *directly* in terms of the thinking relation itself. (This approach is not available to functionalists, such as Lewis, who take self-attribution to be definitionally prior to thinking.) On this approach, self-attribution might be defined as follows: x self-attributes F iff$_{def}$ x thinks that he or she is F. But this just concedes the larger point. For, uncontroversially, this embedded occurrence of 'F' on the right-hand side of the definition is externally quantifiable. So the Self-consciousness Argument goes through in its original form.

to think p, desire q, etc. For example, x thinks p iff$_{\text{def}}$ x is in a state of thinking and that state has p as its content.[15]

Language-of-thought functionalism resembles this approach except that, in step one, tokenings of Mentalese sentences in modules (metaphorically, a Thinking Box, Desiring Box, etc.) take the place of mental state types and, in step two, content is assigned to the Mentalese sentences that might be so tokened.[16] Thus, x thinks p iff$_{\text{def}}$ there is a Mentalese sentence s tokened in x's Thinking Box and s's content is p; x desires p iff$_{\text{def}}$ there is a Mentalese sentence s tokened in x's Desiring Box and s's content is p; and so forth.

The success of step one is incompatible with the metaphysical possibility of a nonphysical, purely mental being.[17] The problem this possibility would create for language-of-thought functionalism is that, for purely mental beings, there could be no physical medium in which the requisite Mentalese sentences could be tokened and no physical modules in which to house these tokens.[18] Accordingly, general definitions of the standard mental relations (thinking, desiring, etc.) would be out of the reach of language-of-thought functionalism.[19] Of course, many language-of-thought functionalists reject the possibility of a purely mental being, so the argument of this section will not turn on it. The reason for mentioning it here is that, as we will see, language-of-thought functional definitions stand no chance of being correct unless they are

---

[15] One instance of this method is just an elaborate form of Ramsification. For example, a state t would be a state of thinking iff$_{\text{def}}$ there exist first-order realizations R satisfying A and $t =$ the state of being related by R_2 to something. And a state t of thinking would have p as its content iff$_{\text{def}}$ there exist first-order realizations R satisfying A and $t =$ the state of being related by R_2 to p. Of course, such Ramsified formulations of the two-step approach are plainly subject to the style of argument given above.

[16] See, for example, Fodor (1987). Incidentally, at certain points in what follows I take the liberty of using ordinary quotation marks where Quinean corner quotation marks are strictly speaking called for.

[17] Not only do many Ramsifying functionalists accept this possibility, but so do various language-of-thought functionalists. For example, Fodor (1981) recognizes "the possibility that systems as diverse as human beings, calculating machines, and disembodied spirits could all have mental states." Furthermore, there are serious *arguments* supporting this possibility: for example, Yablo's (1990) reformulation of the traditional conceivability argument, and my own (1994) reformulation of the traditional certainty argument. Fodor's acceptance of this possibility creates a tension within his overall view.

[18] "Non-physical stuff" is an oxymoron, a metaphysical impossibility: "ectoplasm" and its ilk are just silly—no serious philosopher subscribes to such things. Moreover, the ectoplasm move would not avoid the problem unless it is assumed that some such medium would be necessary for the existence of a purely mental being. But there is no reason to accept this assumption. Indeed, most philosophers who accept the possibility of purely mental beings think they would have to be *simple* beings—not "made" or "composed" of anything.

[19] Here, then, is an advantage of Ramsifying functionalism: it is at least prima facie consistent with this possibility—since, in the case of, say, angels, the requisite first-order realization could be the relation of angel-thinking. Given that language-of-thought functionalism is simply incompatible with the possibility of a purely mental being, it bears a certain *ontological* resemblance to explicitly materialist formulations of Ramsifying functionalism, for example, those in which the first-order realizations are *explicitly* restricted to first-order physical properties and relations.

reformulated as *nonreductive* functional definitions (in the sense of section 4). In this case, however, language-of-thought turns out to be an inessential third wheel.

It is in step two that the problem of self-conscious thought resurfaces. Assume that the content-of relation is somehow defined for Mentalese non-psychological expressions.[20] The question is whether it can be defined for Mentalese *psychological* predicates, specifically, Mentalese predicates ('T,' 'D,' etc.) for the standard mental relations (thinking, desiring, etc.). For, unless this can be done, one will not have defined any of these relations. But the familiar definitional strategies lead to vicious circularity (and other failings)—unless, of course, we return to Ramsified definitions and, with them, some version of our original problem.

The vicious circle is immediately evident in the following candidate definition: the content of 'T' $=_{def}$ the relation of thinking. For the contemplated definition of the relation of thinking (x thinks p iff$_{def}$ there is a Mentalese sentence s tokened in x's Thinking Box and s's content is p) requires that we have already specified the content of 'T'. The same problem besets the following definition: the content of 'T' $=_{def}$ the relation holding between x and q such that a Mentalese sentence s whose content is q is tokened in x's Thinking Box. But this too is circular, for the content-of relation for arbitrary Mentalese sentences s is invoked on the right-hand side: in order to define this relation, one must first define the content-of relation for the primitive predicates that can occur in those sentences s—including, in particular, the predicate 'T' for the relation of thinking.

Another strategy for avoiding the circularity problem would be to adopt a causal account of content. For example, let 'C' be a Mentalese predicate for one or another macroscopic physical property. Then a (highly oversimplified) causal account of its content might go as follows: the content of 'C' $=_{def}$ the property F such that in normal conditions there being an F in the presence of a subject causes '$(\exists x)Cx$' to be tokened in the subject's Thinking Box. (For example, on the assumption that in normal conditions there being a cow in the presence of the subject causes '$(\exists x)Cx$' to be tokened in the subject's Thinking Box—and being a cow is in normal conditions the only macroscopic physical property playing this causal role—the property of being a cow would be the content of 'C'.) The corresponding causal account of the contents of Mentalese psychological predicates (e.g., 'T') would then be something like this: the content of 'T' $=_{def}$ the relation R such that, for any q, if the subject is R-ing q in normal conditions, the subject's R-ing q causes '$i\,T\,s$' to be tokened in the subject's Thinking Box, where s is some Mentalese sentence whose content was previously defined to be q. There are many problems with this approach. I will mention two—each

---

[20] Whether this is feasible is open to serious doubts. One threat comes from the possibility of deviant Quinean interpretations of Mentalese. See Bealer (1984).

of which shows that this approach is incompatible with language-of-thought functionalism and, hence, may not be used to solve its circularity problem.

First, the indicated style of causal account would be correct only if the relation R (i.e., the content of 'T') were the thinking relation itself. But the account must be incorporated into the language-of-thought definition of the thinking relation itself (stated two paragraphs above). So this definition of the thinking relation quantifies over the very relation being defined and, hence, accords to the thinking relation an ontological primacy inconsistent with the primary tenet of functionalism (that mental relations can be defined wholly in terms of the PATTERN of their *ontologically prior* first-order realizations). Indeed, on this account, the causal status of certain events involving the thinking relation is like that of certain events involving physical properties and relations–e.g., the property of being a cow, the relation of being tokened-in–inasmuch as all these events have the power to cause tokenings of relevant Mentalese sentences. The proposed language-of-thought definition would thus qualify as a thoroughgoing non-reductive functional definition, in the sense of section 4 (except that it gratuitously builds in the paraphernalia of language-of-thought).

The second problem with this style of causal account of the content of 'T' is that it explicitly requires *mental-to-physical* causation—specifically, the mental event of the subject's thinking q must cause a certain physical event, namely, the tokening of '$i\ T\ s$' in the subject's Thinking Box. But such mental-to-physical causation violates the causal picture on which language-of-thought functionalism is founded. On that picture, what causes '$i\ T\ s$' to be tokened in a subject's Thinking Box is a physical language-of-thought event, such as the event of s's being tokened in the subject's Thinking Box (where s is a language-of-thought sentence whose content is q).[21] In other words, the property that would be causally relevant to the tokening of '$i\ T\ s$' is not the intentional property of thinking q but rather a physical realizer property.

Let me spell this out. Consider the array of law-governed transitions from mental event to mental event (or mental state to mental states), and consider the corresponding transitions from language-of-thought event to language-of-thought event. The basic language-of-thought causal picture has it that the latter array is not just law-governed but is founded upon genuine physical causal relations holding among these language-of-thought events; in the idiom of causal relevance, it is the associated physical language-of-thought realizer properties (not the intentional properties corresponding to them) that figure in the causal

---

[21] I just spoke as though there is a difference between the tokening of s and the subject's thinking q; this is so on a fine-grained view of events. On certain coarse-grained views of events, there is no such difference; but then the question just shifts to which property is causally relevant, the property of thinking q or a correlated but distinct language-of-thought realizer property. In the text, I employ both idioms to help make clear that no question is being begged.

explanation of these physical-to-physical transitions. For example, suppose the following reports a lawful transition: if a subject is thinking q and is engaging in introspection, he will think that he is thinking q; and suppose that in a given subject's language-of-thought s is a sentence whose content is q. Then, on the language-of-thought causal picture, not only would it be nomologically necessary that a tokening of s in the subject's Thinking Box is followed by a tokening of '$i\,T\,s$', but in the envisaged situation a situation the tokening of s would be the cause of the tokening. The language-of-thought realizer property (having s so-tokened) is the property that is causally relevant to the tokening of '$i\,T\,s$'; the intentional property (thinking q) is causally irrelevant (contrary to the proposed account of the content of 'T').[22]

(Here is Fodor commenting on this basic language-of-thought causal picture (1987, 140): "[E]ven though it's true that psychological laws generally pick out the mental states that they apply to by specifying the intentional contents of the states, it *doesn't* follow that intentional properties figure in the psychological mechanisms. And while I'm prepared to sign on for counterfactual-supporting intentional generalizations, I balk at intentional causation." So, for example, Fodor would hold that the intentional property of thinking q does not figure in any psychological mechanism and thus does not figure causally in producing tokenings of '$i\,T\,s$'; instead, the language-of-thought realizer property is what is causally relevant. He would hold, moreover, that this physical realizer property is causally relevant to subject's thinking that he is thinking q whereas the mental property of thinking q is not. And this generalizes: for Fodor, the causally relevant properties are always physical realizer properties, never intentional properties. Fodor's view is thus a form of epiphenomenalism. By contrast, the sort of nonreductive functional definitions suggested in §4 open up the possibility of an account of mental causation (see Bealer, 2007) that avoids epiphenomenalism and preserves most of our commonsense beliefs about mental causation; this is a further count in favor of this nonreductive functionalism and against Fodorian and other epiphenomenalist functionalisms.)

If these and similar problems block a causal account of the content of the Mentalese psychological predicates ('T,' 'D,' etc.), we are still left with the circularity problem. What alternatives are there? A common technical proposal is to resort to a Tarski-like hierarchy of thinking relations—thinking$_0$,

---

[22] The reason, as I understand it, that language-of-thought functionalists are committed to this causal picture is that it is needed—or at least they believe it is needed—to explain what it is for a system to be a physical realization (or physical implementation) of a psychological system: if causation were not invoked in the indicated way, all manner of physical systems would wrongly qualify as physical realizations (thus undermining the language-of-thought definitions of mental properties). See, e.g., the Appendix in Fodor (1987). David Chalmers (1996b) also provides a nice explanation of the role causation plays for functionalism (and, presumably, he would enlist causation to play the same role in his own functionalist account of intentional properties).

thinking$_1$, . . .—defined as follows: x thinks$_0$ q iff$_{def}$ some nonpsychological Mentalese sentence whose content is q is tokened in x's Thinking Box. The content of 'T_0' $=_{def}$ thinking$_0$. Next x thinks$_1$ q iff$_{def}$ some level 1 Mentalese sentence whose content is q is tokened in x's Thinking Box. The content of 'T_1' $=_{def}$ thinking$_1$. And so on.

But it is now widely recognized that such hierarchy approaches lead to a distorted treatment of our actual psychological attitudes (just as Tarski's hierarchy approach leads to a distorted theory of truth; see Kripke 1975). For example, you might say, "Most people think many things." And I might reply, "I certainly do; in fact, you have just asserted one of them." In this little dialogue, you assert a proposition involving the relation of thinking, namely, the proposition that most people think many things. I reply by affirming a certain *instance* of the proposition you asserted, namely, that I think many things. Then I go on to provide an example of one of the things to which I stand in the thinking relation, namely, the original proposition you asserted (that most people think many things). This, however, is a proposition involving the very relation of thinking just invoked. If this were not so, my *anaphoric* use of 'one of them' would make no sense. Examples like this one are not at all exceptional; they typify our everyday thought and discourse about cognition. Much the same point is tellingly illustrated by Descartes' *Cogito*. Suppose I think that I am thinking something. (In symbols, i Think [($\exists q$) i Think q].) The proposition to which I stand in the thinking relation involves that very relation of thinking. And this proposition is made true just by the fact that I am standing in that very relation to it. This is the point of the *Cogito*—and what is compelling about it. The moral is that, like truth, thinking and other mental relations are *type-free*. The proposed hierarchy picture belies this fundamental fact.

Perhaps, however, the hierarchy picture is still useful theoretically, allowing one to *construct* the thinking relation from the hypothesized relations thinking$_0$, thinking$_1$, etc. The most common proposal is to identify the thinking relation with the *union* of these hypothesized relations. To see why this fails, notice that the thinking relation is distinct from each of the hypothesized relations. For the range of the thinking relation includes such psychological propositions as the proposition that someone thinks something, whereas the range of thinking$_0$ includes, by definition, only nonpsychological propositions. Similarly, the range of thinking$_1$ does not include the proposition that someone thinks something; rather it includes such propositions as the proposition that someone thinks$_0$ something. But these two propositions are distinct, for thinking $\neq$ thinking$_0$, as we have just seen. The argument generalizes in the obvious way. It follows that the proposition that someone thinks something does not belong to the range of any thinking$_n$ relation and so does not belong to the range of the union of the thinking$_n$ relations. Indeed, *not one* proposition involving the thinking relation belongs to the range of the union of the thinking$_n$ relations. But countless such propositions belong to the range of the thinking relation itself. Hence, the thinking relation and the union are *very* different indeed.[23]

The problem with the hierarchy approach is that we can have attitudes toward type-free general propositions that are about nothing other than those very attitudes. This problem also spells defeat for the other standard way of trying to approach mental relations in stages—namely, the standard *recursive* approach. Unlike the hierarchy approach, this approach supposes that there is a single relation of thinking, desiring, etc. It aims to define the content-of relation for Mentalese in inductive stages. At the initial stage, we define the content-of relation for all Mentalese nonpsychological primitives. Then there are two sorts of inductive clauses. One defines the content-of relation for the various categories of complex expressions (existential generalizations, negations, etc.). The other defines the content-of relation for Mentalese psychological primitives ('T,' 'D,' etc.): the content of 'T' $=_{\text{def}}$ the relation holding between x and q such that a Mentalese sentence whose content is q is tokened in x's Thinking Box. And so forth. Superficially, this has the form of an acceptable inductive definition. Our previous discussion, however, reveals what is wrong with it. Type-free Mentalese sentences such as '$(\exists q)\, i\, T\, q$' can be tokened in one's Thinking Box. Accordingly, the above inductive clause fixes the content of 'T' only if the content of '$(\exists q)\, i\, T\, q$' is fixed earlier in the induction. But the content of '$(\exists q)\, i\, T\, q$' is fixed only if the content of 'T' is fixed still earlier in the induction. The inductive clauses thus fail to fix any of these contents.[24]

Once again, the problem is that we can have attitudes toward type-free general propositions that are about nothing other than those very attitudes. They cannot be built up in stages: whether you are thinking that you are thinking something is in principle independent of the other things, if any, you might be thinking; relative to them, it is a primitive fact. This leaves us where we were before the detour into stage-wise approaches, either with a viciously circular definition of the content-of relation or with no definition at all.[25]

---

[23] Thus, the following proposal also fails: x thinks q iff for some n, x thinks$_n$ q. Of course, *within* standard type theories one cannot even quantify over levels n.

Note also that it is possible for me to be thinking that I am thinking something and to be thinking no proposition involving any thinking$_n$ relation. Conversely, for any n, it is possible for me to be thinking that I am thinking$_n$ something and not be thinking that I am thinking something. These things are possible because, as noted earlier, thinking can be highly *focused* in its propositional objects: at a given moment a person can be thinking a specific proposition q and not be thinking any other nearby q. Indeed, someone skilled in meditation arguably can be consciously and explicitly thinking that he or she is thinking something whether or not he or she is at the moment consciously and explicitly thinking anything else.

[24] This difficulty can be overcome by means of a diagonal construction, but the result is just a complicated variant of the sort of nonreductive functional definition considered in the next section and so is subject to the same conclusions.

[25] This discussion also shows that infinitary disjunctive definitions of the standard mental relations fail because they are circular: for example, x thinks q iff$_{\text{def}}$ (x is in physical state S and $q =$ the proposition that something is a horse) . . . or (x is in physical state S' and $q =$ the

There are, of course, alternative language-of-thought proposals. But I know of none that helps to solve the underlying problem of self-conscious thought.[26]

4. NON-REDUCTIVE FUNCTIONAL DEFINITIONS

At this point, there is a very natural response to the problem of self-conscious thought, namely, returning to the original functional definitions but this time suppressing the problematic invocation of realizations and focusing instead on the mental properties themselves. According to the original functional definitions, to be in pain is to have some *first-order realization* of the property of being in pain; to think q is to be related to q by some *first-order realization* of the thinking relation; and so on. The idea is to expunge these restricted quantifications over first-order realizations and to replace them with quantifications that admit as values mental properties themselves. The result would be definitions like the following: to be in pain is to have some property that plays the pain-role in A; to think q is to be related to q by some relation that plays the thinking-role in A. More formally,

x is in pain iff$_{def}$ there exist properties R satisfying A and x has R_1.

x thinks q iff$_{def}$ there exist properties R satisfying A and x is related by R_2 to q.

The crucial difference is that the property expressed by the entire right-hand side is among the values of the variables ('R_1,' 'R_2,' etc.) occurring within the right-hand side. Thus, unlike the original functional definitions, which were formulated in the logical setting of a *predicative type theory* (Putnam, 1970, is very clear on this point), these definitions are formulated in an *impredicative type-free* logical setting. So, if these definitions are correct, the property of being in pain is itself among the properties over which the first definition quantifies; likewise, the thinking relation is itself among the relations over which the second definition quantifies.[27]

Functional definitions of this sort have a significant feature. Since the standard mental properties and relations are themselves satisfiers of A, they are being defined in terms of their interaction with *themselves and one another*. In view

proposition that someone thinks something) or . . . or (x is in physical state S'' and $q =$ the proposition that thinking is a mental relation . . .).

[26] For example, one might attempt a language-of-thought variant on the kind of Ramsified functional definitions discussed in section 2, but then the argument given there can be repeated to show that the content of 'T' would be a first-order realization rather than the thinking relation itself. Alternatively, one might attempt a language-of-thought variant on the kind of nonreductive functional definitions discussed in the next section, but the resulting definitions would be inconsistent with the ontological picture upon which functionalism is based.

[27] Sydney Shoemaker's (2001) response to the Self-consciousness Argument is to reject standard Ramsified functional definitions, which he previously (1981) espoused, and to adopt instead the style of nonreductive functional definitions proposed here and in Bealer (1997).

of the problem of self-conscious thought, this feature is unavoidable in any successful functional definition, for it is this feature that opens up the possibility of getting right the contents of our everyday self-conscious thoughts. The price of this benefit, however, is that these definitions abandon the primary tenet of functionalism, namely, that the standard mental properties be definable wholly in terms of the PATTERN of *ontologically prior realizations*. These definitions are therefore *nonreductive* in the sense that, unlike the original functional definitions, they do not equate mental properties with (second-order) constructions from ontologically prior realizations.[28] On the contrary, these definitions endow mental properties with an ontological primacy inconsistent with the standard functionalist picture: mental properties are now taken to be antecedently given ontological primitives (specifically, first-order irreducibly mental properties) already there waiting to constitute the content of our thought. These definitions merely locate mental properties within the space of ontologically primitive properties.

As indicated, the reason these nonreductive definitions are more promising is that the standard mental properties are admitted as satisfiers of A and (unlike the original functional definitions) they do not *require* that properties besides the standard mental properties (e.g., associated physical realizations) satisfy A. But this does not by itself guarantee that these definitions are successful. For it does not rule out the existence of unwanted satisfiers of A (e.g., physical realizations). To guard against this possibility, our nonreductive definitions might be strengthened in various ways. For example, the initial string of predicate quantifiers in the definitions might be explicitly restricted to properties that are not physical realizations and that are "natural" (i.e., not ad hoc Cambridge properties). In addition, A itself might be strengthened in various ways. For example, A might be strengthened *modally*—for instance, by requiring that its satisfiers satisfy it *necessarily* and by requiring that it be *possible* for its individual clauses to be satisfied nonvacuously. When A is strengthened in this and perhaps other ways, it is plausible that A would *implicitly define* the standard mental properties—that is, A would be *uniquely* satisfied by the standard mental properties. For many people, the resulting definitions are the ideal—what one should strive for in a good functional definition.

Now since successful functional definitions of some sort are a precondition of functionalism's solution to the Mind–Body Problem and since the problem of self-conscious thought evidently forces functionalists to accept some sort of nonreductive definitions, we may assume for the purpose of the remaining discussion that nonreductive functional definitions of some sort are successful. To simplify this discussion, it will be convenient to assume that the simple style of nonreductive definitions given at the outset of the section are correct.

---

[28] The same thing holds true of more complex nonreductive definitions—for example, definitions like those considered in sections 2–3 and accompanying footnotes.

This simplifying assumption is harmless, for it will be evident that each of our remaining points would hold even if some more complicated nonreductive definition were needed (cf., notes 17 and 19).

5. CONSEQUENCES

The adoption of nonreductive functional definitions, however, has a major consequence. Before coming to it, let us take stock.

Mental relations have dual roles. They relate subjects to propositions, and they are commonly contents of those propositions. One and the same relation is involved twice over when a person thinks that he or she is thinking something. Our original argument against functionalism turned on such phenomena: in the original functional definitions, both the embedded and unembedded occurrences of a psychological predicate were quantified with one and the same quantified predicate variable; accordingly, those definitions wrongly implied that propositions involving first-order realizations would be typical objects of thought. Language-of-thought functionalism seemed to avoid these dual quantifications by treating embedded psychological predicates as standing only for representations rather than for mental properties and relations themselves. But this only hid the problem, for then the contents of Mentalese psychological predicates needed to be identified. It turned out that this could not be done without circularity (and other problems). The error of functionalism as traditionally formulated was to think that mental properties and relations are in one way or another *constructible* from ontologically prior realizations. They are not. Functionalists evidently have no alternative but to adopt nonreductive functional definitions, thereby abandoning their primary tenet (that mental properties are definable wholly in terms of ontologically prior realizations). The phenomenon of self-conscious thought teaches us that mental properties must be antecedently given ontological primitives already there waiting to constitute the content of our thought; they must be part of the primitive make-up of the world. Indeed, by virtue of their primitive self-reflexive loops, mental relations might well stand as our very paradigm of irreducibility.

As I noted at the outset, perhaps functionalism's major conceptual attraction for cognitive science was that it promised a materialistically acceptable solution to the Mind–Body Problem. The idea was to employ reductive functional definitions to explain the relationship between physical and mental properties. Specifically, when such definitions are substituted into the following, the result was supposed to be a tautology: if a thing has some system or other of first-order physical properties that fit the PATTERN, then it has the associated mental properties. In this sense, the body–mind relationship would be completely transparent and unmysterious—just a matter of logic and definitions. We have seen, however, that the envisaged functional definitions fail and that functionalists evidently have no choice but to adopt some form of nonreductive functional definition. When this is done, however, the envisaged definitional tie between physical and mental properties is broken. No matter what constellation of first-order physical properties *F* you might have (where *F* may somehow encode physical laws if you wish), it is not a matter of logic and definition that, if you have *F*, you also have the mental properties that you in fact have.[29] From the point of view of pure logic, your first-order physical properties tell us absolutely nothing whatsoever about whether, in addition, you have those distinct, ontologically primitive properties that are defined by the nonreductive functional definitions. On the contrary, the body–mind relationship is a primitive nonlogical relationship. Thus, functionalism's solution to the Mind–Body Problem fails.

To be sure, the highly substantive scientific thesis that (in the actual world) mental properties have only physical realizers is compatible with the foregoing critique. But this (contingent) scientific thesis does not, on its own, illuminate the nature of the body–mind relationship. What accounts of this relationship are there? One view is that it is a nomological relationship: the discovered correlation between physical and mental properties holds as a (contingent) law of nature. Evidently, the only alternative to the nomological view is that the body–mind relationship is a mysterious kind of brute metaphysical necessity, defying any further explanation. But this alternative is unacceptable, given that the nomological account is available. To begin with, the hypothesis of brute metaphysical necessities has no more intuitive support than the nomological hypothesis (on the contrary, it is the other way around, as the much-discussed body of anti-materialist intuitions attests). Nor does the metaphysical hypothesis have any explanatory advantages over the nomological hypothesis; both hypotheses have exactly the same empirical consequences. In addition, the nomological hypothesis is distinctly more economical: nomological necessities need to hold only in a local sphere of worlds whereas metaphysical necessities have to hold in all possible worlds. Viewed another way, the hypothesis of brute metaphysical necessities takes a strong stand in modal metaphysics when none is required. And, what is more, accepting such hypotheses in situations like this is clearly incompatible with standard practice in modal metaphysics.

If this is correct, scientifically minded philosophers and cognitive scientists have no rational alternative but to accept the nomomogical account of the body–mind relationship. Of course, this choice in no way impedes the pursuit of a scientific understanding of the mind. Discovering a law of nature is no less scientific than discovering a property identity (as identity theorists hoped to do)

---

[29] Specifically, it can be shown that, given the nonreductive definitions, the standard sort of logical inference route from *F* to your mental properties is unavailable. Moreover, models can be constructed to show that this relationship cannot be a less direct sort of logical relationship. Such models also show that the body–mind relationship fails to hold as a matter of logic and definition even if one accepts some more complicated style of nonreductive functional definition (such as those considered at various points earlier in the paper). Bealer (1999) develops these points in detail.

or discovering that a certain relationship holds as a matter of logic and definition (as functionalists hoped to do). So on this path nothing scientific is lost; indeed, the project of cognitive science is entirely clear: find the laws. The only casualty is materialism, a metaphysical doctrine to which science was never committed in the first place.

II

ARGUMENTS FROM UNITY
AND IDENTITY

7

You are Simple

David Barnett

I argue that, unlike your brain, you are not composed of other things: you are *simple*. My argument centers on what I take to be an uncontroversial datum: for any pair of conscious beings, it is impossible for the pair *itself* to be conscious. Consider, for instance, the pair comprising you and me. You might pinch your arm and feel a pain. I might simultaneously pinch my arm and feel a qualitatively identical pain. But the pair we form would not feel a thing.[1] Pairs of people *themselves* are incapable of experience. Call this *The Datum*. What explains The Datum? I think the following exhaust the reasonable options. (1) Pairs of people lack a sufficient *number* of immediate parts. (2) Pairs of people lack immediate parts capable of standing in the right sorts of *relations* to each other and their environment. (3) Pairs of people lack immediate parts of the right *nature*. (4) Pairs of people are not *structures* (they are unstructured *collections* of their two immediate parts). (5) Some combination of (1)–(4). Finally, (6) pairs of people are not *simple*.

I defend (6). I argue that none of (1)–(4) is individually sufficient to explain The Datum. Then I argue that no combination is sufficient. I conclude that (6) best explains The Datum.

Although my chapter has the structure of an argument, its real aim is merely to make credible a position that is rarely taken seriously by contemporary philosophers, namely, that conscious beings must be simple.[2] The argument itself has escape routes. Indeed, I do not expect the confident materialist to find it persuasive. Still, it has value. At the very least, it serves as a stalking horse for the materialist. The argument involves a long, slow, development of an intuition pump that is designed to give the reader a certain perspective on key examples. By the end of the argument, the materialists just might find themselves having the intuition that they are wrong.

---

[1] As Chisholm says, 'You could want the weather to be colder and I could want it to be warmer; but that heap or aggregate which is the pair of us (that thing that weighs 300 pounds if you and I each weigh 150 pounds) does not want anything at all' (1991: 172).

[2] Some recent discussions of the position include Bennett (1967), Hart (1988), Chisholm (1991), Foster (1991), Zimmerman (1991, 2005), Taliaferro (1994), Hasker (1999), Lowe (2001), and Barnett (forthcoming).

In the initial sections, as I argue against (1)–(4), I tease out some intuitions related to the intuition behind The Datum, and I introduce some techniques for teasing out further intuitions in more sophisticated settings. Because the main purpose of these early sections is to develop these techniques, the initial examples that I deal with are deliberately simplistic in nature. Only in later sections will I introduce examples that exhibit the requisite degree of complexity for defeating plausible combinations of (1)–(4). Thus, I ask that you withhold your judgment of my ultimate conclusion until you see the whole picture.

1. NUMBER

Do pairs of people lack a sufficient *number* of immediate parts to be conscious?

Perhaps. But this cannot be the full explanation of The Datum. For increasing the number of people in a collection does not have any significant effect on the absurdity of the idea that the collection *itself* might be conscious. For illustration, consider the triplet comprising you, Paul McCartney, and me. Whatever you, McCartney, and I might experience individually, we can be certain that there is no further experience enjoyed by our triplet. Or consider the entire world population. Might this huge collection of people itself be conscious? Might it currently be experiencing, say, the taste of McDonald's French fries? Of course not. For emphasis, try to imagine that each and every human is in excruciating pain, while our collection is itself experiencing pure bliss. This is absurd. No matter how large, a collection of people cannot itself be a subject of experience.

I am not denying that a collection of people might qualify as having an experience in a secondary sense, in virtue of one or more of its members having that experience. Often a whole is said to have a feature in virtue of one of its parts having the feature. For instance, a house is said to be on fire in virtue of its roof being on fire. And a shirt is said to be stained in virtue of its collar being stained. But in these cases it is the part that is the primary bearer of the feature. Perhaps humanity can itself be said to suffer in virtue of one or more of its members suffering. And perhaps a recently divorced couple can itself be said to experience separation anxiety by virtue of its members experiencing this anxiety. Personally, I doubt that there is any legitimate sense in which a whole can 'inherit' an experience in this way from its parts. But in any case this is not what I am denying. What I am denying is that a collection of people might itself be the *primary* bearer of an experience. Hereafter, when I ask whether something might be a bearer of experience, that is, a conscious being, I mean to ask whether it might be a primary bearer of experience.

I conclude that the idea that pairs of people lack a sufficient number of immediate parts to be conscious cannot by itself explain The Datum.

2. RELATION

Do pairs of people lack immediate parts capable of standing in the right sorts of *relations* to each other and their environment to be conscious?

Perhaps. But this cannot be the full explanation of The Datum either. For the only remotely plausible candidate relations are causal-dispositional relations of the general sort borne by the parts of an ordinary human brain (or some other animal brain, or some entire organism) to one another and their environment; these are the relations that things must stand in if they are to jointly function, on a relevant level, like an ordinary human brain. But there is no metaphysical obstacle to two people standing in any such relation.

For illustration, consider the following scenario. Allowing for some radical changes to the laws of nature, imagine that some clever scientists shrink you and me down to the size of McCartney's left and right brain hemispheres, respectively. The scientists then train us to function, at a relevant level, just as our respective hemispheres function: in terms of exchanging signals with the peripheral neurons and each other, we are trained to behave just as our respective hemispheres behave. McCartney's left and right hemispheres are then removed and replaced with you and me, respectively. Someone pinches McCartney's right arm (or his former right arm, should McCartney not survive the ordeal). When the signal arrives at the top of the spinal cord, I identify it; I notify you; we stimulate certain outbound neurons; and we move into a new functional state. As a result, McCartney's head turns and faces his right arm; an irritated look appears on his face; and out of his mouth comes the words, 'Stop that!' On a relevant functional level, you do just what McCartney's left hemisphere would have done. And I do just what McCartney's right hemisphere would have done. At a relevant level, the causal-dispositional relations borne by you and me are those that McCartney's two brain hemispheres would have borne. Together, you and I function like an ordinary human brain.[3]

Given our new relations to each other and our environment, is it any less absurd to think that the pair we form might *itself* be conscious? No. To be sure, there is nothing absurd in the idea that *McCartney* might somehow survive the procedure; though unlikely, perhaps he would remain conscious throughout the ordeal. What seems absurd, rather, is that *the pair comprising you and me* might be conscious. Variation in how two people are related to each other and their

---

[3] This is not quite right, for even if you and I function on a relevant level in the same way that McCartney's two brain hemispheres function, our disposition to function in this way is not law-like in the way that the disposition of McCartney's two brain hemispheres is. To correct for this difference, we can adjust our scenario as follows: it turns out to be a law of nature that when two humans go through the training and shrinking procedure described above, they become disposed—to the same law-like degree—to function, on a relevant level, in the same way that the corresponding brain hemispheres function.

environment has no significant effect on the absurdity of the idea that the pair itself might be conscious.

I conclude that the idea that pairs of people lack immediate parts capable of standing in the right sorts of relations to each other and their environment to be conscious cannot by itself explain The Datum.

3. NATURE

Do pairs of people lack immediate parts of the right *nature* to be conscious?

Perhaps. But this cannot be the full explanation of The Datum either. For varying the nature of the members of the pair does not have any significant effect on the absurdity of the idea that the pair itself might be conscious. It is absurd that a pair of people might itself be conscious. But it is equally absurd that a pair of carrots, rocks, dogs, electrons, or neurons might itself be conscious.

If I tell you only that I have two objects in mind, *a* and *b*, you need more information before you can determine whether *a* is conscious and whether *b* is conscious, but you do not need more information to determine whether the pair comprising *a* and *b* is *itself* conscious. You know by mere reflection that it is not. Pairs of things, we know by mere reflection, cannot themselves be conscious. So there is no need to empirically investigate the individual natures of carrots, rocks, electrons, or neurons to determine whether pairs of them might themselves be experiencing the taste of McDonald's French fries; we know by pure reflection that they are not. In general, the absurdity that any given pair of objects might itself be conscious has nothing to do with the natures of the members of the pair.

I conclude that the idea that pairs of people lack immediate parts of the requisite nature to be conscious cannot by itself explain The Datum.

4. STRUCTURE

How can we know just by reflection that the pair comprising *a* and *b* is not itself conscious? Here is one suggestion: we can know by reflection that *pairs* of things are mere *collections*, and we can know by reflection that *conscious beings* are *structures*. Whereas a collection of things exists whenever those things exist, a structure of things exists only if those things stand in a certain relation required to exhibit the structure. This is not to say that a structure of things is essentially a structure of the particular things that currently exhibit it; some structures can survive the destruction or replacement of some of the things that exhibit them. For an example of a collection, consider the atoms that constitute this clay bowl; for an example of a structure, consider the bowl itself. Intuitively, if we were to spread the atoms evenly throughout the universe, their collection would survive, but the bowl they now form would not. On this informal characterization of a structure, the following entities seem initially to qualify as structures, rather than mere collections: systems, such as a galaxy of stars; certain artifacts, such as a table or a clay bowl; certain non-living natural objects, such as a rock or a planet; and certain living objects, such as an organism, one of its organs, or one of its cells.

Might pairs of people be incapable of experience because they are not structures? Perhaps. But this cannot be the full explanation of The Datum either. To see that it cannot, simply shift your attention from the pair of people inside McCartney's skull to the brain-like system they compose. Unlike the pair, the system is a structure: it would cease to exist if you and I were removed from the skull and placed in isolation chambers (the pair we form would not). Yet this system of people is no better a candidate for being a subject of experience than the pair that constitutes it.

I conclude that the idea that pairs of people are incapable of experience because they are not structures cannot by itself explain The Datum.

5. COMBINATION OF NUMBER, RELATION, NATURE, AND STRUCTURE

Perhaps The Datum is explained, not by any one of *Number, Relation, Nature*, or *Structure* (the four hypotheses considered above) alone, but by some combination of the four. For instance, perhaps a pair of people cannot itself be conscious because it is a *collection* resulting from the *mere existence* of *two* particular *people*, whereas a conscious being is a *structure* resulting from *many organs*, or *billions* of *cells*, or *quadrillions* of *particles*, standing to one another and their environment in certain causal-dispositional *relations*.

Before I evaluate this proposal, I want to discuss an appealing line of reasoning behind it: (i) human bodies—physical structures comprising organs, tissues, cells, molecules, and atoms—are conscious; (ii) the salient differences between human bodies and pairs of people are captured by *Number, Relation, Nature*, and *Structure*; (iii) none of these four hypotheses alone explains The Datum; hence, (iv) some combination of the four must explain The Datum. In particular, I want to discuss the initial—that is, pre-theoretical—appeal of (i). If asked outside a philosophical context whether human bodies are conscious, most of us are inclined to give a positive answer without hesitation. And yet, if my argument is sound, then it is impossible for a human body to be conscious, for it is not simple. Why, then, are we initially willing to ascribe consciousness to human bodies but not to pairs of people? I have two hypotheses.

First, an ascription of consciousness can be interpreted in one of two ways. On the strong interpretation, an utterance of '*x* is conscious' means that *x* is *identical to* a conscious being; on the weak interpretation, it means that x is some conscious being's body—that is, that x *embodies* a conscious being. Pre-theoretically, we interpret ascriptions of consciousness to human bodies in the weak sense. Our initial willingness to accept that human bodies are conscious is simply a willingness to accept that human bodies embody conscious beings. Otherwise we would have difficulty entertaining scenarios involving disembodiment and reincarnation. But we have no such difficulty. For illustration, imagine waking up, looking into a mirror, and discovering that you have swapped bodies with McCartney. No problem. Now imagine waking up and discovering that your favorite chair has swapped bodies with McCartney's favorite chair. Big problem: the scenario does not make sense. We cannot make sense of chairs 'swapping bodies' because our initial conception of them demands that they be *identical* to such bodies. By contrast, we *can* make sense of people swapping bodies, for our initial conception of them does not demand that they be identical to their bodies.

For emphasis, suppose that chairs *are* conscious, as they are depicted in Disney movies. Then we have no trouble making sense of their swapping bodies. But if we have no trouble imagining their swapping bodies on this supposition, then we must be interpreting the supposition in the *weak* sense, as the supposition that chairs *embody* conscious beings (what we imagine, then, is that the embodied beings swap bodies). For, interpreted in the strong sense, the supposition is obviously incompatible with body swapping.

By contrast, we initially interpret the proposal that a pair of people might itself be conscious in the strong sense—as I intend it. For, because we do not consider a pair of people itself to be a body, we never even entertain the idea that it might embody a conscious being.

So one hypothesis as to why we are initially willing to accept that a human body is conscious, but not that a pair of people is conscious, is that we initially interpret the proposal that a human body is conscious in the weak sense, whereas we initially interpret the proposal that a pair of people is conscious in the strong sense. And it seems possible for a human body to embody a conscious being, yet impossible for a pair of people to be identical to a conscious being.

A second hypothesis centers on a difference between the way that a human body is typically presented to our minds and the way that a pair of people is typically presented to our minds. As the human body is typically presented, we are able to ignore its composite aspect. On a daily basis, we see human bodies as single, solid, human-shaped objects. The fact that these objects have left halves, right halves, fingers, hands, arms, and legs is obvious. However, because these parts appear to be spatially continuous with one another, we do not typically see human bodies for what they truly are: structures of organs, tissues, and cells—more fundamentally, structures of quadrillions of tiny particles separated by relatively vast amounts of space. As a result, in certain ways we are able to conceive of our bodies as simples.

Hume makes a related point:

An object, whose different co-existent parts are bound together by a close relation, operates upon the imagination after much the same manner as one perfectly simple and indivisible, and requires not a much greater stretch of thought in order to its conception. From this similarity of operation we attribute a simplicity to it, and feign a principle of union as the support of this simplicity, and the center of all the different parts and qualities of the object. (*Treatise* I.iv.6)

By treating our bodies in many respects as simples, we can take seriously the idea that our bodies are *identical* to subjects of experience.

However, when our bodies are presented to us in a way that makes it difficult to ignore their composite aspect, we resist ascribing consciousness to them. Leibniz makes the point as follows:

If we imagine that there is a machine whose structure makes it think, sense, and have perceptions, we could conceive it enlarged, keeping the same proportions, so that we could enter into it, as one enters into a mill. Assuming that, when inspecting its interior, we will only find parts that push one another, and we will never find anything to explain a perception. And so, we should seek perception in the simple substance and not in the composite or in the machine. (*Monadology*: paragraph 17)

Of course, it is nearly impossible to ignore the composite aspect of a pair of people. And so a second hypothesis as to why we are initially willing to accept that a human body is conscious, but not that a pair of people is conscious, is that human bodies are typically presented to our minds in a way that allows us to ignore their composite aspect, whereas pairs of people are not.

Given the initial plausibility of these two hypotheses, it is important, as we investigate the proposal that some combination of *Number, Relation, Nature*, and *Structure* explains The Datum, first that we focus only on the strict interpretation of the question of whether a given thing is conscious, and second that we not ignore the composite aspect of any composite object that is under consideration. Now, one way to show that no combination of *Number, Relation, Nature*, and *Structure* can explain The Datum is to consider the human body, not as we ordinarily do, as a solid, human-shaped, object, but rather as a structure of many organs, or of billions of cells, or of quadrillions of particles. We need to make salient the composite aspect of the body. The more salient we make this aspect, the less comfortable we will be ascribing consciousness to the body itself, until, at the limit, the whole idea will seem absurd. My strategy is to close the gap between a pair of people and a human body in stages. I will eliminate the difference first in the *number* of parts, then in the *relation* of parts, then in the sort of whole—*structure* versus collection—that comprises the parts, and finally in the *nature* of parts. My motivation for proceeding in stages is to help keep salient the composite aspect of the relevant candidates for consciousness. To ensure that the gap is completely closed, in the final stages we will consider the human body itself, not as we typically do, but rather in ways that make it impossible for us to ignore its composite aspect. By the end of the exercise, we will see that no combination of *Number, Relation, Nature*, and *Structure* can explain The Datum; and we will see that the human body is no better a candidate for being a subject of experience than a pair of people.

First, we eliminate the difference in the *number* of parts. Instead of considering a pair of people, we consider a collection of several billion people. We have already seen that a mere increase in the number of people has no effect on the absurdity of the idea that their collection might itself be conscious.

Second, we eliminate the difference in the *relation* of parts. Here we can borrow any of a trio of examples from Ned Block (1978).

In Block's 'Nation of China' example, we are to imagine that the head of an otherwise normal human contains only miniature two-way radios hooked up to inbound sensory neurons and outbound motor neurons. The radios send and receive signals to and from citizens of China, who are themselves equipped with two-way radios. Block chooses citizens of China because their number is on the order of the number of neurons in a typical human brain. A satellite system displays symbols that can be seen from anywhere in China. Each citizen is given a simple set of instructions: if a given symbol is displayed, then if certain radio signals are received from the sensory neurons, send a given signal to the motor neurons. Together, the billion or so citizens function, on a relevant level, just as a normal human brain functions.[4] Yet the idea that this collection of people might itself be conscious is absurd.

In Block's 'Miniature Men in the Head' example, we are to imagine that the head of an otherwise normal human is filled with a group of little men. Block never says how many men; let us assume that it is several billion. Also inside the head is a bank of lights connected to inbound sensory neurons, a bank of buttons connected to outbound motor neurons, and a bulletin board on which a symbol (designating the current state of the system) is posted. Each man is given a simple set of instructions: if a given symbol is posted, then if certain lights are illuminated, press a given button. Together, the billions of men function, on a relevant level, just as a normal human brain functions. Yet the idea that this collection of tiny men might itself be conscious is absurd.

In Block's 'Elementary-Particle People' example, we are to imagine that the sub-atomic particles in our bodies are gradually replaced with functionally

---

[4] As with our earlier scenario concerning a pair of people in McCartney's cranium, Block's scenario needs to be adjusted to address the fact that the disposition of the population of China to function like a human brain is not law-like to the same degree as the disposition of a typical brain. A further stipulation will suffice: it is a law of nature that, when a group of people aggregate in the way envisaged in Block's example, their collection becomes disposed—to the same law-like degree—to function, on a relevant level, in the same way that a typical brain is disposed to function. This sort of adjustment is required of all three of Block's examples.

equivalent spaceships piloted by tiny aliens. Our brains (or the objects that replace them, should they not survive the procedure) would continue to function, down to the sub-atomic level, just as they ordinarily would. It seems likely that we would continue to have experience just as we ordinarily would. The question arises: might we, or any other subject of experience, be *identical* to the envisaged collection of alien-piloted spaceships? Might this collection *itself* be conscious? If we could see this collection on a greatly magnified level, our visual experience would be much as it would be if we were to witness an invasion of earth by a giant armada of spaceships. The idea that, in addition to the experiences had by the pilots of the ships, there might be a further experience had by the collection comprising the pilots and ships is absurd.

(Block nevertheless concludes that the system constituted by this collection *would* be conscious. This is because Block assumes from the start that we are composite objects. He says, 'Since we know that *we are brain-headed systems*, and that *we* have qualia, we know that brain-headed systems can have qualia' (p. 281). Of course, *supposing* that we are *identical* to brain-headed systems, and supposing that these systems would survive the envisaged alien invasion, *then* the elementary-particle-people system would be conscious. But this begs the question of whether we are, or can be, identical to composite objects. The relevant question is not: supposing that we are identical to composite objects, might such-and-such composite object be conscious? But rather: suppositions and philosophical theories aside, might the collection of elementary-particle-people, or the system that comprises it, itself be a subject of experience? To which the intuitive answer is: *no*.)

Next we shift our attention from collections to the *structures* they sometimes exhibit. Consider again Block's example of the miniature men in the head. Imagine that the miniature men got inside the head as follows. Very gradually, every neuron of a healthy human brain was replaced with a miniature, functionally equivalent man. At the end of the process, billions of miniature men came to constitute a brain-like structure inside the head. Now, there is no problem imagining that the person whose brain undergoes this process survives; however unlikely, the person might remain conscious throughout the ordeal. What seems hard to imagine, rather, is that the structure constituted by the billions of little men might *itself* be conscious. To my mind, the idea that this structure of little men might itself experience, say, the taste of blueberries, seems no less absurd than the idea that the collection of little men which constitutes the structure might itself experience the taste of blueberries. Shifting our attention from the collection of little men to the structure they exhibit does not seem to make any difference. Combining *Number, Relation*, and *Structure* will not, then, suffice to explain The Datum.

Last we eliminate the difference in the *nature* of parts. Here I adapt an example from Peter Unger (1990), who adapts his example from Arnold Zuboff

(1981). Imagine that the neurons of your brain are gradually separated from one another without interrupting the flow of communication within your nervous system. The separation proceeds in stages. First, your brain is removed from your body and separated into halves: the hemispheres are placed in nutrient-rich vats miles apart from each other and the de-brained body; radio transceiver devices are implanted at the interfaces of both hemispheres and the peripheral nervous system. Because radio signals travel at the speed of light, and because ordinary cross-synaptic signals travel at far lower speeds, normal communication within your nervous system can be preserved. In the next stage, the halves are themselves halved: each brain quarter is fitted with transceivers and placed several miles from the others. The process is repeated until each of your neurons sits in its own container, miles from the others, hooked up to a complex radio transceiver. Throughout the procedure the system as a whole maintains its functional integrity. Now, to add a further twist to Unger's Zuboffian story, imagine that each neuron is paired up with an understudy—a person who learns to function, at the level of radio inputs and outputs, just as the neuron does. Mondays are then declared 'Give a Neuron a Break Day'; on this day the neurons are allowed to rest, while their respective understudies operate their radio transceivers for them.

One question is whether you would survive such a procedure. Perhaps you would. Perhaps you would not. We need not take a stance on this question. For the question that concerns us is whether you (or any other conscious being) might be *identical* to the scattered system that controls your body. On Mondays, this system comprises billions of people operating billions of radio transceivers. On other days, it comprises billions of neurons operating billions of radio transceivers. In any case, it comprises billions of objects scattered about the surface of the earth, and it interacts with your body just as your brain would have, had it remained confined to your cranium. Now, the idea that you might be identical to this system on Mondays is absurd. But so is the idea that you might be identical to this system on any other day. Whether the system controlling your body comprises billions of people or billions of neurons seems irrelevant to whether the system might itself be a subject of experience.

One might worry that the scattered state of the system disqualifies it from being a genuine *structure*. To address this worry, and to ensure that we have completely closed the gap between a pair of people and the human body, we now consider the human body itself, with all its parts intact.

We can make salient the composite aspect of the body without envisaging any changes to the body itself. Instead of manipulating the body, we can manipulate our images of it. Imagine for instance that we are fitted with a series of magical goggles. Each pair provides a higher resolution image of McCartney's body than the preceding pair. Without any goggles, McCartney's body looks like a solid, human-shaped, blob. The first pair enables us to see the billions of individual cells that make up McCartney's outer layer of skin. The cells are packed so tightly together that body still looks like a solid blob, though one with an intricate pattern on its surface. The second pair is truly magical: it enables us to see the atoms that make up McCartney's body. Because the atoms are separated by relatively large regions of space, McCartney's body now looks like a scaled-down galaxy of stars. This effect is exaggerated when we don the final pair: it provides us with ultra-fine-grained vision that allows us to see the sub-atomic particles that make up McCartney's body. Our visual experience is now very much like it would be if were to gaze into outer space on a clear night.

With our most powerful goggles on, we ask: might the system of widely scattered particles before us itself be a subject of experience? Here it is easy to heed Hume's warning not to 'attribute a simplicity' to this system, and not to 'feign a principle of union as the support of this simplicity.' It is easy to take the system for what it is: a *structure* of quadrillions of particles. The structure is not some simple object that pops into existence once the particles are so related; at any moment, it *consists* in the particles' being so related. To be sure, a simple object may pop into existence whenever particles are so related, and such an object may itself be a subject of experience. But the idea that this system of particles—considered *as* a system of widely separated objects—might *itself* experience something, say, the taste of McDonald's French fries, seems no less absurd than the idea that a galaxy of stars might itself experience something.

I conclude that no combination of *Number, Relation, Nature*, and *Structure* can explain The Datum.

6. SIMPLICITY

Is a pair of people itself disqualified from being conscious because it is not *simple*?

I think this is the best explanation of The Datum. In all of the hypothetical scenarios we have considered, a composite entity is presented to our minds *as a composite*, and we are asked whether the entity might itself be a subject of consciousness. It does not matter whether the entity has two, two hundred, or two trillion parts; it does not matter whether its parts are people, dogs, neurons, stars, or sub-atomic particles; it does not matter whether its parts bear the relations typically borne by stars of a galaxy, neurons of a brain, or sub-atomic particles of an entire human body; and it does not matter whether it is a mere collection or a structure. What matters is whether the entity is presented to our minds *as a composite*. If so, we find absurdity in the idea that it might be *identical* to a subject of experience. This suggests that what explains The Datum is *Simplicity*: pairs of people are disqualified from being conscious because they are not simple. The only reasonable rival explanations are the various combinations of *Number, Relation, Nature,* and *Structure,* but we have seen that no such combination can explain The Datum. I conclude that *Simplicity* best explains The Datum.

7. CONCLUSION

I have provided an argument that conscious beings must be simple. Granted that we are not simple physical particles, this argument goes against materialism. In addition to my argument, there are a variety of other anti-materialist arguments. Then there are arguments on the other side. While it is admittedly difficult to see which of the arguments is stronger, I want to conclude by giving an initial consideration for thinking that my argument is stronger than what is perhaps the most salient argument in favor of materialism, namely, that the best explanation of the systematic correlations between our mental states and our brain states is that we are identical to our brains.

My argument rests on the following premises:

P1 The Datum (for any pair of people, it is impossible for the pair itself to be conscious).

P2 Something must explain The Datum (there is at least one non-trivial feature that no pair of people could itself have, but which every conscious being must have).

P3 If no combination of *Number, Relation, Nature,* **and** *Structure* **explains The Datum, then** *Simplicity* **explains The Datum.**

P4 No combination of *Number, Nature, Relation,* **and** *Structure* **explains The Datum.**

P1 and **P2** seem obviously true. A reason to accept **P3** is that the various combinations of *Number, Nature, Relation,* and *Structure,* on the one hand, together with their rival, *Simplicity,* on the other, appear to exhaust the reasonable options for explaining The Datum. Reasons to accept **P4** were given in my discussion above.

On the other hand, the correlations between our mental states and the states of our brains give us some reason to identify ourselves with our brains, for this identification would begin to explain the correlations. Of course, if we are identical to our brains, we are not simple. So these correlations give us some reason to think that conscious beings are not simple and thus need not be simple.

I doubt that this reason is strong enough to countervail our reasons to accept **P1–P4**. For imagine a scenario in which it is common knowledge that our heads are filled with little men who, in concert, control our bodies, and that our mental states are correlated with the states of the little men in a way that mirrors the actual correlation between our mental states and the neural states of our brains. Certainly this hypothetical correlation would give us *some* reason to identify ourselves with the systems of little men in our heads. But would it be strong enough to countervail our reasons for accepting **P1–P4**? Could we really take seriously the idea that we were *identical* to collections, or systems, of people? I doubt that we could. For I doubt that we could take seriously the idea that a collection, or a system, of people might itself be a subject of experience. But if this hypothetical correlation would not give us strong enough reason to abandon my argument, then it is doubtful that the actual correlation between our states of mind and the states of our brains gives us such reason. For the only difference between the two cases is a difference in the *nature* of the parts of the candidate systems. And above I gave some considerations for doubting that a difference in the nature of the parts could be relevant.

Evidently, materialists are by and large receptive to these sorts of considerations; for similar considerations are behind the materialist trend to abandon identity-theory in favor of functionalism—a theory on which the nature of the parts of a system is irrelevant to whether the system is itself conscious. One of the main appeals of functionalism is that it respects the idea that a mere difference in the nature of the parts of a system cannot matter to whether the system is conscious. Hilary Putnam defended this idea on empirical grounds, when he first proposed functionalism in 1967. Ironically, Putnam was simultaneously unwilling to swallow the idea that a system of conscious beings might itself be conscious. In the midst of arguing that the nature of the parts of a system is *not* relevant to whether something is in a given mental state, Putnam added to his functionalist analysis a condition that forbids a system of conscious beings from itself being conscious: 'No organism capable of feeling pain possesses a decomposition into parts which separately [are capable of feeling pain]' (Putnam 1967: 227). Why did Putnam do this? The purpose of the condition, according to Putnam, was 'to rule out such 'organisms' (if they can count as such) as swarms of bees as single pain-feelers' (op. cit.). Apparently, Putnam did not see the tension in his own views. He held (a) that the nature of the parts of a system is irrelevant to whether the system is conscious (because it is irrelevant to whether the system has a given functional organization) and (b) that it is impossible for a system of conscious beings to be conscious. But he did not hold what follows: that it is impossible for *any system* of things to be conscious. (To see how this follows, consider a system of people with an arbitrary functional organization. By (b), the system is not conscious. Now replace the people with anything you like, say, neurons. By (a), this change should not matter to whether the system is conscious. So the new system is not conscious. Thus, it is impossible for any system of things to be conscious.) Instead, Putnam added a condition to his functionalist analysis that goes against the very spirit of functionalism. Better, I think, for Putnam to have endorsed what follows from his own convictions—(a) and (b)—namely, that conscious beings must be simple.

I doubt, then, that the systematic correlations between our mental states and our brain states gives us a reason to identify ourselves with our brains that is strong enough to countervail the reasons that I have given to accept that conscious beings must be simple. I leave it as a challenge for the materialist to provide some other countervailing reason.[5]

[5] For helpful comments and discussion, I am grateful to George Bealer and Adam Pautz.

8

Persons and the Unity of Consciousness

William Hasker

We have a conception of human beings as persons. I shall not consider whether it is inevitable that we should have this conception, or whether the conception is present in all human cultures, or whether we ought to conceive of ourselves in this way. It suffices for my purposes that we do have such a conception and that it is deeply embedded in the practices of our daily lives. In reflecting on this conception it is apparent that a person is understood as constituted in part by a self, a unified, coherent center of consciousness that is a rational agent, capable of being responsive, and responsible, to other agents. There are, however, phenomena of empirical disunity that may seem to threaten, both theoretically and practically, the demand for a unified self. The phenomena I will be focusing on are commissurotomy and, even more striking, multiple personality. As a counterpoise to these phenomena, I put forward the unity-of-consciousness argument, deriving from Leibniz and Kant. While this argument might seem to conflict with the empirical evidence of disunity, I maintain that there is no inconsistency between the evidence and the argument. The combination of the two, in fact, both places a barrier in the way of a materialist account of mind and consciousness, and at the same time points out a severe difficulty for standard (especially Cartesian) varieties of dualism. I close by sketching out my own preferred view of the metaphysics of persons, emergent dualism. I shall argue that this view offers the best prospects for taking full account both of the unity of consciousness and of empirical disunity such as is seen, most spectacularly, in cases of commissurotomy and multiple personality.

It is clear that our concept of a person entails the existence of a self, in the sense of a central, relatively coherent and unified focus of the personality. The self must be *rational*, able to comprehend truths of various sorts that are important for the conduct of one's life. A self must also be an *agent*, capable of acting responsibly in relation to other persons. Feeling and emotion play an essential role in life, and the self must be able to *integrate* its emotional responses with its cognitive apprehensions as well as its actions. An important theme in all this is the *centeredness* of the self; the self must somehow be the central unifying focus of the individual as a whole.

1. EMPIRICAL DISUNITY: COMMISSUROTOMY AND MULTIPLE PERSONALITY

Our ordinary notion of a unified, central self is challenged, however, by various phenomena which suggest that we are less unified than we take ourselves to be. Two especially dramatic (though fortunately rare) types of cases will be considered here: commissurotomy and multiple personality. Probably all of us are familiar with the basic facts concerning commissurotomy. In certain hard-to-control cases of epilepsy it has proved beneficial to sever the corpus callosum, the thick sheaf of nerve tissue that forms the main connecting link between the right and left cerebral hemispheres. In many instances this has lessened the severity of epileptic seizures. More surprisingly, this major surgical alteration of the brain has turned out to have relatively slight effects on the patient's normal, day-to-day functioning. However, under controlled experimental conditions some striking results have been obtained. In the interest of brevity I will describe here only two cases, both featuring manipulative skills. One of Roger Sperry's commissurotomy subjects, W. J., was asked to perform a task with his right hand that involved arranging blocks in a predetermined pattern. The right hand, of course, is primarily controlled by the left cerebral hemisphere, which is greatly inferior to the right hemisphere in its ability to perform tasks involving spatial orientation. As a result, the right hand was having difficulty with the assignment. And then,

Slowly and steadily . . . the left hand creeps in, brushes aside the right hand, and starts building rather more efficiently. The experimenter is seen [on Sperry's film] pushing away the intrusive left hand. After a little while, along comes the left hand again. This time we see W. J. grasping the wrist of the left hand with the right, and pushing it away himself. But . . . after another pause, in creeps the irrepressible left hand once again. This time W. J. takes his left hand in his right, pushes it away—and sits on it, to stop it interfering further.[1]

Here is the other case:

L. B., an intelligent eleven-year-old commissurotomy patient, was given a pipe to hold in his left hand; a screen prevented him seeing what he was holding. The pipe was removed, and he was then asked to write, with his left hand, the name of the object he had just held. The left hand is of course primarily controlled by the right hemisphere, which had received the 'pipe' input from the left hand's tactual sensing of the pipe. Slowly and laboriously L. B., with his left hand, wrote 'P' and 'I'. At this point the left hemisphere

---

[1] Wilkes (1988: 139).

took over—using its ipsilateral control over the left hand—and, changing the 'I' into an 'E', swiftly wrote 'PENCIL'. The right hemisphere took over again, crossed out the letters 'ENCIL', and *drew* a pipe.[2]

In each case, there is a conflict between the two cerebral hemispheres, each apparently operating on a different conception of how the assigned task is to be accomplished. Furthermore, a strong impression is created that we have here two *centers of consciousness,* each seeking to pursue its own agenda. This conclusion is not irresistible; it could be that in each case one of the hemispheres is not conscious but is instead proceeding 'automatically,' as one may perform many familiar actions without conscious attention. However, this does not seem at all a natural reading of the situation. The tasks involved are not familiar, routinized procedures like brushing one's teeth or walking along a familiar route. Rather, they involve novel, interesting tasks that receive their point precisely from the special instructions given by the experimenter. The most plausible reading of the situation, surely, is that both hemispheres are somehow conscious, and each is attempting to perform the assigned task in its own way. I submit that any theory about the mind that forces one to deny this incurs a significant empirical burden, by forcing one to reject the most plausible way of understanding the observed facts in cases such as these.[3, 4]

Multiple personality has been somewhat less discussed by philosophers than commissurotomy,[5] and is more likely to elicit a response of skeptical disbelief. Indeed, multiple personality remains a topic of intense controversy among psychiatrists, a fact that should lead us to be cautious in drawing conclusions from contested data. The position taken here will be that there is such a condition, defined as 'two or more personalities occurring in one individual, each of which is sufficiently developed and integrated as to have a relatively rich, unified, and stable life of its own.'[6] I will not take a position on the ultimate causation of the condition, or on the most appropriate method of treatment.

---

[2] Ibid.: 138f.

[3] For me personally one of the strongest pieces of supporting evidence is indirect—essentially, an argument from authority. The neuroscientist John Eccles, whose philosophical leanings were strongly Cartesian, nevertheless admitted that in split-brain cases 'there is remarkable evidence in favour of a limited self-consciousness of the right hemisphere' (John Eccles, *Evolution of the Brain: Creation of the Self* (London: Routledge, 1989), p. 210). Such an admission, which contravened his own prior inclinations (as well as his published views stated in earlier writings) can only have been the result of strong pressure from the empirical evidence.

[4] Tim Bayne and David J. Chalmers have argued in defense of the view that there is in commissurotomy subjects a single consciousness, embracing the data represented in both hemispheres. See the Appendix to this chapter.

[5] The most outstanding exception is Ian Hacking's book, *Rewriting the Soul: Multiple Personalities and the Sciences of Memory* (Princeton: Princeton University Press, 1995). No one interested in multiple personality should miss Hacking's rich and provocative discussion. In chapter 16, 'Mind and Body,' Hacking discusses the ways in which several other philosophers have treated multiple personality.

[6] Confer and Ables (1983: 16). The definition cited is taken from W. S. Taylor and M. F. Martin, 'Multiple Personality,' *Journal of Abnormal and Social Psychology* 39 (1944): 281–300.

Nor is any conclusion drawn here concerning whether the condition has been over-diagnosed as a result of spectacular, widely publicized cases such as those of 'Eve' and 'Sybil.' My discussion is focused on the existence of multiple personality and on its implications for our metaphysical understanding of the mind.

In cases of multiple personality the original personality seems to have become fragmented, leaving parts which are 'separate mental aggregates, each with its own memories, which form the nucleus for new, independently functioning constellations.'[7] Multiple personality may sometimes have its origin in childhood fantasy and role-playing, but the separate personalities gain a degree of autonomy that clearly distinguishes this syndrome from play-acting. The different personalities display different patterns of brain function, as seen by an EEG, and give different, but internally consistent, sets of responses to the Minnesota Multiphasic Personality Inventory.[8] The MMPI is an extremely sophisticated test, with lie-detection scales built in; systematically faking responses without detection is considered virtually impossible. The syndrome may in some cases be exacerbated by unwise actions of the therapist (for instance, by showing excessive favorable attention to alternates that tends to reinforce their distinctness), but it exists outside the therapeutic setting and cannot plausibly be considered to be the result of therapeutic suggestion.

My present concern is not so much with multiple personalities as such, as with the apparent existence of *simultaneously conscious* multiple personalities in the same individual. Sally, the most prominent alternate of Morton Prince's patient Christine Beauchamp,[9] claimed to have been 'intraconscious'[10] with Christine, aware of all of Christine's thoughts as well as actions, since her early childhood. Similarly Jeanne, the main alternate of William Confer's patient Rene, claimed to have been with Rene, and watching over her, virtually all of the time since they first 'met' when Rene was four years old. Here again, as with commissurotomy, we have phenomena which seem to point to the existence of two or more centers of consciousness in the same human individual.

Now, this evidence is not unimpeachable. Alternate personalities have delusions of their own; Jeanne, for example, was for a long time unwilling to recognize that she shared the same body with Rene! So it might be possible to develop a hypothesis according to which, in each multiple personality patient, there is at any given time only one center of consciousness; the different personalities

---

[7] Confer and Ables (1983: 16).   [8] See Wilkes (1988: 111).

[9] This case was originally reported in Morton Prince, *The Dissociation of a Personality* (London: Longmans, Green, 1905); I am relying on the account given by Wilkes.

[10] 'The technical term for a subordinate consciousness that is aware of the primary personalities' actions but not thoughts is "co-conscious"; one aware of both actions and thoughts is "intraconscious"' (Wilkes 1988: 113n.).

alternate, but never co-exist in simultaneous conscious states. But developing such a hypothesis in detail would present a formidable challenge. Among the phenomena to be accounted for are the diverse memories of the different personalities. Sally remembered Christine's thoughts and actions, but emphatically as 'hers' and not as 'mine.' (The name 'Sally' was originally chosen because Sally disliked Christine and objected to being called by her name.) Sally was able to recall Christine's dreams in more detail than Christine herself could. On the other hand, Sally was uninterested in schoolwork and inattentive during lessons; she was quite unable to speak or understand French, a language in which Christine was fluent. (This came in handy when the therapist wanted to communicate with Christine while excluding Sally.)

Another range of data to be explained concerns the apparent interactions between the alternates and the principal personality, and between the alternates themselves. Both Jeanne and Stella, another alternate of Rene, considered that they had a need to protect Rene, which sometimes involved 'taking over' when a situation arose which Rene was unable to handle. On one occasion Stella phoned the therapist to say that Rene, after a traumatic experience, was determined to commit suicide by overdosing on her husband's Seconal and Valium. Stella was asked by the therapist to bring Rene to the emergency ward of the hospital, where he would meet her. Shortly thereafter, Rene did appear at the hospital, in a confused state with no recollection of how she had got there![11]

These few observations merely skim the surface of the phenomena that would have to be explained by a hypothesis that would deny the existence of simultaneous consciousness on the part of two or more personalities. It is my strong impression (subject, of course, to refutation) that any hypothesis that could do this would have to be both ad hoc and extremely complicated, and thus antecedently improbable. Once again, there is an empirical price to be paid, if one is determined to avoid taking the data at their face value.[12]

What conclusions concerning unity and disunity should be drawn from these examples? The most radical conclusion, that we have in these cases multiple distinct *persons*, has been seriously advocated, but there is little to recommend it. In commissurotomy cases, the many-persons interpretation flies in the face of the overall unity and integration of the personality, outside the experimental situations that elicit the anomalous responses. In multiple personality cases, on the other hand, there is an obvious, serious disruption of personal unity, though

---

[11] Confer and Ables (1983: 130).

[12] An alternative solution, of course, might be found in a radically skeptical approach to the multiple-personality data as a whole. Some readers might suppose that such skepticism is to be found in Hacking, but that would be a mistake. Hacking does not doubt that multiple-personality patients are mentally ill, nor does he consider that the illness is caused by the patient–therapist interaction. He does, however, lay heavy emphasis on the way in which not only the interpretation of the condition, but its actual manifestation and symptoms, are shaped by the climate of psychiatric and popular opinion about such cases.

not one that necessarily precludes the assigning of moral responsibility.[13] But the supposition that we have here multiple persons has implications hardly anyone is prepared to accept. It is widely agreed that the objective of therapy for these cases is the re-integration of the original personality, with the fragments that have been 'hived off' making their contribution to the resulting whole. But if we have here literally several different *persons*, then the desired therapeutic result amounts to *ending the lives* of one or more such persons—that is, to homicide. This may actually be the way the situation is viewed by some alternate personalities, but I suspect that no readers of this chapter will be prepared to accept it.[14] The claim that there are multiple persons can perhaps best be viewed charitably, as an expression of wonderment at the strange phenomena encountered in these cases.

But while there may not be multiple persons in these cases, it is hard to resist the conclusion that there are multiple centers of consciousness.[15] And though this is less radical than the 'many-persons' hypothesis, it has major implications of its own. For one thing, it undermines the formulas, 'one person—one consciousness,' and 'one mind—one consciousness,' which seem to be deeply entrenched in our thinking about these matters. Many would claim for these formulas the status of necessary truths, entailed by our concepts of *person* and *mind.* I am not certain whether this is correct or not, but if it is this may be a place where we are forced to revise our concepts under the pressure of experience. Such revisions, however, are far from trivial, nor are they easily accepted. I suspect that it is primarily resistance to this kind of revision that motivates the strong objection felt by many to attributing more than one center of consciousness to commissurotomy and multiple personality subjects.

Beyond this, the notion of multiple centers of consciousness in one person places considerable strain on Cartesian dualist conceptions of the mind, according to which the mind is a 'simple substance' with no internal divisions. How can such a substance be the seat of multiple centers of consciousness and still retain

---

[13] Walter Sinnott-Armstrong and Stephen Behnke discuss this in 'Responsibility in Cases of Multiple Personality Disorder' (*Philosophical Perspectives 14: Action and Freedom* (2000), pp. 301–23). They conclude that multiple-personality patients should be held legally responsible if and only if the personality in control at the time a crime was committed met the requirements for responsibility set out in the Model Penal Code.

[14] I may be overly sanguine. According to Hacking (writing in 1994), 'A few years ago professionals were advising that one should never, in therapy, eliminate a single alter personality, for that would be akin to murder.' But he goes on to add, 'Now the message is, get rid of the personalities altogether' (Hacking 1995: 54).

[15] After work on the present chapter had been completed, I came across the book, *Switching Time,* by Richard Baer (New York: Crown Publishers, 2007). Baer was a psychiatrist in private practice for a number of years, and is currently Medical Director for Medicare in Illinois, Indiana, Kentucky, and Ohio. *Switching Time* recounts the story of the protracted, and successful, psychotherapy of a patient with seventeen alters. The book is highly recommended to readers of this chapter, especially to those who may tend to be skeptical about multiple personality; I think their skepticism is likely to be severely tested by reading it.

its simplicity? Perhaps what could be said here is that the soul has the *potential* for consciousness, but that potential must be actualized through the soul's relationship with a brain and nervous system—and, under some relatively rare circumstances, the potential is actualized simultaneously in conflicting ways by different subsystems of that brain and nervous system. I am not sure whether this move is coherent or not, but even if it is it threatens to demote the soul to the role of a passive bystander, with all the 'real work' of the mental life being done by the cerebral machinery. This, I submit, is a far cry from the proud Cartesian heritage of the 'thinking thing'!

2. THE UNITY-OF-CONSCIOUSNESS ARGUMENT

At this point I will introduce another line of thinking, one that stands in some tension with the empirical evidence we've been surveying—namely, the unity-of-consciousness argument against materialism, derived from Leibniz and Kant. Some readers may tend to think that this argument is contradicted, and refuted, by the empirical data, but I will argue that there is no contradiction. We begin with a familiar passage from Leibniz:

In imagining that there is a machine whose construction would enable it to think, to sense, and to have perception, one could conceive it enlarged while retaining the same proportions, so that one could enter into it, just like into a windmill. Supposing this, one should, when visiting within it, find only parts pushing one another, and never anything by which to explain a perception. Thus it is in the simple substance, and not in the composite or in the machine, that one must look for perception.[16]

This passage is frequently quoted, but often its force has not been appreciated. The difficulty does not lie, as some have thought, in the fact that Leibniz's example was limited by seventeenth-century technology. If instead of his 'parts pushing one another' we fill the machine with vacuum tubes, transistors, or for that matter with neurons, exactly the same problem remains. The problem does not lie in the pushes and pulls but rather in the *complexity* of the machine, the fact that it is made up of many distinct parts, coupled with the fact that *a complex state of consciousness cannot exist distributed among the parts of a complex object.* The functioning of any complex object such as a machine, a television set, a computer, or a brain, consists of the coordinated functioning of its parts, which working together produce an effect of some kind. But where the effect to be explained is a *thought*, a state of consciousness, what function shall be assigned to the individual parts, be they transistors or neurons? Even a fairly simple experiential state—say, your visual experience as you look around this

---

[16] Gottfried Wilhelm Leibniz, *Monadology*, 17, in Nicholas Rescher, *G. W. Leibniz's Monadology: An Edition for Students* (Pittsburgh: University of Pittsburgh Press, 1991), p. 19.

room—contains far more information than can be encoded in a single transistor, or a single neuron. Suppose, then, that the state is broken up into bits in such a way that some small part of it is represented in each of many different parts of the brain. Assuming this to be done, we have still the question: *who or what is aware of the conscious state as a whole?* For it is a fact that you *are aware* of your conscious state, at any given moment, as a unitary whole. So we have this question for the materialist: when I am aware of a complex conscious state, what *physical entity* is it that is aware of that state? This question, I am convinced, does not and cannot receive a plausible answer.

Here is a fairly simple formal presentation[17] of the unity-of-consciousness argument:

1. I am aware of my present visual field as a unity; in other words, the various components of the field are experienced by a single subject simultaneously.

2. Only something that functions as a whole rather than as a system of parts could experience a visual field as a unity.

3. Therefore, the subject functions as a whole rather than as a system of parts.

4. The brain and nervous system, and the entire body, is nothing more than a collection of physical parts organized in a certain way. (In other words, holism is false.)

5. Therefore, the brain and nervous system cannot function as a whole; it must function as a system of parts.

6. Therefore the subject is not the brain and nervous system (or the body, etc.).

7. If the subject is not the brain and nervous system then it is (or contains as a proper part) a non-physical mind or 'soul'; that is, a mind that is not ontologically reducible to the sorts of entities studied in the physical sciences. Such a mind, even if it is extended in space, could function as a whole rather than as a system of parts and so could be aware of my present visual field as a unity.

8. Therefore, the subject is a soul, or contains a soul as a part of itself.

So far as I am able to tell, this is a sound argument, one whose premises are either evidently true or at least highly plausible. Leaving aside the proposed account of the soul in step 7, the most likely place for a materialist to dissent from the argument is step 4, the denial of holism. This, I think, is pretty well where the materialist is forced to go, if he wishes to avoid the anti-materialist conclusion of the argument. (And for what it's worth, I think Peter van Inwagen

---

[17] This version is adapted from a formulation by Paul Draper, who in turn was summarizing the argument as given in chapter 5 of my book, *The Emergent Self* (Ithaca: Cornell University Press, 1999).

is committed to holism at this point, in spite of his expressed reservations about the doctrine.[18])

But is the unity-of-consciousness argument not refuted by empirical evidence of *dis*unity, as found in commissurotomy, multiple personality, and numerous less exotic sorts of cases? In a word, No. The unity-of-consciousness argument takes as its starting point the *experienced fact* of unity—but this is really a very modest sort of unity, consisting merely in the fact that one has at a given moment a phenomenal field (visual and/or auditory and/or tactual and/or . . .) which comprises a large amount and variety of data. That there may in other respects be disunity—even dramatic and surprising disunity—in no way undermines the argument or its conclusion. Nor, let me add in passing, is the argument undermined by the work neuroscientists have done on the so-called 'binding problem.' The binding problem, as they have addressed it, is essentially an engineering problem, the problem of how various sorts of information encoded in the brain are brought together and coordinated so as to enable us to have the coherent, meaningful sorts of experiences we actually do have. (For example, how are the color *red* and the shape *square*, represented in different parts of my visual system, brought together so as to constitute the perception of a red square?) This engineering problem (or cluster of problems) clearly must have an engineering solution, in the actual structure and functioning of the brain, and it is the job of neuroscientists to find out what that solution is. But nothing that has been done or that can be done along these lines constitutes an answer to the question, How can a unitary *state of consciousness* be a state of a complex physical structure, such as the brain?

3. TENSION—AND RESOLUTION?

We can conclude, then, that there is no contradiction between the empirical evidence in commissurotomy and multiple personality cases, and the unity-of-consciousness argument. And it is fortunate that this is so, since both the evidence and the argument seem well established and worthy of our acceptance. However, it cannot be denied that combining the two leaves us with a certain tension. On the one hand, the unity-of-consciousness argument claims to show that the subject of our conscious states *cannot be* a complex material object, such as the brain. On the other hand, the commissurotomy and multiple personality evidence, along with much, much else, strongly suggests that the source of conscious experience *is* to be found in the brain and nervous system. It is evident that the multiple centers of consciousness found in commissurotomy have a physical cause, since

---

[18] See van Inwagen (1990: section 12). For a discussion of van Inwagen's view, see *The Emergent Self,* pp. 140–4.

the phenomena result quite directly from a surgical alteration of the brain. The causation of multiple personality is less well understood. But the distinct patterns of brain activity for the different personalities, as shown by an EEG, strongly suggest that here also a proximate cause is to be found in the existence of several different, largely separate and internally coherent, functional control patterns within the brain. (This is not of course to deny the role of psychological and interpersonal factors in establishing and activating these different functional patterns.) And there is a great deal more evidence that shows the role of the brain in generating conscious experiences of various sorts. This is especially evident in 'localization studies' which point to specific regions of the brain as the locus of specific types of information-processing. I can say as a matter of personal experience that it is very difficult to get Cartesian dualists even to attempt to provide a coherent account of these phenomena. Usually the most one gets is a dogged insistence that there is no logical contradiction, combined with a certain amount of hand waving.[19] In my opinion this body of evidence constitutes a very serious difficulty for dualism of the Cartesian type, far more serious than the (greatly overrated) objection to causal interaction between the body and an immaterial substance. (But why, you may be asking, am I wasting our time by talking about a disreputable, universally despised view such as Cartesian dualism? My answer is that part of my agenda is to point out that dualism in general has been far too quickly dismissed, and the motivations for taking it seriously are more substantial than is usually acknowledged by philosophers. If there are compelling objections to certain dualist views, these need to be spelled out clearly; mere appeal to cultural prejudice is not the method of true philosophy.)

So we have a tension, between an argument that contends that the subject of experience cannot be a material object, and evidence that strongly suggests that consciousness arises as a result of brain function. When the problem is stated in this way, a solution virtually stares us in the face. But it is quite a radical solution, one that exacts a metaphysical price of its own. Put briefly, the solution is that there is indeed an immaterial subject of experience, but one that *emerges from* a complex physical object, namely the brain and nervous system. Normally what is generated by a brain is a single, well-unified conscious subject, but under special conditions, as seen in commissurotomy and multiple personality, the consciousness can divide or fragment.

Stating the proposed view in this way signals immediately that the view is a form of emergentism. But emergentism comes in many different varieties, and

---

[19] The best answer I have seen is from Charles Taliaferro: 'Allow for interaction, and I see no reason why we shouldn't expect the connection to be intricate and many-layered, replete with information processing' (from personal correspondence). This is still very general, but at least it gives us some idea of how the view could be further developed. It also, however, tends to undermine the independence of the mind as the 'thinking thing,' as affirmed by classical Cartesian dualism.

this is one of the stronger ones, holding that a *new individual,* not composed of previously existing 'stuff,' is what emerges from the right configuration of the brain and nervous system. Without doubt, such a strong form of emergentism will seem implausible to a good many philosophers. Still, we need to remind ourselves what the alternatives are. Substance dualisms that make the soul a special divine creation have appealed to many on theological grounds, but they also meet with serious objections—objections which I won't detail here.[20] Reductive versions of materialism encounter serious philosophical difficulties; it was frustration over these difficulties that led to the brief flourishing of eliminativism. 'Non-reductive materialism' has been proclaimed a myth by Jaegwon Kim, and his reasons for saying this appear compelling.[21] Kim has also stated that emergentism has really been the predominant view in philosophy of mind for several decades, though not always under that name. If we consider that some kind of emergence or other is the best way to go, then the main question before us is, what variety of emergentism does the most justice to all the phenomena of our experience? Weak versions of emergence, that maintain the causal closure of the physical domain, make it simply impossible to give a coherent account of our capacity for rational thought, among other things.[22] If our objective is to avoid causal reductionism, we shall have to allow for *emergent laws* and *emergent causal powers*—powers that are *not* the causal consequences of powers exhibited by physical stuff in simpler situations than those in which the emergence occurs. According to this stronger variety of emergence, under certain circumstances the basic physical stuff of which we are made *acts in ways that deviate from the fundamental laws of physics.* And the deviations do not amount to minor modifications, such as some physical constant or other's being altered in the fourth or fifth decimal place. On the contrary, the principles that have to come into play are of a *fundamentally different kind* than the laws of physics as we know them; they will be *teleological* principles, principles which state that certain things happen *in order that some goal may be achieved* (for instance, the goal of arriving at the truth about things), and not merely as prescribed by some impersonal mathematical function. The best statement of this type of emergentism known to me is by Timothy O'Connor, and I salute him for his willingness to take on the physicalist establishment with such a radical proposal.[23] But the question I put to O'Connor, and to others who may be attracted to such a position, is this: is it all that much *more* radical to affirm an emergent *individual substance*—one that is not composed of the ultimate particles of physics? Strong emergentists such as O'Connor have already made a

---

[20] See Hasker (1999: chapter 6).   [21] See especially Kim (1989).
[22] For argument, see Hasker (1999: chapter 3).
[23] See O'Connor (2000); also, O'Connor (1994). See also Hasker (1999: chapter 7).

decisive break with the prevailing direction in the metaphysics of mind; doesn't it make sense for them to take just a step further, and arrive at a view that can really do the job laid out for it? For, absent a radical holism which few philosophers are willing to embrace, even a strongly emergentist materialism such as O'Connor's cannot meet the challenge posed by the unity-of-consciousness argument.

So here is my proposal: emergent dualism, which affirms that a mental substance emerges, under suitable conditions, from a functioning brain and nervous system, is the view that best accounts for the role of the physical organism in generating consciousness as well as for the distinctively 'mental' character of consciousness itself. For those who find this a bit much to swallow, I point out that the view is not in fact altogether novel; an extremely similar view was held by Karl Popper.[24] But in meeting the requirements of philosophical rationality this view also, if I am not mistaken, goes a long way towards meeting the requirements of our conception of a person.

4. APPENDIX: BAYNE AND CHALMERS ON THE SPLIT-BRAIN EVIDENCE

In an important article, Tim Bayne and David Chalmers argue that the split-brain evidence for divided consciousness is at best inconclusive.[25] They begin by making a distinction (taken from Ned Block) between *access consciousness* and *phenomenal consciousness,* defined as follows:

A mental state is *access-conscious* . . . if by virtue of having the state, the content of the state is available for verbal report, for rational inference, and for the deliberate control of behavior. (2003: 28)

A mental state is *phenomenally conscious* when there is something it is like to be in that state . . . [so that] being in that state involves some sort of subjective experience. (2003: 28)

Armed with this distinction, they stipulate two ways in which conscious states may be unified:

Broadly speaking, two conscious states are *access-unified* when they are jointly accessible: that is, when the subject has access to the contents of both states at once. Two conscious states are *phenomenally unified* when they are jointly experienced: when there is something it is like to be in both states at once. (2003: 29)

---

[24] See Popper and Eccles (1977: part I). For a discussion of Popper's views, see Hasker (1999: 185–8).

[25] Tim Bayne and David J. Chalmers, 'What is the Unity of Consciousness?' in Axel Cleeremans (ed.), *The Unity of Consciousness: Binding, Integration, and Dissociation* (Oxford: Oxford University Press, 2003), pp. 23–58.

They go on to formulate a number of theses on the unity of consciousness[26]; for our purposes it will suffice to note the

Access Unity Thesis: Necessarily, any set of access-conscious states of a subject at a time is access-unified (p. 31)

and the

Phenomenal Unity Thesis: Necessarily, any set of phenomenal states of a subject at a time is phenomenally unified. (p. 33)

These theses are related to the split-brain evidence in the following way: that evidence strongly suggests that, for split-brain patients, access unity has broken down (and thus, that the Access Unity Thesis is false). There is a strong inclination, for many people, to conclude from this that phenomenal unity has also broken down for these patients, and thus that the Phenomenal Unity Thesis is also false. Bayne and Chalmers argue against this by presenting a case in which access unity breaks down while phenomenal unity is preserved, showing that a failure of the former need not entail a failure of the latter. They are inclined to affirm the Phenomenal Unity Thesis as a conceptual truth, though they refrain from pronouncing definitely on the matter.

The case they rely on is from an experiment by Sperling, in which a subject is briefly (250 ms.) shown a matrix consisting of three lines of four letters each.[27] Subjects are then asked to report the contents of the matrix. When asked to report the contents of any one row, the success rate is fairly high (3.3 out of four letters). But when asked to report on the entire matrix, the success rate is only 4.5 out of twelve letters. Apparently, after the first few letters have been reported, accurate memory of the others is lost, so that the remaining answers are essentially random. It appears, then, that while any row of the matrix is access-conscious, the subject is not access-conscious of the information in all three rows—that is, the subject cannot utilize all of that information to report correctly on the letters in the matrix. So access unity fails. Yet there is nothing in the experiment that suggests a breakdown of phenomenal unity; it is plausible that the subject was initially conscious of all the letters together.

It seems that this experiment does establish a good deal of what Bayne and Chalmers were hoping to establish. We do have here a breakdown of access unity, as they have defined it, and so the Access Unity Thesis is false. Furthermore, there is no reason in the case to suppose a breakdown of phenomenal unity. So the fact that two conscious states are phenomenally unified does not entail

---

[26] Here and throughout their article, Bayne and Chalmers make a number of technical distinctions which are not pursued here. I do not believe this will affect any of the points made in this note.

[27] Bayne and Chalmers (2003: 35); the source is George Sperling, 'The Information Available in Brief Visual Presentations,' *Psychological Monographs* 498 (1960): 1–29.

that they are access unified, and thus far the Phenomenal Unity Thesis remains unscathed. Applying these results to the split-brain phenomena, they suggest that in split-brain cases we have a breakdown of access unity but not a loss of phenomenal unity. There is, in other words, a single consciousness that embraces the information represented in both cerebral hemispheres, even though the utilization of that information is limited in the ways shown by the experiments.

Let us, however, examine their case a bit more closely. Viewed schematically, Sperling's results fit the following scenario:

1. The contents of states $C_1, C_2, C_3 \ldots C_n$ are phenomenally unified in a subject's experience during a (brief) period of time t.

2. During a (brief) period of time t' (which may or may not coincide with t) any of the C_i can be utilized in the control of behavior, but $C_1, C_2, C_3 \ldots C_n$ cannot all be utilized during that period. (Thus, the states $C_1, C_2, C_3 \ldots C_n$ are all access-conscious, but there is not access unity for these states.)

3. After t' has concluded, the elements of $C_1, C_2, C_3 \ldots C_n$ that were not utilized are lost (not remembered), and can no longer be utilized for the control of behavior.

Viewed in terms of this schema, the Sperling experiment is seen not to be unique but rather to be an instance of a type of scenario often witnessed in life outside the laboratory. Consider, for instance, the situation of a football quarterback as he drops back to throw a pass. Within a few seconds he needs to register and evaluate information concerning (among other things) the pass routes run by his receivers, the positions and movements of the defensive backs, and the movements of the charging defensive linemen, who will seek to tackle him before he can release the pass. It is well known that inexperienced quarterbacks often have difficulty processing this information in the time available. Thus, a quarterback may note that his primary receiver is covered but may still be able to catch a pass if it is thrown accurately, but may fail to realize that another receiver has eluded his cover man and is running unmolested into the end zone—and this in spite of the fact that the latter information is in some way present in his visual field. If we add to this (plausibly enough) that after the play is over the unutilized information is quickly lost from memory, we have a close analogue of Sperling's experiment. And we have a confirmation, from ordinary life, of the results relied on by Bayne and Chalmers.

We can now make the following observations about these two cases:

1. Once we are clear as to what is happening, the results in the two cases are not very surprising. Indeed, these can be seen as the result of principles that plausibly must govern the design of complex biological creatures such as we are. The inability to process and utilize all of the available data in a short space of time reflects what Bayne and Chalmers call a 'bottleneck'; it results from the fact that, given limited neurological resources, any information-processing

system is necessarily limited in its capacity. And the loss of unutilized data reflects the impracticality of retaining in memory vast amounts of low-priority information.

2. These cases do not seem very similar to the split-brain cases; in particular, they have no tendency to make us question the unity of phenomenal consciousness, whereas the split-brain cases unquestionably do have such a tendency, whether or not it is justified.

3. It seems a bit odd to speak of these cases as counterexamples to a principle of the *unity* of consciousness. It would seem that a counterexample to a 'unity principle' should exhibit *disunity* of some significant kind, but that does not seem to be the case here. The only 'split' that occurs in the examples is between the information which happens to be utilized, and the information which could have been utilized but was not because other information occupied the available processing capacity.

4. Notwithstanding point 3 above, the cases are in fact counterexamples to Bayne and Chalmers' Access Unity Thesis. But this may lead us to wonder whether the 'unity' expressed in that thesis captures accurately what is at stake in the debate over the split-brain results. We may, then, be motivated to formulate yet another unity thesis, one that does more justice to the issues in that debate.

Here is my candidate for such a thesis:

New Access Unity Thesis: Any two access-conscious states of a subject at a time, C_1 and C_2, which are such that during a time-period t both C_1 and C_2 can be utilized in the control of behavior, are such that it is possible during t for the conjoined contents of C_1 and C_2 to be utilized in the control of behavior.

This differs from Bayne and Chalmers' Access Unity Thesis, in that it will not allow as counterexamples failures of access that result merely from engineering limitations such as those noted in (1) above. Because of this, the Sperling results and my quarterback example are *not* counterexamples to the New Access Unity Thesis. In those cases, it is not true that, during the relevant time-period, it is possible for both C_1 and C_2 to be utilized in the control of behavior. It is precisely because of this that the experimental subject's recall fails when asked to identify the letters in more than one row of the matrix, and the quarterback is unable to keep track of what is happening to all the receivers and defensive backs at once. The failure, in both of these cases, is readily attributed to the limited capacity for information processing.

However, the split-brain results *are* plausibly seen as counterexamples to the New Access Unity Thesis. Consider the following (relatively simple) case:[28] The

---

[28] See Charles E. Marks, *Commissurotomy, Consciousness, and Unity of Mind* (Montgomery, Vermont: Bradford Books, 1980), pp. 4–6.

words 'key ring' are projected briefly onto a screen, in such a way that 'key' appears in the left visual field and is transmitted to the right hemisphere, while 'ring' appears in the right visual field and is transmitted to the left hemisphere. The subject, asked what he or she saw, says 'ring,' but has no idea what sort of ring in particular. (The speech processes are controlled by the left hemisphere.) But if asked to point with his or her left hand (controlled by the right hemisphere) to what he or she saw, the subject will point to a key and not to a ring. We have, then, a situation in which the subject is able to utilize the word 'key,' and also the word 'ring,' in controlling behavior (and thus is access-conscious of both words), but is not able to utilize the conjoined contents, 'key ring.'

The problem this creates for Bayne and Chalmers is to devise a plausible explanation, consistent with the Phenomenal Unity Thesis, of the subject's inability to utilize the conjoined contents. On the face of it, the most plausible explanation for this would seem to be that there simply *is no* phenomenal awareness of the conjoined contents, 'key ring,' and thus that phenomenal unity has failed. This conclusion, to be sure, is not absolutely forced upon us; it remains logically possible that there is such an awareness, but that for some reason it is not able to be expressed in any form of behavior. But then the burden reverts to Bayne and Chalmers, to explain the causal impotence of this awareness. One explanation that beckons is that *all* awareness is causally impotent; causal efficacy resides solely in the neural connections, which in this case are absent. But if the price that must be paid to uphold the Phenomenal Unity Thesis is epiphenomenalism, many of us will find it excessive.

9

An Argument from Transtemporal Identity for Subject–Body Dualism

Martine Nida-Rümelin[1]

1. SUBJECT–BODY DUALISM

In this chapter I argue for a version of dualism that is stronger than property dualism and that may be taken to be a version of so-called substance dualism. But the latter term invites associations that I would like to avoid. Subject–body dualism as I will use the term includes the claim that there is an individual that has experiences, thinks and is active and is *neither identical* to any material thing *nor constituted* by any material thing. The view is thus incompatible with the claim that—just as the statue is constituted at any moment of its existence by the piece of bronze that makes it up without being identical with that piece of bronze—the subject is constituted by its body.[2] According to subject–body dualism the subject is an individual that exists wholly at any given moment of its existence and persists across time while changing its properties. According to subject–body dualism subjects endure and they do not perdure (subjects exist across time but they are not temporally extended).[3] Subject–body dualism does not imply that conscious subjects can exist without having a body. If the term 'substance' is reserved to entities that do not depend for their existence on the existence of any other entity, then the view proposed cannot be classified as a version of substance dualism.

[1] I would like to thank Max Drömmer, Gianfranco Soldati, Dominic O'Meara, Fabian Dorsch, Gian-Andri Toendury, and Jiri Benovsky for discussions about the topic that helped me a lot to further develop the view here presented. And I would like to thank the participants in my German advanced seminar in the spring semester 2008 at the philosophy department in Fribourg and the participants in my French seminar in the same semester for questions and critical remarks that helped me a lot to see further points to be developed and to be clarified.
[2] For a version of the constitution view see Baker (2000).
[3] The distinction between enduring and perduring objects has been introduced in these terms by Lewis (1986) and Johnston (1987).

Substance dualism is often associated with the view that the person is meta-physically composed of two parts: a body and a soul. According to subject–body dualism the person is not composed. The person has a body and the body is in no sense a part of him or her. There is no difference to be made, according to subject–body dualism between the person and 'the self.' When a person uses the first-person pronoun, or is addressed by the second-person pronoun or is referred to by name, then the reference in each of these cases is the same: the person (the subject of experience). Subject–body dualism rejects many of those ideas that are traditionally associated with the concept of a soul. Souls are often described as composed of some non-material stuff. Subject–body dualism rejects the idea of a non-material stuff. Souls are often described as the immaterial part of a person. The subject–body dualist does not believe in the existence of immaterial parts of people. The experiencing subject is not a *part* of the person—it is the person itself. Persons are subjects: the term 'subject of experience' is only the more general term covering human and non-human conscious beings. Souls are sometimes thought of as literally leaving the body. The capacity to leave the body presupposes spatial location. According to subject–body dualism subjects are located only in a derivative sense: they are where their bodies are.

Substance dualism is often understood as limited to the human domain. All motivations for subject–body dualism with respect to a given being are based on the fact that the being considered is endowed with consciousness. The complexity and the sophistication of the being's conscious life do not play any role in the motivation for subject–body dualism. It follows that subject–body dualism cannot be restricted to the human domain. If it is correct for humans, it must be correct for the most simple organism in which consciousness in the broadest sense arises. Consciousness in the broadest sense is present in a simple creature capable of enjoying warmth or feeling pain.

Since subject–body dualism applies for instance to an elephant, somebody might make the following objection. According to subject–body dualism when I see the huge impressive organism making up the body of an elephant I do not see an elephant, since the elephant is not its body. According to subject–body dualism it is impossible to see elephants, just as it is impossible to see my human friends. I can never see *them*: I can only see their bodies. This is clearly a reductio ad absurdum of subject–body dualism. The subject–body dualist must answer this objection by pointing out that it is based in a mistaken view about what it is to see something. The subject–body dualist will insist that we see the subject by seeing its body or parts of its body.[4]

---

[4] The objection deserves an elaborated answer that will not be developed in the present chapter. The idea that we cannot see the subject according to subject–body dualism is in part based on the mistaken presupposition that the subject is somehow hidden within his or her body and in part on the mistaken idea that the subject cannot be in causal contact with his or her environment. A positive account of seeing that would imply that we see the subject has to develop an account of seeing-as. When we see a smile (a particular movement in a face), we see it as the smile of someone.

Subject–body dualism does not imply the eternal existence of the subject. Subject–body dualism is compatible with the metaphysical hypothesis that it is impossible for a subject to exist without having a body. Subject–body dualism can but need not include the claim that it is metaphysically possible to change one's body.

The dualist view here proposed has no religious motivation. It is compatible with the idea that subjects of experience are products of nature and come into existence without any intervention of any supernatural being. Subject–body dualism is compatible with the plausible assumption that naturally evolved subjects of experience on this and other planets are alone in the universe: no supernatural being causes or knows of or cares about their existence.

2. MOTIVATION FOR SUBJECT–BODY DUALISM

There are, in my view, three main, interdependent motivations for subject–body dualism. The first is based on phenomenal consciousness, the second on the phenomenon of being active, and the third on identity across time.

Here is a brief sketch of how reflecting about phenomenal consciousness may lead to subject–body dualism: a first step consists in the insight that occurrences of phenomenal experience require the existence of a subject who has the experience. One will thereby realize that what is amazing about the emergence of consciousness is not the instantiation of a new kind of properties (phenomenal properties) but rather the beginning of existence of an experiencing subject. One may thereby come to see that no explanation of what it is to be a subject in terms of having experiences is available since any such explanation would be circular. This result can be used in an argument for the claim that no satisfying account of phenomenal consciousness can be given without accepting a specific ontological category for subjects of experience.[5]

A second motivation of subject–body dualism starts from the phenomenological insight that we experience ourselves as active in our doings and that we perceive other conscious individuals as active in their activities. Arguably, these experiences cannot be veridical unless the active subject is itself a cause of certain physical events. In a third step one may see that this kind of causation (the subject is itself a cause) could not possibly exist between a material thing and events occurring within its spatial boundaries. If each of these steps is correct, then subject–body dualism is phenomenologically supported: to deny subject–body dualism would imply that we are constantly the victim of a fundamental illusion

---

The smiling person is directly present in the content of our perceptual experience. Also, the subject is active in its smiling. So we are in causal contact with the subject itself.

[5] This first motivation for subject–body dualism is partially developed in Nida-Rümelin (2008).

in the way we experience our own doings and in the way we perceive the activities of other conscious individuals.[6]

A third motivation of subject–body dualism is based on intuitions concerning the identity across time of conscious individuals. One way to gain the relevant intuitive insight is by reflecting upon cases of so-called duplication where we know of a conscious individual A that it will 'split into' two successors B and C who will stand in symmetrical empirical relation to A. Considering these cases it seems obvious that despite the lack of any difference in the relevant empirical relation obtaining between A and B on the one hand and between A and C on the other, we have a clear positive understanding of the difference between a future course of events that makes the assumption of identity between A and B true and a future course of events that makes the assumption of identity between A and C true. The argument given in the present chapter will be based on this observation. It will be argued in a first step that the clear and positive understanding we have or seem to have of the apparent factual difference between these two possibilities is due to deep conceptual structures present in any thinker who is capable of I-thoughts about the past and the future and who has the cognitive capacities to conceive of others as subjects of experience. On that basis it is argued in a second step that any philosophical theory that denies the factual difference between the two possibilities attributes unavoidable and fundamental illusion to every thinker capable of transtemporal I-thoughts and of conceiving of another being as conscious. This is reason to reject any theory that denies the factual difference. In a third step it will be shown that only subject–body dualism can plausibly fulfill that constraint.[7]

3. GRASPING THE DIFFERENCE BETWEEN TWO POSSIBLE IDENTITY FACTS IN A CASE OF DUPLICATION

Let us consider a case where a person, Andrea, will be operated and thereby 'duplicated' tomorrow: her brain will be divided into two halves, and each of them will be transplanted into a different body. Let us call the woman waking up after the operation with the left hemisphere 'L-Andrea' and the woman waking up after the operation with the right hemisphere 'R-Andrea.' The human organism containing Andrea's left hemisphere will be called the 'L-body' and

---

[6] The argument is based on the idea of subject causation which is similar to Chisholm's thesis of agent or immanent causation (see Chisholm (1976) for a new elaborated version of agent causation, see O'Connor (2000)). The phenomenological observation alluded to is closely related to the claims about phenomenology presented in Horgan et al. (2003). For a development of the argument sketched see Nida-Rümelin (2007).

[7] The argument is developed in detail in the book Nida-Rümelin (2006).

the other organism will be called the 'R-body.' L-Andrea and R-Andrea, let us suppose, will stand in normal psychological continuity with Andrea—each of them feels close to her friends, has Andrea's attitudes towards others, has the same nice humor and the same ideas about what constitutes a good life, etc. Each of them will initially be convinced of being Andrea.

Let us suppose that *there is no relevant empirical difference* in the relation between the original person and her two successors in this sense: there is no difference in these relations that could be responsible for the fact that one of the two successors but not the other is identical to the original person. For the sake of argument let us suppose that the empirical relations of psychological and bodily continuity obtaining directly after the operation between Andrea and L-Andrea on the one hand and Andrea and R-Andrea on the other are perfectly symmetrical. Any such relation either obtains between both successors and the original person or between none of the successors and Andrea.[8]

Let D be a highly complex sentence that describes all the details about the way Andrea divides into two successors. D describes all the details about the way her brain splits and is connected with the two new bodies and all the relevant details about the psychological relation between Andrea and her two successors. From the point of view before the operation we may say that D characterizes the future course of events. According to what I take to be our natural understanding, the possibility described by D can be subdivided in at least three possibilities by adding assumptions about Andrea's identity:

P1: D and Andrea is L-Andrea.

P2: D and Andrea is R-Andrea.

P3: D and Andrea is none of the two.

It is sometimes said in discussions about 'duplication cases' that the original person might be identical with *both* successors. There is a way to make sense of this idea: Andrea might be L-Andrea *and* R-Andrea by having both successor bodies. Since this supposed possibility does not play any role in the argument here presented, I will simply put it aside. In what follows I will focus on the difference between P1 and P2.

In the first step of my argument I would like to convince the reader of what I take to be an insight about our cognitive architecture: we have or seem to have a clear positive understanding of the factual difference (or an apparent factual difference) between P1 and P2. If the future is such that P1 will be rendered true, then Andrea will wake up with the L-body, she will see the world from the L-bodies perspective: *she* will be the one who suffers if the L-body is damaged. But if P2 correctly describes what will happen, then Andrea will have quite different

---

[8] For discussions of the brain division example see Perry (1972); Wiggins (1967: 50); Parfit (1984: 245); Snowdon (1991); Doepke (1996); Hershenov (2004); and Swinburne (2006).

visual experiences when waking up (the ones connected with the R-body): she will act with the R-body, and she will live the life of the person who has the R-body.[9]

In the present first step of the argument my claim is merely conceptual. When we seem to grasp the difference between P1 and P2 we might be under an illusion. It might be that there is no objective difference corresponding to the two different descriptions. But this is not how the situation presents itself to us when we reflect about it. We seem to have a clear conception of an at least apparent factual difference between P1 and P2. The difference appears to be factual in this sense: 'D and Andrea is L-Andrea' and 'D and Andrea is R-Andrea' are not just two legitimate description of one and the same course of events. Rather, there is—according to the way we conceive of the situation—an objective possible feature of the world that makes one of the two descriptions true and the other wrong.

The factual difference may be described pointing out that Andrea will have a different future depending on which of the two possible identity facts will obtain. This is a difference *for* Andrea, in some sense, but it is not only a difference for her; it is not a *merely* subjective difference. It is—or so it seems—an objective feature of the world that Andrea has—at the later moment considered—such and such properties and such and such experiences. We conceive of the difference between P1 and P2 by realizing that Andrea's future is different depending on which of the two possibilities will be realized. If we knew that L-Andrea will have a wonderful life and that R-Andrea will have a horrible life, we can refer to Andrea at her presence and say: if P1 is realized, then *she* will live L-Andrea's happy life and if P2 is realized then *she* will live R-Andrea's horrible life. I take it to be an undeniable fact that we at least seem to understand the difference thus described and that we cannot but conceive of that difference as of a real, factual and quite substantial difference.

It has often been pointed out that the intuition that there is factual difference between P1 and P2 gets much clearer when one imagines oneself being in Andrea's situation. Suppose you wish to know whether you will be the person with the L-body who will live a happy life or the person with the R-body who will live a horrible life. A philosopher might tell you that the answer to your question is under-determined: the real course of future events does not make one of the possible answers true and the other false. It has often been pointed out that the person concerned will not be satisfied by that reply. But it is not easy to spell out what that dissatisfaction consists in. One might think that the person concerned is unsatisfied since he or she does not know what emotional attitudes he or she should take and the person might find it uncomfortable to oscillate between happy expectation and fear. But the dissatisfaction is not just an emotional one. The roots of that dissatisfaction lie deeper. There is a sense

---

[9] I will use the letters 'P1' and 'P2' in a systematically ambiguous way, sometimes to refer to the description of the possibility and sometimes, to refer to the possibility itself. It will be clear from the context which of two is meant.

in which the person concerned cannot make sense of the idea that his or her future is under-determined. There must be—or so it seems—an answer to the question of whether I will lead this life or rather that life; there must be an answer to the question which of two future bodies will be mine. Our conceptual make-up is such that each of us have (or seem to have) a clear understanding of the difference between a world where his or her own I-thought 'I will be happy after the operation,' will be rendered true on the one hand and a world where 'I will be unhappy after the operation' is rendered true on the other. Under the presupposition that there is no possibility that I will be between being happy and being unhappy the world must be such that one of the two I-thoughts is true and the other false, or so it seems. Given our conceptual make-up a person who states the under-determination of the issue seems to be talking nonsense. Our dissatisfaction with his or her claim is cognitive and not or not just emotional.

In what follows I will propose an explanation of why it may help to consider the case from the first-person perspective. However, the insight that taking the first-person perspective in one's reflection about the case makes the relevant intuition more salient can invite a number of misunderstandings. Imagining oneself's being in Andrea's situation helps one to see that there seems to be a factual difference between P1 and P2, and that we seem to be able to grasp that difference. This may invite the idea that empathy is relevant here. One might think that a person who empathizes with Andrea will be able to understand her tendency to insist that there must be an answer to the question of which body will be hers. And one might thus be lead to the hypothesis that we seem to see a difference between P1 and P2 as a result of emotional confusion and that emotion-free reflection about the case will reveal that this as an illusion. But this would be to miss the point. We can realize that there clearly seems to be a substantial factual difference between P1 and P2 even when we think about Andrea's case in a cool and emotionally detached way. We seem to grasp the difference even when we do not care about which of the two possibilities will be realized. To see the difference is not the result of an emotionally colored conception that might be misled for that reason.

Another misunderstanding may occur when we take the exercise to imagine being in Andrea's situation as a case of taking the perspective of another person with the intention to trigger those cognitive processes that the other person is likely to undergo. One may thus be led to the conclusion that P1 and P2 only seem different when considered from the perspective of the person concerned while there is no such impression when we think about the case from the third person perspective. But this is a mistake. We seem to grasp the difference between P1 and P2 when imagining being the person concerned, but we also seem to grasp the difference when thinking about the case as a story concerning somebody else. It is not a case where changing perspectives changes the way things appear: there seems to be a substantial factual difference between P1 and P2 from the first person perspective as well as from the third-person perspective.

Still, being oneself concerned of future duplication would make it particularly difficult to deny that the difference between P1 and P2 is a factual difference. This psychological fact has a number of convergent explanations. One of these makes reference to the fact that I-thoughts play an important role in our grasp of the difference even when we consider the case 'from the outside.' When thinking about Andrea's future we take Andrea's perspective in the following sense: *we use the conceptual resources of self-attribution in considering the question of her identity across time.* This idea will be elaborated in the following section.[10]

4. TRANSTEMPORAL SELF-ATTRIBUTION AND TRANSTEMPORAL SELF-IDENTIFICATION

Suppose you are in Andrea's situation and your brain will be divided and transplanted tomorrow. You wonder if you will ever wake up again after the operation. You wonder if you might wake up with the body of the L-person or with the body of the R-person. You have no difficulty to understand what would have to be the case if you wake up with the body of the L-person. In that case, when looking in the mirror after the operation you will see the L-person's face. You will see what is visible from the L-person's perspective. In that case, when you talk after the operation then you will be moving the L-bodies lips. You understand what would have to be the case for you to be the L-person by understanding the consequences of this assumption for your future. By understanding that being the L-person involves for you having all his or her future properties you gain a clear grasp (or so it seems) of how the world would have to be for the hypothesis 'I will be the L-person' to be true.

If this description is correct then we may say the following: You understand the assumption 'I will be the L-person' on the basis of understanding thoughts like 'I will have property P.' In other words and more precisely: you understand what has to be the case for your utterance 'I will be the L-person' to be true on the basis of your understanding of what would render your self-attribution 'I will have property P in the future moment m' true. We can formulate this claim in a more abstract way: transtemporal self-attributions (thoughts that can be expressed by sentences like 'I will have property P' or 'I had property P') are conceptually prior to self-identifications (thoughts that can be expressed by sentences of the form 'I will be P at moment m' or 'I was P at moment m'). Any person when thinking about his or her own future has an understanding of what makes

---

[10] The idea that we do understand the difference between the two possibilities is present in many discussions of personal identity and it is referred to by those who defend a non-reductionist view about transtemporal personal identity. Instances of this may be found in Chisholm (1970), Madell (1981), Williams (1970), and Swinburne (2006 and 2007). Parfit (1984) repeatedly stresses the intuitive appeal of the claim that there is such a factual difference but he argues that the intuition must be rejected.

thoughts of the second kind true on the basis of his or her understanding of what makes thoughts of the first kind true and only on that basis (and not vice versa).

A second point about transtemporal self-attribution is relevant in the present context. Your understanding of what has to be the case for your I-thought 'I will have property P' to be true in no way depends on the empirical criteria of transtemporal identity of subjects of experience that you implicitly accept. It does not matter if you accept for instance the psychological theory or the bodily theory of transtemporal personal identity. To see this point one may consider Shoemaker's example of the brain state transfer procedure (BST procedure).[11] You live in a society where people regularly get a new body and a new brain cloned from their own genes. They undergo a procedure where the old body is incinerated and the whole brain state of the original brain is transferred to the new brain. Suppose you believe in the psychological theory of personal identity and that you therefore expect that the procedure preserves identity. In that case you believe that for every property P at moment m of the person who will leave the BST machine your corresponding I-thought 'I will have property P at m' is true. Suppose now that one day you change your mind. A brilliant philosopher in debates of several nights has convinced you: the psychological theory of identity cannot be true. The only acceptable theory of personal identity says that your identity across time depends on bodily continuity defined in a sense that is not preserved in the BST procedure. You now think that your existence will come to an end once the BST machine has destroyed your original brain. You think that our conscious experience will stop forever during that procedure. You now believe that you will not have the properties of the person who will leave the BST machine. If P is an arbitrary property of which you know that it will be instantiated by that person at moment m, then before your change of mind about the criteria of transtemporal identity you were convinced that your thought 'I will have property P at m' is true. Now you are convinced that 'I will have property P at m' is false. You have changed your mind about what will be the case. But you have *not* thereby changed your understanding of the content of your own I-thought. Your conceptual grasp of what has to be the case for your I-thought to be true has not changed at all. What has changed is your opinion about the empirical criteria that are necessary and sufficient for your I-thought to be true. If this is true then we may say the following: our understanding of what makes our own I-thought about future properties (transtemporal self-attributions) true is invariant with respect to changes of the empirical criteria of transtemporal personal identity that we implicitly or explicitly accept. Our conceptual grasp of what has to be the case for the self-attribution 'I will smell the odor of basil at m' to be true does not depend on the criteria of transtemporal personal identity that we accept. Empirical criteria of identity across time do not enter the conceptual

---

[11] Shoemaker (1984: 109).

content of transtemporal self-attribution. They do not enter the way we conceive of what must be the case for a given transtemporal self-attribution to be true.

To see this clearly suppose the opposite were true. Suppose that the criteria of transtemporal identity that we accept did enter our conceptual grasp of what would have to be the case for the relevant I-thoughts to be true. It is quite obvious in what way these criteria would have to enter the conceptual content of the relevant I-thoughts. When thinking about your future properties before your change of mind in the example above, your thought 'I will have property P at moment m' would be a thought with roughly the same conceptual content as the thought you might express saying 'There will be a person at m standing in the relevant psychological relation to me who will have property P.' According to this proposal, to think that you will have P is to think that someone standing in a certain empirical transtemporal relation to you will have P. If this was the correct analysis of what you think then after your change of mind about the empirical criteria of transtemporal identity you would think a different thought (a thought with a different conceptual content) when thinking 'I will have property P.' What you then would think after your change of mind in having a thought expressible in these words would roughly given be the different sentence 'There will be a person at m standing in bodily continuity to me who will have property P.' We can see the inadequacy of theses glosses of the conceptual content of your I-thoughts in the following way. When you change your mind about the correct criteria of personal identity then you also change your mind about your own future. For any given property P that you believe will be instantiated by the person who leaves the BST machine you believe your thought 'I will have property P at m' to be true before your change of mind and you believe your thought 'I will have property P at m' to be false after your change of mind. You thereby change your mind about your actual future. There is some possible future fact that you believe to be true before your change of mind and that you believe to be false after your change of mind—or at least this is the way things appear to be according to your understanding of your own I-thoughts. You expect to wake up after the procedure before your change of mind and you do not expect to ever wake up again after your change of mind. You have thereby changed your mind about a specific feature—or so it seems—of the real course of future events. All this would however be wrong if the empirical criteria for transtemporal personal identity accepted by a person did enter his or her conceptual grasp of what has to be the case for his or her transtemporal self attributions to be true. We then would have to say that the thought you expressed saying 'I will have property P at m' before your change of mind is not the same thought that you express saying 'I will have property P at m' after your change of mind. If this was right then there really would be no conflict between the belief you expressed using these words before your change of mind and the apparently contrary belief you express uttering the negation 'I will not have property P at m' after your change of mind. It would be a mistake to think that you changed your mind about your own future. There is, according to that proposal, no fact about the future that you first believe to obtain and then believe not to obtain. If the proposal were correct then in thinking those thoughts it should not even seem to you as if there was such a possible fact that you changed your mind about. The reason is, quite simply, that according to the proposal, in using the same words 'I will have property P at m' you really express quite different thoughts. Before your change of mind you express the thought that there will be someone at m standing in a certain psychological relation to you who has P at m and you still believe this to be true after your change of mind. After your change of mind in using the words 'I will have property P at m' you express a quite different thought, namely, that some person existing at m and standing in a certain bodily relation to you will have property P, and you still believe *this* to be wrong. So there would be no fact or apparent fact about you that is true according to what you believe before your change of mind and that is false according to what you believe after your change of mind. I take this to be a clear reductio ad absurdum of the hypothesis that the empirical criteria of transtemporal identity for people accepted by a thinker enter the conceptual content of his or her I-thoughts about the future.

We thus have arrived at two related claims about the conceptual status of transtemporal self-attribution: transtemporal self-attribution is conceptually prior to transtemporal self-identification, and transtemporal self-attribution is invariant with respect to changes of accepted empirical criteria of transtemporal identity of people. This makes it easy to see why we grasp or seem to grasp a factual difference between P1 and P2 when the case is considered from the first person perspective. Whenever a person in the situation of Andrea thinks about his or her own future, the person has a clear positive understanding of what would have to be the case for his or her thought 'I will be the L-person' to be true. This clear positive understanding is due to his or her clear positive understanding of what has to be the case for certain I-thoughts of the form 'I will have property P' to be true. The latter I-thoughts do not in any way depend in their conceptual content on any empirical criteria of transtemporal identity. No empirical criteria of transtemporal identity enter the conceptual content of these thoughts. This is why we have no difficulty in grasping or at least apparently grasping the difference between the possibilities P1 and P2 when we consider the case from the first person perspective despite the fact that we assume that there is no relevant empirical difference between P1 and P2.

5. THOUGHTS ABOUT IDENTITY ACROSS TIME OF THINGS WITHOUT CONSCIOUSNESS

What has been said about conceptual priority and invariance with respect to changes in the acceptance of empirical criteria for first person thought is quite clearly false when transferred to thought about transtemporal identity of objects that we do not believe to be endowed with consciousness. This point is particularly clear if one considers the special case of socially constituted objects like swimming clubs or restaurants. Suppose a person, Giovanni, accepts as a necessary and sufficient condition for the identity of restaurants across time that the owner, the cook, and the name of the restaurant remain the same. According to his understanding a restaurant may move from Naples to New York. Suppose Giovanni changes his mind later on and now accepts that the surroundings and the interior decoration are essential properties of restaurants. The restaurant Lucia in Naples is closed in April 2008. The owner and the cook move to Little Italy and open a restaurant named 'Lucia' in May 2008. Before his change of mind with respect to the appropriate criteria of identity across time for restaurants Giovanni would have judged that the restaurant Lucia has opened its doors in New York in May 2008. After his change of mind Giovanni judges that the restaurant Lucia does not exist any more. Is there any fact of the matter with respect to which Giovanni has changed his mind? Do we have to assume that Giovanni will be under the impression of having changed his mind with respect to a factual issue? Obviously, the answer to both questions is negative. When Giovanni utters 'The restaurant Lucia will open its doors in May 2008 in New York' before his change of mind and when he utters the same sentence after this change of mind, then on these two occasions he expresses thoughts with quite different conceptual content. The conceptual content associated in Giovanni's thought with the sentence at issue changes with the modification of the criteria of identity for restaurants across time that he presupposes. There is no possible future fact with respect to which Giovanni has changed his opinion when he changed his mind about the appropriate criteria of identity for restaurants. Before his change of mind Giovanni's thought that the restaurant Lucia will open its doors in New York in May 2008 could be paraphrased saying that there will be a restaurant in New York named 'Lucia' and run by the same owner with the same cook that will open its doors in New York in May 2008. Giovanni has not changed his opinion with respect to this detail about the future. After his change of mind the thought expressed by the same words must be paraphrased quite differently: there will be a restaurant named 'Lucia' in the same location in Naples, with the same interior decoration, the same owner and the same chef cook which will open its doors in New York. This thought is trivially false and rejected by Giovanni before and after his change of mind. Reflection on this and further examples motivate the following claims. (1) In the case of thought about non-conscious individuals the conceptual content of transtemporal property attributions and of transtemporal identity statements changes with the accepted criteria of transtemporal identity. The latter can in principle be explained by reference to these criteria. (2) In the case of thought about non-conscious individuals transtemporal identification is conceptually prior to transtemporal property attribution. (1) and (2) explain why, when considering duplication cases for non-conscious individuals, we have no temptation to think that we can grasp a factual difference between the possibilities analogous to P1 and P2 when there is no relevant difference in the relations between the two successors and the original object. When a restaurant splits into two and both successors can be regarded with equal right as the original restaurant (the relevant empirical relations are symmetrical), there is no apparently open factual question about the original restaurant's identity.

6. FIRST-PERSON THOUGHT AND OTHER-DIRECTED THOUGHT

I have argued that transtemporal self-attributions and transtemporal self-identifications have a special conceptual status, which can be summarized by the following claims:

Claim 1: Transtemporal self-attribution is conceptually prior to transtemporal self-identification.

and

Claim 2: Transtemporal self-attribution is conceptually invariant with respect to changes in the thinker's accepted criteria of identity of people across time.

We may add a further claim that has not yet been explicitly mentioned. Since our conceptual grasp of our own transtemporal identity is based on our grasp of what has to be the case for certain transtemporal self-attributions to be true and since the latter are invariant with respect to the thinker's accepted criteria of transtemporal identity, self-identifications exhibit the same conceptual independence. We can thus add:

Claim 3: Transtemporal self-identification is conceptually invariant with respect to changes in the thinker's accepted criteria of identity of people across time.

I will now defend the view that these special traits of first-person thought carry over to other-directed thought.

I argued above that we understand the difference between P1 and P2 by taking Andrea's perspective. Taking her perspective in the relevant sense is a conceptual exercise that is natural for us or even forced upon us in other-directed thought. We use our conceptual resources given by the specific conceptual status of first-person thought in thinking about her. Andrea will have property F just in case her first-person thought 'I will have property F' should be made true by the future course of events. Given the specific conceptual status of first person thought each of us has a clear understanding (or seems to have a clear understanding) not only of how the world would have to be for one's own first person thought 'I will have property F' to be true but also of how the world would have to be for *her* first person thought 'I will have property F' to be true. In other-directed thoughts like 'Andrea will have property F' we fix reference to a particular subject, Andrea in this case, and then consider how the future would have to be for *that subject's* first-person thought 'I will have property F' to be true. To make this point one might say a bit paradoxically: in thinking about future properties of others we use first-person thought applied to them. (I use the phrase 'first-person thought' in the sense of thought in the first-person mode.)

If it is correct that we apply the resources of first-person thought in the sense just explained in other-directed thought, then of course the special conceptual status of first-person thought carries over to other-directed thought. Other-directed thoughts like 'A will have property P' and 'A had property P' are invariant—just like the corresponding first-person thoughts—with respect to changes in the accepted criteria of personal identity or subject identity. Accepted criteria of subject identity do not enter our understanding of what would have to be the case for these other-directed thoughts to be made true by the actual future course of events.

We can and we do use first-person thought applied to others independently of whether these others actually think or can think I-thoughts. It appears obvious that first-person thought applied to others is appropriate with respect to any conscious being independently of whether that subject is sufficiently sophisticated to think I-thoughts. In the case of a baby or a non-linguistic animal we may fix reference to that particular subject and wonder if the future is such that *its* first-person thought 'I will have F' if the subject at issue had that thought would correspond to reality. We then use the conceptual resources of first-person thought in application to a being that does not or cannot have the corresponding I-thought. We clearly are capable of thinking in that way and we clearly do think in that way all the time. Whenever we believe of a being that it is conscious we use the conceptual resources of first-person thought applied to it in the way described. A still stronger thesis appears adequate: to conceive of another being as a subject of experience partially consists in thinking about its past and future in that specific way. A being that is incapable of applying the conceptual resources of first-person thought to others does not have the full concept of a subject and cannot think of another being as a subject of experience.

We can now formulate the claims that state the transfer of the special status of first-person thought about the past and the future to other-directed thought. Given that transtemporal self-attribution is invariant with respect to changes of accepted criteria of personal and subject identity, other-directed thought—via the application of first-person thought to others—is also invariant with respect to changes of criteria of transtemporal personal and subject identity accepted by the thinker:

Claim 4: Transtemporal attribution of properties to other experiencing subjects is conceptually invariant with respect to changes in the thinker's accepted criteria of subject identity across time.

According to claim 4, if we take A to be conscious, then we conceive of what has to be the case for the thought 'A will have (or had) property P at m' to be true in a way that does not apply or presuppose any empirical criteria of transtemporal personal and subject identity. Since (a) we grasp what has to be the case for a conscious being to have the property F at a future moment m by grasping what has to be the case for its corresponding I-thought to be true and since (b) we grasp what has to be the case for another conscious being to be identical with a future subject on that basis, it follows that the conceptual priority of transtemporal property attribution carries over from first-person thought to other-directed thought. For the same reason the invariance of the conceptual content of thoughts about one's own past and future properties carries over to thoughts about transtemporal identity of other conscious beings. The following claims summarize the result of this transfer:

Claim 5: Transtemporal attribution of properties to others is conceptually prior to transtemporal identification with respect to others.

Claim 6: The conceptual content of other-directed transtemporal identitfication is invariant with respect to possible changes of the accepted criteria of subject identity across time. Transtemporal criteria of subject identity do not enter the conceptual content of other-directed transtemporal identification.

The preceding claims explain why we are under the impression that we have a clear positive understanding of the difference between P1 and P2. The cognitive appearance of grasping a factual difference between P1 and P2 has been explained by features of our conceptual architecture. Often in philosophy the explanation of cognitive appearances is intended as an error theory: the appearance is explained in a way that excludes its veridicality. The present explanation is not intended as an error theory. Nothing about the explanation of the appearance undermines the appearance. The explanation given is perfectly compatible with the claim that the cognitive appearance at issue is veridical and that we do grasp a substantial factual difference when comparing P1 and P2.

7. THE ILLUSION THEORY AND WHY IT CANNOT BE ACCEPTED

The following claim is hard to deny: it is appropriate to think about another individual's identity across time and about its past and future using the conceptual resources of I-thought just in case the other individual is conscious. It is precisely in that case that it makes sense to consider the individual's future from its perspective in the sense explained. To resist from thinking about another being in that particular way is to resists from conceiving it as a subject of experience.

In other words: To think of another being as having its own perspective in the sense of being conscious is incompatible with thinking about its identity across time without asking the question of its past and its future using the conceptual resources of first person thought. Using the conceptual resources of first-person thought is part of what it is to be aware in one's thinking of the fact that the other being too has its own 'point of view,' that it is a subject of experience. If this is correct then we are justified to make the following general claim:

> Claim 7: A thinker who conceives of another individual as conscious (as a subject of experience) necessarily uses the resources of first-person thought in his conception of the other individual's identity across time and in his conception of the other individual's past and future.

It is plausible to assume that the specific features of first-person thought pointed out above are essential features of first person thought. When for instance a subject thinks 'There will be someone at m in psychological continuity with me who will have property F,' the subject has a thought about itself, but its thought is not a first-person thought about its future. I propose to assume that fully developed self-conscious beings think about their future and about their past in terms of criterion-free I-thoughts ('criterion-free' in the specific sense given by the conjunction of claims 1, 2, and 3). We may summarize what has just been said in the following way: (a) to be a self-conscious thinker essentially involves thinking about one's own identity and about one's own past and future in a criterion-free manner; (b) to conceive of another individual as a subject of experience essentially involves using the conceptual resources of first-person thought in one's thinking about the other's identity across time and in one's thinking about its past and future. It follows from these two claims together with the explanation developed in the preceding section that a self-conscious individual capable of conceiving of others as subjects of experience cannot free itself from the cognitive impression that there is a factual difference between P1 and P2. In other words: any philosophical theory that denies that there is a factual difference between P1 and P2 attributes unavoidable error to every self-conscious thinker capable of conceiving of another being as an experiencing subject. There is then a sense in which a self-conscious thinker capable of conceiving of another as a subject of experience cannot seriously believe a philosophical account that denies the apparent factual difference between P1 and P2: a thinker of that kind—independently of his or her theoretical convictions—will always be under the impression that P1 and P2 are substantially different possibilities. In order to bring ourselves to seriously believe that the apparent capability to grasp what the difference consists in is illusionary we would have to lose the capacity to think about our own past and future in the first-person mode and we would have to lose the capacity to conceive of others as subjects of experience. There is reason to reject any theory that can only be seriously believed by beings that are conceptually impoverished in such a dramatic and undesirable manner.

To have a convenient term I will call the claim that there really is no factual difference between P1 and P2 the *illusion theory*. The illusion theory is appropriately so called since it says that the unavoidable cognitive appearance of grasping a factual difference between P1 and P2 is a cognitive illusion due to our conceptual architecture as self-conscious beings who can conceive of other beings as experiencing subjects. I just argued that there is good reason to reject the illusion theory since it attributes unavoidable cognitive illusion not just to the contingent human mind but to *any* self-conscious thinker capable of conceiving of someone else as conscious. At this point, however, it might be objected that the error attributed by the illusion theory is rather limited nonetheless. It only occurs when we consider strange science fiction cases. But this objection misses the point.

If the illusion theory is correct then our daily thoughts, perceptions, and emotional attitudes towards others are all infected by the illusion at issue. We have a criterion-free notion of identity across time of conscious individuals in the sense explained earlier. If the illusion theory is correct, then—contrary to what clearly appears to be the case—we cannot use that notion in order to grasp a fact that makes identity statements true. If the illusion theory is correct then our whole thinking about the past and the future of subjects of experience and about their identity across time including our first-person thought is based on an inadequate notion. The corresponding real facts about identity of conscious individuals (if there are any) are then constituted by relations that do not play any role in our understanding of what constitutes our continued existence. In all those cases in which we apply or presuppose that criterion-free notion we only seem to grasp a possible state of affairs.

Once we realize that the criterion-free notion of identity across time for conscious individuals is present not only in our thinking but also in our perceptions and emotions it becomes clear that the illusion at issue is still more general and deeper than one might think at first sight. When a person is touched by meeting a friend whom he or she has not seen since many years, the person perceives that friend *as identical* to the younger person he or she knew so well in the distant past. Perceiving the other person in the way that incorporates the criterion-free notion of identity is an essential component of that emotional experience. Following this line of thought it becomes clear that most of what we value in life would be based on a fundamental cognitive illusion if the illusion theorist were right.

The point that the illusion attributed to human thinking by the illusion theory is not restricted to isolated instances of theoretical reflection but rather concerns our whole cognitive and emotional life which would then be shot through with fundamental error can be made in a different way. It is an essential component of our concept of a subject that the identity of subjects can be grasped in the criterion-free way described. So if the illusion theory is correct then there really are no experiencing subjects in the sense of that notion which is deeply incorporated in our thinking and we are then constantly under a massive illusion when we conceive of ourselves as subjects of experience and when we conceive of the world around us as populated by subjects of experience. It seems clear that this is a fairly radical consequence of a philosophical theory. The evidence in favor of the illusion theory would have to be immense to make it acceptable despite its extreme, unbelievable, and counter-intuitive consequences. Quite obviously, however, there is no such massive evidence in favor of the illusion theory. Philosophers who explicitly or implicitly endorse the illusion theory are motivated by the suspicion that denying the illusion theory will lead quite directly into substance dualism. But the version of substance dualism supported by that denial is subject–body dualism in the sense explained earlier. Subject–body dualism is freed from many suspicious ideas that are usually associated with substance dualism. Furthermore, as briefly sketched at the beginning of the paper, subject–body dualism has independent support by other considerations.

8. HOW A DENIAL OF THE ILLUSION THEORY LEADS TO SUBJECT–BODY DUALISM

It remains to be shown that the acceptance of a factual difference between P1 and P2 has to be combined with subject–body dualism. In a first step we can see that the denial of the illusion theory implies that the subject is not identical with its body. We may assume as a premise that material bodies have empirical criteria of identity across time. According to this premise, the fact that a given material object at m1 is identical to a given material object at m2 consists in the fact that certain empirical relations obtain between the material object at m1 and the material object at m2. Suppose a situation is realized in which the description *D* is satisfied. Suppose that Andrea is identical to her body or some part of her body. Then, according to the assumption that material bodies have empirical criteria of identity across time, there could be a factual difference between P1 and P2 only if there was a difference in the empirical relations between Andrea and her two successors. But we had assumed perfect symmetry in these relations between Andrea and her two successors. So, if Andrea was her body or some part of her body, then P1 and P2 could not be factually different.

   This result is not sufficient to show that the denial of the illusion theory implies subject–body dualism. The result is still compatible with a number of accounts quite different from subject–body dualism. For instance, a functionalist analysis of personal identity is compatible with the claim that the person is not identical to her body or any part of her body since the empirical criteria of identity across time are different for material bodies and for people. Still the functionalist does not posit the existence of non-material individuals. But it is easy to see that the functionalist's analysis of personal identity is incompatible with the idea that there is a factual difference between P1 and P2. For the functionalist, the identity of Andrea with L-Andrea consists in the instantiation of certain causal relations (L-Andrea has memories caused by Andrea's experiences, L-Andrea's actions causally depend on Andrea's earlier intentions, etc.). So if functionalism was correct then there could be a factual difference between P1 and P2 only if there were a difference in the relevant causal relations between Andrea and her two successors. But we had assumed perfect symmetry in all empirical relations between Andrea and her two successors. So, if the functionalist account of personal identity was correct, then P1 and P2 could not be factually different.

A similar argument excludes the view that Andrea is constituted by some material thing just like a statue is constituted by the piece of bronze making it up at any moment of its existence. We may assume that the proponent of the constitution view accepts the following principle. If B is the body of a person P at a given moment m and there are two human bodies $B1$ and $B2$ at a moment m', and if $B1$ but not $B2$ constitutes the person P at m', then $B1$ and $B2$ must be different with respect to their empirical relations to the body B that originally constituted person P. For Andrea to be L-Andrea it is necessary that the L-body constitutes Andrea after the operation. So according to the constitution view there could be a factual difference between P1 and P2 only if there was a difference in the relation between Andrea's body before the operation and the R-body on the one hand and Andrea's body before the operation and the L-body on the other. But we had assumed perfect symmetry in all empirical relations between Andrea and her two successors. It follows that the constitution view too implies the illusion theory.

Obviously, a parallel argument can be repeated for any view about transtemporal subject identity according to which there are some empirical facts that constitute a subject's persistence. The only plausible alternative to any such reductionist account seems to be the view that there is a subject, which is distinct from its body, whose identity across time cannot be reduced to empirical relations, but which can be grasped by employing the resources of first person thought in the way described earlier.

9. WHY FOUR-DIMENSIONALISM DOES NOT HELP

The four-dimensionalist states that people are spatially *and* temporally extended. The four-dimensionalist can make sense of P1 and P2 in the following way. Andrea's use of 'I' and our use of her name do not have a definite referent; they can both be interpreted as referring to (a) Andrea's temporal parts before the operation united with L-Andrea's temporal parts after the operation and (b) Andrea's temporal parts before the operation united with R-Andrea's temporal parts after the operation. The four-dimensionalist may propose a third interpretation: Andrea's temporal parts united with the temporal parts of both successors. For simplicity we may confine the discussion to a version of the theory that states an ambiguity of the reference of 'I' in Andrea's thought and speech only between

(a) and (b). On this view whether we should say that P1 or rather P2 is realized depends on how we interpret the relevant singular terms in their use before the operation. If we interpret both singular terms along the lines of (a), then we may state that P1 is realized. If we interpret them along the lines of (b), then we may state that P2 is realized. Obviously, according to that analysis, there is no conflict between the two descriptions of the real course of events. We may say that P1 is realized when we interpret the name occurring in the corresponding description in one way and we may say that P2 is realized when we interpret the name in another way. So the four-dimensionalist view about the duplication problem is clearly a version of the illusion theory.[12]

Let me note in passing that the four-dimensionalist proposal is clearly inadequate if it is used to describe the cognitive content of I-thoughts and other-directed thoughts involved in reflections about Andrea's case. Any account of the conceptual content of these thoughts has to explain why P1 and P2 when considered from the first-person perspective as well as when considered from the third-person perspective clearly appear to be two substantially different possibilities. No such explanation can be given by reference to an ambiguity in the singular terms used before the operation. Suppose Andrea first believes that she will be L-Andrea and then believes that she will be R-Andrea. It clearly appears to her that she has changed her opinion about the future. When we use the four-dimensionalist account to describe the content of Andrea's thoughts, then we must say that there is no common content she has changed her mind about. What appears to her as a change of mind really would have to be an unnoticed change of the object of reference in her thought. But when considering the two possibilities, there is no change in her concept of herself corresponding to the shift of reference. The analogous observations apply to other-directed thought about Andrea's case. I conclude that the four-dimensionalist cannot explain the conceptual facts about I-thought and other-directed thought within his or her framework.

10. CONCLUDING REMARK

The argument presented in this chapter is not a conceivability argument. Conceivability arguments usually start with the claim that a certain scenario is conceivable without hidden contradictions. They then go on to argue that there is a real metaphysical possibility corresponding to the scenario that we can coherently conceive of. In the second step of conceivability arguments certain principles are evoked and applied which specify under what specific conditions the transition from conceivability to possibility is unproblematic.[13]

---

[12] For a four-dimensionalist treatment of the duplication problem compare Lewis (1976) and Lewis (1983c).

[13] Compare Chalmers (2002).

The first step in the present argument is not a claim about conceivability without hidden contradiction. The first step is an argument for the claim that we seem to grasp a specific factual difference between two possibilities. The second step in the present argument does not appeal to any general principles that allow in specific cases to proceed from conceivability to metaphysical possibility. Rather, the second step is based on the claim that any account that denies the veridicality of the cognitive impression of grasping the difference implies that our self-conception and our conception of others is deeply misguided, and that any self-conscious being capable of conceiving of another being as conscious is necessarily misguided in the same way. The argument proceeds by pointing out that any alternative to subject–body dualism would force us to accept that the most valuable aspects of our life are built upon a deep, permanent, and unavoidable cognitive illusion.

III

INTENTIONALITY, MENTAL CAUSATION, AND KNOWLEDGE

10

Burge's Dualism[1]

Bernard W. Kobes

1. INTRODUCTION AND GOALS

In his 1999 Presidential Address to the Pacific Division of the American Philosophical Association, Tyler Burge contrasted the inflated conceptions of both philosophy and humankind at the ends of the seventeenth, eighteenth, and nineteenth centuries—for example in the works of Leibniz, Fichte, and Bradley—with various twentieth century philosophical deflationisms. A task for philosophy, Burge proposed, is to articulate the specialness of humankind while avoiding the inflations of the past. For example, anti-descriptivism in philosophy of language, anti-individualism in philosophy of mind, and externalism in epistemology, exhibit 'how our natures are determined by norms that reach beyond what we as individuals control. We can better understand the ways that rational beings depend on a universe that is not made up of structures of reason at all.'[2]

An instance of this larger theme is the relation between Burge's anti-individualism about representational aspects of mentality and his proclivity for a weakly dualist position on the mind-body problem. My title, 'Burge's Dualism,' is perhaps hyperbolic, as one does not find in Burge's writings to date any unequivocal affirmation of mind–body dualism. One does find, however, a pervasive set of methodological stances, attitudes, and *dicta* congenial to dualism. One also finds a sharply delineated argument against the physicalist token identity theory, a set of reflections on mental causation that deflate the problem of how mental properties can be causally relevant in a fundamentally physical cosmos, and a more diffuse argument against a weaker materialism that takes the

[1] I wish to thank Torin Alter, David Braun, Derk Pereboom, and Steven Reynolds for helpful discussion of these matters. Most of the relevant papers are collected in Burge, *Foundations of Mind* (Oxford University Press, 2007).
[2] Burge (1999: 30).

mental to be composed of the physical. For these reasons I will continue to refer to 'Burge's dualism,' while acknowledging, in the end, a certain diffidence in his view of the matter.

After gathering Burge's dualist themes and anti-materialist arguments, I will present some prima facie resistance to Burge's doubts about material composition, and explore a way in which his stance might be developed to meet such resistance. I will not attempt a full-dress evaluation of Burge's dualism, which in any case would be premature. My goals are to organize the elements of Burge's dualist stance, to convey a sense of their depth and seriousness, and to gauge what further articulation and empirical confirmation would be needed to set the view among prominently available options for responding to the mind–body problem.

2. BURGE'S METHODOLOGICAL STANCE

Burge's dualism does not focus on phenomenal properties of conscious experience; he does not, for example, appeal to Cartesian or Kripkean intuitions about the conceivability of the physical and the phenomenal coming apart, or to the alleged explanatory gap between them, or to not knowing phenomenal facts despite knowing all pertinent physical facts. Burge's dualism, at least in his published writings to date, concerns intentional or representational aspects of mentality. It may be, however, that some of the considerations he brings to bear on intentional aspects will have analogues for phenomenal aspects of experience.[3]

One manifestation of twentieth century deflationism is the widespread presumption, in the latter half of the century, of materialism as a default presumption — the presumption that we ought to be physicalists if we can — and a preoccupation with physicalist sketches of mentality. Burge rejects the presumption of physicalism, which he sees as a pervasive ideology without clear foundation in either compelling a priori metaphysics or in successful explanatory practices.[4] Of Jaegwon Kim's assumption, typical of much contemporary philosophy, that the world is 'fundamentally physical,' Burge complains that the outlook is under-specified: 'There are many questions to be raised about this

---

[3] Burge has written two articles that include substantial discussion of phenomenal consciousness: 'Two Kinds of Consciousness,' *Foundations of Mind*: chapter 17, and 'Reflections on Two Kinds of Consciousness,' *Foundations of Mind*: chapter 18. Both articles take phenomenal consciousness to be the fundamental notion, but also articulate a distinct notion of rational-access consciousness. On p. 418 of the latter article, Burge rejects the supposition that understanding consciousness will require solving the 'hard problem,' so that consciousness will remain a cosmic mystery unless some sort of functional or neural reduction of the phenomenal is achieved. We do not yet know how to non-reductively systematize and integrate phenomenal consciousness with respect to empirical science. But we are beginning to understand mental representation this way, and we have no reason to doubt that this will be possible for phenomenal consciousness.

[4] See Burge (2007: 360), for strong statements along these lines.

idea and how it is supposed to apply to various cases (the mathematical 'world,' the 'worlds' of value, right and wrong, beauty, rational justification, semantics, indeed mind).'[5] 'It is not obvious to me,' he writes in discussing Descartes, 'that it is mistaken to suppose that mental agents and their mental powers, acts, and states are in no literal sense physical.'[6]

Burge's dualism is naturalistic, in a weak sense of that word:

The theme in naturalism that deserves the status of orthodoxy is not its materialism and not its demand that mentalistic discourse be given some ideologically acceptable underpinning. It is its implicit insistence that one not countenance any form of explanation that will not stand the scrutiny of scientific and other well-established, pragmatically fruitful methods of communal check and testing. (More crudely put, it is the opposition to miracles and to postulation of unverified interruptions in chains of causation among physical events.)[7]

The theme of epistemic reliance on our successful explanatory practices is fundamental and pervasive. Epistemic strength in philosophy derives, Burge insists, from our successful commonsense and scientific explanatory practices. Burge does affirm the possibility of substantial a priori metaphysical knowledge of the nature of the mental. But he holds that metaphysics ought to be pursued in an exploratory spirit, and with a sense of its own fallibility. Metaphysical principle is trumped by consideration of the nature and needs of successful explanatory practice.

The fullest expression of Burge's methodological pragmatism occurs in 'Individualism and Psychology':

Not just questions of supervenience, but questions of ontology, reduction, and causation generally, are epistemically posterior to questions about the success of explanatory and descriptive practices. One cannot reasonably criticize a purported explanatory or descriptive practice primarily by appeal to some prior conception of what a 'good entity' is, or of what individuation or reference should be like, or of what the overall structure of science (or knowledge) should turn out to look like. Questions of what exists, how things are individuated, and what reduces to what, are questions that arise by reference to going explanatory and descriptive practices.[8]

Burge accepts, at least for the sake of argument, a global supervenience of mental facts upon the totality of physical facts.[9] But from this, little of ontological or causal interest follows. Successful explanatory and descriptive practices occur at a variety of levels that, as a matter of empirical fact, proliferate and only occasionally reduce. This entrains a proliferation in our attributions of cause

---

[5] Postscript to 'Mind–Body Causation and Explanatory Practice,' Burge (2007: 368).
[6] 'Descartes on Anti-individualism,' Ibid.: 434.
[7] 'Philosophy of Mind: 1950–2000,' Ibid.: 447.
[8] Ibid.: 232. Burge traces this methodological pragmatism, insofar as it touches ontology, to Frege and to Quine.
[9] Ibid.: 369–70.

and effect and in our presumed ontology. 'The world is a rich and complicated place.'[10]

3. ANTI-INDIVIDUALISM

Burge has famously argued that mental states and events are individuated by broad features of the subject's physical, social, or historical environment. Mental states are not individuated purely by their physical, functional, or phenomenal features, insofar as these can be fully characterized apart from the subject's environment. This view is often described as anti-individualism about mental content, but the point directly concerns the natures of mental states and events as such, not merely their referents, and not merely their contents considered as *abstracta*. According to the view, there are deep individuative relations between features of a subject's environment and her representational mental states, considered in their representational aspect. Not only the referent, but also the *way* in which the referent is thought of or perceived, is environmentally individuated.

Individuation is typically mediated by (perhaps indirect) non-intentional, causal relations to things in the subject's environment. Such causal, non-intentional relations to represented things may be further mediated by the subject's linguistic community, or by the subject's species ancestors. Though causally mediated, individuation is not itself a form of causation, but rather conceptual or metaphysical determination of identity. The laws by which mental states are caused by environmental variables are not at issue here, still less 'nature versus nurture.' Individuation by reference to the environment can give rise to, and explain, failure of local supervenience. That is, neurological, narrow functional, and narrow phenomenal states may be held constant across worlds, while representational states vary in virtue of conceived environmental variation. But anti-individualism is a doctrine of how mental states are individuated, hence a doctrine of their nature, and not fundamentally about the role of a community, deference to experts, or failure of local supervenience.

Burge has developed and defended this view by means of a series of detailed and powerful thought experiments. The thought experiments come in four varieties: those that feature natural kind concepts, those that key on reliance on a linguistic community to fill out incompletely understood concepts, those that feature perceptual contents, and those that highlight the possibility of challenging even fully understood meaning-giving explications. Space limitations prevent detailed exposition of the thought experiments, but I will say a word about each type.

The first type of thought experiment resembles Hilary Putnam's famous Twin Earth thought experiments about the meanings of natural kind terms. In Burge's

---

[10] Burge (2007: 348). The quoted line, taken harmlessly out of context, is from p. 28.

version, a subject on Earth thinks a thought about a natural kind, for example that aluminum is a lightweight metal. We imagine that on Twin Earth a duplicate of the subject exists who is identical to her in all physical, functional, and phenomenal respects, insofar as these can be non-intentionally characterized. On Twin Earth, however, there is no aluminum; instead, there is a distinct metal that is similar to aluminum in superficial respects but that differs from aluminum in microstructure. The microstructural differences make for macro-level differences that could be detected by scientists, but these happen not to causally impact the subject differently from her twin. It is plausible that the twin does not think that aluminum is a lightweight metal. The subject and her twin think different thought types, despite being exactly similar in all individualistic respects. The difference, Burge argues, affects the representational character of thought; it is not merely a difference in reference, and in particular cannot be understood as a difference in indexical reference.

In the second type of thought experiment there are no differences in the environmental natural kinds on Earth as compared to Twin Earth. Instead, the subject thinks that he has arthritis in his thigh, but does not know that the word 'arthritis' correctly applies only to certain rheumatoid ailments of the joints. On Twin Earth, the subject is duplicated in all individualistic respects, but in that linguistic community the word 'arthritis' is standardly applied to a wider class of rheumatoid ailments, including the one that the subject and his twin have in their thighs. It is plausible that the Twin Earth subject does not think that he has arthritis in his thigh. So the subject and his twin think different thoughts, despite being exactly similar in all individualistic respects. The representational difference in this case derives from the subject's dependence on communal experts for the correct application of his concept, which he thinks with but has not completely mastered.

In the third type of thought experiment, Burge imagines a creature that is visually attuned to cracks, while its twin is visually attuned to shadows. The physical, functional, and phenomenal states of the creatures, insofar as these can be individualistically described, are imagined to be exactly similar. Burge argues that there is a difference in perceptual representation—how the creatures visually represent the world to be—and not merely a difference in the objects seen. The creature on Earth perceives cracks as cracks; its twin perceives shadows as shadows. Individuation of representational states is again mediated by non-intentional, causal relations to things in the environment, though in primitive perceptual cases the mediating causal relations may be borne by the creature's species ancestors.

Burge is not committed to the nomological possibility of failure of local supervenience in perceptual cases. For it may be that any environmental difference that makes an individuative difference to perceptual events also makes a correlative difference to neurological processing; thus local supervenience may be underwritten by the tight responsiveness of perceptual neural events to environmental variation. Even so, the thought experiments suggest that environmental differences directly, and not (and not via—hence 'directly') the neural differences, *best explain* the differences in individuation of perceptual states. In any case, vision science, especially in the research tradition emanating from Helmholtz and represented by David Marr, assumes or presupposes perceptual representational contents that are environmentally individuated, or so Burge argues.

In the fourth type of thought experiment, the subject has mastered communally agreed criteria for the proper application of a word or concept. He knows, for example, that competent speakers, including experts, take sofas to be pieces of furniture of such-and-such construction made or meant for sitting. But the subject doubts that these explications are correct, and concocts an alternative theory: the nature of sofas is to be works of art or religious artifacts of a certain sort. The subject's theory is false, but his twin's corresponding theory is correct: the nature of things called 'sofas' on Twin Earth *is* to be works of art or religious artifacts. Burge argues that the subject and his twin think thoughts of different mental types, despite being similar in all non-intentional respects, and despite knowing what are the communally agreed meaning-giving explications for 'sofa.' This thought experiment shows that incomplete mastery of concepts and dependence on experts, which figured in the arthritis thought experiment, are not necessary to exhibit the anti-individualistic phenomena. Meaning-giving explications can be challenged, as they are in the 'sofa' thought experiment, and it can be questioned whether communal patterns of use are as they should be. Mental states are individuated so as to allow for the possibility of such challenges. Meaning-giving explications are empirically substantial; they concern an external, objective subject matter, to which thinkers have independent, causally mediated access.

The four types of thought experiment variously manifest a unitary, deep feature of mental representation, namely, that we represent an objective subject matter, things whose natures are public and independent of any creature's mental events or representational acts. An objective, mind-independent world can be mentally represented only if the relevant mental states derive their natures in part from the natures of things represented. This derivation of natures is not systematically mirrored in the nature of some local neurological or functional substrate, nor in patterns of individual or communal use, nor in conceptual or linguistic mastery. Instead, there is a 'cognitive distance' between thinker and represented objects, so that mental individuation is directly mediated by non-representational relations between perceiver or thinker and represented objects.

4. AGAINST TOKEN IDENTITY

Anti-individualism, so understood, seems incompatible with the strongest kind of mind–body dualism, which employs the traditional conception of a substance as something capable of existing all by itself, without any other contingent thing of an equally basic ontological category. On the other hand, twentieth century materialism militated against recognition of anti-individualist factors in the individuation of mental states; conversely, anti-individualism poses obstacles to certain forms of materialism. Neural states and events are individuated relatively independently of the subject's environment. A neural state, whether type or token, does not partly derive its nature from the natures of things which the subject interacts with and represents. So if a mental state is environmentally individuated in the ways that Burge has argued it is, and if this is not merely a contingent feature of the state but part of its nature, then the relation between the mental state and any underlying neural state coincident with it cannot be identity.

The point is sharpest when local supervenience fails. Subject and twin can be imagined to share their neural states and events, even as their thought contents vary with imagined variation in the environment. A mental state is identified by its intentional content; having the content it has helps make it the mental state it is. The neural state could exist without the corresponding representational mental state. The mental state and the neural state have distinct modal profiles.

A similar modal argument seems to show that mental states cannot be identical to functional states, if functional states are identified narrowly, with the inputs being sensory stimulation and the outputs being muscular activity or bodily motion. For narrow functional states can stay constant across twins, even as mental kinds vary. A broader kind of functionalism that identifies inputs and outputs in terms of environmental kinds, and is also socially and linguistically distributed, might escape the most straightforward objection of this form, but such 'long-arm' functionalist proposals are excessively programmatic.[11]

A weak and widely held form of materialism identifies each mental token, each mental event in a subject on an occasion, with some neural event in the subject on that occasion. The 'token identity theory' is typically combined with a denial that mental types can be identified, or even universally correlated, with neural types. Burge argues, however, that a representational thought token cannot be identical to any neural token. For any plausibly relevant token neural event could occur in a 'twin' environment, construed here as a distinct possible world, such that the content of the thought token in that world differs from the content of the actual thought token, in virtue of environmental differences. The neural event could be the same token across worlds, even as the mental contents differ. In our descriptive and explanatory practices we commonly identify thought tokens by such basic factors as the relevant subject, time, and representational content. By contrast with, say, sentential forms, we have no other standard way to identify thoughts; in particular, we have no way to identify a thought so that it has its

---

[11] On the excessively programmatic nature of an externalized functionalism, see Burge (2007: 454).

content only contingently, and there is no reason to think that a future cognitive science will do so. So it is plausible that no thought token could have had a different content from the one it has. Indeed, Burge suggests that this is evident and a priori, and that to deny it would amount to changing the subject.[12]

I said that according to Burge, anti-individualism is fundamentally a thesis about the individuation of mental states, and not about failure of local supervenience. Anti-individualism is a precondition of mental representation of an objective, mind-independent world. The thought experiments display various kinds of cognitive distance between subjects and represented things. The cognitive distance phenomena show that mental states derive their natures in part from the natures of objective, mind-independent objects to which the subject stands in (perhaps highly indirect) causal, non-intentional relations. The same goes for tokens: a thought token's intentional content is part of its nature, so it derives its nature in part from the natures of objective, mind-independent external objects. But it is implausible to suppose that any neural token derives *its* nature in anything like this way. Our most basic ways of identifying neural tokens are through the descriptive and explanatory practices of neuroscience. This amounts to an anti-token-identity argument that does not exploit failure of local supervenience or distinctness of modal profiles. I am not aware of Burge having argued anywhere against token-identity in precisely this manner. But it seems to me that, for systematic reasons, he ought to be willing to accept this non-modal argument. This argument casts its dialectical net less widely, since it depends on a more theoretically embedded and perhaps less evident metaphysics; fewer may find its premises compelling. On the other hand, the argument may be more illuminating, supplying a deeper explanation of why mental and neural tokens are distinct.

5. MENTAL CAUSATION

Mental causation of physical events, and physical causation of mental events, have been seen as posing difficulties for dualism at least since Descartes. How could two such ostensibly different realms interact causally? Identifying mental events with physical events has often been thought to help solve puzzles of causal interaction. If mental event tokens are identical to physical event tokens, then causal interaction involving mental event tokens is just a species of causal interaction involving physical event tokens.

On the other hand, if mental properties are not reducible to physical properties, as token-identity theorists typically hold, then it can seem puzzling how mental properties can be causally relevant. If the causal efficacy of a mental token is

---

[12] Burge (2007: 157).

due to its physical nature, then it can seem that none of its causal efficacy is due to its mental nature. By such reasoning mental properties can come to seem epiphenomenal—merely along for the ride. Compare the manifestation of a phenotype in a biological parent; this feature does no causal work in effecting the inheritance of the characteristic by offspring. The real causation goes on at the level of genes. The agenda for much recent writing on mental causation has been set by the view that mental causation is underwritten by the physical natures of mental tokens, and that if mental properties are not reducible to physical properties, then their causal relevance is indirect at best.

Burge holds that these worries about epiphenomenalism show a loss of perspective, a set of misplaced epistemic priorities. What we know about mental causation derives primarily from mentalistic explanatory practices, commonsense and scientific. Psychology employs an intentional idiom, deepening and refining its explanations of thought and action in representational terms. This is an adequately robust scientific enterprise, with no serious sign that it will ever be supplanted by any non-intentional explanatory practice, and its explanations are causal on their face. We can be justifiably confident, therefore, that mental causes can have mental effects, and sometimes physical effects, and that mental properties are causally relevant. This is also a presupposition of our status as agents, and a precondition of our rational deliberations having any point. Mental causation does not stand in need of being underwritten by the physical nature of mental tokens.

A variety of metaphysical principles have been employed to cast doubt on the possibility of irreducible mental properties being causally relevant: that, for example, the causal ancestry and causal posterity of a physical event can consist only in other physical events physically described, or that there is a tension between a mental event M's being instantiated *because of* its physical supervenience base, and M's being instantiated *because of* some prior mental event. Kim has argued that such principles pose a credible threat to the causal relevance of mental properties, and has argued further that in responding to the threat we learn that token physicalism is not physicalism enough. We need a reduction of mental properties ultimately to physical properties; mental properties are causally relevant, on Kim's view, but only insofar as they reduce to physical properties.

Burge responds that the appearance of a threat to the causal relevance of mental properties is bogus. What we know from explanatory practice is far more secure than any metaphysical principle that has been employed to conjure up the appearance of such a threat. Burge also subjects the metaphysical principles to specific, searching criticism. Some fail to adequately distinguish distinct levels of explanation and cause, which may coincide on an effect without any objectionable or coincidental kind of over-determination. Some fail due to illicitly treating mental causation as supplying some extra bump or energy that would interfere with physical causation. Some fail to adequately distinguish causation from the kind of determination that characterizes the supervenience relation. Kim holds, for example, that there is a tension between 'horizontal determination,' a mental event M's causing a later mental event M^*, and 'vertical determination.' M^*'s synchronic dependence on its neural supervenience base P^*. Kim's resolution of the tension proceeds by way of the principle that M causes M^* by way of M's supervenience base P causing M^*'s supervenience base P^*. But given anti-individualism this resolution of the alleged tension is not credible, Burge argues, for a belief or thought will typically have an intractably complex supervenience base, spread over large expanses of space and time.[13]

The upshot, according to Burge, is that materialist theories of mind have failed to illuminate mental causation, despite that being advertised as a key point in their favor. Important metaphysical questions about mental causation remain open. Burge acknowledges that physics is gapless, that physical causes do not leave openings for mental causes to fill. The physical asymmetrically sustains the mental, and global supervenience is presumably true. But these weakly naturalistic points show little about the nature of mental–mental or mental–physical causation, and are in any case poorly understood. Mental and physical causes are not basically 'the same,' but neither are they 'in tension.' How mental causation is to be understood in relation to physical causation is a real issue. Mental and physical causes operate systematically in concert, are not in competition, and do not trade in massive coincidences. A metaphysical understanding of how this occurs, from a perspective that encompasses multiple levels simultaneously, is to be desired.

6. DOUBTS ABOUT MATERIAL CONSTITUTION

A still weaker form of materialism than token identity holds that mental states and events are *constituted* or *composed* of physical—presumably neural—states and events. Compositional materialism seems to escape Burge's argument against token identity, because the same neural complex may compose one mental token in the actual world, and a distinct mental token in the twin world. Since composition is not identity, a mental event token may derive its nature in part from the natures of represented things in the environment, while the neural event token that composes it does not. Perhaps compositional materialism about the mental will help us understand how mental and physical causes can operate systematically in concert, without competition or coincidence. Presumably too it will help us understand the asymmetrical dependence of the mental on the physical. Certainly we can manipulate the mental by manipulating the neural in an intricate variety of healing, useful, recreational, nefarious, or tragic ways. This too is a matter of a successful scientific explanatory enterprise.

---

[13] Burge (2007: 374).

In several places, however, Burge expresses doubt about compositional materialism. He notes that the paradigm of decomposition of material objects into physical particles does not apply straightforwardly to properties or events, let alone to numbers, intentional contents, and methods.[14] We do not identify thoughts by their physical compositions or constitutions. The Battle of Hastings, and the emergence of North America as a continent, resemble thoughts in being non-individualistically individuated. But they are plainly physical and are typically identified by their physical parts, and in this respect they contrast with mental events.[15] Some physical events, such as particular 'wars, avalanches, thunderstorms, meal cookings,' may not fall under the kinds of any natural science, yet they, unlike psychological states, explicitly and obviously involve ordinary physical properties that are used in explanations in the physical sciences.[16]

Material constitution is a scientific notion with specific explanatory uses in, for example, chemistry and physiology. We explain how chemical and physiological kinds interact by reference to their physical constitutions. How molecules interact with each other, and how atoms interact with each other, is explained by how their respective component parts interact.[17] But actual successful mentalistic explanations, commonsense or scientific, do not appear, on their face, to refer to material compositions of mental states.[18] Moreover, intentional mental states often serve as explanantia, not merely as explananda; they enter substantially into explanations, with no reference made to their putative material parts.[19]

Burge understands Descartes to hold that the individuation of particular minds is primitive: a mind is an agent of particular mental acts. 'I believe that Descartes may be on to something important in regarding thinkers as consisting not in some special sort of stuff, but in particular instances of the special type of agency, power, consciousness, and point of view involved in thinking.'[20] This suggests a view on which the fundamental sortals in psychology will key on power and point of view, not constitution. The view marks a distinction between psychology and material sciences such as chemistry, physiology, and geology, in which constitution sortals play a fundamental explanatory role. The manipulation of neural events to effect mental changes, and the study of neural activity through imaging technologies such as fMRI, aim to specify the subvening neural events that sustain thought—where thought is conceived as the activity of a mental agent. But it would be a mistake, on the Cartesian conception to which Burge is tempted, to think of such subvening events as what thoughts or mental agents *consist in*. Our most fundamental explanations of mental activity allude to factors such as having reasons, and not explicitly to the matter that thoughts ostensibly comprise, in the manner of chemistry and other sciences of matter.

---

[14] Ibid.: 357, note 14.   [15] Ibid.: 229–30.
[16] Ibid.: 357.   [17] Ibid.: 359.
[18] Ibid.: 230, both main text and note 7 on that page.
[19] Ibid.: 361, note 15.   [20] Ibid.: 433.

There is an epistemic possibility that we will some day make explanatory use of material constitutions of mental states, but Burge sees no positive reason to expect that this will be a feature of a fully developed psychology. To expand our sense of the relevant possibilities, he writes:

Maybe science will never make use of anything more than limited correlations with the lower, more automatic parts of the cognitive system. Maybe identities or part–whole relations will never have systematic use. Maybe the traditional idea of a category difference will maintain a presence in scientific practice.[21]

These remarks convey something of the open, questioning, exploratory nature of Burge's doubts about physical composition of the intentional.

It can seem, however, that these doubts leave us with an enervated conception of the explanatory goals of cognitive neuroscience. It remains less than satisfyingly clear how material composition of intentional events could turn out empirically false, assuming that more basic events can compose or constitute higher level events. Composition is, after all, even weaker than token identity, and the considerations Burge adduces turn on intentionality, not the peculiarities of phenomenal character. Surely some principle of theoretical simplicity or unification favors material composition, even if full-fledged ontological reduction is frustrated by the argument against token identity. There is no shortage of events going on in the brain to do the constituting work, and if our actual future science never makes use of intentional-neural correlations, that may reflect some merely practical limitation. In response to these points of prima facie resistance I will sketch a metaphysical picture that, if it turns out to be empirically accurate, would vindicate, I suggest, Burge's doubts about physical composition.

7. HOW MATERIAL COMPOSITION OF THE INTENTIONAL COULD BE EMPIRICALLY FALSE

Doubts about material composition can be seen as an effort to free our metaphysical and empirical imaginations, to open us up to alternative possibilities in a philosophical climate in which it is difficult to see how cognitive neuroscience could fail to support, at the very least, material composition of intentional tokens. To help make the possibility vivid I invoke a 'mathematical archangel' (C. D. Broad's term), a being with unbounded logical and mathematical abilities, who begins with only the complete facts about fundamental physical objects, events, fields, laws, and causes over all of space and time. This idealized calculator is a (dispensable) heuristic device to depict a conjectured order of metaphysical explanation. The archangel can compute the chemical and physiological facts, I suppose, up to and including the biological and neural facts over a community

---

[21] Ibid.: 360.

of psychological subjects. Assuming global supervenience of the intentional psychological on the physical, and skirting issues of phenomenal character, I further suppose that he can compute the intentional facts over the community of subjects.

The crux is whether in doing so the archangel has available a 'compositional short-cut' at the neural level, that is, whether he could in principle discern at the neural level, prior to attributing propositional attitudes to the subjects, a network of states and events that interact causally, and that are candidates for composing or constituting the intentional states and events to be attributed at a later stage of the computation. Having first identified these discrete neural states and events, the archangel could later see them as constituting intentional mental states and events, identifying the latter by reference to environmental kinds, in anti-individualistic fashion. The actual progress of cognitive neuroscience may support this metaphysical picture—but then again, it may not. It may instead support an alternative picture in which the archangel must first reconstruct the intentional psychology of his subjects, attributing propositional attitudes in something like the way we attribute them in commonsense discourse and in intentional psychology. On this second picture, not even an idealized calculator with perfect knowledge of the basic physical facts could compute, in advance of intentional psychology, particular discrete neural events that compose or constitute particular intentional events.

The suggestion here is not that any sort of mental fact would be forever closed to the archangel, but only that we can understand failure of material composition as the unavailability to the archangel of any prior neural identification of intentional events. Compositional materialism is false just in case the archangel would have to first recapitulate our interpretive practices and intentional psychology, and only then, if at all, seek neural event correlations. The archangel may have initially available no 'handle' on a token intentional event other than such features as its subject, time, and representational content. The intentional theory the archangel constructs may be identical to, or close to, ours. Perhaps, indeed, the archangel must attribute intentional states to the subjects, and simultaneously attribute a systematic practice of intentional *attribution* to those subjects; the intentional events themselves, and subjects' practices of attributing and self-attributing them, may be metaphysically intertwined. But this latter hypothesis is ancillary to the main proposal. If token neural correlates can be found at all for token mental events, the direction of metaphysical explanation is from mental events and their causal patterns to the correlated neural events. By contrast, the archangel first identified chemical and physiological kinds and their instances by their physical components, distinctively arranged.

Indeterminacy of the sought-for neural tokens may frustrate the archangel's search for principled local correlations for particular thoughts; he may not even find plausible candidates for material constitutions of particular thoughts. Given anti-individualism, a thought event m will have no minimal supervenience base *n* within the brain—no smallest neural event *n* such that *m* will occur in any possible world in which *n* occurs. It would be a mistake, moreover, to think of thought tokens as in part environmentally constituted, as smeared out over the world. The individuating factors may involve vast tracts of space and time, without discrete or natural boundaries. Individuation may be mediated by causal factors, such as patterns of deference within a community, distinct from the individual subject's thought. The suggestion of 'smeared constitution' appears to conflate individuation and reference; recall that anti-individualism concerns not only reference, but also the way in which the referent is represented.

Some principle would therefore be required to demarcate the boundaries of the inner neural event that composes a particular thought. But we have no advance guarantee that such determinate boundaries exist. Thoughts often seem to involve mental agency, and mental agency may not be explicable in terms of causal interactions among sentences in a neurally instantiated language of thought. If thoughts are mental acts, it may be unclear how much of the agent to include in the neural composition of the thought. Moreover, if a thought includes the exercise of constituent concepts, then the thought's neural constitution would presumably include neural proper parts corresponding to the exercise of those concepts. But the archangel may lack any principled way of demarcating the boundaries of neural events whose neural part–whole relations respect the thought's conceptual structure. The relation between a thought and its constituent concepts is distinct from the relation between the thought and its putative neural composition, or the relation between an underlying neural event and its neural components. It is an open empirical question whether these can be brought into non-arbitrary alignment.

In any case anti-individualism helps dispel any lingering suggestion that a thought *must* derive its identity and determinacy from its neural constitution. For if an intentional mental event inherits its nature in part from environmental things it is about, then that is an independent source of the event's identity and determinacy. (Here it is worth noting that, while the Kripkean judgment that *this table* could not have been made from a different block of wood has considerable pre-theoretic appeal, the judgment that *this thought* could not have been subserved by a different neural event lacks equivalent pre-theoretic appeal.[22]) The thought is the event that it is, partly because of its having inherited its nature from things it represents, and does not *stand in need* of material constitution to underwrite its status as an entity. An eliminativist strain in American philosophy of mind since Quine holds intentionality hostage to the demand that it stand in a properly disciplined relation to the behavioral or neural realms. Burge's dualism consists partly in his preparedness to jettison even the weakest such

[22] Kripke (1980: 113–14).

demand—material constitution—if it does no explanatory work of a certain kind, and to let intentional explanations stand on their own.

The distinctive kind of explanatory work that, according to Burge, is done by the notion of composition gives rise to an independent doubt about material composition of intentional events, a doubt that could persist even if we assume that the archangel does, in the end, compute principled and determinate correlations between intentional and neural events. Recall the point that we explain the causal interactions of chemical and physiological kinds in terms of their material composition, and similarly for geological, astronomical, and neural kinds. We do not, however, explain the causal interactions of intentional states in terms of their material composition, at least not yet. We can understand the causal necessity of a chemical interaction over time as deriving from the causal necessity of interactions at the atomic level. But mental states are often brought in as explanantia, without explicit reference to underlying neural events. Would the archangel's intentional-neural correlations do any explanatory work analogous to that of composition in familiar sciences of materially constituted things?

This is an open empirical question. The actual progress of cognitive neuroscience may support the following metaphysical picture. The archangel's intentional-neural correlations yield an account of how neural events asymmetrically and synchronically sustain certain intentional mental events, but do not illuminate diachronic causal relations among them. Neural events $n1$ and $n2$ may sustain intentional mental events $M1$ and $M2$ respectively, where $M1$ causes $M2$, but $n1$ may not appear to the archangel as, in any illuminating sense, *the cause* of $n2$. It is compatible with this to suppose that $n1$ is counterfactually relevant to $n2$, in this dime-a-dozen sense: had $n1$ not occurred, $n2$ would not have occurred. Thus $n1$ may be among a plethora of neural events that are *causally* relevant to $n2$, without yet being fore, rounded as *causing $n2$*. It is even compatible with this that $n1$ might be seen by the archangel as being, in a derivative and retrospective sense, *the cause* of $n2$, in light of the previously computed causal relation between $M1$ and $M2$. But if $n1$ had been, in any illuminating sense, the cause of $n2$, then the archangel would have been able to compute that fact prior to computing the subject's intentional psychology, and *ex hypothesi* no such computation was available to him. Only after $M1$ and $M2$ had been anti-individualistically computed did the relation between $n1$ and $n2$ come to the fore.

What is distinctive in this metaphysical picture is that although specific neural events asymmetrically and synchronically sustain corresponding intentional mental events, intentional causal relations stand on their own, without needing or deriving support from causal relations at the neural level. The necessity that attaches to intentional mental causal transactions is *sui generis*, and need not derive from the necessity that attaches to neural causal transactions. The notion of constitution is conceptually linked to distinctive kinds of diachronic causal explanation, so we have depicted a world in which the intentional is not materially constituted. Again, the heuristic device of the mathematical archangel is meant to vividly depict certain possible patterns of metaphysical dependence. The depicted metaphysical dependencies are inspired by, and expand on, Burge's expressed doubts about whether intentional mental events are materially constituted. Whether these possible metaphysical dependencies are actual is an open empirical question.

8. THE INTENTIONAL IN A PHYSICAL COSMOS

The metaphysical picture here sketched conflicts with a physicalist account of the explanatory goals of cognitive neuroscience, and how that discipline illumines the nature of thought and intentional causation. But the worry that it leaves us with an enervated conception of the deepest explanatory goals of cognitive neuroscience is ill-founded. We may hope for a richer understanding of the asymmetric synchronic sustenance of the intentional by the neural; in this sense we gain an understanding of how our mental lives are *possible*. We may particularly hope for a more articulated understanding of the *compatibility* of the intentional and the neural, how it is that they do not pull apart from each other. For the question why they do not pull apart can retain its grip on us even after we acknowledge that the necessity of intentional causation does not derive from that of physical causation, and does *not* depend on physical notions such as energy transfer. Neural events sustain mental events without suffering interference. The physical goes on in the way that it will, without coincidences or inexplicable miraculous parallelism. We may see cognitive neuroscience as fleshing out in satisfying detail these skeletal points, even if the science turns out not to illumine the identity or constitution of mental events, or the nature of mental causation.

It is worth emphasizing that substantial chunks of the physicalist world picture are not being called into question here. A Burgean dualist may hold that (a) there is no old-fashioned mental substance capable of existing by itself, no 'ectoplasm'; (b) the intentional globally supervenes on the physical; (c) the physical is causally gapless at its own level, modulo quantum indeterminacy; and (d) intentional mental events are synchronically and asymmetrically sustained by neural events. An appropriately qualified desideratum of theoretical simplicity in physics and metaphysics may be satisfied by these points. Of course our metaphysics must not depict the world as simpler than it is, given evidence that it is a 'rich and complicated place.'

It will be evident that Burge's position on the mind–body problem is a quite weak form of dualism. Combined with the four theses of the previous paragraph, it could aptly be described as an extremely weak form of physicalism, to contrast it with inflated dualisms of past centuries. Perhaps that accounts for a note of diffidence in Burge's position, as when he writes,

It seems to me that philosophers should be more relaxed about whether or not some form of materialism is true. I think it a thoroughly open—and not very momentous—question whether there is any point in insisting that mental events are, in any clear sense, physical. . . . What matters is that our mentalistic explanations work and that they do not conflict with our physicalistic explanations. But it serves no purpose to over-dramatize the conflict between different ontological approaches. . . .[23]

Of course the particular arguments and positions on individuation, identity, causation, and constitution are what matter. There is nevertheless a certain drama to the larger conception in which these philosophical particulars are set. According to that larger conception we can sketch metaphysical pictures of how irreducibly intentional events and causal processes might arise and persist within a fundamentally non-intentional physical cosmos. We thereby depict a way in which 'rational beings depend on a universe that is not made up of structures of reason at all.'

---

[23] Burge (2007: 360).

11

Modest Dualism[1]

Tyler Burge

I am grateful to Bernard Kobes for his sympathetic and insightful survey, 'Burge's Dualism.' He presents concise sketches of my methodology, my views on mind–body causation, and my argument from anti-individualism against materialist token identity theories. I will comment briefly on each of these three topics before centering on his primary contribution—his discussion of compositional materialism. Then I will present a new line of thought on the mind–body problem.

My methodology requires metaphysical *claims*, as distinguished from metaphysical speculation and heuristic guidance, to be grounded as closely as possible in specific knowledge that resides in explanations and judgments in science and common sense. The history of philosophy has shown that a metaphysics that either goes it on its own or takes off from insufficiently specific features of science and common sense tends to be wayward.

Our best understanding of causation comes from reflecting on good instances of causal explanation and causal attribution in the context of explanatory theories. Similarly, our best understanding of what sorts of things exist comes from reflecting on ontological commitments of explanations in science, or clear-cut judgments in common sense. Ontological commitments are what must be the case if such explanations or judgments are to come out true. Of course, both scientific explanations and common-sense judgments are fallible. And sometimes they are reduced to other forms of explanations or judgments. Science and common sense remain our best epistemic routes to understanding both causation and ontology.

Understanding mind–body and body–mind causation is philosophically important and difficult. But such understanding has regularly been distorted by antecedent metaphysical commitments. Thus Descartes' account of mind–body causation as a relation between two self-sufficient substances over-dramatized the problem, to the detriment of nearly all subsequent discussions. The claim of some modern materialists that mental events, properties, and kinds must be associated with a physical mechanism if they are to have causal upshot raises

---

[1] I thank Ned Block for several astute critical comments on an earlier draft.

the concern that mental attributes are in themselves irrelevant to mind–body or body–mind causation. Neither approach sufficiently grounds its metaphysics in what is known from psycho-physical explanation. We should start with our knowledge that there are causal interactions among psychological events and between psychological events and physical events, and try to understand the interactions in light of scientific explanations and common-sense judgments.[2]

I continue to think that my old argument against the materialist token identity theory is sound. Indeed, it seems to me decisive. Any given token physical neural event that is a candidate for being identical with a mental event could have been associated with different causal antecedents in the distal environment from those it in fact had. The different causal history could have been part of a pattern of physical or social environmental relations that constitutively determined a different kind of mental event, with different representational content. Mental events are different events if they have different representational contents. Such differences in distal causal history are not constitutively determinative of the identity and kind of the neural event. The same type and token neural event could have derived from various causal histories, of the sort that determine different mental events, type and token. So the given neural event could exist in a situation in which the mental event with which it is supposed to be identified did not occur, and in which some other mental event (with a different representational content) occurs instead. So the neural event is not identical with the original mental event. The argument is general. So token neural events are not identical with token (representational) mental events.[3]

Kobes expounds a closely related argument: token physical events in the brain are not constitutively dependent for having the natures that they have on relations to specific attributes in the physical or social environments. Representational mental events are constitutively dependent for having the natures that they have on such relations. Token events are different if their natures are. So token physical events in the brain and representational mental events are not identical.

I think that this argument is implicit in the argument that I gave against token identity theories in 'Individualism and the Mental.' The modal points made in the first argument were grounded in my view of the natures—or basic explanatory attributes—cited in the second. Kobes in effect emphasizes the different forms of individuation in different sciences, and emphasizes that the modal argument that I gave has its underpinnings in the different identity conditions of basic explanatory kinds referred to in the sciences.

---

[2] For elaboration of these points see my 'Mind–Body Causation and Explanatory Practice' and 'Postscript to "Mind–Body Causation and Explanatory Practice,"' both in Burge (2007).

[3] The argument was first given in 'Individualism and the Mental,' section IV, in Burge (2007). The argument is further defended and elaborated in 'Mind–Body Causation and Explanatory Practice.'

I focus now on Kobes's interesting and, I think, successful attempt to give some substance to my doubts about a materialist view that does not maintain *identities* between mental and physical states or events, but holds that mental states and events are *composed* of physical entities. Call this view *compositional materialism*. This view is less committal than the materialist token identity theory. A statue could be composed of marble. The statue is not identical with the marble. The same marble could have composed a different statue, or no statue at all. Then the marble would have existed but the statue would not have existed. The statue is materially composed of the marble. So identity is a stronger relation than material composition.

The natural sciences are built on the view that more complex material entities, such as planets, crystals, and plants are materially composed of material parts. Chemistry and physics were conceived in terms of material composition from the beginning. Some biologists once thought that explaining life would be a problem for compositional materialism in biology. But that view was never a majority position. The idea that plants are to be understood in terms of some soul or entelechy within them that is not composed of material entities has never had a serious foothold in western thinking, at least since early-modern science; nor should it have.

Because the framework of material composition has been explanatorily successful in the natural sciences, it is prima facie reasonable as a heuristic strategy to explore whether relations of material composition hold between psychological entities and neural or chemical entities. But *belief* in compositional materialism at this stage of inquiry seems to me not to be reasonable. The difference is between heuristic worth-trying and having reason for belief.

In the first place, the entities that psychology theorizes about (psychological states and events) are not perceived as material in the way that planets, salt crystals, and plants are. Although much of the *evidence* for psychology is physical movement conceived functionally (more specifically, as behavior), what psychology tries to understand and explain, and what it theorizes about, is not perceived or introspected as material.

In the second place, there are prima facie differences between psychology (sociology, economics, and so on), on one hand, and the natural sciences, on the other, that ground caution about *assuming* that material composition is the right relation between psychological events and brain events, merely on the basis of the success of the framework of material composition in the natural sciences. There are widely articulated problems in understanding how consciousness and qualitative states can be understood as materially composed. And there are attributions of reason in parts of psychology that have no analog in the natural sciences. Material composition is not a relation that grounds theorizing in mathematics or logic. As will emerge later in this chapter, I think that because psychology makes essential reference to structures from these disciplines, there is some question whether a framework of material composition applies within relevant areas of psychology. In sum, the prima difficulties in construing psychology in terms of a material-compositional framework—difficulties that have concerned philosophers for centuries—are much more substantial than they ever were in biology.[4]

In the third place, there are large areas of psychology in which compositional materialism has literally no positive support in the explanations or methods of the science. Although there are limited correlations between neural events and low-level sensory states, which give some hope to a material-compositionalist view about them, the view has no positive support in science as applied to propositional thought, and nearly none as applied to consciousness.

I believe that there is no good reason to believe compositional materialism. I think, however, that it is the least implausible form of materialism about the mind. I will pursue critical discussion of the view as applied to *propositional thought*, an area where it seems to me to be particularly doubtful. Kobes concentrates his attention on this area, and I join him in this focus.

I like Kobes's approach. He explores ways the world could empirically turn out to be, avoiding strong commitment to any of the ways. Unlike most authors who have written on this topic, Kobes does not claim more than he or anyone has good and specific reason to believe.

Kobes introduces a highly knowledgeable mathematical archangel as a heuristic device. He proposes two scenarios. On both, the archangel can use facts about fundamental physical entities over all of space–time to compute chemical and biological facts, including neural facts, regarding a community of psychological subjects. On both scenarios, Kobes stipulates that assuming global supervenience of the representational aspects of psychology on the physical, and bracketing issues regarding phenomenal character, the archangel can also compute the representational facts over the community of subjects. The two scenarios differ over what neural states and events that systematically correlate with the representational facts are computed *from*.

On the first, the archangel can discern at the neural level, prior to attributing propositional attitudes to the subjects, a network of states and events that interact causally, and that are candidates for composing the intentional [representational] states and events to be attributed at a later stage of the computation.

The idea is that the archangel computes certain salient, discrete neural states and events in a causal network. At a later stage of the computation—a stage that invokes psychological kinds and principles—the already distinguished neural states and events can be seen as specifically correlating with representational

---

[4] There have been massive attempts in mainstream philosophy since the 1950s to show that worries about materialism are just mistaken. I think that in some cases the attempts succeed in showing that certain a priori arguments in favor of dualism are unsound. And in some cases, the attempts set out prima facie empirically possible materialist pictures regarding *certain* psychologically relevant phenomena. The attempts have, in my view, failed to give good reasons for believing any form of materialism about the mind.

states and events that are individuated anti-individualistically. And at this later stage the correlated neural states and events can be seen as materially composing the representational states and events.

On the second scenario, the archangel cannot compute, without using principles from representational psychology, neural events that form patterns that naturally correlate with the representational states and events. The archangel cannot, independently of psychological concepts and principles, identify a pattern of neural events that correlates structurally with states and events in the psychologically identified structure.

Kobe proposes, 'compositional materialism is false just in case the archangel would have to first recapitulate . . . intentional psychology, and only then seek neural event correlations.' In the second scenario, 'if neural correlates can be found at all for token mental events, the direction of metaphysical explanation [would be] from mental events and their causal patterns to the correlated neural events.' In the first scenario, just as the archangel first identifies 'chemical and physiological kinds and their instances by their physical components, distinctively arranged,' so the archangel identifies, without using psychological kinds or principles, distinctively arranged material items that can later be seen to correlate with and compose instances of psychological kinds.

The key issue for Kobes is whether there are principles, other than psychological ones, for independently demarcating boundaries of neural events and states that are the units out of which psychological events and states are (and are later seen to be) composed. Kobes holds that if demarcation of neural correlates is possible only with help of psychological principles, compositional materialism is false. I believe that his idea is that if ideal non-psychological explanations in science do not independently identify the material complexes that correlate with (and compose) psychological states and events, there is reason to believe that compositional materialism is not true. He holds that the explanatory question is empirically open.

A second issue, which Kobes takes to be independent, is this. Even if the archangel 'computes principled and determinate correlations between [representational] and neural events,' would the correlations do explanatory work analogous to that of compositions in familiar material sciences? If the correlations did not illuminate diachronic causal relations in a way analogous to diachronic relations among materially composed things, then correlation would not suffice to establish material composition. Kobes insightfully supposes, for example, that the neural correlates of psychological causes might be *causally relevant* to the neural correlates of a psychological effect of that cause, without being a neural *cause* of the neural correlate of the psychological effect. In such a case, neural causation would not line up with psychological causation in the way that would be required by compositional materialism.

Again Kobes holds that the facts are empirically unknown. Our actual neural and psychological theories do not provide us with relevant correlations or with parallel causal structures—neural and psychological. Perhaps the situation is simply a product of our ignorance. Kobes's point is that nothing that we now know makes the situation postulated by compositional materialism an explanatorily illuminating or distinctively likely situation.

Kobes's suggestions are insightful, intriguing, and provocative. I do not see my way to the bottom of these issues. I will, however, hazard some tentative comments.

One doubt starts very far back. Kobes assumes that the archangel can compute biological facts from a starting point of 'only the complete facts about fundamental physical objects, events, fields, laws, and causes over all of space and time.' The archangel can identify 'chemical and physiological kinds and their instances by their physical components, distinctively arranged.'

In contrast to Kobes, I doubt that it is possible to identify the material components of biological kinds and compute the behavior of the components that causally correlates with the behavior of instances of biological kinds, relying entirely on entities' *distinctive arrangement and behavior as described by physics alone.* If, for example, the physical components of biological species or the physical mechanisms of phenotypic expression of genotypes could be identified purely by distinctive physical arrangement and physics-described behavior of physical components, then biological kinds and laws would be reducible to physical kinds and laws much more simply than they seem to be.[5] I think that to identify the physico-chemical components of biological kinds and compute the physico-chemical behavior of the components of biological kinds, one must make use of biological principles.

I am not certain that these points are correct. The issues are very abstract, and Kobes grants the archangel large powers. What seems to me hard to believe is that biological kinds in general coincide with independently identifiable, 'distinctive' patterns of arrangement and movement of physical particles. I find it doubtful that generalizations of physics that apply specifically to the physical components of distinctively biological transactions, can be derived from independent physical observations and independently identifiable principles of physics that govern 'distinctive' movement of those components. Biological kinds are individuated by theoretical notions in biology. I doubt that their components can be picked out as 'discrete' or salient patterns among entities identified in physics.

Like specifications of all kinds and principles, specifications of biological kinds and principles are inevitably intensional. They are not reducible to specifications of finite groupings of particles, for example. I doubt that an effective procedure can compute the component physical behavior of instances of the kinds governed by those principles—even relative to an intensional base of physics-kinds and physics-principles. I think that the relevantly distinct component kinds and movements are distinctive only in light of biological categorization and

---

[5] I know of no clear sense in which all of biology is reducible to physics.

explanation, not—or at least not in general—independently. The supervenience, and even the compositional dependence, of the subject matter of biology on the subject matter of physics, do not entail that one can *compute* the physical behavior distinctively associated with biological entities from the behavior of entities described in physics together with principles of physics.

Let us suppose that these points are correct. Then it would *not* be a sufficient condition for rejecting compositional materialism that the archangel could not, prior to using psychological kinds and principles, identify physical components of psychological kinds. It would *not* be a sufficient condition for rejecting compositional materialism that the archangel could not compute distinctive patterns of neural states and events that could be slotted into a psychological network, once representational psychological kinds were individuated in an anti-individualistic manner. For instances of biological kinds are *composed* of entities identified in physics, even though (by hypothesis) the distinctive components of biological kinds cannot be identified as salient and distinctive types through concepts and principles available only in physics.[6]

A second doubt concerns the alleged independence of Kobes's two worries about compositional materialist theories. Kobes takes the question whether the archangel can establish representational-neural correlations that show how neural events 'asymmetrically and synchronically sustain representational events' to be independent of a second question. The second question is whether the correlations illuminate diachronic causal relations involving representational events. I do not see how synchronic correlations could be of any ontological interest or integrity if they did not track diachronic causal relations at the level of representational events. So I think that Kobes's two worries are not independent.

Of course, as Kobes recognizes, the key issue regarding compositional materialism is not merely a generic correlation and coincidence, even between causal sequences of neural events and causal sequences involving propositional representational events. It is whether the correlated neural events explain their effects in a way that illuminates causation at the psychological level 'in the manner of familiar sciences of materially constituted things.' As I have long emphasized, composition is a *specific* theoretical relation. The issue is not only whether the two levels of causal structure can be correlated, but also—as Kobes rightly emphasizes—whether they can be correlated *in a manner familiar from sciences that make use of causal aspects of material components to illumine causal aspects of higher level composed kinds.*

Are there the relevant event-by-event, structure-preserving correlations? Do they ground explanations that use the causal powers of the candidate neural and chemical components to explain the causal behavior of the psychological propositional events in a compositional manner?

6 Ned Block noted that the same point can be made about computations between different levels within physics.

Many philosophers will be inclined to ask, dismissively, how *could* answers to these questions not be affirmative. I believe that such philosophers allow ideology to turn them dogmatic about a very complex and not very deeply explored empirical matter.

Psycho-physics gives us no such correlations. There are promising correlations in pre-perceptual aspects of the perceptual system. For example, firings of banks of neurons in the retina correlate with registered information regarding the spatial distribution of proximal stimulation from light arrays. This registered information forms the first input into the psychological mechanisms that yield visual perception. There are even some nice correlations between aspects of genuine visual *perceptual* representation (such as edge representations) and firings of lines of neurons. Moreover, there are correlations between the timing of neural occurrences in areas of the brain and the timing of certain stages in the formation of visual perceptions. There is certainly the beginning of a massive scientific effort to correlate processes in perceptual systems with neural processes. Correlation and perhaps even composition present a natural paradigm for research in these areas. Still, correlations are currently quite generic, except at the periphery of psychological processes. More importantly, correlation is far from explaining all psychological causation in the compositional manner of the material sciences.

With regard to *propositional* psychological events, there is not even a serious beginning in establishing the correlations needed to support compositional materialism. Propositional thinking is known to have a variable correlation with brain processes, both over time in given individuals and across individuals. This situation is compatible with compositional materialism. But if there is little stability or uniformity in the types of physical events that underlie types of propositional thoughts, there will be limited scope for explanations of patterns of psychological causation in terms of (putatively composing) patterns of neural causation.

In the natural sciences, relative stability and uniformity in relations between kinds of components and kinds of things that they compose facilitates part–whole causal explanation. Of course, science can appeal to many levels of kind specifications that might be used to carry out compositional explanations of psychological states. And we are in the earliest stages of understanding the brain, not to say its relation to psychology. So it would be premature to take the lack of established correlations between neural events and propositional attitude events to show that compositional materialism is false. It seems possible, however, that the plasticity of the brain and the genetic and developmental differences among individuals may prevent compositional forms of explanation from being viable for psychological science. More crucially, neural occurrences may not match up well with propositional attitude occurrences, *even in individual cases*. There might turn out to be no clear correlations, even in individuals at specific times, between particular propositional occurrences (among the propositional occurrences at any given time) and particular neural occurrences (among the neural occurrences at the same time) that could provide the beginning of a compositional materialist account. If science does not provide correlations, there will remain no reason to believe in compositional materialism.

Kobes delineates one way in which a failure of correlation could emerge. As noted earlier, he holds that psychology could provide explanations that feature psychological events as causes of a given physical or psychological event, and could cite further psychological states and events as part of the causal *enabling* conditions for the transaction. At the same time, neural science could cite a complex of neural and chemical causes of the physical event, and a background of causal *enabling* neural and chemical events. There could be a general correlation between causally *relevant* events at the two levels, where causally relevant events include both causing and enabling events. But there could turn out to be no illuminating correlation of any subset of the *causing* neural events with the *causing* psychological events. Yet each theory, psychological and neuro-chemical, could provide a true and illuminating account of why certain effects, including physically specified effects, occur. It seems to Kobes, and to me, an open question whether the two types of causal explanation will line up so that causation at neural/chemical levels is correlated with causation at the psychological level, even in given contexts, in the way required by compositional materialism.

The burden on compositional materialism is heavy. It must correlate neural causes and their effects with psychological causes and their effects. And it must illuminate *psychological* causation, of both physical and psychological effects, in ways familiar from the material sciences. I will not try to formulate a precise assumption about physical causation entailed by compositional materialism. However, causation at the level of wholes must be a physical composite of causation at the level of material parts, for some natural division of the material parts. Of course, causation at the level of the parts can capitalize on physical *relations* among the parts. For the psychological causing event to be composed materially, *psychological* causation must depend on the causation of the material parts in one of the ways familiar from causation in the natural (material compositional) sciences. To *know* that such causation occurs, we must have explanations that take psychological causation to operate in such ways.

For example, can one explain the psychological causation of an occurrent thought that is the conclusion and causal effect of a piece of reasoning in such a way that the inference to that thought, including the inference's causally relevant *rational* aspects, are illuminated by the composite causation of the components of an antecedent chemical or neural event? As I elaborate shortly, it is hard to see how the rational aspects of psychological causation can be illuminatingly explained as a material composite of the causal operations of putative neural or chemical components of the inferential process, even taking into account the physical relations among those components in their causal operation.

Some philosophers claim that appeal to a language of thought is assumed in the psychology of propositional attitudes.[7] The idea is that there is a level of psychological activity that is 'purely syntactical.' Representational content is taken to be a further matter attributed at a different stage of explanation. It is frequently also assumed that the tokens of the syntactical, 'linguistic' items are brain events. (Here one often hears intoned the portentous but utterly misleading slogan that the brain is a syntactic engine.) It is concluded that a language of thought illuminates how occurrences of thoughts—inner 'linguistic' episodes—could be composed of brain processes. The language of thought picture is sometimes said to indicate that compositional materialism is already in place in psycho-physical science.

Such reasoning skates too fast at each turn. In the first place, except perhaps in psycho-linguistics, there is no autonomous account of syntactical processing in cognitive psychology. Theories of perception and perceptual belief, theories of natural inference and practical reasoning, do not attribute a syntax *except* as a structure *in* the representational contents of psychological states. There is no purely syntactical level of explanation in most of cognitive psychology. Even in the syntactical part of psycho-linguistics, syntax appears to be an abstraction from—and the structure of a capacity embedded in—capacities to understand meaningful sentences.

Thus the view that psychology contains a theory of an autonomous 'purely syntactical' level of processing—one that operates independently of a representational capacity—is misleading even as applied to syntactical aspects of psycho-linguistics. It is without *any* solid grounding as applied to perceptual or propositional attitude psychology, indeed the whole representational part of psychology. The idea that all of propositional thinking is, at some level, a processing of syntactical symbols that in themselves are neutral as regards representational content has no scientific basis. Propositional psychology is about thought. Thought has a structure. One can abstract that structure and study its properties. Some thinking—for example, certain deductive proofs—but probably not very much thinking, hinges purely on that structure. Even then, the structural elements are not content-neutral. In fact, the structural elements have representational content that is relevant to rationality-based explanations. The category of logical constant or predicate, for example, gets its content from roles in reasoning with representational contents. Even in purely deductive thought, the logical constants have representational content.[8] The structure has no psychological status apart from its association with representational thought.

In the second place, since syntactical elements in psychology are associated with attributions of contentful representational states, they have no specific

---

[7] The picture that I will criticize is substantially that of Jerry Fodor (1979).

[8] Hilbertean proof theory is an abstraction from reasoning that uses the representational contents of logical constants.

association, in current psychological theory, with brain states or brain events. Correlating brain states with syntactical states is just as much an open empirical problem as correlating brain states with representational states. In fact, these are different specifications of substantially the same problem, insofar as we have any clarity about what the syntactical states are (to wit, aspects of representational states). So appeal to a language of thought gets us *no* closer to material correlates that are supposed to constitute the compositional material of the syntactical states, or the representational states. It is just part of the materialist ideology, not part of scientific theory, that 'syntactical' states or events are instantiated by specific neural states or events.

Thus in our present state of knowledge, the language of thought hypothesis cannot make compositional materialism more plausible. The hypothesis is not even a plausible gloss on psychology unless standard presentations of it are severely qualified.

One important difference between representational psychology, on one hand, and neuro-physiology and chemistry, on the other, is brought out by anti-individualism. Representational kinds are partly individuated through patterns of causal relations that they bear to entities in an environment that lies well beyond them. Neural and chemical kinds are not individuated in ways that rely on these long-range patterns.

A further difference between representational psychology, particularly the psychology of propositional attitudes, and the neural and bio-chemical sciences is that the part–whole relation of material composition plays no evident role in psychological theorizing. Propositional psychological structures are compositional in a different way. They are broadly rational structures. They include predication and structures of deductive inference. These structures are notoriously not assimilable to physical structures. The bonds between elements in rational structures are not physical but propositional. Since the seventeenth century, it has been evident—in fact, virtually axiomatic in the natural sciences—that the physical world, as described by the natural sciences, does not have the form or content of a text. It is not made up of rational structures at all. It is not a direct expression of reason. The brute nature of physical relations—the difference, for example, as Kant put it, between resisting force and logical negation,[9] or between property inherence and predication—should, I think encourage puzzlement about how physical structures *per se* could compose instances of propositional attitudes.

There have been ways of trying to blunt this concern, insofar as it is ever raised. One might, for example, say that rational structures are relevant only to *norms* governing psychological transactions; material composition is relevant to the ontology and the causal transactions among psychological events that may or may not fulfill the norms. This line is not plausible. Psychological explanation takes the propositional structure of propositional attitudes to be fundamental to

---

[9] Immanuel Kant (1968: 175–6).

what they are. Psychological explanation gives the rational, propositional aspects of psychological states a causal role. It is not that we are infallibly guided by reason. Obviously we often fall short. Rather, both common sense and scientific explanation indicate that rational, propositional aspects of psychological states and events figure both in the ontological individuation and in the causal powers of psychological occurrences. Indeed, I think that any psychological science that did not acknowledge a role for rational elements in psychological identity and psychological causation could be reasonably counted inadequate.[10]

Let us reflect on examples involving the causal powers of propositional attitudes with rational structure. The thought occurrence that is the conclusion of an individual's deductive inference is caused by transitions involving premise thoughts that incorporate competence with the logical structures of the premises. The rational-structural aspects of the premise attitudes figure causally in drawing the conclusion. An individual's predicating a concept of a perceived particular, in a perceptual judgment, is part of the cause of the individual's practical reasoning about how to deal with the particular. These rational aspects of psychological causation—deductive inference and predication—are not construed as summations of material forces.

Similar examples support a constitutive role for rational structure in the ontology of propositional attitudes. What it is to be an occurrent thinking *since all humans are mortal, if that human is Socrates, then Socrates is mortal* depends constitutively on the propositional structure of the thought. Any event occurrence that lacked that structure would not be the same event.

I have two concerns about compositional materialism, beyond concern about lack of evidence for it. First, it is hard to see how material compositional structures could ground causation by propositional psychological states or events. Second, it is hard to see how material compositional structures are consistent with the nature of propositional psychological states or events. I shall elaborate the causal point first.

Rational, propositional structures are fundamental aspects of psychological causation by propositional states and events.[11] Rational, propositional structures do not appear to be identifiable with structures of material composition. Everything we know about causation by material composites indicates that such causation is not rationally structured. In fact, as noted, this point is a virtual axiom in the natural sciences (physics, chemistry, biology, including neuro-physiology). Moreover, scientific reduction of rational, propositional structures to material compositional structures has little prospect of success. For such a reduction to succeed, natural science would have to show that a *constitutive* aspect of causation

---

[10] For a discussion of this point, see the end of 'Mind–Body Causation and Explanatory Practice,' in Burge (2007).

[11] The psychological cause could have a psychological effect. Or it could have a physical effect, for example a physical activity motivated by propositional reasoning.

by propositional psychological states and events—their rational structure—is fully *explainable* in terms of the causal properties of brute material composition. There is not the slightest reason to think that such a reduction can succeed. These points derive as much from fundamental commitments of the natural sciences as from fundamental commitments of psychology.

Earlier, I did not attempt a precise formulation of the sort of physical causation produced by material composites. But any such causation must be a physical composite of causation by the material parts (on some natural division of those parts), where the parts operate through their physical relations to one another. Since nature is not a text, such causation does not have rational or propositional structure. And as noted, rational, propositional structures do not appear to be explainable in terms of brute material compositional structures. Thus causation that depends on rational, propositional structure appears not to be identifiable with or reducible to causation by material composites, or by material components of material composites operating through their physical relations to one another. So material composites, such as chemical and neural composites, appear not to exhaustively constitute causation by rational, propositional states or events. Causation by states or events that are material composites is purely causation of material composites. So rational, propositional states or events appear not to be material composites.

More simply: reason is a constitutive structural feature of causation by propositional psychological states and events. According to the natural sciences, reason is not a structural feature of material composites. The causation by material parts of material composites, operating in their physical relations to one another, must suffice to alone compose causation by material composites. It is hard to see how the causal powers and causal structure of material components could alone compose the causal powers and causal structure of causal transactions that hinge on the rational, propositional structures of propositional states and events. So it appears that rational, propositional, psychological causation is not the causation of a material composite. Propositional psychological states and events are material composites only if their causation is purely that of a material composite. So it appears that propositional psychological states and events are not material composites.

The second concern about compositional materialism is similar, but does not feature causation. Here it is: the physical structure of material composites consists in physical bonds among the parts. According to modern natural science, there is no place in the physical structure of material composites for rational, propositional bonds. The structure of propositional psychological states and events constitutively includes propositional, rational structure. So propositional states and events are not material composites.[12]

---

[12] There is a distant kinship between these arguments and the argument for the simplicity of the soul that Kant criticizes in the second Paralogism. Cf. Immanuel Kant, *Critique of Pure Reason*,

Both arguments depend on a structural contrast between material composites and propositional psychological states and events. Psychological causation hinges often, but then constitutively, on rational propositional structure. And the nature of propositional psychological states and events constitutively involves rational, propositional structure. Causation associated with material composites is, to all appearances *constitutively, not* causation that involves rational, propositional structure. And it is a principle of physical nature that physical structures of material composites are constitutively *not* rational, propositional structures. So it appears that psychological causation by propositional states and events is constitutively not causation by material composites. And it appears that propositional psychological states and events are constitutively not material composites.[13]

These arguments are, of course, very abstract.[14] Perhaps developments in empirical science will show how to overcome them. But the developments would have to be fundamental. At present, the arguments seem to me to support provisional rejection of compositional materialism—independently of doubt that derives from the absence of the correlations and of the explanations of psychological causation that compositional materialism requires.

What are we to say about demands for a *mechanism* for psychological causation? Such demands are often just question-begging insistence on physical mechanism, specified by the natural sciences. Postulating such mechanisms is warranted if and only if they enhance empirical explanation. We want to understand relations between respective explanations and subject matters in representational psychology and the biological and chemical sciences. It does no good to insist that empirical explanation in psychology conform to explanations in very different sciences. There may be no deeper way to explain *how* psychological events cause

---

A351–361. The argument that Kant criticizes does appeal to the propositional unity of thought, in effect predication, which is one of the rational, propositional structures that my arguments appeal to. But the argument Kant criticizes aims to establish the simplicity of thinkers, and by (alleged) extension, their exemption from dissolution (A356). My arguments are not for simplicity, only against *material* compositeness. And my arguments center not on the thinker but on psychological states and events. They also center on a basic feature of modern natural science—that natural physical relations do not include rational, propositional structures. I believe that my arguments are not subject to any of the objections that Kant raises.

[13] These arguments differ in two respects from the arguments, discussed early in this chapter, against the materialist token identity thesis. First, the earlier arguments depend essentially on anti-individualism and on the view that the identity of neural/chemical events in the brain does not depend on the sorts of long-range patterns of relations to the distal environment that the identities of representational states do. The arguments against compositional materialism do not depend on anti-individualism or on denying that the identities of neural/chemical events in the brain depend on the same long-range causal patterns that the identities of representational states do. Second, the earlier arguments do not center on the causal or constitutive roles of rational, propositional structures, whereas the later arguments do.

[14] It should be obvious that both of the arguments could be modified into additional arguments against materialist token *identity* theories. Such arguments would supplement the two arguments against such theories that I discussed near the beginning of this chapter.

psychological or physical events than to specify the law-like patterns by which they do so, and the neural or chemical patterns some of which seem necessary to those psychological patterns' occurring. The most popular way of indicating how psychological causation could be composed of physical causation has been to appeal to computers. Computers are claimed to be physical machines that 'instantiate' reason. This claim does not solve the problem. Computers' processes express reason only insofar as we give them programs and interpret their processes in accord with those programs. There is nothing in the computer's physical processes *per se* that makes the computer reasonable, or explains whatever rational causation might occur in computers. Actual computers do not reason autonomously. They go through a sequence of states that were fashioned to express and amplify our rational states. In them, we simply mimic physical symbolization of our own reasoning, and amplify our reasoning by relying on the computers' processing of those symbols.

I leave open whether more sophisticated robots could reason autonomously. It would, however, not follow from the assumption that a robot reasons autonomously that rational causation in the robot is explained by material composition, even on the further assumption that there are known correlations between its physical states and its propositional states. One still needs to explain rational causation in terms of a composition of physical causal relations. That is what we have some reason to believe cannot be done. Supposing that a robot could reason autonomously does not entail supposing that its reasoning events are *composed* of material processes. The robot's reasoning events would depend for their existence on material processes, just as ours appear to. Its supposed rational propositional events would appear not to be materially composed any more than ours appear to be. Only a cartoonish view about what rejecting material composition amounts to—a view that would see the rejection as postulating immaterial soul stuff in the robot—would have to be embarrassed by a reasoning robot.[15]

The language of thought hypothesis is often conjoined with the computer analogy to try to support materialism. The idea is that reasoning in computers hinges causally on the shape, size, and physical configuration of symbols. In addition to the difficulties with this hypothesis that I catalogued earlier, there is a further one. The argument I gave regarding rational causation applies to any attempt to use the language of thought hypothesis to support compositional materialism. Psychological causation depends on the rational, hence representational, aspects of psychological states. Insofar as the language of thought hypothesis tries to account for psychological causation in terms of the shapes,

---

[15] I am abstracting from issues about consciousness. I think that robots that have the *sorts* of material bases that they commonly have would not and could not be conscious. I am doubtful about counting such beings autonomous reasoners, without serious qualifications. I claim that even if one *lays aside* issues about consciousness, supposition of autonomously reasoning robots does not threaten objections to compositional materialism about propositional reasoning.

sizes, and configurations of symbols, it fails to connect with the type of causation that is referred to by common sense and psychological explanation in science. Psychological causation that hinges on the rational, propositional properties of psychological states is not independent of representational content in the way that causal processes that hinge on the physical properties of symbols are. As I have indicated, there is no scientific basis for an explanation of psychological causation in terms of an autonomous syntax realized in neural or chemical entities. Even if there were, the account of causation provided by such explanation would fail to explain psychological causation that hinges on the rational aspects of the form and content of psychological events. The language of thought hypothesis is not only ungrounded in scientific explanation. It is irrelevant to explaining the central feature of psychological causation by propositional psychological states and events. Kobes cites my interest in Descartes' apparent view that psychological states and events are distinctive in that their being or nature is grounded in consciousness, activity, power, and point of view, not in substance, soul stuff, or composition. Let us reflect on that list.

With Kobes, I have bracketed consciousness. I think that consciousness is constitutively associated with our psychological being. Constitutive relations between consciousness and specific types of psychological states are complex. I will not take on these issues here.

Not all representational psychological states or events, even propositional ones, are active. But all propositional states and events are *constitutively associated* with activity. For all propositional psychological states and events are constitutively associated with inference—the exercise of the capacity to make use of propositional structure. Inference is activity.

Propositional psychological states and events seem to be constitutively associated with at least generic causal vulnerabilities and powers, including some active powers. Those states and events seem to be constitutively associated with points of view that mark them—representational contents. Unlike material entities, propositional psychological states and events are not identifiable through their material substance, stuffings, or compositions. This conception of the natures of propositional psychological states and events accords with what we now know about them. I see no good reason to believe that such psychological states and events are materially composed. I think it reasonable to think that they are not.

Kobes highlights elements in my dualism that are at odds with traditional dualisms. First, it is not a substance dualism, in the early-modern sense of 'substance.' I have no reason to believe, alas, that psychological events can exist *self-sufficiently*, or *independently* of physical material. Representational psychological events seem to depend for their existence on physical events and material that 'sustain' them. A lot of physical states do not depend on psychological states, but all psychological states seem to depend on physical states. (It may be that the particular underlying physical states could not be what they are if they did not sustain, underlie, or otherwise associate with psychological states.) Second, a strengthening of this first point: although I am not committed to a belief in global supervenience of the psychological on the physical, I incline toward such a belief, pending better reasons against it than any that I know of. Third, the physical world is without gaps in physical causation, modulo quantum indeterminacy. It is *approximately* causally deterministic. Most or all of these points are uncongenial with most early-modern forms of dualism. My dualism is not only conjectural; it is modest and undramatic. It does not encourage belief that our souls can soar out of the material world.

On the other hand, it is not merely a dualism of concepts. Nor is it merely what is often called a property dualism. It is a dualism of occurrent events as well as states, kinds, and properties. For now, I leave open how to think of psychological *agents*. I am not convinced by Strawsonian claims that one *must* conceive of *every* such agent as having material properties, at least if material properties are not comprised of *relations* of dependence on matter.

Kobes speculates that my modest dualism might be counted an 'extremely weak' form of physicalism. I am inclined to resist this speculation. Psychological states and events depend on the physical. But I see no intellectual substance in counting them physical. They are unlike numbers and logical forms in that they have causal powers and vulnerabilities, and in that they occur in time. They are like numbers and logical forms in seeming to lack material composition, mass, physical force, and physical energy. In fact, propositional psychological states and events are what they are through their having logical forms. None of the primary attributes that we cite in theorizing about them–including logical forms—are cited as physical structures in the natural sciences. I see no clear sense in which propositional psychological states or events are physical. Supervenience is consistent with dualism. To be materialist (or physicalist), a view must claim that psychological entities are themselves material (or physical), not merely that they vary with or depend on material (or physical) entities.

So I do not think that counting my view a weak form of physicalism accounts for the diffidence in my position in recommending—in the passage that Kobes quotes—that philosophers be more open and relaxed about whether some form of materialism (or physicalism) is true.[16] I am no type of physicalist or materialist. But I recommend—not sloth or indifference, but—disinterested, open reflection on the issue.

On relaxation: I think that the question whether something like my form of dualism or some non-reductive form of materialism is true is not momentous. At least, it is not momentous for traditional reasons for caring intensely about

---

[16] From 'Mind–Body Causation and Explanatory Practice,' in Burge (2007: 360), 'It seems to me that philosophers should be more relaxed about whether or not some form of materialism is true. I think it a thoroughly open—and not very momentous—question whether there is any point in insisting that mental events are, in any clear sense, physical . . . What matters is that our mentalistic explanations work and that they do not conflict with our physicalistic explanations. But it serves no purpose to over-dramatize the conflict between different ontological approaches.'

whether dualism is true. Traditional issues of life after death, the existence of freedom and moral responsibility, and the explanatory powers of natural science within its own domain, do not seem to hinge on the answer to the question.

On openness: I think that we do not know enough about the relation between psychology and the natural sciences to take hard lines for or against materialism. I believe that at this point a modest dualism is clearly more reasonable than materialism. But I think that materialistically motivated empirical research is heuristically tenable. The key to any view in this area is openness to empirical exploration and philosophical reflection. Both positions should be developed in a dialectically open spirit.

A modest dualism, however, cleaves more closely to what we know. It does not make warrantless claims. It is more reasonable than compositional materialism, or other sorts of materialism or physicalism, partly through abnegation, and partly through appreciation of the deep differences between rational structures and physical structures. Psychological events have not been shown to have any attributes that are distinctive of physical events. Their primary attributes are not those cited in the natural sciences.

I confess to a more psychological influence on my dualism. I was educated in philosophy in a climate in which materialism had become smug ideological dogma. It dripped with the more supercilious aspects of blind religious orthodoxy. It was not just that herd instinct in philosophy was itself a danger signal. I thought that there was an implicit hypocrisy in the climate. What concerned me was that many philosophers saw any doubt about materialism as *ipso facto* irrational and unscientific. Many still do. Many philosophers exuded a certainty that was out of line with the speculativeness and lack of force in the grounds supporting their positions. Many still do. Such philosophers assume the mantle of science while contravening its letter and spirit. I hope that new generations of philosophers will do better.

12

Descartes' Revenge Part II: The Supervenience Argument Strikes Back

Neal Judisch

1.

For nearly three decades Jaegwon Kim has argued that antireductionist theories of mind are inconsistent with mental causation. Here I aim to show that if Kim's charge against antireductionism is correct his own reductionist view falls prey to the same plight. Specifically, I argue that (i) Kim's theory salvages mental causation only if mental properties are multiply realizable, physically reducible, and have instances that are causally efficacious in virtue of being *mental* property instances, but (ii) his theory is unable jointly to satisfy these conditions. In section 2 I present the Supervenience Argument designed by Kim to prove that psychophysical causation requires reductionism. In section 3 I highlight two principles upon which Kim's charge against nonreductive physicalism essentially relies, and in section 4 I show how a consistent application of these principles places demands upon theories of mental causation that Kim's reductive functionalism cannot meet. The result is that no theory of mind other than type physicalism is consistent with mental causation if Kim's case against antireductionism holds up. If, on the other hand, Kim's reductive functionalism does the trick, antireductive physicalism has nothing to fear from the Supervenience Argument.

2.

The Supervenience Argument incorporates three central assumptions. The first one specifies that the physical world is causally closed:

Closure. If a physical event has a cause at t, then it has a physical cause at t. (Kim 2005: 15)

The second one stipulates that mental properties supervene upon physical properties:

Supervenience. If any system s instantiates a mental property M at t, there necessarily exists a physical property P such that s instantiates P at t, and necessarily anything instantiating P at any time instantiates M at that time. (p. 33)

And the third is an exclusion principle expressing the prohibition of systematic overdetermination:

Exclusion. If an event e has a sufficient cause c at t, no event at t distinct from c can be a cause of e (unless this is a genuine case of causal overdetermination). (p. 17)

According to Kim, if we further assume that mental properties are neither reducible to not identifiable with physical properties, what results is a set of propositions inconsistent with the causal relevance of mental properties:

The problem of mental causation. Causal efficacy of mental properties is inconsistent with the joint acceptance of the following four claims: (i) physical causal closure, (ii) causal exclusion, (iii) mind–body supervenience, and (iv) mental/physical property dualism—the view that mental properties are irreducible to physical properties. (pp. 21–2)

The reasoning behind this contention is as follows. Suppose we wish to identify a mental property instance, M, as the cause of a subsequent physical property instance, P. By *Supervenience* we know that there must be some physical property instance upon which M supervenes and by *Closure* we know that if P has a cause at a time t, it has a physical cause at t. Let us suppose that P has a cause at t and that the physical cause of P (at t) is P_0, and let us assume that P_0 is the physical property instance upon which M supervenes.[1] By *Exclusion* we know that P has no cause other than P_0 unless this is a case of genuine causal overdetermination, which, we will assume, it is not. From this it follows that M is the cause of P only if $M = P$. But given that no mental property is identical with or reducible to any physical property, it follows that the putative mental cause, M, is not in reality a cause of P.[2] Since there is nothing special about M, P, or P_0, the argument generalizes to show that instances of irreducible mental properties do not have physical effects, so that nonreductive physicalism entails epiphenomenalism: 'That then is the supervenience argument against mental causation, or Descartes's revenge against the physicalists' (Kim 1998: 46).

---

[1] The assumption is innocuous: if M's supervenience base is some physical property instance distinct from P_0, the closure and exclusion principles still kick in to screen off any causal influence M might exercise with respect to P.

[2] It follows, that is, on Kim's supposition that the irreducibility of mental to physical properties entails the nonidentity of mental and physical property instances. More on this just below.

3.

I am not interested in disputing the validity of this argument or any of the assumptions it deploys. Instead I want to make explicit two principles Kim relies upon to force the choice between reductionism and epiphenomenalism. After laying them out I will argue that Kim's theory of mental causation is untenable in light of the parameters they set.

It is crucial to keep clear on the distinction between *properties* and *property instances*. Kim himself is quite explicit that properties are 'causal' in virtue of their *instances* being causal:

Properties as such don't enter into causal relations; when we say '*M* causes *M**,' that is short for 'An instance of *M* causes an instance of *M**' or 'An instantiation of *M* causes *M** to instantiate on that occasion.' (Kim 2005: 39)

And he is just as clear concerning the intended reading of the premiss that 'Mental properties are not reducible to, and are not identical with, physical properties' (p. 34) as it functions within his argument. According to him, just as the claim that '*M* causes *M**' is short for 'An instance of *M* causes an instance of *M**,' the assumption that '*M* ≠ *P*' 'only means that this instance of *M* ≠ this instance of *P*' (p. 42, n. 9). As is well known, however, not all antireductionists endorse this assumption. For these theorists the nonidentity of mental and physical phenomena enters into the picture at the level of *properties*, not at the level of property *instances*. Indeed, Kim's initial formulations of the Supervenience Argument were targeted precisely at such 'token identity' theories. He claimed then, as now, that not just any theory according to which mental and physical property instances are identical suffices to vindicate mental causation, since mental causation requires that mental events produce their effects *in virtue of being the sorts of* mental *events they are*.[3] But if mental properties cannot be reduced to physical properties any mental property instance identical with a physical property instance is causal only as regards its *physical* characteristics, which is epiphenomenalism near enough. To save mental causation, therefore, what is required is either reduction or identity of mental with physical properties themselves.

Why then does Kim specify that the assumption *M* ≠ *P* 'only means that this instance of *M* ≠ this instance of *P*?' As he realizes, this qualification evidently leaves open a question Kim has tried to close:

Does this mean that a Davidsonian 'token identity' suffices here? The answer is no: the relevant sense in which an instance of *M* = an instance of *P* requires either property

---

[3] Thus when we say 'that mental events cause physical events' we intend 'that an event, *in virtue of its mental property*, causes another event to have a certain physical property,' which requires the reduction of mental to physical properties (Kim 1989: 279).

identity $M = P$ or some form of reductive relationship between them . . . The fact that properties M and P must be implicated in the identity, or nonidentity, of M and P instances can be seen from the fact that 'An M-instance causes a P-instance' must be understood with the proviso 'in virtue of the former being an instance of M and the latter an instance of P.' (Ibid.)

So if a mental property instance is identical to a physical property instance it must be either that the *properties* instantiated are identical or that one of them reduces to the other, otherwise it would not be causal in virtue of its mental features. In the 'relevant sense,' then, no theory according to which mental properties are nonidentical with or irreducible to physical properties can lay claim to the identity of mental with physical property instances either. Thus we have the following principle on *Property instance identification*:

(PII)   For any property instances x and y, if $x = y$ then there exist properties z and w such that x is an instance of z and y is an instance of w and either $z = w$ or there is a reductive relation $\mathfrak{R}$ such that z bears $\mathfrak{R}$ to w.

What conditions constrain the relationship $\mathfrak{R}$? According to Kim the 'root meaning of reduction' may be summarized as saying that 'if Xs reduce to Ys, then Xs are nothing over and above the Ys.' Thus if a property exists but is 'nothing over and above' a physical phenomenon it must be identical with something physical: 'if anything is physically reduced, it must be identical with some physical item' (p. 34). Since $\mathfrak{R}$ is a relation of physical reduction it follows, in accordance with Kim's stipulation, that any reducible property must conform to this *Reducibility principle*:

(RP)   For any x and y, if x bears $\mathfrak{R}$ to y then there exists some z such that z is physical and $x = z$.

A question emerges: Does (RP) imply that (PII) contains a superfluous disjunct? From (PII) it follows that an instance of a property M is identical to an instance of a property P only if either $M = P$ or M bears $\mathfrak{R}$ to P. But if M bears $\mathfrak{R}$ to P it follows from (RP) that $M = $ some physical item. And what could this 'physical item' be if not P, given that the properties M and P must be implicated in the identity of M and P instances? The identification of M with some other physical item, P^*, looks to underwrite the identity of M-instances and P^*-instances, which is of no obvious use to the identity of M-instances and P-instances unless P-instances *are* P^*-instances. But if P-instances are P^*-instances then, by (PII), either P and P^* are identical, in which case (by transitivity of $=$) $M = P$ after all, or P and P^* stand in relation $\mathfrak{R}$, in which case a precisely similar series of questions arises.[4]

---

[4] The question becomes all the more pressing when we consider that Kim's theory of events itself seems to entail the superfluity of the last disjunct in (PII)'s consequent. On that picture any event is an ordered triple consisting of an object, a property and a time, and an event $\langle O, x, t \rangle = $ an

The answer must be that there are two nonequivalent ways in which mental and physical property instances may be legitimately identified. The first is via an identification of the relevant properties. But Kim does not accept type physicalism for reasons involving the assumed multiple realizability of the mental within the physical. Still, he believes his approach entitles him to identify mental and physical property instances by way of a reductive relationship between mental and physical properties, and further that this relationship suffices to secure mental causation:

It may be true—I think it is true—that type physicalism will vindicate mental causation, but it may not be the only position on the mind-body problem that can do this. In my view, functional reduction . . . which, unlike . . . type physicalism, is immune to the notorious multiple realization argument, can also ground mental causation.   (p. 148)

So Kim's (PII) does not demand type-type identities: if a property M bears $\mathfrak{R}$ to a property P we may conclude that any M-instance is a P-instance, and this does not require that $M = P$. What it does require (in the absence of such identities) is that M be *functionally reducible* to P.

I shall have more to say about functional reduction in section 4. For now what requires our attention is the importance of (PII) and (RP) to Kim's strategic posture. Given his insistence that antireductive physicalism entails epiphenomenalism in view of its failure to satisfy (PII), Kim must show how his theory does not run afoul of that principle. But given that type physicalism falls victim to the multiple realization argument he cannot satisfy (PII) by effecting type-type identifications between mental and physical properties. Rather, he must outline a theory of reduction that does not entail such identities, but which nevertheless respects the specification in (RP) that property reduction requires the identification of reduced properties with something physical. To steer a course between type physicalism and antireductionism, therefore, Kim's theory must entail that a mental property M can be (a) multiply realizable and (b) physically reducible, where (b) demands the existence of a physical item with which M may be identified. Further, if the theory is to avoid epiphenomenalism it must entail that (c) instances of M are causally efficacious in virtue of being M-instances, for the failure to satisfy (c) has been his chief complaint against antireductive physicalism from the start. In what follows I argue that Kim's theory cannot satisfy these three conditions.

4.

If Kim can ensure the identity of mental and physical property instances and the antireductionist cannot he must posit as a condition on property instance

event $\langle O^*, y, t^* \rangle$ iff $O = O^*$ and $x = y$ and $t = t^*$. But then there is no hope of identifying mental and physical events by way of the reductive relation $\mathfrak{R}$ unless it's true that M bears $\mathfrak{R}$ to P only if $M = P$, in which case the qualifier concerning $\mathfrak{R}$ once more appears idle. See Kim (1976).

identification the physical reducibility of mental properties. Moreover, the reduction of a mental property M demands that M be identified with some physical item, and the physical item must be such as to imply that M-instances are causal in virtue of instantiating M. What could this physical item be? Because M is multiply realizable it cannot be identified with any singular physical type that realizes M. But according to Kim, if M is a functional property a *reduction* of M to its physical realizers can be accomplished and this will preserve its causal efficacy. Functional reduction involves three steps. First, we assign the property targeted for reduction a functional definition specifying the typical causal conditions under which the property is exemplified and the typical effects of its instantiation. Second, we search the reduction base domain for properties that implement the causal role definitive of the functionalized property. Third, we construct a theory explaining how the realizers of this property perform the specified causal tasks (pp. 101–2). Then, when a physical property instance p satisfies the causal profile of a functionalized property M we may be confident that p is an *instance* of M, in which case the causal powers of this instance of M will be identical to the causal powers of p: 'if pain can be functionalized in this sense, its instances will have the causal powers of pain's realizers . . . [and] the problem of mental causation has a simple solution for all pain instances' (pp. 25–6).

　Conspicuously absent from this description is any specification of which 'physical item' it is with which the mental property (pain) has been reductively identified. Curiously, while Kim's outline of the procedure begins with the aim of reducing the *property* pain it moves directly into a discussion of the conditions under which pain is *instantiated*, which then (in recognition of pain's multiple realizability) leads him to remark that 'Neural bases may differ for different instances of pain, but *individual* pains must nonetheless reduce to their respective neural/physical realizers,' and the process terminates with the result that 'all pain *instances* are reduced to the *instances* of their realizers' (pp. 24–5, italics mine). This is confusing in several respects. To begin, it makes little sense to say that one property instance 'reduces' to another if reduction requires functionalization, since token, non-repeatable events aren't the sorts of things that admit of definition in terms of their 'typical' causes and effects. But if the 'reduction' of an M-instance to P-instance simply amounts to their identification, (PII) licenses the identification only if there is 'some form of reductive relationship' between the properties M and P themselves. Yet the identification of 'individual pains' with their 'respective realizers' has no tendency to suggest that pain itself has been reduced to anything, still less that it has been successfully identified with 'some physical item' as (RP) demands. Indeed, nothing in the above serves noticeably to demarcate Kim's picture from classical functionalist construals of the 'token-identity' theory, which he has repeatedly alleged entail epiphenomenalism.[5]

The crucial questions for Kim then are these: have mental properties been eliminated? If not, are they epiphenomenal (are their instances causal, but not in virtue of their mental aspects)? If not—if mental properties may be reductively identified with causally efficacious items—which physical things are they? If either of the first two questions is answered affirmatively Kim's theory can hardly be supposed to ensure that mental events are causal 'in virtue of being *mental* property instances,' and he gains no ground over the antireductive views he has long opposed. But those two questions can be answered in the negative only if he has a suitable reply to the third: for the conjunction of (RP) and (PII) tells us that unless a mental property is identical with something physical it cannot be reduced, in which case its instances cannot be identified with physical property instances. And from this, according to the Supervenience Argument, epiphenomenalism results.

Kim seems aware that these questions are pressing. Unfortunately, he answers the first two without directly addressing the third:

> But what of the causal efficacy of pain itself? . . . The answer is that as a kind pain will be causally heterogeneous . . . Pain, as a kind, will lack the kind of causal/nomological unity we expect of true natural kinds, kinds in terms of which scientific theorizing is conducted. This is what we must expect given that pain is a functional property . . . If the term 'multiple' in 'multiple realizations' means anything, it must mean causal/nomological multiplicity . . . On this reductive account, pain will not be causally impotent or epiphenomenal; it is only that pain is causally heterogeneous.   (p. 26)

So according to Kim a mental property M, upon its functionalization and reduction, is causally heterogenous and ill-suited to figure into scientific laws, but M is not thereby eliminated or rendered ineligible as a cause. And since the reduction of M requires its identification with something physical there must be some physical item that matches the profile Kim depicts.

I know of one item that perfectly fits the bill: M could be identified with the disjunctive property each disjunct of which is a physical realizer of M. But this evidently is not a suggestion Kim is prepared to endorse:

> [If] we insist on having M as a disjunctive property, we may end up with a property that is largely useless. What good would it do to keep it as a property when it is not a projectible kind that can figure in laws, and cannot serve in causal explanations?, . . . Ex hypothesi,

---

[5] For example, Robert Van Gulick's antireductive functionalism is almost word for word identical to the 'reductive' theory Kim presents here. See Van Gulick (1992: 172) and compare the discussion of nonreductive functionalism in Kim (1998: 51–6).

[diverse realizers of M] are heterogeneous kinds, and if heterogeneity is going to mean anything significant, it must mean causal/nomic heterogeneity. Now . . . this means that instances of M are not going to show the kind of causal/nomological homogeneity we expect from a scientific kind. In short, [these properties] are causally and nomologically heterogeneous kinds, and this at bottom is the reason for their inductive unprojectibility and ineligibility as causes.   (1998: 109–10)

So disjunctive properties are ruled out. Unfortunately, it seems, everything else is too. For if the heterogeneity and unprojectability of disjunctive properties is 'at bottom' the reason for their ineligibility as causes (and, indeed, is grounds for their elimination), and if *any* physical item with which M might be identified will inevitably display these features, there can be no suitable physical candidate for M's identification—no candidate that would make M-instances efficacious in virtue of instantiating M.

At this point we confront two options: we may eliminate mental properties or we may attempt to retain them. Taking the first option first, suppose we agree with Kim that while there are disjunctive and functional *concepts* which make possible the application of psychological predicates to physical phenomena, these concepts correspond to no real properties (Kim 1998: 103 ff). If a mental 'property' M is identified with such a concept then M has not been identified with any physical item relevant to mental causation (since 'the problem of mental causation does not concern the causal efficacy of *psychological concepts*' (p. 106)), in which case, as we know from (RP) and (PII), M has not been reduced and therefore has no causally efficacious instances. But clearly this does not solve the problem of mental causation as Kim wields it against the nonreductivist. For according to him any solution to this problem must entail that mental events are efficacious in virtue of their mental properties, and *eliminating* mental properties hardly implies that events psychologically described are efficacious in virtue of 'instantiating' them.

So suppose we admit the existence of heterogeneous, non-nomic kinds and identify mental properties with them. This will be of no use either. For even if mental properties were identified with such kinds we cannot by sheer fiat decide that the considerations militating against their causal status can simply be ignored, least of all in this context. As Kim has repeatedly stressed, the competition between irreducibly mental and physical causes is generated by the central role properties occupy within the problem of mental causation, 'for it is in terms of properties and their interrelations that we make sense of . . . concepts that are crucial in this context, such as law, causality, explanation and dependence' (1989: 270). On his reckoning, any causal transaction must be grounded in a law citing the causally homogeneous physical types those events instantiate. Now if no mental property is identical with a causal/nomic physical property, any physical event instantiating a heterogeneous mental kind M will also instantiate a causal/nomic physical property P such that $M \neq P$. Clearly, any such event will be causal in virtue of instantiating P. But even granting this event is both an

M-instance and a *P*-instance it does not follow that *its being an instance of M* is enough to deliver mental causation. Specifically, this maneuver cannot solve the problem of mental causation *as formulated by Kim against the nonreductivist*. So, I claim, neither does it solve the problem as it confronts Kim.

Recall that from Kim's perspective the fundamental problem with 'a Davidsonian token identity' is its implication that '*the very same network of causal relations would obtain in Davidson's world if you were to . . . [remove].. . mentality entirely from the world* (1989: 269), and it entails this because mental events—despite their identity with physical events—are causal in virtue of the *causal/nomic physical kinds they are* but not in virtue of their *mental* properties. Yet what is true at 'Davidson's world' is equally true at Kim's if mental properties cannot be identified with causal/nomic physical kinds. Thus, even conceding that Kim can guarantee the identity of mental and physical events this does not vindicate mental causation, because the 'relevant sense' in which mental and physical property instances must be identified *was intended to ensure what nonreductive 'token identity' theories cannot*: that such events are causal in virtue of their mental properties. Of course, it may be that the functionalization of mental properties allows for the identification of their instances with physical events in a principled way. But this does not accomplish the aims for which Kim's psychophysical reduction was originally introduced. What motivated the reductionism was not its potential for delivering property-*instance* identities—*those* identities have never been enough to secure mental causation according to Kim—but rather its promise as a means of resolving the causal competition between distinct mental and physical *properties* and the apparent redundancy of the former as opposed to the latter, so that mental events may be causal *in virtue of* their mental aspects. And Kim's strategy for identifying mental with physical events does nothing to alleviate these difficulties at all. Yet if this is reason enough to deny the compatibility of mental causation and antireductionism, it is reason enough to deny its compatibility with Kim's reductive functionalism as well.

5.

If the Supervenience Argument demonstrates that nonreductive physicalism entails epiphenomenalism it does so only by way of (PII) and (RP). Kim's theory either fails to satisfy these principles or satisfies them in a way that leaves the causal competition between mental and physical properties unresolved. Consistently applied, therefore, the principles constraining the Supervenience Argument's reasoning lead to the conclusion that type physicalism alone is consistent with mental causation. On the other hand, if Kim judges his theory a success he cannot consistently claim that nonreductive token identity theories entail that 'mentality does no causal work' (p. 269). Either way, Kim's reductive functionalism is no better (and no worse) off than the nonreductive theories he has labored so strenuously against.

13

Nonreductive Physicalism or Emergent Dualism? The Argument from Mental Causation

Timothy O'Connor and John Ross Churchill

Throughout the 1990s, Jaegwon Kim developed a line of argument that what purport to be *nonreductive* forms of physicalism are ultimately untenable, since they cannot accommodate the causal efficacy of mental states. His argument has received a great deal of discussion, much of it critical. We believe that, while the argument needs some tweaking, its basic thrust is sound. In what follows, we will lay out our preferred version of the argument and highlight its essential dependence on a causal-powers metaphysics, a dependence that Kim does not acknowledge in his official presentations of the argument.[1] We then discuss two recent physicalist strategies for preserving the causal efficacy of the mental in the face of this sort of challenge, strategies that (ostensibly) endorse a causal powers metaphysics of properties while offering distinctive accounts of the physical realization of mental properties. We argue that neither picture can be satisfactorily worked out, and that seeing why they fail strongly suggests that nonreductive physicalism and a causal powers metaphysics are not compatible, as our original argument contends. Since we also believe that robust realism concerning mental causation should not be abandoned, we take the argument of this paper to strongly motivate an account on which the mental is unrealized by and ontologically emergent from the physical. In a final section, we sketch what an ontologically emergentist account of the mental might look like.

---

[1] While Kim does not officially endorse a causal powers metaphysic, he has noted his reliance upon a certain view of causation in making his case, a view that, on the surface, bears some similarity to the view we endorse. See for example Kim (1998: 45–56); Kim (2002: 674–5); and Kim (2005: 17–18, 30, 45, and 47 note 12). However, there is some ambiguity in the way Kim uses the term 'cause.' See Kim (1998: 43) and Kim (2005: 20 and 41). And see especially Kim (2002: 677), where he speculates that causality may supervene on fundamental laws (and, perhaps, initial conditions), or that it could 'emerge' at macro-levels ('Could Hume be right about fundamental physics but wrong about macro-objects and events?'), or that it might be 'implemented' or 'realized' by something more basic, like energy flow or momentum transfer.

1. A CAUSAL POWERS ONTOLOGY

Let us first explain what we mean by the term 'causal powers.' One way of using this term is merely a loose manner of describing the causal features of a property, entity, or kind independently of any definite commitments on the metaphysics of causation. A person using the term this way might say, for example, that a defoliant has the causal power to kill plants, where this claim is neutral as to whether (a) the presence of the defoliant can produce or generate the death of a plant; (b) there is a law of nature that relates properties of the defoliant and plant death; (c) plants regularly die after being sprayed with the defoliant; (d) there are subjunctive conditionals relating the properties of the defoliant and the death of plants in a certain way; (e) citing the presence of the defoliant satisfactorily explains the occurrence of plant deaths in certain contexts; or some (f) fitting a still different analysis of causation.

We do not use the term in this neutral manner. Our usage corresponds to the first of these: a power to produce or to generate, where this is assumed to be a real relation irreducible to more basic features of the world. Our favored technical term for this is 'causal oomph.' So understood, causation is not amenable to analysis in non-causal terms, but instead involves the exercise of ontologically primitive causal *powers* or *capacities* of particulars. Powers are either identical to, or figure into the identity conditions of, certain of the object's properties, which are immanent to those things as non-mereological parts. (Whether one thinks of these as immanent universals or tropes is not crucial in this context.)

It bears emphasis that this view is *not* committed to assuming that all causation must amount to something like 'pushing,' or 'pulling,' or 'knocking,' or 'the exertion of a force.' What is assumed, rather, is solely this: when an instance of a property — the event of the particular's having the property — is a cause, the world unfolds in a certain way after the instance of that property, and that property instance is one of the factors that jointly *make* the world unfold this way. This is just another way of saying what's come before, that the property instance, and others besides, jointly *produce* or *generate* certain effects; they jointly oomph the world into going on in *this* way rather than *that*. Because of this, there are certain counterfactuals true of the world ('were the property not to have been instanced, such-and-such effects would not have occurred'). But these counterfactuals are derivative from, and not to be equated with, or seen as the basis of, the causal facts themselves: it's *because* the property instance was among the factors that jointly produced the relevant happenings that certain corresponding counterfactuals are true. Causally efficacious properties have the power to make the world unfold in ways that it otherwise would not, and this is a fundamental feature about these properties upon which all else (counterfactuals true of them, regularities and patterns that encompass them, explanations that cite them) is derivative.

There is much debate, and not a little confusion, over how to delineate the finer points of this general picture. While we cannot delve deeply into these matters, we make the following two remarks to forestall confusion that might infect understanding of our subsequent argument. First, there is a pervasive manner of speaking that appears on the surface to say that *objects* have and exercise causal powers. (Witness our example above with respect to defoliants.) In our view, such talk should be construed by the causal powers metaphysician as a shorthand way of expressing the claims that:

i) the having of the property is the having of the causal power;

ii) the event of the property's being had by the object in appropriate circumstances causally contributes to the effect; and

iii) the exercise of the causal power just is this causal contribution.[2]

Second, a single property may contribute to a very wide array of effects, depending on the context in which it is instanced. A particle's being negatively charged may contribute to its accelerating at varying rates away from a similarly charged nearby particle, accelerating toward an oppositely charged nearby particle, even accelerating towards a similarly charged particle (though at a slower rate than would occur were the particle not to have been so charged), and countless other manifestations, all depending on the context of its occurrence. But in ordinary speech, again, there is a tendency to talk of a corresponding array of causal powers being exercised, 'each' of which is identified through the effect actually manifested. This sort of speech has encouraged some metaphysicians to posit a multiplicity of properties, or worse, to posit a distinct type of entity (a causal power), any number of which are 'conferred by' a single property. We should resist such moves on grounds of parsimony, and here science is a much better guide to property/power identifications.[3] The key is to understand a basic power or disposition not in terms of this or that salient manifestation, but rather in terms of a unitary causal influence, something that is constant across circumstances while its manifestations will vary.

While we cannot undertake here a defense of this understanding of causation, we will summarize what we take to be some key advantages over two very general rival approaches. The first is the class of broadly Humean reductionist accounts. While details differ considerably, on all Humean accounts, whether one event

---

[2] One *might* hold to a philosophical view leading one to insist that in certain cases, it is indeed the object that exercises the power, and not the event of the object's having the property/causal power. Such is the claim of the agent causationist, e.g., with respect to the forming of a free decision. But this is a substantive and controversial thesis, not a spelling out for one sort of case what is common to every case of causation. (For a discussion of the relationship of agent causation to the more usual 'event causation' within a causal powers metaphysics, see Timothy O'Connor, 'Agent-Causal Power,' forthcoming in Toby Handfield (ed.), *Dispositions and Causes* (Oxford: Oxford University Press).

[3] We are influenced here by Richard Corry. See 'A Causal-Structural Theory of Empirical Knowledge' (PhD thesis, Indiana University, 2002) and 'Scientific Analysis and Causal Influence,' in Handfield (2008).

causes another is a massively nonlocal matter, insofar as causal relations supervene on the global pattern of events across space and time. Should the pattern of future events turn out to be very different from what our best theories now predict, it might 'turn out' that what we thought to be an obvious causal interaction—never mind the details of its nature, the very existence of any causal relationship at all—was no such thing. But this is implausible. What happens in the distant reaches of space and time cannot nullify whether a causal transaction occurs here and now. (To focus, one's intuitions, consider rational agency as a special case. Actions are a special kind of causal process. If a Humean picture of causation more generally is correct, then should the future pattern of events unfold in certain ways, and nothing that has happened thus far will keep it from doing so, we should have to say none of us ever undertook an action at all. Mind, we are not speaking here of 'free' actions in the sense of free will, just plain-old actions.) The causal powers metaphysician has no such implausible nonlocality commitment. Furthermore, by grounding causal relationships, ultimately, in the contingent global distribution of noncausal facts, certain kinds of explanations become unavailable in principle. For example, if, in seeking an explanation for the occurrence of token event y, we're seeking knowledge of *what made y occur*, then the Humean must deny that there is any such item of knowledge. And while, e.g., X- and Y-type events may conform to a pervasive pattern of a specified sort (whether actual or counterfactual), for Humeans there will either be no explanation as to why that pattern holds, or else the explanation will itself bottom out in unexplained pattern facts. For anyone who shares our temperament vis-à-vis explanation, these consequences are bound to disappoint.[4] The account of causation we favor, on the other hand, invites neither of these two disappointments. This should be obvious in the first case, given what we have proposed concerning the causal relation. As for the second case, noting that X-type events all manifest a common property that is disposed to bring about Y-type events in specified sorts of circumstances provides us with an explanation as to why X- and Y-type events conform to the pattern they do, an explanation that does not bottom out in unexplained pattern facts. (And whatever else we might think of them, Humean complaints that dispositions introduce a 'mysterious modality' into the world are hardly founded in scientific practice, where functional methods of specifying theoretical properties is standard. On the causal powers view, where such identifications are accurate, they capture something about the nature of the property itself. Whereas for the Humean, they merely describe contingent patterns of instantiation of the property, while being forever silent concerning its intrinsic character.)

The second rival approach, developed in somewhat different ways by Michael Tooley and David Armstrong, involves associating particular causal relations in

---

[4] We are aware that not everyone shares our temperament with respect to explanation, so not everyone will share our disappointment. For more on causal explanation, to include thorough discussion of extant theories of causal explanation, see Woodward (2003).

the world with a contingent, higher-order, nomic relation among universals, a relation that Armstrong dubs 'necessitation.' The central idea is that the obtaining of a nomic fact of the form $N (F, G)$ grounds and explains the fact that a particular instance of F is followed by a particular instance of G. But, as many have pointed out, it's not at all transparent how a second-order relation among universals can constrain particular first-order F-G sequences.[5] Both Tooley and Armstrong have tried to complicate the account in order to overcome the difficulty. Here we restrict our attention to Armstrong's (1997) strategy. It is to conjecture that the second-order relation among universals is identical to the causal relation among its instances—causation is a relation not among particular, first-order states of affairs, but of types of states of affairs. But now the appearance of an advantage over the brute conjecture of the Humean theorist has vanished. For each occurrence of G is ontologically and so explanatorily prior to the immanent, co-occurring $N (F, G)$ fact. So the posit of the N relation is gratuitous, as it can only be put into the world consequent upon the regularity. It is merely a baroque adornment to Humeanism—enough so that we might with justice call it 'second-order Humeanism.'[6] This is so, that is, unless we make the stronger claim that F by its very nature is disposed to bring about G, in which case we are back to the primitive dispositionality of the causal powers metaphysics.

Such, in outline form, are a few central reasons we have for thinking a causal powers metaphysics to be preferable to its main rivals. In considering the prospects for a nonreductive physicalist view of the mental, we are assuming, rather than arguing for, this causal powers metaphysic. We are investigating its implications for the question at hand. Can the (by our lights) right-thinking metaphysician who has seen his way clear to this view of causation make out a nonreductive physicalist view on which mental states are causally efficacious in this sense? We will try to persuade you that the prospects are bleak.

2. CAUSAL POWERS AND THE DILEMMA OF REDUCTION OR CAUSAL EXCLUSION OF THE MENTAL

We will now present our preferred version of a Kim-style argument for the reducibility of mental properties to physical properties.[7] We begin with three related premises concerning causation and properties:

1) Causation is a real relation irreducible to more basic features of the world. (*causal nonreductionism*)

---

[5] See van Fraassen (1988: chapter 5), and Lewis (1983a: 40).
[6] Mumford (2004) includes an extended discussion of this problem for the Armstrongian approach. See pp. 99–103 and 148–49.
[7] See Kim (1993b, 1997, 1998, 1999, 2003, 2005).

2) Causation involves the exercise of causal powers or capacities of particulars. *(production account of causation)*

3) Properties are individuated in terms of causal powers, such that there are no distinct properties that confer exactly the same causal powers. *(causal theory of properties)*

The next three premises flow from the distinctive commitments of non-reductive physicalists:

4) Mental properties supervene on physical properties. *(supervenience thesis)*

The hoary slogan, of course, is 'no mental difference without a physical difference,' intended to capture an appropriate dependence relation. What exact form the supervenience relation should take in this context, however, is a difficult and controverted issue. We will follow Kim in supposing that complication arising, e.g., from mental content externalism can be safely ignored. If this is correct, we may assume for the sake of argument that mental properties 'strongly supervene' on the physical properties of the individual (or on the physical properties and relations of the individual's parts). Next we have:

5) Mental properties are realized by physical properties: a particular event M of a person S's having mental property M is either 'constituted by' (a kind of onto-logical posteriority) or is identical to various physical particulars—possibly including portions of the person's environment—having certain physical properties and standing in certain physical relations. *(realization thesis)*

We will be noncommittal on whether the realization of mental properties by physical properties involves constitution or identity of the corresponding events, since non-reductive physicalists' pronouncements on this matter are varied and often obscure.[8] Finally, physicalists typically wish to assert:

6) Every *physical* event that has a cause has a complete physical cause.[9] *(causal completeness of physics)*

According to (6), nothing non-physical is *required* in order to causally account for the occurrence of any physical event, where the latter consists in the instantiation of fundamental physical properties and relations by fundamental physical entities. Whatever their particular views concerning the status of special science laws and causes, including those pertaining to psychology, the typical physicalist maintains that any fundamental physical event (including large-scale distributions of fundamental properties and relations) that has a cause has a cause that is equally fundamental and physical in character. The true physics is causally complete.

---

[8] See, for example, the variation among Fodor (1974); Pereboom and Kornblith (1991) and Pereboom (2002); Shoemaker (2001 and 2007); and Gillett (2002).

[9] We will ignore the complication of indeterministic causation, which would require us to formulate the completeness thesis in terms of fixing the chances of the effect.

We now contend that (1)–(6) are inconsistent with supposing

7) A mental property, **M**, is distinct from its physical realizer property (or properties), **P**, and each event that consists of **M**'s being instanced exercises a distinctive form of causality that one way or another impinges the realm of physical events.[10] *(assumption for reductio)*

Premise (7) is the supposition that there are mental properties that do not reduce to physical properties and whose causal efficacy does not reduce to the causal efficacy of some physical properties. This means, in the schema used in (7), that the singular causal action of the mental event of **M**'s being instanced does not reduce to the singular causal action of some physical event or events (say, the instancing of the physical property **P** that realizes **M** in the circumstances). In short, the commitment expressed by (7) is what puts the 'non' in 'non-reductive' physicalism. The argument that (7) is inconsistent with (1)–(6) proceeds as follows.

8) The instance of **M** either

    (a) directly produces a subsequent mental event, M^*, or

    (b) it directly produces a wholly physical event, P^*.

The realization thesis (5) and production account of causation (2) together strongly suggest that option (a) is a nonstarter. On this view, mental events are ontologically dependent on their subvening realizers, wholly constituted by (if not identical to) them, and this is no less true of mental *effects* as of mental *causes*. Bringing about such a mental event *eo ipso* involves causally affecting the physical event which realizes it. So

9) Not (8a).

But the thesis of causal completeness (6) implies that

10) If 8b, then the physical event P^* is overdetermined by M and some other physical event.

Now, if we accept the production account of causation, it will seem passing strange to suppose that, in regular fashion, there are physical events that are systematically 'overoomphed' by distinct events, even if—indeed, *especially* if—these causes might stand in a supervenience relation. If, say, a physical event P, the realizer of the mental event M, produces or oomphs P^*, what causal work is left over for M? It would be at best a gross violation of parsimony to posit two distinct productive relations for a single event every time mental events supervene

---

[10] We will, for the sake of convenience, continue to refer only to **P**, the single realizer of **M**, though it should be understood that on some accounts of realization **M** may be realized by multiple properties ('the **P**s,' say) each time it is instanced. As we'll see below, Gillett (2002) is one such account.

on the fundamental physical cause. Note that on reductive accounts of causation, on which causal facts are not something additional to the totality of noncausal facts, the situation looks very different. Suppose, for example, that our effect P^* is counterfactually dependent on both P and M. If we accept something like the counterfactual analysis of causation, there is nothing strange or objectionable about deeming M, as well as P, to be a cause of P^*. For in doing so we are not making a commitment to anything additional—M's status as a cause of P^* falls out of the facts that we already accept along with our analysis. It comes for free. By contrast, on the nonreductive productive account, we would be positing an additional fundamental relation between M and P^*, when doing so is entirely unnecessary for accounting causally for P^*. Thus, we should conclude that:

11) There is not systematic mental-physical overdetermination, as the consequent of 10 implies.

But this is the end of the road. We are forced to conclude, therefore, that:

12) **M** does not make a distinctive contribution to occurrences in the physical world, whether wholly physical or supervening mental occurrences. *(completing Reductio of 7)*

Finally, the causal theory of properties (premise 3) both rules out an epiphenomenalist retreat and suggests the proper ultimate conclusion: we ought either to reductively *identify* **M** with **P** or *deny* that **M** is a bona fide property—one that earns its causal keep—in the first place.

Nonreductive physicalists see an obstacle to the first option, reductionism, in the fact that, as functional properties, intentional properties are multiply realized. What counts as a belief that Q in humans may be quite distinct, at any physical level of description, from what counts as that same belief in, say, an intelligent extraterrestrial or a sophisticated artificial machine built out of steel and silicon. In reply, Kim recommends that we seek local, species-specific reductive identities for intentional properties—*human* belief that such-and-such as identical with physical property so-and-so—and so preserve the status of these intentional properties as causal powers. That is, we characterize both **M** and **P** in terms of *highly* specific mental and physical types, respectively, and move to a type-type identity theory.

The second, eliminativist option is to interpret apparent reference to mental properties as properly denoting mental *concepts* only. There are far fewer properties had by an object than the vast number of concepts it falls under. As indicated in premise (3), *properties* are immanent to their instances and make a nonredundant difference to how the objects act in at least some circumstances. (They answer to what Kim calls 'Alexander's dictum.')

The argument just presented, like earlier relatives, seeks a reductionist or eliminativist conclusion by way of arguing for the *exclusion* of irreducibly mental causation. Yet it does this by explicitly invoking the thesis of causal powers realistically construed. So let us refer to it hereafter as the *power exclusion argument*.

As critics of Kim have observed, this argument appears to generalize beyond mental properties to all properties posited in the special sciences (sciences other than basic physics).[11] And since, contra Kim, it is highly plausible that special science categories are not ontologically reducible (owing in part to their own multiple realizability),[12] the eliminativist conclusion the argument ultimately invites here is often taken as a *reductio ad absurdum*: surely the terms of well-established biological and chemical theory pick out genuinely efficacious properties!

Owing to length constraints, we shall not be able to treat this sort of indirect criticism of the argument in detail. We will rest content with the following two-fold response.

First, notice that a rejection of premises (5) and (6), the realization and causal completeness theses, suffices to block the final conclusion of the power exclusion argument. As we discuss later on, we believe the best way to maintain a robust, nonreductive view of the mental is to reject these two premises. Similarly, one might reject the corresponding premises in an exclusion argument directed at special science properties that one takes to be irreducible and efficacious. Recent philosophy of science has seen significant challenge to the completeness thesis in particular.[13]

But second, for one who takes the case for the completeness of physics with respect to some or all special sciences to be convincing, it would not be absurd to accept a causal exclusion conclusion from a corresponding form of argument. For so-called 'high level' theories can be enormously useful and illuminating, and even necessary to the progress of human knowledge of how the world works, without answering to ontological 'levels' or layers populated by distinctive properties and their objects.[14] And the further fact that such theories are not generally reducible to more fundamental theories is a highly interesting fact about our world (and one necessary for science to get off the ground, as in practice we inevitably work our way in, not out), but it cuts no ontological ice. An alternative to the levels picture of physical reality has already been hinted at above: there is a vast array of microphysical entities (for simplicity, 'the particles') bearing primitive, dynamical features and standing in primitive relations. Talk of composite objects and their properties, at least in the general case, is the imposition of a conceptual scheme that selectively picks out coarse-grained patterns running through the vast storm

---

[11] For discussion, see Baker (1993); Burge (1993); van Gulick (1993); Kim (1996, 1997, 1999, 2003, 2005); Block (2003); Ross and Spurrett (2004).

[12] See Fodor (1974); Dupré (1993); and Rosenberg (1994).

[13] See Cartwright (1999) and Dupré (1993 and 2001). And for a powerful challenge to the case for completeness in the special scientific domain of chemistry in which it is widely thought to be most secure, see Hendry (2006).

[14] On this point, see Heil (2000: chapters 2–7).

of particles. These concepts really are (*objectively*) satisfied by the world, but not in virtue of a one–one relation between general concepts and properties, or individual concepts and particulars.

This second response might be thought to entail the devaluation of the special sciences. Such a conclusion would be too hasty, however. For it is simply false that science is of value only as a source of representing the world in more and more accurate ways. It is, in addition, a source of means for intervening and manipulating the world so as to change it for the better, and much of its value is due to this rather than its representational fruits. We value science—we fund it, prioritize it, give special social status to many of its practitioners, etc.—because of its role in improving the world, and not just because of its role in representing the world. (The development of methods for effectively preventing and treating myriad diseases serves as just one example of such improvement.) But *qua* sources of improvement, some of the special sciences are at least as valuable, and perhaps more so, than fundamental physics. For we are very often *better* able to intervene and manipulate in ways that improve the world by using the resources of the non-fundamental special sciences.

Returning to the status of mental properties, here, then, is where we are left. The commitments that drive the power exclusion argument—the causal powers metaphysics along with the supervenience, realization, and causal completeness theses of nonreductive physicalism—appear to generate the conclusion that mental properties are either reducible or eliminable. This is serious trouble for philosophers who are neither reductionists nor eliminativists with respect to the mental, and they are legion. Thus, if we wish to preserve the mind as irreducibly efficacious, we must reject one or another of the commitments driving the argument above.

Or so we believe. Sydney Shoemaker, however, disagrees, and has recently attempted to provide a way out for the nonreductive physicalist who is a realist with respect to causal powers. Since Shoemaker has *bona fides* as both a causal powers metaphysician and as a physicalist, it is fitting that we investigate his approach in detail.

3. SHOEMAKER ON NON-REDUCTIVE MENTAL CAUSATION

Shoemaker thinks that the key to vindicating the causal efficacy of mental properties without reduction lies in a distinctive account of the *realization* of mental properties by physical properties. In broad strokes, his proposal is that mental and other realized properties are *disjunctive* properties, with their disjuncts as their realizers: the relation of realizer to realized is simply the relation of disjunct to disjunction.[15] This ensures that realized properties have a proper subset of each of their realizers' *forward-looking causal features*—what instances of the properties can causally suffice for—while having a superset of their realizer properties' *backward-looking causal features*—what can causally suffice for instances of the properties. Shoemaker then exploits the conclusion that realized properties have a subset of their realizers' powers to argue that mental causation is not reducible to causation by the physical realizers, owing to a certain proportionality thesis explained below concerning what counts as a cause of what. The following schema captures Shoemaker's picture.

(C1 v C2) is a property realized by each of **C1** and **C2** just in case:

C1 → *E1*	*C1* → (*E1* v *E2*)	*B1* → *C1*	*B1* → (*C1* v *C2*)
C2 → *E2*	*C2* → (*E1* v *E2*)	*B2* → *C2*	*B2* → (*C1* v *C2*)
	(*C1* v *C2*) → (*E1* v *E2*)		(*B1* v *B2*) → (*C1* v *C2*)

('→' denotes causal sufficiency)

How is accepting this picture of realization supposed to make things easier for non-reductive physicalism? We begin by observing that if the realized property has a subset of the forward-looking causal features of the realizer, then the realizer property event is causally sufficient for everything the realized property event is causally sufficient for, *plus more*. So, for example, *C1* is causally sufficient for (*E1* v *E2*), just as (*C1* v *C2*) is, but unlike the disjunctive cause it is also sufficient for an instance of **E1**. Now, if *C1* and (*C1* v *C2*) overlap in this way in what they causally suffice for, and if causal considerations ought to drive our conclusions about the identity of properties, a natural conclusion is that (*C1* v *C2*) is a proper *part* of *C1*. More generally: events which instance realized properties are parts of those instancing the corresponding realizers, and so are not identical to them.

From here, Shoemaker invokes a version of Stephen Yablo's 'proportionality' constraint[16] on what we ought to count as 'the cause' in a causal interaction: while it is true that *C1* is causally sufficient for (*E1* v *E2*), (*C1* v *C2*) is, Yablo and Shoemaker say, a *better candidate* for being the cause. For (*C1* v *C2*) is also causally sufficient for the specified effect, but only 'just so'—it causally suffices for the effect *and nothing more besides*. The only features of *C1* that contribute to the 'bringing about' of (*E1* v *E2*) are features had by (*C1* v *C2*), a 'part' of *C1*. And

---

[15] For key passages in support of this interpretation, see Shoemaker (2007: section II of chapter 2 (especially pp. 17–18), pp. 55–6, and section V of chapter 4 (especially p. 79 and 82)). See also the remark that Lenny Clapp has proposed a view similar to his own in Shoemaker (2001: 93 note 3, and 2007: 11). (Clapp (2001) is explicit in his construal of realized properties as disjunctive properties with their disjuncts as the realizers.)

[16] Shoemaker (2001: 81). See Yablo (1992).

as with a more familiar sort of case, such as Jones's single shot in a firing squad, just ahead of the others, killing the condemned, we are invited to conclude that it is best to say that while the whole (*C1*; the firing squad's firing) was causally sufficient for the effect ((*E1* v *E2*); the death of the condemned), proportionality constraints argue in favor of counting a particular part ((*C1* v *C2*); Jones's firing) rather than the whole as *the cause*.[17] This is how realized events in general—and realized *mental* events in particular—qualify as causes in certain scenarios, such that it is *false* in these scenarios that the (physical) realizer events are likewise causes of the very same effects.

We now have Shoemaker's account of realization laid out before us, as well as the way it is supposed to provide for non-reductive mental causation. But how, we may wonder, does the account underwrite a response to the power exclusion argument? Notice, first, that there is no rejection of the supervenience, realization, or completeness theses (premises 4–6). And, of course, Shoemaker intends (7), the anti-reduction premise, to come out true as well. Thus, one who takes our exclusion argument above to be cogent will naturally suspect that Shoemaker's commitment to the causal powers metaphysics (as expressed in premises 1–3) is less than it appears.

To bring the problem into focus, consider first that, for all his distinctive claims, Shoemaker clearly gives ontological priority to the physical realizer event. He tells us that P realizes M just in case P is metaphysically sufficient for (but not identical to) M and 'constitutively makes [it] real' (Shoemaker 2007: 6, 10). He goes so far as to say that realized states are 'nothing over and above' their realizers (Shoemaker 2007: 2). If all this is so, then how is a case of M's causing an effect, E, not also a case whereby P, M's constituting realizer, is likewise causing E? Indeed, how is this not a case where P is causally prior to M, so that, by the power exclusion argument, we should conclude that P is the sole true cause?[18] It seems that only a retreat from a causal powers metaphysics could allow you to say that P is somehow 'merely' causally sufficient whereas M is the proper cause. If P is ontologically prior to M, *able* to bring about E, and in the circumstances necessary to do so, how can it get out-oomphed by M?

The only way for us to make sense of this is by ignoring Shoemaker's talk of P's constitutively making real M and focusing instead on his notion that M is a part of P, owing to the subset-of-powers thesis and the causal theory of properties. (This line of interpretation is encouraged by his invocation of the

---

[17] See Shoemaker (2001: 81) and (2007: 13–14).

[18] A bolstering consideration comes from certain indeterministic scenarios. We take it to be evident that, *assuming the causal completeness of physics*, the chance of E given M cannot be greater than the chance of E given a total physical cause (here, our P). But there seems to be no reason to think that it cannot be less. Now consider a case where Pr (E/M) is significantly less than Pr(E/P). Surely in such a case, where E in fact occurs, it is highly implausible to insist nevertheless that M, not P, is the cause of E. While this is a special case, if our conclusion from it is accepted, it indicates further that there is something wrong about Shoemaker's method for assigning causes.

firing squad analogy (Shoemaker 2007: 53) and also by such statements as 'It is only because the C-fiber stimulation instance realizer contains the pain instance realizer that it has the relevant effects.' (Shoemaker 2007: 48)) We might then suppose that Shoemaker is proposing what amounts to a radical inversion of the reductionist's vision, such that it is the *physical* properties that resolve into an assemblage of mental properties plus some non-mental remainder.[19] Now, even if that could make sense of how mental causation would be genuine, it has the substantial drawback that it is just plain weird. The physical property is thereby conceived as (or as closely bound up with) a cluster of causal features, a subset of which are the features that define an associated mental property. Making this picture out perhaps requires us to analyze the physical property as a structural property, the instancing of which just consists in the instancing of properties of the object's parts and relations between them. The mental property then comes out, on Shoemaker's view, as an overlapping structural property, perhaps somehow abstracted from the full physical structural property. Waiving considerable doubts we should have about the plausibility of this picture of the mental-physical relationship, it still has the result that *both* mental properties and the larger structural physical properties in which they are embedded turn out to be derivative structures, entities that are constructions out of *micro*physical properties and relations. The specter of reductionism again menaces.

Shoemaker attempts to resist the reductive identification of mental (or other macro-level) properties with microphysical states of affairs by giving an analysis of microphysical realization on which there is only constitution, not identity. However, his case for this rests on two claims about property identity that should be unacceptable to a causal powers theorist (Shoemaker 2007: 48–9). First, he lays down that, in general, a property instance has just one constituent object and one constituent property, so a mental property instance can't be identical to a state of affairs involving many distinct properties and objects. He seems to put this forward as a definitional truth or platitude. But a causal powers theorist does not take quasi-grammatical considerations to be final arbiters concerning the structure of reality. One might just as well take Shoemaker's supposed platitude together with facts (assumed for now) about microphysical constitution and draw the conclusion that there are not, strictly speaking, mental properties at all—not in the sense of entities that contribute directly to how the world unfolds. Shoemaker's second claim is that the modal properties of macro-level property instances and their microphysical realizers will generally differ. (Consider familiar claims made in discussions of the statue of Goliath.) This claim rests on intuitive judgments about possible variation in the material constitution of composite objects. But the status of composite objects, no less than that of 'their' properties, is very much in question on the powers metaphysics. One cannot simply assume

---

[19] We've recently come across a paper where a similar interpretation of Shoemaker is entertained. See Heil (2003: 24).

that there are robustly *objective* modal facts about them and use these to ward off what otherwise appears to be a powerful reductionist challenge.

It is time to take stock. We have defended a power exclusion argument for the untenability of nonreductive physicalism. It is a variant of Kim's argument that makes explicit an assumption of a causal theory of properties. We have tried to show that Sydney Shoemaker's recent attempt to harmonize the two positions fails. We believe that such failure was inevitable, given Shoemaker's unusual combination of physicalist commitments, a causal theory of properties, and an abundant, rather than sparse, ontology of such properties. It is an unstable compound. The causal theory requires that properties earn their keep. This appears inevitably to push the philosopher in one of two directions when it comes to macroscopic structures: reduction or elimination, on the one hand (we needn't here adjudicate the claims of these two), or a rejection of one or more of the characteristic claims of physicalism, on the other.

A typical rejection of physicalism includes the denial of the realization, causal completeness, and the supervenience premises. (We'll here set aside the question whether the rejection of physicalism requires rejecting all forms of supervenience, as it is not resolved easily and is not important for our purposes here anyway.[20])

But before we consider what form a rejection of physicalism might take, we must consider an alternative and original proposal defended in a number of places by Carl Gillett. Gillett contends that we can best reject the Kim-style argument against non-reductive physicalism not by rejecting physicalism itself, but by weakening it. He suggests that we may retain realization and supervenience, and reject only completeness.

4. GILLETT'S 'STRONG EMERGENCE'

Gillett dubs his view 'strong emergentism.' On this view, mental properties, like all macro-level properties, are realized microphysically. That is to say, an instance of a mental property is identical to a combination of *other*, microphysical property instances and relations among them, where the other properties are, in the circumstances, the property's realizers.[21] Strong emergence occurs where *microphysical* properties contribute *different* fundamental causal powers to their microphysical individuals precisely when these properties realize certain properties.

A schematic example: microphysical property L confers upon the microphysical entity that bears it only powers α, β, and γ in all circumstances *except* when it

[20] See the discussion in O'Connor and Wong (2005).
[21] See Gillett (2006b: 275, 280, 281, 282). See also Gillett (2002) for the proposal and defense of his preferred account of realization.

realizes property H, in which case it confers power δ. Now, notice that it's still the case that only microphysical properties contribute the fundamental, irreducible causal powers. (We'll hereafter let the qualifiers 'fundamental' and 'irreducible' be implicit.) But Gillett argues that the realized property H is nevertheless causally *efficacious*, for three reasons:

i) H *non-causally determines* L to contribute the δ power to its bearer,

ii) H is a necessary member of a set of factors jointly sufficient for the contribution of δ to an individual, and

iii) positing H as a causally efficacious property is necessary if we are to 'account for' the relevant microphysical individual's having power δ.[22]

Furthermore, since in cases of strong emergence, we have realized properties, such as H, determining the contribution of causal powers (like δ) by their micro-level realizer properties (L), these count for Gillett as cases of 'downward determination' by H.[23]

Such, in brief, is Gillett's suggested picture of 'strong' emergence. How does it fare as an explication of robust nonreductionism, and is it preferable to non-realizationist varieties of emergence? Notice first that since H is a realized property, the microphysical property L whose activity it non-causally determines is part of H itself. This may seem to result in an objectionable circle of determination relations, but it does not. While an instance of L contributes to the constitutive determination of an instance of H, the latter is not thought to similarly bear some kind of ontological priority to the former. Instead, H determines which causal powers L shall confer in the context.

Our basic criticism is this: Gillett's strong emergence provides at best a very attenuated form of causal efficacy for mental properties. They do not produce (non-derivatively) any event or even trigger some other causal power into activity. They seem to be simply the occasion on which microphysical properties act in unusual ways (i.e., ways departing from their nearly ubiquitous manner of activity). In fact, from the perspective of a causal powers theorist, H in our example seems but a handy name for the sort of circumstances in which L confers δ; it answers one sort of 'when' question. But it's hard to see what's gained in explanation by insisting on accepting an emergent realized property into our ontology. In fact, this insistence plausibly obscures, for (when combined with 'determination' talk) it makes it look as if there's some light being shed on *how* and *why* L confers δ when there's not. The sober metaphysical truth seems to be that whenever L is co-instanced with certain other properties in a certain way—where that way and those other properties can be wholly specified in microphysical terms—then L confers δ. We can introduce the term 'H' as a label for this type of scenario. But in doing so, we wouldn't be accounting for anything that we

---

[22] Gillett (2003: 102); Gillett (2006b: 274, 281, 282, 287).   [23] Gillett (2003a).

hadn't previously accounted for in speaking only of microphysical properties and relations, and we wouldn't have gotten one step closer to understanding how or why L confers δ in the relevant scenarios. Hence, we don't think we ought to accept Gillett's contention that H, understood as an emergent realized property, is a necessary posit in 'accounting for' the contribution of δ by L.[24]

Some will be inclined to reply at this point along the lines of Jerry Fodor's brief on behalf of the standard, non-emergentist variety of nonreductionism: we must recognize H as a real, multiply realized, and explanatory property in its own right because otherwise we will fail to capture the commonality of the many different scenarios, microphysically described, in which L confers δ. Only here the case for H would be bolstered by the fact (*ex hypothesi*) that the *fundamental* dynamics are distinctive in nonreductive scenarios. We are unmoved, but suppose one is inclined to concede the point. Even so, all we would have embraced are mental properties that play a kind of structuring role in the world's dynamics. They do no distinctive causal work—provide no extra causal oomph. There is, indeed, a strong analogy here to the role played by spatial and temporal relations in Newtonian mechanics, as construed by a causal powers theorist.[25] Such relations, one might say, provide a necessary framework for the interplay of dispositional entities, while themselves having no dispositional nature. Surely our nonreductionist physicalist wants more than this by way of the causal relevance of the mental. More than being local, nondispositional constraints on the way fundamental physical causes operate, our beliefs, desires, and intentions themselves directly contribute to the unfolding dynamics of our behavior.

5. A BETTER ACCOUNT OF EMERGENCE

It thus appears that a rejection of the causal completeness tenet of mainstream physicalism will not in itself suffice to secure a robust efficacy for mental properties. We must also reject the realization thesis, and in the context of mental

[24] Gillett buttresses his claims about a non-causal determination relation by comparing the case of emergent properties (like H) to what he counts as other cases where there is non-causal determination. Such cases include parts–wholes, realization, constitution, and properties that contribute conditional powers. See Gillett (2003a: 109, 2006a: 6–7, 2006b: 268). Though more deserves to be said in response, we'll here say only that a causal powers theorist is under no obligation to accept, and may have good reason to reject, each of the four additional candidates for non-causal determination relations Gillett proposes. The grounds in favor of this response are, in brief, that (i) questions about which properties count as causally efficacious (in a causal nonreductionist sense) ought to be settled prior to any commitment concerning the first three proposed relations, and (ii) a causal powers theorist inclined toward 'sparseness' with respect to properties will reject the sort of conditional power-conferring properties Gillett invokes (in his 2003a: 101 and 2006b: 279–80, 285–6) as the *relata* of the fourth proposed relation.

[25] Gillett anticipates this analogy by deeming spatial relations entities that (if they exist) 'do not contribute powers themselves' but 'may still determine the contributions of powers to individuals by other properties and relations' (Gillett 2003b: 35).

causation, at least, that is clearly a rejection of physicalism altogether. In our judgment, the best avenue for developing an anti-physicalist view rooted in the rejection of realization and completeness involves a stronger variety of emergence, what is often termed *ontological emergence*.

The term 'emergence' is used to cover a multitude of sympathies (in some cases, sins). So we want to indicate in clear, albeit very abstract, terms what an emergentist picture would look like, in our way of thinking.

Properties are *ontologically emergent* just in case:

(i) They are ontologically basic properties (token-distinct from, and unrealized by, any structural properties of the system).

(ii) As basic properties, they constitute new powers in the systems that have them, powers that non-redundantly contribute to the system's collective causal power, which is otherwise determined by the aggregations of, and relations between, the properties of the system's microphysical parts. Such non-redundant causal power necessarily means a difference even at the microphysical level of the system's unfolding behavior. (This is compatible with the thesis that the laws of particle physics are applicable to such systems. It requires only that such laws be supplemented to account for the interaction of large-scale properties with the properties of small-scale systems.)

In respects (i) and (ii), emergent properties are no less basic ontologically than unit negative charge is taken to be by current physics. However, emergent and microphysical properties differ in that

(iii) emergent properties appear in and only in organized complex systems of an empirically specifiable sort and persist if and only if the system maintains the requisite organized complexity. The sort of complexity at issue can be expected to be insensitive to continuous small-scale dynamical changes at the microphysical level.[26]

We are inclined to further suppose (though this may depend on our inclination to accept a controversial, strong causal explanatory principle) that

(iv) the appearance of emergent properties is *causally originated and sustained* by the joint efficacy of the qualities and relations of some of the system's fundamental parts. (This would involve fundamental properties having latent dispositions to contribute to effects, dispositions that are triggered only in organized complexes of the requisite sort.)

---

[26] Concepts of emergence have a long history—one need only consider Aristotle's notion of irreducible substantial forms. Their coherence is also a matter of controversy. For an attempt to sort out the different ideas that have carried this label, see O'Connor and Wong (2002). And for a detailed exposition and defense of the notion we rely on in the text, see O'Connor and Wong (2005).

One cannot give uncontroversial examples of emergent properties, of course. Though there are ever so many macroscopic phenomena that seem to be governed by principles of organization highly insensitive to microphysical dynamics, it remains an open question whether such behavior is nonetheless wholly determined, in the final analysis, by ordinary particle dynamics of microphysical structures in and around the system in question.[27] Given the intractable difficulties of trying to compute values for the extremely large number of particles in any medium-sized system (as well as the compounding error of innumerable applications of approximation techniques used even in measuring small-scale systems), it may well forever be impossible in practice to attempt to directly test for the presence or absence of a truly (ontologically) emergent feature in a macroscopic system. Furthermore, it is difficult to try to spell out in any detail the impact of such a property using a realistic (even if hypothetical) example, since plausible candidates (e.g., phase state transitions or superconductivity in solid state physics, protein functionality in biology, animal consciousness) would likely involve the simultaneous emergence of multiple, interacting properties. Suffice it to say that if, for example, a particular protein molecule were to have emergent properties, then the unfolding dynamics of that molecule *at a microscopic level* would diverge in specifiable ways from what an ideal particle physicist (lacking computational and precision limitations) would expect by extrapolating from a complete understanding of the dynamics of small-scale particle systems. The nature and degree of divergence would provide a basis for capturing the distinctive contribution of the emergent features of the molecule.

Now, many contemporary philosophers seem to think that such a view is too extreme to be plausible. When pressed, such critics often cite the alleged consequence that an emergentist view compromises *the unity of nature*. But unity does not require the reductionist vision of the world as merely a vast network binding together local microphysical facts, with a pervasive and uniform causal continuity underlying all complex systems. It is enough that at every juncture introducing some new kind of causally discontinuous behavior, there is a causal source for that discontinuity in the network of dispositions that underlie it. In short: unity in the order of the unfolding natural world need not involve causal continuity of behavior, only continuity of dispositional structure.[28] For the emergentist, the seeds of every emergent property and the behavior it manifests are found within the world's fundamental elements, in the form of latent dispositions awaiting only the right context for manifestation.

---

[27] For numerous examples of such phenomena, see R. B. Laughlin et al. (2000).

[28] This is not to concede that it is ipso facto a theoretical virtue for a metaphysics that it entails greater unity in nature, nor that it is ipso facto a theoretical vice if the converse is true. The issue of the unity of nature, and the related issue of unity in science, are deep and complex. Our point in the text is that there is *a* kind of unity in nature if the emergentist account we have proposed is correct. For more on the topics of unity in science and nature, see Cat (2007).

We make no assertion one way or the other as to whether anything is like this for any chemical or biological properties, though we note that present evidence allows for the possibility that some perfectly respectable biological and chemical features are ontologically emergent in this way.

We do, however, propose that the conscious intentional and phenomenal aspects of the mind strongly favor an emergentist account. A human person's experiences and other conscious mental states exhibit features quite unlike those of physical objects, whether as revealed in ordinary sense perception or as uncovered in the physical and biological sciences. And the maximally direct nature of our first-person awareness of the intentional and phenomenal features of our conscious states prohibits the a posteriori ascription to them of underlying physical micro-structure hidden to introspection. The upshot of this familiar reflection, if it stands, is that our experiences and other conscious mental states have fundamentally distinctive characteristics. But these very characteristics are also *prima facie* causally efficacious. (Indeed, on a causal powers metaphysics, to countenance them as properties is to accept them as efficacious.) Thus, certain mental properties appear to be (1) resistant to analysis in terms of physical structural properties and so plausibly ontologically basic; (2) causally efficacious; and (3) borne only by highly organized and complex systems. Though we cannot argue the matter at length here, we find extant materialist attempts to overcome this prima facie case to be implausible.[29] (It goes without saying that we take the grounds for an emergentist account of the mental to be defeasible.)

Some philosophers acknowledge that the sort of broadly 'Cartesian' picture sketched above captures how we naively think about conscious experience but contend that it is an illusion. For our part, we think that such philosophers underestimate the difficulties for a theory of empirical knowledge that maintains that we are subject to a radical and pervasive cognitive illusion at the very source of all our empirical evidence. And if the central argument of this paper is correct, then for any of these philosophers likewise committed to a causal powers metaphysic, the seemingly *paradoxical* position of denying the causal efficacy of mental states must be added to those difficulties.

---

[29] For extended argument on this point, see Timothy O'Connor and Kevin Kimble (manuscript), 'The Argument from Consciousness Revisited.'

14

Epistemological Objections to Materialism[1]

Robert C. Koons

1. THE DEFINITION OF 'MATERIALISM'

The term 'materialism' has covered a variety of theses and programs. It has quite a long history, dating back at least to Aristotle's objections to the 'earlier thinkers' who over-emphasize the 'material element' in Book Alpha of his *Metaphysics*. It is relatively easy to identify a chain of paradigmatic materialists: Democritus, Empedocles, Lucretius, Hobbes, d'Holbach, Vogt, Büchner, Feuerbach, Marx, J. C. C. Smart, David Lewis, and David Armstrong. Materialism encompasses much more than a thesis or set of theses in the philosophy of mind. It would not be adequate, for example, to identify materialism with the thesis that human beings (or indeed all possible persons) are essentially embodied. This would incorporate only a small part of what materialists have affirmed, and it would include some anti-materialists, like Aristotle or Leibniz (at least with respect to finite and sublunary persons).

Materialism entails the affirmation of at least four central theses:

(1.1) Everything that exists and has real causal efficacy or an inductively discoverable nature can be located within space and time. Nature forms a causally closed system.

(1.2) All genuine causal explanation has a factual basis consisting of the spatial and kinematic arrangement of some fundamental particles (or arbitrarily small and homogenous bits of matter) with specific intrinsic natures. All genuine explanation is bottom–up.

(1.3) These intrinsic natures of the fundamental material things (whether particles or homogeneous bits) are non-intentional and non-teleological. The intentional and teleological are ontologically reducible to the non-intentional and non-teleological.

[1] My thanks to Cory Juhl, Alvin Plantinga, and Michael Rea for their insightful comments on an earlier draft of this chapter.

(1.4) The existence, location, persistence-conditions, causal powers, and de re modal properties of the fundamental material things are ontologically independent of the existence or properties of minds, persons or societies and their practices and interests. Ontological and metaphysical realism.

Given these four principles, there is a relatively simple and homogeneous backing for all veridical causal explanation, and this foundation is independent of and prior to all intentionality, teleology and normativity. Understanding the world consist simply in decomposing all complex phenomena into their constituent parts and uncovering the causal powers of those parts. These parts and their causal powers are of a relatively familiar and unproblematic sort, harboring no mysteries of merely intentional existence or impenetrable subjectivity.

Anti-materialism falls into several distinct varieties, depending which of these theses are rejected. Interactionist substance-dualism rejects (1.1) and (1.2), as does any sort of theism. The various kinds of anti-realism, including ontological relativity, pragmatism, and idealism, reject (1.4). Finally, theses of so-called 'strong' emergence, including the standard interpretation of Aristotle's hylemorphism, entail the denial of (1.2) and (1.3).

To the extent that materialism represents, not a doctrine or set of doctrines, but something much definite, such as a kind of attitude or orientation toward problems in philosophy, I will have little to say against it, although raising difficulties for the combination of the four theses does make the corresponding attitude less attractive. In the concluding section 7, I will explain why I take thesis (1.4) to be an essential part of the materialist package. In brief, making the material world (including the natures and capacities realized in it) in any way dependent on the human mind undermines in a radical way the monistic simplicity of the realist version of materialism.

2. EPISTEMOLOGICAL OBJECTIONS

The epistemological objections to materialism that I will raise fall into two categories: transcendental arguments, and arguments from no-defeater conditions on knowledge. A transcendental argument takes a familiar form:

(2.1) If materialism is true, then human knowledge (or human knowledge of a particular subject matter) is impossible.

This counts as an objection to materialism, as opposed to merely the drawing out of one of its consequences, when this thesis is combined with an anti-skeptical assumption:

(2.2) Human knowledge is possible.

A special case of the transcendental argument is one that charges materialism with being epistemically self-defeating:

(2.3) If materialism is true, then human knowledge of the truth of materialism is impossible.

If thesis (2.3) could be established, we would have shown that materialism is either false or unknowable. Since knowledge entails truth, we can detach the further conclusion that no one knows that materialism is true.

The second category of epistemological objection is that of the violation of no-defeater conditions for knowledge:

(2.3) Anyone who believes in materialism violates the no-defeater condition for knowledge of subject matter M.

A *defeater*, as developed by Chisholm, Pollock (1986), Plantinga (1993), and Bergmann (2000, 2005), for one's belief that p is a fact that overrides or neutralizes all of one's prima facie reasons for believing that p. In other words, suppose that I have various putative reasons $r_1, \ldots, r_n$ for my belief that p: my belief that p is based upon my taking the conjunction of r_1 through r_n to provide good reason for believing that p. A defeater for this belief would be a fact q that is such that the conjunction of q with r_1 through r_n provides no reason for believing that p. This could be either because q provides reasons for believing the negation of p that overrides the reasons for believing p provided by r_1 through r_n (a 'rebutting' defeater), or because the fact that q makes each of r_1 through r_n to be no reason at all (all things considered) for believing that p (an 'undercutting' defeater).

A person S violates the no-defeater condition for knowing that p whenever the world as S believes it so be contains a defeater for all of what S takes to be reasons for believing that p. Thus, thesis (2.3) is equivalent to (2.3.1):

(2.3.1) Anyone S who believes in materialism takes the world to include a fact that would, if all of S's beliefs were true, defeat what S takes to be his or her own reasons for believing anything about subject matter M.

Satisfying the no-defeater condition is a necessary condition of knowledge:

(2.4) Necessarily, if S knows that p, S does not violate the no-defeater condition for p.

Consequently, a successful no-defeater argument establishes that belief in materialism is incompatible with knowledge of subject matter M. That is, (2.3) and (2.4) entail (2.5):

(2.5) Anyone S who believes in materialism lacks knowledge of subject matter M.

A special case of the no-defeater violation argument takes the subject matter M to be the truth of materialism or one of its constituent theses. In this case, the argument's conclusion would be that anyone who believes in materialism does not know materialism to be true. Since belief is a necessary condition of knowledge, this would be a second route to the conclusion that materialism is unknowable.

I will make use of one particular kind of no-defeater violation objection, in which the defeater in question will take the following form:

(2.6) S's belief that p was the product of cognitive processes with a low objective probability of producing true beliefs.

I take the reliability of the underlying cognitive process to be a necessary condition of epistemic warrant. If I believe that my belief that p is unwarranted, then the world as I take it to be contains no reason for my believing that p, and I have thereby violated the no-defeater condition of knowledge. Since an alethically reliable mode of production is a necessary condition of warrant, then I cannot know that p if I believe that my belief that p was formed in an alethically unreliable way.[2]

This sort of reliability constraint raises the generality issue: the process producing any given belief is a token of many different types, and alethic reliability applies at the level of types, not tokens. My response is to follow Alvin Plantinga who proposed, in *Warrant and Proper Function* (Plantinga 1993), that the relevant type is drawn from the 'design plan' of the believer's cognitive faculties (defined by means of a teleological notion of proper function). This response is also available to the materialist, since it does not entail that teleology is a fundamental feature of reality.

There are connections between the two sorts of objection (transcendental and no-defeater violation arguments). For example, we might suppose the following principle:

(2.7) If knowledge of subject matter M is possible, and the fact that q is a sufficiently robust truth (something that would remain true if S were to come to believe it), then it follows that it is possible to know something of M while believing that q.

Materialism, if true, would certainly be a highly robust truth. Hence, a successful argument of the no-defeater violation sort would, together with the robustness of materialism and thesis (2.7), provide us with a new transcendental argument against materialism.

Moreover, any valid transcendental argument would, if its premises are believed by S, provide a defeater for S's belief in materialism.

---

[2] There are two kinds of defeaters: *rationality* defeaters (that provide grounds that undermine the rationality of a basing a belief on certain grounds) and *knowledge* defeaters (that provide grounds that undermine the legitimacy of a claim to knowledge on behalf of a belief based on certain grounds). The two kinds are not mutually exclusive: some defeaters function at both levels, including those that challenge the objective alethic reliability of one's actual grounds.

3. CONCERNING OUR KNOWLEDGE OF NATURES AND NATURAL LAWS

(3.1) A preference for simplicity (elegance, symmetries, invariances) in the hypothesized fundamental laws of nature is a pervasive feature of scientific practice.

(3.2) Our knowledge of the natures of material things depends on our knowledge of the fundamental laws of nature.

(3.3) Given 3.1, our knowledge of the laws of nature depends on the existence of a causal connection between the simplicity (et al.) of a possible fundamental law and its actuality.

(3.4) Materialism entails that there can be no such causal connection.

Consequently:

(3.5) Materialism entails that we have no knowledge of the natures of material things.

3.1. The Pervasive Role of Simplicity

Philosophers and historians of science have long recognized that quasi-aesthetic[3] considerations, such as simplicity, symmetry, and elegance, have played a pervasive and indispensable role in theory choice. For instance, the heliocentric model replaced the Ptolemaic system long before it had achieved a better fit with the data because of its far greater simplicity. Similarly, Newton's and Einstein's theories of gravitation won early acceptance due to their extraordinary degree of symmetry and elegance. The appeal of the electroweak theory was grounded the internal symmetry that it posited between electrons and neutrons.[4]

In *Dreams of a Final Theory*, physicist Steven Weinberg (1993) detailed the indispensable role of simplicity in the recent history of physics. According to Weinberg, physicists use aesthetic qualities both as a way of suggesting theories and, even more importantly, as a sine qua non of viable theories. Weinberg argues that this developing sense of the aesthetics of nature has proved to be a reliable indicator of theoretical truth.

The physicist's sense of beauty is . . . supposed to serve a purpose—it is supposed to help the physicist select ideas that help us explain nature. Steven Weinberg, *Dreams of a Final*

---

[3] My argument does not depend on simplicity's being genuinely aesthetic in character. All that is essential is that we rely on some criteria of theory choice other than mere consistency with observed data.

[4] See, for example, van Fraassen (1988).

Theory: The Scientist's Search for the Ultimate Laws of Nature (New York: Vintage Books, 1993), p. 133.

. . . we demand a simplicity and rigidity in our principles before we are willing to take them seriously. (Weinberg 1993: 148–9)

Weinberg notes that the simplicity that plays this central role in theoretical physics is 'not the mechanical sort that can be measured by counting equations or symbols.' (Weinberg 1993: 134) Theory choice involves recognizing form of beauty by a kind of aesthetic judgment. As Weinberg observes,

There is no logical formula that establishes a sharp dividing line between a beautiful explanatory theory and a mere list of data, but we know the difference when we see it. (Weinberg 1993: 148–9)

In claiming that a form of simplicity plays a pervasive and indispensable role in scientific theory choice, I am not claiming that the aesthetic or quasi-aesthetic sense involved is innate or a priori. I am inclined to agree with Weinberg in thinking that 'the universe acts as a random, inefficient and in the long-run effective teaching machine. . .' (Weinberg 1993: 158) Nonetheless, even our aesthetic attunement to the structure of the universe is not mysteriously prior to experience, there remains the fact that experience has attuned us to *something*, and this something runs throughout the most fundamental laws of nature. Behind the blurring' and buzzin' confusion of data, we have apparently discovered a **consistent** aesthetic running through the various fundamental laws. As Weinberg concludes,

It is when we study truly fundamental problems that we expect to find beautiful answers. We believe that, if we ask why the world is the way it is and then ask why that answer is the way it is, at the end of this chain of explanations we shall find a few simple principles of compelling beauty. We think this in part because our historical experience teaches us that as we look beneath the surface of things, we find more and more beauty. Plato and the neo-Platonists taught that the beauty we see in nature is a reflection of the beauty of the ultimate, the *nous*. For us, too, the beauty of present theories is an anticipation, a premonition, of the beauty of the final theory. And, in any case, we would not accept any theory as final unless it was beautiful. (Weinberg 1993: 165)

This capacity for 'premonition' of the final theory is possible only because the fundamental principles of physics share a common bias toward a specific, learnable form of simplicity.

We can come to know the natures of material things only because they fall into repeatable natural kinds, whose causal powers are delineated by the fundamental laws of nature. Hence, our knowledge of those natures depends critically on our use of simplicity and elegance as a guide to the truth. This *epistemic* priority of laws over intrinsic natures would hold true, even if, *metaphysically* speaking, it was the laws that supervened on the individual natures.

3.2. The Need for a Causal Connection

Gettier's celebrated thought experiments (Gettier 1972) demonstrated justified true belief is not enough for knowledge. There must also be a real, non-accidental connection between the belief and the fact believed in. This remains true when the fact in question concerns the holding of a fundamental law of nature.

Consider the following Gettier-like thought experiment. Suppose that the planets in our local system are moving on invisible rails by means of nuclear-powered engines, with the apparent orbits of the planets fixed as they are in order to satisfy religious rituals completely unrelated to gravity. In this scenario, Newton, building on Kepler's laws of planetary motion, would have had justified true belief but no real knowledge of the laws of nature.

Even more to the point, suppose that the fundamental laws of nature had been designed by an omnipotent God, in order to encode certain dietary laws, when those laws were expressed by means of a certain mathematical language. In this scenario, it is sheer, dumb luck that the laws share a common aesthetic quality. Scientists who, as Weinberg described above, used this aesthetic quality as a guide for theory selection would acquire thereby true and justified beliefs about the laws, but no knowledge. Whatever characteristics we use as a screen for viable theories about the laws of nature (as a set that is a sine qua non) must have some real connection to the actual holding of those laws. To count as knowledge, our scientific theorizing must track a causal structure that lies beneath or behind the laws, and this is incompatible with the materialist thesis (1.1).

It is the lack of causal connection, and not the contingency of the coincidence, that matters. Even if God's intention to encode certain dietary rules were a metaphysically necessary one, and even if our disposition to prefer certain aesthetic qualities were equally robust, any coincidence between the two would remain merely accidental, in a way that would be incompatible with knowledge.

A materialist who believes in immanent universals might be able to make sense of a causal connection between the natures of material things and the flow of events, and so could perhaps insist that our scientific knowledge of laws be causally connected to the natures involved in those laws. However, a materialist cannot suppose that the laws themselves are products of some causal process that gives to them a common aesthetic quality, since this would be to extend the reach of the causal nexus beyond the realm of space and time.[5] Only such a deep causal structure would establish a non-accidental connection between the laws and the aesthetic qualities, and such a connection is required for genuine knowledge.

---

[5] Even if the universals are immanent, and so located in space and time, the interactions between universals that would be required for some common aesthetic to pervade them would require causal interactions unlimited by spatiotemporal propinquity. Connections between universals that correspond to the fundamental laws of nature have to be eternal and, if caused at all, caused atemporally.

There are three historically prominent alternatives to materialism, each with its own account of our knowledge of the laws of nature:

- Theism
- Aristotelianism, with a cosmic order of forms
- Nomological anti-realism

The first two posit causal connections between the deep structure of the laws of nature and that of the human mind, either transcending or immanent to nature; the third rejects both causal connections and the mind-independent reality of the laws.

According to theism, the creator of the universe actualized the world's natural laws. In doing so, God revealed a stable preference for simple, elegant laws.

On the Aristotelian picture, material things instantiate Forms or essences, which form a tightly integrated cosmic system. The Forms of sublunary things derive their natures from a common source, the 'separate' intelligences (associated by Aristotle with the celestial spheres). This Aristotelian picture (reflecting the mature Aristotle of the middle books of the *Metaphysics*) is thoroughly anti-materialist, since the forms or essences are not spatiotemporally located individuals and yet form a causally connected system, with the Aristotle's 'god' playing the central, unifying role, drawing the other forms into imitating it through final causality.

A final alternative is nomological anti-realism. The most relevant version would be the Ramsey-Lewis account of natural laws. A proposition L is a natural law just in case it belongs to that axiomatized system of propositions that best combines comprehensiveness, accuracy and axiomatic simplicity. Here is the dilemma: either this fails to solve the problem, or it fails to comply with the metaphysical realism of materialist thesis (1.4).

In order to solve the epistemological problem, the Ramsey-Lewis account must take the following form:

(3.6) A proposition L is a natural law just in case it belongs to that system of propositions that, given the actual empirical facts, best satisfies our conventional standards of lawlikeness.

We can know our own conventional standards in ways fully compatible with materialism. Hence, if materialists who accept (3.6) can explain in a materialistic-ally acceptable way how it is possible that we know the laws of nature. However, any view that makes the laws of nature depend on our epistemic practices violates principle (1.4) and thereby counts as a version of anti-materialism. Our knowledge of the nature and powers of material objects comes entirely from our scientific knowledge of the laws connecting the natural kinds: for example, all that we know about the natures and powers of electrons comes from our knowledge of the laws that assign dynamical properties (like charge and mass) to those particles and that describe the influence of those properties on the behavior of electrons and other particles. If the laws lack mind-independence, then so do the natures of the material things, insofar as they are scrutable by us.

What if the Ramsey-Lewis definition is rigidified, as in (3.7)?

(3.7) A proposition L is a natural law just in case it belongs to that system of propositions, given the actual empirical facts, best satisfies the standards that are in Alpha (the actual world) the conventional standards for lawlikeness.

In this version (which was Lewis's), the account is metaphysically realist. However, in order to know (3.7), we would have to know that Alpha is an exceptional world: one where the character of the actual laws and the conventional standards of lawlikeness happen to coincide. The problem of accounting for how we could know that Alpha is such a world is exactly the problem materialism cannot solve. Moreover, our conventional standards of theory choice, as they vary from world to world, would not track the features of those worlds' laws.

3.3. Materialism as a Defeater of Scientific Knowledge

In addition to the simple argument that materialism fails to provide a Gettier-proof account of theoretical knowledge, I would add that the lack of connection between the laws and our standards of theory choice that materialism entails provides us with an effective defeater of any claim to scientific knowledge. This is essentially the application of Plantinga's 'evolutionary argument against naturalism' to the case of theoretical knowledge of the fundamental laws (Plantinga 1993; Beilby 2002).

(3.8) If materialism is true, then there is no connection between the simplicity of a possible law and its actuality, or, more generally, between the character of the actual laws and the contingent standards of lawlikeness (including the aesthetic sensibilities of humans).

(3.9) Given (3.8), if materialism is true, then the objective probability that these standards of lawlikeness coincide accurately with the character of the actual laws is quite low.

(3.10) Given (3.9), anyone who believes in materialism has a defeater for all knowledge pertaining to the natures of material things.

(3.11) Given (3.10), no one who believes in materialism knows the nature of any material thing.

(3.12) No one who doesn't know the nature of any material thing knows that any material thing exists.

(3.13) No one who believes in materialism knows that any material thing exists.

Since materialism implies the existence of material things, and since knowledge implies belief, we can conclude that no one knows that materialism is true.

4. CONCERNING OUR ONTOLOGICAL KNOWLEDGE
OF MATERIAL BEINGS

As Michael Rea has argued (Rea 2002), anyone who believes in material things and who is a metaphysical realist must believe in individual persistence conditions and individual essences. A persistence condition is a proposition laying out either necessary or sufficient conditions for the continued existence of some material thing. Let's stipulate that these conditions are logically non-trivial ones. Since it is very hard to see how we could know the persistence conditions pertaining to particulars as such without knowing that the same condition pertains to all the particulars in the same natural kind, we can focus on our knowledge of the persistence conditions corresponding to natural kinds of material things.

If a natural kind of thing has non-trivial persistence-conditions, it is very plausible to assume that they have de re modal essences as well. In fact, a persistence condition is itself a kind of modal proposition, stating that it is impossible for something to survive or fail to survive under specified conditions.

One cannot avoid the commitment to non-trivial persistence conditions by adopting either mereological universalism or mereological nihilism, nor does the commitment disappear by combining mereological universalism with a perdurance account of persistence (resulting in a world of arbitrarily disconnected spacetime worms). Here are a range of possible ontologies of persistence:

(4.1) Nothing persists, and simples never compose anything. (Persistence nihilism plus mereological nihilism: a world of space–time punctual things.)

(4.2) Nothing persists, and every set of simultaneous objects compose something. (Persistence nihilism plus mereological universalism: a world of instantaneous time-slices, each arbitrarily connected or disconnected in space.)

(4.3) Every set of simultaneous objects composes something, and every sequence of time-slices of objects constitutes the history of a persisting thing. (Persistence universalism plus mereological universalism: a world of arbitrarily connected or disconnected space–time worms.)

(4.4) Simultaneous simples never compose anything, and every sequence of time-slices of atoms constitutes the history of a persisting thing. (Persistence universalism plus mereological nihilism: a world of temporally extended space–time strings, each arbitrarily connected or disconnected through time.)

These four positions represent the four extremes: our common sense ontology lies somewhere in between, with some composite and enduring things, but with significant necessary conditions on both composition and persistence. It is important to bear in mind that one doesn't avoid the burden of ontological commitment by adopting one or another of the extreme views. Nihilists and universalists bear exactly the same epistemological burdens as do defenders of more common sense ontologies.[6]

4.1. Knowing the Persistence Conditions and Individual Essences of Material Things

Materialism excludes the possibility of our knowledge of the composition and persistence conditions of material beings, because it entails the causal inertness of the identity and distinctness of material particulars. According to materialist thesis (1.2), it is only the arrangement of certain *kinds* of material bodies that can play a causal-explanatory role. The identity and distinctness of these bodies with bodies that have existed in the past or will exist in the future are otiose. In addition, it is only the *arrangement* of fundamental particles (or arbitrarily small, homogenous masses) that do all the causal work: whether these simples or masses *compose* anything can make no difference, and neither can it make any difference whether there are particles that persist through time or merely continuous sequences of instantaneous particle-stages, nor whether or not the instantaneous particle-stages compose a four-dimensional 'worm.'[7]

Since, as the Gettier-like thought-experiments demonstrate, causality is an essential component of knowledge, the lack of any causal connection between our ontological beliefs and the corresponding facts is fatal to a materialist epistemology of the ontology of material beings. Suppose, to re-use an earlier example, that we inferred true ontological beliefs from a false theological theory. Even if the process were perfectly reliable—the false theory hardwired into our brains, and the ontological truths all necessary—and even if the beliefs were formed in a perfectly reasonable way, the result could not constitute knowledge. Only if the ontological facts figure some way in the formation of our beliefs can those beliefs constitute real knowledge. Moreover, the lack of real connection, on the materialist's story, between the ontological facts and our intuitions gives us

---

[6] I am setting aside the issue of endurance vs. perdurance: that is, the issue of whether persisting things persist by being "wholly present" (in some sense) at each moment, or whether they do so by having temporal parts or counterparts at each moment (see Sider 2001). The very same epistemological issues will apply in either case. It is hard to see how materialism could be compatible with knowing either of these positions to be the true one, but materialists might well be able to live with agnosticism on this issue.

[7] The issue of what is commonly called 'Aristotelian' or 'scientific essentialism' (as in Ellis) is irrelevant, as Rea has pointed out (Rea 2002). Scientific essentialism is the thesis that there are natural kinds with real essences: that there are clusters of properties that must be co-instantiated if any of their members are instantiated at all. What I am focusing on here concerns the existence and persistence conditionals of *individuals*. Even if, for example, water has a scientific essence (viz., being H_2O), it does not follow that each watery individual is essentially watery, nor that each watery individual persists so long as it remains watery, nor that any contiguous mass of water molecules does (or does not) compose a single watery thing.

good grounds to doubt the reliability of those intuitions, resulting in a defeater (both of knowledge and of rationality).

Some anti-materialists can fare much better. Theists can appeal to the epistemic benevolence of the human mind's designer, together with the omnipotence of that designer with respect to the existence, composition, and persistence of material things, to provide the requisite causal connection. Similarly, Aristotelian forms make composition, generation and destruction, and their contraries, causally relevant to the histories of material things. Simples that compose an organism of a certain kind behave differently than they would if they failed to do so (a strong emergence of biological powers). On an Aristotelian picture, the causal laws governing such composition are diachronic: there are substantial, empirically discoverable laws of the persistence (as well as the generation and destruction) of things of the various natural kinds.

Anti-realists can argue that the composition and persistence conditions are determined by our linguistic conventions, or by features of our concepts (understood as contingent features of the human mind). On such a view, we could know the conditions by examining social practices or introspecting the workings of the human mind. However, any such conventionalism or conceptualism would be inconsistent with materialist thesis (1.4), making material entities into mind-dependent things, as Michael Rea has argued (Rea 2002: 85–96).

4.2. The Unavailability to the Materialist of Mind/Brain Identity

Since materialists have no knowledge, either of the intrinsic natures nor of the persistence and composition conditions, concerning material objects, no materialist can have de re knowledge of any material thing. As Michael Rea has argued (Rea 2000: 81–5), there seems to be no argument available to the materialist for the claim that there exist any material things at all, given that the materialist can point to no single instance. For the materialist, the category of material things corresponds to a bare epistemic possibility: a domain of we-know-not-what that may, for all we know, exist.

Each human being knows that he or she exists. The materialist must claim that each human being is identical to some material being, although he is ignorant of what material thing it is to which the human being in question is identical. In fact, the supposed identity of the material thing with a conscious human being is the only thing the materialist can claim to know about it. This puts the materialist in an impossibly weak dialectical position with respect to the mind/brain (or person/body) identity thesis. Any plausibility of the identity thesis depends on our being able to identify, antecedently, the two things that are to be identified. This is just what the materialist cannot do. He can identify the mind or person, in the usual Cartesian way, but he lacks epistemic access to the supposed material counterpart.

Ironically, it is only anti-materialists, such as theists or Aristotelians, who are in a position to articulate and defend such an identity thesis, since they can legitimately claim to have knowledge of the material side of the ledger, and they can justify the identity thesis on familiar Ockhamist grounds, as effecting a simplification of their ontology. Without a positive ontology of the material, the materialist can make use of no such rationale. The materialist can employ Cartesian grounds for positing the existence of the conscious self but lacks any grounds for positing the existence of any *body* with the sort of composition and persistence that would be needed to match the boundaries and survival conditions of the human mind. Without independent grounds for believing in such bodies, the materialist lacks the resources to defend a mind/brain or self/organism identity thesis.

5. CONCERNING OUR KNOWLEDGE OF MATHEMATICS AND LOGIC

5.1. The Unavailability of Mathematical Platonism

A materialist who posits mathematical objects (such as the numbers) as real, immaterial entities is barred from supposing that mathematical knowledge is possible, since the required causal connection will always be absent. At best, the materialist can suppose that we have justified true belief about mathematics. Gettier thought-experiments reveal the gap between such justified true beliefs and real knowledge. For example, suppose a mathematician believes the axioms of Peano arithmetic because they can be derived as theorems from an extremely plausible but false set theory (like Frege's inconsistent theory of extensions). The mathematician's beliefs would be true and justified but fall short of knowledge, in a way exactly analogous to the original Gettier cases. Mathematical knowledge depends on our somehow grasping or seeing (note the causal idioms) the facts that verify our axioms. This would be true even if the mathematical beliefs of humans had no chance of being false: if, for example, humans derived their mathematical beliefs from a false but biologically hard-wired theory.

Similarly, suppose that a mathematician accepts the axioms of arithmetic as self-evidently true as a result of post-hypnotic suggestion (and suppose further that the hypnotist wrongly believes the axioms to be false, intending to deceive the mathematician). Such a mathematician would be in exactly the same phenomenological state and inclined to grasp the very same fundamental truths as a mathematician who knows arithmetic to be true and yet would lack this knowledge.

Since the materialist cannot accept the existence of a causal connection between mathematical facts and human intuition, materialist must embrace some form of anti-realism about mathematics. As Hartry Field has pointed out (Field 1980,

1985), the usefulness of mathematics for theoretical science depends simply on its logical consistency (or, to be more precise, on its being a *conservative extension* of the nominalistic version of the physical theory). Thus, to gain knowledge through applied mathematics, all that is required is knowledge of the logical consistency of mathematics.

This Fieldian strategy could be fleshed in either of two ways: Field's own fictionalist approach, which treats mathematical theories as false but useful because consistent, and modal-structuralist approaches, which treat mathematical assertions as true because asserting merely the (logically) possible existence of certain kinds of mathematical structure.

However, Field and other materialists have provided no explanation of our knowledge of the logical consistency of infinitary mathematical theories. How, for example, could we know that the axioms of Peano or Robinson arithmetic are mutually consistent? It cannot be by being able to find physical models of the axiom systems, since we are acquainted only with finite systems of material things. We know from Gödel's work that any mathematical theory powerful enough to prove the consistency of arithmetic must be at least as strong as arithmetic, with the result that any such proof would be question-begging. In fact, we are confident that the theory of arithmetic is possibly true simply because we believe that it has an actual model, viz., the natural numbers themselves. As Frege puts it in *The Foundations of Arithmetic*: 'Strictly, of course, we can only establish that a concept is free from contradiction by first producing something that falls under it' (Frege 1959: 106).

Field's response is to claim that we can know the axioms of arithmetic to be logically possible on the basis of our failure over a large number of attempts to derive any explicit contradiction from them (Field 1984: 520, 524). It is obvious that such 'evidence' falls woefully short of supporting any claim to knowledge. If we think of our attempts to find a contradiction as some kind of random sample of the theory's consequences, we face a number of objections: (i) we have no reason to think that our attempts are genuinely a random sample; (ii) even if the sample justified the claim that the ratio of successful derivations of a contradiction to failures to do so was extremely low, this would give us no good reason to suppose that the ratio is equal to zero; and (iii) Field's evidence presupposes our knowledge of the completeness of first-order logic, which is simply another piece of supposed mathematical knowledge.

To know that the axioms of arithmetic are logically consistent or logically possible is itself a piece of *mathematical* knowledge, knowledge at least as strong in content as the knowledge of arithmetic itself. Hence, retreating to consistency or logical possibility offers no epistemological advantages whatsoever. The mystery of mathematical knowledge is left precisely where it was.[8]

---

[8] For more details, see *Realism Regained* (Koons 2000: 169–93) and my review of Field's book (Koons 2003).

Once again, we can deploy Plantinga's evolutionary defeat argument here. Since there is no connection between our beliefs in the truth, possible truth, or logical consistency of our mathematical theories and the corresponding mathematical facts, the objective probability that our beliefs correspond to the facts is extremely low. In addition, since natural selection is interested only in reproductive fitness, and there is no plausible linkage between reliable mathematical intuition about infinitary systems and the reproductive fitness of our ancestors in the remote past, we have good grounds for doubting whether the human brain is a reliable instrument for detecting such mathematical truths. As long as the inconsistencies in our mathematical beliefs do not reveal themselves in the sort of simple situations encountered regularly by primitive human beings, mistaken intuitions of consistency would be biologically harmless.

5.2. Knowledge of Logical Implication and Necessity

In the case of our knowledge of logical necessity (and the associated properties of implication and inconsistency), the materialist is in a somewhat stronger position but still faces serious obstacles. Here again, if materialism is true, there is a lack of causal connection between the logical facts and our beliefs and practices. Consider, for example, someone who believes the law of excluded middle only because of the assurances of astrology, or because the law is deducible from an inconsistent logic. Such a reasoner would lack knowledge of the law, on Gettierian grounds.

Are logical beliefs subject to Gettier-like conditions? It is plausible to argue that some are not: the core principles of a minimal logic, the common ground between classical and 'deviant' logicians (e.g., defenders of intuitionist, relevantists, substructuralist, paraconsistentist, or quantum logics). These core beliefs cannot be reasonably doubted, and the combination of unvarying belief with necessary truth might be considered adequate to secure a non-accidental connection. However, this supposition will not secure all of the logic required for classical mathematics: the law of excluded middle, double negation removal, distribution of conjunction over disjunction, *ex falsum quodlibet*. These 'peripheral' principles of logic are not indubitable. We know that they can be doubted, because reasonable people have in fact doubted them.

Moreover, even in the case of the stable core of minimal logic, the materialist faces a problem of defending our knowledge of the *modal status* of logical truths. We not only know that the law of excluded middle is true: we also know that it is true as a matter of logical necessity. The materialist, however, cannot ward off a Plantinga-style defeater for this modal knowledge. The materialist cannot suppose there to be any causal connection between logical necessities and the bounds of human conceivability. Natural selection could very easily have resulted in a brain that is bound by some constraints of conceivability that do not correspond to any logical necessity. In fact, it almost certainly has done so: inconceivability is, in general, a fallible guide to impossibility. Thus, the objective probability that any given constraint of conceivability does correspond to a logical necessity is low or inscrutable, resulting in a defeater of our modal beliefs about core logical truths.

An anti-materialist, in contrast, can take inconceivability as a reliable indicator of logical impossibility, by relying on the supposition that we can (through intro-spection or reflection on our thoughts) discern that certain things are *absolutely* unthinkable (following Aristotle's argument for the law of contradiction). This assumption in turn depends on conscious thought's having a real *nature*, and this the materialist must deny. For the materialist, introspection can, at best, reveal something about the constraints on the physical realization of thought in the human brain, but absolute unthinkability does not follow from being merely unthinkable-by-us. There are a variety of possible explanations of the fact that we find the denial of the law of contradiction to be unthinkable, many of which have nothing to do with its truth.

The materialist might reply that we wouldn't count something as *thought* if it didn't follow the core principles of logic. However, this distinction between thought and near-thought cannot be supposed to cut nature at the joints, since it is in itself causally otiose. On this view, if I recognize the unthinkability of the denial of the law of contradiction, I am merely reflecting on our conditions for the use of the word 'thought,' and this cannot secure the relevant sort of reliability. Although I cannot *think* the law of contradiction to be false, I can *nearly-think* so, where nearly-thinking involves a physical structure close to the actual structure of the brain that fails merely to satisfy all the conventional standards for *thinking*.

In contrast, the anti-materialist can suppose that conscious thought has a real essence, one that could reveal itself in through introspection and the exercise of imagination. One could then discover that it is absolutely unthinkable (by any form of consciousness) that certain laws fail to hold. If truth lies in a correspondence between the mind and the facts, then absolute unthinkability excludes the possibility of falsehood and could secure the reliability of a judgment of logical necessity.

If materialism lacks the resources for an account of our knowledge of logical possibility and necessity, then it cannot be combined with any account of mathematical objectivity (such as fictionalism or modal structuralism) that relies on logical modality. Tarski's work is thought to have de-mystified logical modality for materialists by showing that claims about logical necessity or possibility can be understood as ordinary mathematical claims (about the existence or non-existence mathematical models of certain kinds). Fictionalists and structuralists hope to de-mystify claims about mathematical object by showing that they can be understood as assertions of the logical consistency of sets of axioms and of the logical implication by those axioms of mathematical theorems. However, one cannot simultaneously claim that talk of logical modality is merely talk about mathematical objects in disguise, and that talk of mathematical objects is merely talk about logical modality in disguise. Once again, the materialist is trapped in a vicious circle.

6. CONCERNING THE CONSTITUTION OF EPISTEMIC NORMATIVITY

Epistemology is inherently normative. A non-normative 'epistemology' (such as Quine's naturalized epistemology) is merely a branch of empirical psychology and abandons any attempt to answer the unavoidable questions of epistemology, such as: what does rationality in respect of our opinions and affirmations? Epistemological notions such as *knowledge, justification*, and *rationality* are all normative in essence. If the price of materialism were the utter disavowal of all epistemology, this price would be unacceptably high, as Jaegwon Kim has argued (Kim 1988).

Here is the problem: what, for materialists, do facts about normativity consist in? A materialist could embrace G. E. Moore's non-naturalism, asserting that normative facts involve properties and relations that are fundamentally non-physical. However, this creates two difficulties: first, by making normative facts both causally inert and independent of all physical facts, the materialist could have no account of how we might come to know them, and, second, by positing a weird and inexplicable dichotomy within the world, with inexplicable metaphysical connections (i.e, the strong supervenience of the normative on the non-normative) between the two realms.[9]

In addition, the combination of Moorean non-naturalism with materialism undermines the possibility of normative knowledge, for the same kind of reasons discussed above. Without a causal connection between objective norms and our normative beliefs, justified normative beliefs, even if true, fall short of knowledge on Gettier grounds. In addition, we would have good grounds for doubting the reliability of our normative beliefs, resulting in a universal defeater of claims to normative knowledge, including knowledge about what constitutes good scientific and philosophical practice.

---

[9] Isn't it *chutzpah* for the anti-materialist to charge the Moorean materialist with a 'weird' metaphysics? It's not the case that normative facts are inherently weird: the weirdness I'm pointing to lies in the mismatch between normative facts and all the other facts acknowledged by the materialist. Irreducibly normative facts have a much more natural home within an anti-materialist cosmos, whether theistic, dualistic or Aristotelian. In addition, if there are strongly emergent biological entities (organisms) and activities (behaviors, modes of exploiting the environment), of a sort incompatible with materialism, then the prospects of a reduction of the normative to the non-normative along the lines of Wright and Millikan are much greater.

6.1. The Impossibility of Constructivist or Projectivist Accounts

Besides normative anti-realism and Moorean dualism, the materialist has only two remaining options: to claim that all norms are somehow a projection of human practices and preferences, or to provide a physical basis for normativity that it s independent of our deeds and attitudes. There is a simple and compelling objection to all projectivist and constructivist accounts of normativity:

(6.1) Some doxastic or prescriptive intentionality is ontically prior to all social conventions, practices, attitudes, preferences, etc. (since the existence of social conventions, practices, etc., depends on certain beliefs and intentions on the part of the participants).

(6.2) All doxastic or prescriptive intentionality is such that there is some normativity that is prior to everything the intentionality is prior to.

(6.3) Ontic priority is transitive and well-founded.

Therefore:

(6.3) Some normativity is posterior to no social convention, practice, attitude, or preference.

By 'doxastic' intentionality I mean the intentionality of states of belief, opinion and knowledge, while 'prescriptive' intentionality is that which characterizes intentions, preferences, wants and desires. Thesis (6.1) is clearly true, I think. Only doxastic and prescriptive intentional states or practices incorporating such intentional states are capable of projecting or constructing normative facts. Brute behavior, described in physical terms, does not such thing. The argument turns, then, on the plausibility of thesis (6.2): the inherent normativity of all doxastic and prescriptive intentionality.

In both cases, there is a proper fit between the state and the world: beliefs are supposed to be true, and intentions are *supposed to be* carried out (at least prima facie so, and provided that they are not themselves normatively defective in some way), desires are (other things being equal and with similar provisos) *supposed to be* satisfied, and so on. The normative aspects of these states are almost certainly essential to them and play an indispensable role in our folk-psychological specifications of them.

Moreover, the only possible accounts of intentionality that are available to the materialist ensure that some normativity is not posterior to all intentionality. A materialist account of intentionality must secure the distinction between veridical representation and misrepresentation. This distinction must be grounded either in some form of pre-representational normativity (such as biological teleology) or in the conventional norms of interpretation (that is, the norms governing the best assignment of content to representational states). The first alternative corresponds to the teleosemantics (e.g., Millikan, Dretske, and Papineau) and the second to David Lewis's best-interpretation semantics. In both cases, there are normative facts that are explanatorily prior to the facts about intentionality, as (6.2) requires.

There is, however, a devastating problem for the best-interpretation model: vicious circularity. If we are supposed to be in a position to know what the canons of good interpretation are, these must be founded on social convention or prescription. This contradicts (6.2). If, on the contrary, the canons of good interpretation are consist in fully objective facts about certain functions, and these functions are merely picked out rigidly by our conventions in the actual world, then we have no reliable knowledge of them, since our transworld conventions of 'good interpretation' don't track these objective facts. Thus, the materialist is left with some form of naturalized teleology as the only viable account of normativity.

6.2. Problems for the Materialist with Naturalized Accounts of Normativity

Accounts of naturalized teleology all make use of causation. For example, on the account first developed by Larry Wright (1972) and followed, in general terms, by Millikan (1984) and Papineau (1993):

(6.4) The property P of organism O is *supposed to* bring about effect E iff the complete causal explanation of O's existing and having property P includes the fact that being P tends to cause E (Wright 1972).

A variant of (6.4) applies the same idea to the carrying of information by, for example, beliefs and perceptual states.

(6.4.1) The property P of organism O is *supposed to* carry the information that E iff the complete causal explanation of O's existing and having property P includes the fact that P carries (or tends to carry) the information that E.

An alternative, more Skinnerian approach, connects normativity with positive reinforcement:

(6.5) The property P of organism O is *supposed to* bring about effect E iff O's being P tends to cause E, and the complete causal explanation of O's being P (or having been P in the past, or being disposed to be P in the future) includes the fact that O's being P tends to cause E.

(6.5.1) The property P of organism O is *supposed to* carry the information that E iff O's being P carries the information that E, and the complete causal explanation of O's being P includes the fact that O's being P carries the information that E.

In both cases, causation plays a dual role: linking P as cause to E as effect (or linking P with the information that E), and linking the P to E connection to O's being (or continuing to be) P. At this stage, I will propose a dilemma for the materialist, and I will argue that on either horn of the dilemma, the materialist account of normativity must fail.

Humean vs. Anti-Humean Accounts of Causation

The dilemma turns on the question of whether the materialist embraces a Humean or anti-Humean conception of causation. On the Humean account, a causal connection between two events or between the aspects or properties of two events consists simply in a relation between the event-types or property-types in question. On the anti-Humean account, there is, in addition to and not supervenient upon all such facts about types, a connection or *nexus* at the level of token-events or token-properties (or tropes). This non-Humean causal tie could consist in a primitive sort of entity, as in Michael Tooley's (1987) *Causation: A Realist Account*, or it might consist in the persistence of a trope, as in Douglas Ehring's (1997) *Causation and Persistence*, or in some token-token modal connection, such as the asymmetric necessitation of the existence of the cause-token by the existence of the effect-token, as in my own *Realism Regained* (Koons 2000). A causal-powers metaphysical theory would also count as anti-Humean, with the connection between tokens provided by the primitive, irreducible relation of *the exercise of a causal power*.

For Humeans, there are no such token–token causal ties. Instead, the existence of a causal connection between two events or event-aspects consists entirely in some kind of counterfactual covariation of the events (without reference to non-qualitative individual haecceities), or some regular or nomic concatenation[10] of the two types. For example, David Lewis's (1973, 2001) counterfactual theory of causal influence is paradigmatically Humean. Event C causes event E just in case, had C not occurred, E would not have occurred either. The semantics of the Lewisian counterfactual makes no reference to the individual essences or non-qualitative haecceities of the two events: instead, we look at worlds that are similar to the actual world, both in exact match in the distribution of qualities over regions of space and time, and in the law-like regularities that are more or less perfectly observed. Thus, the presence or absence of a causal connection between two events, for the Humean, turns only on their intrinsic qualities, their spatial and temporal proximity, and on the laws of nature (both strict and non-strict) in which the events' types figure.

---

[10] It's enough, as David Lewis (1973a) noted, for the two types to be linked by a defeasible, ceteris-paribus law.

The Difficulty with Humean Materialism: Radical Indeterminacy

The central problem with a Humean-materialist account of teleology is that of a radical indeterminacy of content. The indeterminacy has two sources: (i) the mismatch between insensitivity of the causal context and the fine-grainedness of the content of norms; and (ii) the circularity of the account.

The charge of indeterminacy based on the insensitivity of causation to subtle distinctions of content is not a novel one: it is simply to point out that 'natural selection' is merely a metaphor. Its literal sense would require a reified, purposeful Nature to do the selecting. Once we unpack the metaphor, realizing the 'Nature' is nothing but a name for the totality of physical factors, we should see that Nature cannot select for features with the kind of fine-grained sensitivity that is required for an adequate account of human intentionality (as Jerry Fodor (2007) has argued in a recent paper).

If understood in Humean terms, causation is a relatively crude instrument, a blunt weapon incapable of distinguishing features that co-vary in a regular way across nearby worlds. If feature A and feature B are co-extensive in the historically relevant situations across the set of relevantly close possible worlds, then one can be substituted *salve veritate* for the other in a counterfactual conditional, and, for the Humean, in a causal context. The result is an intractable mismatch between the semantics of causation, on the one hand, and the hyper-intensional notion of intentional content.

It is the liberality with respect to substitution that gives the Humean a ready solution to the problem of mental causation. Even if mental types are not identical to physical types, and even if all causal laws involve only physical types, the instantiation of a mental type can still (for the Humean) be causally relevant by virtue of the substitutability of mental terms for physical terms within the relevant counterfactuals. This liberality is a virtue in the case of mental causation, but a damning vice in the case of providing a causal account of normativity and intentionality. As Fodor (1990: 73) argued in an earlier essay:

. . . appeals to mechanism of selection won't decide between cases of *reliably equivalent* content ascriptions; i.e., they won't decide between any pair of equivalent content ascriptions where the equivalence is counterfactual supporting. To put this in the formal mode, the context: *was selected for representing things as F* is transparent to the substitution of predicates reliably coextensive with *F* . . . In consequence, evolutionary theory offers us no contexts that are as intensional as 'believes that. . .' If this is right, then it's a conclusive reason to doubt that appeals to evolutionary teleology can reconstruct the intentionality of mental states.

When this limitation on the Humean approach is run through the purported reductions of normativity in propositions (6.4) and (6.5), the result is that all norms are radically indeterminate in content. If N is a norm, A is a property involved in N, and property A and B are nearly co-extensive in relevant situations across nearby worlds, then N' will also count as a norm, where N' results from replacing A with B in N. The Humean account of normativity falls into the grip of what Fodor has called the 'error problem' or the 'disjunction problem': 'such theories can't distinguish between a true token of a symbol that means something that's disjunctive and a false token of a symbol that means something that's not' (Fodor 1990: 59).

Suppose, for example, that there is an epistemic norm that, when one believes that there a m A's that are B, and n A's that are not B, one should believe that there are at least $m + n$ A's altogether. The property of there being $m + n$ A's is co-extensive in the historically relevant situations with the property of there being m $quus$ n A's, where $quus$ differs from $plus$ only on pairs of numbers that human beings have never before added before (see Kripke 1982). As a result, the Humean account entails that there is a norm enjoining quaddition in such situations.

Again, suppose that there is an epistemic norm that, when one is appeared to greenly, one should believe (in the absence of contrary evidence) that one is seeing something green. The property of being grue (Goodman 1973) is co-extensive in historically relevant situations in nearby worlds with the property of being green. There would be, therefore, a norm enjoining belief in one's seeing something grue under those conditions. Similarly, if there is an epistemic norm that enjoins believing that one sees a horse when one is appeared to horse-ly, so there will be a counterpart norm enjoining that one believe that one is seeing a horse-or-equine-looking cow when one is appeared to horse-ly, so long as the disjunctive type of horse-or-equine-looking cows and the type of horses have been co-extensive in the historically relevant situations across nearby worlds. The Humean is thus forced to recognize in each case two, mutually inconsistent norms as equally binding. Any particular belief that violates an epistemic norm will also accord with a counterpart of that norm, and vice versa. The Humean will be unable to distinguish epistemically normal from epistemically abnormal beliefs and inferences, rendering the account of normativity vacuous.

The second source of indeterminacy of the Humean-materialist account of normativity and intentionality is this: the Humean account of *causation* is an ineliminably mind-dependent one. As I have argued in section 6.3, the materialist must adopt an anti-realist conception of the laws of nature: what counts as a law of nature depends on what we take to be an adequately eloquent formulation of a possible law. Moreover, as David Lewis (1973b) showed in *Counterfactuals*, the standards of relative 'closeness' of possible worlds are determined by our own interests and intentional practices.[11] However,

---

[11] Could the Humean materialist deviate here from Lewis and posit an ontologically primitive, metaphysically privileged relation of counterfactual closeness? No, for two reasons. First, such an account would leave us no explanation for the epistemic role of our beliefs about scientific laws

as we have seen, the normativity that is constitutive of intentionality cannot be ontically posterior to any intentionality. The Humean materialist offers a viciously circular reduction, making intentionality depend on causation, and causation depend on intentionality.

The Humean-materialist account of normativity is circular in a second way: by its tacit appeal to phenomenologically grounded properties and event-types. Given materialist thesis (1.2), it is only the fundamental, microphysical types that truly carve nature at the joints. Only they correspond to natural properties. However, the causal account of normativity must appeal to macroscopic features of human behavior and the human behavior: response-dependent features like color, visible shape, basic bodily movements. All of these types are, for the materialist, mere projections of human intentionality. Since intentionality is inherently normative, the materialist cannot legitimately make use of such types in providing a reductive account of normativity.

The Humean can avoid this circularity, as indeed David Lewis did,[12] by insisting that our practices of picking the 'best' system of laws and the 'appropriate' transworld similarity relation fix the reference of these terms *rigidly*—picking out a fully objective fact about those systems and those relations (e.g., the fact that they correspond, as inputs, to the maxima of some fixed utility function). This avoids the ontic circularity, but it introduces a new semantic or metalinguistic circularity (with the result of a radical indeterminacy of content). Since we are attempting to fix the reference of terms in our theory that are prior to and constitutive of intentionality itself (namely, 'proper function' and 'causation'), there had better be something in the world that is especially 'eligible' (to use David Lewis's term)[13]—a reference magnet on the side of the world that provides the terms with reasonably determinate extensions. However, a Humean account of causation and a Lewisian account of counterfactuals and laws provide no such magnets, and neither does the microphysicalist's account of macroscopic properties. The functions that pick out (from the point of view of the actual world) the best laws, similarity relations and macro-properties belong to continua of functions without sharp boundaries. (For obvious reasons, the materialist cannot appeal here to an ontological primitive intentional reference relation.)

One might try to render the semantic circularity harmless by proposing a **simultaneous** definition of *law, counterfactual closeness, macroscopic similarity* and *normativity*. We would then use a fixed-point construction to identify the acceptable interpretation of the set of simultaneously-defined terms. However, fixed points don't always exist, and, when they do, they are typically not unique. In this case, there is real doubt about whether any fixed point exist, since it is

---

in shaping our judgments about counterfactual conditionals. Second, because such primitive facts about relations between worlds would themselves have no causal efficacy and so would leave our supposed knowledge of them vulnerable to Gettier-like refutation.

[12] This was pointed out to me by Michael Rea.   [13] In Lewis (1983a and 1984).

unclear (as I argued earlier) that nature could select for the capacity to recognize the actual laws of nature and (consequently) the causal powers of things. If we assume, however, that nature can select for this capacity, then we have good grounds for believing that there are an infinite number of fixed points, which together span the entire space of possible norms.

This strategy of simultaneously defining causation, counterfactuals, laws, normativity and content is vulnerable to Hilary Putnam's (1981) model-theoretic argument for the radical indeterminacy of content. There are infinitely many, widely divergent functions that fit our actual practice equally well and that are mathematically and (on Humean grounds) ontologically on a par. For each bizarre, 'gruesome' assignment of lawlikeness and counterfactual closeness, there is a correspondingly bizarre interpretation of mental content and norms such that it is plausible to suppose that (under the stipulated theory of laws and causal relations) nature has selected humans for the capacity to form beliefs with the corresponding content. The fundamental problem for the Humean materialist is that the facts left in the ontological basis of the theory (the 'Humean mosaic' of microphysical qualities distributed across spacetime) is simply too thin to constrain in any meaningful way the vast superstructure of scientific laws, causation, intentionality, and normativity (to say nothing of phenomenology).

The Difficulty with Anti-Humean Materialism: The Causal Irrelevance of the Macrophysical

A popular idea in recent philosophy, the introduction of so-called 'truth-makers', can be enlisted in the construction of a non-Humean alternative account of causation. These truth-makers are concrete parts of the world that are responsible for grounding the truth-values of statements and propositions. They can be conceived of as either situations or states of affairs (something like the atomic facts of the logical atomism of Russell and Moore) or as tropes (abstract particulars, scholastic individual accidents). For my purposes here, further specification of these truth-makers, states of affairs, or tropes is not needed.

If, on this non-Humean view, there are non-physical aspects of events that genuinely enter into causal explanations of physical events, then the physical domain cannot be causally complete. This means that materialism is inconsistent, thanks to theses (1.1), (1.2), and (1.3), not only with mental causation, but with causation associated with any of the special sciences (i.e., with anything except fundamental microphysics).

Consider again the teleofunctional account of normativity of the Wright-Dretske-Millikan variety. Teleofunctional accounts of proper functions assume that gross, macroscopic properties can be causally explanatory. For example, the teleofunctionalist's explanation for why the proper function of the wing is to support flight depends on the assumptions that having wings is part of the causal explanation for flight, and that flight is part of the causal explanation for the successful survival and reproduction of birds, bats, insects, and so on.

However, as Trenton Merricks (2001) has argued, a materialist (who rejects any emergent causation at the macroscopic level) should reject the existence of all macroscopic objects (including wings). All the considerations that motivate physicalism also motivate microphysicalism, the view that the *microphysical* world is causally closed. All the causal work supposedly to be done by wings is actually done by a large number of fundamental particles arranged wing-wise. Analogously, the macroscopic *property* of being arranged flight-wise or being arranged wing-wise does no causal-explanatory work, given the anti-Humean view of causation. For the anti-Humean materialist, all of the real explanatory work is done by simply aggregating the microphysical properties of a large number of particle-trajectories. Macroscopic properties like being wing-shaped or flying do not cut the world at its causal joints. They are, for the anti-Humean materialist, grue-like, massively disjunctive, gerrymandered properties. They seem natural to us only from an anthropomorphic perspective. When we describe a bird as flying, we are thinking of it from the perspective of reverse engineering: we are imposing upon the bird a hypothetical design plan. We are projecting upon the bird the intentions that we would have if we were trying to design such a creature for the tasks of survival and reproduction. The anti-Humean materialist cannot imagine (given thesis (1.3)) that describing natural things in this way reveals genuine, mind-independent causal connections.

Thus, except for microscopic functions, like hemoglobin's function of binding and releasing oxygen molecules, the teleofunctional account cannot account for biological proper functions, if anti-Humean materialism is assumed. A fortiori, it cannot account for the mental functions of brain states.

The materialist must suppose that natural selection and operant conditioning work on a purely physical basis (without presupposing any prior designer or any prior intentionality of any kind). According to anti-Humean materialism, only microphysical properties can be causally efficacious. Nature cannot select a property unless that property is causally efficacious (in particular, it must causally contribute to survival and reproduction). However, few, if any, of the biological features that we all suppose to have functions (wings for flying, hearts for pumping bloods) constitute microphysical properties in a strict sense. All biological features (at least, all features above the molecular level) are physically realized in multiple ways (they consist of extensive disjunctions of exact physical properties). Such biological features, in the world of the anti-Humean materialist, don't have effects—only their physical realizations do. Hence, the biological features can't be selected. Since the exact physical realizations are rarely, if ever repeated in nature, they too cannot be selected. If the materialist responds by insisting that macrophysical properties can, in some loose and pragmatically useful way of speaking, be said to have real effects, the materialist has thereby returned to the

Humean account, with the attendant difficulties described in the last sub-section. Hence, the materialist is caught in the dilemma.[14]

7. CONCLUSION

Apparently, the majority of Anglophone philosophers would accept (1.1), (1.2), and (1.3), but reject (1.4) (metaphysical realism). Is it coherent to combine metaphysical anti-realism (which amounts to a form of idealism) with a thoroughgoing materialism about the contents of the phenomenal (constructed or projected) world? Surely this involves some sort of vicious circularity. If A totally depends on B, then B cannot be wholly constituted by A.

To put this in another way, the causally fundamental features of the world must be intrinsic to the things that bear them. They cannot be simultaneously fundamental (in the causal order) and mere projections (metaphysically speaking). What is a mere projection can do no real causal work. If the existence and fundamental nature of the whole realm of material things depends on some features of the human mind, then it is those features of the mind, and not the so-called 'natures' of material things, that must carry the load of causal explanation. Neither the causally fundamental features of a thing, nor the very existence of the thing bearing these fundamental features, can consist in some extrinsic facts about other things, like human minds or societies.[15] Given these principles, thesis (1.2) must entail (1.4), ruling out the hybridizing of materialism and idealism. The failure of many to see this is due to a failure to step back and simply look at the big picture.

---

[14] I am not claiming that all macroscopic properties are *equally* unnatural. Some are definable in terms of microphysical properties in relatively simple and direct ways: primary qualities (like mass, velocity, shape, and net electric charge), mineralogical properties (crystalline structure), thermodynamic features (entropy), or chaos-theoretic features (within a strange attractor). There are two reasons why such relatively natural microphysical properties are of no use to the materialist. First, the features of behavior, organic processes, and ecological factors that are relevant to the definition of macroscopic biological functions (and, a fortiori, of psychological functions) are not even remotely natural. Second, even though the macrophysical properties are *relatively* natural, their instantiations still consist in nothing over and above the arrangement of microphysical tropes, and, for the anti-Humean, it is only the latter that can stand in causal relations to each other.

[15] In addition, Michael Rea has developed a fascinating argument to the effect that any form of anti-realism entails the truth of something in the neighborhood of theism (Rea 2002: 147–55).

IV
ALTERNATIVES TO
MATERIALISM

15

Materialism, Minimal Emergentism, and the Hard Problem of Consciousness

Terry Horgan

My project in this chapter is as follows. I will begin, in section 1, by setting forth my current favored articulation of the metaphysical doctrine of materialism. In section 2, I will describe an alternative metaphysical position I call *minimal emergentism*, which has two versions; and I will contrast it with stronger kinds of emergentism. In section 3, I will set forth what I take to be some very powerful challenges to materialism—challenges involving features of human consciousness. In section 4, I will argue that, in light of these challenges, minimal emergentism is a viable and theoretically appealing non-materialist metaphysics of mind.[1]

1. MATERIALISM CHARACTERIZED

The pre-theoretic idea of materialism, as a metaphysical worldview, is somewhat vague and inchoate. How best to explicate this notion is itself a challenging and important philosophical question. Here I will briefly set forth and motivate the explication I favor.

In seeking a satisfactory formulation of materialism, it helps to employ the notion of a *possible world*. Possible worlds are plausibly construed not literally as universes other than the single real universe (i.e., not as *cosmoi*), but rather as *total ways the cosmos might be*—i.e., maximal *properties* instantiable by the single real world (the single cosmos). On this usage, the item designated as the actual world—considered as one among the various possible worlds—is not itself the cosmos either, but rather is the total cosmos-instantiable property that is *actually* instantiated by the cosmos. But it will be convenient in practice to speak as though the actual world is the cosmos and as though other possible worlds are other such cosmoi—a harmless enough manner of speaking, as long as one bears

---

[1] I will draw in part on material in Horgan and Tienson (2001) and Horgan (2006a, 2006b).

in mind that it is not intended literally. (The various claims made below in terms of possible worlds can all be reformulated in terms of the language of maximal cosmos-instantiable properties, but I will not bother to do so.)

The possible worlds we are interested in are *physically* possible worlds—that is, worlds in which obtain all the same physical laws that actually obtain in the cosmos.[2] In order to hone in on the physically possible worlds we are interested in, it is useful to borrow from Frank Jackson (1998) the idea of a *minimal physical duplicate* of a physically possible world: if w is a physically possible world, then w^* is a minimal physical duplicate of w just in case (i) w^* is *physically just like w*, (ii) w^* contains no entities other than those required for it to meet condition (i), and (iii) no properties or relations are instantiated in w^* other than ones whose instantiation in w^* is required to meet condition (i). (A minimal duplicate of a physically possible world does not contain—alongside various physical entities like quarks, electrons, and composites entirely composed of such physical parts—any such entities as immaterial Cartesian souls. Nor are any properties or relations instantiated in a minimal-physical-duplicate world that are not also instantiated in any other physically indistinguishable possible world.) Drawing upon the idea of physically possible world and the idea of a minimal duplicate of such a world, I propose the following thesis as a characterization of materialism:

(M)   (1)   The actual world is a minimal physical duplicate of itself,

   (2)   for any physically possible worlds w_1 and w_2, if (i) $w_1{}^*$ is a minimal physical duplicate of w_1, (ii) $w_2{}^*$ is a minimal physical duplicate of w_2, (iii) r is a spatiotemporal region of $w_1{}^*$, (iv) s is a spatiotemporal region of $w_2{}^*$, and (v) r and s are intrinsically just alike in all physical respects, then r and s are just alike in *all* intrinsic respects, and

   (3)   there are no brute inter-level relations of either (i) nomic necessitation or (ii) metaphysical necessitation linking physical particulars or properties to non-physical particulars or properties.

Let me add some explanatory comments, by way of elucidation and motivation. First, the point of clauses (2.iii) and (2.iv) is to preclude a putative possible world that (1) is physically possible, (2) is a minimal physical duplicate of itself, but nonetheless (3) contains two spatio-temporal *regions* that are just alike in all intrinsic physical respects yet are not just alike in all intrinsic respects. Also to be precluded are such pairs of regions in two *different* physically possible worlds, where each of the two worlds is a minimal physical duplicate of itself.

---

[2] If one construes the semantics of counterfactuals in such a way that the possible worlds pertinent to evaluating ordinary counterfactuals can be worlds in which minor deviations from the actual physical laws occur—what Lewis (1979) called 'divergence miracles'—then the scope of physically possible worlds will need to include these kinds of worlds too. But I will ignore this complication, for simplicity.

The metaphysical hypothesis of materialism, pre-theoretically understood, surely should preclude such putative regions within such worlds.

Turn now to clause (3). The motivation for part (3.i) is that materialism, pre-theoretically understood, surely should not countenance any fundamental, *sui generis* laws or nomic relations other than those that figure in fundamental physics. Higher level laws, and also inter-level laws, should be ontologically derivative in some way, rather than being additional fundamental laws that 'dangle' outside of physics. J. J. C. Smart nicely expressed this idea some sixty years ago, in the following frequently quoted passage:

Why do I wish to resist this suggestion [viz., that sensations are phenomena that are not physically explicable]? Mainly because of Occam's razor. It seems to me that science is increasingly giving us a viewpoint whereby organisms are able to be seen as physicochemical mechanisms: it seems that even the behavior of man himself will one day be explicable in mechanistic terms. There does seem to be, so far as science is concerned, nothing in the world but increasingly complex arrangements of physical constituents. All except for one place: in consciousness . . . I just cannot believe that this can be so. That everything should be explicable in terms of physics (together of course with descriptions of the ways in which the parts are put together—roughly, biology is to physics as radio-engineering is to electromagnetism) except the occurrence of sensations seems to me to be frankly unbelievable. Such sensations would be 'nomological danglers,' to use Feigl's expression. It is not often realized how odd would be the laws whereby these nomological danglers would dangle . . . Certainly we are pretty sure in the future to come across new ultimate laws of a novel type, but I expect them to relate simple constituents . . . I cannot believe that ultimate laws of nature could relate simple constituents to configurations consisting of perhaps billions of neurons (and goodness knows how many billion billions of ultimate particles) . . . Such ultimate laws would be like nothing so far known in science. They have a queer 'smell' to them.   (Smart 1959: 61)

So the thought is that the only metaphysically fundamental properties and laws should be properties and laws within physics itself, with all else about the world being ultimately explicable on that basis. It would be a radical violation of Occam's razor to hold that although *almost* all else is so explicable, some small pocket of reality is not—e.g., consciousness.

One way to motivate part (3ii) of clause (3) is to consider, for instance, G. E. Moore's metaethical position (Moore 1903, 1922). Moore held that *intrinsic goodness* is an objective, non-natural, property. He held that its instantiation is supervenient on the instantiation of certain natural properties (although he did not use the *term* 'supervenient'), in a modally very strong way: in *any* possible world in which thus-and-such natural property is instantiated by an individual *i* at a time *t*, the non-natural property of intrinsic goodness is thereby instantiated by *i* at *t*. He also held that the metaphysically necessary supervenience connection linking the pertinent natural property to intrinsic goodness is itself fundamental and sui generis—rather than being derivative from any other facts. (He held that we know such metaphysically fundamental, synthetic, necessary truths by a special faculty of moral intuition.) Moorean non-naturalism in metaethics surely should not be considered consistent with metaphysical materialism. Yet, because of the modal strength of the metaphysically fundamental necessary connections that supposedly obtain between certain natural properties and intrinsic goodness—connections that obtain in *all* possible worlds, even though they are synthetic—Moorean non-naturalism entails that even a *minimal* physical duplicate of any physically possible world, or of any spatio-temporal region of such a world, will be just like that world (or region) with respect to how the non-natural property of intrinsic goodness is instantiated. So part (3ii) of clause (3) is needed in our characterization of materialism, in order to render materialism incompatible—as it surely should be—with doctrines like Moorean metaethical non-naturalism.[3]

Perhaps clause (3) could itself be further explicated; I leave open whether this is so, and also whether it would be worthwhile seeking such an explication. Meanwhile, I propose (M) as an articulation of the thesis of materialism.

2. MINIMAL EMERGENTISM

Assuming that (M) is—or at least approximates being—an adequate articulation of materialism, two alternative potential metaphysical positions suggest themselves immediately. Both are versions of what I will call *minimal emergentism*. The first variant, *nomic* minimal emergentism, embraces as metaphysically fundamental certain properties and/or relations other than those that figure in the fundamental laws of physics; it also affirms that there are unexplainable, metaphysically brute, inter-level relations of necessitation between certain physical properties and the metaphysically brute non-physical properties; and it affirms that the modal strength of these inter-level necessitation relations is nomic. So, according to nomic minimal emergentism, Smart was wrong about the scope of fundamental laws governing the cosmos: the full class of such laws includes 'nomological danglers' of the kind he found so hard to believe in, and the class of metaphysically fundamental properties instantiated in the cosmos includes fundamental non-physical properties that 'dangle' outside the realm of the physical.

How should thesis (M) be altered, in order to yield an articulation of nomic minimal emergentism? To begin with, let me introduce a partial kind of minimal duplication among physically possible worlds: if w is a physically possible world, then w^* is a *substantivally minimal physical duplicate* of w just in case (i) w^* is physically just like w, (ii) w^* contains no individuals other than those

---

[3] A further need for clause (3) is that clauses (1) and (2) are actually compatible with a version of full-fledged Cartesian dualism, viz., a version asserting that there are brute relations of metaphysical necessity linking human physical composition to possession of a human soul.

required to meet condition (i). (This leaves it open that some individuals in w^* might instantiate certain *properties* or *relations* that are not instantiated by these individuals in w.) We can now formulate minimal nomic emergentism this way, (with the label 'ME' for 'minimal emergentism', the subscript 'n' for 'nomic,' and with some words boldfaced to highlight the key differences from thesis (M)):

(ME_n) (1) The actual world is a **substantivally** minimal physical duplicate of itself,

     (2) for any physically possible worlds w_1 and w_2 **in which all the same fundamental laws obtain**, if (i) w_1^* is a **substantivally** minimal physical duplicate of w_1, (ii) w_2^* is a **substantivally** minimal physical duplicate of w_2, (iii) r is a spatiotemporal region of w_1^*, (iv) s is a spatiotemporal region of w_2^*, and (v) r and s are intrinsically just alike in all physical respects, then r and s are just alike in *all* intrinsic respects, and

     (3) there **are**, in the actual world, brute inter-level relations of **nomic** necessitation linking physical **properties** to certain non-physical **properties**.

On this view, the actual world is not a *completely* minimal physical duplicate of itself, because nomically emergent properties are instantiated in the actual world but not in a minimal physical duplicate of the actual world; hence the weakening of clause (1) in (ME_n), in comparison to clause (1) of (M). Also, exact intrinsic physical similarity, between two spatiotemporal regions either in distinct physically possible worlds or in the same one, makes for *complete* intrinsic similarity only when both worlds are substantivally minimal and all the same fundamental laws (including any inter-level ones) obtain in both worlds; hence the alterations in clause (2) of (ME_n), in comparison to clause (2) of (M). And in the actual world, certain brute inter-level laws obtain linking physical properties to non-physical properties, as expressed in clause (3) of (ME_n).

The second variant of minimal emergentism is a position I will call *Moorean* minimal emergentism, because it affirms that certain metaphysically brute inter-level supervenience relations obtain with metaphysical necessity rather than with mere nomic necessity. (As noted above, Moore held that this kind of stronger-than-nomic supervenience relation held between certain natural properties, e.g., aesthetic pleasure, and certain non-natural moral properties, e.g., intrinsic goodness.) Because of the modal strength involved, there is evidently no need for this view to back away from either clause (1) or clause (2) of the materialist thesis (M); for, in any physically possible world w^* in which the posited emergent properties are instantiated, those same properties will be instantiated (and in the same ways) even in a physically possible world w that is a *fully* minimal duplicate of w^*. So Moorean minimal emergentism can be formulated as follows, as a modification of the materialist thesis (M) in which only the third clause of (M) gets altered (with the subscript 'm' for 'metaphysical'):

(ME_m) (1) The actual world is a minimal physical duplicate of itself,

(2) for any physically possible worlds w_1 and w_2, if (i) w_1^* is a minimal physical duplicate of w_1, (ii) w_2^* is a minimal physical duplicate of w_2, (iii) r is a spatiotemporal region of w_1^*, (iv) s is a spatiotemporal region of w_2^*, and (v) r and s are intrinsically just alike in all physical respects, then r and s are just alike in *all* intrinsic respects, and

(3) there **are** brute inter-level relations of **metaphysical** necessitation linking physical **properties** to certain non-physical **properties**.

On this view, even though the actual world is a completely minimal physical duplicate of itself, such complete minimality does not comport with materialism. Rather, metaphysically fundamental emergent properties are instantiated too, because of the brute, metaphysically necessary, supervenience relations that obtain between physical properties and the emergent ones.[4,5]

I call these two versions of emergentism *minimal* because they do not include certain additional theses that often have accompanied metaphysical positions called emergentist. One such additional thesis I will call the *nomological openness of physics*—the negation of a thesis (often espoused in recent metaphysics and philosophy of mind) that I will call the nomological *closure* of physics. The latter thesis, which is usually called the *causal* closure of physics, says that for every phenomenon P that occurs in the world, the occurrence of P is determined by prior phenomena and laws of nature—to whatever extent it is thus determined at all—by purely *physical* phenomena together with the laws of *physics*. (I call this the *nomological* closure of physics, rather than the *causal* closure of physics, because it does not mention causation per se. One can envision approaches to causation under which temporally antecedent physical phenomena that nomically determine (modulo the laws of physics) a specific phenomenon do not necessarily count as *causing* that phenomenon.)

The thesis of the nomological closure of physics has strong empirical support; moreover, I take it that there is no credible empirical evidence against it. Hence, the thesis of the nomological *openness* of physics is a very shaky plank to stand on, evidentially speaking: to advocate the latter thesis is to place oneself in a highly dubious position epistemically, a position that is very significantly challenged by the ongoing progress of science. Minimal emergentism does not take that epistemically dubious step, but instead is entirely consistent with the thesis of the

---

[4] The two versions of emergentism have been formulated in a way that assumes there are no emergent individuals involved, just emergent properties. One could allow for emergent individuals too, and one would then need to alter the theses accordingly. But I will not try to do that here.

[5] Several recently proposed explications of materialism, notably those in Jackson (1998) and Levine (2001), are inadequate by my lights, because they are actually consistent with Moorean emergentism.

nomological closure of physics—which is a very good thing, given how strong is the ever-mounting evidence in support of the closure thesis.

Another doctrine often embraced by positions classified as emergentist is what I will call the thesis of *emergent-force generation*. This is the claim that certain non-physical properties, when instantiated, generate fundamental forces over and above the fundamental forces generated by properties described by physics. This thesis does not assert that the laws of physics are *falsified* when emergent properties are instantiated; it need not assert this, because the laws of physics do not themselves assert or entail that the only fundamental forces at work in any given situation (as physicalistically described) are *physical* forces. Rather, the thesis of emergent force-generation says that when an emergent force-generating property is instantiated in a specific situation, the *total* net force in that situation is different from the total net *physical* force: a further, non-physical, force is operative, which can combine with the net physical force to produce a subseqent outcome that is different from the outcome that would have resulted from net physical force by itself.

The thesis of emergent-force generation, I take it, is closely conceptually intertwined with the thesis of the nomological openenness of physics. Exactly how these theses interconnect is a delicate question, involving the question of how the notions of *fundamental force* and *fundamental law* are interconnected. Fortunately, we need not settle that issue here. This much seems uncontroversial, in any case: the thesis of emergent force-generation entails the thesis of the nomological openness of physics. The idea here is straightforward: if there are fundamental non-physical forces that can combine with the net physical force (at time t) to render the net total force (at t) different from the net physical force (at t), then the fundamental laws of physics cannot themselves determine the future course of events (after t); hence, there are other fundamental laws in play too, involving the emergent properties themselves and the forces they generate.

Given this entailment relation, the strong empirical evidence against the thesis of the nomological openness of physics also constitutes, mutatis mutandis, strong empirical evidence against the thesis of emergent force-generation. The latter thesis is no less epistemically dubious than is the former.

So the minimality of minimal emergentism is significant, in light of how tendentious and dubious are these further doctrines that minimal emergentism does not embrace. Minimal emergentism is entirely consistent with the hypothesis that physics is nomologically closed—and therefore is also entirely consistent with the hypothesis that the only fundamental forces in nature are physical forces. This means that the substantial empirical evidence *against* doctrines like the nomological openness of physics, and against emergent force-generation, does not constitute evidence against minimal emergentism. On the contrary, minimal emergentism *fits smoothly* with the hypothesis of the nomological closure of physics, and with the hypothesis that all fundamental forces in nature are physical forces.

It does need to be acknowledged, nonetheless, that minimal emergentism posits metaphysically fundamental modal relations between physical and non-physical properties that are 'danglers' in the Feigl/Smart sense. Such principles are *nomological* danglers under nomological minimal emergentism, and are what I will call *Moorean* danglers under Moorean minimal emergentism. Also, it should also be acknowledged that Smart's invocation of Occam's razor is both appropriate and epitemically powerful, as a reason to repudiate both dangling non-physical properties and metaphysically fundamental inter-level necessitation relations (either nomic or metaphysical) between physical properties and non-physical ones; *ceteris paribus*, a metaphysical position is surely better if it confines the range of fundamental properties and fundamental laws to physics, and also eschews Moore-style relations of synthetic, metaphysically basic necessitation. I myself continue to resonate strongly to the 'nomological dangler' argument for metaphysical materialism (and to a parallel version of the argument applicable to 'metaphysical danglers'); nowadays I call myself a 'wannabe materialist.' But the trouble is that *cetera* are not all *paria*, insofar as the hoped-for avoidance of nomological or Moorean danglers is concerned. The fly in the ointment is phenomenal consciousness.

3. THE PROBLEM OF IRREDUCIBLY PSYCHIC PROPERTIES

The above-quoted passage from Smart occurs early in his classic 'Sensations and Brain Processes,' a paper defending the claim that sensations are identical to brain processes. The nomological dangler argument was his principal positive consideration in support of this identity theory—although in my view, what the argument really supports is a more generic materialist thesis along the lines of (M). (One could embrace (M) without embracing either a type-type or a even a token-token psychophysical identity theory—e.g., by treating mental types as multiply realizable functional-role properties, and by treating token mental processes as constituted by, but not identical to, token physical processes.) The bulk of Smart's paper consisted of various objections then in the air, together with Smart's replies. The objection that he himself considered most difficult to rebut was what he called the problem of 'irreducibly psychic properties.' In my view, essentially the same objection has resisted successful refutation for all the years since Smart's paper, and continues to do so today. Let me explain.

3.1. Smart's Formulation of the Problem and his Original Reply

The problem involves the properties of sensations in virtue of which one introspectively identifies a given sensation and introspectively classifies it. Smart formulated the objection this way:

[I]t may be possible to get out of asserting the existence of irreducibly psychic processes, but not out of asserting the existence of irreducibly psychic *properties*. For suppose we identify the Morning Star with the Evening Star. Then there must be some properties which logically imply that of being the Morning Star, and quite distinct properties which entail that of being the Evening Star. Again, there must be some properties (for example, that of being a yellow flash) which are logically distinct from those in the physicalist story . . . [C]onsider the property of 'being a yellow flash.' It might seem that this property inevitably lies outside the physicalist framework within which I am trying to work . . . by being a power to produce yellow sense-data, where 'yellow,' in this second sense of the word, refers to a purely phenomenal or introspectable quality.   (Smart 1959: 63–4)

Smart replied to this objection by appeal to the idea that first-person sensation-reports are translatable into reports that deploy 'topic-neutral' language. As he put it,

My suggestion is as follows. When a person says, 'I see a yellowish-orange after-image,' he is saying something like this: '*There is something going on which is like what is going on when I have my eyes open, am awake, and there is an orange illuminated in good light in front of me, that is, when I really see an orange.*'   (Smart 1959: 64)

But the inadequacy of this reply is fairly obvious, and was soon pointed out by various critics: viz., that in order for such a translation to be even in the ballpark of capturing the meaning of the original report, it would need to be supplemented with a specification of the *respect of similarity* between the after-image experience and the perceptual experience. And the relevant respect of similarity, evidently, is just this: both mental episodes instantiate the very same *phenomenal quality*. So the problem of irreducibly psychic properties arises all over again. The problem is that the property of my yellowish sensation by virtue of which I introspectively identify and classify this experience *as* a yellowish sensation seems different from any property by which I would identify and classify a brain process of a certain kind *as* such-and-such a brain process. And, as Smart says, it seems that this property 'inevitably lies outside the physicalist framework.'

3.2. The Persistence of the Problem

In the sixty years since Smart's paper, much effort has been expended in philosophy of mind in the attempt to find a satisfactory materialist account of phenomenal consciousness in general, and of sensory 'qualia' in particular. Earlier attempts included functionalist accounts of mentality, which treated each mental-state concept as the concept of a state (type) with a specific, definitive, causal role—a syndrome of most typical causal connections to sensory inputs, behavioral outputs, and other such functionally characterizable state-types. (Vicious circularity can be avoided by first characterizing the whole system of states, and then identifying each specific mental state with some particular state within that system.) 'Role-functionalism,' as advocated for instance by Hilary Putnam (1973), identified mental states with multiply realizable functional states, whereas 'filler functionalism,' as advocated for instance by David Lewis (1966, 1980) and D. M. Armstrong (1968), identified mental states (for creatures of a given creature-kind) with whatever physical states occupy the relevant causal roles (in creatures of that kind). A persistent objection to functionalist approaches, however, was that they construed the essence of mentality to be entirely relational and non-instrinsic, whereas mental states like sensations have an intrinsic phenomenal character—an intrinsic 'what-it's-like-ness'—that functionalism seems to leave out altogether. Yellowish sensations are introspectively identifiable by virtue of their *intrinsic phenomenal yellowishness*—a property that persistently seems to lie outside the physicalist framework, and that functionalism seems to overlook entirely. One introspectively identifies a sensation of yellowness by noting this intrinsic feature of the experience—not by noting anything about functional features or by characterizing it physically.

More recent attempts to provide an explanatory reduction of phenomenal consciousness include, inter alia, higher order thought theory, externalist representationalism, and internalist representationalism. In effect, each of these is a sophisticated variant of functionalism—in some cases, a 'long-armed' form of functionalism asserting that the pertinent, constitutive, causal-role connections include linkages between the cognitive agent and the agent's wider environment. But to my mind, these approaches are subject to powerful and persuasive objections, which are very effectively articulated by Joseph Levine (2001). The basic problem, as Levine so clearly demonstrates, is the familiar one about the intrinsicness of phenomenal character being left out by functionalism—a problem that persists despite all the bells and whistles in recent reductionist theories. 'It seems to me,' Levine says,

> that a lot of the literature about qualia over the past two decades can be seen as a pendulum, with various proposals bouncing back and forth between treating qualia as intrinsic and treating them as relational, but none overcoming the basic structure of this dilemma: qualia as intrinsic properties can't be integrated into a naturalistic framework, but no proposal to treat them as relational seems at all compelling. (p. 93)

So Smart's problem of irreducibly psychic properties remains with us. The problem, again, is that the property of my yellowish sensation by virtue of which I introspectively identify and classify this experience *as* a yellowish sensation seems different from any property by which I would identify and classify a brain process of a certain kind *as* such-and-such a brain process, or *as* a process with such-and-functional role. It is a what-it's-like property that is *intrinsic* rather than relational, and whose very essence is this intrinsic qualititative character, this what-it's-like-ness. The worry, as Smart says in formulating the problem, is that this property 'inevitably lies outside the physicalist framework.'

3.3. The Explanatory Gap

Essentially the same worry is the conundrum that Joseph Levine (1983, 2001) calls the 'explanatory gap' and David Chalmers (1996) calls the 'hard problem' of phenomenal consciousness. That problem, in a nutshell, is that there seems to be no way to explain, on the basis of physics and/or the other natural sciences, why it should be that undergoing a given kind of brain process (e.g., a certain pattern of neural firings in the visual cortex), or instantiating a physically realizable functional property, should have a specific phenomenal character (e.g., phenomenal yellowishness), rather than having some other phenomenal character (e.g., phenomenal blueishness) or none at all (visual zombiehood). Such an explanation seems not to be forthcoming because physical explanations of worldly phenomena are virtually always explanations of *structure* and/or *function*—and neither kind of explanatory format seems capable of addressing the question at hand.

A familiar symptom of the explanatory gap—of the hard problem—is the fact that we seem easily able to conceive of phenomenal inverts, and to conceive of zombies. A phenomenal invert is someone whose neural circuitry is physically (and hence functionally) just like that of an ordinary human being, but whose experiences are qualitatively inverted relative to a human's, along some dimension (e.g., the color spectrum). A zombie is someone whose neural circuitry is physically (and hence functionally) just like that of an ordinary human being, but who lacks phenomenal consciousness—i.e., intrinsic what-it's-like-ness—altogether. If we had on hand a way of physicalistically explaining why specific physical processes in the neural circuitry implement phenomenal properties, in the ways they actually do, then the explanatory story should preclude the very possibility of phenomenal inverts, or of zombies. (Compare: once one has on hand an explanatory story about the intermolecular forces and connections in the kinds of stuff we classify as liquids, one cannot coherently conceive of some stuff that exhibits such intermolecular forces and connections and yet fails to exhibit the behaviors and behavioral tendencies that constitute liquidity.) But, fill in the structural-functional details about neural circuitry as fully and specifically as you wish, and it *still* seems coherently conceivable that a creature could possess such circuitry and still be either a phenomenal invert or a zombie. (Call this *robust* conceivability, the idea being that the scenario remains coherently conceivable no matter how much structural-functional physicalistic detail gets filled in.)

Now, why exactly does this hard explanatory problem pose a challenge to materialism? Some claim that it does so because the robust conceivability of zombies and phenomenal inverts establishes that such beings are *metaphysically possible*, and that their metaphysical possibility goes contrary to materialism. (Thesis (M) above certainly repudiates their metaphysical possibility.) Others contest this inference from robust conceivability to metaphysical possibility, and seek to explain why and how a materialist can plausibly resist it. (More on this in section 3.iv.) My own view is that although the robust conceivability of zombies and inverts does not *entail* that they are metaphysically possible, it does ground a very powerful-looking abductive argument in favor of their metaphysical possibility. The reasoning goes as follows. One question that looms very large is *why* the daunting, epistemologically recalcitrant, explanatory gap exists. And one obvious potential answer is this: the explanatory gap, as an epistemological phenomenon, reflects an underlying *metaphysical* explanatory gap, constituted by the fact that there are metaphysically brute necessitation relations between certain physical or functional properties on one hand, and associated phenomenal properties on the other hand—either brute inter-level *laws* or brute inter-level relations of *metaphysical necessitation*. This answer provides a needed *explanation* of the epistemological explanatory gap, and an explanation is needed. The explanation of the epistemological gap is that the linkages between physical or functional properties and phenomenal properties are unexplainable *in principle*, because they are metaphysically brute facts about the world, alongside the fundamental laws of physics: these linkages are unexplainable explainers. The hypothesis of a metaphysical explanatory gap thus can be plausibly advanced as the best available explanation (some might think the *only* coherent available explanation) of the epistemological explanatory gap; and so the existence of the epistemological gap supports this metaphysical hypothesis, via non-demonstrative 'inference to the best explanation' (some might think, 'inference to the *only* available explanation').

Of course, non-demonstrative reasoning about the truth or falsity of materialism needs to take account of a full range of evidentially relevant considerations, including those considerations that support the view. Perhaps a good case can be made that all things considered, the evidence favoring materialism tips the evidential scales fairly decisively in its favor, the explanatory gap notwithstanding. Concerning the anti-materialist reasoning just advanced, for instance, the materialist might say this to the anti-materialist:

> I admit that I cannot explain why there is an epistemological explanatory gap, whereas you can explain this fact via the metaphysical explanatory gap that you posit. This is a theoretical cost faced by my materialism, and a theoretical advantage of your anti-materialism. However, this cost I face is outweighed by the strength of the various considerations that non-demonstratively *support* materialism. And although I cannot explain why there is an epistemological explanatory gap, I contend that the unexplainability of the explanatory gap is a reflexive aspect of this very gap itself—another *epistemological* dimension of a merely epistemological gap. Why the epistemological explanatory gap exists is just another part of what we humans are unable to explain.

This kind of non-demonstrative, equilibratory, reasoning fully acknowledges the substantial evidential support that the epistemological explanatory gap provides for the hypothesis of a metaphysical explanatory gap, while nonetheless concluding that all things considered, the net evidential weight of the various relevant considerations tips the epistemic scales in favor of materialism. I myself am strongly tempted by this line of thought. But I worry that hoped-for scale-tipping considerations in *favor* of materialism might be lacking—a theme I will take up in the section 4.

3.4. New Wave Materialism to the Rescue?

Recently, some materialists—notably Hill (1997), Loar (1997), Hill and McLaughlin (1999), and McLaughlin (2001)—have sought to defuse anti-materialist arguments that appeal to the intrinsicness of phenomenal character and/or the robust conceivability of zombies and phenomenal inverts, by claiming that the conceptual gap involved here involves no genuine *explanatory* gap—no genuine hard problem of phenomenal consciousness. Phenomenal *properties*, they maintain may yet turn out to be multiply realizable functional properties—or, instead, first-order physical properties that fill certain functionally specifiable cognitive roles. But phenomenal *concepts* should be not be construed as functional or physical concepts. Instead they should be construed in a way that renders them conceptually *independent* of functional and physical concepts, and in such a way that their introspective deployment is grounded in intrinsic features of the token states to which they are introspectively applied. Phenomenal concepts also should be construed in a way that fully accommodates the robust conceivability of zombies and inverts, and does so in a manner that is consistent with the metaphysical impossibility of such scenarios.

John Tienson and I have dubbed this approach 'new wave materialism' in Horgan and Tienson (2001). Three key ideas are involved. First, phenomenal concepts are a species of so-called 'recognitional' concepts: their functional role in human cognitive economy is to enable the cognitive subject to self-ascribe certain internal states just on the basis of undergoing those states.[6] Second, genuine phenomenal concepts are not presentationally blank—as would be the corresponding recognitional concepts of zombies, whose self-ascriptions would be like those of a self-ascribing 'super-blindsighter.' (Blindsighters lack visual experience but process retinal information subliminally, and thus score better than chance when they are asked to say what kinds of objects are in front of them.) Third, genuine phenomenal concepts operate via phenomenal 'modes of presentation': the modes of presentation are the phenomenal properties themselves, as currently instantiated in the experiencing subject.

The new wave materialists are offering an account of phenomenal concepts that is very different from a functionalist account—even though their ideological treatment of phenomenal *concepts* is consistent with the claim that

---

[6] It bears emphasis that invididuating recognitional concepts via their functional roles in cognitive economy is a very different matter from proposing a *functionalist conceptual analysis* of these concepts. New-wave materialists are not doing the latter at all.

phenomenal *properties* are indeed either functional role-properties or physical role-filling properties. (Adapting the conveniently terminology in Loar (1997), I will hereafter use the blanket expressions 'physical/functional property' and 'physical/functional concept.') Their account, I take it, is not supposed to be a conceptual analysis of phenomenal concepts. Rather, it triangulates these concepts in terms of the distinctive role they play in human cognitive economy—a non-blindsighter-like recognitional role, vis-à-vis certain internal physical/functional properties. These properties themselves are identical to phenomenal properties, according to the new wavers. And, because phenomenal concepts play a role in human cognitive economy that is independent of the roles played by physical/functional concepts, zombies are robustly conceivable. Nevertheless, zombies are not metaphysically possible, because phenomenal concepts refer to the very same properties as do certain physical/functional concepts.

But on close inspection, unfortunately, this story appears to be incoherent. Here I will summarize the problem very briefly. (For a more extended presentation, see Horgan and Tienson (2001); for a reply by a new waver, see McLaughlin (2001).) Consider the following argument.

Deconstructive Argument

1. When a phenomenal property is conceived under a phenomenal concept, this property is conceived otherwise than as a physical-functional property.

2. When a phenomenal property is conceived under a phenomenal concept, this property is conceived directly, as it is in itself.

3. If (i) a property P is conceived under a concept C, otherwise than as a physical-functional property; and (ii) P is conceived, under C, as it is in itself, then P is not a physical-functional property.

Hence,

4. Phenomenal properties are not physical-functional properties.[7]

The argument is valid, and the new wave materialists are committed to premises 1 and 2. Yet premise 3 does not appear to be credibly deniable; on the contrary, it seems virtually tautologous, given that the pertinent form of direct conceiving is supposed to be not presentationally blank (and thus not *nakedly* referential, as in the case of the introspective, recognitional, direct conceiving of the 'super-blindsighter') but rather is supposed to work via the phenomenal property P as a self-presenting *mode of presentation*. If indeed phenomenal properties, when conceived under phenomenal concepts, not only are conceived otherwise

---

[7] This argument is similar in spirit to the 'property dualism argument' presented in White (1986: 353). Note well that premise 1 does not say that phenomenal properties are conceived, under phenomenal concepts, as non-physical-functional properties. Conceiving a property *otherwise than as* a physical-functional property is different from, and weaker than, conceiving it *as otherwise than* a physical-functional property.

than as physical-functional properties, but also are conceived under a mode of presentation that self-presents them *as they are intrinsically*, then how can could these properties fail to *be* otherwise than physical-functional? In other words, how could it be that they are not physical-functional properties?

Since the deconstructive argument is valid, the new wavers are obliged to reject at least one premise. And since they are committed to premises 1 and 2, they are obliged to reject the tautologous-looking premise 3. Furthermore, they acknowledge three explanatory tasks that a credible version of materialism should simultaneously accomplish:

A: Explain the differences between phenomenal concepts and associated physical-functional concepts in a way that renders them conceptually independent, and thereby renders separatibility scenarios (e.g., scenarios involving creatures physically just like humans who are zombies or whose qualia are inverted) coherently conceivable.

B: Explain the differences between phenomenal concepts and associated physical-functional concepts in a way that fully respects the phenomenology of conscious experience.

C: Explain the differences between phenomenal concepts and associated physical-functional concepts in a way that is consistent with the claim that phenomenal properties are identical to physical-functional properties.

But the problem is to see how to one could deny premise 3 while still simultaneously meeting all three explanatory tasks. The only way to clearly meet tasks A and C is to deflate the idea of conceiving a property *directly* under a phenomenal concept—and thereby to deflate to idea of a phenomenal property functioning as self-presenting *mode of presentation*—to the point where these notions (as thus deflationally construed) would be applicable to zombies whose experience is phenomenally empty. And the cost of such deflation, of course, is a failure to meet task B.[8]

At present I see no cogent way for new wave materialism to avoid the deconstructive argument. On the contrary, this deductive argument seems to reinforce the above-described abductive argument from the epistemological explanatory gap to the denial of materialism about phenomenal consciousness. The deconstructive argument reveals why the abductive argument seems so epistemically powerful: the epistemological explanatory gap seems to reflect a metaphysical explanatory gap because the what-it's-like of phenomenal properties

---

[8] The new wave response to the deconstructive argument offered by McLaughlin (2001) seems to me to encounter this fate. It is telling that McLaughlin says nothing about why or how the new wave account would fail to apply to zombies who recognitionally conceive their own physical-functional states in a phenomenally empty 'super-blindsighter' manner. By contrast, Loar (1997) explicitly seeks to articulate the new wave position in a way that excludes introspective 'super-blindsighters'; but, as is argued in Horgan and Tienson (2001), Loar does so at the cost of losing any clear way to simultaneously meet explanatory demands A and C.

(a) is the very essence of these properties; (b) is directly presented in experience (rather than being presented via some contingent mode of presentation); and (c) is presented in experience otherwise than as physical. How then *could* phenomenal what-it's-likeness have a physical/functional essence? Abduction gets converted to deduction by explicitly affirming a premise to the effect that it could not, given (a)–(c)—viz., premise 3 of the deconstructive argument. The problem of 'irreducibly psychic properties' thus remains very much alive and well, and continues to be a very daunting challenge to materialism about phenomenal consciousness.

3.5. Phenomenal Intentionality and the Whole Hard Problem

Let me conclude this section with some brief remarks about what I take to be the scope of the explanatory gap, a.k.a. the hard problem, a.k.a. the problem of irreducibly psychic properties. Smart himself, and also his fellow pioneer psycho-physical identity theorist U. T. Place, regarded the problem of consciousness as confined primarily to sensory experience (and perhaps certain related phenomena such as sentory mental imagery); they regarded other mentalistic notions as susceptible to the kind of behaviorist account championed by Gilbert Ryle in *The Concept of Mind*. When behaviorism fell by the wayside in philosophy of mind and functionalism became popular, it was often noted that functionalism was somewhat similar in spirit to behaviorism—the main difference being that the functionalist held that the definitive causal role associated with any given mental notion involves its place within a web of causal connections that includes not only behavior and behavioral dispositions, but also sensory inputs and other internal mental states that have their own definitive causal role within the whole system of states. (This affinity to behaviorism has been noted not only with respect to the role functionalism once championed by Putnam, but also with respect to the filler functionalism about mental concepts, combined with an across-the-board type-type psychophysical identity theory about mental properties, that was championed by Armstrong and Lewis.)

One prominent theme in philosophy of mind in recent decades has been what George Graham and John Tienson and I call *separatism*—the view that mental phenomena can be fairly cleanly partitioned into two categories: (1) phenomena that exhibit intentionality and do not exhibit phenomenal character; and (2) phenomena that exhibit phenomenal character but to not exhibit intentionality. Occurrent beliefs and desires are often cited as paradigm examples of phenomena of type (1), and sensory experiences as paradigm examples of type (2). Some separatists have held that phenomena of type (1) are amenable to functionalist construal (in terms of either filler functionalism or role functionalism), but that phenomena of type (2) are recalcitrant and are subject to the hard problem. On this view, the fact that much of mentality is amenable to a functionalizing treatment (although not all of it is) gives us what Jaegwon

Kim calls (in the title of a recent book of his) 'physicalism, or something near enough.'

In my view, separatism is profoundly mistaken. In a number of recent papers, Graham and Tienson and I have been arguing that the scope of phenomenal consciousness includes much more than just sensory experience and related phenomena like sensory imagery. In addition, it includes virtually all of one's conscious (as opposed to unconscious) mental life.[9] Phenomenal consciousness, we maintain, is also richly and pervasively *intentional*: there is a kind of intentionality that is entirely constituted phenomenologically (we call it *phenomenal* intentionality), and it pervades people's mental lives. Among the different aspects of phenomenal intentionality are the following. First, there is the phenomenology of perceptual experience: the enormously rich and complex what-it's-like of being perceptually presented with a world of apparent objects, apparently instantiating a rich range of properties and relations—including one's own apparent body, apparently interacting with other apparent objects which apparently occupy various apparent spatial relations as apparently perceived from one's own apparent-body centered perceptual point of view. Second, there is the *phenomenology of agency*: the what-it's-like of apparently *voluntarily controlling* one's apparent body as it apparently moves around in, and apparently interacts with, apparent objects in its apparent environment. Third, there is *conative and cognitive* phenomenology: the what-it's-like of consciously (as opposed to unconsciously) undergoing various occurrent propositional attitudes, including conative attitudes like occurrent wishes and cognitive attitudes like occurrent thoughts. There are phenomenologically discernible aspects of conative and cognitive phenomenology, notably (i) the phenomenology of *attitude type* and (ii) the phenomenology of *content*. The former is illustrated by the phenomenological difference between, for instance, *occurrently hoping* that Hillary Clinton will be elected US President and *occurrently wondering* whether she will be—where the attitude-content remains the same while the attitude-type varies. The phenomenology of content is illustrated by the phenomenological difference between occurrently thinking that Hillary *will* be elected and occurrently thinking that she will *not* be elected—where the attitude-type remains the same while the attitude-content varies.

If the non-separatist approach to phenomenal consciousness just sketched is on the right track, then the hard problem of consciousness is much more pervasive than it is sometimes thought to be. It extends to virtually of conscious (as opposed to unconscious) mentality. Indeed, it may well extend indirectly to unconscious mentality too, because it is arguable that unconscious states can only be genuinely mental, with genuine intentionality, insofar as they are suitably

---

[9] See, for instance, Horgan and Tienson (2002), Horgan, Tienson and Graham (2004). Others who have been arguing along similar lines include Uriah Kriegel, Colin McGinn, David Pitt, Charles Siewert, and Galen Strawson.

causally interconnected to phenomenally conscious states within a cognitive agent.[10] But I will not pursue this theme here. The hard problem makes serious trouble for materialism in any case—whether or not separatism is true.

4. MINIMAL EMERGENTISM AND MENTAL CAUSATION

It is often maintained that materialism about mentality is the only viable way to fend off epiphenomenalism. Joseph Levine, who argues in favor of materialism despite his dissatisfaction with extant treatments of phenomenal consciousness in philosophy mind, puts the point this way: 'It seems to me that so long as we take mental properties to be causally relevant to the production of behavior, and accept the principle that the fundamental physical properties provide the only causal bases there are for changes in physical properties, we have reason to believe [materialism] must be true' (Levine 2001: 16). The leading ideas here are (1) that there is very strong, and constantly mounting, scientific evidence for the metaphysical hypothesis that in section 2 above I called the nomological closure of physics, and (2) that if this hypothesis is true, then mental properties can be causally efficacious only materialism is true.

On the other hand, it also is often maintained that a viable version of materialism about mentality should eschew the view that mental state-types are outright identical to physical state-types. A familiar argument against such type-type psychophysical identities is that mental properties are *multiply realizable* by different kinds of physical state-types in different kinds of physically possible creatures. Moreover, although Lewis (1980) was able to parry this argument by urging that according to Lewis-Armstrong filler functionalism, mental-state names should be construed as *nonrigid designators* that denote different physical properties relative to different populations of creatures (humans, Martians, robots, etc.), the fact remains that an adequate version of materialism should accommodate the physical possibility of mental properties being multiply realizable within a *single* creature-kind (or within a single individual creature, or within a single individual creature at a specific moment in its life); this is what I call *strong* multiple realizability. So I think that the multiple-realization argument against type-type psychophysical identities is fundamentally sound, notwithstanding the wiggle room afforded by appeals to kind-relative nonrigid designation.

Levine is among those who maintain that because mental properties are multiply realizable, materialism should repudiate type-type psychophysical identities. Concerning the claim that pain is identical to some neurological property B, he says, 'identifying pain with state B is inconsistent with the claim that pain can be realized in different ways, as in Martians or robots' (p. 26). But any version of

---

[10] See Graham, Horgan, and Tienson (2007) and Horgan and Graham (in press).

materialism that backs away from such type-type identities faces the well-known conundrum that Jaegwon Kim calls the problem of 'causal exclusion.' Levine describes the problem this way:

Consider . . . the pain's causing my hand to withdraw from the fire. My instantiating the mental property, being in pain, is supposed to be causally relevant to the subsequent motion of my hand. We know that a certain brain state, call it *B*, set in motion the nerve impulses which ultimately moved the muscles in my hand. My instantiating *B* was clearly causally relevant. *B* also realizes the pain. It's supposed to be because the pain is realized in *B*, which causes my hand to move, that we get to say that the pain caused my hand to move. However, from the description I just gave, it seems that my (or my brain's) instantiating pain adds nothing to the causal power relevant to producing a hand motion. All the causal work is none by the neurological property *B*. So it looks as if being physically realized can't help to secure causal efficacy for the mental.   (p. 26)

How then can a materialist who embraces the multiple realizability of mental properties, and who rejects the type-type psychophysical identity theory on this basis, fend off the threat that mental properties are 'causally excluded' by physical properties and are therefore epiphenomenal? Levine has this to say about the matter:

The answer I favor includes two elements. First, we have to be satisfied with perhaps a lesser grade of causal efficacy than we might want. There is no way around it . . . [I]f by 'causal efficacy' one means the kind of role that, according to materialism, only basic physical properties can play—and I won't deny that one can plausibly use the phrase that way—then of course it will turn out that mental properties, along with all other non-basic physical properties, are not causally efficacious. But so long as we recognize another sense of 'causal efficacy' . . . then there will be a sense in which mental properties are causally efficacious . . . [Second] When we say that believing it's going to rain and wanting to stay dry cause one to take an umbrella, I don't think we intend that this is a case of basic causation . . . Rather, what makes it a genuine case of causation is the fact that there is a lawful regularity that holds between beliefs and behaviors of the relevant kinds . . . It supports counterfactuals, is confirmed by instances, and, I believe, grounds singular causal claims . . . The regularity view may not give us all that we want, intuitively, by way of mental causation, but it is all that materialism allows. Is it enough? I think so, but I will not attempt to provide any further defense here.   (pp. 28–9)

Suppose that this reply to the causal-exclusion argument, or some similar reply, is adequate—that some 'lesser grade of causal efficacy' is enough to keep epiphenomenalism at bay. Well then, why can't an advocate of minimal emergentism embrace the very same reply? Consider a view that makes these claims: (1) materialism (characterized as in thesis (M) of section 1) is false; (2) the instantiation of phenomenal properties is necessitated by the instantiation of fundamental physical properties; (3) this necessitation involves inter-level supervenience connections, linking physical properties to phenomenal properties, that are fundamental and explainable; (4) phenomenal mental properties are causally relevant to the physical domain; and (5) their causal relevance is grounded in the (fundamental, unexplainable) necessitation relations between physical and phenomenal properties. Call this view *minimal-emergentist causal naturalism* (for short, MECN). The view has two variants: *nomic* MECN, which asserts that the inter-level necessitation relations obtain with nomic necessity, and *Moorean* MECN, which asserts that they obtain with metaphysical necessity. Either version of MECN could take on board Levine's response to the causal-exclusion argument—which means, apparently, that one need not embrace materialism in order to accommodate the causal efficacy of mental properties. Materialists are thereby deprived of one of the principal arguments they typically wield in support of materialism, the argument from the causal efficacy of mental properties.

Could a materialist respond that treatments of non-basic causal efficacy like Levine's are too lax, and that genuine causal efficacy of supervenient properties requires a form of 'metaphysical glue' between fundamental physical properties and the supervenient ones that is stronger than mere nomic necessitation? Perhaps so. I myself argued in Horgan (1987) that nothing less than *metaphysically* necessary supervenience relations, between underlying physical properties and non-physical properties, will suffice to secure the causal efficacy of the non-physical ones. My argument was in the spirit of the following remarks of David Lewis concerning the contention that mental properties could be causally efficacious by virtue of being suitably nomically related to underlying physical properties, remarks that seem applicable to the lately quoted passage from Levine:

> The position exploits a flaw in the standard regularity theory of cause. We know on other grounds that the theory must be corrected to discriminate between genuine causes and the spurious causes which are their epiphenomenal correlates. (The 'power on' light does not cause the motor to go, even if it a lawfully perfect correlate of the electric current that really causes the motor to go.) Given a satisfactory correction, the nonphysical correlate will be evinced from its spurious causal role . . .   (Lewis 1966: 106)

Suppose, then, that in order to be genuinely causally efficacious, non-physical properties must supervene with metaphysical necessity on underlying physical properties—rather than merely supervening on physical properties with *nomic* necessity. That would preclude the nomic version of MECN. But it would not thereby secure the argument from the causal efficacy of mental properties to materialism. For, the *Moorean* version of MECN would still remain a viable theoretical option—a theoretically viable way of allowing for the causal efficacy of the mental without embracing materialism.

5. CONCLUSION

Let us take stock. Minimal emergentism about phenomenal consciousness is a metaphysical position that looks to be entirely consistent with current scientific theory. It fits smoothly with scientifically well-supported theses like the nomological closure of physics and the thesis that all fundamental force-generating properties are physical properties.

A major theoretical advantage of minimal emergentism, in comparison to materialism, is that minimal emergentism provides an explanation for the epistemological 'explanatory gap,' whereas materialism seems to lack the resources either to explain epistemological gap or to explain it away. The emergentist explanation is that the epistemological explanatory gap reflects a *metaphysical* explanatory gap: there are supervenience connections linking physical properties to phenomenal mental properties are metaphysically basic, sui generis, and unexplainable.

One principal argument often used in support of materialism—viz., the argument from the causal efficacy of the mental—fails to provide any clear advantage of materialism over minimal emergentism. For, once it is acknowledged that mental properties, being multiply realizable, are not 'ground-level' causal properties, it appears that whatever strategies the materialist might deploy in an effort to secure some suitable kind of causal efficacy for the mental can be mimicked by the minimal emergentist. If nomic supervence is good enough, then both the nomic and the Moorean versions of minimal emergentism can rightly claim that mental properties are causally efficacious; it doesn't matter that the physical-to-mental supervenience connections are metaphysically brute, rather than being materialistically explainable. On the other hand, if the modal strength of the supervenience connections needs to be metaphysical (rather than merely nomic) in order for mental properties to be causally efficacious, then Moorean minimal emergentism is still available as a non-materialist position that secures the causal efficacy of mentality.

It remains true that minimal emergentism posits inter-level relations that are theoretical 'danglers' in the Feigl/Smart sense—either nomological danglers or Moorean danglers. Many of us, myself included, find ourselves unable (as did Smart) to believe in such metaphysically brute inter-level connections. But Smart's problem of irreducibly psychic properties remains as virulent a challenge to materialism as ever, and minimal emergentism meanwhile deserves to be recognized as a seriously viable alternative position.

16

Dualizing Materialism

Michael Jubien

The 'identity theory' of mind was under intense discussion when I was a graduate student. It was widely taken to be a 'materialist' doctrine, but I have never felt entirely comfortable with this understanding. It is also true that although I've never found any variant of the theory plausible, I haven't been particularly comfortable with this appraisal. My worry has been that what I think are the best known objections to the best versions have often been seen by materialists either to miss the point or to beg the question. Thus I want to begin by setting down my own reactions to the identity theory and drawing some conclusions about 'materialism'—something I have so far never done.[1] I hope to be able to dismiss the theory without seeming either to misunderstand it or to beg the question.

I will consider only the 'token(-token)' variant of the theory, which has generally been thought to be superior to 'type-type' versions because these seem defeated by the familiar problem of 'multiple realizability.' I believe that some of the typical objections to the token theory were on the right track but perhaps were not given their sharpest possible statements, so that identity theorists were often able to respond in ways that many materialists found satisfactory. As a general comment, it seems to me that the early discussion was impaired by the very way the theory was typically stated. It was usually presented as the claim that every specific 'mental state,' or 'event,' or 'process' (of ours) is identical with some specific 'brain state,' or 'event,' or 'process.' (Early theorists, for example Herbert Feigl, U. T. Place, and J. J. C. Smart, often spoke of 'processes,' but in this context I think we may safely assume that a process would be a certain sort of event. At any rate I will avoid talk of processes.) Then what exactly is meant here by 'state' or 'event'?

---

[1] I am grateful to George Bealer and Rob Koons for inviting me to contribute to this volume and for affording me the freedom to express my views in the summary fashion that will be noticed in what follows. I should add that the literature on these topics is vast and it is likely that much of what I will say has been said before in one way or another by other philosophers. In at least some cases I will be able to give examples.

There can be no doubt that we speak and act as if there are entities called 'states' and 'events.' Perhaps most people think of states as events of a certain kind, and for simplicity I will use 'event' in a way that reflects this. But it isn't easy to say just which things are events, that is, to mark out a class of undoubted *entities* to which the term 'event' (and so 'state') clearly applies.

As I see it, the material world consists of physical matter—physical objects—instantiating properties and standing in relations. So far this is virtually a truism. I favor elaborating it by adopting W. V. Quine's naturalistic and mereologically liberal conception, according to which a physical object '. . . comprises simply the content, however heterogeneous, of some portion of space-time, however disconnected and gerrymandered.'[2,3] I think, as Quine did, that this view combines best with a four-dimensionalist treatment of ordinary physical objects like tables and dogs, and for clarity I'll presuppose this in what follows. At the same time I think nothing ultimately hinges on it and, despite the assumption, I will sometimes speak in the everyday three-dimensionalist way.

Quine, perhaps surprisingly, recognized no distinction between physical objects and *events* (presumably including states). Thus, to pick a familiar example, the intuitive event of a ball's rotating over a certain time interval is, on the Quinean conception, just the temporal part of the ball determined by that interval—a certain mereological sum of matter in a spacetime region whose temporal span is the interval in question. For most four-dimensionalists who aren't picky about wide-open mereology, this counts as a clear enough *entity* but, to repeat a familiar complaint, it isn't a very plausible candidate for being the intuitive *event* because, on Quine's account, it might also have to be, say, the event of the ball's warming up over the same interval. Intuitively, the ball has countless properties over this interval and Quine's conception in effect fuses these myriad circumstances into a single 'event.'

Our intuitive talk of events thus appears instead to favor Jaegwon Kim's well known suggestion that we think of an event, roughly, as the instantiation of a *property* by an *object* at a *time*.[4] Let's call this the *OPT* conception of events (including states). Because *rotating* and *warming up* are distinct properties, OPT more closely captures our 'fine-grained' intuitive thinking about events than does Quine's 'coarse-grained' conception. But, as so far elaborated, it does so *without* isolating any specific *entities* to which talk of events could comfortably be claimed to refer.

The standard grammar of event talk reinforces this. We make seeming reference to specific events by employing possessive constructions like 'the ball's rotating.' (Here I'll suppress times.) What makes these constructions seem to refer is our

---

² Willard van Orman Quine (1960).
³ I offer a more detailed account of the contents of the physical world in Jubien (2009: chapter 1).
⁴ For example, see Jaegwon Kim (1973).

employment of them in subject- and object-positions in complete sentences like 'The ball's rotating caused it to curve in its flight.'[5] We cannot take 'the ball's rotating' simply to refer to the ball, as if it were interchangeable with 'the ball, which was rotating.' Nor can we take it simply to refer to the property of rotating, as if it were interchangeable with 'rotating, which the ball exemplified.' Either of these would result in a dramatically false or even incoherent causal claim. But the only ingredients we have to go on in the phrase are 'the ball,' the possessive, and 'rotating.' The causal claim works only if this combination is somehow or other taken to unite the object and the property so that what is being claimed isn't simply about a ball which is incidentally rotating or simply about a property which is incidentally exemplified by the ball. But now we have an ontological problem.

The problem is that there are many conceivable ways in which to bring these two entities together into a single, third entity to play the role of the intuitive event. Quine's way of course does bring them together but, as we saw, with many unwelcome tagalongs. Most other ways appeal to abstract entities (in addition to the given property). For example, we could bring the ingredients together into a *set* or into an *ordered pair* (or *triple* when considering the time). Or we could invoke a further property (for example, the 'disjunctive' property: *being either the ball or (the property of) rotating*). But there is nothing in the mere use of the possessive that points definitively toward any particular such abstract treatment of events. An alternative that avoids further abstract entities is to treat the event as the mereological sum of the object and the property. But again, it is hard to see such a treatment as dictated simply by our use of the possessive. Our options here are many, and one is reminded of the many equally serviceable options for 'treating *natural numbers* (or, for that matter, *ordered pairs*) as sets.'[6,7]

In a formal setting, say in discussing causation, we might follow Kim by enlisting ordered triples of objects, properties, and times to *play the role of* events, but it cannot be seriously maintained that in our everyday, pre-theoretic talk of events we are actually referring to *ordered triples*.[8] And even if we could get beyond that, there would remain the fact that there are six different ways to put three entities into an ordered triple. How could any one of them enjoy pride of place over the others?

---

[5] Unfortunately the possessive is often dropped in colloquial speech, yielding grammatically incoherent offerings like 'The ball rotating caused it to curve.' Charity requires us to restore the possessive in our interpretation of such tokens.

[6] And also reminded, of course, of the argument of Paul Benacerraf (1965). Similar points are made about *propositions* in my 2001 paper, 'Propositions and the Objects of Thought,' *Philosophical Studies* 104: 47–62.

[7] Another possibility, which I view as metaphysically suspect, is inspired by the dubious idea of a 'bare' particular—an object somehow taken in isolation from its properties. Instead of a bare particular, we might think here of a 'scantily clad' particular: a particular draped in one but only one of its properties. I will not detail reasons for avoiding this option.

[8] George Bealer makes a similar point about propositions in 'Propositions,' *Mind*, 107 (1998): 1–32.

In the end, strictly as a matter of ontology, there may be no ultimate need to postulate events or states. Apparent talk of events and states might be seen simply as an often convenient (if ontologically misleading) manner of speaking about objects, properties, and times. In fact this is the view I favor, but I won't try to defend it here. What is crucial, I believe, is that whether we include events in our ontology or not, ordinary fine-grained event talk is deeply committed to objects, properties, and times (as it would obviously be if events really were, say, ordered triples of these entities). Speaking a bit loosely, the reason is that the fine-grainedness of the talk depends on the implicated properties. What makes (the event of) the ball's rotating distinct from (the event of) the ball's heating up is nothing other than the fact that *rotating* and *heating up* are different properties. Whereas a Quinean physical object comes 'saturated' with a plurality of intuitive events and states in which the object participates, when we ordinarily speak of specific events or states, we generally limit our attention to some one of these and deliberately disregard the others. We're talking only about, say, the ball's *rotating, not* about its *warming up*. So it seems to me that if an account of states is to reflect this undoubted aspect of typical state talk, then it must somehow incorporate Kim's OPT conception. In what follows I will assume this is correct. An immediate and crucial consequence of OPT is that any claim of state- or event-identity entails underlying claims of object-, property-, and time-identity. (In the interest of simplicity I am going to set aside complex intuitive events that may have no obvious single object constituent.)

Now let's think about the token identity theory of mind. In accordance with its early proponents' intentions, the theory is that any specific occurrent mental state is identical with (i.e., nothing but) a certain specific occurrent brain state. Let's consider this with the help of an example. There is good evidence that in 1934 Lorenz Hart spent some time thinking about the moon. Intuitively, and in conformity with how we normally speak and indeed just spoke, *Hart himself* was the entity doing the thinking. I think this is very awkward for the identity theory. For whereas the mental state consists in *Hart's* having a certain property, the brain state evidently consists in a *brain's* having a certain property. The brain of course is Hart's. But surely the theory need not include the very doubtful claim that Hart is identical with his brain.[9] What the theory clearly does claim, when taken literally, is that this fortunate mental episode of Hart's was identical with a certain brain state. But, given OPT, that could not be true unless Hart were identical with his brain. Again, states can be identical only if their constituent objects, properties, and times are (respectively) identical.

There are two ways of patching this up. One would be to reconstrue the theory so that by 'brain state' we now understand a state in which, in the terms

---

[9] It would be more plausible to hold that he is identical with his body, so that his brain would be but one among his many parts. Of course the theory, as stated, is not automatically committed to this particular identity either.

of our example, Hart himself is the relevant object and the relevant property is *having a brain that instantiates such and such (physicochemical) property*, say *P*. (I continue to omit times for simplicity.) This would bring the intuitive subjects of the mental state and the brain state back into line by making Hart the object constituent of both, thus preserving the possibility of mental state/brain state identity. A different way would be to work from the other side, so that the brain would be the object constituent of both states. Then, in our example, the property constituent of the mental state would be *being the brain of someone who is thinking about the moon*.

I believe we are now able to put the commitments of the identity theory into very sharp focus. Suppose we take the former of the two options just mentioned, so that Hart is the object constituent of both the mental and the physical state. Then the claim that the mental state is identical with the brain state entails, under OPT, that the property of *thinking about the moon* is identical with the property of *having a brain that instantiates P* (and of course that the relevant time constituents are also identical). On the second option, where Hart's brain is the object constituent of both states, the state-identity claim entails that the property *P* is identical with the property of *being the brain of someone who is thinking about the moon*.

But these are obviously *type-type* identity claims, and one of the key virtues of the token identity theory was supposed to be its insulation from the well known problems of type identity theories, prominently including the above mentioned problem of multiple realizability. Thus, by making explicit the ontological underpinnings of the cloudy notion of *states*, OPT has enabled us to see that the supposedly more flexible and sophisticated token theory is actually a type identity theory in disguise.[10]

But I think difficulty looms quite independently of the realizability problem. I believe that on any reasonable conception of *properties*, neither of these claims of property identity is even remotely plausible. Thus consider the property of *thinking about the moon*. Intuitively, it has the *thinking (about)* relation and the property of *being the moon* as constituent parts.[11] This is because any *analysis* of *thinking about the moon* must, somehow or other, involve both this simpler property and this relation. It might involve them directly if the analysis were comparatively unrefined, or indirectly if it were more refined and so incorporated analyses of one or both of these intuitive constituents. But the property of *having a brain that instantiates P* has no such constituent properties or relations. No analysis of *P* would involve either *thinking* or *being the moon*. The constituents of the 'brain state' property are then *having a brain* and the simpler physicochemical properties and relations that are the natural constituents of *P*. It is these properties

---

10 Others have made similar criticisms. For example, see Horgan (1981).
11 It would not involve the moon itself because we are able to think about things that don't exist, like unicorns and the Fountain of Youth.

that would appear, directly or indirectly, in any analysis of *having a brain that instantiates P*. I believe these claims would be true even if nothing ever instantiated either of these properties without also instantiating the other. Essentially the same comment applies in the case of the other property identity. So, each of these two pairs of properties is a pair of distinct properties, and this just as a matter of the *ontology* of complex properties.

A likely objection to this line of thinking is that it's plausible only if we accept something like the outmoded doctrine of *conceptual analysis*. For I seem to be claiming that we know that *thinking about the moon* has no purely physicochemical constituents (and this is something that could only be known *a priori*). This is indeed what I'm claiming. I think we know such things because our understanding of our own language guarantees, more or less, that we know what concepts our words express, and 'thinking about the moon' and 'having a brain that instantiates P' are clear examples of phrases that express different concepts (with different analyses).

Early identity theorists would have viewed the supposed identity of these sorts of properties as *contingent*. But now it is all but universally accepted that the relation of genuine (numerical) identity never holds contingently. Further, as we all know, Hilary Putnam and Saul Kripke famously argued (separately) that familiar 'scientific identities' are subject to empirical discovery. So the necessity of an identity would not guarantee its triviality. The best known—and now very widely accepted—example of such an '*a posteriori* necessity' is the supposed identity of water and H_2O (which surely is best construed as a claim of *property* identity). Although Kripke argued against 'contingent identity' versions of the identity theory, the Putnam-Kripke arguments and examples were actually a boon for identity theorists. For they could now cheerfully hold that *thinking about the moon* and *having a brain that instantiates P* are necessarily identical, while at the same time finessing their apparent distinctness by holding the identity to be of the nontrivial scientific variety.

But, for reasons too involved to discuss here, I don't think Putnam and Kripke were right. I think their conclusions rested on an incorrect, overly idealized understanding of the workings of natural language. I also think no reasonable account of natural language supports the doctrine of necessity *a posteriori*. So I remain a proponent of conceptual analysis and it is from this standpoint that I claim the properties we've been considering are distinct. (In fact I believe the property originally expressed by 'water' is *not* identical with that expressed by 'H_2O', and I believe this original use of the term survives in the language. I also think there is now a further use of 'water' which *does* express the property of *being H_2O*, but that the corresponding claim of property identity is not *a posteriori*.[12])

---

[12] Detailed reasons for these views may be found in the above mentioned *Possibility*.

Notice that the claim of distinctness does not depend on any specific theory or analysis of property constituency. It depends only on the idea that properties like thinking about the moon and *P* are complexes of simpler properties and relations (including logical relations), and that we have insight into the nature of these properties directly from our understanding of the language. This 'ontological' point is of course related to the Cartesian claim that, in effect, we can easily conceive of thinking about the moon without having a brain that instantiates the physical property *P*, indeed, without having a brain at all. It is similarly related to the claims of 'zombie' theorists that we can easily imagine a being's having a brain instantiating *P* but doing no directed thinking at all, indeed, having no mental states at all. But the ontological point is really prior to these because it doesn't exploit what we are able to conceive or imagine.

We thus have what I think is a devastating dilemma for the token identity theory quite apart from its apparent commitment to dubious type identities. Either it posits the identity of states whose constituent objects are distinct, or else it posits the identity of states whose constituent properties are distinct. But states can be identical only if all of their constituents—objects, properties, and times—are (respectively) identical.

It has often been argued, independently of the niceties of OPT, that states like Hart's thinking about the moon cannot be identical with states like Hart's (brain's) instantiating *P* because Hart's thinking about the moon is an *intentional* state while the other state is not. (Or because one is a 'purely physical' state while the other is not.) Such arguments never convinced committed materialists. From their perspective these critics were begging the question. (And from the critics' perspective, the charge of begging the question could only be made by someone who was denying the obvious. An impasse.) It was common for identity theorists to insist that phrases with overtly intentional language and phrases with seemingly purely physical language might differ dramatically in meaning, but that it would not follow that they didn't refer to the very same states. If the two phrases pick out the same state, and one phrase picks out (say) an intentional state, then so does the other after all. There was frequent appeal to '*The Morning Star*' and '*The Evening Star*' in an effort to seal this point.

The ontological objection is not an 'intentionality' objection (any more than it is a 'conceivability' objection). Like the intentionality objection, it relies on the indiscernibility of identicals, but there is no reliance on the idea that some properties are 'irreducibly intentional' while others are 'purely physical.' The key property that *thinking about the moon* has, but *having a brain that instantiates P* lacks, again, is simply the property of *having the relation of thinking* (or *the property of being the moon*) *as a constituent*. Similarly, a property that *having a brain that instantiates P* has, but *thinking about the moon* lacks, is *having C as a constituent*, where *C* is any physicochemical property that is a constituent of *P* (and so of *having a brain that instantiates P*). (And on the second option, we have two properties, one of which also has *thinking* (or *being the moon*) as a constituent while the other does not.) Here we are not relying on intuitions about the intentionality or lack of intentionality of various properties.[13]

Despite this claim, there might be a lingering suspicion that intentionality is somehow playing a covert role because the *thinking (about)* relation is a constituent of the intuitive mental state, and this relation is plainly intentional. But I think the intentionality of this relation is beside the point. To see why, consider the property of *having a visual image*. The having of a visual image surely counts as an intuitive mental state, but there is nothing intentional about it (in itself), even though it might be part of a more complex, intuitively intentional state. But no physicochemical property of the brain has an analysis involving the property of *having a visual image* (or any of its natural constituents).

The ontological objection relies only on OPT, on a straightforward effort to bring the intuitive object constituents of a mental state and a brain state into agreement, and on an intuitively compelling conception of complex properties as complexes of simpler properties and relations. Thus it is hard to see that it begs the question or misses the point. If there is anything wrong with it, it is either OPT or the idea that typical properties are complexes involving simpler properties (or that they have analyses involving simpler properties). But surely these are positions that one would think at the outset have no built-in bias one way or the other on the matter of the identity theory.

Thus it seems to me that OPT has brought a welcome dose of clarity to the discussion by shifting it from the cloudy arena of states to the relatively crystalline realm of properties. As a further example of the newfound clarity, we may now easily see a problem with the just mentioned meaning/reference response to the intentionality objection. It is of course right to distinguish the (supposed) meaning of, say, '*The Morning Star*' from its referent, for its referent, after all, is a physical object while its (supposed) meaning is a certain property. So it is no surprise that '*The Evening Star*' might have a different meaning and yet refer to the same object.[14] But when we are liberated from overt state talk, the phrases playing the key individuative roles are now phrases that denote *properties*, not *states*, and here it is entirely reasonable to think that their meanings and referents *do* coincide. If this is right, then the meaning/reference strategy does not appear to offer a promising response to the intentionality objection.

But maybe it isn't right, and the meanings and referents of such property-denoting expressions need not coincide. Is this a coherent position for an

---

[13] The objection applies with equal force to 'functionalist' variations on the (token) identity theory, in particular to those that hold that a given physical state gets its 'mental' character from its causal role in the subject's interactions with the external world. We are not relying on the mental character of Hart's thinking about the moon, whatever its source might be. At the same time I would not deny either the mental or the intentional character of this intuitive state.

[14] This is surely the case if the terms are taken as definite descriptions rather than proper names. If they are taken as names the matter is trickier. On my own view names do express properties, but as a rule distinct names with the same bearer ('Twain' and 'Clemens,' for example) express the same properties. (See *Possibility* for details.)

identity theorist to take? It seems to me to be at least awkward and perhaps even inconsistent. An identity theorist adopting the 'meaning/reference' strategy would hold that both (1) and (2) are true:

(1) The meaning of 'thinking about the moon' ≠ the meaning of 'having a brain that instantiates *P*.'

(2) The referent of 'thinking about the moon' = the referent of 'having a brain that instantiates *P*.'

Suppose we assume that the meanings of the phrases are *properties*. Then just which properties *are* these two meanings? One very natural and tempting possibility is given by (3) and (4):

(3) The meaning of 'thinking about the moon' = (the property of) *thinking about the moon.*

(4) The meaning of 'having a brain that instantiates *P*' = (the property of) *having a brain that instantiates P.*

But accepting (3) and (4) is not an option for an identity theorist. The reason is that (1), (3), and (4) together entail

(5) Thinking about the moon ≠ having a brain that instantiates *P*,

whereas (2) entails

(6) Thinking about the moon = having a brain that instantiates *P*.

To persist in the strategy, then, appears to require rejecting (3) and (4) and postulating that the meanings of the phrases are further properties that have not yet come under discussion, or else claiming that the meanings are not properties at all. But what further properties? Would one of them be intuitively mental and the other intuitively physical? And if the meanings *aren't* properties, what sorts of entities are they? Concepts? And what exactly are these?[15] Perhaps they aren't entities at all, and our talk of meanings is just a manner of speaking. What I believe is clear at this point is that there are several different options for backing up the meaning/reference strategy, and that any of them would require abandoning the intuitively straightforward notion that 'thinking about the moon' means *thinking about the moon.* I won't consider the possible backup strategies here.

Leaving the full subtleties of OPT aside, I have concluded that the property of *thinking about the moon*, and *P* (or any other physicochemical property you like that is denoted by a phrase couched entirely in the language of physics

---

[15] I hold that when we speak of concepts as publicly available entities (e.g., 'the concept of mass'), as opposed to our individual subjective representations of concepts, these nonsubjective concepts are in fact properties (e.g., *having mass*) and relations. For more on this topic see my 1997 *Contemporary Metaphysics* (Oxford: Blackwell Publishers), chapter 1.

and chemistry) *must* be distinct. I believe intentionality-free considerations are always enough to show the distinctness of the property constituents in mental-state/brain-state identity claims, and I believe they do so without inviting charges of begging the question or missing the point.

Now let's return briefly to the question why we should think the identity theory is a 'materialist' position in the first place. When we applied OPT to bring the subjects of the states into line, we wound up having either Hart or Hart's brain as the subject (and nothing of great consequence seemed to depend on the choice since the states wound up being distinct either way). But of course if one chooses *Hart*, then there is ample room to hold that the subject of the two intuitive states is not a physical object. And even if we go with the *brain* option, the property constituent of the intuitive mental state (*being the brain of someone who is thinking about the moon*) clearly has *being a person* as a constituent, and there is nothing in the theory so far that entails that this property may only be instantiated by something physical. So, even ignoring the problem of the distinctness of the property constituents, it remains that the theory, construed literally but in accordance with OPT, is compatible with Cartesian dualism. I think this was easy to overlook when the discussion was taken to be fundamentally about *states*, and states were thought to be unproblematic.

The natural fix for this problem is to adjoin to the theory the claim that each person is a physical object, or more generally that no concrete (i.e., non-abstract) entity is immaterial. That, at any rate, seems to be a core materialist belief, so we might as well put it into the theory. We may then state the revised theory, as it applies in the case of Hart and the moon, as follows (again suppressing times):

T: (1) Some physical object instantiates *being Hart, thinking about the moon,* and *having a brain that instantiates P,* and (2) *thinking about the moon* and *having a brain that instantiates P* are identical.

In my preferred way of translating English into the language of first-order logic,[16] we would have:

T*: $\exists x[Ixp \,\&\, Ixh \,\&\, Ixm \,\&\, Ixb \,\&\, m = b]$,

where '*I*' is a two-place predicate letter expressing the instantiation relation, '*p*' denotes the property of *being physical,* '*h*' denotes the property of *being Hart,* '*m*' denotes the property of *thinking about the moon,* and '*b*' denotes the property of *having a brain that instantiates P.*

A Cartesian dualist, of course, will deny that Hart instantiates *p* and also that $m = b$. But, as we have seen, it isn't necessary to be a Cartesian dualist to reject T*, for we found an ontological reason for rejecting $m = b$ that doesn't rely on Cartesian premises.

---

[16] See *Possibility* for reasons and details.

But let us probe a little more deeply, by bringing times and the four-dimensional account of ordinary objects into play. For this we need a binary predicate letter, 'P,' to express the part–whole relation; 'Pxy' will mean that x is part of y. We also need a unary function symbol, 'F,' mapping an arbitrary (Quinean) physical object to the time over which it exists. Here a time may be an instant; a continuous (open, closed, or mixed) interval; or it may be a discontinuous (mereological) sum of instants and/or intervals. We now have something fairly complicated:

T′: $\exists x \exists y [Ixp \;\&\; Ixh \;\&\; Pyx \;\&\; Fy = t \;\&\; Iym^* \;\&\; Iyb^* \;\&\; m^* = b^*]$.

Here 'm^*' denotes the property of the 't-part' of Hart that makes it true that Hart is thinking about the moon at (or during) t, and 'b^*' denotes the property of the t-part of Hart that makes it true that Hart has a brain that instantiates P at (or during) t. To avoid further complication I've refrained from building into T′ that y is the most extensive part of Hart that exists over the time t. But doing that would be straightforward enough, so let's just pretend it's been done. Now, since I have already rejected the claim that $m = b$, I am committed to rejecting the claim that $m^* = b^*$. Thus it seems reasonable to wonder about the plausibility of the theory, call it T′, that results from replacing '$m^* = b^*$' by '$m^* \neq b^*$' in T′. To put it a little differently, how plausible is what we might call 'materialism about people'—the 'core claim' that people are physical objects—if we reject the apparent type-type consequence of the token identity theory (and so the theory itself)?

Recall that it isn't that m and m^* are distinct from b and b^* because the latter are the *wrong* physical properties, where there might be some others that would do the trick. We have seen that no purely physical property can have the same constituents as m (or m^*). (Nothing potentially prejudicial was ever assumed about m and b (or m^* and b^*), so we are entitled to generalize.) It evidently follows that m and b (etc.) are fundamentally different and incompatible *kinds* of properties. And what would the different kinds be if not *mental* and *non-mental* or *not purely physical* and *purely physical*? Of course as soon as someone says that m is a mental property and b is not, a defender of the identity theory may be tempted to declare that we are begging the question. But in the present case I believe we are not. We concluded that $m \neq b$ for ontological reasons involving no premises about the mental and the non-mental or the purely physical and the not purely physical. It follows from that reasoning that m and b are fundamentally different sorts of properties and that the sorts are incompatible in the sense that no property could be of both sorts. Now we are merely giving labels to the different sorts. We could just as easily call them X-type properties and non-X type properties, but the fact is that we already have terms available that do the job. As long as we use these terms carefully there can be no serious objection to doing so.

Presumably any materialist is content to speak of properties that are expressible in the language of physics and chemistry. So for the moment let's call these properties *purely physical*.[17] I also believe that a materialist—at least one who is willing to speak of properties in the first place—should agree that not all properties enjoy this distinction, for example, the properties of *being a ghost* or *being a natural number*. This should be conceded even if one thinks neither ghosts nor natural numbers exist. So now we merely seem to have found yet another property that isn't purely physical—the property *m*—along with any other property that counts intuitively as *mental*.

We have arrived at (a version of) the familiar theory known as 'property dualism.' Many philosophers have found it just as untenable as (Cartesian) substance dualism.[18] I have always had quite the opposite reaction. It seems to me to be entirely obvious that we have properties like *thinking about the moon*. (So I would reject 'eliminativism' out of hand.) If the claim that such properties are identical with purely physical properties is rejected, then property dualism looks like the best alternative for anyone who is inclined to think that human beings are complicated physical entities.

Still there is considerable resistance. I suspect that it flows partly from a conviction that 'non-physical' properties are just as mysterious as non-physical substances. For example, in criticizing property dualism, John Searle writes, 'We really do not get out of the postulation of mental entities by calling them properties. We are still postulating nonmaterial mental things.'[19] But this is really not a sound objection. On typical accounts, *all* properties, including foursquare, purely physical properties like *having mass* and the recent *P*, are 'nonmaterial' entities—they are not located in space-time or made of matter (or energy). And we have just seen that to call a property like *thinking about the moon* 'mental' need mean no more than saying that it isn't expressible in the language of physics (including chemistry).[20]

---

[17] There are of course different conceptions of 'physical properties.' For example we might speak of the properties expressible in the *ultimate* language of physics, or we might want somehow to divorce the notion from physics entirely. I believe the present notion is relatively clear and that it suffices for immediate purposes. I will offer a broader notion of *physical property* below.

[18] Smart is a good example of an early identity theorist who recoiled at the idea of 'irreducibly non-physical' properties. At the same time, he does not hesitate to speak of properties in general. (See Smart (1970: 160). Some 'materialists' may reject abstract entities, but it doesn't seem to me that (as it were) the spirit of the view requires it. Of course nowadays philosophers are much more comfortable with (abstract) properties than they were in the 1960s. As far as properties like *being a ghost* are concerned, it's worth noting that if we reject this property (etc.) we then need a semantical account of 'There are no ghosts' that differs dramatically from the natural account of 'There are no Martians.'

[19] See John Searle (2004: 46).

[20] Of course on accounts of properties that somehow locate them in space–time, either the charge that they are 'nonmaterial' loses its force or else the trait is once again shared by purely physical properties. A similar point can be made about nominalist treatments of property talk—the issue of nonmateriality no longer has any grip, but it remains that the propositions expressed by the nominalist rewrites of mental property claims are not expressible in the language of physics and chemistry.

The mental properties, like the purely physical ones, are entirely natural properties, in the sense that they are instantiated by natural beings—on this theory by certain complicated physical objects. The tendency to see these properties as mysterious seems to me to be a case of guilt by association. Philosophers decided it was mysterious to think that it's a nonmaterial entity that is thinking about the moon, but then they promptly assumed that there is something mysterious about the property of thinking about the moon. But how could there be anything mysterious about thinking about the moon? I would say it's something that all of us have done many times, and that often it's not a bad thing to do at all.

We really need to ask why we should think that any property a physical object might have would automatically be describable in the language of physics as we know it. We don't think every property a *biological* entity might have is describable in the present language of biology; nor do we think every property a *mathematical* object might have is describable in the current language of mathematics.

Even a sketchy reminder of the history of physics and its languages may be useful here. Early physics—specifically Aristotle's—was primarily a theory about the motions of physical bodies. The basic vocabulary included terms for the five different (presumed!) substances (including the postulated substance ether) and for the explanatory principle of natural place. There was of course no talk of such matters as magnetism, electrons, or quanta. So at the time it would have been dramatically incorrect to think that all properties of physical objects were expressible in this very limited language. Eventually Galileo and others (for the most part) discarded the Aristotelian concepts in favor of the familiar notions that would later receive grand theoretical expression in Newton's physics. But still there was no theorizing (for example) about magnetism and electricity. It would again have been dramatically wrong to think that all properties of physical objects were expressible in the Newtonian language of physics. Today, of course, the language of mainstream physics includes extensive additions to and revisions of the Newtonian language. It easily expresses properties of physical objects that might have seemed mysterious in the seventeenth century. But there is no good reason to think this language is 'complete' (in the sense of being able to express all future developments in physics). Physics, after all, still has its share of mysteries, and we may need entirely new notions (and language) to cope with them.

I want to suggest that a property dualist should maintain that physics, or at least physical science, should ultimately include a theory of the mental. Mental properties are of course not *purely physical* in our present sense, but it does not follow that they lie outside the proper subject matter of physical science or even physics proper. I suggest that we construe *physical science* as the theoretical study of those properties of physical entities that are related in law-like ways to (the current) *purely physical* properties, and that we regard any such properties as *physical* whether they are among the (current) purely physical properties or not.

Many of the properties that we call *mental* are evidently so related to purely physical properties (though of course I've been arguing that the relation is not identity). It also seems clear that there are law-like relations among the mental properties themselves. Thus, given that we do take mental properties to be instantiated by physical entities, we should expect that ultimate physical science would include an account of the mental. Mental properties would ultimately stand shoulder-to-shoulder with once-mysterious properties like electric charge and magnetic attraction. In this environment the intuitively mental properties would have ascended to the status of physical properties because they would be expressible in the expanded vocabulary of physical science. It would of course remain that their analyses would not include anything like the sorts of properties encountered in the analyses of properties like the recent P.

Why should there not be 'psychophysical' laws? A familiar objection is that we cannot easily see 'causation' occurring in either direction, or even, for example, that 'mental causation' (of physical action) is inherently mysterious. I believe a property dualist should say three things about these complaints. First, echoing Hume, we cannot easily see 'causation' at work even in the interactions of billiard balls or in planetary motion. Second, echoing Russell, it is far from obvious that physics concerns causation in the first place. When we happen to find the word 'cause' (etc.) in a physics book, we find it only in informal remarks, not in what counts as the actual physics. Third, as partly evidenced by the silence of physics on the matter, the concept of cause is an everyday notion (even a 'folk' notion). The many painstaking (and ingenious) efforts of philosophers to analyze it have in fact resulted in widely divergent and incompatible accounts. (Though part of the reason may be that there is really more than one everyday notion of cause.) There is nothing like general agreement upon some one of the resulting technical concepts as playing a central role in science.[21]

These considerations provide a basis for responding to an influential line of resistance to property dualism that may seem more persuasive than the charge of mysteriousness. The resistance takes root in the widespread conviction that 'physical' effects are always explicable by reference to 'physical' causes. If one takes this view and accepts the apparent fact that 'mental' events may and do enter into the production of 'physical' effects, and if one also rejects the possibility of parallel mental/physical overdetermination, it is very tempting to infer that

---

[21] Here a comparison with the intuitive notion of (physical) force may be worthwhile. To the extent that we have a single such notion, it doesn't seem to be captured by the notion of force codified in Newton's '$F = ma$.' A bowling ball dropped from 20 feet applies more intuitive force to the ground than one dropped from 2 feet, but both are accelerating at the same rate. So intuitive force seems more akin to the Newtonian notion of kinetic energy ($\frac{1}{2} mv^2$), where it is velocity rather than acceleration that supplies the juice. What is clearly true may only be that the laws of physics do apply in cases where we intuitively think force is being applied, but without there necessarily being some specific physical concept that corresponds to the intuitive one in the complete description of such a case. The case for a specific physical concept corresponding to intuitive causation is of course yet more tenuous than the case for force.

'mental' properties are identical with 'physical' properties. Those who make this inference of course reject property dualism.

I won't consider every possible variation on this theme. But an initial and general difficulty is that it is couched in the everyday vocabulary of event causation (or in similarly unclear terms). I suggested earlier that *events* are dubious entities that may be avoided by switching to talk of individuals, properties, and times. And I just endorsed the Russellian view that *causation* is essentially a folk notion that plays no clear role in physics proper.

Against this background let's briefly consider the two key claims. The first may perhaps be construed in a friendly, event-free, deductive-nomological way as the view that the instantiation of specific physical properties by objects at times is a consequence of general laws in which physical properties are appropriately linked, in company with specific prior instantiations of physical properties. If that is accepted, then the remaining business is to settle just what is meant by 'physical properties.' There is more than one possibility.

One would be to take physical properties to be properties describable in the (current) language of physics—what I have been calling purely physical properties. But under this interpretation the claim is unpersuasive. At least it seems that there have been times when 'effects' describable in the then-current language of physics would not be 'covered' by laws and 'initial conditions' that could be stated in the same terms. Consider the earlier example of a ball curving in its flight. Although Newton had the vocabulary to describe the curved path of the ball, its 'explanation' would have to wait a half-century for Bernoulli's introduction of hydrodynamics and its generalization to gasses. Are there good reasons to think that every effect describable in today's physics is covered by a theory stated in the same terms? At the very least this is an optimistic thought. The first claim is then far from obvious on the present interpretation.

Another reading would take physical properties to be properties describable in the 'ultimate' or 'ideal' language of physics. This interpretation collapses into the idea, urged above, that a physical property is simply any property that a physical object may possess and which is related in law-like ways to (current) purely physical properties, and that it is the ultimate business of physical science to investigate and theorize about such properties. But under this reading a property dualist may readily endorse the principle. Thinking about the moon is then a physical property in the new sense, and if having it should inspire someone to wax lyrical and put pen to paper, then ultimate physical science should have laws covering such successions of intuitive 'mental' and 'physical' events.

The second claim, so interpreted in the 'ultimate' way, then poses no serious threat to the intuitive distinctness of 'mental' properties from those properties of parts of the brain that, as it happens, actually are describable in the current language of physics.

So a property dualist should insist that at bottom it is the business of theoretical physical science to investigate law-like connections between properties of physical entities. The fact that we do not presently have a clear arsenal of well established, law-like 'psychophysical' connections should be seen as nothing worse than ignorance, not as evidence of mysteriousness.

Nor should the ignorance be surprising, for it is pretty clear that general psychophysical laws would have to be forbiddingly complicated. Imagine, as might be true, that it was the hearing of a certain melody pecked out by Richard Rodgers that got Hart to thinking about the moon one day in 1934, so that certain stimulations of his auditory apparatus resulted in neural activity that issued in the thinking. For this scenario to fall under an appropriate psychophysical law requires a general law connecting neural activity with directed thinking. As a result of multiple realizability, it is unreasonable to think that this law would merely connect occurrent neural activity with such thinking. It would have to be much more complex, in particular highly relational, with relata stretching well into the past, perhaps (in the present case) reflecting Hart's original acquisition of the term 'moon', any evolution in the structures that represent, for Hart, the property of being the moon, and of course also the initial development and subsequent evolution of his ability to engage in directed thought. Further, the fact that no law worthy of the name would apply only to Hart requires, in effect, that the law in question somehow incorporate all physically possible brain structures and histories that would support such directed thought in a human subject.

Plausible psychophysical laws, then, would seemingly have to capture enormously complex type-type connections, where the 'physical' types in question would generally not simply be intrinsic features of occurrent neural activity as envisaged by early type identity theorists. This is just the inevitable result of multiple realizability. It is important to emphasize that although I have rejected token identity theory partly because of the realizability problem, the connections postulated in psychophysical laws would not be identities. They would simply be law-like regularities. The connections would not be metaphysically necessary, so suspicions about the identity theory that are grounded in worries about necessity would have no traction here. It seems to me that we may never arrive at anything more impressive than fairly small pieces of such laws, that the laws themselves—thought of as certain very general propositions—may be too complex for us to handle. But that is irrelevant. It does not make the thesis that there really are such laws in any way mysterious.

So I am advocating a slightly tweaked version of the theory that is commonly called 'property dualism.' It is a theory that philosophers who think of themselves as materialists all too reflexively reject. Perhaps this is because they are by now allergic to the very word 'dualism'. But the theory seems to me to be much more plausible than any of the standard 'materialist' theories of the mental, and moreover that it is compatible with a more evolved version of 'materialism': one that claims simply that the non-abstract world includes no immaterial entities, or, more to the present point, simply that human beings are physical entities.

The strain of materialism that produced the identity theory in the mid-twentieth century was a predilection of philosophers who had been heavily influenced by positivism and by the teachings of Quine. They shared a strong nominalistic tendency even while freely engaging in overt property talk. For the most part they were not theorizing about properties or worrying about Platonism; they were theorizing about human beings and mental activity. Since the later part of the century the grip of nominalism has loosened considerably (along with phobias about serious modality). Perhaps we are now ready for a softer form of materialism, one that earns its name merely by making the above claim about human beings, and has a more liberal attitude about the remaining contents of reality, specifically about the postulation of Platonic properties. It seems to me that that's all it would take to render 'property dualism' a respectable species of a more relaxed brand of materialism. Well, that along with an acceptance of the everyday truth that people think about the moon.[22]

---

[22] I am very grateful to Gina Calderone, David Copp, and Gene Witmer for probing questions and insightful comments on earlier versions of this chapter.

17

Dualistic Materialism[1]

Joseph Almog

Materialism has not been waning, nor is dualism on the wane. Both are thriving and, dare one predict, will go on thriving *conjointly*. Therein lies the point of the chapter. All of us, marketplace people, or to echo Descartes, 'in life and conversation and without philosophizing (*sans philosopher*),' are both, and at the same time, materialists and dualists. It is not merely logically consistent and even really possible to be both; it is necessary—stronger yet, it is of our very *nature*—to be both materialists and dualists.

Obviously much turns here on what is meant by the mutually *sustaining* marketplace dualism and materialism as contrasted with the mutually *exclusionary* philosophical dualism and materialism.

The fundamental idea that marketplace materialism and dualism are not antagonistic and exclusionary but symbiotically interdependent, is encapsulated in a little remark Descartes makes to Princess Elizabeth in a letter of June 28

[1] Thanks to the editors, Robert Koons and George Bealer, who have been supportive and kind through and through. I owe thanks to recent joint teaching about essence and necessity (in Descartes and Spinoza) to John Carriero and Barbara Herman. Both have helped me understand my own views in a way I was not capable of before. Sarah Coolidge produced admirable notes of the joint teaching. I am grateful to earlier conversations (1985–97) on essence and/or the mind/body problem (especially Kripke's work on pain) to Kit Fine, Keith Donnellan, the late Rogers Albritton, David Kaplan, Tony Martin (for the analog case of mathematical/physical duality mentioned repeatedly below), Tyler Burge, Tom Nagel, Saul Kripke, and, finally, to my inventive ex-student Dominik Sklenar whose ideas changed mine (1992–7). A special debt is owed to Moriel Zelikowsky for conversations, back in 2001 and onwards, about work in contemporary experimental psychology about fear and pain in animals and humans. This is a sequel to my 2002 'Pains and Brains,' *Philosophical Topics*, 30, and my 2005 'Replies: The Human Mind, Body and Being,' *Philosophical and Phenomenological Research*, 70: 717–34. When it comes to Descartes' inspiration, the present piece extends ideas broached in my 2002 book *What am I?* and my 2008 *Cogito?* I see the mental/physical duality problem as raising deep structural analogies to the mathematical/physical duality. The analogy is mentioned repeatedly below and dissected in detail, including a path to a common unified solution, in my 2007 'The Cosmic Ensemble—The Mathematics/Nature Symbiosis,' *Midwest Studies in Philosophy*, 31: 344–71. In a similar vein, the present considerations on whatness-essence-nature vs. modal necessity (truth in all possible worlds) in the mind–body arena extend to a general such comparison of nature and necessity. See the references below to earlier work of mine on the distinction.

1643. I will dub this as the *two-in-one ensemble axiom*, or in a nutshell, *the ensemble axiom*:

(**Two in one Ensemble**) Finally, it is by relying on life and ordinary conversations, and by abstaining from meditating and studying things that exercise the imagination, that we learn how to conceive the union of mind and body . . . the notion of the union that each of us has inside him- or herself without philosophizing: that he or she is a single person that has together ('ensemble') a body and thought, that are of such nature so that the thought can move the body and feel the accidents that happen to it.[2]

The last sentence in the quote, past the colon, is literally what I call the two-in-one *ensemble axiom—each of us is a single person that has ensemble . . .* On some occasions, I will also allude to it as *Descartes' natural life axiom*, because it strikes me both (i) as a very natural—'life and ordinary conversation' view of what each of us is but also (ii) because he uses the vocabulary *of such nature*. The phrase 'of such nature' alludes here to the nature of the things involved—the person, his or her mind and his or her body.

So much for Descartes' optimism reflected in the ensemble axiom. A few lines earlier in his letter, Descartes, forgetful of life and ordinary conversation and in a more philosophical, darker and sophistical, mood foists on the princess what I will call the *Either-one-or-two-dilemma*:

(**Either one or two Dilemma**) It does not seem to me that the human mind is capable of conceiving and distinctly at the same time the distinction between the mind and the body and their union because for this one has to conceive them as one thing and as two (things), which is contradictory.[3]

Thoughts of this kind feed into the idea that materialism and dualism are contradictory; that we must make a painful choice between materialism and dualism; that the initial optimism of the ensemble axiom was unfounded. My task below is to engage (the darker, dilemma-bound) Descartes, and with him, most contemporary philosophical dualists and materialists. I would like to argue that they are overly pessimistic with their sense of an impending contradiction and the reign of an either-one-or-two dilemma and the hard choice it forces.

---

[2] See Descartes (1991). In the French original: 'Et enfin, c'est en usant seulement de la vie et des conversations ordinaires, et en s'abstenant de méditer et d'étudier aux choses qui exercent l'imagination, qu'on apprend à concevoir l'union de l'âme et du corps . . . la notion de l'union que chacun éprouve toujours en soi-même sans philosopher; à savoir qu'il est une seule personne, qui a ensemble un corps et une pensée, lesquels sont de telle nature que cette pensée peut mouvoir le corps, et sentir les accidents qui lui arrivent.'

[3] Descartes (1991, fn. 2). In the French original we read, 'Ne me semblant pas que l'esprit humain soit capable de concevoir bien distinctement, et en même temps, la distinction entre l'âme et le corps, et leur union; à cause qu'il faut, pour cela, les concevoir comme une chose et comme deux, ce qui se contrarie.'

What I put forward under the title of 'dualistic materialism' and the ensemble axiom is an account of each of us—a human being adhering to the following four desiderata. The first pair reflects our natural attraction to a pre-philosophical ('sans philosopher') form of dualism:[4]

(**D1**—**numerical difference**) Pain and FCF are two (numerically) different kinds of phenomena.

(**D2**—**nature difference**) Pain and FCF differ in nature (essence).[5]

The second pair reflects our holding on, again in life and ordinary conversation, to a *structural* mind–body connection and an embedding of the connection within material nature:

(**M1**—**necessary connection**) Pain and are FCF are necessarily inter-dependent —no real possibility of one without the other.

(**M2**—**by nature (essential) connection**) Pain and FCF are *by nature* (essentially) inter-dependent—in specifying the nature of each, we allude to its structured relation to the other.[6]

Before we put forward such a picture of dualistic materialism, I would like to trace the contemporary philosophical senses of dualism and materialism. Where do we get the stronger—antagonistic forms of dualism and materialism, one that excludes the joining together of our four desiderata?

1. ANTAGONISMS—PHILOSOPHICAL DUALISM AND MATERIALISM

Materialism and *dualism*, like many other 'isms,' are theoretical terms (of philosophy). Such theoretical uses may *radicalize* the marketplace conceptions. Philosophical meditation leads us to adopt more 'ideological' and antagonistic forms of dualism that exclude materialism; dualism becomes anti-materialism and materialism is cast as anti-dualism.

Striking examples of such philosophical antagonistic radicalizations are offered by what are probably the two most historically famous examples of dualism/materialism debates. The first is due to Descartes' 1641 sixth meditation

---

[4] I state here, as in the aforementioned 'Pains and brains,' the theses in terms of the contemporary debate between Saul Kripke, David Lewis, and Jack Smart about the connection between the sensation-kind pain and the brain-process kind, the firing of C-fibers (FCF). See Smart (1959), Lewis (1966) and Kripke (1980).

[5] I here work the guiding principles for *psychophysical kinds*—e.g., the sensation kind Pain—and the brain processes kind, FCF. In the more general case and back to Descartes' letter, the analog (D1) and (D2) assert that (my) mind and (my) body differ in number and in nature (essence).

[6] Again, when our focus is not on kinds of sensations and brain processes but, as in Descartes' letter, the mind/body connection, the analog (M1) and (M2) assert a necessary and, stronger yet, by nature (essence), connection between (my) mind and body (as in Descartes' ensemble axiom).

so-called *substance dualism* 'real distinction' argument. The second instance is due to Saul Kripke's 1970's 'refutation' of the Smart-Lewis materialist *identity theory* of the sensation-type (kind) pain with the brain-process type (kind) the firing of C fibers (FCF).[7]

1.1. Radicalization I: Substance Dualism and Real Distinctions

On a common and classical *philosophical* reading, Descartes tells us that a mind–body dualist is one who asserts a mind–body *substance dualism*—a real distinction of mind and body ('real distinction' is a technical term here). Given, e.g., Descartes' mind (DM) and Descartes' body (DB), we assert that (i) DM and DB are each a *substance* and (ii) they (on a variant reading: at least one of them) *can exist* without the other. Thesis (i) involves the technical term 'substance.' Claim (ii) involves the locution 'can exist without the other.' Both (i) and (ii) require some elucidation.[8]

As for (i), 'substance' is understood to mean: the candidate item can exist all by itself (except for God, who is needed as its creator). Claim (ii) involves the same mysterious 'can exist.' In earlier work, I separated two readings of the 'can.' The first is the alethic *modal* reading of *real possibility*—e.g., it is really possible for DM to exist without DB. The second reading—the *by nature* reading is weaker and merely asserts a logical consistency claim (with the nature of the items involved), without thereby asserting a real possibility: it is consistent with what (the nature of) DM is—Descartes is said in this argument to make it just the 'principal attribute' *being a thinking thing*—that DM exists without DB (or any body around).

On either reading, we are goaded to view dualism as contradicting any structural by-nature connection—between DM and DB. And so, the ensemble

---

[7] Both Descartes' argument(s) for mind/body real distinction and Kripke's Pain/FCF argument invoke a highly complex *theoretical* apparatus. In Descartes' discussion with Arnauld (the fourth objections/replies of the Meditations, and studied in detail in the abovementioned *WAI*, part I), critical use is made of *conceivability*, seeming and real (successful), the notion of possibility, the notion of complete idea and the notion of substance. Kripke's discussion is cluttered with technicalia: there is a whole line of argument involving *de dicto* indirect discourse locutions, as when we move from 'I seem to imagine that: Pain exists but FCF does not' to 'I really imagine that: Pain exists but FCF does not,' and on to 'It is modally possible that: Pain exists but FCF does not.' Also, key use is made of linguistic hypotheses about the terms 'Pain' and 'FCF'—they are rigid designators. The notion of 'epistemic counterpart' and 'qualitatively given evidential situation' (sometimes 'possible world') are also repeatedly deployed (and there's more, as running through Kripke (1980: 146–55) or its detailed exposition in Almog (2002b) will convince the reader). I have resolved to expose Descartes' and especially the Kripke-materialists' debate with minimal involvement of such technicalia (most of which I anyway view as a distraction). The reader interested in delving into the technical scaffolding may consult Almog (2002a) (for a comparison of Descartes and Kripke and of de dicto vs. de re arguments). Almog (2002b) lingers over Kripke's various arguments and his use of the imagination, possibility, rigidity, reference-fixers, and other such. In the present work, we try to get onto the essentials without the technical gadgets.

[8] For pedantic details regarding 'real distinction,' see Almog (2002a).

axiom is in shambles—the idea that body and thought are connected by nature must go by the board.

This is starkly clear on the modal reading: it must be possible, e.g., for DM to exist all by itself, absent DB or any other material (extended) body. But now, if we understand 'structured connection' as, at the very least, a modally necessary connection in all possibilities, we must give up on this last. We end up having a modally contingent connection—as we like to say, merely in the *actual* world between DM's existence and DB's.

On the *by-nature* reading, it must be consistent with DM's nature—assumed to be *being-a-thinking-thing*—that it exists without DB. Very well: there *can* be no (viz., it is not logically consistent that there should be) *by nature* connection between DM and DB. There is a setup, a model, consistent with what DM's nature is in which it is *un*-connected to DB. No connection *by nature* between the two may be had.

In all, we are in a bind: we cannot both hold to (i) the *duality* intuition—DM and DB are two in number and of two different natures and (ii) the *structural connection* intuition—a fundamental necessary and *by nature* connection binds DM (mind) and DB (body).

It is either/or. The dualist elects the duality intuition and thus gives up the structural connection intuition, demoting it to a mere contingent (and not by nature) connection, of the contingent kind we find, to use Kripke's own example, between Benjamin Franklin and the invention of bifocals.[9]

The materialist, e.g., Descartes' critic in the fifth objections Pierre Gassendi (or for that matter, fourth objections Arnauld, who plays materialist-devil's advocate) primes the idea of a structural connection. And so he is forced now to give up the duality intuition—if fundamental connection there is between the mental and the material, it must be within this one single substance. The connection is reduced to *identity*. The materialist is not allowed to hold on to a sense of deep connection while segregating two substances. Where we have two *substances*, there can be no such structural connections.

Descartes, who is classically presented as believing in such a dilemma, in fact offers and very vividly his own version (only to dismiss it rather in the way he gracefully dismisses the threat in his ensemble axiom).[10] In his fourth replies, Descartes speaks of the relation between the arm and the full body (of a man) as the model of the mind/body conundrum (as I explain, in the above mentioned work, I prefer to replace the arm by the still fully material, man's *brain*). On the one hand, says Descartes, we may *prove too much,* if we show that the two candidates—the body and the brain (arm)—may exist without one another;

---

[9] As explained in 'Pains and Brains,' for Kripke the notion of *by nature* or essential feature (connection) reduces to the modal idea of necessity.

[10] See the arm/body, prove too much/too little discussion in fourth replies, Descartes (1985: 2: 160). This case is the centerpiece of Almog (2002a), as well as my replies to critics in Almog (2005).

for their stitching back together into a man would make the full man a mere derivative and contingent composition. Thus over-independence threatens the sense that the human being is a *real being*. On the other hand, we may *prove too little*, if we view the brain (arm) as *by nature* (Descartes' own term) bound to the body. For now, we are threatening the sense the brain (or arm) are genuine beings (substances). They seem more like mere features (*modes*) of an underlying being (substance). Thus, if we prime the idea of a deep structural connection, we endanger the sense of having two real substances on hand.

1.2. Radicalization II: Kripke's Purely Qualitative Sensation of Pain[11]

Kripke operates within a framework that assumed the relation of identity as the key relation. He responds to the idea that just as (the chemical kind). Water is identical with hydrogen hydroxide so is (the sensation kind) pain identical with FCF. Kripke's argument is that the cases are not symmetrical because we have on hand a genuine possibility of pain without FCF and of FCF without pain.

What strikes one as fundamental among Kripke's moves are his claims that (i) the sensation of pain is pain and that (ii) the sheer (full) essence of the sensation of pain is what he calls the *purely qualitative* feel, the *quale* Q. This is the *full* nature-essence (for Kripke identifies essence with modally necessary feature) of the sensation of pain and thus of pain. This sets the scene for a strong separability, a strong form of independence, between Pain and FCF.

Again, we may discern here a stronger, Kripke's own, *modal* reading and a *by-nature* reading. On the former, it is really possible that (i) Pain occurs in me without FCF and that (ii) FCF occurs in me without Pain. For (i), we need a possibility in which the Q feeling is felt but the FCF are dormant. For (ii) we have the FCF occur but no Q is being felt. Of course, if Pain may so exist without FCF (or vice versa), Pain cannot be numerically identical with FCF. But note well: Kripke's premise, that possibly FCF exists without Pain is much stronger a claim than his conclusion of mere numerical distinctness. Surely, they may be distinct phenomena (kinds), perhaps of distinct natures, and yet not be modally separable, simply because they are necessarily connected.

Not for Kripke. *By-nature* is glossed for him by way of a modally necessary feature (for the phenomenon's existence). Thus, if the sole nature of pain is

---

[11] As mentioned (and dissected in detail in Almog (2002b)), Kripke's discussion involves heavy baggage of philosophy of language and other inherited technical notions (types and tokens of mental states). I view the notions as a distraction (e.g. the very idea of a type and of a token, which must be given as the token-of-a-type, just like a denotation for Frege is the denotation-of-a-sense). I am not here bent on deconstructing these notions. I try to state Kripke's main ideas in technology-free terms. To separate this particular pain I have at 6 am from the general phenomenon, Pain, I speak of the particular vs. the sensation-kind (or kind of sensation) just as I would in discerning this particular animal, Fido, from the kind of animal it makes, Dog. This is all the terminology we need. For the dispensability of the rigid designators, possible worlds, seeming and real imaginings, etc., see Almog (2002b).

having Q, it cannot be necessarily connected to FCF, whose necessary features do not include being felt as Q. So, for Kripke, the (modal) essence-nature difference of Pain and FCF entails the modal *independence* of Pain and FCF. Any connection between Pain and FCF is accidental (not by nature).

But even if we read 'essence' or 'nature' as distinct from mere modal necessity, we are trapped. For Kripke's idea is now that Pain *by nature* is Q and that this is its sole by-nature feature. So, we can construct a *model* (if not a real possibility) in which we have pain without a by-nature connection to FCF (or vice versa: where FCF occurs but no by-nature connection to Pain is forced). It might still be the case on this attenuated reading that psychophysical connections are necessary (as it were, they are necessary co-variances). But the connections are not by-*nature*, not essential to the phenomena.

As with Descartes and Gassendi, Kripke and the modern materialists offer us a stark choice. Follow Kripke and we have protected the dualism (of number and nature) of Pain and FCF but lost the sense of psychophysical connections running deep and being by nature (necessary). The modern materialist—of the kind displayed classically by Jack Smart and David Lewis faces the opposite choice. Priming as he does the sense of a by-nature connection, he is forced to argue for an identity theory. There could be, for Lewis, no necessary (and thus essential) connections between distinct existences (phenomena). But, by assumption, we do have here a necessary connection. Thus, we have only one fundamental existence/phenomenon, with two appellations (just as in the Water/hydrogen hydroxide case).

Either way, we are denied the possibility of dualistic materialism: numerical and nature distinction of Pain and FCF coupled with their necessary and by nature inter-dependence. It is either nature-independence or full identity.

2. REGAINING THE PRE-PHILOSOPHICAL ENSEMBLE AXIOM

2.1. Marketplace-Dualism Regained—Substances vs. Real Subjects

Let me say again in the language of ordinary life and conversation, what dualistic materialism is after. I am a common sense dualist in thinking my pain and my firing of C fibers make a duo of numerically distinct kinds of phenomena. Whether they make two substances or kinds or properties is a further, more theoretical issue, of logical grammar. But in whatever level of the type hierarchy we end up, they make *two* items of that level.

And there is more to pre-philosophical dualism. Not only are they—the pain and the FCF distinct in number, they are distinct in nature (essence, what-each-is). This nature-distinctness is not the much stronger and more abstract and regulative claim that their two natures are *independent*. Not at all. It may well be, in this case, as in many others, that the very distinction in nature is complemented by the *correlative* nature of the natures, their inter-dependence.

This separation of nature distinction from nature independence is upon us quite separately of the mind–body (sensation/brain process) difficult case. For example, if Max and Moritz are two 'identical' twins, I see them, as any two distinct things, as differing in nature due to a difference in the generation process responsible for each one's coming into being. The processes are similar, closed under invariants, up to a point, *where* and *when* the two processes take two different paths resulting in two different individuals (and different natures). But these two have *correlative co-ordinated* natures, with the dash in 'co-ordinated' to remind us there is simultaneous cosmic 'ordination' in producing such inter-dependent items.

Such correlative coordinated natures pervade nature. We find it at the minutest scale of the structure of elementary particles, where pairs of different ('opposite') natures are by nature inter-dependent (e.g. electron-positron pair annihilation leading to photon-pair creation). We find it in the proton/electron (coulomb force) relation in a hydrogen atom. We find it in the symbiosis of a dog body's and the dog's brain. And so it goes: when you consider two sides of the same coin, say a quarter, you consider things of a different nature (and different in nature from the coin whose sides they are), but they are nonetheless two things of correlative natures, and essentially so. The North Pole and South Pole present us with another such pair: different natures but, by nature, correlative natures. Indeed symmetric systems abound in nature and often they consist of items of different natures that *must* be correlative natures. If we consider more than two components, as in delicately balanced n-body systems, again we may get n different natures, all correlative.

Cases of correlative-coordinated but different natures also abound in mathematics. The natural numbers (or more generally, the ordinals) offer a vivid example. Each item in the sequence 0,1,2,3,4 . . . has its own nature. Nonetheless, they are all inter-dependent, by nature. And so it goes—the kind of numbers, primes, and the kind of numbers, composites, have each its own nature. But they—the two number kinds have correlative natures (just in case you doubt it, I take it as of the nature of primes that they generate composite numbers).[12]

Philosophers like to view all mathematics foundationally, as a branch of set theory (rather than the other way round, with set theory as a mere late branch

---

[12] A very interesting such case from more advanced number theory (in effect algebraic geometry) connecting elliptic curves and modular forms comes for close examination in Almog (2007). The case lies behind a very fundamental conjecture in number theory—now a theorem called the *modularity theorem*—(that had as one of its consequences the settling of Fermat's last theorem). Another case of such deep coordination that the paper discusses, based on the Belyi'd theorem, connects algebraic curves (curves over the algebraic numbers) and compact Riemann surfaces. Mathematics is full of such deep correspondence results unfolding coordinated natures. I hope to return to the theme in part II of 'The Cosmic Ensemble,' where the case of the many (algebraic, topological, complex analytic) 'lives' of Riemann surfaces is discussed as an example.

of mathematics). Very well, then, set theory abounds with such correlative cases. Consider a given finite subset F of the natural numbers and its cofinite complement CO(F). F and CO(F) differ in nature but their natures are correlative. At a slightly higher level of abstraction, consider the notions of *finite* and *natural number* (and in turn, finite set vs. inductive set). Here, again, the natures are different but coordinated.

An interesting example, on the edge of *mathematical* set theory (for it involves *impure* sets), is provided by Kit Fine in his discussion of the Eiffel Tower and its singleton, the set whose sole member is the Eiffel Tower. Fine suggests that the two necessarily co-exist. With this, I agree. He suggests that they have different natures; with this, I agree too. But he also claims, most famously, that though the essence of the singleton alludes to the Eiffel Tower, the essence of the Eiffel Tower makes no mention of the singleton.[13]

Some may merely mean by this (Fine does not) that in giving an answer to the immaculate Paris tourist's question 'What is the ET?,' no mention of sets is likely to come up. No doubt. One level deeper, if we seek in an Aristotelian vein, to provide *real definitions* of things, or to *sort* things into fundamental categories, yet again we are not likely to *classify* the object Eiffel Tower by way of sets. But such questions derive from how we *understand* the thing; how we make it, by way of a *formal cause*, intelligible; what would be a fundamental *sorting concept* for it.

Unfolding our classification system and how the human understanding works is not unfolding the *thing's* own nature and what processes, *in* cosmic nature, are an integral part of its coming into cosmic existence. If we are assessing not our classification and understanding modes but the nature of the two items proper, the Eiffel Tower and its singleton, what features they have *by nature*—then I beg to differ with Fine. It is of the nature of the Eiffel Tower, indeed of any object's nature, to generate its singleton, as part of its coming into being. For it is part of what it is to be an object, any kind of object, that one's existence engenders the existence of a set whose sole member it is.

And so it goes. The set theoretic-*pair* of the Eiffel Tower and the Notre Dame Cathedral, {ET, ND} differs in nature from the Eiffel Tower's nature, from the Notre Dame Cathedral's nature and from the nature of the twosome plurality—uncollected into a set of ET-and-ND. But it is of the nature of the uncollected plurality of objects ND and ET that it engenders the set theoretic pair {ET, ND}. And it is of the nature of the single object ET to have the conditional feature that, if the ND exists, then it, the ET, and the ND together engender the set theoretic pair.

I submit that it is *only because* it is in the nature of (non-set) objects to engender singletons that it is in the nature of singletons to have the object as

---

[13] See Kit Fine (1994). I enlarge upon the idea of correlative natures and fitting in the cosmic grid (the cosmic well-foundedness of each real being) in Almog, 'Everything in its right place,' (forthcoming).

their sole *members*. If we *could*, in the *by-nature* sense of could, have an object *x* without generating {*x*}, it would not be written into the nature of {*x*} that it is so ontologically dependent on *x*. For on my understanding of the *real* object {*x*}, it is not the *logical object* (Frege), the extension of the predicate 'identical with *x*.' Extensions—more generally logical constructs—may be defined and given as it were by a formal cause. An extension may be given simply by a logical-semantical condition, the truth (satisfaction) of a predicate. A real object, on the present intra-cosmic understanding, cannot be made-to-*be* by mere satisfaction of a condition. It could only be *made* to be by a generative process involving other cosmic objects. In this vein, it is only the *existence* of an object *x* that can engender the *existence* of the object {*x*}; nothing else could. That the nature of {*x*} involves *existential* dependence on *x* is a *result* of the fact that the very existence of *x contains* and brought about that of {*x*}.[14]

For a similar example of correlative natures consider the emergence of the first individual tigers and the co-emergence of the species tiger. I would like to say: the species exists only if generated by individual animals. But this is true only because the individual animals cannot come into existence without thereby bringing, by their very nature, the species they are of. It is not as if the animals could exist without thereby making the species exist. And so, it is not only that the species needs some interbreeding animals to come into existence (a mere one-way existential dependence); this much is true only because for the *animals* to exist, they must exist as members of the species.

2.2. Summary—Nature Difference and Nature Independence

We should not presuppose that nature difference forces nature independence. The nature-independence metaphysicians start with an atomist or rather *island-ist* (an 'island-like') conception of 'things,' as if the grid of cosmic *relations* between them is imposed ex post facto. I propose here an alternative on which we may come to see the nature *inter-dependence* of things as vouchsafing their really-being

---

[14] It seems to me that Fine reads the essence of his singleton in the logical (and logicist) way—real definition—rather than the intra-cosmic way of generation-process. This generalizes to sets vs. predicate-extensions in general. Consider the separation axiom of modern set theory and a given subset S, consisting of items a,b,c, . . . This subset exists as a real object, as a set, quite independently of the satisfaction (truth) of some defining predicate F, by each of its (already existing) *members*. For S to exist as an object its members must engender it and no amount of predicate-satisfaction can substitute for the members making-up the set in the efficient—what Frege would call *wirklich* (actual)—sense of making. Subsequently, we may round up that existing set by means of a predicative condition, just as we may round up the already existing Bill Clinton by means of the predicative condition '42nd president.' But the extension of '42nd president' and the real man BC are very different kinds of entities. Only a cosmic generative process can bring BC into existence. Only a logico-semantical definition by way of truth (predication) can define the extension. I expand on this distinction and other differences with Fine in Almog (2003); and Almog (forthcoming).

in nature, their being real—it is only because one is nature-embedded, related by nature to other of nature's items, that one is part of nature too. The nature-distinctness of a given real item rests in the distinct *relations* to other nature items that were nature's way of bringing it about.

Thus the Eiffel Tower is a distinct item, with its own distinct nature. But it is only its emergence from a process relating it to others-in-nature that makes for the numerical and nature distinctness of the product. If, *per impossibile* (modally and by-nature impossible as it were), there was some funny jump object, call it Bozo, that appeared from nowhere, unrelated to others by an intra-nature *making* process, we would have the seeds of a worry about the basis of the numerical distinctness and nature distinctness of Bozo. There'd be nothing in Bozo to differentiate it from another such hypothetical Shmozo and we'd be on our way to turning a model-theoretic hypothetical island existence into a real metaphysical possibility.

An idle worry. For real cosmic existence is not island-existence in a model. To each real existent there is by nature a cosmic root, grounding it in others. Indeed, any real existent has such a well-founded root running all the way back to the origination of the cosmos itself, however exactly that origination took place (be it by a Divine act or by the Big Bang or . . .). However the origination took place, it did take *place* and set in *motion* a long series of intra-nature processes, eventually culminating in the coming into existence of the numerically distinct and nature-distinct Eiffel Tower.

Everything just said about the object ET applies *salva veritate* to the object {ET}, if it is to be a real, and not a mere logical, object (in the sense that Frege's extensions of concepts were). {ET} too has its own distinct cosmic root culminating in its coming into existence as a distinct set and with a distinct nature, e.g., when contrasted with {ND}. Both the numerical and nature distinctness of {ET} are *determined* by the distinct nature process bringing this item *into* the cosmos.

So much then for pulling back marketplace dualism from an overly abstrac-tionist and independent-ist notion of nature. Dualism should not entail in the mind-body arena, as it should not in other cosmic domains, that nature-distinct items are nature-independent. We are, I urge, all dualists about the number of items the mind and body make and about the number of natures they have. But we also view them as *by-nature* coordinated.

3. MARKETPLACE MATERIALISM REGAINED—REDUCTIONIST MATERIALISM VS. STRUCTURED CONNECTIONS

Two ideas guide what I see as the natural pre-philosophical materialism lurking in the back of the ensemble axiom. Both ideas leave us very far from the contemporary philosophical forms ridden by reductionism and identity theories (of the mental or the mathematical or the moral). The ideas allow the materialist to preserve—not to eliminate—the distinctness in number and nature of these non-'physical' phenomena while embedding them in the material cosmos. The first idea is not specific to the mind–body domain; it is about *real objects* in general. The second concerns the mind–body connection.

The first tenet of ordinary pre-philosophical materialism is that nature, the cosmos around us, is the *sole* realm of being—to be is to be part of the material cosmos. Various philosophies have suggested a second realm (or 'world') of mental items; and Frege (and to a certain extent a variety of Platonists, ancient and modern) have separated three realms—the physical, the subjective-psychological (or phenomenal), and the abstract-objective third realm of abstracta. Materialism insists that the material cosmos, the spatio-temporal manifold saturated by causal relations, is all there is to being.

To be, for the common sense materialist, is to be part of the one and only material cosmos. And so, consider a candidate entity or kind of property that is moral or mental or mathematical. If it is to be at all, it *must* be *of* and *in* nature, related to other cosmic items by generative relations. To be (and thus, as we just said—to be of nature), any such item has to *come* into being by an intra-cosmic generation process. There is no being *outside* nature and there is no being without *coming* into being *in* it by one of *its* processes.

Thus if we hold on to mental realism, to the real existence of pains and imaginings and thinkings, to mental phenomena being *real*, we must *place* them in this cosmic grid. A pain, an imagining, a thinking, is made into a real phenomenon by being engendered by a causal process in history. Grounding such goings on in the history of the material cosmos is not eliminating or reducing or demoting them. Quite the contrary—we so authenticate the pains being as real as rivers and trees and tables and brains. Like other matters real, my pain and my imagining must answer to 'when?' and 'where?' and 'how?,' viz., how did it—that pain or imagining come into cosmic existence? There is no being without coming into it; and there is no coming into it except by a process involving other already actively placed beings that make a new being: one being (or more) making another.

So much applies, on marketplace materialism, to any *real being* as such, including mathematical entities, be they numbers or elliptic curves or Riemann surfaces or infinite sets. But, in addition, the marketplace materialist holds specific theses about (i) the *by-nature* connection of the human body and the human mind and (ii) the *by-nature* connection between sensations and brain processes. We mentioned a moment ago that a candidate real mental existent—a pain—must, like any other real, show when and where and how it came into existence. Our second thesis is that mental kinds and particulars of the kind, the sensation kind Pain and my particular pain this morning at 6am, are generated by specific intra-cosmic generative processes.

Consider for contrast, an 'ordinary' natural non-mental kind, e.g., the species of tigers and a specific particular of the kind, Shirkhan. We would like to say that this specific species originated at a particular *place* (planet Earth, in Africa). And this did not happen yesterday or five billion years ago but a few million years back. And it happened by an efficient causal process between animals and their environmental niche (food, water, etc.) in which energy was transferred (by way of the ur-group sexual reproduction, etc.). In like way, the specific particular tiger, Shirkhan, originated last year, in a particular place (on this planet and in no way on Neptune) and yet again by a particular energy expanding process of sperm and an egg (of two tigers) engendering a baby tiger.

In a similar vein we find that the sensation kind Pain and this specific pain of mine this morning at 6 am, I will call it 'Nixon,' have nature-properties embedding them in space, time and the cosmic causal grid. Nixon had to come into existence in me, JA; thus it came into being on planet Earth or close enough to its surface; it had to occur at the time in question, not a year earlier; it had to be engendered by a firing of my C-fibers. If yours had fired or if my T-fibers had fired (those engendering the Thirst sensation), Nixon would not have come into existence.

At the kind of level, we face the question of what kind of species was complex enough (in terms of nervous system wiring and resulting sensing) to be the first in which the sensation of pain was taking place. Primal bacteria, living in deep vents in the ocean floor, were not the early producers of pain. And if there were only worms around, perhaps no such sensation kind would have come into existence. If we think human pain is a distinct kind (I believe so), then the sensation-kind had to await the emergence of the species and is bound, in its nature-features, to it—in time, in place and in the causal processes that took place *in* humans to bring about the first felt pains.

And so it goes: in the way the specific tiger Shirkhan is discernible in number and nature from specific tiger Tony by the corresponding generative processes leading to their coming into being, specific human pain Nixon and specific human pain Agnew (one occurring in you at 10 am today) differ in nature in virtue of their distinct intra-cosmic generative processes (in your and my brains). Just as the tigers, as one species, differ in nature from the horses, a different species in virtue of distinct generation processes, so do the (human) sensation kinds Pain and Thirst. These two sensation kinds differ in their natures, including the feel they induce in humans. This difference is real enough and anything but *purely* qualitative (nothing, no thing, that would be *purely* qualitative would be real; indeed, nothing *could* be purely qualitative, period). The difference traces to different generative processes in human brains.

In all, the relationship between the sensation-kind Pain and the neuro-physiological kind FCF is not unlike what we found about ET and its singleton. The candidate kinds are (i) indeed numerically distinct kinds and (ii) of different nature (roughly: *hurtful sensation engendered* (in humans) *by their FCF*;

neurophysiological process engendered by brain electrical activity . . . and engendering pain). As in the case of {ET}, it might seem at first that though its nature involves reference to ET, ET's nature involves no citing of {ET}. As before, on marketplace materialism, this reaction runs two facts together: the question of what generates what; the fallacious inference that if *x* generates *y*, *x*'s nature cannot include allusion to its generating *y*.

No doubt it is the brain firing that engenders the pain. But it is not as if the brain firings are *purely* material, free of any engendering of the sensation. We think we can specify in purely molecular—or geometrical-topological terms pertaining to molecular shape—what FCF is. But this is an illusion. It is of the nature of certain complex molecular reactions to have *in* them sensations. We imagine the physics as it were occurring without any sensation (thus the imagining of Zombies). As if something additional has to be added (as Kripke says: 'God had to do an additional thing') for these to be felt as pain or thirst or . . . Not so, when the physics of the cosmos attains a certain complexity and is embedded in a certain niche, *it*—any further acts of God aside—is the engenderer of the emergent phenomena. Thus, when the molecules are large enough and niche-embedded rightly, they are *living* systems; when they are brain-embedded and wired in the way FCF to the rest of the body-system, they are—a *sensation*. There is nothing further God should or could do. Thus the firing has *in* it the feeling. And it is only for this reason, as with {ET}, that the sensation *must* be given in terms of what generated it—just because there is, for these kinds of complex molecules inside a human brain, no bare physics, no sheer clustering of molecules, just because that molecular alignment has *in* it the sensation, the sensation that has in its nature the allusion to the brain firing: nothing but the brain firing could bring it about, make it—the sensation—come into the world. For the sensation to come into existence nothing but the FCF's existence would do. And for the FCF to come into existence is, ipso facto, for pain to be brought in.[15]

4. CONCLUSION

I opened with Descartes' pre-philosophical ensemble axiom and I will close with it. Guided by it, I submitted a conception I dubbed 'dualistic materialism,' articulated by our four theses—two were driven by dualism and asserted numerical and by-nature distinctions of the mental and the physical. They are complemented by another pair, driven by materialism, insisting on structured mental-physical connections: modal (necessary) and by-nature inter-dependence.

---

[15] A further pertinent example of such correlative physical-mental natures is Russell's famous discussion of sense data: e.g., this yellow after-image of mine and that red after-image of yours. Their particular differences as well as their differences in kind trace to the essentially distinct causal generative processes bringing them into existence.

I urged that both philosophical radicalizations—the reductionism of the modern identity theory and the abstractionism and purely qualitative entities of the modern dualist—miss the mark. Philosophy forces on us a sense of crisis that we don't encounter in ordinary life, in what Descartes called 'l'union vecu' (translatable as both—and both are poignant—the union as *experienced* and the union as *lived*). As he reminds us, after all, it is by *relying on life and ordinary conversations, and by abstaining from meditating and studying things that exercise the imagination, that we learn how to conceive the union of mind and body* . . . the notion of the union that each of us has inside himself without philosophizing: that he or she is a single person that has together ('ensemble') a body and thought, that are of such nature that the thought can move the body and feel the accidents that happen to it.

18

Varieties of Naturalism

Mario De Caro

1.

'Materialism' is a very common term of art in contemporary philosophy. It is the label for a metaphilosophical view, which has become very common both in the United States and Australia, and is increasingly popular in many other countries, including some that traditionally were dominated by openly anti-materialist philosophies.[1] As is sometimes noticed, however, today's use of the term 'materialism' may be misleading, because of the peculiar technical sense that the word 'matter,' from which it derives, has assumed in contemporary physics.[2] Traditionally, in fact, under the influence of the mechanics of Galileo and Newton (neither of whom, by the way, was a materialist), matter was conceived as the sole ontological component of the universe, and as solid, extended, isotropic, inert, impenetrable, and ubiquitous. It was thought that it could not be transformed into something else and that it obeyed strictly deterministic laws.[3] Finally, as noticed by Philipp Pettit (1992a: 297), the category of the material was believed 'to be given intuitively.'

The situation with contemporary physics, however, is very different. Today, physicists estimate that the percentage of matter in the universe, compared to the so-called 'dark matter,' is surprisingly small. Moreover, few of the classic intuitions linked with the traditional concept of matter have survived the radical shift of physical paradigms that took place in the first half of the twentieth century. Consequently, when contemporary philosophers employ the term 'matter,' they use it, or should use it, in a new sense, which is very loosely related to the old sense; predictably, however, some of the old intuitions still lurk in the

---

[1] See Moser-Trout (1995); Gillett- Loewer (2001).

[2] According to the *Webster's Ninth New Collegiate Dictionary* (1991), the term 'materialism' was introduced in written English in 1748, i.e., in the golden age of Newtonianism.

[3] More details, and some caveats, on these issues are in Earman (1986: chapter 3), and Papineau (2001).

background, sometimes generating confusion. Today, at any rate, most often the term 'materialism' is used interchangeably with the term 'physicalism,' which denotes the view that all existing things are physical, or that, as David Papineau (2001: 3) puts it, 'anything with physical effects must in some sense be physical.'[4] This is an ontological view; but some interesting epistemological consequences easily follow from it—such as the absolute primacy of physics over the other sciences and cognitive fields. Hartry Field (1992: 271), for example, writes: 'When faced with a body of doctrine. . . that we are convinced can have no physical foundation, we tend to reject that body of doctrine.'

As has often been remarked, however, it is not self-evident exactly how the term 'physical' should be interpreted in such contexts. Since, of course, one cannot assume that present-day physics explains correctly and completely what 'the physical' is, frequently this term is explained by referring to 'an idealization from contemporary physics.' (Pettit 1992a: 297, 1992b) But, again, it is controversial to what the actual content of such an idealization would amount exactly, and even whether we can really make sense of it.[5] For the purposes of this chapter, however, the reference to physicalism is less useful than reference to the broader metaphilosophical concept of *scientific naturalism*. While physicalism is based on the thesis of the absolute epistemological and ontological primacy of physics (a view that many philosophers, even of a naturalistic orientation, find unpalatable, and which, at any rate, is not very relevant in the present context),[6] scientific naturalism is not committed to that thesis, even if it is compatible with it. More precisely, scientific naturalism maintains the absolute ontological and epistemological primacy of the natural sciences *as a whole*, whether the other natural sciences are reducible to physics or not—and this, arguably, is what most contemporary philosophers really care about. Therefore, in my use of the terms, all physicalists are scientific naturalists, but not vice versa. In the following, I will evaluate the philosophical credentials of scientific naturalism, and compare it with a more liberal form of naturalism.

2.

Scientific naturalism is a metaphilosophical view whose connotation, scope and perspectives can be understood by discussing several claims to which most of its advocates would subscribe.[7] The first of those claims is the most resolute

---

[4] See, for example, Armstrong (1980), Kim (1989: 266 n.), Field (1992), van Inwagen (1993: chapter 9), Moser-Trout (eds.) (1995: 1), Gillet (2001).

[5] See Hempel (1970), Crane and Mellor (1990), Robinson (1993), Gillett-Loewer (2001), Stoljar (2001).

[6] On the meaning of this 'absolute primacy' see Barry Loewer's remarks in (2001: 41–8).

[7] De Caro and Voltolini (forthcoming) explore the possibility of a more inclusive definition of naturalism than the one offered here.

refusal of non-naturalism or supernaturalism, on the grounds that 'there are only natural things: only natural particulars and only natural properties' (Pettit 1992a: 296), or that 'nature is all there is and all basic truths are truths of nature' (Audi 1996: 372). The vast majority of contemporary philosophers who would define themselves as 'naturalists,' including the liberal ones who criticize scientific naturalism, endorse this thesis; so it could be named 'the Constitutive thesis of naturalism.'[8]

How this claim should be interpreted and what consequences it has, however, are very controversial matters within the naturalistic field. If it is interpreted as only denying the legitimacy, both in philosophy and science, of the appeal to spiritual entities, Intelligent Designers, immaterial and immortal minds, entelechies and prime movers unmoved, then the thesis is in fact acceptable to the vast majority of contemporary philosophers, including some who like to preserve some space for some religious belief—as long as belief does not interfere with science and philosophical reasoning (even if of course it can *motivate* such reasoning).[9] In this reading, the only commitment that derives from the Constitutive thesis of naturalism is the idea that our experience dictates that there is no supernatural 'gulf between nature and man,' as John Dewey (1927: 58) put it.

Even so, interpreting the Constitutive claim becomes controversial as soon as one moves beyond the simple cases toward more problematical ones, such as values, abstract entities, modal concepts, or conscious phenomena. As long as these posits are seen as resisting all the attempts to naturalize them, the question obviously arises, in a naturalistic framework, whether they should be considered non-natural—and consequently discarded from our 'first-grade conceptual system.'[10] The crucial point here is that the extension of the category of the *non-natural* depends on how one defines the complementary category of the *natural*, i.e., the category that includes everything that belongs to nature. And this is exactly what is at stake in the debate that opposes the advocates of scientific naturalism to the supporters of the more liberal forms of naturalism. Thus, in order to understand what view of 'the natural' is proper of scientific naturalism—and distinguishes it from more liberal forms of naturalism—it is useful to refer to two other claims, which, sometimes implicitly, characterize scientific naturalism by compelling a narrower reading of the Constitutive claim of naturalism mentioned above.

---

[8] Some philosophers of a theistic orientation sometimes use the term 'naturalism' in a different sense, to label a view according to which science and religion can be epistemically well integrated (see Draper 2005; on this, also Audi 2000; Papineau 2007). This way of using the term, however, is peculiar.

[9] See Putnam (2005) and Kitcher (2007) for two ways of defending a tolerant naturalistic point of view on religion. However, there are also scientific naturalists, including Nielsen (2001) and Dennett (2006), who interpret naturalism as implying, or at least recommending, atheism.

[10] On the idea of first-grade and second-grade conceptual systems, see Quine (1960, 1969).

The first of those claims is ontological in character. It states that our ontology should be shaped by science, and by science alone (so that a complete natural science would in principle account for all accountable aspects of reality).[11] So, for example, writes Alan Lacey (2005: 640), 'everything is natural, i.e. . . . everything there is belongs to the world of nature, and so can be studied by the methods appropriate for studying that world, and the apparent exceptions can be somehow explained away.'

This claim implies that, in principle, discourses appealing to non-scientific entities, events, processes or properties that are not directly accounted for by the natural sciences could be either *reduced* (perhaps after undergoing a 'revisionary' treatment) to discourses that only refer to scientifically kosher posits[12] or should be treated as mere *fictional* language, and thereby treated as such—that is, either retained as helpful, although illusionary, beliefs or eliminated altogether, depending on whether or not they play a useful (and perhaps indispensable) social function.[13] The many naturalization projects so fashionable today are the clearest expression of the spectacular fortune of this idea.[14]

The second claim through which scientific naturalism interprets the Constitutive claim of naturalism is *methodological* in character. According to it, 'philosophy is continuous with natural science.'[15] This claim can, in turn, be interpreted in different ways. In the blandest reading, it only states that philosophical views should be compatible with the best scientific theories—a thesis that was advocated (alongside a vast majority of philosophers until the nineteenth century) by John Dewey (1944: 2), who wrote, 'a naturalist is one who has respect for the conclusions of natural science.' But this is not much more than a reformulation of the above-mentioned constitutive claim of naturalism, according to which philosophy should not appeal to non-natural or supernatural entities or properties—and, as said, even the most liberal naturalists would agree on that.

There are, however, also some more interesting, and increasingly more controversial, readings of this claim. According to those readings,

---

[11] On this, see Williams (1978, 1985).

[12] A typical strategy for treating properties defiant to naturalization attempts is to argue that they supervene on physical properties; however, this strategy, if common, has not reached uncontroversial results. It is also contentious what forms of supervenience are really suitable for naturalization attempts. McDowell (2006), for example, argues that 'global supervenience' is weak enough for being acceptable to liberal naturalists (and consequently too weak for scientific naturalists!). Notice, however, that according to some philosophers who sympathize with liberal naturalism, even 'global supervenience' is useless to account for evaluative or mental properties. Thus, Dupré (1996, 2007) argues that this notion is epistemically vacuous and Bilgrami (2006) that, in general, talking of supervenience with regard to those items is a mere categorical mistake.

[13] See, for example, Nolan (2002), Ramsey (2003), Eklund (2007).

[14] A critic of scientific naturalism wrote: 'The flood of projects over the last two decades that attempt to fit mental causation or mental ontology into a "naturalistic picture of the world" strike me as having more in common with political or religious ideology than with a philosophy that maintains perspective on the difference between what is known and what is speculated' (Burge 1993: 117).

[15] Quine (1990: 281).

(a) Philosophy should not be treated as a Superdiscipline anymore—that is, as the *Philosophia Prima* or *Regina Scientiarum* of ancient metaphysics, which played the privileged role of evaluating the legitimacy and ranking of all the other disciplines, including the sciences.

(b) Philosophers should stop pursuing the classic project of foundational epistemology, which aimed at finding *a priori* the basic, self-evident, beliefs that could justify all other beliefs—including the scientific ones.

(c) When philosophers reach a point in dealing with a problem in which science has something to say, then philosophy should submit to the authority of science. In this light, Huw Price (2004: 71), for example, writes that, 'to be a philosophical naturalist is to believe that philosophy is not simply a different enterprise from science, and that philosophy properly defers to science, where the concerns of the two coincide.'

(d) Philosophy should adopt the methods of the natural sciences, according to Quine (1986: 430–1), since it is 'a part of one's system of the world, continuous with the rest of science.' (Notice the use of the term 'the *rest* of science'!) In this light, David Papineau (1993: 5), a strong supporter of scientific naturalism has written, for example, that philosophical research is 'best conducted within the framework of our empirical knowledge of the world.'

Generally, these claims are taken for granted, without much explanation or support. Sometimes, however, some detail is offered, and something like the following remarks may be read or heard:

• The scientific empirical method is also apt for dealing with philosophical problems—or, at least, with *genuine* philosophical problems. That is, in essence philosophical theories are 'synthetic theories about the natural world, answerable in the last instance to the tribunal of empirical data' (Papineau 2007).

• Beyond some 'relatively superficial' differences, 'philosophy and science [are] engaged in essentially the same enterprise, pursuing similar ends and using similar methods' (ibid.). The 'superficial differences' include philosophy's greater generality (which supposedly explains the perpetual lack of consensus about which of some competing philosophical theories is the best), differences in the way in which science and philosophy gather their respective data, and the fact that the philosophical issues tend to generate 'some kind of theoretical tangle' (ibid.). Also, philosophers can hope to offer a (mildly) specific contribution by organizing and clarifying scientific results (Quine 1990: 281; Dennett 2003: 15).

• When it is said that philosophy is continuous with science, this should be interpreted to mean that philosophy is continuous only with the sciences of nature—since the social and human sciences are taken to be in an obvious state of intellectual minority (this state reasonably will be overcome when those 'semi-sciences' undergo the naturalization process, nowadays emphatically announced in many humanistic fields).[16]

• In this light, it is reasonable to expect that, if philosophical research is developed in continuity with the natural sciences, it will eventually be able to emulate the majestic success obtained by Modern Science (this has been called 'Great Success of Modern Science Argument').[17] The continuity thesis, by the way, is compatible with both the claim that philosophy depends on the actual results obtained by using the scientific methods or that it has directly to employ scientific methodology (Leiter 2007).

• The empirical methods of the natural sciences, which philosophy should adopt, are clearly devoid of relevant intentional and normative features.[18]

• The empirical method characterizes the *only* legitimate way of philosophizing, even when philosophy deals with issues concerning ethics, rationality, freedom, consciousness, etc. Therefore philosophers should recognize that they are given no special method of investigation. In this light, scientific naturalists either ban those methods that they traditionally considered as peculiar to philosophy (e.g., the analytic method, a priori conceptual analysis, thought experiments, reflections on counterfactual scenarios, the appeal to intuitions, phenomenological investigations, *Verstehen*)[19] or grant that some of those methods are indeed legitimate, but only because they actually embody relevant empirical information about the world (and so can be considered *lato sensu* scientific).[20]

• The scientific attitude will eventually generate a complete professionalization of philosophy. It is also reasonable to expect that philosophy, by abandoning the humanistic field in this way, will finally obtain a scientifically respectable status—with the many appealing practical consequences that this may have.

3.

Unsurprisingly, liberal naturalists disagree with most of the claims, either explicitly or implicitly made, that characterize scientific naturalism. First of

---

[16] The idea of the 'state of minority' of the social sciences is of course both traditional and very controversial. Many interesting classic contributions to the discussion are collected in Martin-McIntyre (1994).

[17] Cf. De Caro and Macarhur (2004a: 4–6).

[18] This view is harshly criticized by Putnam (1992).

[19] Kitcher (1992). For a view more sympathetic with conceptual analysis (one that is, however, conceived of as fallible), see Jackson (2000).

[20] Williamson (2005).

all, they refuse the ontological thesis according to which the only legitimate reference of the terms 'nature' and the 'natural' comes from the ontology of the natural sciences, as unreasonably restrictive and puritanical. (Couldn't this view be summed up by a new Rutherfordean slogan, 'There is natural science, and there is stamp-collecting'?). In the liberal naturalist perspective, it is simply not true that what cannot be naturalized is, *ipso facto*, non-natural or super-natural, and should therefore be treated as a fiction or an illusion.[21] In this regard, for example, John McDowell (1994), one of the leading liberal naturalists, is happy to recognize that the 'space of reasons'—to which the concepts of knowing and thinking, and the normative notions and properties belong—cannot be subsumed under scientific laws, i.e., it cannot be subsumed under the space of the natural as defined by the natural sciences. In his view, however, this is far from meaning that the concepts of the space of reasons should be viewed as unnatural or supernatural. What one should say, instead, is that, as animals, we are part of nature, but by sharing a culture with other human beings (by participating in the space of reasons), we also acquire a 'second nature.' And a second nature is still nature.

In addition, the cluster of epistemological claims with which scientific naturalists flesh out the idea that philosophy is continuous with science is generally rejected by liberal naturalists. Not only do liberal naturalists think that the traditional methods of philosophy are perfectly legitimate, but also that they are essential in defining the philosophical enterprise. In this light, viewing the famous Heideggerian claim 'Science does not think' as evidently wrong does not mean that philosophy should annihilate itself by trying to mimic scientific procedures. Not *only* science thinks, so to say.

Liberal naturalists also tend to disagree with the other claims that characterize scientific naturalism. For example, even if they would be ready to grant that legitimizing science as a whole is not one of philosophy's prerogatives, they would deny the illegitimacy of conceptual analysis as a philosophical method, as claimed by scientific naturalists; they would consider the idea of the Unity of Science (in method, subject, and/or purpose), which is cherished by many scientific naturalists, as a philosophical myth;[22] they would prize the social sciences even when they appear irreducible to the natural sciences, or perhaps even *because* of

---

[21] Macarthur (2004). Philosophers who understand 'naturalism' in a generous sense include John McDowell (1994), David Chalmers (1996), Barry Stroud (1996), Jennifer Hornsby (1997), John Dupré (2004).

[22] The *locus classicus* of this view is Oppenheim and Putnam (1958). However, it is still very common today: see, for example, Tooby and Cosmides (1992), Cat (2007). For harsh criticisms of this view, see Galison and Stump (1996) and Dupré (2001). It should be noticed, however, that on the issue of the unity of science, Quine was more sensible than many of his followers. In Quine (1990: 285), for example, he argued that naturalism 'is noncommital on this question of unity of science.'

that; several of them would not agree that epistemological foundationalism is completely bankrupt.[23]

More generally, given their common refusal of supernaturalism, scientific and liberal naturalists diverge on two major issues—on which all their other points of disagreement seem to depend. One concerns the kind of 'respect' (to repeat Dewey's term from the quotation above) philosophers should manifest toward science. While scientific naturalists think that philosophy is not genuinely autonomous from the sciences, the *compatibility* of a philosophical view with the best scientific theories of the period is all liberal naturalists hold that one should ask for. So, for example, Hilary Putnam has recently advocated a form of naturalism that is 'a modest nonmetaphysical realism squarely in touch with the results of science' (2004: 66). In this light, philosophers should certainly avoid making claims that, although they once had a period of glory, are now inconsistent with the scientific view of the world, such as that biological species (including ours) do not evolve or that randomness does not play a fundamental role in evolution; that physical vacuum cannot be real; that minds and bodies are ontologically unrelated; that the physical world is necessarily Euclidean. That granted, however, liberal naturalists wholeheartedly reject the idea that philosophy should borrow its subject matters, ends or methods from science.[24]

However, related to the issue of the continuity of philosophy with science, there is also another, even more relevant, point of general disagreement between scientific and liberal naturalists. It concerns how great a role to the concepts of the so-called 'space of reason' (to use McDowell's (1994) term), 'manifest image' (to use Wilfrid Sellars's (1962) term), or 'agential perspective' (to use Stephen White's (2004) term, which I will employ here) philosophy should recognize.[25] Are such concepts really in need of reduction or elimination? Or, to put it differently, how seriously should those concepts be taken by philosophers? In short, the question is how to deal with the deep and seemingly structural differences between the scientific and the agential perspectives. Scientific naturalists tend to think that the latter can and should be taken over, absorbed or substituted by the former, while liberal naturalists think that the agential perspective is irreducible, ineliminable and, above all, intellectually precious. Discussion on this question is vast and deep, and has many stimulating implications.

[23] See McDowell (1994), for a defense of a weak foundationalism centered on the idea that perceptual experience plays an essential warranting role.

[24] A brilliant defense of philosophy as a humanistic, non-scientific discipline is offered by Williams (2000). Putnam (forthcoming) judiciously argues that philosophy is characterized both by a humanistic side, which is irreducible to science, and a side that overlaps with science. Examples of the latter are offered by the debates on the epistemological credentials of crucial scientific theories (such as set theory, quantum mechanics and string theory) and by the discussion on the mind–body problem.

[25] It is not, of course, that there are no differences on how McDowell, Sellars, and White conceive the human perspective on the world; however, those differences are substantially irrelevant here.

An important part of this controversy concerns the issue of normativity. John Mackie (1977: 36), with his 'error theory' famously voiced the deep suspicions of scientific naturalism against normative notions: 'If there were objective values, then they would be entities of a very strange sort, utterly different from anything else in the universe.' Mackie wrote, '*If* there were,' because for him, as for many other scientific naturalists, there is no place for such 'queer' things in the world. As a consequence, normative judgments, which do pretend to be objective, are indeed to be considered irretrievably false.[26]

Putnam (2004: 70) sees this kind of anti-normativism as the ideological mark of scientific naturalism. In Putnam's view, in fact, the same wide appeal of this view is 'based on *fear*,' and the fear in question is 'a horror of the normative'—a horror that can only make sense, however, if one is in the grip of a misleading, scientistic metaphysics. Also John McDowell is very critical of the anti-normativist ideology of scientific naturalism. In (1996: 187), for example, he wrote that 'nothing but bad metaphysics suggest that the standards in ethics must be somehow constructed out of facts of disenchanted nature.' In an analogously critical spirit, Christine Korsgaard (1996: 166) wittily replied to John Mackie,

It's true that they are queer sorts of entities and that knowing them isn't like anything else. But that doesn't mean that they don't exist. . . For it is the most familiar fact of human life that the world contains entities that can tell us what to do and make us do it. They are people, and the other animals.

In this passage, Korsgaard clearly presupposes a version of the view—previously advocated by P. F. Strawson (1962) and Thomas Nagel (1986), and even earlier by Kant—that human beings can be looked at from two perspectives: the objective, scientific perspective, through which we only see *happenings*; and the subjective, agential perspective, through which only we can see *doings*.[27] By adopting the latter perspective, i.e., by looking at us as agents—and, according to Kant, Korsgaard, Strawson, and Nagel, *only* in that case—our responsiveness to norms and values makes perfect sense, while norms and values lose their appearance of queerness. In this light, one can see what is really at stake when scientific and liberal naturalists discuss the legitimacy and the autonomy of the

---

[26] On this issue, see Villanueva (1993) and De Caro and Macarthur (forthcoming). Recently it has been argued, on the ground of empirical ('ethnoepistemological') research, that common people's intuitions about crucial philosophical issues are deeply culturally laden. So these intuitions cannot be considered universal or a priori (see, for example, Winberg, Stich, and Nichols 2001). One could wonder, however, why the fact that, say, a Korean and an Italian undergraduate, possibly with no particular attitude or even interest toward philosophy, disagree on the significance of the Twin-earth scenarios should throw any clear light on the validity of the related intuitions. Whether mathematical intuitions are universal and a priori or not—to make a comparable case—is not an issue that one would try to evaluate asking random undergraduates! Analogously, in order to evaluate the validity of philosophical intuitions, one should test people with some philosophical sophistication.

[27] See Nagel (1991) for the doing/happening distinction. Cf. also Hornsby (2004).

agential perspective. The crucial question is how seriously philosophy should take the idea of conceiving humans *as agents*.

Nowadays the discussion between scientific and liberal naturalists is very alive and its stakes are clear. Scientific naturalists' goal is to offer adequate treatment of the concepts included in the agential perspective (beginning, of course, with the concept of being an agent), i.e., to show that these concepts are either reducible to naturalistic concepts or illusory. The success of such a strategy would prove, at the very least, that philosophers should stop taking the agential perspective so seriously. Liberal naturalists have the opposite goal: they want to vindicate the agential perspective as a whole, by proving that their concepts (or at least most of them) are legitimate, necessary, ineliminable, and that they cannot be reduced to scientific concepts.[28] And this shows that the controversy between scientific and liberal naturalists is a zero-sum game. If the concepts of the agential perspective—with all their references to normativity, responsibility, and intentionality—survive the assault, scientific naturalism fails as global metaphilosophical view. If, on the contrary, scientific naturalists' attempts to naturalize and take over the agential perspective do work, then liberal naturalism collapses.[29]

John Earman (1992: 262) presents this alternative in a fair way when he writes, 'It seems that the attempt to locate human agents in nature either fails in a manner that reflects a limitation on what science can tell us about ourselves, or else it succeeds at the expenses of undermining our cherished notion that we are free and autonomous agents.'

To reformulate this contentious matter bluntly, the question is whether the concept of being a human agent can survive the admirable progress of human agents' scientific philosophy. It is not unreasonable to think, however, that the burden of proof is on those who think it cannot.[30]

---

[28] Within liberal naturalism there are two main tendencies as to the question of what relation the agential perspective has with the scientific perspective. Some liberal naturalists, such as John Dupré (1993) and Tim O'Connor (2000), argue that the reconciliation of these two perspectives is possible—provided that the agential perspective is taken seriously and that the natural sciences are conceived in a much more open-minded way than scientific naturalists normally do today (so, for example, agential properties are seen to *emerge* from physical and biological properties and causal pluralism is granted). Other liberal naturalists, such as McDowell (1994), Hornsby (1997), and White (2007) think on the contrary and in a mildly Kantian spirit, that looking for a reflective equilibrium between the two perspectives is a categorical mistake. According to these views, the two perspectives speak irreconcilably different languages; but this does not mean that they *contradict* each other (as both non-naturalists and scientific naturalists instead think). On the distinction between these forms of liberal naturalism, see the introduction to De Caro and Macarthur (forthcoming).

[29] Of course, as always in philosophy, it can simply happen that the struggle about the philosophical legitimacy of the agential perspective will go on indefinitely. However, in principle, what is at stake is the same survival of scientific and liberal naturalism as acceptable metaphilosophical paradigms.

[30] I thank David Macarthur, Hilary Putnam, and Stephen White for several useful conversations concerning the issues discussed here.

19

Against Methodological Materialism

Angus J. L. Menuge

1. INTRODUCTION

Many of the discussions about the legitimacy of teleology and design in science center on the validity of Methodological Naturalism as a principle for doing science. I will briefly explain why I believe that this is not the pivotal issue, since the real opposition is between design and purpose, on the one hand, and Methodological Materialism, on the other. Then I will explore the main arguments employed to defend Methodological Materialism, and show that none of them succeed. Finally, I argue that while both Methodological Materialism and Methodological Teleology have significant provisional value, the best overarching principle for science is Methodological Realism: this principle sets scientists and teachers free to evaluate the evidence for and against design.

2. METHODOLOGICAL *MATERIALISM* IS THE REAL ISSUE

According to Methodological Naturalism (MN), science must proceed as if nature is all there is. While it is certainly tendentious to assume that *no* scientific evidence could be best explained by a supernatural cause, another difficulty with MN is the ambiguity of 'nature.' Does nature include only the blind, undirected causes of chance and law, as the materialist claims? Or might it also contain teleological (goal-directed) processes and programs? If the former, then MN excludes any form of teleology from science, even a non-theistic, Aristotelian approach. If the latter, then teleological science is legitimate science so long as it restricts itself to goal-directed processes within nature, and does not make the final step of implicating the divine. Some proponents of a teleological or design inference in science who are also theists would be quite happy with this restriction, as they agree that it is not the job of science alone, but also of metaphysics and theology, to identify the designer and to build a case for the designer's attributes. That is, teleological science is primarily interested in discerning empirical patterns of teleological causation, not in resolving the question of whether these patterns ultimately derive from immanent principles (part of nature) or from a supernatural being.

It therefore confuses the discussion to define teleological or design-theoretic science (popularly known as 'intelligent design' theory) by opposition to MN. While some may insist that explicitly supernatural causation should be recognized by science, it is possible to defend teleological science but maintain that science proper can only detect the *presence in nature* of teleology, remaining neutral as to whether its *ultimate* source is natural or supernatural. In any case, most of science is concerned with proximal causes, not ultimate causes, and both human artifacts and such processes as embryogenesis and protein synthesis evidence proximal teleological causes operating fully within nature. Teleological science therefore need not oppose MN—at least most of the time, when only proximal causes are being investigated[1]—*so long as 'nature' is liberalized to include teleological causes.* What teleological science necessarily opposes is Methodological Materialism (MM), the claim that science should only recognize the undirected causes of chance (random events) and necessity (law-governed events).

3. METHODOLOGICAL MATERIALISM AND DEMARCATION

A longstanding project in the philosophy of science has been the articulation of demarcation criteria that would provide a principled distinction between science and non-science.[2] These criteria, it was hoped, would state necessary and sufficient conditions for a theory or activity to be scientific and thus offer a clear boundary between science and non-science. The impulse to find demarcation criteria is entirely understandable, since the very word 'science' connotes knowledge, and the rise of modern science depended on rigorous observation and experiment absent from other intellectual disciplines (such as poetry, for example), suggesting that it has a distinctive methodology.

Today, however, there is a curious dissonance between the views of working scientists and those held by philosophers of science. The virtual consensus view of the philosophers is that substantive demarcation criteria do not work because they are vulnerable to counterexamples. Either they fail to state necessary conditions

---

[1] It may of course be argued that in the case of the fine-tuning of the cosmological constants, the best scientific explanation is a supernatural being quite independently of philosophical or theological interpretation.

[2] In the modern period, demarcation criteria were proposed by members of the Vienna Circle, and by the Logical Positivists of the first half of the twentieth century.

for science, implying that some non-controversial science is not really science,[3] or they fail to state sufficient conditions, and cannot exclude obvious non-science.[4] This explains why the eminent philosopher of science Larry Laudan asserted, 'If we could stand up on the side of reason, we ought to drop terms like "pseudo-science" . . . They do only emotive work for us.'[5]

On the other hand, many scientists subscribe to demarcation criteria. In particular, many scientists would agree that commitment to MM is at least a necessary condition for a theory or activity to be scientific. But why do scientists subscribe to MM? There are a number of quite specific reasons, but behind them all, I suspect, is a largely unexamined mental picture of a typical scientist, busily searching for general, observable regularities by conducting laboratory experiments.

This picture naturally suggests that the primary focus of legitimate science is the discovery of laws that connect observable, quantifiable, physical properties. If this is all there is to science, then MM seems quite reasonable, since there is no reason to expect anything other than undirected physical causes of the phenomena under investigation. Not only that, a number of objections, ranging from the naïve to the sophisticated, naturally arise for design. This is the reason many scientists think it is obvious that design has no place in legitimate science. I will consider twelve of the most common objections (O1–O12) and provide replies for each of them (R1–R12).

O1. Teleology and design are unobservable.

R1. Uncontroversial science frequently invokes unobservables. In any case teleology can work through observable intermediaries (design vehicles).

The fact that typical experiments relate observable material quantities distracts us from the many examples in which unobservable entities are postulated by theoretical science. Examples include: forces, fields, subatomic particles, mental states (available to first-person introspection, but not observable in a third-person experimental sense), and mathematical and formal constructs that coherently organize observables but cannot themselves be observed. In many cases, scientists make a tentative commitment to an unobservable entity because the supposition of its existence is the best of the competing explanations for the currently available data. In the same way, teleological science claims that design is the best explanation of phenomena that exhibit specified complexity, and thus there is

---

[3] Many proposed criteria have the consequence that historical sciences, such as geology and paleontology (mostly) do not count as science, since (many of) their claims fail to be repeatable and fail to generate specific, testable predictions.

[4] If only careful observation and recording is required, then perhaps journalism is a science or perceptive novelists like Charles Dickens are scientists. A definition of science that is this broad seems quite unhelpful.

[5] Larry Laudan (1988: 349).

warrant for postulating design as a theoretical entity, even if a designer is not observable.

But in any case, it is not necessary to concede that *all* candidate designers are unobservable. O1 assumes that we are talking about some ultimate unobservable designer, such as a transcendent deity. As will be further developed in subsequent replies, the ultimate designer(s) can work through intermediaries—design vehicles—such as design programs or plans, and these may indeed have observable dimensions, at least if we recognize the degree to which observations are theory-laden. For example, if the genome really is a vast database of instructions or an instruction manual (i.e., this is not merely a useful fiction), and it is responsible for assembling proteins, then here is an example of an observable design vehicle. Evidently, the real problem is not 'observability,' but the much deeper problem of how we interpret what we observe. The real question is whether the structure we observe is teleological or non-teleological. Consider an analogy with human writing. One can choose to say that all we observe are marks with certain shapes, and decline to interpret the structure (syntax) or meaning (semantics) of the marks. But most will say that we observe meaningful words, or perhaps even a message that conveys information. Teleological science claims that the genome really does contain information that has a purpose: the goal of this information is the construction of various functional biological systems. More often than not, the focus of teleological science is not on the ultimate designer but on interpreting observations in a different way.

O2. **Appeal to teleology is religious, but religion cannot be mixed with science because science recognizes a 'publicity condition': scientific results and theories must be accessible to the entire scientific community regardless of ideological and/or faith perspective.**

R2. **Within teleological science as a research program, the role of teleology is strictly limited to accounting for observable events and qualities: religious interpretations of the ultimate source of natural purpose are irrelevant to this role.**

When teleology is postulated in science, its only salient characteristics are those necessary to explain phenomena, generating the phenomena in accordance with some pre-existing plan. The metaphysical status of the source of purpose is a further question, to which additional scientific evidence may be relevant, but which ultimately belongs in philosophy and theology. To see this, consider the case of human design. When a forensic scientist detects signs of foul play and infers the existence of a murderer, the scientist does not thereby claim to settle deep metaphysical questions about whether human beings are merely complex material objects or whether they have (what some would call) a supernatural dimension, such as an immortal soul. What he does claim is that these particular evidential traces would not have occurred were it not for the action of an intelligent cause, a designer.

Likewise, in non-human cases, a teleological or design inference will not by itself tell us whether the ultimate source of purpose is part of nature (such as an alien being or an immanent teleology or logos) or beyond nature (a transcendent principle, power or being). Thus, no particular religious or metaphysical inter-pretation of the source of purpose is required to make a teleological inference.[6] Scientists are not required to undergo a religious conversion in order to detect purpose or design in nature. As a result, teleological science conforms to the requirement that scientific evidence is accessible to all scientists regardless of their faith and ideological commitments.

O3. Miracles do not provide general scientific explanations.

R3. Miracles usually do have limited explanatory value within science, but a teleological inference is not the same as an inference to a miracle.

Suppose we observe an obviously crippled person interact briefly with a faith-healer and then walk normally. This may provide excellent scientific reason to infer that a miracle occurred, but it is quite true that saying 'it was a miracle' has limited explanatory value, as it does not help us to predict similar phenomena. However, intelligent and purposive causes are clearly at work *within* nature in the case of human actions. No one would claim that inferring the existence of the intelligent humans who created the cave paintings at Lascaux, France involves an appeal to a miracle.

Likewise, the outworking of immanent teleology need not be supernatural. Even if God is the ultimate source of nature's immanent purposes, God's ongoing contribution to nature is not restricted to miracles. The proximal cause of some biological feature might be a natural process or program (understanding 'natural' as including teleology), a design vehicle acting as a fully natural agent. Only additional, metaphysical argument would allow someone to infer that this design vehicle is itself the product of divine action. If God normally works through design vehicles fully within nature, design can be detected without implying a special miracle. If the Darwinist insists that a design program for assembling a biological structure is entirely the result of natural selection, the teleological paradigm predicts that this also will turn out to be false. If, as teleological theory maintains, teleology is *sui generis*, and not derived from the non-teleological, any explanation that suffices to account for a teleological system will itself appeal to teleological processes or entities.

O4. Design is a 'Science stopper' that commits the 'God-of-the-gaps' fallacy.

R4. Teleological inferences need not be science stoppers and some 'gap' arguments are legitimate.

---

[6] Of course, in some cases, additional evidence, beyond the design inference may make some interpretations of the designer more plausible than others. For example, immanent teleology seems ill suited to explain apparent design of the initial conditions of the formation of the entire universe.

It should be evident from the last reply why inferring teleology or design does not necessarily stifle further scientific investigation. Even if God or some other transcendent power or principle were ultimately responsible for a phenomenon, the proximal cause actually inferred, a design vehicle, might be a natural entity. For example, the assembly of an irreducibly complex molecular machine appears to require a goal-directed program to ensure that the production of necessary parts is synchronized and the various stages of the assembly properly coordinated.

Complex, functional structures such as the cilium and flagellum . . . demand intricate construction machinery and control programs to build them.[7]

How this design vehicle itself works is then a tractable question, which may in turn lead to the question of whether the program itself was designed, and if so, by what means. In the end of course, we may reach a 'science stopper,' but this is no less of a problem for the materialist who must eventually assert that at least some material causes or processes are brute facts. Normally, however, design encourages further investigation into exactly how a designing system works. By contrast, because of its pessimism about the quality of natural 'teleology,' Darwinian theory is itself often a 'science stopper,' or at least a 'science retarder.' It has encouraged scientists to give up prematurely, by claiming that some structures are nonfunctional though they were later shown to have an important function (e.g. 'junk DNA'[8]).

Further, Del Ratzsch has shown that 'God of the gaps' arguments have been vastly overrated.[9] The objection behind these arguments rests on the two false assumptions that (1) only theists make gap arguments and (2) that all gap arguments are bad. In fact, entirely materialistic science employs gap arguments routinely when explaining unlikely historical events. The most widely accepted explanation of the geologically rapid, widespread extinction of dinosaurs invokes a rare, but fully materialistic event: asteroid impact.[10] Part of the evidence for this event is that none of the processes believed to be going on at the time (including likely diseases—initially a competing hypothesis) are sufficient to account for such a catastrophic extinction. In other words, there is a gap between these processes and the fact of extinction. Asteroid impact was then hypothesized as a possible cause, leading to independent predictions of shocked quartz in the Cretaceous-Tertiary boundary, which were subsequently confirmed. Not only is this gap argument completely materialistic,

---

[7] Behe (2007: 100).

[8] See, for example, 'Scientists Explore Function of "Junk DNA",' http://www.physorg.com/news82661803.html; 'Identification and Analysis of Functional Elements in 1% of the Human Genome by the ENCODE Pilot Project,' *Nature*, 447 (June 14, 2007), 799–816; and 'Exploring "Junk DNA" in the Genome' *Science Daily*, June 16, 2007.

[9] Del Ratzsch (2001: 47–49 and 118–20).

[10] This example is discussed in some detail by Cleland (2002).

it is also a good one, because it depends on the confirmation of independently testable predictions that discriminate between the asteroid hypothesis and its competitors.

In fact, historical science of all kinds is filled with gap arguments. There is a gap between the unloaded military antique mounted on a wall and the deceased Colonel Mustard who was somehow killed using the antique, and this gap may be best explained by the intelligent agency of a murderer. There is a horrific numerical gap between the population records for Jews and Slavs before and after the Second World War that is best explained by deliberate genocide. There may be a gap between a student's own creative ability and the spectacular slide show on impressionism he presented, best explained by the artistic skill of impressionist artists. Evolutionary scientists themselves frequently employ gap-arguments, claiming that there must have been intermediary creatures between those whose fossils have actually been discovered, for otherwise there is no suitably gradual explanation of the presumed transitions. In general, a good gap argument is based on a careful assessment of what the normal course of nature is capable of doing, thereby providing evidence of an objective gap in nature, not merely a gap in our knowledge, and this leads to the postulation of some additional factor or agency whose causal powers are known to be capable of filling the gap. Good gap arguments are therefore not arguments from ignorance but arguments from knowledge, both of what nature is normally capable of doing, and of the resources capable of doing more.

O5. Appeals to teleology are based only on ignorance.

R5. Appeals to teleology are based on knowledge, not on ignorance.

The previous reply also answers O5. Bad teleological arguments may indeed be based on ignorance, taking the form: we do not know how nature can do this; therefore, it was designed. However, good teleological arguments are based on knowledge of what purposeless natural processes cannot do and knowledge of what designers or design vehicles can do to account for deviation from the norm.

O6. Teleology cannot be subsumed under natural law.

R6. Teleology is most at home in historical science, not operations science. However, there may still be laws relevant to facts about natural purpose, e.g., laws governing the origin and transformation of complex specified information in which natural purposes are implicated.

Objection O6 hails back to the famous testimony of Michael Ruse at the Arkansas creation-science trial of 1981–2.[11] According to Ruse's testimony,

---

[11] See Michael Ruse (1988).

teleology and design cannot provide a scientific explanation because they do not explain by natural law. If all scientific explanations must invoke laws and the only laws are those nonteleological laws connecting material properties, then MM is perfectly reasonable and design is excluded from science. Unfortunately, as many have argued, laws are not required by all scientific explanations.[12] In so-called *operations science*, where one investigates a repeatable effect, it is natural to appeal to a natural law to explain the connection between cause and effect. However, historical science deals with singular past events that are not repeatable in all their specificity. Murders may happen all too frequently, but the murder of Abraham Lincoln happened only once, and so it is futile to search for a law specifying the conditions under which Abraham Lincolns are murdered. Instead, as Carol Cleland has shown,[13] historical science investigates the evidential traces surrounding a particular event, formulates competing causal narratives and then selects the best current explanation. Laws may indeed be relevant, e.g., laws of ballistics may tell us something about where Lincoln's assassin must have been when he fired. But the primary explanation of Lincoln's assassination is not a law, but the particular non-repeatable actions of an intelligent agent. Laws do provide a framework for explanation, but even in materialistic science, they may not be *the* explanation of a particular event, as is shown by the example of asteroid impact explaining dinosaur extinction. All sorts of laws are of course implicated in the behavior of the asteroid and in the demise of the dinosaurs, but there are no interesting laws whose specific job it is to explain dinosaur extinctions.

On the other hand, even though it is particular designs that are invoked to explain particular events, it does not follow that we cannot move up a level and discover laws that specify what natural purposes in general are capable of doing. In particular, Dembski's work argues that new complex specified information only arises from intelligence,[14] and that we may also be able to measure how much information has been added by design to the materialistic processes at work in a given situation. The case is analogous to psychology, which has been notoriously unsuccessful in providing accurate predictions of individual behavior, but can still find laws connecting personality types or compulsive disorders with characteristic behaviors. A causal narrative is appropriate in the individual case, while laws are guides to the kind of things one can typically expect. Likewise, teleological explanations can provide particular causal narratives for particular features, and can also make generalizations about the sorts of things design programs tend to do (e.g. employ top–down, modular design) without being able to predict the specific details of as yet unexamined designed objects: to discover this, an engineering analysis is required.

---

[12] See Carol Cleland (2002).   [13] Ibid.   [14] William Dembski (2002).

O7. Teleology does not provide a mechanism.

R7. Teleology does not provide a materialistic mechanism, but it does not follow it provides no mechanism at all.

'Mechanism' is actually a very slippery word. It is sometimes used in a metaphysically tendentious way with the connotation of a *materialistic* process. But this begs the question against teleological science, since teleological science postulates a teleological causal agency that does not reduce to materialistic processes. Or 'mechanism' can be used in a metaphysically neutral way to mean *well-defined causal process*. In that case, however, there is no reason to deny that teleological science provides mechanisms. If the ultimate designing principle or entity works through design vehicles, then even if the ultimate designer remains occult and ill defined as a causal process, there is no reason why empirical investigation will be unable to show how the design vehicles work. Regularly, biologists decode 'programs' for development, intracellular communication, and the regulation of vital processes. If it can be shown that the teleological specification of these programs is essential to understanding their operation, and not merely a convenient fiction for the more complex materialistic processes doing the real work, then indeed design is providing a mechanism. The difference is that teleological science allows genuinely teleological mechanisms capable of top–down causation, while materialism allows only blind, bottom–up processes. As we will see, this leads to clear differences in the predictions made by the methodologically materialistic neo-Darwinian theory and teleological science.

O8. The designer is intractable: science should not postulate causes that cannot be further investigated.

R8. The ultimate designer may be 'intractable' at least within science, but not only are the design vehicles tractable, they are sometimes *more* tractable than those postulated by materialism.

It is quite true that neither a deity nor an immanent teleological principle can be directly investigated by scientific methods. But intermediary design programs and plans (design vehicles) can be investigated, and the assumption that they really function as programs and plans (in a robust teleological sense) will make the explanation of biological assembly, communication, and regulatory activities much more tractable than will dropping down to the level of underlying physics and chemistry.

Here there is a helpful analogy with work in the philosophy of mind. Action theorists, including Dennett, have pointed out that an 'intentional stance' is enormously helpful in predicting actions. If we drop down to the underlying neurophysiological level, then we lose the ability to capture higher level patterns. For example, an agent may greet someone in an indefinite number of physically different ways: by saying 'Hi,' 'Hello,' or 'Good morning,' all requiring different neural signals to the vocal chords; by nodding his or her head, smiling, or raising his or her eyebrows; by holding up or waving his or her hand; by making a telephone call or sending an email; by asking a classmate or the waiter to pass on a note, etc., etc. There are enormous differences between these bodily movements and they all require quite different neurophysiological explanations. Yet all the movements constitute actions of greeting and all are most naturally explained by an intention to greet.

Similarly, in biology, there are all sorts of physically different methods for intracellular communication (transmitting information from one part of a cell to another), because the messengers and their recipients have highly specific interfaces. What teleological science does is to keep us focused on the fact that these methods are all in place in order to communicate, providing the abstraction necessary to distinguish these processes from many others that are going on in the cell. Design therefore helps biologists to find high-level patterns that organize and make sense of the myriad biochemical processes. In fact, Darwinists and other scientific materialists mostly agree that 'Methodological Design' (treating the system as if it is designed) is indispensable in practice, even though they suppose that the idea of a designer is a metaphor. For example, in his recent book, *Darwin and Design*, the prominent Darwinian philosopher Michael Ruse agrees that:

> We treat organisms—the parts at least—as if they were manufactured, as if they were designed, and then try to work out their functions. End-directed thinking—teleological thinking—is appropriate in biology because, and only because, organisms seem as if they were manufactured, as if they had been created by an intelligence and put to work.[15]

In a frequently cited paper, Bruce Alberts, former President of the National Academy of Sciences, and no friend of teleological science, argues that twenty-first century biologists must be trained in engineering (design) concepts to understand the stunningly complex machinery inside each cell:

> The entire cell can be viewed as a factory that contains an elaborate network of interlocking assembly lines, each of which is composed of a set of large protein machines. Why do we call the large protein assemblies . . . machines? Precisely because, like the machines invented by humans . . . these protein assemblies contain highly coordinated moving parts.[16]

But the fact that Darwinists may endorse Methodological Design does not mean there is no empirical difference between the predictions of Darwinism and teleological science. A metaphorical designer who uses such bottom–up processes as random point mutations, gene duplication and co-optation together with natural selection will not 'design' things in the same way as a teleological top–down designer or design vehicle.

---

[15] Michael Ruse (2003: 268).
[16] Bruce Alberts, 'The Cell as a Collection of Protein Machines: Preparing the Next Generation of Molecular Biologists,' *Cell*, 92 (1998: 291).

O9. The designer is not controllable: one cannot 'put the designer in a test-tube.'

R9. An entity or process can be scientific without being controllable and in any case, there is no reason to deny that at least some design vehicles are controllable.

Objection O9 is closely linked to O8. The thought is that a tractable entity or process is one that can be studied in the laboratory, and, by careful experimental design, we can see whether, and under what conditions, it is able to produce a particular effect. But first, historical science does not require entities or processes to be controllable in this way. The most sophisticated labs in the world could not (even if they wanted to) engineer an asteroid impact capable of mass dinosaur extinction, and in any case, *those* dinosaurs are already extinct. Furthermore, even in operations science, inferences can be made to entities that are not fully controllable. Quantum mechanics infers the existence of subatomic particles whose individual behavior is not controllable. Control is only possible at the higher level of statistical regularities in the behavior of populations of particles. Again, one might correctly infer that a madman must have killed someone, even though his subsequent behavior is ungovernable and unpredictable. Thus if some design activities are 'uncontrollable' (either because they produce unique historical events or because the designer is unpredictable in character) this will not show that a teleological inference is unscientific.

At the same time, there are plenty of design programs and plans in operation today whose operation is highly controllable. For example, an embryologist trying to discover the elements actually involved in an organism's developmental program can see what happens when certain elements are modified or removed, or if substitutions are made: is development normal, viable but abnormal, or non-viable? Likewise, at the biochemical level, protein knock-out experiments, modification of existing material and the insertion of novel material, can determine which elements are necessary for a molecular machine to function, and how much perturbation of the system is possible whilst retaining various levels of functionality. In this sense, the design of biological systems is controllable in the laboratory, and much of modern biology is concerned with exploiting that knowledge.

O10. A designer is empirically sterile: postulating a designer generates no interesting predictions, and is therefore neither testable nor falsifiable.

R10. Some specifications of a designer are empirically uninteresting; but others yield significantly different predictions than those based on materialist assumptions. Properly specified design theories are actually easier to test and falsify than some materialistic theories.

Some opponents of teleological science grant that a designer may be at work 'behind it all,' but insist that this has no value to scientists because the designer is free to do whatever he or she (or it) wants. With no basis for determining which choices will be made, no interesting predictions follow from postulating a designer. Indeed, if there is no specification at all of the characteristics of the designer so that certain types of choice are more likely than others, a designer is an empirically vacuous concept, since the designer might choose to do precisely those things that could have just as well arisen without design. In that case, nothing could count as evidence against the design hypothesis.

It should be conceded that some invocations of a designer are empirically vacuous. For example, some theistic evolutionists claim that God has 'designed' the diversity of life by working through Darwinian evolution.[17] Since Darwinian evolution claims to be an unguided, automatic process, this postulation of a 'designer' adds no predictions to those that already follow from Darwinian theory.[18]

Likewise, it is easy to see that some conceivable versions of teleological science generate no empirical predictions. Consider, for example, a designer like a modern artist who punctures sacks of paint and twirls them above a canvass. Although such an artist almost certainly does not know how his or her 'art' would work out, the artist has intelligently designed the method of producing it. Unfortunately, the results are scarcely distinguishable from the accidental spills of a house painter. Postulating a designer like this is therefore empirically sterile. Likewise, it is pointless to invoke a designer like Forrest Gump, who decides to do things, like running across America, 'for no particular reason.' Designers who choose to emulate undirected processes are not worth postulating because no empirical test will decide between design and its absence.

However, there is already empirical warrant for proposing a more robust designer. The fact that many biologists feel compelled to employ models from engineering and computer software and hardware in order to account for the biological 'machines' they discover suggests that a more fruitful portrait of the designer is a rational, top–down engineer. Unlike Forrest Gump, this designer does do things for a particular reason. And unlike our modern painter, the principles of top–down design are employed to develop a number of modules mutually adapted to accomplish an overall task.

This perspective makes important predictions about the organization of any biological system, many of which directly contradict the predictions of the

---

[17] Others argue that God guides evolution in detectable ways, and so their view is an example of teleological science, rather than an alternative.

[18] In fact, the viewpoint is also self-contradictory, since it claims that God does something intentional (He produces life's diversity) through entirely unintentional means (Darwinian evolution). This would be like my claiming that I had intentionally repaid you a loan of $20 because a random gust of wind from Hurricane Dennis blew one of my $20 bills into your car. Note that I might even have risked the proximity of the tornado because I intended to repay you, so that, in some sense, my intention caused you to receive the $20. It still does not follow that I repaid you intentionally. Interestingly enough, theistic evolutionists of this stripe have fallen foul of the causal deviance recognized by action theory, where an agent's intention may cause a result that was intended but still fails to produce an intentional action.

methodologically materialist, Darwinian account. Darwinism predicts messy, makeshift 'designs,' dependent on the fortuitous co-optation of components developed for other purposes. And it predicts vestigial organs, 'junk' DNA and other useless memorabilia of a species' voyage through evolutionary history. Indeed Darwinists frequently claim to have found just such evidence. By contrast, the hypothesis of a rational top–down designer predicts that modules are not merely co-opted and may have a dedicated function as they are designed to play a specific role in contributing to a particular type of system. Components may of course be re-used, and a rational designer may develop components that have a wide range of uses to avoid 're-inventing the wheel,' but in the long run, bad design would only occur if the original design had degenerated or been upset in some way. Rational, top–down design is not the same as optimal design, and mutations or copying errors might lead to a loss of crucial information and hence functionality, but the prediction would still be that in normal, functioning systems, there would be less conspicuously bad design than is predicted by Darwinism.

O11. Teleology makes no practical difference to science: it does not generate any research programs, or if it does, they are not substantively different from those already pursued employing MM.

R11. Teleology can make an enormous practical difference to science: it prompts different questions, novel techniques, and novel research programs drafting in principles from such sciences as engineering and computer science. If successful, these research programs are likely to discover more than Darwinism, which has a built-in reason for 'giving up' when systems prove difficult to analyze.

As we have seen, design can make a difference to science, because, so long as the designer is adequately specified, design generates predictions incompatible with those of Darwinism. More than that, design prompts different design-related questions such as:

(1) 'What are the modules of the system and what does each contribute to overall function?'
(2) 'Can we reverse-engineer the system to see how it was assembled?'
(3) 'How robust is the system in the face of perturbations or manipulation?'

Design suggests that modern biologists are well-advised to search for analogs to biological systems in engineering and computer science, using an analysis of the elements required in the latter cases to predict biological structures playing a similar role in the former case. (Interestingly, the assumption that biologists are investigating engineered systems has spawned a whole new area of science called *biomimetics*, in which engineers look for design principles in living systems to improve their own machines.) While Darwinism may stop short, satisfied with a messy and illogical compromise, design will prompt scientists to look for underlying mechanisms that unlock order in the seeming chaos. Perhaps the true function of much DNA wrongly identified as 'junk' and of organs wrongly labeled vestigial would have been discovered far earlier if more scientists had followed design.

Not too long ago man was imputed to have 180 vestiges. Organs like the appendix, tonsils, thymus, pineal gland and thyroid gland were on the list. Today, all former vestigial organs are known to have some function during the life of the individual. If the organ has any function at any time, it cannot be called rudimentary or vestigial . . . As man's knowledge has increased the list of vestigial organs decreased. So what really was vestigial? Was it not man's rudimentary knowledge of the intricacies of the body?[19]

The first concerted effort to understand all the inner workings of the DNA molecule is overturning a host of long-held assumptions about the nature of genes and their role in human health and evolution . . . The findings, from a project involving hundreds of scientists in 11 countries and detailed in 29 papers being published today, confirm growing suspicions that the stretches of 'junk DNA' flanking hardworking genes are *not junk at all* . . . the vast majority of the 3 billion 'letters' of the human genetic code are busily toiling at an array of previously invisible tasks . . . regulating genes, keeping chromosomes properly packaged or helping to control the spectacularly complicated process of cell division.[20]

The discovery of unsuspected function in non-coding DNA and of so-called vestigial organs powerfully supports teleological science and refutes the predictions of Darwinism, according to which living systems are make-shift compromises riddled with non-functional elements.

O12. **Natural teleology was scientific until Darwin, but Darwin decisively eliminated the design paradigm.**

R12. **Teleology cannot both be unfalsifiable and falsified. Even if a theory is knocked out on the basis of the evidence available at a given time, new evidence, and a more sophisticated formulation, may allow the theory to compete again on more favorable terms.**

Objection O10 claims that design makes no difference to science, and so could not be falsified. O12 contradicts this by claiming that design has been falsified. Obviously if something has been falsified, it can be, so these objections are actually inconsistent.

But let us suppose that Darwin's theory defeated the natural teleology of Darwin's era on the basis of the evidence available in 1859. The problem is that there is now abundant data (about the inner workings of the cell

---

[19] Wysong (1976: 397).
[20] Rick Weiss, 'Intricate Toiling Found in Nooks of DNA Once Believed to Stand Idle,' *Washington Post*, June 14, 2007, http://www.washingtonpost.com/wp-dyn/content/article/2007/06/13/AR2007061302466_pf.html

and many other matters) that was completely unavailable to Darwin, and the mathematics of the design inference has recently undergone a sophisticated reformulation, employing a rigorous empirical test to distinguish designed from non-designed features.[21] The failure of an older version of a theory with a relatively small amount of data shows nothing about the prospects of a newer version of the theory developed to account for a large number of later discoveries. This is simply a logical consequence of the instability of abductive inference: today's best current explanation may not be the best explanation tomorrow, when new data is discovered or new competitor theories are proposed.

4. WHAT'S THE ALTERNATIVE?

Some proponents of MM will grant that there is no way to defend MM as an *a priori* principle for science and science education, but will argue instead that MM has such an impressive track-record that alternatives are unmotivated. It must be conceded that MM has been very successful in science. However, a number of important things do not follow from this:

(1) That the success of MM can *only* be explained by assuming that MM is universally valid.
(2) That MM is without scientific limitations.
(3) That MM has been the *only* successful paradigm employed by science.

In fact, teleological science can easily explain why MM has been very successful. In many areas, no intelligent cause is relevant to the explanation of a phenomenon, because no one is asking for a teleological explanation (e.g., we want a chemical, not a psychological explanation of the formation of a chemical compound), or we are witnessing what nature does when left to its own devices. Teleology is only worth wheeling out of our intellectual armory if our interests happen to focus on the activity of intelligent agents or if we are witnessing something that undirected processes would not do by themselves, and believe there is strong evidence that natural materials have been intelligently configured or redirected in specific ways. Since teleological science studies the contrast between what unaided matter can do and what requires the assistance of purpose, it can affirm correct materialistic explanations as falling within the known limitations of undirected causes, but also has the potential to explain phenomena that transcend materialistic categories. If successful in the latter case, teleological science's relation to MM is aptly described by Lakatos' phrase 'incorporation with excess content,' since teleological science can account for anything MM is right about as well as more that MM cannot account for.

---

[21] Dembski (1998).

It is also important to notice that MM's success is partly the result of the fact that much of modern science made a practical choice, in the interests of the simplicity and tractability of its object, to limit itself to impersonally described objects and processes, a choice that necessarily keeps agents, including scientists themselves, out of the picture. The focus is typically on such questions as what those chemicals typically do when combined and not on why the chemist is combining them. MM does not supply the right categories for explaining the phenomena studied by many special sciences of the human (forensics, cryptography, archaeology, psychology). These special sciences also show that MM is not the only successful paradigm. Teleological explanation has been quite successful in the social sciences, and, as I argue at length in *Agents Under Fire*, does not seem to have a workable replacement.

Further, if what matters is the results of methodology and not its literal truth, it is easy to see that Methodological Teleology (MT) has been a very effective paradigm in biology, where human design is not normally involved. As we saw, the prominent philosopher of biology Michael Ruse agrees that 'teleological thinking... is appropriate in biology because, and only because, organisms seem as if they were manufactured, as if they had been created by an intelligence and put to work.'[22] Ruse himself thinks that the teleological concepts are metaphorical and that they can all ultimately be explained away. But we do not have detailed, materialistic accounts that actually show how this can be done, and so the confidence that it can be done really rests on a prior commitment to MM. A neutral observer of the same evidence would have to conclude that it is just as reasonable to take the success of MT, and the persistent failure to develop convincing materialistic explanations, as pointing to a real teleology that is not reducible to law and chance. At the very least, the existence of real teleology in biology would be seen as a hypothesis that further evidence might tend to confirm or disconfirm.

The case for real teleology is strengthened by the fact that modern advances in many areas of biology have depended on an engineering (design) perspective far more than on Darwinism. The vocabulary of genetic codes, intracellular communication systems, assembly programs and, in general, molecular machines, is all drawn from a design paradigm, frequently borrowing technical terms of computer science and electrical or mechanical engineering. It is not just that this way of talking is useful shorthand: a design approach has led to an explosion of discoveries about the complex machinery with the cell, and within various multi-cellular structures. There is a fundamental contrast between a Darwinian approach and this engineering paradigm. Darwinian accounts of complex systems are bottom-up: they assume that a complex system was built by recruiting simpler systems that originally served quite different functions. This approach is pessimistic about the formation of functional complex systems, since

22 Michael Ruse (2003: 268).

they are cobbled together in an opportunistic way without plan or foresight. By contrast the increasingly successful engineering paradigm is optimistic that the functionality of the higher level system is achieved in a coherent (not necessarily optimal) way. The assumption that the system was assembled in a top–down manner leads scientists to look for tightly integrated modules that contribute efficiently to the overall function of the system, and which do not resemble reconditioned parts from a recycle bin. It is this approach, and not Darwinism, that seems to be doing all the real work in many areas of biology today.

This fact is frequently obscured by the large number of articles that contain an obligatory reference to Darwinian evolution even though it plays no substantive role in the analysis given. The rest of the chapter is functional analysis that treats the biological system as a designed machine and uses clever techniques to try to figure out how the system works. Adam Wilkins, editor of the journal *BioEssays*, supports this conclusion:

The subject of evolution occupies a special, and paradoxical, place within biology as a whole. While the great majority of biologists would probably agree with Theodosius Dobzhansky's dictum that nothing in biology makes sense except in light of evolution, most can conduct their work quite happily without particular reference to evolutionary ideas. Evolution would appear to be the indispensable unifying idea and, at the same time, a highly superfluous one.[23]

In other words, the scientific analysis in no way depends on the assumption that the system evolved in a Darwinian fashion. It does, however, frequently depend on the assumption that the system can be treated as if it were designed (MT). When critics of design point to the relatively small number of peer-reviewed articles that explicitly mention design, they unfairly neglect to mention the vast number which employ a design (engineering) perspective throughout, but which do not mention anything so *verboten* as teleological science, or which even claim without serious supporting argument that the results can be understood from a Darwinian perspective.

5. METHODOLOGICAL REALISM

It might help to go back to basics. If we ask a typical citizen why science is so highly regarded, he or she would likely reply, 'Because its findings are objective.' But just what is it for science to be objective? Scientists, like everyone else, have biases, but, we are told, the methods of science, like those employed in a court of law, are carefully designed to counteract bias. The use of control experiments to rule out possibly interfering factors is an obvious example. However, MM decides in

---

[23] Wilkins (2000).

advance that there are certain conclusions science may not derive, no matter what the evidence is. This is not a means of counteracting bias. It is the incorporation of a bias, a tendentious assumption about metaphysics and epistemology, into scientific activity. MM makes the metaphysical assumption that if any teleology is operative in nature, it is irrelevant to natural phenomena, and it makes the epistemological assumption that we can fully understand nature without recourse to teleological categories. To be sure, science cannot proceed without some metaphysical and epistemological assumptions: for example, scientists must assume that the world is somewhat orderly and that the human mind is capable of learning something about its systematic operation. Call any such philosophical biases, required for a rational person to engage in science, 'feasibility assumptions.' What we have seen in this chapter is that there is no good reason to say that MM is a feasibility assumption. None of the standard arguments against recognizing teleology as a legitimate category in science are convincing, and in fact teleology (design) is assumed as a working hypothesis all the time. Teleology was permitted in science for at least 2000 years, and despite excesses and mistakes, has an undeniable track record of impressive results from Aristotle to the pioneers of the scientific revolution.[24]

There is no warrant, therefore, for science assuming MM as a starting point. Scientists should allow that either MM or MT may be valuable in their field, and should let the results of their investigation determine which is the more appropriate paradigm. There is no doubt that MM is both fruitful and appropriate in many areas, where no question of teleology is even raised. But where that question is raised, the answer should not be prejudged by dogmatically assuming that only one of MM and MT is the right approach. The conviction that only an impartial assessment of the results of applying MM and MT as working methodologies can fairly adjudicate their evaluation may be termed 'Methodological Realism' (MR). MR asserts that it is the iconoclastic nature of reality itself that must judge the effectiveness of our methodologies. Beyond science's inevitable feasibility assumptions, any additional scientific methodology must vindicate itself through scientific practice. Indeed, it is unscientific to claim that these additional presumptions about how science should proceed are immune to revision by the findings of science. MM is not to be identified with science. It is in some respects an anti-scientific ideology that attempts to fossilize science in the rigid categories of nineteenth century materialistic metaphysics and epistemology. Those who hold a particular, tendentious worldview that was not required for science in antiquity, or for the rise of modern science, and is not the true foundation of many of its most striking contemporary results,

---

[24] For details of the importance of design thinking in ancient and modern science, see the contributors to my 2004 collection of essays, Angus Menuge (ed.), *Reading God's World: The Vocation of Scientist* (St. Louis, MO: CPH), especially essays by Barker, Harrison, Menuge and Pearcey.

have attempted a monolithic identification of this worldview with 'the scientific method.' The antidote to this malaise is not to mandate the exclusive employment of some equally tendentious methodology, such as MT. The antidote is a return to intellectually honest vulnerability to the truth about reality, whether it supports our expectations or not, in other words, a return to MR.

Francis Bacon, himself a powerful critic of the misuse of design in science, is helpful here. In his important work on scientific method, *The New Organon,*[25] Bacon may have been naïve in supposing that scientists can really free their minds of various human, individual, social, and linguistic biases (which he called 'idols of the mind'). But he did make an enormously important distinction between anticipating nature and interpreting it. In his critique of Aristotelian science, Bacon's most telling point is that the scholastics used *a priori* metaphysics to anticipate how nature must be. As a result, they did not carefully examine the evidence to see if these anticipations were correct, and any recalcitrant evidence they did stumble across was coerced to fit a preconceived mold, even if it would be better explained by rival paradigms. MM works in just the same way, assuming that no teleology can be involved and coercing any evidence of apparent teleology into materialistic categories even if they fail to do justice to the phenomena, and even if more illuminating accounts could be provided by rivals of MM.

Bacon insisted that it is not up to the scientist to dictate what nature must be like. Rather, the scientist must humbly allow himself to be dictated to by nature itself. The scientist's job is not to dogmatically anticipate nature, but to interpret what nature is doing. Methodologies may be helpful, but they are rules of thumb, fallible instruments. Consider an analogy with home improvement. One finds by actually trying various tools that some are helpful and others are not. Suppose that a salesman for a particular screwdriver insisted that it is the best solution for all of your home improvement projects, but you learn from experience that other tools are sometimes much more effective. In fact, suppose that on some projects you never use the screwdriver, because it is only other tools that seemed to work. It would be quite absurd to continue to insist that the screwdriver defined legitimate home improvement. And yet this is just the way proponents of MM argue, because they insist that only materialistic explanations are valid (anticipating nature in materialistic terms) even when experience shows that teleological approaches are sometimes much more helpful. Bacon's call to scientists mired in scholasticism is a call to return to MR. The call is just as valid today for scientists who have learned from experience that MM is not effective in every area of their work. Scientists have not ceased to be scientific because experience teaches them that MT is sometimes the right toolkit for the project. And if those scientists discover powerful reasons for thinking that MM really *cannot* do the job, they have not stopped being scientific because they infer that

---

[25] For an excellent, recent edition, see Bacon (2000).

teleology is probably real. MR forbids scientists from simply assuming that the design in nature is real, but it does not prohibit them from *concluding* that that is the case. Once MR is acknowledged, there is no doubt that teleological science has potential as a legitimate scientific program, and the only fair way to evaluate it will be to examine its proposals and to test them empirically.

6. CONCLUSION

In summary, a survey of the typical reasons advanced in favor of MM shows that none of them is compelling. Granted MR, however, scientists can explore the case for and against design without prejudice, and teachers are set free to present all of the relevant evidence.

20
Soul, Mind, and Brain

Brian Leftow

The most prominent recent dualists have been avowedly Cartesian.[1] And when materialists trouble to wave dualism a quick, none-too-fond farewell, the form they consider is also Descartes'.[2] But dualism has other forms, some of which are fairly represented as hybrids with materialism. For Aquinas, each human has a soul, which lives on when its body dies.[3] As it lives without a body, the soul is immaterial. So for Thomas,

(1) Humans have souls which are live immaterial particulars.

Aquinas also claims that:

body and soul are not two actually existing substances; instead one actually existing substance comes from the two.[4]

The one substance which 'comes from' body and soul is a human being. A human is a kind of animal. For Thomas, 'body is the genus of animal.'[5] Bodies are material substances. So for Thomas,

(2) A human is a single material substance.

This, despite having an immaterial soul. Cartesian dualists assert precisely that 'body and soul are two actually existing substances.'[6] So Thomas flatly denies a characteristic claim of Cartesian dualism. Further, (2) certainly sounds materialist. Yet usually materialists deny (1). So (1) and (2) seem incompatible. Thomas's position seems inconsistent, and one may well wonder what led Thomas to this odd conjunction of views.

An explanation some favor goes this way. Thomas uses 'form,' in one sense, as a term for live immaterial particulars—angels, souls, and God.[7] So Thomas can and does put (1) as:

(1a) human have souls which are forms.

¹ So, e.g. Foster (1991) Swinburne (1986).
² For one of innumerable examples, see Kim (1996: 2–5), and Kim (2001).
³ S. Thomae Aquinatis, *Summa Theologiae* (Ottawa: Studii Generalis, 1941) (henceforth *ST*) Ia 75, 6.
⁴ *SCG* II, 69: 164.   ⁵ *EE*, 3: 149.   ⁶ See the final section below.   ⁷ *EE*, 5.

Thomas holds (2) because he treats the soul as a form in another sense:

something one in nature can be formed from an intellectual substance and a body.
Now a thing one in nature does not result from two permanent entities unless one has
the character of substantial form and the other of matter.[8]
The intellectual soul is the form of the body.[9]

Most Thomist substantial forms are states of material things—and so abstract.
Thinking of a soul as a living form, Thomas asserts (1). Thinking of a soul as a
form in the abstract sense, Thomas asserts (2). (1) and (2) are in fact inconsistent,
but Thomas did not see this because he puts (1) as (1a), takes (2) to presuppose
that the soul is the body's form, and overlooks the ambiguity in his usage of
'form.' Thus William Hasker suggests that Thomas purchases (2) only by treating
the soul as a 'form' in the sense of a state of a body, but 'God and the angels
are not 'states of' anything... and neither is the human soul.'[10] Again, David
Braine writes that Thomas

may have been deceived by confusing two different uses of the word 'form' of quite
different origins: on the one hand... the use... to refer to... God and... angels;
and, on the other hand... 'form' as a correlate of matter originating with the idea of
shapes... as forms of material things.[11]

In what follows, I explicate Thomas's views and argue that Thomas can hold
(1) and (2) consistently and without equivocating. I also tackle a second charge
Hasker levels against Thomas.

1. THE SOUL AS FORM

Aquinas explains the terms 'matter' and 'form' this way:

matter... of itself exists incompletely... form gives existence to matter... just as
everything which is in potency can be called matter, so everything by which a thing has

---

[8] *SCG* II, 56. This text is just a dozen chapters before the denial, quoted above, that body
and soul are two 'actually existing' substances. So while Thomas here calls the soul an intellectual substance, this is compatible with the prior text *if* we understand this as not entailing
being an actually existing substance, but rather one potentially existing. Thomas later suggests that for a human to come to exist is for a body to come to participate in an existence
that belongs primarily to the soul (*Quaestiones de Anima*, 1 *and* 17). So if this is something he also thought at the time of *SCG* II, he will not be denying that the soul exists.
Rather, the texts harmonize if he holds that the soul while incarnate is only potentially a substance.
[9] *ST* Ia, 76: 1.
[10] Hasker (1999: 168). Hasker actually discusses Thomas not *propria persona* but as presented
in Stump (1995). Still, as Hasker discusses Stump only as a way to get at Aquinas's position
in contemporary terms (Hasker 1999: 161–2), he means to make a claim about Aquinas's views,
not Stump's.
[11] Braine (1992: 499n.).

(substantial) being . . . can be called (a substantial) form . . . sperm which is potentially a human is made actually a human by the soul.[12]

'Matter,' for Thomas, is actually shorthand for a relative term, matter of *x*.[13] The matter of *x* is what is potentially *x*, the stuff of which *x* is made or the parts from which *x* is assembled. Save for prime matter, what is potentially *x* is actually something on its own. What is potentially human, in Thomas' example, is actually sperm. Sperm 'exists incompletely' only in the sense that it is incompletely *human*. An item is matter insofar as it is *potentially* some thing or some way. Something is matter insofar as it can be or come to be of a different kind, or all or part of a different individual, than it actually is.

Thomas defines substantial form by its function: *x*'s form is that, intrinsic to *x*, which 'makes' *x*'s matter constitute *x*—i.e., makes *x*'s matter to be actually what it could have been or had been merely potentially.[14] If *x* is a substance composed of matter, *x*'s existing consists in *x*'s matter's being in a particular state—call it *F*; *x*'s substantial form is that, intrinsic to *x*, by which *x*'s matter is *F*. More precisely, it is that whose presence in x *is* *x*'s being *F*: the form of water is that whose presence in some matter *is* that matter's being water. For the matter to be water is for the form of water to be present in it. Aquinas writes that

per se, forms can be wholes and parts as regards completeness of essence. Speaking of this kind of wholeness . . . any form . . . is whole in (its) whole (bearer) and whole in each of (the bearer's) parts, for just as . . . the whole nature of whiteness is in the whole (white) body, so also it is in each part of it.[15]

So the substantial form of x is that y such that y is present as a whole in each part of *x*,[16] and for y to be so is for all of *x*'s matter to be *F*. Often *y* is a state—say, being alive. For the state of being alive to be present as a whole in each part of a live thing *x* is for each part of *x* to be in the state of being live matter. But Thomas's account of form above is abstract enough to leave room for a *y* that is not a state.[17]

---

[12] *De principiis naturae*, c. 1: 8.

[13] This is so even for prime matter, which cannot exist save as the prime matter of some substance or other (*ST* Ia, 66, 1c *et ad* 3). Thomas distinguishes 'matter from which' from 'matter in which' (for an explanation, see my 'Souls Dipped in Dust,' in Corcoran (2001: 123–5)). This text explains 'matter from which.'

[14] Efficient and final causes also 'give existence' to matter in their own way. Thomas rules them out by saying 'by which': efficient and final causes are causes from which, not by which—extrinsic, not intrinsic causes.

[15] *SCG* II, 72: 167. One could quibble with the example.   [16] *ST* Ia, 76: 8; *SCG* II, 72.

[17] Thus I agree with Braine that Thomas's notion of form here is 'not . . . determinate as to category' (Braine 1992: 510–11).

Where *x* is a human and *y* is a human soul, *x*'s matter's being live human tissue consists in *y*'s being wholly present in each part of *x*.[18] Thus *y* is *x*'s form, on Thomas's account: for Aquinas, the human soul is a human being's substantial form.[19] This is so whether or not the soul is a state. If a form is a state, for the form to be present is for the matter to be in a state. And for the human soul as Aquinas conceives it to be present in a body is equally for that body to be in a state—being human.[20] This is so whether the soul just is that state or is instead a particular thing whose presence puts the body into that state. *Contra* Hasker and Braine, if Aquinas holds that a live immaterial particular is also a substantial form, nothing misleads him. He instead just takes advantage of a wide, univocal definition of 'substantial form.' In that case, it simply turns out that some single thing is a form in two clearly distinct senses. Of course just how the soul is present in the body is a long story; I've discussed it elsewhere.[21]

2. THING AND FORM

But even if there is no equivocation or inconsistency in the claim that Thomas's soul is a form in two senses at once, the claim is hard to understand. How *can* something be both a substantial form and a particular? In *ST*'s treatment of human nature, Thomas first argues that the soul is 'the act' of a body[22]—i.e., its form—and then turns at once to his most careful exposition of the claim that it is a concrete particular thing.[23] Again, in his disputed question on the soul, Thomas tackles the form/thing claim first.[24] This might suggest that Thomas sees the soul's being both form and live particular as his toughest nut to crack.

There are three basic approaches to understanding Thomas's view. One takes as given that the soul is a live immaterial particular, then tries to show how such a thing can be a substantial form: call this a Platonic or Augustinian reading of Thomas. Another takes it as given that the soul is a substantial form, then tries to show how such a thing can be a live immaterial particular: call this an Aristotelian approach. A third would take it as primitive that the soul has some other unitary nature, and try to show how this nature allows it to be both: call this a 'neutral monist' reading of Thomas.[25]

---

[18] *ST* Ia, 76: 8; *SCG* II, 72.   [19] *ST* Ia, 76: 1.
[20] For a full account of this, see my "Souls Dipped in Dust," in Kevin Corcoran (2001: 120–38).
[21] Leftow (2001).   [22] *ST* Ia, 75: 1.   [23] *ST* Ia, 75: 2.   [24] *QD de An.*, 1.
[25] The term is of course Russell's. A fourth approach would simply take as primitive the conjunction of substantial form and particular thing, i.e,. not attempt at all to explain how the two roles can be conjoined. But as I see it, this would not be an attempt to *understand* the view, or show how it could possibly be true.

I have elsewhere defended a Platonic reading, as closest to the text and not wholly beyond hope philosophically. Eleonore Stump once offered an Aristotelian reading of Thomas. She has since taken a different tack, closer to the Platonic reading, but I'd like to suggest that Stump's original Aristotelian approach at least presents a broadly coherent position some might find appealing. She wrote that for Aquinas,

the soul is (a) configurational state which is . . . subsistent, able to exist on its own apart from the body.[26]

Here she takes it as basic that the soul is a state, then adds that it is a thing ('subsistent' confers thinghood, in Aquinas's lexicon) and able to outlast its body.[27]

Now for Aquinas, all states are 'tropes.' They are not universals, but particulars individuated by their bearers: what Socrates has is not a universal, wisdom, but a particular, Socrates' wisdom.[28] Stump's claim on Aquinas's behalf seems to be, then, that some tropes—human souls—can 'float free' of their initial bearers. Now it is not implausible that tropes can leave their first bearers. If my iris is the only green part of me, and my eye is transplanted to you, and you have no other green parts, you now have my greenness. For the greenness of my eye is now the greenness of your eye, and the greenness of your eye is yours. Philosophers routinely deal in brain-transplant thought experiments. So suppose that Socrates' wisdom consists in various dispositional qualities of his brain; suppose too that Socrates' brain-contents are so distributed that those aspects of his psychology continuance of which are necessary for his survival (if any) are in one part of his brain and those qualities which make him wise are segregated from these. Then it seems at least as conceivable as any other transplant scenario that a mad Athenian surgeon splice just the wisdom-bearing parts out of Socrates' brain, leaving Socrates otherwise intact and alive, and transplant Socrates' wisdom-bearing brain-tissue into Thrasymachus. If this occurs, Thrasymachus is not Socrates, but Thrasymachus now has the very token brain-states having which made Socrates count as wise. These brain-state tropes just *are* the wisdom that was Socrates'. So it seems conceivable that Socrates' wisdom leave Socrates.

But Stump's claim on Aquinas's behalf is that the soul at death floats free of all bearers, lingering like the Cheshire Cat's grin when the Cat has gone. (We do not quite have this in transplant cases. The greenness inheres in the eye while

---

[26] Stump (1995: 12, 519.)
[27] Stump *may* be basing the soul's thinghood on its ability to outlast its body. This would sit ill with Aquinas' argument for the soul's immortality (i.e., ability to outlast its body), which takes the soul's being a thing as a premise (*ST* Ia, 75: 6).
[28] *EE*, 3.

between persons.) Hasker objects that states must always belong to something:
they can't exist at a time if nothing bears them at that time.[29] But Stump may just
want to deny this.[30] She reminds us of Shoemaker's brain-state transfer (BST)
device,

which transfers a person's brain states from one body to another . . . there is an interval,
however small, in which the states are in the process of being transferred and so are no
longer in the first body and not yet in the second, and yet the states don't go out of
existence in this interval. On Aquinas' view, the interval may be much longer, and in that
interval the state can continue to operate . . . Nevertheless, on both Aquinas' account and
Shoemaker's, the imposition of the . . . state on new matter preserves the identity of the
person.[31]

The suggestion seems to be that if Shoemaker's BST-device is conceivable,
this suggests that states can exist for a while between owners. And Stump
seems to ascribe to Aquinas the view that the soul just is an exception to
Hasker's metaphysical rule, a unique sort of state that at some times has no
bearer.

If this is Stump's point, the BST-device will not really help her make it.
According to Shoemaker, the device effects it that a later brain has states that are
type-, not token-identical with an earlier brain's.[32] If so, the device as originally
conceived does not transfer tropes. It would take some doing to show that
it could. But for Aquinas, my soul when I am resurrected is token-, not just
type-identical with my earlier soul: that very trope returns. Again, Shoemaker
himself thinks that while brain-states are in the BST-device between brains,
they are states of something, namely the BST-device.[33] This seems correct: they
qualify its memory banks, though they perhaps can't have there the functional
role they have in a human psychology. Further, one can explicate the transition
without allowing for a gap in which the (type or token) state is unborne: one
can say, for instance, that there is a last instant at which the brain-state is in its
donor, and that at every instant between that state and the last instant t in which
it is in the machine, it is in the machine, and at every instant after t, for however
long it persists, it is in another human. If so, it's not clear why we should think
that the transfer-scenario involves a gap in which the state has no bearer. So
the BST analogy fails just where it is most needed, at the claim that the device
keeps numerically the same state in existence between bodies and while nothing
bears it.

[29] Hasker (1999: 168). Stump could accept a weaker reading of Hasker's 'a state must be a state
of something': even a discarnate soul is the soul of someone- just not of someone who then exists.

[30] Here and throughout, I use the 'historical present,' speaking of Stump at the time she wrote
the article.

[31] Stump (1995: 516–17).

[32] Thus Shoemaker writes that via the BST-device 'mental states existing immediately before
a body-change produce the functionally appropriate *successor*-states' (Shoemaker (1984: 111), my
emphasis).

[33] Shoemaker (1984: 110–11).

Still, the claim that states can persist between owners may not be untenable. States are attributes. On some views, an attribute can exist first as a state of something else and thereafter on its own. Suppose, for instance, that attributes are immanent universals with the Platonic property of being able to exist uninstanced. Immanent universals exist *in* their bearers. So immanent *state*-universals exist as their bearers' very states: *a*'s state of being a proton is the very entity which also exists in *b* as *b*'s state of being a proton. Suppose, then, that there have always been protons, but in the far future, all protons decay away. If it is an immanent but Platonic universal, then at that time protonhood, the very entity that was a state of every proton, persists though it is no longer a state of any proton. If still later some quarks form protons again, the very item that was a state of some protons will have existed 'between' owners. Now I have no argument that 'immanent Platonism' is the *right* theory of universals. But it seems a perfectly coherent theory. Nothing in the theory itself seems to rule it out, even though it features a claim very like the one Stump may make on behalf of Aquinas's soul.

There are also disanalogies here, of course. Were souls *just like* immanent Platonic universals, the whole human race would have the same soul, and it would be an abstract entity. But we get closer to Thomas if we suppose that there are haecceities, or individual essences, and they are immanent and Platonic. Thomas holds that a fetus in a womb became Jones because it received the soul it did,[34] and that in the Resurrection, a body will receive Jones' soul, and this will effect it that Jones lives in that body.[35] So as Stump notes, Thomist souls have the metaphysical roles of haecceities:

the soul makes matter be not just human, but also *this* human being . . . the . . . soul . . . is what makes a human being this particular individual.[36]

According to Robert Adams, before Jones exists, there is no haecceity of Jones, but there comes to be at least one when Jones comes to exist[37]—e.g., being Jones. So too, for Thomas, Jones' soul cannot pre-exist Jones.[38] While Jones exists, being Jones is a state of Jones: Jones is in the state of being Jones. So too, on Stump's reading, while Jones exists, Jones's soul is a state of Jones. Can being-Jones outlast Jones, as Thomist souls outlast their bearers? On many views of haecceities, it does. So being-Jones may have just the traits Stump finds in Jones' Thomist soul: it begins to exist as a state of Jones, but persists after his demise. Aristotle held that 'forms' are immanent, Plato says that they exist even if nothing bears them. 'Immanent Platonism' seems a consistent way to assert both things. So the conjunction of immanent Platonism and belief in haecceities seems consistent too. Perhaps an entity which is a state of something at some times may not be so at all times, and so may not be in every sense a state at all

---

[34] *Quaestione de Anima* a., 1: *ad* 1.   [35] So, e.g., *In I Cor., 15*.   [36] Stump (1995: 520).
[37] Adams, 'Actualism and Thisness,' (1981).
[38] *ST* Ia, 118: 3. The analogy is not perfect. For Adams, the individual's existence accounts for the haecceity's. For Thomas, the soul's existence accounts for the individual's.

times—though given its origin, and the fact that it can again have a bearer, it will always be a state in some senses.[39] And so perhaps in their general metaphysical status, Thomist souls should be no more (if no less) controversial than immanent Platonist haecceities.

Of course, the most basic objection to an 'Aristotelian,' state-based reading of Thomas is yet to be faced: how can a state, a trope, be something living? States are abstract. Nothing abstract is alive. So the soul on an 'Aristotelian' reading goes from being abstract to being concrete and alive at death. If it does not make this transition, then even while a state it is something concrete, or neither abstract nor concrete. The first consequence is unlovely. The second may be tolerable, since it is compatible with saying that while it is a state, the soul is non-concrete. For even if abstract and concrete are mutually exclusive, Thomas does not think they are jointly exhaustive. He thinks that in God's case the distinction does not apply.[40] God is identical with His own nature: 'God' and 'deity' refer to the same entity.[41] So Thomas might reply that his soul is another entity that slips between the horns of the abstract/concrete dilemma. It's not obvious that nothing can do so: just what the abstract/concrete distinction amounts to and what the criteria are for falling on one or the other side of it are notoriously unclear.[42] Nor is it clear that Aquinas's claim about God in particular is indefensible.[43] So too, Thomas's God is identical with a nature—a trope—and yet is alive. This is not as odd as it sounds. If God is identical with a trope, then He does not have all the properties we would expect God to have and all the properties we would expect a trope to have, since many standard divine- and standard trope-attributes are incompatible. But if God is identical with a trope, one entity has all the properties *really* possessed by the referent of a concrete term, 'God,' and all the properties *really* possessed by the referent of an abstract term, 'deity,' and these do not include all the properties we would *expect* in both cases—but they do, according to Thomas, include being alive. So too, perhaps, for Thomas read the Aristotelian way the soul has all properties really possessed by a referent for a term for a concrete entity ('soul of Jones') and all properties really possessed by the referent for a term for an abstract entity ('substantial form of Jones'), and these don't include everything we would expect in each case, but do include being alive.[44] I suggest, then, that there is at least more work to do before we can conclude that Aquinas read in the Aristotelian way holds an incoherent view of the soul's nature or metaphysical status.

---

[39] So perhaps *QD de Anima* a., 1: *ad* 10.   [40] *In VII Meta.*, l., 5: # 1380.
[41] *ST* Ia, 3: 3 and 50.   [42] See, e.g. Lewis (1986: 82–5).
[43] For a recent treatment, see Stump (1993: 92–130).
[44] This move veers close to a neutral monist approach to Aquinas. If it becomes one, perhaps the moral is simply that the Aristotelian reading must adopt a bit of another approach at just this point. A neutral monist account could still be strongly Aristotelian, if it (say) kept more trope- than other features in its picture of the soul.

Stump's treatment of the soul's role as substantial form centers on a molecule, C/EBP,

which when . . . bound in the right way to DNA . . . helps to unravel the DNA molecule, thereby (giving a new form to) the DNA . . . before it is bound to DNA, C/EBP isn't (giving form to) anything . . . Nonetheless, it doesn't undergo any radical transformation, or hop any categories, when it changes from being unbound to DNA and non-(giving form) to being bound and (giving form to DNA). C/EBP was all along . . . a . . . molecule with a capacity to (give form to) other molecules, and it nature doesn't change when it exercises that capacity . . . Like the angels, the human soul is itself (a thing); but like the forms of other material things, the human soul has the ability to (give form to) matter . . . Consequently, in the transition from (giving form to) matter to not (giving form to) matter, the human soul doesn't undergo any radical metaphysical transformation or category switching, any more than the molecule C/EBP does when it goes from (not giving form to) to (giving form to) DNA.[45]

One problem here is that C/EBP's relation to DNA is a case of ordinary efficient causation, whereas Thomas's soul is a 'formal' cause—a cause as forms are, one whose 'activity' consists in matter's being in a state, not in bringing matter to be in a state.[46] Another is that Thomas does think that the soul is in a broad sense part of us, as forms generally are broad 'parts' of the things whose forms they are.[47] The C/EBP analogy does not catch this note of parthood: the C/EBP molecule is not part of the DNA whose structure it causes.[48] So perhaps a better analogy might run this way.

Consider a free chemical radical in an unstable state. This is not a fugitive from the 1960s, but rather a sort of molecule. A radical is a combination of elements that acts as a single unit in chemical reactions. A free radical is such a unit currently not bound into any larger molecule. A radical in an unstable state has a free 'place' in its structure which another atom or molecule can fill, and if it meets an atom or molecule that can occupy this 'place,' will bind with that item and form a compound. An unstable radical, then, is one prone to form a molecule of a compound, by its very chemical nature. Think, then, of a large, complex free radical with one empty 'place' for a hydrogen atom, which then meets a hydrogen atom and forms a stable molecule. The radical persists as an undetached part of the resulting molecule. It is in a clear sense the structuring part of that molecule: the molecule has the structure and powers it does because the radical had the structure and powers it did. And while there are efficient-causal bonds between the radical and the atom that completes the resulting molecule, there are none

---

[45] Stump (1995: 514–15).
[46] Stump herself notes that 'C/EBP configures something which is a matter-form composite itself; the soul configures unformed matter' (Stump 1995: 514 n. 43). This is part of the difference between formal and efficient causes.
[47] For the general claim, see *ST* Ia, 3: 2.
[48] Stump notes this disanalogy herself (Stump 1995: 514 n. 43).

between the radical and the resulting molecule. Their relation is part/whole, and arguably the radical is the whole's formal cause: it gives the whole its structure, and for the whole to have that structure is for the radical to be part of it. To get a full analogue for the life-story of the Thomist soul, take it that God creates a stable molecule (human being) initially,[49] death 'breaks off' a part which leaves an unstable radical, and resurrection returns that part, forming the very molecule one had before.

3. HUMAN BEING: MATERIAL THING?

Thomas speaks of material things as 'composed of' form and matter.[50] Thus he sees items' forms and matter as in a broad sense part of them. Thomas would say, then, that a body of water has an immaterial part, in a broad sense of 'part': the water's form is a broad-part of it, and its form is a state, an abstract particular. But the body of water is one material thing all the same. For Thomas, there being water just is a water-form being wholly present at each point in a parcel of matter. Similarly a human just is the human form (a soul) wholly present at each point in a parcel of matter. If Thomas is not a dualist about water, then on the Aristotelian reading he is likewise not a dualist about humans.

For Descartes, the soul's complement is a material substance, a body which can exist unensouled. For Thomas, subtract the soul and the complement left behind is prime matter—which cannot exist on its own. Thomas is so far from being a dualist that there is no second actual thing for the soul to pair with. This is because for Thomas there is at one level of analysis almost nothing to us but a soul: a human is a soul wrapped in prime matter. And all the same, a human being is one material thing, as much so as a body of water. Involvement with prime matter might seem to make this aspect of Thomas's position simply unavailable to contemporary philosophy. But the key feature here is just that minus the soul, there is no second thing that is or was the body. A number of recent views would let a dualist reproduce this feature, if it seemed desirable. For a number of contemporary views entail either that there are no composite material objects at all or that a dead body would not count as a single composite object.[51] On any such view, we amount to a soul somehow related to a cloud of quarks: what 'pairs' with the soul is not one thing but a plurality of things.

---

[49] As Thomas sees it, the fetus in one's mother's womb before God ensouls it is numerically distinct from the human who exists there after the ensoulment: and so the soul first exists as included in the body-soul 'molecule.'

[50] E.g., *ST*, Ia, 3: 2.

[51] For the first see Rosen and Dorr (2002). For the second see Peter van Inwagen (1990).

4. DUALISM AND THE BRAIN

Thus I claim that Thomas has not equivocated on or been misled by 'form,' and that his metaphysical account of the soul may be defensible when taken the Aristotelian way. But Hasker adds a second charge that Thomas's account of our mental life differs too much from his account of other animals' mental life:

If the apparently rich mental and emotional lives of dogs, dolphins and chimpanzees can be fully explained in terms of the function of . . . their bodies, where is the plausibility of arguing that the cognitive activity of human beings requires an immaterial soul? Especially when the principal argument for such an immaterial soul has rested on the contention, now scientifically discredited, that there is no neural correlate for the higher rational processes? This . . . raises serious questions about the internal coherence of Thomistic dualism. Consider the account which is to be given of sense perception for humans and other animals. In the case of animals, the subject of perception is the . . . brain and nervous system. For humans the subject is the composite consisting of the brain and nervous system *and the immaterial soul*. This contravenes what seems to be strong evidence that perception works in very much the same way in humans and in animals. And it means that the metaphysical analysis of perception in the two cases is going to have to be radically different, in spite of the empirical similarities.[52]

Here Hasker misreads Aquinas. If it were true that the subject of perception is the brain and nervous system, these things would *include* the soul, in both dogs and humans. The soul would be present in dog and human brains and nerves as their form: and so the subject would be the composite in both cases. In fact, the only difference involved on the Aristotelian reading would be that the state involved can float free in one case but not the other—which is not a factor that generates a different metaphysical account of perception. But for Aquinas, in both humans and (say) chimps, the subject of perception—correctly—is the whole animal, not any sub-system: 'one can say that the soul understands as one can say that the eye sees, but it is more proper to say that the human understands through the soul.'[53] Again, Aquinas does not say that 'higher rational processes' have no neural correlate. He instead makes the somewhat different claim that they have no bodily organ.[54] I now explicate the no-organ claim and suggest that it is not the sort of thing science *could* discredit. On my account of Thomas, the root difference between human and non-human mental lives does not lie at the level of anything empirical, nor even in the fact that the soul involved can in one case float free. It lies instead (say I) in the account to be given of the content of our and other animals' mental states.

Thomas does contend that intellectual activity—mental activity using universal concepts—has no bodily organ.[55] But by this he means to deny no obvious

---

[52] Hasker (1999: 169).   [53] *ST* Ia, 75: 2 *ad* 2, 441a.   [54] *ST* Ia, 75: 2.
[55] *ST* Ia, 75: 3. Thomas adds willing as another such act at *ST* I-IIa, 22: 3.

facts. Thomas is aware that differences in one's body affect one's power of intellectual understanding.[56] He explains this as partly because lower powers relevant to thought (memory, imagination) have functions that are fully embodied (i.e., have organs) and partly because differences in a thing's matter do generally affect the way its matter realizes its substantial form. In fact, for Thomas, our thinking always involves the brain. Even the most 'intellectual' thoughts always are based on and include the brain's generating 'phantasms,' physically encoded and realized 'images' which our sense-faculties (powers *inter alia* of the brain) replay.[57] So firm is Thomas in this conviction that he holds that for our souls to think in a discarnate state, God must intervene miraculously to provide content our brains can no longer generate.[58] For Thomas, phantasms do not exhaust our intellectual states' content, but these states can fail to include them only by a miracle—for realizings of phantasms are (as it were) the medium in which embodied thinking takes place.[59]

Hasker charges that for Thomas intellectual operations have 'no neural correlate.'[60] Thomas's insistence on the role of brain-generated phantasms gives this claim the lie—the correlation may not be 1:1, but that's not required for there to be, in fact, a correlation. We must distinguish between saying that such thinking has no *organ* and saying that it does not involve the brain, or has no neural correlate or component.[61] We can do so by looking at how Thomas thinks of organs generally.

Thomas writes that:

if a bodily organ carries out an operation of the soul . . . the power of the soul which is that operation's source is the act of that part of the body which carries out its operation, as vision is the act of the eye.[62]

Thomas sees sense organs in particular as the body-parts in which sense powers are sited.[63] He writes that

sensation and the consequent operations of the sensitive soul are evidently accompanied with change in the body; thus in the act of vision, the pupil of the eye is affected by a reflection of color . . . Hence . . . the sensitive soul has no *per se* operation of its own, and . . . every operation of the sensitive soul belongs to the composite.[64]

Thomas uses this passage to flesh out the claim that intellectual thinking has no organ. Thus he appeals to the eye precisely because it is the organ of sight. His point is at least that certain kinds of change in the eye, sight's organ,

---

[56] *ST* Ia, 85: 7   [57] *ST* Ia, 84: 7 and 85: 1 *ad* 3.   [58] *ST* Ia, 89: 1 *ad* 3.
[59] *In Boeth. de Trinitate*, 6: 2 *ad* 6.   [60] Hasker (1999: 169).
[61] Even if for Thomas some mental states 'are implemented in the brain together with the immaterial, subsistent mind' (p. 168), they are still brain-implemented. Placing them even partly in neural stuff distinguishes Aquinas's position from Descartes's, and counts as a materialist *part* of his view.
[62] *SCG* II, 69: 164.   [63] *In II De Anima*, l. 24: #555.   [64] *ST* Ia, 75: 3.

correlate non-accidentally with seeings. But shortly thereafter, Thomas writes that anger too is 'accompanied by' bodily change.[65] Now anger is a propositional attitude—one is angry about something—and so becoming angry is a mental event, one moreover involving mental content. Yet Thomas *defines* anger as a type of physical process—a kind of change in the blood around the heart.[66] So for Thomas, anger is *by nature* a kind of bodily change. For Thomas, then, bodily change 'accompanies' becoming angry because one event *is* both a bodily change and a mental event. I suggest that the like holds for some events in the eye, for Thomas: they are bodily events which *are* sensings of color. To put this another way, for Thomas, an animal's sensing is the animal's sense-organs coming to be and being in a particular state. Thus some sorts of mental event correlate 1:1 with physical events because they *are* physical events. Thomas's argument here is that the intellective soul *has* a '*per se* operation of its own' and so need not be 'accompanied' by a physical change. But this doesn't imply that they're not correlated with and do not involve physical changes. What follows is only that the correlation is not necessarily 1:1. Later, Thomas writes that:

the act of the intellectual appetite [will] requires no bodily change, because an appetite of this kind is not a power of an organ.[67]

Again, what does not require—entail—any particular bodily change (because it is not identical with any) might nonetheless be correlated with bodily changes without a 1:1 correspondence.

It seems, then, that if a body-part is an organ for an animal's *G*-ing, the animal's power to *G* is sited in the organ (the power of sight in the eye,[68] of movement in the heart[69]), thus the animal *G*s by using a power sited in that organ, the state of *G*-ing is a state of the organ and so when the animal begins to *G*, the organ changes.[70] Sensing changes sense-organs in that when we sense, they become subjects of received, cognized forms: our seeing (etc.) is or includes our sense-organs' being in a particular state.[71] For Thomas, normally functioning sense-organs fully embody or encode sensed forms.[72] That is, their being in a particular state suffices for us to have 'taken in' that form: the whole form we sense is there. Putting it another way, the sort of information the senses take in is fully realized in physical states of the sensory system.

I suggest, then, that Thomas's account of organs for animal activities goes something like this:

B is an organ for *A*'s *G*-ing iff

(a) *A* is an animal,

---

[65] *ST* Ia, 75: 3 *ad* 3.   [66] *ST* I-IIa, 22: 2 *ad* 3.   [67] *ST* Ia I-IIa, 22: 3, 844a.
[68] *DSC* 4 ad 11.   [69] *DSC* 4 ad 1.
[70] Organs are for Thomas the bodily instruments of the soul's powers (*In I De Anima*, l. 13: #208). So they change if the power which uses them acts.
[71] *In II De Anima*, l. 14: #418.   [72] *ST* Ia, 85: 2 *ad* 3; 17: 2; 85: 6.

(b) B is a proper part of A's body;

(c) A can G;

(d) G-ing is a use of a power sited in B;

(e) A's G-ing is or includes B's being in a particular state or process, and so pairs
     1:1 with B's coming to be or being in this state or process, and;

(f) if B is a *cognitive* organ, B fully embodies or encodes received forms (the
     media and/or content of cognition[73]).

If this reading of Thomas is on the right track, then when Thomas denies
that intellectual activity—mental activity which uses universal concepts—has
an organ, we can infer that this sort of activity fails to satisfy at least one
clause of the definition. Absent more specific textual evidence, we cannot say
which, or whether it fails more than one—though we've already seen reason to
suspect that (e) is involved. There are at least three ways the brain in particular
could fail to satisfy some of (b)–(f) for thinking, and so fail to be an organ
of thought in Thomas's sense, even given what we now know of its role in
thought.

One involves failing (b). Suppose that our brains do what matters most
causally in our thinking. Behaviorists know that this is so. But despite this, on
their account, thinking is not the sort of thing to have what Thomas would
call a particular bodily organ. For on behaviorism, such terms as 'thinks P'
or 'wills P' apply to us primarily due to dispositions to behavior which are
not localized in the brain. Coming to think P is coming to be disposed to
speak and act in certain ways. These dispositions involve one's whole body:
thinking P is the whole body's being in a certain state, not just the brain's
doing so. If this is so, then even if the brain matters more causally to one's
thinking than the rest of one's body, no proper part of one's body is an
organ of thought, in Thomas's sense. But failing only (b) is compatible with
the body being as a whole as the organ of thought, and this is probably not
Thomas's view—though he does sometimes speak of the body as the organ of
the soul.

A second involves (e): it is plausible that states with intellectual content fail
the 1:1 correspondence condition. Quine asks us to:

Consider...the totality of truths of nature, known and unknown, observable and
unobservable, past and future...the indeterminacy of translation withstands all this
truth.[74]

We meet a speaker of a language we've never heard. The speaker points at a
rabbit and says 'Gavagai!' This might assert (in effect): 'Here's all of a 3D rabbit!'

---

[73] On this, see Pasnau (1997), *passim*.   [74] Quine (1969a: 303).

or 'Here's a time-slice of a 4D rabbit!' or 'It's rabbiting over there!' Which is meant? Quine suggests that we couldn't tell given even all truths about matter in space—and so in particular all truths about the speaker's brain states. There are many issues here, but a great many philosophers think there's something to this. Suppose it's true, and now let's switch back to Thomist cognitive psychology. Then in particular, which phantasm the material cognitive system is realizing and replaying—or perhaps which phantasm of a sentence-token one is mentally hearing—won't 'fix' the content of the thought the sentence expresses. The same phantasms would be the medium of thinking 'Here's a rabbit!,' 'Here's a rabbit time-slice!' or 'It's rabbiting over there!'—just as in fact, the same sensory presentation would appear to us, no matter what the truth is about rabbit ontology. The correlation between determinate thoughts and replays of phantasms is many–one, not 1:1.

Thomas's argument that the mind is a *hoc aliquid*, a particular thing, points toward (f):

by means of the intellect, man can have knowledge of all corporeal things. Now whatever knows certain things cannot have any of them in its own nature, as that which is in it naturally would impede the knowledge of anything else. Thus we observe that a sick man's tongue being vitiated by a feverish and bitter humor, is insensible to anything sweet, and everything seems bitter to it. So if the intellectual principle contained the nature of a body it would be unable to know all bodies. . . . It is likewise impossible for the intellect to understand by means of a bodily organ; since the determinate nature of that organ would impede knowledge of bodies: as when a certain determinate color is not only in the pupil of the eye, but also in a glass vase, the liquid in the vase seems to be of that same color.[75]

Taken at face value, this argument is not one of Thomas's better moments. But the general point it tries to make may deserve a bit more regard. For Thomas's idea, however odd his way to suggest it, is plainly that the sort of information in which the intellect deals cannot be adequately encoded physically, and so intellectual content cannot be localized at any point within the body, nor even in the body as a whole (though Thomas doesn't draw this further moral). Consider Quine again. We think there is a difference between a speaker of an unknown tongue's holding an ontology of 3D rabbits and the speaker's holding one of undetached rabbit-parts or slices of 4D rabbits. Quine suggests that as we try to translate the language, we cannot tell which ontology is in fact being held, given even all truths about matter in space—i.e., that not even all of physical fact suffices to let a translator determine that (say) a 3D translation of the speaker's utterances is correct and a 4D translation is not. From this Quine concludes that there is no fact of the matter about which *is* correct. There are plenty of assumptions to question in this, but what I'll note now is just that Aquinas might

[75] *ST* Ia, 75: 2.

instead turn things on their head and say: there *is* a difference in content between belief in 3D rabbits and belief in 4D rabbit slices.[76] If the totality of physical fact doesn't determine this, this means only that not all thought-content is physically encoded. If the difference depends precisely on which universal concepts one in fact uses, then mental states involving such concepts have a content for which no state of one's brain can account. Not all of this content consists in the brain's being in a particular state—in which case the brain fails condition (f) for being the organ of such thought. For the brain to be what Thomas would call the organ of thought, its states would have to embody on their own the full contents of our mental states. The full form the intellect grasps—the full content of its information—would have to be there, as the full form the senses grasp is in sense-organs. I add that if this is correct, then any externalist account of mental content also entails that the brain flunks (f) and so is not on Thomas's terms the organ of thought. As most philosophers of mind are externalists these days, if I'm right, most would in fact endorse Thomas's claim about the brain, though they wouldn't put it in his terms. It's worth noting, though, that the possibility of a purely physicalist externalism blocks any Thomist attempt to move from information's not being physically encoded in the brain to its not being physically encoded at all, and so to there being a spiritual host for the information. Information not present in the brain could be present in a physical sum, the brain plus its physical environment.

Is Thomas a behaviorist, or an externalist? Is there a Quine in Aquinas? I have not said so. My point is the more modest one that Aquinas's doctrine that there is no 'organ of (intellectual) thought' may not simply be a bit of outdated science. It may instead involve serious theses about the nature of mental states and their content. If this is so, Thomas's claim that we have no organ of intellectual thought may well be defensible. And the claim that intellectual thinking is an act of the soul may assert only that such thinking has no organ. My suggestions naturally make one curious about Thomas's full account of how intellectual states have their content. But Thomas holds that a state has mental content of the sort the intellectual soul deals in just in case our being in that state involves the nature of some thing existing in the mind.[77] What to make of natures' mental existence is too large a question to tackle here, and so I cannot go further.

5. TAXONOMY: THE MENTAL AND THE PHYSICAL

Let us now ask just where Thomas's views may fall on the map of current debate. Thomas holds that at least some events have both mental and physical properties.

---

[76] I owe this thought to James Ross's treatment of Aristotle in Ross (1992).
[77] So *ST* Ia, 85: 1–2 and *De Ente*, 3.

Getting angry is a mental process. Yet Thomas defines anger as a type of physical process—a kind of change in the blood around the heart.[78] So for Thomas, some event is both a getting angry and (say) a heating of blood. Again, the sensing of a color is a mental event.[79] Yet Thomas explicitly calls the sensing of color a modification of the eye.[80] And while Thomas treats the eye alone as the organ of sight, we today can surely be allowed to correct his physiology and include, e.g., the optic nerve and the brain. More generally, following Aristotle, Thomas defines a sense-organ as an area of the body which receives an 'immaterial' sensed form.[81] That the event takes place in the organ makes it physical. That the event is reception of an 'immaterial' form amounts to saying that in the event, this part of the body enters a state with mental content.[82] For such events, then, Thomas is a property-dualist. So for a wide range of cognitive states, Thomas offers an account which is recognizably materialist. Finally, Thomas is explicit that for some kinds of sensing—those not involving the use of universal concepts, i.e., cases of non-'intellectual' cognition[83]—the cognitive apparatus and causal or metaphysical story for humans and other animals is identical, down to both involving organs located in the brain.[84] This story in neither case entails a subsistent soul, though in our case the soul that plays the soul's causal role is in fact subsistent. Thomas makes the further claim that the story for other sorts of human mental states differs only because their content involves universal concepts. If he were to admit that other sorts of animals also employ such concepts, he'd apply the same sort of story to them. There is a genuine, non-arbitrary distinction between mental states with and mental states without such content. If Thomas makes the break between non-subsistent and subsistent souls according to where such states are and are not found, his distinction tracks a genuine difference between kinds of animal.

---

[78] *ST* I-IIa, 22: 2 *ad* 3.

[79] Though some sensings are not also *intellectual* events. Thomas speaks of the senses, not just the intellect, as making judgments, e.g. of *sense* as seeing of a particular first that it is a body, then an animal, then a man, then Socrates (*ST* Ia, 85: 3), that the sun is a foot in diameter or this is honey (*ST* Ia, 85: 6), and more generally as judging the presence of proper, common and accidental 'sensibles' (*ST* Ia, 78: 4 *ad* 2). These examples involve the wielding of universal concepts, if they involve recognizing that the particular being sensed falls under what is in fact such a concept. Since universal concepts are the intellect's province, strictly speaking here sense and intellect co-operate. But Thomas also classes among our sensory powers what he calls the *particular reason*, which he says 'compares' individual 'intentions' (concepts) as 'intellectual reason' does with universal concepts (*ST* Ia, 78: 4)—perhaps the sort of thing involved in noticing of two red patches that *this* is like *that*, without conceptualizing in any way their respect of likeness. This is a case of cognition, a case of acquiring knowledge of something, and so certainly a mental event. Yet it is not *intellectual* cognition.

[80] *ST* I-IIa, 22: 2 *ad* 3.   [81] *In II de Anima*, l. 24: #555.

[82] For the immateriality/content tie, see e.g. *SCG* I, 44. One must distinguish the claim that the form received is immaterial from the claim that the form is received immaterially: Thomas allows that the air transmitting '*species in medio*' to our sense-organs also receives forms immaterially (*In II de Anima*, l. 14, #418).

[83] *ST* Ia, 86: 1; 78: 1.   [84] *ST* Ia, 78: 4.

In sum: no philosophical mistakes need lie behind Thomas's account of the soul, and an Aristotelian reading of this seems at least tenable. Nor does Thomas's account force him to overplay the difference between ourselves and other animals. To this extent, at least, one can save Thomas's soul.

6. THE SOUL: SUBSTANCE?

There is another puzzle in a text quoted at our outset. Descartes took concrete immaterial particulars to be substances.[85] Most current dualists follow him in this. Yet Aquinas asserts that:

(3) Though human souls are immaterial particulars, they are not substances.

(3) is at best hard to interpret. One also wonders just what beyond a bit of metaphysical terminology might be at stake between Thomas and Descartes here. I think more than this is at stake. I also think that those who see what it is will incline to agree with Thomas.

Thomas sometimes does call human souls substances.[86] But his most considered view is that they are not.[87] To explain the denial, I must treat what Thomas means by 'substance.' Thomas writes that:

A substance is a thing suited not to exist in a subject . . . in the notion of substance is understood, that it has a nature to which existence not in another is suited.[88] An individual in the genus of substance . . . is . . . complete in some species and genus of substance, whence . . . a hand and a foot and the like are called parts of substances rather than substances . . . because . . . they do not have a complete nature of some species.[89]

One point to note here is that for Thomas, items are substances due to their natures. If so, items are non-substances due to their natures. Again,

'this something' is properly said of an individual in the genus of substance.[90] 'This something' can be taken in two ways: in one, for anything subsistent, and in the other, for a subsistent complete in the nature of some species. Taken in the first way, it excludes

---

[85] Descartes (1985a), v. 1, 52.

[86] So *SCG* II, 56 and 68, and the *proem* to *ST* Ia's 'Treatise on Man.'

[87] Or else that the term substance is used analogically in calling them substances. In either case, thus the careful distinctions of *ST* Ia, 75: 2 *ad* 1 *et ad* 2. *SCG* II calls the soul a substance throughout; this is no occasional 'slip.' As *SCG* II predates *ST* Ia, it is possible that Thomas's view changed: that in *SCG* he just does see the soul as a substance, and in *ST* he does not. If this is so, I treat only the *ST* view.

[88] *SCG* I, 25: 27.

[89] *De Anima*, in S. Thomae Aquinatis (Turin: Marietti, 1931), v. 2 (henceforth *QD de Anima*), a. 1, p. 368.

[90] *Ibid.*

the inherence of an accident or a material form. Taken in the second, it excludes the imperfection of a part. For this reason one can call a hand 'this something' in the first way but not the second.[91]

Accidents and material forms are attributes. For Thomas, then, something is a substance only if it is a non-attribute and is not by its very nature part of some other thing. Further, for Thomas, attributes can exist only if they are exemplified,[92] and attributes are parts (in a broad sense) of the items which have them.[93] So for Thomas, attributes by their natures can exist only as parts of other things, and we can reduce the necessary condition to: something is a substance only if it is not by its nature part of some other thing.

Descartes's conception of substance has a similar note:

In the case of created things, some are of such a nature that they cannot exist without other things, while some need only the ordinary concurrence of God in order to exist. We make this distinction by calling the latter 'substances.'[94]

In other words, leaving God out of the picture (as we did with Aquinas), substances are those things whose natures are such that they could exist even if nothing else but their parts and attributes did those things which are not by their very natures parts of some larger whole (at least a created universe containing them and other items). For Descartes, the immaterial mind is a substance.[95] For Thomas, the soul is no substance, for it is by nature part of a larger thing, a human.[96]

More is at stake here than a bit of abstruse ontological classification. Hands act only in that animals act by them. If we say 'the ball moved because a hand threw it,' then since a hand is by definition a part of an animal who grips (and throws with it), our claim entails that the ball moved because some animal threw it. The latter explanation is in an obvious sense more basic; one can and should 'cash in' any explanation invoking a hand's motion for one invoking an animal's act. Thus a by-nature part is not a basic explainer.[97] On the other hand, it is not the case that any explanation invoking a substance entails one invoking a larger whole of which it is part. A substance can act on its own, rather than by some more inclusive thing's acting.

Thus when Descartes asserts that mind and body are substances, he asserts (*inter alia*) that each can act apart from the other. For him,

man's body (is) a kind of mechanism . . . composed of bones, nerves (etc.) in such a way that even if no mind existed in it, the man's body would still exhibit all the same motions

---

[91] *ST* Ia, 75: 2 *ad* 1, p. 441a.   [92] So, e.g., *De Ente et Essentia*, c. 3.
[93] So, e.g., *ST* Ia, 3: 2 and 3: 6.   [94] Descartes (1985): I, 51: 210.
[95] *Ibid.*, I, 52: 210.   [96] *DP* 3: 10; *ST* Ia, 75: 2 *ad* 1.
[97] Nor is an exemplified quality—our other example of a Thomistic-nature part—a basic explainer. Shapes do not reflect light. Shaped things do, due to their shapes.

that are in it now except for those motions that proceed either from a command of the will, or, consequently, from the mind.[98]

For Descartes, the body does some things reflexively, without input from the mind. And as the *Meditations* show, Descartes thinks his mind could process 'ideas' just as it actually does even if the physical world (and so his body) did not exist[99]—which entails that the mind's idea-processing does not even now depend in any essential way on the body. Further, for Descartes, a human being is a defined entity, composed by nature of two more basic substances, a body and a mind. Because this is so, human actions are for him always decomposable into more basic acts by a mind and a body. Descartes had from his Scholastic education a concept of body and soul as 'incomplete substances' that descends directly from Thomas's treatment of the soul. But while he is willing to let us *call* body and soul incomplete substances when we consider them as composing a further substance, a human,[100] this is just a concession to received usage. Descartes does not think that body and soul lack anything if not conjoined in a human: he does not think they have any intrinsic *need* to compose any further thing.[101]

On the other hand, in asserting that soul and body are not substances, Thomas asserts *inter alia* that neither can act fully independently of the other while the soul is incarnate. So too, for Thomas, human activities are basic, soul- and body-activities (if treated as distinct from human activities) derivative: again, 'one can say that the soul understands . . . but it is more proper to say that the human understands through the soul.'[102] Thomas insists that a soul on its own lacks a 'complete nature.'[103] A thing with a complete nature can under natural circumstances do the actions natural to its kind. In nature, says Thomas, the soul cannot do its peculiar action without a body.[104] For its act is to understand, but the soul cannot do this naturally without a body to supply 'phantasms,' the data and *media* of its understanding.[105] If the soul cannot understand on its own, it cannot be fully a soul on its own. If the soul can understand only in a body (naturally), the soul can fully be itself only when in a body (naturally). So if the soul is a soul by itself, it is *incompletely* a soul. So too, a severed but still live eye, unable to see, would be incompletely an eye.

The disagreement between Descartes and Thomas, then, really turns on whether the soul's nature lets it act on its own, apart from input or aid by body

---

[98] Descartes (1993: 55).   [99] Descartes (1993: 2, 6).

[100] Descartes (1985b) *Fourth Replies*.

[101] Descartes (1985*b*) 'Letter to Regius'. I owe this and the previous reference to Cover and O'Leary-Hawthorne (1999: 48).

[102] *ST* Ia, 75: 2 *ad* 2, 441*a*.   [103] Ia, 75: 2 *ad* 1; *QD de An:* 1 *et ad* 4.   [104] *QD de An* 1.

[105] *QD de An*, 1; *St* Ia, 75: 2 *ad* 3.

or brain, without a miracle. Descartes says, yes, Thomas, no. With the disagreement explained this way, most dualists these days will side with Thomas. But the more basic point here is that while Thomas denies that the brain is the organ of thought, he thinks the soul's dependence on it is profound enough to help determine the soul's metaphysical category.

21

Materialism Does Not Save the Phenomena—and the Alternative Which Does

Uwe Meixner

Usually, materialism is attacked by way of a priori arguments: deductive arguments that make crucial use of a priori premises. But 'a priori premise' can mean one of two things. An a priori premise *in one sense* (the strict sense) is a premise that can be shown to be true without recourse to empirical data; an a priori premise *in another sense* (the loose sense) is a premise that—though true or false—cannot be shown to be false, but cannot be shown to be true either (with or without recourse to empirical data). The anti-materialistic argument of René Descartes (particularly as I construe it[1]) and the anti-materialistic argument of David Chalmers[2] are built on a priori premises in the second sense, which means: it cannot be shown to be false that there is a possible world in which I exist without anything physical existing—Descartes' master premise—and it cannot be shown to be false that there is a possible world in which everything physical is just like it is in the actual world, but without anything conscious existing—Chalmers' master premise—but neither is it the case that either Descartes' or Chalmers's master premise can be shown to be true—in such a manner that every rational person had better believe that it is true on taking cognizance of the demonstration, which, by the way, might simply consist in the presentation of what is self-evident. Obviously, a priori arguments that are based on a priori premises in the second sense—one might call them *metaphysical premises*—are vulnerable to rational doubt. What cannot be shown to be true *can* be rationally doubted—even if it may so turn out that it cannot be shown to be false either. Materialists, of course, have widely availed themselves of this rational possibility for doubt.

What I will offer here is not another a priori argument against materialism. Rather, my aim is to point out some empirical data—empirical phenomena—that quite strikingly militate against materialistic views regarding human

---

[1] See Descartes (1985a) and the Neo-Cartesian Argument in Meixner (2004).
[2] See Chalmers (1996).

nature. But it should be kept in mind from the start that these data, though empirical, are relevant for conceptual decisions (hence for matters that are traditionally regarded as falling within the province of the a priori), as will become rather apparent in the last section of this chapter. These data are of such a fundamental nature that they, unlike the usual empirical data, affect the choice between various conceptual frameworks, not just the choice between various theories within a given conceptual framework.

1. WHERE AM I?

In *Philosophical Foundations of Neuroscience* (Bennett and Hacker 2003), the two authors attack what they call 'the mereological fallacy' in neuroscience. According to them, psychological predicates can only apply—for conceptual reasons—to human beings as wholes, *not* to parts of them, in particular *not* to their brains. I am far from having Bennett's and Hacker's utter self-assurance in adjudicating what is conceptually correct or incorrect. Their judgments seem problematic to me in many cases, even if it is presupposed that the standard of conceptual correctness is to be set by ordinary (or natural) language. What seems absolutely certain to me is that some psychological predicates apply—in their primary, literal, non-analogical, non-metaphorical sense—*to me*. But what am *I*? What are *we*? This is a deep and difficult question, and Bennett and Hacker do not seem to have fully appreciated the full extent of its depth and difficulty, or they would not be so dismissive of the recent materialistic attempts to answer it, as well as of the earlier, dualistic ones. I submit, if these attempts fail, something more than just a neglect of 'conceptual hygiene' (ibid.: 116) is responsible for it.

But rather than dwell on this, I will, first, consider a question that seems much easier to answer than the question of what is the ultimate nature of my (and our) being: *Where am I?* Well, I am now here, of course. And *where* is *here* where I am now, at t_0, for example? A true answer seems to be this: I am at t_0 precisely where my body is at t_0. However, this answer is not without difficulties. Prima facie, the further question, 'Where is my body (now, at t_0)?,' is taken to ask for *the* place in which my body is at t_0. But there is no such unique place. *Places* (for three-dimensional objects) are three-dimensionally extended regions in space—located, undivided volumes of space—and hence there certainly are infinitely many places in which my body is a t_0. In all of these infinitely many places I am, too, if I am a t_0 precisely where my body is at t_0. This, surely, is much more than I ask for when I ask, 'Where am I?'

It seems that this difficulty can easily be overcome. 'The place in which my body is at t_0' is, of course, intended to mean the same as 'the *smallest* place in which my body is at t_0,' or in other words: 'the place which is at t_0 *exactly occupied* by my body.' Yet, is there any such place? A place l_0 is at t_0 exactly occupied by my body if, and only if, (1) every part of my body is at t_0 in l_0, *and* (2) there is no part of l_0 in which there is at t_0 no part of my body. The first condition *alone* is certainly satisfied, by many places; but the first and second condition *together* may easily be unsatisfiable. Suppose my body has at t_0 isolated proper parts: proper parts of it that are surrounded by empty space. Then there is *no* place which fulfills conditions (1) and (2) together. And is it not true that my body has at t_0 isolated proper parts? It seems otherwise only as long as we do not descend to the micro-level of mereological composition.

Another difficulty for the idea that I am at t_0 precisely where my body is at t_0—a difficulty of a quite different nature than the one just described, and a difficulty which remains even if it be decreed that I am at t_0 precisely in what is *for all practical purposes* the smallest place in which my body is at t_0 (that is, the place where the water would not go if my body, mouth closed, were at t_0 submerged in water)—is the following difficulty: I can look at my feet resting at t_0 on the seat of a chair, and I can look at my hands resting at t_0 on my thighs, and there is a sense in which the following two questions and two assertions make perfect sense (the two assertions being even *true* in that sense): 'How far away from me is at t_0 the tip of my left big toe?'—'How far away from me is at t_0 the tip of my right pinkie?'—'My hands [*or* my gloves] are at t_0 nearer to me than my feet [*or* my shoes].'—'My head [*or* my cap] is at t_0 nearer to me than my feet [my shoes], and even nearer to me than my hands [my gloves].'[3] But how can this be if I am a t_0 precisely where my body is at t_0? Obviously, I must be somewhere else at t_0 than my body is. But *where am I*, then?

Here is an experiment that will determine where I (really) am at a certain time. Its central idea is that I am in the location—place or point in space—from which I am looking at the world (or rather: at whatever it is in the world that I am looking at). Thus, the experiment determines from which location I am looking at the world at a certain moment of time. I am sitting upright on a chair with my head immobilized (for, clearly, the location from which I am looking at the world may change when I move my head). I am looking straight ahead, at a white wall on which there is, at the height of my eyes, a pattern of black dots, like this:

```
. . . .
. . . .
. . . .
. . . .
```

---

[3] A few months after I wrote this, I discovered that at least one other philosopher had had such convictions: G. E. Moore. In van Inwagen (1995: 121), Moore is quoted as saying, 'I am closer to my hands than I am to my feet,' and the source of this is indicated to be White (1960). Van Inwagen calls Moore's conviction 'extraordinary' (van Inwagen 1995: 177). The conviction seems commonplace to me, and presumably seemed so also to Moore. Interestingly, Moore also drew a similar conclusion from it. The original passage in White (1960: 806) is this: 'He [Moore] insisted that he was quite distinct from his body, and one day said that his hand was closer to him than his foot was.' White describes Moore as a believer in Cartesian dualism (ibid.).

In front of the white wall, at a certain distance from it and from me—namely, just within my arm's reach—there is a very thin but rigid transparent screen. I am looking at the wall and at the pattern on the wall through that screen. I close my left eye, and with a fine marker I mark the location on the screen where the tip of the marker seems to me to coincide with a dot on the wall. I do this with regard to all sixteen dots. This yields a dot-by-dot projection of the sixteen dots on the wall onto sixteen dots on the screen. Next, sixteen straight lines are drawn, each line being uniquely determined by a dot on the wall and by the dot that corresponds to it on the screen. The point in space where these lines intersect or the region in space where they maximally converge, *there* I was during the experiment.

Consider also the following, somewhat more exciting way of determining where I am: If I—without non-negligible fault: *accurately*—aim a rifle at the colored center of a glass ball sitting on a pedestal, then a certain straight line is uniquely picked out: it is determined by the center of the ball and by the point in space where the bead of the rifle is located when it seems to me to coincide both with the center of the ball and with the rifle's rear sight. I—the subject of this action of aiming a rifle and, at the same time, the subject of the visual experience *through which*, so to speak, that action takes place—am somewhere on that line, or at any rate very near to some point on it. But can my location be known more precisely? Yes, it can. Let the former line be recorded (by measuring the coordinates of its determining points), and let me now aim the rifle accurately at the center of another glass ball sitting on a pedestal, so near to the first one that, in aiming the rifle, I do not need to move my head. Hence there is a second aim-line, which is determined in a way completely analogous to the way in which the first aim-line was determined. I am—as long as the aiming lasts—where the two lines intersect, or at any rate within the region where the two lines—and others generated just like them—come nearest to each other.

There are four possible general results: either my location (at a certain time) that is determined by these experiments—by increasing the number of dots on the walls, or the number of acts of aiming the rifle, the accuracy of my localization can be increased to any desired degree—is entirely inside of my body (though possibly encompassing points of its surface), or merely *in*[4] its surface, or entirely outside of my body (though possibly encompassing points of the surface), or partly inside and partly outside of it. In all four cases, I do not spatially coincide with my entire body. Therefore, I am not identical to my body, nor am I identical to a psychophysical unity from which my entire body can be abstracted as its physical constituent (for then, too, I would have to spatially coincide with my body). If I am merely in the surface of my body, or entirely outside of my body, or partly inside and partly outside of it, then it is clear that I cannot be a physical entity. For *nothing physical* that is

---

[4] Though unusual, 'in' is more accurate than 'on' here.

merely in the surface of my body or at least partly outside of that body can be *me*. If I am to be a physical entity, I must be entirely inside of my body. Yet, whatever it is that is physical and occupies the location in my body that the experiments might conceivably determine as my location, it will certainly not be a likely candidate for being *me*. Therefore, wherever I am found to be located by the described experiments, nothing physical located there could with any likelihood be me. I am, therefore, not a physical entity (discounting the possibility that I might be a physical entity that is not located where I am found to be located by the experiments, but somewhere else; regarding this possibility, see below). Hence, since I certainly exist, I exist non-physically (though, of course, *not* independently of my body, not now and, in all likelihood, not ever).

Some, instead of accepting this conclusion, will undoubtedly prefer to conclude that since I am not a physical entity, I do not really exist, but have the same ontological status a center of gravity has: the status of a useful fiction.[5] *For me*, with my subjective certainty of my real existence, this conclusion can hardly be acceptable, of course. But there are some further considerations—which are independent of my physical or nonphysical status—that may also convince other people than me that I really exist. (1) It cannot be denied that it seems to me that I really exist. Hence, if one assumes that I do not really exist, then one must also assume that I am under the illusion that I really exist. But, doubtless, whatever is under an illusion really exists. (2) It is simply not plausible that I do not really exist, since I am operative in carrying out the experiments which determine my location—experiments that depend crucially on how specific aspects in my experimentally prepared environment *visually seem to me* when *I complete doing* certain specific things with my instruments (the marker, the rifle), which *doings are persistently intended by me* to bring about precisely those visual seemings of mine—*doings I persistently direct* so as to make it really happen that *I have these visual seemings* (visual seemings that may, moreover, lead to dramatic consequences, as is evident if I aim my rifle—loaded, with the safety catch off—*and* pull the trigger).

The described experiments are meant to determine my location by determining my *eye-point*, my *center of perspective*, assuming that where my center of perspective is, that there, precisely, I am myself. This might be disputed. Perhaps I am not where my center of perspective is (but am a physical entity after all and located somewhere else). However, these doubts can be allayed. *Perspective* is standardly defined as the art of picturing objects in such a way as to show them as they 'appear to the eye' (with regard to shape).[6] But this definition, *taken literally*, is faulty, for nothing whatever 'appears to the eye,' just as nothing whatever appears to a camera. The perfect definition of perspective—the literal

5 See the views on the self in Dennett (1991).
6 Cf. *Webster's New World Dictionary*, the Second College Edition of 1976.

expression of what is non-literally conveyed by the previous definition—is that perspective is the art of picturing objects in such a way as to show them as they *appear to us from where we are in space*. (Our eyes are instruments necessary for having objects visually appear to us and they are approximately where we are—this is the basis of the metaphorical expression 'as they [objects] appear to the eye.')

It might, finally, be objected that, as a matter of principle, *anything that is literally located in space must be physical*. Therefore, either the experiments do not determine where I am literally located in space, or I am, after all, something physical. Anti-materialists, if they were forced to accept this purported dilemma, would still be happy to embrace its first horn. But the objection flies straight in the face of the fact that the experiments do seem to determine where I am literally located in space, and the fact that at this location no physical entity seems to be available that, with any plausibility, might be me. Clearly, one has a choice here: *either* to stick to the above principle—considering it an a priori premise—*or* to accept the conclusions which the phenomena, straightforwardly interpreted, strongly suggest. I would advocate the latter—also because there are *other* phenomena that point to *strictly analogous* (but not identical) conclusions. These other phenomena are addressed in the next section.

2. WHERE IS THIS ITCH?

Experience is full of illusions. Some of them are actually constitutive of an entire region of experience, of visual experience, say—for example, the all-pervasive visual illusion that certain (actually separate) points coincide, of which the illusion that the moon is a luminous disk that is as big as a silver dollar (or smaller) is just one particular outcome. Pervasive illusions—and illusions that result from pervasive illusions under particular circumstances—are not normally taken notice of by us when we have grown up. Hardly anybody but a child, I suppose, would be fascinated by the illusion that, between tracks seen from a fast-moving train, there is a dirt-colored torrent that runs in opposite direction to the train's movement. But some illusions—non-visual ones—are so extraordinary that one can never fail to notice them as long as one labors under them: phantom itch, phantom pain. The designations 'phantom itch' and 'phantom pain' are somewhat amiss, since phantom itches and phantom pains are real enough—and so are their locations: the person who has a phantom itch or pain can tell (and point to) where the itch sits, or the pain. The only thing *phantom* about phantom itch and phantom pain is this: where these bodily sensations are, there is no human bodily part *in which* they are (but, usually, just thin air), though there seems to be such a part as long as one does not look or (try to) touch; this alone is what makes phantom itch and pain *illusions*.

Phantom itches and phantom pains only bring out in a particular striking manner what holds true of all bodily sensations: Since they are *where* they are, they cannot be physical entities, because, obviously, none of the physical entities (that is, living tissue, cells, nerve-endings—or just molecules of nitrogen, oxygen, and carbon dioxide) that are *where* the bodily sensations are can be identical with them. (The analogy of this reasoning to the reasoning employed in section 1 should be evident.)

Bodily sensations are nonphysical entities; but, of course, they are not independent of the body: without certain physical things going on in the brain of the person who has them, they would not exist. This, however, should not foster the idea that bodily sensations might be identified with those cerebral goings-on. The former cannot be the latter, because the latter do not have the right location for that. I do not have an itch in my brain, I have it in the middle of the palm of my left hand. And I can make the itch go away by rubbing the palm of my left hand. In this, I am fortunate; there is no such easily obtainable relief for the person who experiences a phantom itch.

I and my itch—both nonphysical—are depending for our nonphysical existence on the body, specifically the brain. The difference between my itch and me—*besides* the obvious difference (and its consequences in the given setting): that the itch is an *event* and I a *substance*—is this: the location of my itch is rather distant from its main causal source (the brain), while my own location is rather near to it. Now, the reality of phantom itches suggests the *metaphysical possibility* of *phantom selves*. Like a phantom itch, a phantom self would be real enough—and so would be its location: a phantom self would still see the world (at a time) from *where* it is (at that time). The only thing *phantom* about a phantom self would be this: where this self is, there is no human bodily part *in which* it is (but, say, only thin air).

The ontological coherence of this idea is rather convincingly argued in (Hart 1988). Moreover, if out-of-body experiences *really* occur—out-of-body experiences *in the strong sense,* which are such that the person who undergoes them sees (*veridically* sees) things that it could only have seen from a location, say, a few meters away from her body (such experiences have been alleged by near-death patients)—then the subject that has these experiences is certainly a *real* (and not only a possible) phantom self as long as these experiences last. Further, if the experiments described in Section 1 located me *entirely outside* of my body, my everyday existence would be that of a phantom self (in the described sense)—and this would be our common lot (since there is certainly nothing special about me and what the experiments determine with regard to me).

As this last consideration shows, even a phantom self is not *ipso facto* a self that is independent of the body—just as not even a phantom itch is *ipso facto* an itch that is independent of the body. As a matter of fact, phantom itches and phantom pains—to the extent that their real occurrence is indisputable—depend for their existence on a functioning brain. And the same is more than likely to be true of phantom selves—if there really are such things—even of the phantom selves in out-of-body experiences (taken in the strong sense, if there be such experiences): they would be selves 'with a long tether,' so to speak, but be causally linked to a functioning brain nonetheless. It must, however, be admitted that the nature of the non-local psychophysical causation that would be involved in such phenomena is quite unknown.

3. WHEN I REMOVE MY GLASSES, WHAT HAPPENS?

For some time, I have been sitting and looking fixedly at a white wall with the black silhouette of a human figure on it. Being told to remove my glasses and to keep looking at the wall as before, I do so. Instantly, the silhouette in front of me looks different to me from what it looked when my glasses were still appropriately positioned on my nose. The silhouette looks *blurred* to me. Before I removed my glasses, in contrast, it looked *sharp* to me, although I did not, then, pay any attention to this. I put on my glasses again. Instantly, the *blurredness* goes away and is replaced by the former *sharpness*.

What is the ontologically correct description of what is going on here? It turns out that this description is surprisingly hard to find, for there are several alternative descriptions, all of them with some initial plausibility:

(1) Sharpness and blurredness succeed each other as properties of the silhouette I am looking at: first, this silhouette is *sharp*, then it is *blurred*, then it is *sharp* again—However, it is rather unlikely that the mere removal of my glasses from their customary place, and their subsequent restoration to that place, should have such remarkable effects on the silhouette (four meters in front of me). Moreover, the alleged succession of properties is only observed by *me*, while other observers (needing no glasses) do not perceive it.

(2) It's not that sharpness and blurredness succeed each other as properties of the silhouette, but there is, nonetheless, a succession of properties with regard to the silhouette: *looking sharp to me* and *looking blurred to me* succeed each other as (relational) properties of the silhouette—This is certainly correct, but far from answering all the questions. The main question is this: during the whole episode, is there anything that is first *sharp* (that is, first has the property of *sharpness*), then *blurred* (that is, then has the property of *blurredness*) and then *sharp* again—or is there not?

(3) During the whole episode there is *nothing* that first has the property of sharpness, then the property of blurredness, and then, once more, the property of sharpness—However, this does not seem plausible, since it seems to be clearly the case that *something* that is sharp becomes blurred when I remove my glasses, and becomes sharp again when I put them on again.

(4) During the whole episode *something* has the property of sharpness at first, then the property of blurredness, then the property of sharpness once more. But it is not the silhouette on the wall (cf. (1)); it's my *visual experience*, conceived of as an ongoing process (without an inherent terminus).

(4.1) Alternatively, the matter can also be described as follows: first (in the order of time), there is a section of my visual experience that is sharp, then comes a section of my visual experience that is blurred, and then again comes a section of my visual experience that is sharp.

If (4) and (4.1) are correct descriptions, how do they square with the equally correct description (2)? The general relationship that is relevant to answering this question is captured by the following schema:

(S1) The silhouette looks F_{obj} to me if, and only if, my visual experience[7] of the silhouette is F_{exp}.

This is correct. But the following, similar schema is incorrect (if taken at face value: with the predicate F meaning the same on the left side of the 'iff' and on the right):

(S2) The silhouette looks F to me if, and only if, my visual experience of the silhouette is F.

But, notoriously, predicates are used *homonymously*, first with an *objectival* and then with an *experiential meaning*, to express an (S1)-relationship, making it *seem* as if an (S2)-relationship is being asserted. And equally notoriously, philosophers will point out to the conceptually unwary that they are speaking nonsense. Thus, though the silhouette looks black (or colored, or thin, or . . .) to me, my visual experience of the silhouette is of course not black (or colored, or thin, or . . .). But this does not refute what was really meant: that the silhouette looks $black_{obj}$ (or $colored_{obj}$, or $thin_{obj}$, or . . .) to me if, and only if, my visual experience of it is $black_{exp}$ (or $colored_{exp}$, or $thin_{exp}$, or . . .). Indeed, 'black' and '$black_{obj}$' are synonyms—but not, of course, also 'black' and '$black_{exp}$': 'black' and '$black_{obj}$' each stand for the property of blackness, whereas '$black_{exp}$' stands for that property of my visual experience of the silhouette that makes the silhouette look black to me (that is, makes it seem to me as if the silhouette had the property of blackness—as I have described matters, *correctly so*, since the silhouette was assumed to be black in fact).

Although (S2) is false, it looks as if it had some true instances, for example, the following two:

(S2.1) The silhouette looks blurred to me if, and only if, my visual experience of the silhouette is blurred.

---

[7] Alternatively: '*the current section of* my visual experience . . .'

(S2.2) The silhouette looks sharp to me if, and only if, my visual experience of the silhouette is sharp.

But on, closer inspection, it seems more appropriate to say that in these instances of (S2), too, predicates—'blurred,' respectively 'sharp'—are being used *homonymously* (first in the objectival sense and then in the experiential). Hence, what (S2.1) and (S2.2) are *meant* to say is more adequately expressed as follows:

(S1.1) The silhouette looks blurred$_{obj}$ to me if, and only if, my visual experience of the silhouette is blurred$_{exp}$.

(S1.2) The silhouette looks sharp$_{obj}$ to me if, and only if, my visual experience of the silhouette is sharp$_{exp}$.

Two comments (before I come to the conclusion of this section):

(i) If (S1.1) is to be true, then it is crucial that—other things held constant—we stick to one particular objectival meaning of 'blurred': the one *corresponding* to the experiential effect of removing one's glasses. For it may easily be that the following is *not* true: the silhouette looks to me (for example) *as if it had a ('physically') smeared outline* (that is, looks to me *blurred in another objectival sense* than the one just mentioned) if, and only if, my experience of the silhouette is blurred in the experiential sense heretofore solely considered and held constant (that is, in the sense of the experiential effect of removing one's glasses).

(ii) In the case of 'blurred'—in contrast to the case of 'black'—the experiential meaning seems to be the primary one, such that 'blurred' and 'blurred$_{exp}$' are synonyms and 'blurred$_{obj}$' is a derived predicate (whereas in the case of 'black,' 'black' and 'black$_{obj}$' are synonyms and 'black$_{exp}$' is a derived predicate). For can an object be blurred$_{obj}$ that nobody ever looks at? It seems not. (Note, in contrast, that there is no difficulty in assuming that an object is black$_{obj}$ that nobody ever looks at.)

Now the conclusion: while I sit looking at the white wall with the black silhouette on it and remove my glasses and put them on again, not taking my eyes away from the scene in front of me, something that is sharp$_{exp}$ is caused by this action to become blurred$_{exp}$, and then to become sharp$_{exp}$ again: my visual experience. But no physical entity is caused by this action of mine to become either blurred$_{exp}$ or sharp$_{exp}$. In all of space–time nothing could with any likelihood be physical and become blurred$_{exp}$ or sharp$_{exp}$, brain-events not excluded—although, of course, something physical is happening in my visual cortex that has causally to do with the observed succession of experiential properties and although, indeed, some physical entity—for example, the silhouette—that looks sharp$_{obj}$ to me is caused by the described action of mine to look blurred$_{obj}$ to me and then to look sharp$_{obj}$ again. Hence, my visual experience, an ongoing process, is not a physical entity. Nor can the successive sharp$_{exp}$ and blurred$_{exp}$ and sharp$_{exp}$ sections of my visual experience be physical entities: these sections are events, but physical events cannot be sharp$_{exp}$ or blurred$_{exp}$. In consideration of the fact that I, the subject of my visual experience and of any section thereof, exist nonphysically (see section 1), these results can only be considered *befitting*. As a matter of fact, blurredness, and sharpness—or better: blurredness$_{exp}$ and sharpness$_{exp}$—are straightforward examples of what philosophers have become accustomed to call *qualia*. Nothing physical has qualia. No wonder qualia are denounced as *epistemically inaccessible* ('mysterious') by materialists (implying their ontological dubiousness), but, as I hope the above considerations have shown, quite wrongly so.

Some, rather than accept the nonphysical nature of my visual experience and its sections, will undoubtedly prefer to deny that there is such an ongoing process as visual experience and that there are such events as its sections, which stance is, for example, adopted by Daniel Dennett: see his eliminativist rejection of 'real seemings' in Dennett (1991). But I would urge that straightforward phenomena be not denied. Some philosophers, however, *apparently* do not wish to deny subjective experiential processes and events—episodes of being appeared to in a certain way—but do not wish to admit their existence either; nor can such philosophers be regarded as being agnostics regarding the matter in question. The attitude described seems to be a rather difficult one (to say the least), an attitude that, in the absence of positive evidence, one would not believe that anyone might be attracted to. But in the following quotation it seems to be adopted:

If *A* perceives an object *O*, then there was a perceiving of an *O* by *A*, and *A* had a perception of *O*. But these nominals introduce no new entities other than those already presented by the simpler sentence '*A* perceives *O*'; they merely introduce convenient *façons de parler*, abstractions from the familiar phenomena. This does not mean that there are not really any perceptions (or that pains, tickles or twinges do not really exist, or that there are no hopes or fears). It means that there are, but that they are not 'entities' or kinds of things.   (Bennett and Hacker 2003: 296)

This, on the face of it, is incoherent, since the statements 'there are perceptions (pains, tickles, . . .)' and 'perceptions (pains, tickles, . . .) exist' just means (in ordinary language) that *there are entities* which are perceptions (pains, . . .), respectively, that *entities exist* which are perceptions (pains, . . .). However, I take it what Bennett and Hacker—and other Wittgensteinians who, qua Wittgensteinians, believe in the universal sufficiency and/or necessity of behavioral criteria for the mental—*really* mean to say is simply this: that there really are no such things as *Cartesian perceptions and pains*—namely, perceptions and pains qua subjective experiential episodes (though there are certain *façons de parler* that make it seem otherwise). Just like Dennett, they deny the inner or subjective world (textual evidence for this is ample throughout Bennett and Hacker's book, but can be found especially in chapters 10 and 11).

But one will not be able to do without the assumption of that inner world, since behavioral criteria are neither sufficient nor necessary for perceptions, pains, tickles, twinges, fears, and hopes, while the occurrence of certain subjective experiential episodes is certainly at least *necessary*—that is, at least a *conditio sine qua non*—for all of these things. And this is not an invention of Descartes, but a mere matter of the semantics ('the grammar') of ordinary language. Let me make this plain.

The mind of a solitary woman who lies motionless in the middle of a flowering meadow, deep in the woods, on a sunny day is far from being empty. However, of what is going on in her mind, only the tiniest fraction is shown in her face or posture. She—Lady Jane—*sees* (the blinding light of the sun when her eyes are open, a uniform redness when her eyes are closed); *hears* (the voices of the birds and the sound of the gentle wind); *smells* (the fragrance of flowers and crushed plants); *tastes-and-feels* (her own spittle); *feels tactilely* (the texture of the leaves and stalks of grass and herbs pressing into her thinly clad backside); *feels bodily* (the relative dryness of her mouth, the sun's heat, the relieving instant coolness from the evaporation of her sweat, when one of those light gusts of wind goes over her body); *feels bodily-emotively* (a sharp sexual yearning for John Thomas); *recalls* (details of her last being together with John Thomas); *fears* (that someone might come by and see her who is not John Thomas); *hopes* (that John Thomas will come to her soon); *thinks* (fleetingly about what to tell Clifford, later, when she returns home)—all of this, and much more, is manifestly going on in her mind as she lies motionlessly. And she is still lying motionlessly, her heart pounding in her ears, when, on hearing someone approach through the grass, she feels the experiential kick of the adrenaline that is released into her body: feels as if she is falling into herself, into a bottomless pit which exhales a metallic tasting coolness.

This story is told in ordinary English—a story that offers glimpses of a physical environment and of a subjective mental life (of a 'stream of consciousness') in contact with that environment. A description of behavior does not occur in that story (except rudimentarily; there really is nothing properly behavioral there to be described)—and yet every adult English-speaking reader (I trust) perfectly understands the mental descriptions that occur in it, which descriptions refer to complex inner episodes. They perfectly understand them because they have had inner episodes similar to those described, or can easily imagine having them.[8]

---

[8] Further criticism of Wittgenstein's all too influential ideas on psychological language can be found in Meixner (2004).

4. A DEEP DIFFICULTY

Straightforward phenomena should not be denied. But perhaps the phenomena are not as straightforward as they seem to be. If my visual experience is nonphysical, it yet remains true that it is experience *of* physical entities. Physical entities are, as one is wont to say, *intentional objects* of my (and everyone else's) visual experience. How can this be? Obviously, physical objects cannot literally be parts of something that is nonphysical. But if this tree, for example, is not literally a part of the visual experience in which it appears to me, how, then, am I and, in a more direct way, my experience *intentionally* (in the philosophical sense) related to it? There is a tempting answer to this question: the tree is not literally a part of my experience, but a *representation* of the tree is; this is how I am intentionally related to the tree.

From the days of John Locke (at least) to this day, philosophers and scientists have succumbed to the temptation of *representationalism*, the only modification in the course of time being that representationalism, following the profound change in metaphysical taste during the last century, was adapted to the requirements of materialism. In other words, a neuronal representation of the tree is nowadays held to be a literal part of a certain brain-process, and it is supposed that my seeing the tree—my being in this way intentionally related to it—*consists in* that tree-representation being a part of this brain-process. But all that can be legitimately held on the basis of the empirical data is this: a neuronal causal trace of the tree—a firing-pattern of neurons—is, at the end of a long and complicated causal chain, a literal part of a brain-process *without the occurrence of which* I would not be seeing the tree.

As Edmund Husserl has repeatedly emphasized,[9] in visual experience we are dealing directly with the visually experienced objects themselves, not with representations of them. Note that we *cannot* (on pain of epistemological absurdity) adopt the position that we are merely *thinking* that we are dealing directly with the objects themselves, whereas in reality we are not doing so but are dealing directly only with their representations; for if that were so, the route to total skepticism regarding the physical world would be very short, since we could never, as it were, get behind the screen of representations to check on their veridicality. Representation in some sense—a causal sense, not in the sense of semantic signification—must surely be involved in the causal mechanism that makes visual intentionality possible; but it is not involved in the end-product,

---

[9] A brief account of Husserl's theory of intentionality, and a favorable comparison of it with modern representationalist conceptions (of Fred Dretske and others), can be found in Meixner (2006a).

neither overtly (unless, of course, we are looking at a painting, a photograph, a movie, etc.) nor in a hidden way. But the problem how physical objects can be intentional objects of nonphysical visual experience is still with us. That nonphysical images of physical objects are, in a literal sense, parts of experience fails to do the trick, hardly less so than the idea that the object themselves are, in a literal sense, parts of experience. What else can do the trick?

Husserl, without his ontological idealism, may be our inspiration here. The following ideas are essentially Husserlian.[10] Visual experience is the nonphysical medium *through which* (by the organization of its *hyletic* content) the physical objects of vision—normally existent, but sometimes non-existent—are intentionally attained, visually grasped, so to speak. But that grasp is always only partial: the physical objects of vision always *transcend* the visual experiences, since these experiences *give* or *present* (*not* represent) those objects only in a perspectival, aspectual manner, in other words: always give or present only a *moment* or *side*, an abstract part of them (an *Abschattung*, says Husserl). In *perspectival presence* and in the transcendence of perspectival presence—a transcendence, indeed, that is implied at each moment by the perspectival presence itself—physical objects are the intentional objects of nonphysical visual experience.

5. I, THE SAME YESTERDAY, TODAY, AND TOMORROW

Yesterday, I did U and felt V; today, I do W and feel X; tomorrow, I will do Y and feel Z. This is shown by experience to be true for many U, V, W, X, Y, and Z, and for many dates of temporal reference. Experience also shows it to be true *in the straightforward sense*, namely, *without* a temporal counterpart of me[11]—of *now-me*, as it were—or a temporal part (stage) of me[12]—of *me-the-temporal-aggregate*, so to say—being required for its truth to do U or Y or feel V or Z. The next question is *how* the first sentence of this section can be true in this straightforward sense. Clearly, for that sentence to be true in the straightforward sense, I must be able to exist as numerically the same entity yesterday, today, and tomorrow, without needing temporal parts or counterparts for this. What must be my nature if I am to be able to exist in this way?

First, there must be a certain *analogy* between me and existing universals, for example, the property of being human. Clearly, that property is able to exist—that is: to be exemplified by something existing—as numerically the same entity yesterday, today, and tomorrow, without needing temporal parts or counterparts for this. And in fact, that property existed yesterday, exists today, and will exist tomorrow *without having* either temporal parts or temporal counterparts—just like me.

---

[10] See Husserl (1966).   [11] Temporal counterparts are explored in Meixner (2002).
[12] For advocacy of this approach, see Lewis (1986), for example.

Second, there must be a certain *disanalogy* between me and existing universals, the example being again the property of being human. That property can be, and is, exemplified (every human being is an exemplifier of it), while *I* neither am exemplified nor can be. The simple truth of the matter is that the property of being human is a universal, and hence can be exemplified, while *I* am not a universal but an *individual*, and hence cannot be exemplified.

An individual that in its manner of existence through time is analogous to existing universals may be called an *endurant*.[13] I am an *endurant*; this has been established in the three previous paragraphs. I am, moreover, a *subject of experience and action*. This, too, has already been established: it is certainly true that yesterday I did *U* and felt *V*, that today I do *W* and feel *X*. An endurant that is a subject of experience and action has every right to be called a *sentient agent-substance*. Hence, I am a sentient agent-substance—and a nonphysical one at that, as was shown in section 1.

What is the basis of my nonphysical existence as a sentient agent-substance, or in other words: as an endurant that is a subject of experience and action? As is known, no atom in my body is part of my body during the entire span of my existence. Hence the basis of my *endurance* cannot be purely material. It is known that a certain structure is maintained in my brain during the entire time of my existence; if that structure is no longer there, I have ceased to exist (in all likelihood), even though my body, with outward assistance, may yet go on living for a long time. But that structure is a complex universal that, in principle, is capable of *multiple exemplifications*. Hence the basis of my endurance—of my being an *enduring individual*—cannot be purely structural (or formal) either.

Clearly, the basis of my nonphysical existence as a sentient agent-substance is, so to speak, *material-formal* (or *formal-material*). But this, by itself, does certainly not answer all the important questions. One would—or at any rate *should*—like to know the nomological foundation of the causal potential of the basis of my nonphysical existence as an enduring subject of experience and action, in other words: the psychophysical laws that made *my existence* come about when the world took a singular turn and prepared the basis for this existence. But, so far, that nomological foundation is in its entirety *terra incognita*.

Moreover, the union of *this* matter—a certain huge collection of atoms—with *this* form—a certain mind-bogglingly complex manner of arranging atoms in space—first brought forth the physical object in which my nonphysical existence as a sentient agent-substance was, so to speak, *kindled*, in accordance with the psychophysical laws of nature. Now, if, say, after a fairly long time but still within my span of existence, *those* atoms and *that* manner of arrangement were miraculously brought together again, then, *in a sense*,[14] the very same physical

---

13 The source of this terminology is Mark Johnston, as is indicated in Lewis (1986: 202).

14 The emphasis is appropriate: remember *the Ship of Theseus*. Would the ship rebuilt from the old parts that were collected and safely stored over many years be the Ship of Theseus? *In a sense*,

object would be reconstituted that had once been brought forth already. But the *soul* that would be kindled in that physical object would certainly not be *me* (since, obviously, it would not be where I am at the time); rather, it would be *comparable* to the soul of a belated identical twin of mine.[15] What, then, *individuates* me? The answer is ready at hand: the place-and-time of my origin is essential for my individuation; equivalently, my temporally specified history is essential for my individuation. Therefore, *this* origin (or *this* history), in addition to *this* matter and *this* form, are needed to differentiate me from every other soul.[16]

6. IS THIS CARTESIANISM?

Yes and no. Yes, since what I have been arguing for in this chapter has some, not inessential aspects in common with Cartesianism. No, since (1) Cartesianism makes some substantial claims that are not condoned in this chapter; and (2) some substantial claims are made in this chapter that contradict Descartes or are entirely outside of his ken.

Against (what they regarded to be) the suspicion of being guilty of dualism, various philosophers have reacted—in conversation with me—with the bizarre claim that they are not dualists but *pluralists*. Presumably, this is directed against the Cartesian dichotomy, according to which every *res* is either *cogitans* or *extensa*. But, in a perfectly straightforward sense, even a dualist like Descartes is a pluralist. For Descartes did not teach that *cogitans* and *extensa* are the only subdivisions of the domain of *res*: doubtless there are, also for Descartes, among the *res extensae* such that are *alive* and such that are *not*. Hence there are, also for Descartes, at least three kinds of *res*: *cogitans*, *extensa et vivens*, *extensa et non-vivens*. Evidently, Descartes, too, is a pluralist (indeed, how could he not be a pluralist?)—and yet he is a dualist.

This being said on behalf of Descartes, it should be noted that the kind of dualism here advocated is *not* a dichotomous dualism in the Cartesian tradition. It is *not* claimed that every entity is either mental or physical (for this, in my eyes, is obviously false: the number 0 is neither mental nor physical). Nor is it claimed that everything mental is nonphysical, because, for making such a claim,

---

yes. But in another sense, no. Consider that there is *another* ship, a ship afloat: the ship from which the parts were gradually taken and replaced by new ones. That ship has as at least as good a right to be the Ship of Theseus as the rebuilt ship.

[15] But note that, normally, even identical twins are built from *entirely distinct* collections of atoms. Clearly, more than just identical twinhood is involved in this doppelganger scenario. In Peter van Inwagen's more dramatic version of the thought-experiment, the man is confronted with the reconstituted boy, each claiming—apparently with equal justification—that he is Peter van Inwagen; see van Inwagen (1997).

[16] The usefulness of the concept of *soul*, also for scientific purposes, is defended in Meixner (2006c) and in greater depth and detail in Meixner (2004).

the meaning of the word 'mental' is far too fuzzy (in the obnoxious manner that makes every precisification look more or less arbitrary). I claim, however, that *some existing mental entities are nonphysical entities* (or, a different way to say the same thing, that *there exist nonphysical mental entities*). And this is the thesis that I stipulate be here referred to by the designation 'psychophysical dualism,' or 'dualism' for short (no other dualism than psychophysical dualism can be meant in the present context). Moreover, in order to dissociate the discussion in the philosophy of mind from misleading historical baggage (which has been a vast disadvantage for dualists in the struggle with materialism), I *recommend as a general practice* that psychophysical dualism be taken to consist in the thesis that some existing mental entities are nonphysical entities, nothing more and nothing less.[17]

This thesis of psychophysical dualism is vague also to the extent that the term 'physical' remains unanalyzed. I will not here offer such an analysis, but proceed on the assumption that the term in question is sufficiently well understood. A few elementary remarks, however, are absolutely necessary in order to avoid confusion:

(i) 'Physical' may mean (1) *entirely (or purely) physical*; or (2) *at least partly physical*; correspondingly, 'nonphysical' may mean (1) *at least partly nonphysical*; or (2) *entirely (or purely) nonphysical*. Obviously, *nonphysical$_1$* is the negation of *physical$_1$*, *nonphysical$_2$* the negation of *physical$_2$*. In all purely ontological contexts of this chapter, 'physical' (if occurring without the mentioned modifiers) is to be taken in the sense of 'physical$_2$' and 'nonphysical' (if occurring without the mentioned modifiers) in the sense of 'nonphysical$_2$.'

(ii) 'Physical' is, taken literally, an ontological term, but it can also be used in an analogical sense, for example, as a semantic term when speaking of 'physical predicates.' Interestingly, the distinction made in (i) is also valid for the semantic use of 'physical.' Thus, by saying that a predicate is physical, one can mean (1) that it is a *purely physical* predicate: that it has a *purely physical meaning* (this latter phrase containing another analogical application of the term 'physical'); or (2) that it is an *at least partly physical* predicate: that it has an *at least partly physical meaning*. Below, 'physical' will be used semantically (hence analogically) with the *first* of the two meanings just indicated.

Perhaps some may worry that the suggested conception of (basic) psychophysical dualism is, regarding propositional (or logical) content, too weak to be interesting. But it is easily seen that this is not so. The label 'dualism' is well-deserved by the thesis that is proposed to express psychophysical dualism, since that thesis entails that there is a nonphysical side of being—a *second* and *complementary* side, since

---

[17] A detailed discussion of the question of what is to be understood by the designation 'psychophysical dualism' can be found in Meixner (2004).

it can be taken for granted that there is also a *physical* side of being and that every entity is either physical or nonphysical. Materialists (or, to use the modern term, physicalists), though they take themselves to be opposed to 'dualism,' often do not have a clear idea of what they take themselves to be opposed to. If it turned out, on reflection, that they take their own position *not* to be opposed to the thesis that some existent mental entity is nonphysical, then one may well wonder whether their position can properly (or honestly) be called 'materialistic.'[18]

That psychophysical dualism consists in the indicated thesis does of course *not* preclude that it can be *enriched* in all sorts of ways; *one* such enrichment of psychophysical dualism is Cartesian dualism; *another* such enrichment is the kind of psychophysical dualism that I have defended in this chapter on empirical grounds. I call this dualism 'empirical dualism.'

Both according to empirical dualism and Cartesian dualism, I am an existent nonphysical mental substance (*mental* I am qua being a subject of experience). And both according to empirical dualism and Cartesian dualism, my experiences are existent nonphysical mental events (although, it must be noted, *event-dualism* is not as explicit in Descartes' work as substance-dualism; event-dualism can, however, be rather effortlessly distilled from his main work, the *Meditations*).

Descartes is notorious for not according the status of (dualistically conceived) mentality to other than human animals. Empirical data show, however, that he was wrong in this: experience—which cannot be without a subject of experience, which subject, in turn, is more than likely to function also a subject of action—is widespread throughout the animal kingdom.[19]

Since the time Cartesian dualism made its appearance on the stage of the history of philosophy, many have felt that psychophysical dualism is burdened with a huge load of demands for *explanation*—a load so heavy that psychophysical dualism can only sink under it. For this overly critical attitude, empirical ignorance is in part responsible, and in part philosophical unfairness. Even Descartes himself asserted that the body is very closely joined to the self or soul—*mihi valde arcte coniunctum est*.[20] Knowing next to nothing about psychophysical correlations, Descartes was, like everyone else for a long time to come, not in a position to make good on this assertion. But it is true, nonetheless, that body and soul, though distinct, are very closely joined, so closely as to form

---

[18] The point just made is urged in Meixner (2005 and 2008a).

[19] An evolutionary explanation of this is provided in Meixner (2006b) and in greater depth and detail—embedded in a theory of *decision makers*—in Meixner (2004). Objections are answered in Meixner (2008b).

[20] See *Meditations*, VI: 9. It is worth mentioning that Descartes explicitly distances himself from that ancient analogy—see Aristotle's query in *De anima*, II: 1; Thomas Aquinas in *S. c. G*, II: 57, connects the analogy doctrinally with Plato—which even to these days is thought to be representative of substance-dualism: *the-navigator-in-the-ship analogy*. Descartes: 'Docet etiam natura, per istos sensus doloris, famis, sitis &c., me non tantum adesse meo corpori ut nauta adest navigio, sed illi arctissime esse conjunctum & quasi permixtum adeo ut unum quid cum illo componam' (*Meditations*, VI: 13; quoted from Descartes (1986)).

a *unified entity*—still an *unum quid* (compare the quotation from Descartes in footnote 20), though not the *unity* that the psychophysical *unitarians* assume the human person to be (see below). And for the first time in human history we are beginning to be able to *show* that Descartes' assertion is true. With the increasing amount of knowledge about psychophysical correlations, the feeling that psychophysical dualism unduly separates the mental and the physical—to the point that, absurdly, the two seem to have nothing whatever to do with each other, that there seems to be an unbridgeable gulf between them—is bound to diminish. Of course, this positive effect of increasing empirical knowledge will only be felt by those who give dualism a chance to begin with, and do not safeguard themselves against it by philosophical unfairness.

What is it, in particular, that I mean by 'philosophical unfairness' here? It is philosophically unfair—and misguided—to demand explanations that go beyond the indication of lawful correlations, and then to complain that psychophysical dualism can't provide such explanations, and then to urge that psychophysical dualism must, therefore, be discarded. One might as well demand an explanation of gravity that goes beyond the indication of the precise lawful correlation between the masses of physical objects and their distance from each other on the one hand, and the gravitational force they exert on each other on the other. No such explanation is forthcoming (the general theory of relativity does *not* provide it). Does this make it incumbent upon us to give up the idea that a physical object and its gravitational field are distinct entities (insofar as they could, metaphysically (*not* nomologically), each exist, such as they are in themselves, without the other)? Certainly not. And in fact nobody is complaining that physics is making a misplaced mystery out of the relationship between material objects and their gravitational fields just by considering them distinct entities (in the indicated sense). *Neither* should anyone complain that dualism makes a misplaced mystery out of the relationship between certain living bodies and *their mental fields*, so to speak, just by considering them distinct entities (insofar as they could, metaphysically (*not* nomologically), each exist, such as they are in themselves, without the other).

Another frequent complaint against Cartesian-type psychophysical dualism—and empirical dualism, though not Cartesian, is certainly of Cartesian type—is the complaint that it makes the direct and literal ascription of physical predicates to, for example, *me* impossible. But, first, this is not invariably impossible: as we have seen, a predicate of being at a certain spatial location (at a certain time) can be literally and directly ascribed to *me*, although I am a nonphysical entity. Second, with regard to other cases, where indeed a physical predicate cannot be literally and directly ascribed to me, which predicate, however, one would nevertheless want to ascribe to me (for example, 'to have a mass of 85 kg'), it should be remembered that nothing is wrong with the following biconditional:

I [analogically] φ if, and only if, my body [literally] φs—for all physical predicates φ that cannot be literally and directly ascribed to me.

The empirical dualist takes this biconditional to formulate a rule of analogical predication, which governs the analogical and indirect (that is, secondary) ascription of physical predicates to me that cannot literally and directly (that is, in the primary way) be ascribed to me, but which one would nevertheless want to ascribe to me. For the empirical dualist, the analogical ascription of such predicates is good enough.

It should be noted that for those materialists who identify me with my body the above biconditional is not a rule of analogical predication, but, *for all predicates* φ, a consequence of Leibniz's Law: the predicate-ascriptions on both sides of the biconditional are regarded as literal and direct. Those materialists, however, who identify me with my brain or some part thereof are also forced to resort to analogical ascriptions, according to the rule of analogical predication stated above (but now being referred to the context that is created by *their hypothesis* about my nature); for the predicate 'to have a mass of 85 kg,' which one would want to ascribe to me, obviously cannot be literally and directly be ascribed to me if I am my brain or some part thereof. Finally, for those who take me to be a psychophysical unity, the above biconditional is also not a rule of analogical predication, but nevertheless *true for all physical predicates* φ, with the predicate-ascriptions being literal and direct on both sides of the biconditional. Like the *body-materialist*—but unlike the *brain-materialist*—the *psychophysical unitarian*[21] believes that my mass is as literally and directly 85 kg as the mass of my body is literally and directly 85 kg. This may seem a very attractive option. However, its attractiveness cannot suffice to dislodge empirical dualism, which can speak of my mass being 85 kg only in an analogical and secondary way, but nevertheless *can speak of it*. It cannot suffice in consideration of the fact that empirical observations (see section 1) show me to be literally *where* neither body-materialists nor brain-materialists, nor psychophysical unitarians have any means—either analogical or literal ones—of saying truly that I am *there*.

Besides predicates that are physical—that is: *purely* physical—there are predicates that are indeed not physical, but not psychological—that is: *purely* psychological—either; this is just a matter of the semantics of ordinary language. The most important one of these predicates is truthfully ascribed to me in the next sentence. *I am a human being.* For materialists, 'human being' can only be a physical predicate after all, meaning as much as the predicate 'human body.' Then, 'human being' can be literally and truthfully ascribed to me according to the body-materialist (because it is literally true that my body—which I

---

[21] Modern hylemorphists like to see themselves as psychophysical unitarians—and Thomas Aquinas as well (for example, Klima (2007)), which, however, does not quite seem to do justice to the historical truth. An epitome of modern psychophysical unitarianism, in any case, is P. M. S. Hacker. Psychophysical unitarianism is *not* a monism (since psychophysical unitarians will acknowledge that there also exist purely physical entities), and it is *not* a form of psychophysical dualism either (since psychophysical unitarians will deny that there exist nonphysical—that is, *purely* nonphysical—mental entities).

am identical to, according to the body-materialists—is a human body), not, however, according to the brain-materialist (obviously). But is it true that 'human being' is a *physical* predicate, or that it should be taken to be such a predicate? Psychophysical unitarians deny this—rightly. For them, 'is a human being' logically entails 'is a psychophysical unity.' Psychophysical dualists do not quite follow the unitarians in this, although 'human being' is, of course, also for dualists not a physical predicate, and although, normally, it is for them not a psychological predicate either (an exception being Plato and his followers—at least in the eyes of Thomas Aquinas;[22] in their own way, *such* dualists contradict the conceptual framework of ordinary language as much as the materialists do). For dualists (leaving aside Aquinas's Platonic dualists), 'is a human being' logically entails *only* 'is a *unified* entity of *physis* and *psyche*,'[23] and *not* 'is a psychophysical *unity*.' However, the dualistic conceptual option does remain within the bounds of the semantics of ordinary language (the naturalness of dualism within natural language is, as a rule, grossly underestimated by unitarian Wittgensteinians, like P. M. S. Hacker). Moreover, the dualistic option seems to be better adapted than the unitarian one to what the empirical phenomena (some of which have been described in this chapter) tell us about *us*—so much better that we can well accept that 'human being' is only being analogically and indirectly ascribed to me when I say of myself 'I am a human being,' my *literal* meaning being that I am the nonphysical substantial core of a *unified* entity of *physis* and *psyche* that is of human kind.

---

[22] See *S. c. G.*, II: 57, 'Plato posuit quod homo non sit aliquid compositum ex anima et corpore: sed quod ipsa anima utens corpore sit homo.'

[23] It should be carefully noted that it is, according to Cartesian as well as empirical dualists, essential (that is, *conceptually existence-essential*) for a human being to be a *unified* entity of physis and psyche: it is conceptually (and hence metaphysically) impossible for a human being to exist without being such an entity. This does not mean, however, that it is essential for the physis and the psyche of a human being to be unified and constitute the unified entity which is a human being: according to Cartesian as well as empirical dualists, it is metaphysically (and hence conceptually) possible for the psyche, and for the physis, of a human being to exist without being a constituent of any human being. (For my views on essentiality and on metaphysical and conceptual (im)possibility, see Meixner (2006d).)

22

Substance Dualism: A Non-Cartesian Approach

E. J. Lowe

Substance dualism in the philosophy of mind is, naturally enough, commonly thought of on a Cartesian model, according to which it is a dualism of two radically different kinds of substance, one (the 'body') purely material and the other (the 'mind') wholly immaterial in nature. This view is subject to many familiar difficulties. However, the almost universal rejection of Cartesian substance dualism has blinded many philosophers to the possibility of formulating other and more plausible versions of substance dualism. Non-Cartesian substance dualism (NCSD), as it may most perspicuously be called, is a dualism not of *minds* and bodies, but of *persons*—or, more generally, of *subjects of experience*—and their 'organized' bodies. This is an ontological distinction that is chiefly motivated not by some fanciful notion that there could be disembodied persons—although NCSD does not rule out that possibility—but by much more solid considerations which require us, for instance, to distinguish between the *identity-conditions* of persons and their bodies. Much of the intuitive appeal of Cartesian dualism is retained and explained by NCSD, without any of the former's counterintuitive features and metaphysical difficulties. NCSD is, however, still a *non-materialist* position, because it is incompatible even with very weak forms of non-reductive physicalism. In what follows, I shall begin, in section 1, by explaining and justifying NCSD's distinctive ontology of persons, before moving on, in section 2, to present and argue for its novel anti-physicalist account of the metaphysics of mental causation.

1. NCSD'S ONTOLOGY OF PERSONS

1.1. Non-Cartesian Substance Dualism Defined

Dualism in the philosophy of mind is customarily divided into two chief kinds: *substance* dualism and *property* dualism, the former maintaining the distinctness of mental and physical *substances* and the latter maintaining the distinctness of mental and physical *properties*. But what are we supposed to understand by a mental or physical 'substance' in this context? I shall take it that by a *substance*, here, we should simply mean an *individual object*, or *bearer of properties*. I shall further take it that by a *mental* substance we should mean a bearer of mental or psychological properties, and that by a *physical* substance we should mean a bearer of physical properties. Thus, whereas the property dualist holds that mental and physical properties are distinct, the substance dualist *additionally* holds that certain *bearers* of those properties are distinct—the implication being that substance dualism entails property dualism but not *vice versa*. I assume, incidentally, that both kinds of dualism entail dualism with regard to mental and physical *states* and *events*, since I take these to consist in the exemplification of properties by objects at times.[1] All this being so, what is needed at this point is a defensible account of the two key concepts of a *mental* property and a *physical* property. These, it seems clear, are distinct *concepts*, although whether the *properties* of which they are concepts are themselves distinct is, of course, one of the main issues under dispute. However, it is one thing to say that these concepts are distinct and quite another to provide an account of that conceptual distinction that would satisfy everyone. In fact, it has proved remarkably difficult to produce an uncontentious characterization of either concept.[2] Fortunately, it is much easier to provide *paradigm examples* of mental and physical properties that almost all parties to the debate will be happy to accept as such. For instance, *pain* and *desire* are universally recognized as being mental properties, while *mass* and *velocity* are universally recognized as being physical properties. In what follows, therefore, I shall take it for granted that the conceptual distinction now at issue is a genuine one and that for practical purposes it can be captured by appeal to such paradigm examples.

Now, substance dualists contend that certain bearers of mental properties, such as pain and desire, are distinct from—that is, are not to be *identified* with—certain bearers of physical properties, such as mass and velocity. What *are* these 'bearers,' though? The bearers of mental properties may be called, quite generally, *subjects of experience*—understanding 'experience' here in a broad sense, to include not just sensory and perceptual experience, but also introspective and cognitive states or, in other words, 'inner' awareness and thoughts.[3] *Human persons*—we ourselves—provide prime examples of subjects of experience, but no doubt we should also include examples drawn from the 'higher' reaches of the non-human animal domain. As for the bearers of *physical* properties, for the purposes of the present discussion I shall mostly be referring to *bodies*, or

---

[1] See Kim (1980).   [2] See Crane and Mellor (1990).
[3] See further Lowe (1996: chapter 1).

parts of bodies—on the understanding that what we are talking about here are not mere lumps or masses of matter, but *organized* bodies and their parts, the paradigm examples being the human body and its organic parts, such as the brain and the neurons and other kinds of cell making up the brain and central nervous system. In these terms, then, the substance dualist may be construed as holding that a person is not to be identified with his or her body, nor with any part of it, such as the brain. On this view, a *person—not* the person's body or brain—feels pain and has desires, even if it is true to say that a person feels pain or has desires *only because* his or her body or brain is in a certain physical state. The physical state in question—a certain pattern of excitation in nerve cells, say—is not to be *identified* with the pain or desire consequently experienced by the person, according to the substance dualist. It is at this point that I want to introduce a key distinction between two different types of substance dualism. An implication of what I have said so far concerning substance dualism might seem to be that, according to it, a bearer of mental properties—a subject of experience—*only* bears mental properties, whereas a bearer of physical properties, such as a human body or brain, *only* bears physical properties. This was indeed the view of the most famous substance dualist of all, René Descartes, for whom the human self or ego is an *immaterial* substance.[4] However, even if I am distinct from—not to be identified with—my body or any part of it, as Descartes held, it does not automatically follow that I can have only mental, not physical properties. And, indeed, there is a modern form of substance dualism—which may be called, aptly enough, *non-Cartesian substance dualism*—which differs from Cartesian substance dualism precisely over this point. According to NCSD, it is *I*, and *not* my body or any part of it, who am the bearer of mental properties, just as Descartes maintained. However, unlike Descartes, the advocate of NCSD does not make the further claim that I am not the bearer of any physical properties whatsoever. This sort of substance dualist may maintain that I possess certain physical properties *in virtue of* possessing a body that possesses those properties: that, for instance, I have a certain *shape* and *size* for this reason, and that for this reason I have a certain *velocity* when my body moves.[5] It doesn't follow that such a substance dualist should allow that *every* physical property possessed by my body is also possessed by me, however, for the possession of some of these properties may entail that the thing possessing them is a *body*—and the advocate of NCSD wants to deny, of course, that I am a body. One such property, for instance, would appear to be the property of being *wholly composed of bodily parts*, which is possessed by my body but presumably not by me.

---

4 See Descartes (1985a) and, for prominent modern sympathizers, Swinburne (1986) and Foster (1991).
5 Compare Lowe (1996: chapter 2), and also Baker (2000).

1.2. The Inadequacy of Neo-Cartesian Arguments for Substance Dualism

Setting aside, for the time being, the distinction between Cartesian and non-Cartesian substance dualism, what sorts of arguments can be advanced in favour of such dualism, and how good are they? Some of the best-known arguments have been inherited from Descartes himself and hence their contemporary versions may be described as 'neo-Cartesian.' Two neo-Cartesian arguments in particular are worthy of consideration: the argument from the conceivability of disembodiment and the argument from the indivisibility of the self. For brevity's sake, I shall call them the *conceivability argument* and the *indivisibility argument* respectively.

The conceivability argument has both a strong and weak version, the difference in strength being a difference in the strength of their premises—that is to say, the premises of the strong version of the argument entail those of the weak version, but not *vice versa*. That being so, one might suppose that the weak version is to be preferred, because it assumes less. The *weak* version may be reconstructed as follows.

(1) It is clearly and distinctly conceivable that I should exist without possessing a body.

(2) What is clearly and distinctly conceivable is possible. Hence,

(3) It is possible that I should exist without possessing a body.

(4) If it is possible that I should exist without possessing a body, then I must be distinct from my body. Therefore,

(5) I am distinct from my body.

The *strong* version of the argument replaces premise (1) by

(1*) It is clearly and distinctly conceivable that I should exist without any body whatever existing,

which clearly entails (1).[6] The historical source of (1*) is, of course, Cartesian doubt about the very existence of the physical world in its entirety—a doubt which at least appears to be coherent and therefore to describe a possible state of affairs. As I say, one might suppose the weak version of the argument to be preferable to the strong version because it assumes less. However, it could be contended that (1) is only plausible, or at least is most plausible, in the context of (1*), on the grounds that it is difficult to conceive of oneself as existing in a disembodied state save under the hypothesis that the existence of the entire physical world is an illusion.

Whether we consider the strong or the weak version of the conceivability argument, it presents certain difficulties. Particularly controversial is premise

---

6 Compare Meixner (2004: chapter 3).

(2), that what is clearly and distinctly conceivable is possible.[7] Let us grant the truth of premise (1*), that it is clearly and distinctly conceivable that I should exist without any body whatever existing, basing this claim on the coherence of Cartesian doubt about the existence of the physical world. The content of such doubt is something like this: Perhaps, for all that I know, the entire physical world as it seems to be presented to me in perception is non-existent and that perception is wholly illusory. This is a doubt about the nature of the *actual* world, amounting to a surmise that the actual world contains no physical objects although it does contain me and my mental states. I am inclined to think that the surmise is at least a coherent, or logically consistent one. But the question is whether this is enough to establish that there is a possible world in which I and my mental states exist but no physical objects exist. Of course, if the surmise is *correct*, then the actual world is just such a world. But we are not given that the surmise is correct, only that it is *coherent*. To this it may be replied that it suffices that the surmise *could* be correct—it doesn't have actually to *be* correct. But the trouble, I think, is that *we simply don't know* whether or not it could be correct, because there may, for all we know, be some reason why it *couldn't* be correct—a reason that we haven't yet thought of. For instance, it might be that there simply couldn't be a world containing no physical objects, whether or not it also contained me and my mental states.

We might sum up this response to the conceivability argument by saying that the trouble with premise (2) is that it illicitly conflates 'real' or *metaphysical* possibility with mere *epistemic* possibility. That is to say, (2) together with either (1) or (1*) does not serve to ground the truth of (3), that it is *possible* that I should exist without possessing a body, in the requisite sense of 'possible.' The most that can be established by these means is that I *might* actually exist without possessing a body, in an epistemic sense of 'might.' This is the sense of 'might' in which we can say, for instance, that there *might* be an even number greater than 2 which is not the sum of two prime numbers, because we don't know whether or not Goldbach's conjecture is true. But in the *metaphysical* sense of 'necessary', it is either *necessarily the case* or else *necessarily not the case* that every even number greater than 2 is the sum of two prime numbers, so the matter is not in this sense a contingent one. Likewise, then, we cannot assume that it is a contingent matter whether or not I possess a body just because it is true that, in the epistemic sense, I *might or might not* possess a body.

Let me pass on now, rather briefly, to the *indivisibility argument*. This may be reconstructed as follows.

(6) I contain no parts into which I am divisible.

(7) My body is composed of parts.

Therefore, (5) I am distinct from my body.

---

[7] For well-informed discussion of this issue, see Gendler and Hawthorne (2002).

I take it that (7) is uncontentiously true. Premise (6), however, may appear to be straightforwardly question-begging, since it simply denies that I possess a property that (7) uncontentiously attributes to my body—namely, the property of being a composite entity—and hence, it may be said, already presumes the truth of the conclusion, (5), that I and my body are distinct. Certainly, if the indivisibility argument is to acquire any persuasive force, an independent reason needs to be advanced in support of premise (6). My own view, I should at once declare, is that premise (6) is indeed *true*, but that the most plausible argument for its truth requires (5) as a premise, so that (6) cannot without circularity be appealed to in an argument for the truth of (5). If (5) is to be successfully argued for, then, we need to look elsewhere than to the indivisibility argument. I shall suggest an alternative shortly. What we can conclude so far, however, is that neither of the two neo-Cartesian arguments for substance dualism that we have just examined is particularly compelling.

1.3. An argument for the simplicity of persons

Now I need to explain my chief reason for thinking (6) to be true, that is, for holding *myself*—and, by the same token, any other person—to be a *simple* or *non-composite* entity. This is that I consider the following argument—and note that its first premise includes (5) as a conjunct—to be not just valid but sound.[8]

(8) I am not identical with my body nor with any part of it.

(9) If I am composed of parts, then all of those parts must be parts of my body.

(10) Anything that is wholly composed of parts of my body must either itself be a part of my body or else be identical with my body as whole. Hence,

(11) I am a simple entity, not composed of any parts.

(11), notice, is just another way of expressing (6). The crucial premise here is, of course, (8), to which I shall return shortly. As for premise (9), this should be uncontentious in the context of a debate between substance dualism and its physicalist opponents, since those opponents will naturally agree with (9), holding as they do that I am identical with my body or some part of it, such as my brain. Premise (10) seems equally uncontentious—but more of that in a moment. I should acknowledge, however, that not *all* substance dualists will be happy to assert premise (9). Some, for instance, adopt the following view of the self: they hold that I am distinct from—not identical with—my body, but am *composed* of it and another, immaterial entity, my *soul*. On this view, I am a *body–soul composite*.[9] Such a composite is still a 'substance'—that is, an

---

[8] For a fuller account, see Lowe (2001).
[9] For discussion and criticism, see Olson (2001) and Kim (2001).

individual object or property-bearer—but one which, in violation of premise (9), contains both parts of my body *and something else*, my soul, as parts. Indeed, Descartes himself sometimes writes as if he endorses this view. I can only say that I find it implausible and unattractive myself.

Another kind of substance dualist will reject premise (10), holding that I am wholly composed of parts of my body and yet am not identical with any part of it nor with my body as a whole. This kind of substance dualist sees the relation between me and my body as being analogous to that between a bronze statue and the lump of bronze of which it is made. On this view, I am *constituted by*, but not identical with, my body.[10] And, indeed, the example of the bronze statue may be seen as posing a threat to a generalized version of (10). For doesn't it show that it simply *isn't true* that anything that is wholly composed of parts of an object *O* must either itself be a part of *O* or else be identical with *O* as a whole? For *the bronze statue*, it may be said, is wholly composed of parts of *the lump of bronze* and yet is neither itself a part of the lump of bronze nor identical with the lump of bronze as a whole. However, here a great deal turns on the question of how, precisely, we are to understand the assertion that the bronze statue is 'wholly composed of parts of the lump of bronze.' If the assertion is taken to mean that we can *decompose* the statue into parts all of which, without remainder, are parts of the lump of bronze, then it is certainly true. For we can decompose the statue into bronze particles, all of which are parts of the lump. But if, instead, the assertion is taken to mean that *all of the parts of the statue are also parts of the lump of bronze*—which is, *mutatis mutandis*, the interpretation that I was assuming in proposing premise (10)—then it is far from evident that it is true. For example: the *head* of the statue—assuming it to be a statue of a man—is a part of the statue and yet is not, plausibly, a part of the lump of bronze.[11]

However, is it not open to the constitution theorist to *agree*, now, with premise (10), interpreted in the manner I intend and instead reject premise (9), although not for the same reason that this was rejected by the proponent of the body–soul composite theory? Cannot the constitution theorist say that, just as the statue has parts, such as its head, that are not parts of the lump of bronze, so *I* have parts that are not parts of my body—but not because I have any *immaterial* part or parts, any more than the statue has? In principle, I agree, the constitution theorist *could* say this. However, I simply don't see what these 'additional' parts could at all plausibly *be*. The reason why the statue has parts that are not parts of the lump of bronze is that it has parts—such as its head—that are, like the statue, *constituted by*, but not identical with, a portion of bronze. If, analogously, I were to have parts that are not parts of my body, they would have to be parts that are *constituted by*, but not identical with, parts of my body—just as, according to the constitution theorist, *I* am constituted by my body as a whole. But there are, surely, *no* such parts of me—no parts of me that are related to parts of my

<hr>

[10] See especially Baker (2000).   [11] See further Lowe (2001).

body in the way that I am related to my body as a whole. As a self or subject of experience, I do not, for example, have lesser or subordinate selves or subjects as parts of me, each of them associated with different parts of my body—as though I were a kind of collective or *corporate* self, on the model of a company or club.[12] At least, it certainly doesn't seem that way to *me*!

1.4. Identity-Conditions and the Replacement Argument

Now I need to return to unfinished business—the search for a plausible argument in favour of the main claim of substance dualism, that *I am not identical with my body nor with any part of it.* This was premise (8) of my argument for the simplicity of the self. We have seen that neither the conceivability argument nor the indivisibility argument is satisfactory for the present purpose. I believe, however, that a much more compelling consideration in favour of (8) is this:

(12) My identity-conditions differ from those of my body or any part of it.

Entities possessing different identity-conditions cannot be identified with one another, on pain of contradiction.[13] But what *are* 'identity-conditions'? Speaking quite generally, the identity-conditions of entities of a kind *K* are the conditions whose satisfaction is necessary and sufficient for an entity *x* of kind *K* and an entity *y* of kind *K* to be identical, that is, for them to be *one and the same K*. Thus, for example, the identity-conditions of *sets* are these: a set *x* and a set *y* are *one and the same set* if and only if *x* and *y* have exactly the same members. In the case of things that *persist through time*, their identity-conditions will also provide their *persistence*-conditions, since a thing persists through time just in case *that same thing* exists at every succeeding moment during some interval of time. Now, there are, of course, notorious difficulties attaching to the question of personal identity, and particularly to the question of what conditions are necessary and sufficient for the identity of the self over time. However, even without being able to settle this question, we may well be in a position to determine that the identity-conditions of the self, whatever they may be, are *different* from those of the body or any part of it, such as the brain.

    Here is one sort of consideration that seems quite compelling in this respect. We know already that parts of the human body can be replaced by artificial substitutes that serve the same function more or less equally well, as far as the person possessing that body is concerned. For example, a 'bionic' arm can replace a natural arm and serve the person who owns it pretty much as well as the original did. And, indeed, it seems perfectly possible *in principle* that *every* part of a person's biological body should, bit by bit, be replaced in this fashion, with nerve cells gradually being replaced by, say, electronic circuits mimicking their

---

[12] For more on the latter notion, see Scruton (1989).
[13] See further Lowe (1989: chapter 4).

natural function.[14] If such a procedure were carried out completely, as it seems it could be, the *person* whose biological body had been replaced by an entirely artificial one would, very plausibly, *survive* the procedure and so *still exist* at the end of it. And yet, clearly, neither that biological body nor any part of it would have survived and still exist. If correct, this shows that the persistence-conditions of human persons are different from those of their biological bodies and their various parts, such as their biological brains, and hence that such persons—*we ourselves*—are *not identical with* those bodies nor with any of their parts. In short, it establishes the truth of (8), the main claim of substance dualism.

This argument—which may aptly be called the *replacement argument*—can be set out rather more formally as follows. Its first premise is:

(13) I could survive the replacement of every part of my body by a part of a different kind,

where by a part of a different 'kind' I mean one that is alien to the kind of thing that my body is, in the way that a bionic arm, say, is alien to the kind of thing that a biological human body is. Equally, of course, a *biological* arm would be, in this sense, 'alien' to a wholly bionic body, in the case of a person with such a body. The second premise is:

(14) My body could not survive the replacement of every part of it by a part of a different kind,

the reason for this being that such a process would leave me with *a body of a different kind*, and an object cannot undergo a change with respect to the kind of thing that it is—not, at least, with respect to the *highest* kind to which it belongs.[15] And here I take it that biological organisms and bionic artefacts, for example, are things which clearly do *not* belong to the same highest kind. Now, (13) and (14) together entail (12)—that I and my body (or any part of it) have different identity-conditions—and thereby entail (8), that I am not identical with my body (or any part of it). Of course, (8) may be inferred *directly* from (13) and (14) by an application of Leibniz's Law: but it is nonetheless important to notice that they entail (12), which itself entails (8), because this renders more perspicuous the relevant difference between persons and their bodies that precludes their identification with one another, namely, the difference in their *identity-conditions*.

Notice, however, that the foregoing argument for substance dualism, while it serves the purposes of *non-Cartesian* substance dualism well enough, is not sufficient to establish the truth of *Cartesian* substance dualism, since the latter

---

[14] Compare Lowe (1989: 120) and Baker (2000: 122–3).

[15] This claim is central to the sort of 'individuative essentialism' that is defended by David Wiggins in Wiggins (2001: chapter 4), with which I am broadly in agreement: see Lowe (1989). I don't mean to imply, however, that Wiggins himself would have sympathy for the replacement argument.

maintains that the self possesses *only* mental properties, not any physical ones. For the replacement argument doesn't show that the self could survive in a completely *disembodied* state and hence doesn't show that the self might exist even in circumstances in which no physical properties whatever, such as shape or mass, could possibly be attributed to it. The conceivability argument *does* purport to show this, of course, but has been found wanting in persuasive force. As for the indivisibility argument, it, like the replacement argument, cannot be used specifically in support of *Cartesian* dualism, even setting aside the other difficulties that attach to it—for its conclusion is only that I am *distinct* from my body, not that I lack, or could lack, any physical properties whatever.

1.5. The Unity Argument

Although, as we have seen, the indivisibility argument is unsatisfactory, there is another argument that is in some ways reminiscent of it but which, I think, deserves considerably more respect. I also think that it is even more compelling than the replacement argument, since it does not depend upon speculations which at present, it might be said, belong only to the realm of science fiction. I call this the *unity* argument—the unity in question being the unity of *the self* as the unique subject of all and only its own experiences. The first premise of the unity argument is:

(15) I am the subject of all and only my own mental states.

which is surely a self-evident truth. The second premise is:

(16) Neither my body as a whole nor any part of it could be the subject of all and only my own mental states.

The conclusion is, once again, (8) I am not identical with my body nor with any part of it.

Of course, (16) is the crucial premise, so let us see how it might be defended. First, then, observe that my body *as a whole* does not need to exist in order for me to have *every one* of the mental states that I do in fact have. If, for instance, I were to lack the tip of one of my little fingers, I might as a consequence lack *some* of the mental states that I do in fact have, but surely not *all* of them. I might *perhaps* lack a certain mildly painful sensation in the finger tip—a sensation that I do in fact have—but many of my other mental states could surely be exactly the same as they actually are, such as the thoughts that I am in fact having in composing this essay. Indeed, I *could* still even have that sensation 'in my finger tip', because the phenomenon of 'phantom' pain is a well-attested one. However, I venture to affirm that no entity can qualify as the *subject* of certain mental states if those mental states could exist in the absence of that entity. After all, *I* certainly qualify as the subject of *my* mental states, as (15) asserts, but for that very reason *those* mental states could not exist in my absence. Mental states must always *have* a subject—some being whose mental states they are—and the mental states that in fact belong to one subject could not have belonged to another, let alone to no subject at all.[16] But, as we have just seen, very many and quite possibly *all* of my own mental states could exist even if my body as a whole were not to exist—that is to say, even if certain parts that my body actually possesses were not to exist. This, I suggest, indicates that my body *as a whole* cannot qualify as the subject of all and only my own mental states and so cannot be identified with *me*. Now, many physicalists may agree with my reasoning so far, but draw the conclusion that, rather than being identical with my body *as a whole*, I am identical with some *part* of it, the most obvious candidate being *my brain*. However, it is easy to see that the foregoing reasoning can now just be repeated, replacing 'my body as a whole' by 'my brain as a whole' throughout. For it seems clear that, although I may well need to *have* a brain in order to have mental states, neither my brain as a whole nor any distinguished part of it is such that *it* in its entirety needs to exist in order for me to have *every one* of the mental states that I do in fact have. Indeed, even if every one of my mental states depends in this fashion upon *some* part of my brain, it by no means follows, of course, that there is some part of my brain upon which every one of my mental states thus depends. (To suppose that this does follow would be to commit a so-called 'quantifier-shift' fallacy.) And yet I, being the subject of all and only my own mental states, am such that every one of those mental states *does* depend upon *me*. Hence, we may conclude, neither my brain as a whole nor any part of it can qualify as the subject of all and only *my* mental states and so be identical with *me*. Putting together the two stages of this train of reasoning, we may thus infer that (16) is true and from that and (15) infer the truth of (8), the main claim of substance dualism.

I should perhaps stress that it is important to appreciate, when considering the foregoing argument, that I am by no means denying that there may be some part of my brain that is such that, *were it to be completely destroyed*, all of my mental states would thereby cease to be. After all, I am happy to concede that this may very well be true of my brain as a whole—that if *it* were to be completely destroyed, all of my mental states would thereby cease to be. All that I am denying, in effect, is that there is any part of my brain that is such that, were *any part of it*—such as one particular neuron—to be destroyed, all of my mental states would thereby cease to be. That is to say, neither my brain *as a whole*, nor any distinguished part of it *as a whole*, is something with which I can be identified—any more than I can be identified with *my body* as a whole—because no such entity is such that all and only *my* mental states can be taken to depend on it, in the way that they clearly do depend on *me*.

---

[16] See further Strawson (1959: chapter 3), and Lowe (1996: chapter 2).

However, here it may be objected that the foregoing defence of premise (16) depends upon an illicit assumption, namely, that if my body as a whole were to lack a certain part, such as the tip of one of my little fingers, then *it*—my body as a whole—would not exist. This assumption, it may be said, is unwarranted because it presupposes, questionably, that every part of my body is an *essential* part of it, without which it could not exist. As it stands, this may be a fair objection—although it should be acknowledged there are some philosophers who *do* hold that every part of a composite object is essential to it.[17] However, I think that the reasoning in favour of premise (16) can in fact be formulated slightly differently, so as to make it independent of the truth of this assumption. The initial insight still seems to be perfectly correct—that, as I put it, my body as a whole does not need to exist in order for me to have every one of the mental states that I do in fact have. Thus, to repeat, the thoughts that I am having in composing this essay plausibly do not depend upon my body including as a part the tip of one of my little fingers. Call these thoughts *T*. Consider, then, that object which consists of my body as a whole *minus* that finger tip. Call this object *O* and call my body as a whole *B*. (It should be conceded here that there are some philosophers who would deny that any such object as *O* exists[18]—but that is, to say the least, a controversial claim.) Suppose, now, that it is proposed that I am identical with *B*, and hence that *B* is the subject of the thoughts *T*. Then we can ask: on what grounds can *B* be regarded as the subject of *T* *in preference to O*, given that *T* do not depend upon *B*'s including the part—the finger tip—that *O* does not include? Isn't the material difference between *B* and *O* simply *irrelevant* to the case that can be made in favour of either of them qualifying as the subject of *T*? But in that case, we must either say that *both B and O* are subjects of *T*, or else that *neither* of them are. We cannot say the former, however, because *B* and *O* are numerically distinct objects, whereas the thoughts *T* have just *one* subject—*myself*. We may conclude, hence, that neither *B* nor *O* is a subject of *T* and thus that I, who *am* the subject of *T*, am identical with neither of them. This sort of reasoning can then be repeated, as before, with respect to any specific *part* of *B*, such as my brain.

However we exactly formulate the defence of premise (16), the basic point of the unity argument, as I call it, is that my mental states do not all depend on my body as a whole or on any part of it in the unified way in which they all depend upon me as their subject. This point, it seems to me, is a good one. Indeed, between them, the unity argument and the replacement argument provide, I think, fairly compelling grounds for belief in the truth of non-Cartesian substance dualism.

---

[17] See, for example, Chisholm (1976: chapter 3).   [18] See, for example, van Inwagen (1981).

2. NCSD AND THE METAPHYSICS OF MENTAL CAUSATION

2.1. The Causal Closure Argument Against Interactive Dualism

In this second half of my essay, I want to explore certain *causal* considerations that inevitably arise in the debate between dualism and its opponents. For dualism—whether we are talking about substance dualism or property dualism—is traditionally divisible into interactionist, epiphenomenalist, and parallelist varieties. Perhaps the most powerful argument against *interactive* dualism is the so-called *causal closure argument*.[19] By *interactive dualism* I mean the doctrine that mental events or states are not only *distinct* from physical events or states, but are also included amongst the *causes and effects* of physical events or states. Of course, the causal closure argument can have no force against either *epiphenomenalist* or *non-interactive parallelist* dualism, but since even the first and more credible of these positions has relatively few modern advocates, I shall not consider them here.[20] In any case, even those who do support them would presumably concede that they would prefer to endorse interactive dualism if they thought that it could meet the physicalist's objections, so let us concentrate on seeing how those objections can indeed be met, focusing on the causal closure argument.

The key premise of the causal closure argument against interactive dualism is the principle of the causal closure of the physical domain. This principle has received a number of different formulations—some of which are really too weak for the physicalist's purposes[21]—but the relatively strong version of the principle that I shall chiefly consider here is this:[22]

(17) No chain of event-causation can lead backwards from a purely physical effect to antecedent causes some of which are non-physical in character.

It may be objected on behalf of interactive dualism that (17) is simply question-begging, because it rules out by *fiat* the possibility of there being non-physical *mental* causes of some physical effects. However, as we shall see, (17) does not in fact rule out this possibility. Dialectically, it is in the dualist's interests to concede to the physicalist a version of the causal closure principle that is *as strong as possible*—provided that it still falls short of entailing the falsehood of interactive dualism—because if the causal closure argument in its strongest

---

[19] For further background, see Lowe (2000a: chapter 2).
[20] But see, for example, Robinson (2004).
[21] See further Lowe (2000b).   [22] Compare Kim (1993a).

non-question-begging form can be convincingly defeated, the physicalist will be left with no effective reply. Weaker versions of the causal closure principle can, of course, be countered by interactive dualists relatively easily, but tend to be countered by them in implausible ways which leave the physicalist with a telling response.

To illustrate the latter point, consider the following widely advocated version of the causal closure principle:

(18) Every physical effect of a mental cause has a sufficient physical cause.

An interactive dualist may accommodate (18) by, for example, espousing the doctrine of *interactive parallelism*, which maintains that there is a *one-to-one correlation* between the mental and physical causes of any physical event that has a mental cause, such that *both* the mental *and* the physical causes of any such event are *sufficient* causes of it.[23] (By a *sufficient* cause of a given event, I mean an event or conjunction of events that *causally necessitates* the event in question.) The physicalist may object that this doctrine has the highly implausible implication that every physical effect of a mental cause is *causally overdetermined* by that mental cause and the physical cause that is, suppposedly, one-to-one correlated with it. To this the interactive parallelist may reply that such causal overdetermination is no mere accident but, rather, the upshot of psychophysical laws, so that the fact that it occurs is a matter of nomic or natural necessity. However, it may nonetheless appear surprising to the impartial bystander that psychophysical laws of this character should be thought to govern the causal interactions of mind and body, when so many other possibilities are compatible with interactive dualism. The *non*-interactive parallelist has, it seems, much better reason to suppose that there is a one-to-one correlation between the *apparent* mental causes of physical events and their *actual* physical causes, because (traditionally, at least) they see this as being the upshot of a divinely instituted *pre-established harmony* between the mental and physical domains. Equally, the *physicalist* has a perfectly good reason to suppose that there is a one-to-one correlation between the mental and physical causes of physical events, because they *identify* those causes, and identity is a one-to-one relation *par excellence*. But the interactive parallelist, it seems, must simply regard it as a *brute fact* that psychophysical laws sustain such a one-to-one correlation—a fact that is all the more remarkable because so many other arrangements are consistent with the truth of interactive dualism. Neutral parties to the debate could be forgiven for suspecting that the interactive parallelist postulates the one-to-one correlation of mental and physical causes simply in mimicry of the physicalist's position, with a view to denying the physicalist recourse to any empirical evidence of a causal character that could discriminate between the two positions. For wherever the physicalist claims to find evidence of *one and the same cause* of a certain

---

[23] For an exposition and defence, see Meixner (2004: chapter 8).

physical effect—a single cause that is both mental and physical—the interactive parallelist will be able to reply that we in fact have *two distinct but correlated causes*, one of them mental and the other physical. However, this is a dangerous game for a dualist to play, because the physicalist can very plausibly urge that their *identity* theory provides a much more economical explanation of the one-to-one correlation of mental and physical causes that both they and the interactive parallelist believe to obtain.

Let us now consider a version of the causal closure argument against interactive dualism that appeals to the very strong formulation of the causal closure principle embodied in premise (17)—that no chain of event-causation can lead backwards from a purely physical effect to antecedent causes some of which are non-physical in character. Two additional premises are needed. First,

(19) Some purely physical effects have mental causes,

which the interactive dualist accepts as true, of course. Second,

(20) Any cause of a purely physical effect must belong to a chain of event-causation that leads backwards from that effect.

These three premises entail the conclusion,

(21) All of the mental causes of purely physical effects are themselves physical in character,

which contradicts the defining thesis of interactive dualism. My defence of interactive dualism will rest upon a challenge to premise (20). Moreover, it will endorse a version of interactive dualism that combines it with the sort of non-Cartesian substance dualism defended earlier.

2.2. Two Different Perspectives on the Causal Explanation of Voluntary Action

In order to keep matters relatively simple and to confine my discussion to manageable proportions, I shall concentrate, in what follows, on issues concerning voluntary and deliberative human action, where it is most obviously pressing that some coherent story needs to be told as to how mental and neurophysiological causes interrelate with one another. So let us focus on a specific case of such an action, such as an agent's deliberate (that is, premeditated and entirely voluntary) raising of an arm, for whatever reason (for instance, in order to catch a lecturer's attention with a view to asking a question). Now, what seems relatively uncontroversial, on the purely neurophysiological side of the causal story involved in such a case, is that if we were to trace the purely *bodily* causes of the relevant peripheral bodily event—in this case, the upward movement of the agent's arm on the given occasion—backwards in time indefinitely far, we would find that those causes *ramify*, like the branches of a tree, into a complex maze of antecedent events in the agent's nervous system and brain—many of the neural events in the agent's brain being widely distributed across fairly large areas of the motor cortex and having no single focus anywhere, with the causal chains to which they belong possessing, moreover, no distinct *beginnings*.[24] And yet, intuitively, the agent's mental act of *decision* or *choice* to move the arm would seem, from an introspective point of view, to be a *singular* and *unitary* occurrence that somehow *initiated* his or her action of raising the arm. The immediate question, then, is how, if at all, we can reconcile these two apparent facts. It seems impossible to *identify* the agent's act of choice with any individual neural event, nor even with any combination of individual neural events, because it and they seem to have such different causal features or profiles. The act of choice seems to be unitary and to have, all by itself, an 'initiating' role, whereas the neural events seem to be thoroughly *disunified* and merely to contribute in different ways to a host of different ongoing causal chains, many of which lead independently of one another to the eventual arm-movement.

I believe that NCSD can enable us to see how *both* of these causal perspectives on deliberative physical action can be correct, without one being reducible to the other and without there existing any sort of rivalry between the two. First of all, the act of choice is attributable to the *person* whereas the neural events are attributable to parts of the person's *body*: and a person and his or her body are, according to this conception of ourselves, *distinct* things, even if they are not *separable* things. Moreover, the act of choice *causally explains* the bodily movement—the upward movement of the arm—in a different way from the way in which the neural events explain it. The neural events explain why the arm moved *in the particular way* that it did—at such-and-such a speed and in such-and-such a direction at a certain precise time. By contrast, the act of choice explains why a movement *of that general kind*—in this case, a rising of the agent's arm—occurred around about the time that it did. It did so because shortly beforehand the agent decided to raise that arm. The decision certainly did not determine the precise speed, direction, and timing of the arm's movement, only *that* a movement of that general sort would occur around about then. The difference between the two kinds of causal explanation reveals itself clearly, I suggest, when one contemplates their respective *counterfactual* implications. If the agent had not decided to raise his or her arm, there wouldn't have been an arm-movement of that kind *at all*—the arm would either have remained at rest or, if the agent had decided to make another movement instead, it would have moved in a quite different way. It doesn't seem, however, that one can isolate any neural event, or any set of neural events, whose non-occurrence would have had *exactly the same consequences* as the non-occurrence of the agent's decision. Rather, the most that one can say is that if this or that neural event, or set of neural events, had not occurred, the arm-movement might have proceeded in a

---

[24] See, e.g., Deecke, Scheid, and Kornhuber (1969) and Popper, and Eccles (1977: 282–94).

somewhat different manner—more jerkily, perhaps, or more quickly—*not* that the arm would have remained at rest, or would instead have moved in a quite different kind of way.

2.3. A Counterfactual Argument Against Psycho-Neural Causal Identity

This last point is an extremely important one and requires further elucidation. It is now standard practice amongst philosophers of logic and language to interpret counterfactual conditionals in terms of possible worlds, very roughly as follows.[25] A counterfactual of the form 'If it were the case that *p*, then it would be the case that *q*' is said to be true if and only if, in the *closest* possible world in which *p* is the case, *q* is also the case—where the 'closest' possible world in question is the one in which *p* is the case but otherwise *differs minimally* from the actual world. Now, suppose that a physicalist in the philosophy of mind were to propose that the agent's decision, *D*, to raise his or her arm on a given occasion—the agent's mental act of choice—is identical with a certain neural event, *N*, which is correctly identifiable as being a *cause* of the subsequent bodily event, *B*, of the arm's rising. Here I must stress that *D*, *N*, and *B* are, each of them, supposed to be *particular events*, each occurring at a particular moment of time, with *B* occurring at least an appreciable fraction of a second later than *D* and *N*, since our decisions to act do not take effect immediately—and the physicalist must suppose, of course, that *D* and *N* occur at the *same* time, since they hold them to be identical. And let me add, too, that I do not wish to get embroiled here in the debates concerning Benjamin Libet's celebrated but highly controversial experiments on the precise timing of volitions,[26] as this would sidetrack me from my present concerns. Let us concede, consequently, that the following counterfactual is true: 'If *N* had not occurred, then *B* would not have occurred.' All that I am presupposing here is that if *N* was indeed a cause of *B*, then the foregoing counterfactual is true. The physicalist cannot, I think, have any quarrel with me on this account. I am not taking any advantage, then, of the various reasons that have been advanced for doubting, at least in some cases, whether causal statements entail the corresponding counterfactuals.[27] What I am now interested in focusing on is the following question: what sort of event *would* have occurred, instead of *B*, if *N* had not occurred? In other words: in the closest possible world in which *N* does not occur, what sort of event occurs instead of *B*? My contention is that what occurs in this world is an event *of the same sort as B*, differing from *B* only very slightly. The reason for this is as follows.

---

[25] See, especially, Lewis (1973b), although I do not replicate every detail of his account, but only those that are germane to the issues now under discussion.

[26] Libet (1985). Note, in any case, that Libet's experiments were not concerned with *premeditated* actions, but only with 'spontaneous' ones.

[27] For discussion of this, see Lowe (2002a: chapter 10).

It seems evident, from what we know about the neural causes of an event such as B, that N must be an *immensely complex* neural event: it must be, in fact, the sum (or 'fusion') of a very large number of individual neural events, each of them consisting in some particular neuron's firing in a particular way. Recall, here, that N must be supposed to occur an appreciable amount of time *before* B, at a time at which the neural antecedents of B are many and quite widely distributed across the agent's cerebral cortex. It would be utterly implausible for the physicalist to maintain, for example, that the agent's decision D is identical with the firing of just a *single* neuron, or even of a small number of neurons. If D is identical with any neural event *at all*, it can surely only be identical with an extremely complex one, consisting in the firing of many neurons distributed over quite a large region of the agent's cerebral cortex. However, it seems indisputable that if N is, thus, the sum of a very large number of individual neural events, then the *closest* world in which N itself does not occur is a world in which *another* highly complex neural event, N^*, occurs, differing *only very slightly* from N in respect of the individual neural events of which it is the sum. In other words, N^* will consist of *almost exactly the same* individual neural events as N, plus or minus one or two. Any possible world in which a neural event occurs that differs from N in *more* than this minimal way simply will not qualify as the *closest* possible world in which N does not occur. This is evidently what the standard semantics for counterfactuals requires us to say in this case. But, given what we know about the functioning of the brain and nervous system, it seems clear that, in the possible world in which N^* occurs, it causes a bodily event *very similar* to B, because such a small difference between N and N^* in respect of the individual neural events of which they are respectively the sums cannot be expected to make a very big difference between their bodily effects. There is, we know, a good deal of redundancy in the functioning of neural systems, so that the failure to fire of one or two motor neurons, or the abnormal firing of one or two others, will typically make at most only a minimal difference with regard to the peripheral bodily behaviour that ensues. Thus, the answer to the question posed earlier—what sort of bodily event would have occurred instead of B, if N had not occurred?—is this: a bodily event *very similar to B*. In other words, if N had not occurred, *the agent's arm would still have risen in almost exactly the same way as it actually did.*

Now, I hope, we can see the importance of this conclusion. For, if we ask what sort of bodily event would have occurred instead of B if *the agent's decision, D,* to raise his or her arm had not occurred, then we plausibly get a very different answer. Very plausibly, if D had not occurred—if the agent had not made the very act of choice that he or she did to raise the arm—then the arm *would not have risen at all*. It is, I suggest, quite incredible to suppose that if the agent had not made *that* very decision, D, then he or she would have made another decision virtually indistinguishable from D—in other words, *another* decision to raise the arm in the same, or virtually the same, way. On the contrary, if the agent had not made *that* decision, then he or she would either have made a quite different decision or else no decision at all. Either way—assuming that there is nothing defective in the agent's nervous system—the arm *would not* have risen almost exactly as it did.

I suppose that a convinced physicalist might try to challenge the claim that I have just made and contend that, indeed, if *D* had not occurred, then *another* decision to raise the arm in virtually the same way would have occurred instead, giving rise to a slightly different bodily event of the same kind.[28] But, on the face of it, this would appear to be a purely *ad hoc* maneuver designed solely to save the envisaged physicalist's position. One serious problem with it is that contentful mental acts such as decisions are, very plausibly, *individuated* at least partly by their contents—and yet their contents surely cannot be as fine-grained as the physicalist's conjectured contention would appear to demand. How, exactly, would the *content* of the decision that, supposedly, would have occurred if *D* had not occurred, have differed from the content of *D*? If the putative difference in their contents is to match the *very slight* difference between the bodily events that are supposed to ensue from them, then a degree of *fine-grainedness* must be attributed to those contents that, it seems to me, is utterly implausible from a psychological point of view. For instance, we must suppose that *D* is a decision to raise the agent's arm along a quite specific trajectory *T*, whereas if *D* had not occurred then the agent would instead have decided to raise his or her arm along the very slightly different trajectory *T**, where the spatiotemporal differences between *T* and *T** are of the same order of magnitude as the very slight differences between the *actual* arm-movement *B* and the arm-movement that would have occurred if neural event *N** had occurred instead of neural event *N*. But the contents of our decisions to act are surely *never* as fine-grained as this—not, at least, if our conscious introspective awareness of those contents is to be relied upon. And to propose that they always have much finer-grained contents that are *inaccessible* to consciousness seems a desperate recourse on the part of the physicalist. When, for instance, I decide to raise my arm in a lecture in order to ask a question, I may indeed decide to raise it *quickly* and *vertically*, but never—surely—along a quite specific trajectory at a quite specific speed. Quite apart from anything else, I simply don't possess sufficient *voluntary control* over my limb-movements to be able to decide to execute them with such precision.

If all of this reasoning is correct, then it follows unavoidably that the decision *D* cannot be identical with the neural event *N* with which the physicalist proposes to identify it, for the counterfactual implications of the non-occurrence of these two events are quite different. If *D* had not occurred, the agent's arm would not have risen at all, but if *N* had not occurred, it would have risen almost exactly as it did. One fundamental reason for this—according to the conception of human persons that I favour as an advocate of NCSD—is that a mental act of choice

---

[28] I am grateful to José Bermúdez for pressing this line of response.

or decision is, in a strong sense, a *singular* and *unitary* event, unlike a highly complex sum or fusion of independent neural events, such as N. N^* differs from N only in excluding one or two of the individual neural events composing N or including one or two others. That is why N and N^* can be so similar and thus have such similar effects. But D, I suggest, cannot intelligibly be thought of, in like manner, as being *composed* of myriads of little events—and that is at least partly why, in the closest possible world in which D itself does not occur, there does *not* occur another decision D^* which differs from D as little as N^* differs from N. Note that this strong *unity* of our mental acts, whereby they resist decomposition into lesser parts, nicely parallels our own strong unity as 'simple' substances, revealed by the unity argument of section 1.5 above.

I should perhaps add that, although I do not have space enough to demonstrate this in detail here, the foregoing line of argument sustains not only the conclusion that the mental and neural causes of voluntary bodily movements must be numerically *distinct*, but also the stronger conclusion that those mental causes cannot even be taken to be 'realized by' any of those neural causes—where 'realization' is taken to be a relation distinct from identity itself, in virtue of which realized events or states inherit their causal features entirely from those of the events or states that realize them.

2.4. Intentional Causation Versus Physical Causation

So far, I have tried to explain why the mental and neural causes of voluntary bodily movements must be distinct, consistently with allowing, as I do, that such movements have *both* mental *and* neural causes. Now I want to say a little more about the respects in which mental causation is distinctively different from bodily or physical causation. Most importantly, then, mental causation is *intentional* causation—it is the causation of an *intended* effect *of a certain kind*. Bodily causation is not like this. All physical causation is 'blind,' in the sense that physical causes are not 'directed towards' their effects in the way that mental causes are. *Both* sorts of causation need to be invoked, I believe, in order to give a full explanation of human action and NCSD's conception of human persons seems best equipped to accommodate this fact. The very *logic* of intentional causation differs, I venture to say, from the *logic* of bodily causation. Intentional causation is *fact* causation, while bodily causation is *event* causation.[29] That is to say, a choice or decision to move one's body in a certain way is causally responsible for the *fact* that a bodily movement *of a certain kind* occurs, whereas a neural event, or set of neural events, is causally responsible for a *particular* bodily movement, which is a particular *event*. The decision, unlike the neural event, doesn't causally explain why that *particular* bodily movement occurs, not least because one cannot *intend* to bring about what one cannot *voluntarily*

---

[29] For more on this distinction, see Bennett (1988) and also Lowe (2002a: chapter 9).

control—for, as I pointed our earlier, one cannot voluntarily control the *precise* bodily movement that occurs when one decides, say, to raise one's arm.

As I have just implied, the two species of causal explanation, mental and physical, are both required and are mutually complementary, for the following reason. Merely to know why a *particular* event of a certain kind occurred is not necessarily yet to know why an event of *that* kind occurred, as opposed to an event of some other kind. Intentional causation can provide the latter type of explanation in cases in which bodily causation cannot. More specifically: an event, such as a particular bodily movement, which may appear to be merely *coincidental* from a purely *physiological* point of view—inasmuch as it is the upshot of a host of independent neural events preceding it—will by no means appear to be merely coincidental from an *intentional* point of view, since it was an event *of a kind* that the agent intended to produce.[30]

Notice, here, that the aforementioned fact—that a mental decision, *D*, to perform a certain kind of bodily movement, cannot be said to cause the *particular* bodily event, *B*, of that kind whose occurrence renders that decision successful—is already implied by the argument that I developed a little while ago in section 2.3. For, given that *D* is *not identical* with the actual neural cause, *N*, of *B*, the closest possible world in which *N* does not occur *is still a world in which D occurs*—but in that world a slightly different bodily movement, *B**, ensues, being caused there by a slightly different neural cause, *N**. (Clearly, if *D* is not identical with *N*, then there is no reason to suppose that the closest world in which *N* does not occur is also one in which *D* does not occur, for a world in which *both* of these events do not occur evidently differs more from the actual world than a world in which just *one* of them does not occur, other things being equal.) However, this means that the occurrence of *D* is causally compatible with the occurrence of two *numerically different* bodily movements of the same kind, *B* and *B**, and hence does not causally determine *which* of these occurs, but only that *some* bodily movement of their kind occurs.

2.5. Reasons, Causes, and Freedom of Action

Much more can and should be said on these matters, but since I have discussed many of them extensively elsewhere,[31] I shall rest content with the foregoing remarks for present purposes. Here, however, it may be asked: *But what about the causes of an agent's acts of decision or choice?* Are *these* bodily or mental, or both? My own opinion is that an act of decision or choice is *free*, in the 'libertarian' sense—that is to say, it is *uncaused*.[32] This is not to say that decisions are simply *inexplicable*, only that they demand explanations of a non-causal sort. Decisions are explicable in terms of *reasons*, not causes. That is to say, if we want to know

---

[30] See further Lowe (1999).   [31] See again, in particular, Lowe (1999).
[32] See further Lowe (2003a).

why an agent *decided* to act as they did, we need to inquire into *the reasons in the light of which* they chose so to act.[33] Since decisions are, according to NCSD's conception of the mind, attributable to the person and not to the person's body or any part of it, there is no implication here that any *bodily* event is uncaused. It's not that I want to exclude altogether the idea of causal explanation in terms of mental states in favour of purely rational explanation in the psychological sphere—as my earlier arguments make manifest. However, I do want to help to reinstate the idea that reason-giving explanation is *not* a species of causal explanation and that it is one form of explanation that is distinctive of the psychological sphere.

But now it may be wondered: how is it really possible for mental acts of decision to explain anything in the physical domain, if that domain is *causally closed*, as many contemporary philosophers of mind—and just about all physicalists—assume? This takes us back to the earlier concerns of section 2.1 above. As we observed there, much turns on precisely how the putative causal closure of the physical domain is to be defined, for this is no simple matter.[34] According to one popular view,[35] the thesis of physical causal closure amounts to the claim that no chain of event-causation can lead backwards from a purely physical effect to antecedent causes some of which are *non*-physical in character. This was premise (17) of the version of the causal closure argument presented in section 2.1. But intentional causation according to NCSD's conception of human persons, as I have tried to characterize it earlier, does not violate the thesis of physical causal closure just stated, since it does not postulate that mental acts of decision or choice are events *mediating between bodily events* in chains of causation leading to purely physical effects: it does not postulate that there are 'gaps' in chains of physical causation that are 'filled' by mental events. Thus, NCSD's model of mental causation is consistent with premise (17) of the causal closure argument and avoids the conclusion of that argument by repudiating, instead, premise (20).

As we have seen, according to NCSD's conception of human persons, a decision can explain the fact that a bodily movement *of a certain kind* occurred on a given occasion, but not the *particular* movement that occurred. Even so, it may be protested that if physical causation is *deterministic*, then there is really no scope for intentional causation on the model that I am defending to explain anything physical, because the relevant counterfactuals will all simply be *false*. It will be *false*, for instance, to say that if the agent had not decided to raise his or her arm, then a rising of the agent's arm would not have occurred: rather, precisely the same bodily movement *would* still have occurred, caused by precisely the same physical events that actually did cause it—for if physical determinism is true, there was never any real possibility that those physical events should not

---

[33] Compare Dancy (2000).   [34] See Lowe (2000).
[35] Endorsed, for example, by Kim (1993a).

have occurred, nor that they should have had different effects. Maybe so. But, in view of the developments in quantum physics during the twentieth century, we now know that physical causation is *not* in fact deterministic, so the objection is an idle one and can safely be ignored. The model of intentional causation that I am proposing may nonetheless still seem puzzling to many philosophers, but if so then I suggest that this will be because they are still in the grip of an unduly simple conception of what causation involves—one which admits only of the causation of one event by one or more antecedent events belonging to one or more chains of causation which stretch back indefinitely far in time. Since this seems to be the only sort of causation that is recognized by the physical sciences, intentional causation on NCSD's model is bound to be *invisible* from the perspective of such a science.[36] To a physicalist, this invisibility will seem like a reason to dismiss NCSD's conception of intentional causation as spurious, because 'non-scientific.' I hope that to more open-minded philosophers it will seem more like a reason to perceive no genuine conflict between explanation in the physical and biological sciences and another, more humanistic way of explaining our intentional actions, by reference to our choices or decisions and the reasons for which we make them.

[36] Compare Lowe (2003b).

Bibliography

Adams, Robert M. (1981), 'Actualism and Thisness,' *Synthese* 49:3–41.

Almog, Joseph (2002a), *What Am I? Descartes and the Mind–Body Problem* (New York: Oxford University Press).

——— (2002b), 'Pains and Brains,' *Philosophical Topics* 30:1–30.

——— (2003), 'The Structure-in-things: Existence, Essence and Logic,' *Proc. Aristotelian Society* 103:197–225.

——— (2005), 'Replies: The Human Mind, Body and Being,' *Philosophy and Phenomenological Research* 70:717–34.

——— (2007), 'The Cosmic Ensemble—The Mathematics/Nature Symbiosis,' *Midwest Studies in Philosophy* 31:344–71.

——— (2008), *Cogito? Descartes and Thinking the World* (New York: Oxford University Press).

——— (forthcoming), 'Everything in its Right Place.'

Antony, Louis (2007), 'Everybody Has Got It: A Defense of Non-Reductive Materialism,' in Brian McLaughlin and Jonathan Cohen (eds.), *Contemporary Debates in the Philosophy of Mind* (Oxford: Blackwell).

Aquinas, T. (1982), *Summae contra gentiles libri quattuor*, bk. II, ed. by K. Albert and P. Engelhardt (Darmstadt: Wissenschaftliche Buchgesellschaft).

Armstrong, David M. (1968), *A Materialist Theory of Mind* (London: Routledge and Kegan Paul).

——— (1980), 'Naturalism, Materialism and First Philosophy,' *The Nature of Mind and Other Essays* (St. Lucia: University of Queensland Press), pp. 149–65.

——— (1997), *A World of States of Affairs* (Cambridge: Cambridge University Press).

Audi, Robert (2000), 'Philosophical Naturalism at the Turn of the Century,' *Journal of Philosophical Research*, 25:27–45.

Austin, David (1990), *What's the Meaning of 'This'?* (Ithaca: Cornell University Press).

Baars, Bernard (1988), *A Cognitive Theory of Consciousness* (Cambridge: Cambridge University Press).

——— (1996), *In the Theater of Consciousness* (New York: Oxford University Press).

Bacon, Francis (2000), *The New Organon*, ed. Lisa Jardine and Michael Silverthorne (New York: Cambridge University Press).

Baker, Lynne Rudder (1993), 'Metaphysics and Mental Causation,' in Heil and Mele 1993, pp. 75–95.

——— (2000), *Persons and Bodies: A Constitution View* (Cambridge: Cambridge University Press).

Balog, Katalin (1999), 'Conceivability, Possibility, and the Mind–Body Problem,' *Philosophical Review* 108:497–528.

Barnett, David (forthcoming), 'The Simplicity Intuition and Its Hidden Influence on Philosophy of Mind,' *Noûs*.

Barwise, Jon and John Perry (1983), *Situations and Attitudes* (Cambridge: MIT Press/Bradford Books).

Bealer, George (1984), 'Mind and Anti-mind,' *Midwest Studies in Philosophy* 9:283–328.

―― (1994a), 'Mental Properties,' *The Journal of Philosophy* 91:185–208.

―― (1994b), 'The Origins of Modal Error,' *Dialectica* 58:11–42.

―― (1997), 'Self-consciousness,' *The Philosophical Review* 106:69–117.

―― (1998), 'Propositions,' *Mind* 107:1–32.

―― (2007), 'Mental Causation,' *Philosophical Perspectives* 21:23–54.

―― (forthcoming a), 'The Mind–Body Problem.'

―― (forthcoming b), 'Ramsification and Intensionality.'

―― and Uwe Mönnich (1989), 'Property Theories,' *Handbook of Philosophical Logic*, vol. 4. ed. by Dov Gabbay and Frans Guenthner (Dordrecht: Kluwer), pp. 133–251.

Behe, Michael (2007), *The Edge of Evolution: The Search for the Limits of Darwinism* (New York: Free Press).

Beilby, James (2002), *Naturalism Defeated? Essays on Plantinga's Evolutionary Argument Against Naturalism* (Ithaca: Cornell University Press).

Benacerraf, Paul (1965), 'What Numbers Could Not Be,' *Philosophical Review* 74:47–73.

Bennett, Jonathan (1967), 'The Simplicity of the Soul,' *Journal of Philosophy* 64:648–60.

―― (1988), *Events and Their Names* (Oxford: Clarendon Press).

Bennett, M. R. and Hacker, P. M. S. (2003), *Philosophical Foundations of Neuroscience* (Oxford: Blackwell).

Bergmann, Michael (2000), 'Deontology and Defeat,' *Philosophy and Phenomenological Research* 60:87–102.

―― (2005), 'Defeaters and Higher Level Requirements,' *Philosophical Quarterly* 55:419–36.

Bilgrami, Akeel (2006), 'Some Philosophical Integrations,' in Cynthia Macdonald and Graham Macdonald (eds.), *McDowell and His Critics* (Oxford: Blackwell), pp. 50–66.

Block, Ned (1978), 'Troubles with Functionalism,' in Ned Block (ed.), *Readings in Philosophy of Psychology 1980*, (Cambridge: Harvard University Press), pp. 268–305.

―― (1990), 'Can the Mind Change the World?' in George Boolos (ed.), *Meaning and Method: Essays in Honor of Hilary Putnam* (Cambridge: Cambridge University Press), pp. 137–70.

―― (1995), 'On a Confusion About a Function of Consciousness,' *Behavioral and Brain Sciences* 18:227–87.

―― (1997), 'Anti-Reductionism Slaps Back,' *Philosophical Perspectives 11: Mind, Causation, and World*, pp. 107–32.

―― (2002), 'Concepts of Consciousness,' reprinted in Block (2007).

―― (2003), 'Do Causal Powers Drain Away?' *Philosophy and Phenomenological Research* 67:133–50.

―― (2007), *Consciousness, Function, and Representation: Collected Papers, Volume 1* (Cambridge, MA: MIT Press).

BonJour, Laurence (1998), *In Defense of Pure Reason* (Cambridge: Cambridge University Press).

―― and Sosa, Ernest (2003), *Epistemic Justification* (Oxford: Blackwell).

Borg, G., Diamant, H., Strom, L. and Zotterman, Y. (1967) 'The Relation Between Neural and Perceptual Intensity,' *Journal of Physiology* 192:13–20.

Boyd, Richard (1980), 'Materialism Without Reductionism: What Physicalism Does Not Entail,' in Ned Block (ed.), *Readings in Philosophy of Psychology*, vol. 1 (Cambridge, MA: Harvard University Press), pp. 67–106.

Braine, David (1992), *The Human Person* (Notre Dame, IN: University of Notre Dame Press).

Burge, Tyler (1978), 'Belief and Synonymy,' *Journal of Philosophy* 75:119–38.

—— (1979), 'Individualism and the Mental,' in P. A. French, T. E. Uehling, and H. K. Wettstein (eds.), *Midwest Studies in Philosophy* 4:73–121.

—— (1993), 'Mind–Body Causation and Explanatory Practice', in John Heil and Alfred Mele (eds.), *Mental Causation* (Oxford: Clarendon Press), pp. 97–120.

—— (1999), 'A Century of Deflation and a Moment About Self-Knowledge,' *Proceedings and Addresses of the American Philosophical Association* 73:25–46.

—— (2007), *Foundations of Mind* (New York: Oxford University Press).

Byrne, Alex and Hilbert, David (1997), 'Colors and Reflectances,' in Alex Byrne and David Hilbert (eds.), *Readings on Color, Vol. 1: The. Philosophy of Color* (Cambridge, MA: MIT Press), pp. 263–88.

—— and Tye, Michael (2006), 'Qualia Ain't in the Head,' *Noûs* 40:241–55.

Campbell, J. (1993), 'A Simple View of Colour,' in John Haldane and Crispin Wright (eds.), *Reality, Representation and Projection* (Oxford: Oxford University Press), pp. 257–68.

Carnap, Rudolph (1966), *The Philosophy of Physics* (New York: Basic Books).

Carruthers, Peter (2000), *Phenomenal Consciousness: A Naturalistic Theory* (Cambridge: Cambridge University Press).

—— (2001), 'Who is Blind to Blindsight?' *Psyche* 7(04), http://psyche.cs.monash.edu.au/v7/psyche-7-04-carruthers.html

Cartwright, Nancy (1983), *How the Laws of Physics Lie* (Oxford: Clarendon Press).

—— (1989), *Nature's Capacities and Their Measurement* (Oxford: Clarendon Press).

—— (1999), *The Dappled World: A Study of the Boundaries of Science* (Cambridge: Cambridge University Press).

Cassam, Quassim (1992), 'Reductionism and First-Person Thinking,' in David Charles and Kathleen Lennon (eds.), *Reduction, Explanation, and Realism* (New York, NY: Oxford University Press), pp. 361–80.

Cat, Jordi (2007), 'The Unity of Science,' *Stanford Encyclopedia of Philosophy*, http://plato.stanford.edu/entries/scientific-unity/

Chalmers, David (1982), 'Partial Character and the Language of Thought,' *Pacific Philosophical Quarterly* 63:347–65.

—— (1995), 'Facing up to the Problem of Consciousness,' *Journal of Consciousness Studies* 2:200–19.

—— (1996), *The Conscious Mind: In Search of a Fundamental Theory* (Oxford: Oxford University Press).

—— (1996), 'Does a Rock Implement Every Finite-State Automaton?,' *Synthese* 108:309–33.

—— (2002a), *Philosophy of Mind: Classical and Contemporary Readings* (Oxford: Oxford University Press).

—— (2002b), 'Consciousness and its Place in Nature,' in Chalmers (2002a), pp. 247–72.

—— (2002c), 'Does Conceivability Imply Possibility?' in Tamar Szabo Gendler and John Hawthorne (eds.), *Conceivability and Possibility* (New York: Oxford University Press), pp. 145–99.

—— (2005), 'Representationalism Showdown,' http://fragments.consc.net/djc/2005/09/representationa.html

Chalmers, David (2006), 'Perception and the Fall from Eden,' in T. S. Gendler and J. Hawthorne (eds.), *Perceptual Experience* (Oxford: Oxford University Press).

Charles, David and Kathleen Lennon (eds.) (1992), *Reduction, Explanation, and Realism* (New York, NY: Oxford University Press).

Chisholm, Roderick M. (1966), *Theory of Knowledge* (Englewood Cliffs, NJ: Prentice-Hall).

_____ (1970), 'Identity Through Time,' in Howard E. Kiefer and Milton K. Munitz (eds.), *Language, Belief and Metaphysics* (Albany: SUNY Press), chapter 4.

_____ (1976), *Person and Object: A Metaphysical Study* (London: George Allen and Unwin).

_____ (1981), *The First Person* (Minneapolis: University of Minnesota Press).

_____ (1989), *On Metaphysics* (Minneapolis: University of Minnesota Press).

_____ (1991), 'On the Simplicity of the Soul,' *Philosophical Perspectives* 5:167–81.

Chomsky, Noam (1959), 'A Review of B. F. Skinner's *Verbal Behavior*,' *Language* 35:26–58.

_____ (1988), *Language and the Problems of Knowledge* (Cambridge, MA: MIT Press).

Churchland, Paul M. (1981), 'Eliminative Materialism and the Propositional Attitudes,' *Journal of Philosophy* 78:67–90.

Churchland, Paul M. and Patricia S. Churchland (1998), *On the Contrary: Critical Essays, 1987–1997* (Cambridge, Mass.: MIT Press).

Clapp, Lenny (1998), 'Senses, Sensations, and Brain Processes: A Criticism of the Property Dualism Argument,' *Southwest Philosophy Review* 14:139–48.

_____ (2001), 'Disjunctive Properties: Multiple Realizations,' *Journal of Philosophy* 98:111–36.

Cleland, Carol (2002), 'Methodological and Epistemic Differences between Historical Science and Experimental Science,' *Philosophy of Science*, 69:474–96.

Coghill, R., Sang, C., Maisog, J., and Iadarola, M. (1999), 'Pain Intensity Processing within the Human Brain: A Bilateral, Distributed Mechanism,' *Journal of Neurophysiology* 82:1934–43.

Confer, William N. and Abbes, Billie S. (1983), *Multiple Personality: Etiology, Diagnosis, and Treatment* (New York: Human Silences Press).

Corcoran, Keith (ed.) (2001), *Soul, Body, and Survival: Essays on the Metaphysics of Human Persons* (Ithaca, NY: Cornell University Press).

Corry, Richard (2002), 'A Causal-Structural Theory of Empirical Knowledge,' PhD thesis, Indiana University.

_____ (2008), 'Scientific Analysis and Causal Influence,' in Handfield (2008), pp. 158–88.

Cover, Jan and John O'Leary-Hawthorne (1999), *Substance and Individuation in Leibniz* (New York, NY: Cambridge University Press).

Craig, William L. and Moreland, J. P. (2000), *Naturalism: A Critical Analysis* (London: Routledge).

Crane, Tim and Mellor, D. H. (1990). 'There is No Question of Physicalism,' *Mind* 99:185–206.

Crick, Francis (1994), *The Astonishing Hypothesis: The Scientific Search for the Soul* (New York: Scribners).

_____ and Cristof Koch (1990), 'Towards a Neurobiological Theory of Consciousness,' *Seminars in the Neurosciences* 2:263–75.

Crisp, Thomas and Ted Warfield (2001), 'Kim's Master Argument: A Critical Notice of *Mind in a Physical World*,' *Noûs* 35:304–16.

Dancy, Jonathan (2000), *Practical Rationality* (Oxford: Clarendon Press).

Davidson, Donald (1980), *Essays on Actions and Events* (Oxford: Clarendon Press).

——(1984), 'Radical Interpretation,' *Inquiries into Truth and Interpretation* (Oxford: Clarendon Press), pp. 125–39.

Dawkins, Richard (1976), *The Selfish Gene* (Oxford: Oxford University Press).

De Caro, Mario (forthcoming), *Normativity and Naturalism* (New York: Columbia University Press).

——and Macarthur, David (eds.) (2004a), *Naturalism in Question* (Cambridge, MA: Harvard University Press).

——and Macarthur, David (eds.) (2004b), 'Introduction: The Nature of Naturalism,' in De Caro and Macarthur (2004a), pp. 1–17.

De Valois, R. and De Valois, K. (1993), 'A Multi-Stage Model of Color Vision,' *Vision Research* 33:1053–65.

Deecke, L., Scheid, P. and Kornhuber, H. H. (1969), 'Distribution of Readiness Potential, Pre-Motion Positivity and Motor Potential of the Human Cerebral Cortex Preceding Voluntary Finger Movements,' *Experimental Brain Research* 7:158–68.

Dembski, William (1998), *The Design Inference: Eliminating Chance through Small Probabilities* (Cambridge: Cambridge University Press).

——(2002), *No Free Lunch: Why Specified Complexity Cannot Be Purchased without Intelligence* (Lanham, MD: Rowman and Littlefield).

Dennett, Daniel C. (1987), *The Intentional Stance* (Cambridge, MA: MIT Press).

——(1991), *Consciousness Explained* (Boston: Little, Brown and Company).

——(1993), 'Living on the Edge,' *Inquiry* 36:135–39.

——(1996), *Darwin's Dangerous Idea: Evolution and the Meanings of Life* (New York: Simon & Schuster).

——(2003), *Freedom Evolves* (New York: Viking).

——(2006), *Breaking the Spell: Religion as a Natural Phenomenon* (New York: Viking).

Descartes, René (1985a), *The Principles of Philosophy*, in John Cottingham, Robert Stoothoff and Dugald Murdoch (eds.), *The Philosophical Writings of Descartes* vol. 1 (New York: Cambridge University Press), pp. 177–292.

——(1985b), *Meditations on First Philosophy*, in John Cottingham, Robert Stoothoof and Dugald Murdoch (eds.), *The Philosophical Writings of Descartes*, vol. 2 (Cambridge: Cambridge University Press), pp. 1–399.

——(1986), *Meditationes de Prima Philosophia*, ed. G. Schmidt (Stuttgart: Reclam).

——(1991), 'Letter to Princess Elizabeth,' June 28, 1643, in John Cottingham, Robert Stoothoff and Dugald Murdoch (eds.), *The Philosophical Writings of Descartes* vol. 3 (New York: Cambridge University Press), pp. 214 ff.

——(1993), *Meditations on First Philosophy*, trans. Donald Cress, 3rd edn. (Indianapolis: Hackett).

Dewey, John (1927), 'Half-Hearted Naturalism,' *Journal of Philosophy* 25:57–64.

——(1944), 'Antinaturalism in Extremis,' in Y. H. Krikorian (ed.), *Naturalism and the Human Spirit* (New York: Columbia University Press), pp. 1–16.

Doepke, Frederick C. (1996), *The Kinds of Things: A Theory of Person Identity Based on Transcendental Argument* (Chicago: Open Court).

Draper, Paul (2005), 'God, Science, and Naturalism,' in W. Wainwright (ed.), *The Oxford Handbook of Philosophy of Religion* (Oxford: Oxford University Press).

Dretske, Fred I. (1997), *Naturalizing the Mind* (Cambridge, MA: MIT Press).

Dupré, John (1993), *The Disorder of Things: Metaphysical Foundations of the Disunity of Science* (Cambridge, MA: Harvard University Press).

—— (1996), 'Metaphysical Disorder and Scientific Disunity,' in Galison and Stump (1996), pp. 101–17.

—— (2001), *Human Nature and the Limits of Science* (Oxford: Oxford University Press).

—— (2004), 'The Miracle of Monism,' in De Caro and Macarthur (2004b), pp. 36–58.

—— (forthcoming), 'How to be Naturalistic without being Simplistic in the Study of Human Nature,' in De Caro and Macarthur (forthcoming).

Earman, John (1986), *A Primer on Determinism* (Dordrecht: Reidel).

Ehring, Douglas (1997), *Causation and Persistence: A Theory of Causation* (New York: Oxford University Press).

Eklund, Matti (2007), 'Fictionalism,' *Stanford Encyclopedia of Philosophy*, http://plato. stanford.edu/entries/fictionalism/

Field, Hartry (1980), *Science without Numbers* (Princeton, NJ: Princeton University Press).

—— (1984), 'Is Mathematical Knowledge Just Logical Knowledge?' *Philosophical Review* 93:509–52.

—— (1985), 'On Conservatives and Incompleteness,' *Journal of Philosophy* 82:239–59.

—— (1992), 'Physicalism,' in J. Earman (ed.), *Inference, Explanations, and Other Frustrations: Essays in the Philosophy of Science* (Berkeley: University of California Press), pp. 271–91.

—— (2001), *Truth and the Absence of Fact* (Oxford: Clarendon Press).

—— (2006), 'Truth and the Unprovability of Consistency,' *Mind* 115:467–605.

Fine, Kit (1994), 'Essence and Modality,' *Noûs Supplement* 8:1–16.

Fodor, Jerry (1974), 'Special Sciences,' *Synthese* 28:97–115.

—— (1978), 'Propositional Attitudes,' *The Monist* 61:501–23.

—— (1979), *The Language of Thought* (Cambridge, MA: Harvard University Press).

—— (1981a), 'The Mind–Body Problem,' *Scientific American* 244:114–23.

—— (1981b), *Representations* (Cambridge, MA: MIT Press).

—— (1987), *Psychosemantics* (Cambridge, MA: MIT Press).

—— (1990), *A Theory of Content and Other Essays* (Cambridge, MA: MIT Press).

—— (2000a), *In Critical Condition: Polemical Essays on Cognitive Science and the Philosophy of Mind* (Cambridge, MA: MIT Press).

—— (2000b), *The Mind Doesn't Work That Way* (Cambridge, MA: MIT Press).

—— (2007), 'Against Darwinism,' http://ruccs.rutgers.edu/faculty/Fodor/Fodor_ Against_Darwinism.pdf

Foster, John (1991), *The Immaterial Self: A Defense of the Cartesian Dualist Conception of the Mind* (London and New York: Routledge).

Galison, Peter and Stump, David J. (eds.) (1996), *The Disunity of Science, Boundaries, Contexts, and Power* (Stanford: Stanford University Press).

Gardner, Howard (1985), *The Mind's New Science* (New York: Basic Books).

Gendler, Tamara S. and Hawthorne, John (eds.) (2002), *Conceivability and Possibility* (Oxford: Clarendon Press).

Gettier, Edmund L. (1973), 'Is Justified True Belief Knowledge?' *Analysis* 23:121–3.

Gillett, Carl (2001), 'The Methodological Role of Physicalism,' in Gillet and Loewer (2001), pp. 225–50.

_____ (2002), 'The Dimensions of Realization: A Critique of the Standard View,' *Analysis* 62:316–23.

_____ (2003a), 'Strong Emergence as a Defense of Non-Reductive Physicalism: A Physicalist Metaphysics for "Downward" Determination,' *Principia* 6:83–114.

_____ (2003b), 'Non-Reductive Realization and Non-Reductive Identity: What Physicalism Does Not Entail,' in Walter and Heckmann (2003), pp. 31–57.

_____ (2006a), 'The Hidden Battles over Emergence,' in P. Clayton (ed.), *Oxford Handbook of Religion and Science* (Oxford: Oxford University Press), pp. 801–18.

_____ (2006b), 'Samuel Alexander's Emergentism: Or, Higher Causation for Physicalists,' *Synthese* 153:261–96.

_____ and Loewer Barry, (eds.) (2001), *Physicalism and Its Discontents* (New York: Cambridge University Press).

Goldman, Alvin (1970), *A Theory of Human Action* (Englewood Cliffs, NJ: Prentice Hall).

Goodman, Nelson (1973), *Fact, Fiction and Forecast* (Indianapolis: Bobbs-Merrill).

Graham, George, Horgan, Terry, and Tienson, John (2007), 'Consciousness and Intentionality,' in M. Velmans and S. Schneider (eds.), *The Blackwell Companion to Consciousness* (Oxford: Blackwell), pp. 468–84.

Handfield, Toby (ed.) (2008), *Dispositions and Causes* (Oxford: Oxford University Press).

Hardin, C. L. (1988), *Color for Philosophers* (Indianapolis: Hackett).

Harman, Gilbert (1973), *Thought* (Princeton, NJ: Princeton).

_____ (1990), 'The Intrinsic Quality of Experience,' *Philosophical Perspectives* 4:31–52.

Hart, W. D. (1988), *The Engines of the Soul* (Cambridge: Cambridge University Press).

Hasker, William (1999), *The Emergent Self* (Ithaca, NY: Cornell University Press).

Heil, John (2000), *From an Ontological Point of View* (Oxford: Oxford University Press).

_____ (2003), 'Multiply Realized Properties,' in Walter and Heckmann (2003), pp. 11–30.

_____ and Mele, Alfred (eds.) (1993), *Mental Causation* (Oxford: Clarendon Press).

Hellman, Geoffrey (1989), *Mathematics without Numbers: Toward a Modal-Structural Interpretation* (Oxford: Clarendon Press).

Hempel, Carl (1970), 'Reduction: Ontological and Linguistic Facts,' in S. Morgenbesser et al. (eds.), *Philosophy, Science, and Method: Essays in Honor of Ernest Nagel* (New York: St Martin's Press), pp. 179–99.

Hendry, Robin (2006), 'Is There Downward Causation in Chemistry?' in D. Baird, L. McIntyre and E. Scerri (eds.), *Philosophy of Chemistry: Synthesis of a New Discipline, Boston Studies in the Philosophy of Science Volume 242* (New York: Springer), pp. 173–89.

Hershenov, David (2004), 'Countering the Appeal of the Psychological Approach to Personal Identity,' *Philosophy* 79:447–75.

Hill, Christopher (1991), *Sensations: A Defense of Type Materialism* (New York: Cambridge University Press).

_____ (1997), 'Imaginability, Conceivability, Possibility, and the Mind–Body Problem,' *Philosophical Studies* 87:61–85.

_____ and McLaughlin, Brian (1999), 'There are Fewer Things Than Are Dreamt of in Chalmers' Philosophy,' *Philosophy and Phenomenological Research* 59:445–54.

Hirsch, Eli (1986), 'Metaphysical Necessity and Conceptual Truth,' *Midwest Studies In Philosophy* 11:243–56.

Horgan, Terence (1981), 'Token Physicalism, Supervenience, and the Generality of Physics,' *Synthese* 49:395–414.

——(1984), 'Jackson On Physical Information and Qualia,' *Philosophical Quarterly* 34:147–51.

——(1987), 'Supervenient Qualia,' *Philosophical Review* 96:491–520.

——(2002), 'The Intentionality of Phenomenology and the Phenomenology of Intentionality,' in D. Chalmers (ed.), *Philosophy of Mind: Classical and Contemporary Readings* (Oxford: Oxford University Press), pp. 520–33.

——(2006a), 'Critical Study of Joseph Levine, *Purple Haze: The Puzzle of Consciousness*,' *Nous* 40:579–88.

——(2006b), 'Materialism: Matters of Definition, Defense, and Deconstruction,' *Philosophical Studies* 131:157–83.

——and Graham, George (in press), 'Phenomenal Intentionality and Content Determinacy,' in R. Schantz (ed.), *Prospects for Meaning* (Amsterdam: de Gruyter).

——and Graham, George (2003), 'The Phenomenology of First-Person Agency,' in Walter and Heckmann (2003), pp. 323–40.

—— ——and Graham, George (2004), 'Phenomenal Intentionality and the Brain in a Vat,' in R. Schantz (ed.), *The Externalist Challenge* (Amsterdam: Walter de Gruyter), pp. 297–317.

——and Tienson, John (2001), 'Deconstructing New Wave Materialism,' in Gillett and Loewer (2001), pp. 307–18.

Hornsby, Jennifer (1992), 'Physics, Biology, and Common-Sense Psychology,' in Charles and Lennon (1992), pp. 155–77.

——(1997), *Simple Mindedness: In Defense of Naïve Naturalism in the Philosophy of Mind* (Cambridge, MA: Harvard University Press).

——(2004), 'Agency and Alienation,' in De Caro and Macarthur (2004a), pp. 173–87.

Hunt, R. G. W. (1982), 'A Model of Colour Vision for Predicting Colour Appearance,' *Color Research and Application* 7:95–112.

Husserl, E. (1966), *Analysen zur passiven Synthesis*, vol. XI of the *Collected Works*, ed. by M. Fleischer (Den Haag: Martinus Nijhoff).

Jackendoff, Ray (1992), *Languages of the Mind* (Cambridge, MA: MIT Press).

——(1997), *The Architecture of the Language Faculty* (Cambridge, MS: MIT).

Jackson, Frank (1982), 'Epiphenomenal Qualia,' *Philosophical Quarterly* 32:127–36.

——(1986), 'What Mary Didn't Know,' *Journal of Philosophy* 83:291–95.

——(1998), *From Metaphysics to Ethics: A Defense of Conceptual Analysis* (Oxford: Oxford University Press).

——(2003), 'Mind and Illusion,' in Anthony O'Hea (ed.), *Minds and Persons*. Royal Institute of Philosophy Supplement: Volume 53 (Cambridge: Cambridge University Press), pp. 251–71.

Johnson-Laird, Philip (1988), *The Computer and the Mind* (Cambridge, MA: Harvard University Press).

Johnston, Mark (1987), 'Is There a Problem about Persistence?', *Proceedings of the Aristotelian Society* 61:107–35.

——(2004), 'The Obscure Object of Hallucination,' *Philosophical Studies* 120:113–83.

——(MS) *The Manifest*.

Jubien, Michael (1997), *Contemporary Metaphysics* (Oxford: Blackwell Publishers).

_____ (2001), 'Propositions and the Objects of Thought,' *Philosophical Studies* 104:47–62.

_____ (2009), *Possibility* (Oxford: Oxford University Press).

Kalderon, M. (2007), 'Color Pluralism', *Philosophical Review* 116:563–601.

Kant, Immanuel (1968), 'Attempt to Introduce the Concept of Negative Magnitudes into Philosophy' (1763), *Kants Werke*, A.K. II (Berlin: Walter de Gruyter & Co.).

Kaplan, David (1989), 'Demonstratives,' in Joseph Almog, John Perry, and Howard Wettstein (eds.), *Themes from Kaplan* (New York: Oxford University Press), pp. 481–564.

Kim, Jaegwon (1973), 'Causation, Nomic Subsumption and the Concept of Event,' *Journal of Philosophy* 70:217–36.

_____ (1976), 'Events as Property Exemplifications,' in Myles Brand and Douglas Walton (eds.), *Action Theory* (Dordrecht: Reidel), pp. 159–77.

_____ (1988), 'What is "Naturalized Epistemology"?' *Philosophical Perspectives* 2:381–405.

_____ (1989), 'The Myth of Nonreductive Materialism,' *Procedural Address of the American Philosophical Association* 63:31–47; reprinted in Kim (1993b) *Supervenience and Mind* (Cambridge: Cambridge University Press), pp. 265–84.

_____ (1993a), 'The Non-Reductivist's Troubles with Mental Causation,' in John Heil and Alfred Mele (eds.), *Mental Causation* (Oxford: Clarendon Press), pp. 189–210.

_____ (1993b), *Supervenience and Mind* (Cambridge, MA: MIT Press).

_____ (1996), *The Philosophy of Mind* (Boulder, C.: Westview Press).

_____ (1997), 'Does the Problem of Mental Causation Generalize?', *Proceedings of the Aristotelian Society* 97:281–97.

_____ (1998), *Mind in a Physical World* (Cambridge: Cambridge University Press).

_____ (1999), 'Supervenient Properties and Micro-based Properties: A Reply to Noordhof,' *Proceedings of the Aristotelian Society* 99:115–18.

_____ (2001) 'Lonely Souls,' in Corcoran (ed.) (2001), pp. 30–43.

_____ (2002), 'Responses,' *Philosophy and Phenomenological Research* 65:671–80.

_____ (2003), 'Blocking Causal Drainage and Other Maintenance Chores with Mental Causation,' *Philosophy and Phenomenological Research* 67:151–76.

_____ (2005), *Physicalism, or Something Near Enough* (Princeton, NJ: Princeton University Press).

Kitcher, Philip (1992), 'The Naturalist Return,' *Philosophical Review*, 101:53–114.

_____ (2006), *Living with Darwin: Evolution, Design, and the Future of Faith* (New York: Oxford University Press).

Klima, G. (2007), 'Thomistic "Monism" vs. Cartesian "Dualism",' in U. Meixner and A. Newen (eds.), *Logical Analysis and History of Philosophy* 10 (Paderborn: mentis), pp. 92–112.

Koons, Robert C. (2000a), *Realism Regained: An Exact Theory of Causation, Teleology and the Mind* (New York: Oxford University Press).

_____ (2000b), 'The Incompatibility of Naturalism and Scientific Realism,' in Craig and Moreland (2000), pp. 49–63.

_____ (2003), 'Review of *Truth and the Absence of Fact*, by Hartry Field,' *Mind* 112:119–26.

Korsgaard, Christine M. (1996), *The Sources of Normativity* (Cambridge: Cambridge University Press).

Kripke, Saul A. (1971), 'Identity and Necessity,' in M. K. Munitz (ed.), *Identity and Individuation* (New York: NYU Press), pp. 162–63.

Kripke, Saul A. (1975), 'Outline of a Theory of Truth,' *Journal of Philosophy* 72:690–716.

———— (1980), *'Naming and Necessity* (Cambridge, MA: Harvard University Press).

———— (1982), *Wittgenstein on Rules and Private Language: An Elementary Exposition* (Cambridge, MA: Harvard University Press).

———— (1999), 'Identity and Necessity,' in Jaegwon Kim and Ernest Sosa (eds.), *Metaphysics* (Oxford: Blackwell).

Lacey, Alan (2005), 'Naturalism,' in T. Honderich (ed.), *The Oxford Companion to Philosophy* (Oxford: Oxford University Press), pp. 296–97.

Laudan, Larry (1988), 'The Demise of the Demarcation Problem,' in Michael Ruse (ed.), *But Is It Science? The Philosophical Question in the Creation/Evolution Controversy* (Buffalo, NY: Prometheus Books), pp. 337–50.

Laughlin, R. B., D. Pines, J. Schmalian, B. Stojkovic, and P. Wolynes (2000), 'The Middle Way,' *Proceedings of the National Academy of Sciences* 97:32–37.

Leftow, Brian (2001), 'Souls Dipped in Dust,' in Corcoran (2001), pp. 120–38.

Leiter, Brian (2007), 'Legal Naturalism,' *Stanford Encyclopedia of Philosophy*, http://plato.stanford.edu/entries/lawphil-naturalism/

Levine, Joseph (1966), 'An Argument for the Identity Theory,' *Journal of Philosophy* 63:17–25.

———— (1970), 'How to Define Theoretical Terms,' *Journal of Philosophy* 67:427–46.

———— (1972), 'Psychophysical and Theoretical Identifications,' *Australasian Journal of Philosophy* 50:249–58.

———— (1973a), 'Causation,' *Journal of Philosophy* 70:556–67.

———— (1973b), *Counterfactuals* (Oxford: Blackwell).

———— (1976), 'Survival and Identity,' in Amelie Rorty (ed.), *The Identity of Persons* (Berkeley: University of California Press), pp. 17–40.

———— (1979a), 'Attitudes *De Dicto* and *De Se*,' *Philosophical Review* 88:513–43.

———— (1979b), 'Counterfactual Dependence and Time's Arrow,' *Nous* 13:455–76.

———— (1980), 'Mad Pain and Martian Pain,' in Ned Block (ed.), *Readings in the Philosophy of Psychology, Vol. I*, (Cambridge, MA: Harvard University Press), pp. 216–22.

———— (1983a), 'New Work for a Theory of Universals,' *Australasian Journal of Philosophy* 61:343–77.

———— (1983b), 'Radical Interpretation' and 'Postscripts to "Radical Interpretation"' in *Philosophical Papers*, Vol.1 (New York: Oxford University Press), pp.108–21.

———— (1983c), 'Postscript to "Survival and Identity",' *Philosophical Papers* Vol. 1, (Oxford: Oxford University Press), pp. 73–77.

———— (1983d), 'Materialism and Qualia: The Explanatory Gap,' *Pacific Philosophical Quarterly* 64:354–61.

———— (1984), 'Putnam's Paradox,' *Australasian Journal of Philosophy* 62:221–36.

———— (1986), *On the Plurality of Worlds* (Oxford: Blackwell).

———— (1988), 'What Experience Teaches,' in J. Copley-Coltheart (ed.), *Proceedings of the Russellian Society* (Sydney: University of Sydney), reprinted in Chalmers (2002a), pp. 281–94.

———— (1993), 'On Leaving Out What It's Like,' in M. Davies and G. Humphreys (eds.), *Consciousness* (Oxford: Blackwell), pp. 137–49.

———— (1994), 'Humean Supervenience Debugged,' *Mind* 103:473–90.

———— (2001a), 'Causation as Influence,' in Hall, J., Collins, E., and Paul, L. (eds.), *Causation and Counterfactuals* (Cambridge, MA: MIT Press), pp. 75–106.

_____ (2001b), *Purple Haze: The Puzzle of Consciousness* (Oxford: Oxford University Press).

Libet, Benjamin (1985), 'Unconscious Cerebral Initiative and the Role of Conscious Will in Voluntary Action,' *Behavioral and Brain Sciences* 8:529–66.

Loar, Brian (1981), *Mind and Meaning* (New York: Cambridge University Press).

_____ (1997), 'Phenomenal Concepts,' in Ned Block, Owen Flanagan, and Guven Güzeldere (eds.), *The Nature of Consciousness* (Cambridge: MA: MIT Press/Bradford Books), pp. 597–616.

Loewer, Barry (2001a), 'From Physics to Physicalism,' in Gillet and Loewer 2001, pp. 37–56.

_____ (2001b), 'Review of J. Kim, *Mind in a Physical World*,' *Journal of Philosophy* 98:315–24.

Lowe, E. J. (1989), *Kinds of Being: A Study of Individuation, Identity and the Logic of Sortal Terms* (Oxford: Blackwell).

_____ (1996), *Subjects of Experience* (Cambridge: Cambridge University Press).

_____ (1999), 'Self, Agency, and Mental Causation,' *Journal of Consciousness Studies* 6:225–39.

_____ (2000a), *An Introduction to the Philosophy of Mind* (Cambridge: Cambridge University Press).

_____ (2000b), 'Causal Closure Principles and Emergentism,' *Philosophy* 75:571–85.

_____ (2001), 'Identity, Composition, and the Simplicity of the Self,' in Corcoran (2001), pp. 139–58.

_____ (2002a), *A Survey of Metaphysics* (Oxford: Oxford University Press).

_____ (2002b), 'Phenomenal States,' in Chalmers (2002a), pp. 295–310.

_____ (2003a), 'Personal Agency,' in Anthony O'Hear (ed.), *Minds and Persons* (Cambridge: Cambridge University Press), pp. 211–27.

_____ (2003b), 'Physical Causal Closure and the Invisibility of Mental Causation,' in Walter and Heckmann (2003), pp. 137–54.

Ludlow, Peter, Yujin Nagasawa, and Daniel Stoljar (eds.) (2004), *There's Something About Mary* (Cambridge, MA: MIT Press).

Lycan, William (1987), *Consciousness* (Cambridge, Ma: MIT Press).

_____ (1997), *Consciousness and Experience* (Cambridge, MA: MIT Press).

_____ (2006), 'Pautz vs. Byrne & Tye on Externalist Intentionalism,' http://garnet.acns.fsu.edu/~tan02/OPC%20Week%20Four/

Macarthur, David (2004), 'Naturalizing the Human or Humanizing Nature: Science, Nature and the Supernatural,' *Erkenntnis* 61:29–51.

Mackie, J. L. (1977), *Ethics: Inventing Right and Wrong* (New York: Penguin).

Madell, Geoffrey (1981), *The Identity of the Self* (Edinburgh: Edinburgh University Press).

Martin, R. M. (1966), 'On Theoretical Constants and Ramsey Constants,' *Philosophy of Science* 31:1–13.

Martin, Martin, and McIntyre, Lee C. (eds.) (1994), *Readings in the Philosophy of the Social Science* (Cambridge, MA: MIT Press).

Maund, Barry (2003), *Perception* (Montreal: McGill-Queen's University Press).

Maxwell, Grover (1970), 'Structural Realism and the Meaning of Theoretical Terms,' in M. Radner and S. Winoker (eds.), *Minnesota Studies in the Philosophy of Science* 4:181–92.

McConnell, Jeff (1994), 'In Defense of the Knowledge Argument,' *Philosophical Topics* 22:157–87.

McDowell, John (1994), *Mind and World* (Cambridge, MA: Harvard University Press).

——— (1996), 'Two Sorts of Naturalism,' in *Mind, Value, Reality* (Cambridge, MA: Harvard University Press), pp. 167–97.

McGinn, Colin (1989), 'Can We Solve the Mind-Body Problem?' *Mind* 98:349–66.

——— (1996), 'Another Look at Color,' *Journal of Philosophy* 93:537–53.

McLaughlin, Brian (1997), 'Review of *The Unity of the Self*,' *Journal of Philosophy* 94:638–44.

——— (2001), 'In Defense of New Wave Materialism: A Response to Horgan and Tienson,' in C. Gillett and Loewer (2001), pp. 319–31.

Meixner, Uwe (2002), 'Change and Change-*Ersatz*,' in A. Bottani, M. Carrara, and P. Giaretta (eds.), *Individuals, Essence and Identity. Themes of Analytic Metaphysics* (Dordrecht: Kluwer), pp. 427–49.

——— (2004), *The Two Sides of Being: A Reassessment of Psycho-Physical Dualism* (Paderborn: mentis).

——— (2005), 'Physicalism, Dualism, and Intellectual Honesty,' *Dualism Review* 1:1–20.

——— (2006a), 'Classical Intentionality,' *Erkenntnis* 65:25–45.

——— (2006b), 'Consciousness and Freedom,' in A. Corradini, S. Galvan, E. J. Lowe (eds.), *Analytic Philosophy Without Naturalism* (London: Routledge), pp. 183–96.

——— (2006c), 'The Indispensability of the Soul,' in B. Niederbacher and E. Runggaldier (eds.), *Die menschliche Seele. Brauchen wir den Dualismus?* (Frankfurt am Main: ontos), pp. 19–40.

——— (2006d), *The Theory of Ontic Modalities* (Frankfurt am Main: ontos).

——— (2007), 'The *Reductio* of Reductive and Non-Reductive Materialism—and a New Start,' in A. Antonietti, A. Corradini, E. J. Lowe (eds.), *Psycho-Physical Dualism Today: An Interdisciplinary Approach* (Lanham, MD: Rowman and Littlefield).

Menuge, Angus J. L. (2004a), *Agents Under Fire: Materialism and the Rationality of Science* (Lanham, MD: Rowman and Littlefield).

——— (2004b), *Reading God's World: The Vocation of Scientist* (St Louis, MS: Concordia Publishing House).

——— (2008), 'New Perspectives for a Dualistic Conception of Mental Causation,' *Journal of Consciousness Studies* 15:17–38.

Merricks, Trenton (2001), *Objects and Persons* (Oxford: Clarendon Press).

Meyer, Stephen (2000), 'The Scientific Status of Design Science,' in Michael Behe, William A Dembski, and Stephen C. Meyer (eds.), *Science and Evidence for Design in the Universe* (San Francisco, CA: Ignatius Press).

Millikan, Ruth G. (1984), *Language, Thought and Other Biological Categories: New Foundations for Realism* (Cambridge, MA: MIT Press).

——— (1989), 'Biosemantics,' *Journal of Philosophy* 86:281–97.

Minsky, Marvin (1985), *The Society of Mind* (New York: Touchstone).

Moore, G. E. (1903), *Principia Ethica* (Cambridge: Cambridge University Press).

——— (1922), 'The Conception of Intrinsic Value,' in *Philosophical Studies* (New York: Harcourt, Brace, and Co.).

Moser, Paul and Trout, J. D. (eds.) (1995), *Contemporary Materialism: A Reader* (London: Routledge).

Mumford, Stephen (2004), *Laws in Nature* (New York: Routledge).

Nagel, Thomas (1974), 'What Is It Like to Be a Bat?,' *Philosophical Review* 83:435–50.

—— (1986), *A View from Nowhere* (Oxford: Oxford University Press).

—— (1991), 'Agent-relativity and the Doing–Happening Distinction,' *Philosophical Studies*, 63:167–85.

Nemirow, Laurence (1989), 'Physicalism and the Cognitive Role of Acquaintance,' in William Lycan (ed.), *Mind and Cognition* (Oxford: Basil Blackwell), pp. 490–9.

Newell, Alfred (1990), *Unified Theories of Cognition* (Cambridge, MA: Harvard).

Nida-Rümelin, Martine (2006), *Der Blick von innen: Zur transtemporalen Identität bewusstseinsfähiger Wesen* (Frankfurt am Main: Suhrkamp).

—— (2007), 'Doings and Subject Causation,' *Erkenntnis* 67:147–372.

—— (2008), 'Experiencing Subjects,' in Antonella Corradini *et al.* (eds.), *Emergence in Science and Philosophy*.

Nielsen, Kai (2001), *Naturalism and Religion* (Amherst: Prometheus).

Nolan, Daniel (2002), 'Modal Fictionalism,' *Stanford Encyclopedia of Philosophy*, http://plato.stanford.edu/entries/fictionalism-modal/

Nozick, Robert (1981), *Philosophical Explanations* (Cambridge, MA: Harvard University Press).

O'Connor, Timothy (1994), 'Emergent Properties,' *Americal Philosophical Quarterly* 31:91–104.

—— (2000), *Persons and Causes: The Metaphysics of Free Will* (New York: Oxford University Press).

—— (2008), 'Agent-Causal Power,' in Handfield, pp. 189–214.

—— and Kevin Kimble (unpublished), 'The Argument from Consciousness Revisited.'

—— and H. Y. Wong (2002), 'Emergent Properties,' *Stanford Online Encyclopedia of Philosophy*. http://plato.stanford.edu/entries/properties-emergent/

—— and H.Y. Wong (2005), 'The Metaphysics of Emergence,' *Noûs* 39:659–79.

Olson, E. T. (2001), 'A Compound of Two Substances,' in Corcoran (2001), pp. 73–88.

Oppenheim, Paul and Putnam, Hilary (1958), 'Unity of Science as a Working Hypothesis,' *Minnesota Studies in the Philosophy of Science* 2:3–36.

Papineau, David (1993), *Philosophical Naturalism* (Oxford: Blackwell).

—— (2001), 'The Rise of Physicalism,' in Gillett and Loewer (2001), pp. 3–36.

—— (2007), 'Naturalism,' *Stanford Encyclopedia of Philosophy*, plato.stanford.edu/entries/naturalism/notes.html#1

Parfit, Derek (1984), *Reasons and Persons* (Oxford: Clarendon Press).

Pasnau, Robert (1997), *Theories of Cognition in the Later Middle Ages* (New York: Cambridge University Press).

Pautz, Adam (2003), 'Have Byrne and Hilbert Answered Hardin's Challenge?' *Behavioral and Brain Sciences* 26:44–45.

—— (2006), 'Sensory Awareness is not a Wide Physical Relation,' *Noûs* 40:205–40.

—— (2007a), 'Intentionalism and Perceptual Presence,' *Philosophical Perspectives* 21:495–541.

—— (2007b), 'A Simple View of Consciousness' (longer version), http://webspace.utexas.edu/arp424/www/simple.viewpdf

—— (2008), 'The Interdependence of Phenomenology and Intentionality,' *The Monist*.

Pautz, Adam (MSa), 'Color Eliminativism.'

——— (MSb), 'Variation in Color Vision.'

——— (MSc), 'Why Explain Experience in Terms of Content.'

Peacocke, Christopher (1983), *Sense and Content* (Oxford: Clarendon Press).

——— (2001), 'Does Perception Have a Nonconceptual Content?' *Journal of Philosophy* 98:239–64.

Pereboom, Derk (2002), 'Robust Non-Reductive Materialism,' *Journal of Philosophy* 99:499–531.

——— and Hilary Kornblith (1991), 'The Metaphysics of Irreducibility,' *Philosophical Studies* 63:125–45.

Perry, John (2001), *Knowledge, Possibility and Consciousness* (Cambridge, MA: MIT Press).

Pettit, Philip (1992a), 'Naturalism,' in Jonathan Dancy and Ernest Sosa (eds.), *A Companion to Epistemology* (Oxford: Blackwell), pp. 296–7.

——— (1992b), 'The Nature of Naturalism,' *Proceedings of the Aristotelian Society* Supplementary vol. 66:245–66.

Plantinga, Alvin (1982), 'How to be an Anti-Realist,' *Addresses and Proceedings of the American Philosophical Association* 56:47–70.

——— (1993), *Warrant and Proper Function* (New York: Oxford University Press).

Pollock, John L. (1986), *Contemporary Theories of Knowledge* (Totowa, NJ: Rowman Littlefield).

Popper, Karl R. and Eccles, J. C. (1977), *The Self and its Brain: An Argument for Interactionism* (Berlin: Springer).

Price, Huw (2004), 'Naturalism without Representationalism,' in De Caro and Macarthur (2004b), pp. 71–105.

Putnam, Hilary (1967), 'The Nature of Mental States,' in W. H. Capitan and D. D. Merrill (eds.), *Art, Mind and Religion* (Pittsburgh, PN: University of Pittsburgh Press), pp. 37–48.

——— (1970), 'On Properties,' in N. Rescher *et al.* (eds.), *Essays in Honor of Carl G. Hempel* (Dordrecht: D. Reidel).

——— (1973), 'Psychological Predicates,' in W. H. Capitan and D. D. Merrill (eds.), *Art, Mind, and Religion* (Pittsburgh: University of Pittsburgh Press).

——— (1975a), 'The Meaning of "Meaning",' in K. Gunderson (ed.), *Language, Mind and Knowledge*, Minnesota Studies in the Philosophy of Science, Volume IX (Minneapolis: University of Minnesota Press).

——— (1975b), *Mind, Language and Reality* (Cambridge: Cambridge University Press).

——— (1981), *Reason, Truth, and History* (Cambridge, MA: Cambridge University Press).

——— (1988), *Representation and Reality* (Cambridge, MA: MIT Press).

——— (1992), *Renewing Philosophy* (Cambridge, MA: Harvard University Press).

——— (2004), 'The Content and Appeal of "Naturalism",' in De Caro and Macarthur (2004), pp. 59–70.

——— (forthcoming), 'Science and Philosophy,' in De Caro and Macarthur (forthcoming).

Pylyshyn, Zenon (1984), *Computation and Cognition* (Cambridge, MA: MIT Press).

Quine, Willard van Orman (1960), *Word and Object* (Cambridge, MA: MIT Press).

——— (1969a), 'Reply to Chomsky,' in D. Davidson and J. Hintikka (eds.), *Words and Objections* (Dordrecht: D. Reidel), p. 303.

_____ (1969b), 'Epistemology Naturalized,' in *Ontological Relativity and Other Essays* (New York: Columbia University Press), pp. 69–90.

_____ (1986), 'Reply to Putnam,' in Lewis Hahn and Paul Schillp (eds.) *The Philosophy of W. V. Quine* (La Salle IL: Open Court), pp. 427–31.

_____ (1990), 'Naturalism; Or, Living within One's Means,' *Quintessence* (Cambridge, MA: Harvard University Press), pp. 275–86.

Ramsey, Frank P. (1931), 'Theories,' in R. B. Braithwaite (ed.), *The Foundations of Mathematics* (London: Routledge and Kegan Paul).

_____ (1978), *Foundations: Essays in Philosophy, Logic, Mathematics and Economics* (Atlantic Highlands, NJ: Humanities Press).

Ramsey, William (2003), 'Eliminative Materialism,' *Stanford Encyclopedia of Philosophy*, http://plato.stanford.edu/archives/fall2003/entries/materialism-eliminative/

Ratzsch, Del (2001), *Nature, Design, and Science: The Status of Design in Natural Science* (Albany, NY: SUNY Press).

Rea, Michael C. (2002), *World Without Design: The Ontological Consequences of Naturalism* (Oxford: Clarendon Press).

Robinson, Howard (ed.) (1993), *Objections to Physicalism* (Oxford: Clarendon Press).

Robinson, W. S. (2004), *Understanding Phenomenal Consciousness* (Cambridge: Cambridge University Press).

Rosen, Gideon and Dorr, Cian (2002), 'Composition as a Fiction,' in Richard Gale (ed.), *The Blackwell Guide to Metaphysics* (London: Basil Blackwell), pp. 151–74.

Rosenberg, Alexander (1994), *Instrumental Biology or the Disunity of Science* (Chicago, IL: University of Chicago Press).

Rosenthal, David M. (2002), 'Explaining Consciousness,' *Revue Roumaine de Philosophie* 46:109–31; reprinted in Chalmers (2002a).

Ross, James (1992), 'Immaterial Aspects of Thought,' *Journal of Philosophy* 89:136–50.

Ross, David and Spurrett, David (2004), 'What to Say to a Skeptical Metaphysician: A Defense Manual for Cognitive and Behavioral Scientists,' *Behavioral and Brain Sciences* 27:603–47.

Ruse, Michael (1988), 'A Philosopher's Day in Court' and 'Witness Testimony Sheet,' in Michael Ruse (ed.), *But is it Science? The Philosophical Question in the Creation/Evolution Question* (Buffalo, NY: Prometheus Books), pp. 386–94.

_____ (2003), *Darwin and Design: Does Evolution Have a Purpose?* (Cambridge, MA: Harvard University Press).

Russell, Bertrand (1948), *Human Knowledge: Its Scope and Limits* (New York: Simon & Schuster).

_____ (1971), 'The Philosophy of Logical Atomism,' in Robert C. Marsh (ed.), *Logic and Knowledge* (New York: Putnam), pp. 175–281.

Sainsbury, R. M. (1979), *Russell* (London: Routledge and Kegan Paul).

Schiffer, Stephen (1978), 'The Basis of Reference,' *Erkenntnis* 13, 171–206.

Scruton, Roger (1989), 'Corporate Persons,' *Proceedings of the Aristotelian Society*, Supplementary 63:239–66.

Searle, John R. (1980), 'Minds, Brains, and Programs,' *Behavioral and Brain Sciences* 3:417–24.

_____ (1992), *The Rediscovery of the Mind* (Cambridge, MA: MIT Press).

_____ (2004), *Mind: A Brief Introduction* (Oxford: Oxford University Press).

Sellars, Wilfrid (1962), 'Philosophy and the Scientific Image of Man,' *In the Space of Reasons* (Cambridge, MA: Harvard University Press), pp. 369–408.

Shoemaker, Sydney (1980), 'Causality and Properties,' in Peter van Inwagen (ed.), *Time and Cause* (Dordrecht: D. Reidel), pp. 109–35.

—— (1981), 'Some Varieties of Functionalism,' *Philosophical Topics* 12:93–119.

—— (1984), 'Personal Identity: A Materialist's Account,' in Sydney Shoemaker and Richard Swinburne (eds.), *Personal Identity* (New York: Basil Blackwell), pp. 67–132.

—— (1994), 'The Mind–Body Problem,' in R. Warner and T. Szubka (eds.), *The Mind–Body Problem: A Guide to the Current Debate* (Oxford: Blackwell), pp. 55–60.

—— (1998), 'Causal and Metaphysical Necessity,' *Pacific Philosophical Quarterly* 79:59–77.

—— (2001), 'Realization and Mental Causation,' in Gillett and Loewer (2001), pp. 74–98.

—— (2002), 'Kim on Emergence,' *Philosophical Studies* 108:53–63.

—— (2007), *Physical Realization* (Oxford: Oxford University Press).

Sider, Theodore (2001), *Four-Dimensionalism: An Ontology of Persistence and Time* (Oxford: Clarendon Press).

Siewert, Charles (1998), *The Significance of Consciousness* (Princeton: Princeton University Press).

—— (2001), 'Spontaneous Blindsight and Immediate Availability: Reply to Carruthers,' *Psyche* 7(07), http://psyche.cs.monash.edu.au/v7/psyche-7-08-siewert.html

—— (2003), 'Eliminativism, First-Person Knowledge, and Phenomenal Intentionality: Reply to Levine,' *Psyche* 9(03), http://psyche.cs.monash.edu.au/v9/psyche-9-06-siewert.html

Smart, J. C. C. (1959), 'Sensations and Brain Processes,' *Philosophical Review* 68:141–56.

—— (1970), 'Materialism,' in C. V. Borst (ed.), *The Mind/Brain Identity Theory* (London: Macmillan), pp. 159–70.

Smith, D., John, S. and Boughter, J. (2000), 'Neuronal Cell Types and Taste Quality Coding,' *Physiology and Behavior* 69:77–85.

Snowdon, P. F. (1991), 'Personal Identity and Brain Transplants,' in David Cockburn (ed.), *Human Beings* (Cambridge: Cambridge University Press), pp. 109–26.

Soames, Scott (2005), *Reference and Description* (Princeton, NJ: Princeton University Press).

Sober, Elliott (1984), *The Nature of Selection* (Cambridge, MA: MIT Press).

Stevens, Stanley (1975), *Psychophysics: Introduction to its Perceptual, Neural, and Social Prospects* (New York: John Wiley and Sons).

Stoljar, Daniel (2001), 'Physicalism,' *Stanford Encyclopedia of Philosophy*, http://plato.stanford.edu/entries/physicalism/

Strawson, P. F. (1959), *Individuals: An Essay in Descriptive Metaphysics* (London: Methuen).

—— (1962), 'Freedom and Resentment,' *Proceedings of the British Academy* 48:1–25.

Strawson, Galen (1994), *Mental Reality* (Cambridge, MA: MIT Press).

Stroud, Barry (1996), 'The Charm of Naturalism,' *Proceedings of the American Philosophical Association* 70:43–55.

Stump, Eleonore (1993), *Aquinas* (New York: Routledge), pp. 92–130.

—— (1995), 'Non-Cartesian Substance Dualism and Materialism Without Reductionism,' *Faith and Philosophy* 12:505–31.

Swinburne, Richard (1984), 'Personal Identity: The Dualist Theory,' in Sidney Shoe-maker and Richard Swinburne (eds.), *Personal Identity* (Oxford: Basil Blackwell), pp. 1–66.

_____ (1986), *The Evolution of the Soul* (New York: Oxford University Press).

_____ (2006), 'Wodurch ich ich bin—Eine Verteidigung des Substanzdualismus,' in B. Niederbacher (ed.), *Die menschliche Seele: Brauchen wir den Dualismus?* (Frankfurt am Main: ontos Verlag), pp. 41–59.

_____ (2007), 'From Mental/Physical Identity to Substance Dualism,' in Peter van Inwagen and Dean Zimmerman (eds.), *Persons* (Oxford: Oxford University Press), pp. 142–64.

Taliaferro, Charles (1994), *Consciousness and the Mind of God* (Cambridge: Cambridge University Press).

Tooby, John and Cosmides, Leda (1992), 'The Psychological Foundation of Culture,' in Jerome Barkow, Leda Cosmides, and John Tooby (eds.), *The Adapted Mind* (New York: Oxford University Press), pp. 19–136.

Tooley, Michael (1987), *Causation: A Realist Approach* (Oxford: Oxford University Press).

_____ (1993), 'Causation: Reductionism versus Realism,' in E. Sosa and M. Tooley (eds.), *Causation* (Oxford: Oxford University Press), pp. 172–92.

Tye, Michael (1986), 'The Subjective Qualities of Experience', *Mind* 95:1–17.

_____ (1990), 'A Representational Theory of Pains and Their Phenomenal Character,' in James Tomberlin (ed.), *Philosophical Perspectives*, Vol. 9 (Atascadero: Ridgeview Publishing Co.), pp. 223–39.

_____ (1995), *Ten Problems of Consciousness* (Cambridge, MA: MIT Press).

_____ (2000), *Consciousness, Color and Content* (Cambridge, MA: MIT Press).

_____ and Bradley, M. (2001), 'Of Colors, Kestrals, Caterpillars, and Leaves,' *Journal of Philosophy* 98:469–87.

Unger, Peter (1990), *Identity, Consciousness, and Value* (New York: Oxford University Press).

Van Fraassen, Bas (1988), *Laws and Symmetry* (Oxford: Clarendon Press).

Van Gulick, Robert (1992), 'Nonreductive Materialism and the Nature of Intertheoretic Constraint,' in A. Beckerman *et al.* (eds.), *Emergence or Reduction? Essays on the Prospects of Nonreductive Materialism* (Berlin: Walter de Gruyter), pp. 157–78.

_____ (1993), 'Who's in Charge Here? And Who's Doing All the Work?' in Heil and Mele (1993), pp. 233–56.

_____ (2004), 'So Many Ways of Saying No to Mary,' in P. Ludlow, Y. Nagasawa, and D. Stoljar (eds.), *There's Something About Mary* (Cambridge, MA: MIT Press), pp. 365–405.

Van Inwagen, Peter (1981), 'The Doctrine of Arbitrary Undetached Parts,' *Pacific Philosophical Quarterly* 62:123–37.

_____ (1990). *Material Beings* (Ithaca: Cornell University Press).

_____ (1993), *Metaphysics* (Boulder, CO: Westview Press).

_____ (1997), 'The Possibility of Resurrection,' in P. Edwards (ed.), *Immortality* (Amherst, NY: Prometheus Books), pp. 242–6.

Viger, Christopher (2000), 'Where Do Dennett's Stances Stand?' in Don Ross, Andrew Brook and David Thompson (eds.), *Dennett's Philosophy: A Comprehensive Assessment* (Cambridge, MA: MIT Press).

Villanueva, Enrique (ed.) (1993), *Naturalism and Normativity* (*Philosophical Issues*, 4), (Atascadero: Ridgeview).

Walter, Sven, and Heinz-Dieter Heckmann (eds.) (2003), *Physicalism and Mental Causation: The Metaphysics of Mind and Action* (Exeter: Imprint Academic).

Weinberg, Steven (1993), *Dreams of a Final Theory: The Scientist's Search for the Ultimate Laws of Nature* (New York: Vintage Books).

Weinberg, J. Stich, S., and Nichols, S. (2001), 'Normativity and Epistemic Intuitions,' *Philosophical Topics* 29:429–60.

Weiskrantz, Lawrence (1986), *Blindsight: A Case Study and Implications* (Oxford: Oxford University Press).

—— (1997), *Consciousness Lost and Found: A Neuropsychological Exploration* (Oxford: Oxford University Press).

Werner, J. S., and Wooten, B. R. (1979), 'Opponent Chromatic Mechanisms: Relation to Photopigments and Hue Naming,' *Journal of the Optical Society of America* 69:422–34.

White, Morton (1960), 'Memories of C. E. Moore,' *Journal of Philosophy* 57:805–10.

White, Stephen L. (1986), 'Curse of the Qualia,' *Synthese*, 68:333–68.

—— (1991), 'Narrow Content and Narrow Interpretation,' *The Unity of the Self* (Cambridge, MA: MIT Press/Bradford Books, 1991), chapter 2.

—— (1999), 'Consciousness and the Problem of Perspectival Grounding,' presented at the Workshop on Consciousness Naturalized, Certosa de Pontignano, Siena, May 28.

—— (2004), 'Subjectivity and the Agential Perspective,' in De Caro and Macarthur (2004b), pp. 201–27.

—— (forthcoming), 'Subjectivity and the Agential Perspective,' in De Caro and Macarthur (forthcoming).

Wiggins, David (1967), *Identity and Spatio-temporal Continuity* (Oxford: Blackwell).

—— (2001), *Sameness and Substance Renewed* (Cambridge: Cambridge University Press).

Wilkes, Kathleen (1988), *Real People: Personal Identity Without Thought Experiments* (Oxford: Clarendon Press).

Wilkins, A. S. (2000), 'Evolutionary Processes: A Special Issue,' *BioEssays* 22:1051–2.

Williams, Bernard (1970), 'The Self and the Future,' *Philosophical Review* 79:161–180.

—— (1973), *Problems of the Self* (Cambridge: Cambridge University Press).

—— (1978), *Descartes: The Project of Pure Enquiry* (Harmondsworth: Penguin Books).

—— (1985), *Ethics and the Limits of Philosophy* (Cambridge, MA: Harvard University Press).

—— (2000), 'Philosophy as a Humanistic Discipline,' *Philosophy* 75:477–96.

Williamson, Timothy (2005), 'Armchair Philosophy, Metaphysical Modality and Counterfactual Thinking,' *Proceedings of the Aristotelian Society* (Presidential Address) 105:1–23.

Woodward, James (2003), *Making Things Happen: A Theory of Causal Explanation* (Oxford: Oxford University Press).

Wright, Larry (1973), 'Functions,' *Philosophical Review* 82:139–68.

Wysong, R.L. (1976), *The Creation–Evolution Controversy* (East Lansing, MI: Inquiry Press).

Yablo, Stephen (1990), 'The Real Distinction Between Mind and Body,' *Canadian Journal of Philosophy, Supplementary* 16:149–201.

—— (1992), 'Mental Causation,' *The Philosophical Review* 101:245–80.

Zimmerman, Dean (1991), 'Two Cartesian Arguments for the Simplicity of the Soul,' *American Philosophical Quarterly* 28:217–26.

_____ (2006), 'Dualism in the Philosophy of Mind,' in D. M. Borchert (ed.), *Encyclopedia of Philosophy* 2nd Edition (New York: Macmillan).

Zuboff, Arnold (1981), 'The Story of a Brain,' in Daniel Dennett and Douglas Hofstadter (eds.), *The Mind's I* (New York: Basic Books), pp. 202–11.

Index

Index